LOURDES COLLEGE LIBRA
3 0379 1003 708

D1221502

CRIMINAL INVESTIGATION

Nelson-Hall Series in Law, Crime, and Justice

Consulting Editor: Howard Abadinsky
Saint Xavier University, Chicago

Michael J. Palmiotto

ARMSTRONG STATE COLLEGE

CRIMINAL INVESTIGATION

NELSON-HALL PUBLISHERS/CHICAGO

Project Editors: Becky Strehlow and Richard Meade
Photo Research: Nicholas Communications
Illustrator: Bill Nelson
Cover Painting: *Untitled* by Paul Sierra
Cover Design: Dorothy Anderson

LIBRARY OF CONGRESS CATALOGING-IN-PUBLICATION DATA

Palmiotto, Michael.
Criminal investigation / Michael J. Palmiotto.
p. cm.
Includes bibliographical references and index.
ISBN 0-8304-1180-1
1. Criminal investigation. 2. Criminal investigation—United States I. Title.
HV8073.P25 1994
363.2'5—dc20 92-14264
CIP

Manufactured in the United States of America

10 9 8 7 6 5 4 3 2 1

The paper used in this book meets the minimum requirements of American National Standard for Information Sciences—Permanence of Paper for Printed Library Materials, ANSI Z39.48-1984.

CONTENTS

Chapter 3

Legal Issues 39

Chapter 4

Sources of Information 57

Chapter 5

Interviewing and Interrogation 75

Chapter 6

Informants 97

Chapter 7

Writing Reports and Field Notes 121

Chapter 8

Surveillance and Undercover Operations 135

Chapter 12

Sex Offenses 243

Lyle L. Shook

Chapter 13

Death Through Violence 273

Chapter 14

Assault and Robbery 311

Chapter 15

Burglary 333

Chapter 16

Larceny 359

Chapter 17

Acident Investigation 401

Chapter 18

Narcotics and Other Drugs 423

Chapter 19

Special Investigations 473

Chapter 20

The Police/Prosecutor Relationship 519

Chapter 21

Investigative Trends 531

ACKNOWLEDGMENTS

A large number of individuals deserve a note of appreciation for their assistance in getting this book published. Valuable reviewers include James Hendricks, Christopher Hertig, James Farris, and Howard Tritt.

A special acknowledgment belongs to Lyle Shook for writing the chapter on Sexual Investigation. Sheldon Arenberg deserves a special thanks for providing the information on Link Analysis. Eugene R. Hunyadi provided information on Robbery Analysis for Investigative Links. My good friend David Kramer provided information on informants as did Kelvin McLaughlin. David King gave information on tracking down fugitives.

Chief David Gellathy and Major Dan Reynolds of the Savannah Police Department provided support. Savannah Detective Robert Roy of the Auto Theft Bureau was also helpful. Sergeant C. D. Brown of the Savannah Traffic Divisions rendered valuable assistance for the Accident Investigation chapter. Corporal David Dixon did the diagrams for the Auto Theft section.

Major Rubin Young and Sergeant Roy Willis of the Chatham County Police Department provided pictures for the text. Corporal R. L. Hoyser gave support for the Accident Investigation chapter. Major Dennis King of the Chatham County Sheriff's Department was extremely helpful in obtaining pictures for our book. Roger Parian of the Georgia Bureau of Investigation Crime Lab offered valuable information on Forensic Science.

A note of appreciation goes to my wife Emily and my sons Michael Joseph and Vincent James for their strong support and confidence.

Note

An instructor's resource manual and a test bank, both in print and on disk, are available with this book. Please contact the publisher for information.

CHAPTER 1

Historical Review of Criminal Investigation

The practice of investigating individual conduct can be traced to antiquity. When a society, tribe, group, or family establishes laws, customs, or rules, it expects members to obey them. All cultures recognize that when rules are violated, someone must determine who and what has been violated and who committed the violations. In order to find the answers, an investigation must be conducted. Although information on early investigative activities is clouded within an historical maze, some knowledge of its development does exist.

Roots of Investigation

In early tribal and clan life, the people performed the police task. When behavior occurred that violated the rules of the clan, all members were responsible for identifying the violator and determining the means and degree of sanctions to be imposed. This was known as **kin policing**. The process was often swift, certain, and absolute. Offenses considered serious usually resulted in torture, banishment, or death. Lesser offenses led to flaying or a similar corporal punishment or giving property to the offended family as atonement for the transgression. To prevent future violations and identify the offender, it was not uncommon for the tribe to brand or mutilate the culprit.

Among the ancient Hebrews, the kings, high priests, and elders had the law enforcement responsibility. Individuals were appointed to apprehend and punish law violators. This process continued even under Roman rule. For example, the decision to arrest Jesus was made by the chief priests and elders. Also, the high priest and elders gave Paul the authority to arrest and commit to prison Christians he apprehended.

Ancient Babylon codified its customs into the **Laws of Hammurabi**, which dealt with individual responsibilities to groups and private dealings between individuals. **Messengers** were assigned the responsibility of carrying out the law. A judicial system was established and violation became a crime against the state. The early Greek city-states developed the precursors of today's police. Pisistratus, the ruler of Athens, established a security system to protect the highways, the tower, and the ruler. Sparta developed police called *epohi* whose members were appointed by the ruler. They were given almost unlimited powers, including the authority to investigate, try, and punish individuals.

During the fifth century B.C. the Romans adopted their first written laws. The **Twelve Tables** dealt with legal procedures, property ownership, building codes, and punishment for crimes. After the Twelve Tables were approved, specialized police officials called *Quaestorees Parricidi* were appointed to track murderers. These were the forerunners of the modern detective. It was their responsibility to "track down" murderers for the state. (Thorwald, 1964, p. 4) Through their conquest of the Mediterranean world, the Romans influenced the legal and law enforcement systems of western Europe.

From the collapse of the Roman Empire through the early Middle Ages, formal law enforcement and criminal investigation were almost nonexistent as tools for social control. Various noninvestigative methods were devised to identify individuals who committed offenses. In **trial by ordeal**, accused persons were required to submit to some ordeal, such as placing their hands in boiling water. If their hands were burned, they were considered guilty. If their hands were uninjured, they were thought to be innocent—but possibly witches. In **trial by combat**, the victor was deemed to be telling the truth. Another method was the court of the **Star Chamber**, which derived its authority from the king and used brutal, legalized methods or torture to force confessions from suspects.

By the thirteenth century, the emerging European powers began to develop their own structured legal and law enforcement systems. One important concept was the classification of crimes. The English also defined the legal age of reason. Enforcement methods included the hue-and-cry system, the watch-and-ward system, and the office of sheriff.

In 1750 **Henry Fielding**, a London magistrate, established an

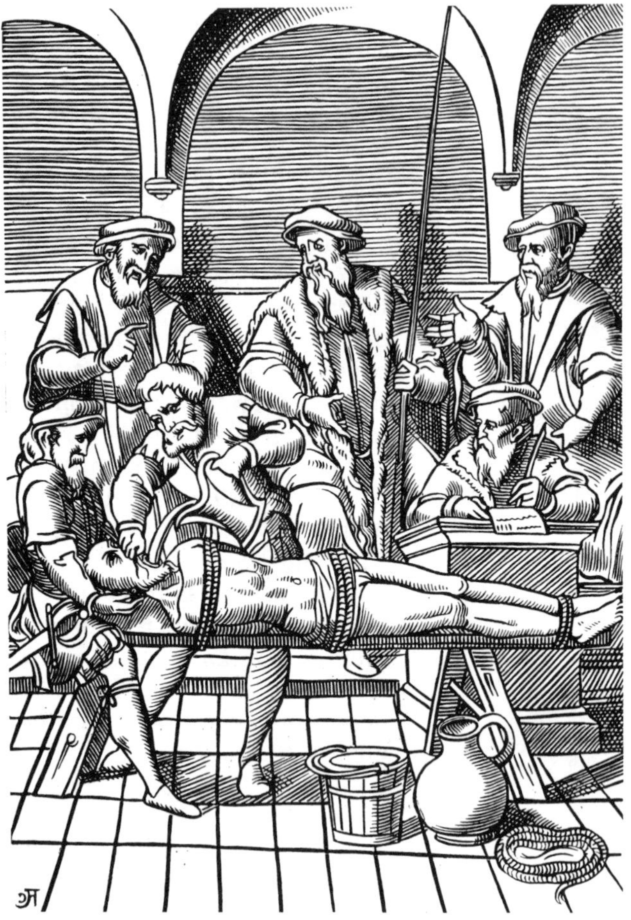

Trial by torture was one of the Star Chamber's legalized methods of forcing confessions from suspects.

investigative force known as the **Bow Street Runners** or **Thief Takers.** The group accepted cases only from those who could afford their fees. (Pringle, 1958) In 1753, John Fielding succeeded his brother Henry. Many of the practices they developed are still in use, such as hiring informants and conducting criminal raids.

Although the Metropolitan Police of London were established in 1829, it was not until 1842 that an investigative unit was founded. Due to a series of brutal murders, twelve police officers were taken out of uniform and made detectives. (Thorwald, 1964, p. 35)

Most studies of American law enforcement emphasize our English heritage while neglecting the investigative contributions of the French. The first formal use of the detective in modern times began in 1810 with the establishment of the French **Sûreté** (security). Its founder, **François-Eugène Vidocq,** was a convicted criminal who believed that only criminals could fight crime. In a single year Vidocq and his twelve investigators "arrested 812 murderers, thieves, burglars, robbers, and embezzlers, and cleaned a den of criminals into which no inspector would ever have dared to venture." (Thorwald, 1964, p. 4)

Vidocq believed in obtaining intimate knowledge of criminals' habits and methods of committing crime. He planted undercover investigators in prison to obtain information. Long after Vidocq's time, the Sûreté continued to use ex-convicts as informants and to plant undercover agents in prison. The Sûreté maintained accurate records of every known criminal's name, aliases, crimes, and sentences.

Investigations in America

The evolution of American criminal investigation has been greatly influenced by our social, political, economic, and legal needs. Exactly when the first detective was appointed in America is unknown. However, in 1789 the U.S. government appointed investigators, known as the Revenue Cutter Service, to prevent smuggling. In 1829, the U.S. Postal Service appointed detectives to investigate mail fraud.

At the municipal level, **Francis Tukey,** head of the Boston police department, appointed three detectives in 1846. Tukey's men recovered $16,000 worth of stolen property in 1850 and $62,000 in 1860. In the city of Boston, detective work was becoming an essential component of the police department. (Lane, 1967, p. 109)

In 1857 the New York City Police Department designated twenty police officers "detectives." This force was divided into squads responsible for specific crimes. Each squad maintained records of complaints and arrests. Each detective was required to submit daily reports on the progress and disposition of cases. (Costello, 1972, pp. 402–404)

Philadelphia initiated a detective unit in 1859, Chicago formed a bureau in 1860, and Massachusetts established a state investigative agency in 1865. The Detective Bureau of New York City was created by an act of the legislature in 1882. The bureau was placed under the authority of **Thomas Byrnes,** who led it to national and world recognition. Byrnes assigned a detective to Wall Street to curtail forgeries, pickpocketing, and larceny. He used informants, emphasized the need for detectives to learn the

Allan Pinkerton, shown here walking behind President Abraham Lincoln, warned the President in 1861 about a plot to assassinate him and thereby saved his life.

criminal's procedures for committing criminal acts, and required discipline and secrecy during investigation. (Costello, 1972, pp. 416–417)

The most successful investigative agency during the nineteenth century was not associated with a public law enforcement agency. **Allan Pinkerton's** initiation into investigation occurred in 1847 when he assisted a local sheriff in arresting a band of counterfeiters. In 1849 Pinkerton became Chicago's first detective. The next year he was appointed a special mail agent by the U.S. Postal Service to investigate post office thefts and robberies in Chicago. In the early 1850s Pinkerton opened a private detective agency, which eventually became known as the National Detective Agency. According to James D. Horan:

> They were the nineteenth-century prototype of the present Federal Bureau of Investigation and a forerunner of Interpol. By 1872, they had established a liaison with the important police organizations of Europe, for the exchange of information about international crime and criminals, and most of the frontier sheriffs and heads of metropolitan police in the United States sought their assistance. Though it is

> a little-known fact, the Pinkerton's pioneering Rogues' Gallery formed a basis for the modern FBI's Criminal Identification Bureau, the largest in the world. (Horan, 1967, p. x)

Pinkerton developed an excellent system of underworld informants. His investigators, known as **operatives**, infiltrated criminal gangs. They also investigated a case for Western Union in which messages were being intercepted before they reached their destinations. Pinkerton operatives required that all suspects arrested be stripped and all body cavities be checked. The Pinkertons are also credited with employing the first female detective, in 1856.

The Role of Patrol Officers

In municipal police departments, the patrol officer plays an important role in the investigative process. Usually the patrol officer arrives at the crime scene first. How he or she handles the initial investigation may affect how the case proceeds through the criminal justice process. Depending on departmental policy and the number of personnel, the patrol officer may conduct the entire investigation, assist the investigator, or be assisted by the investigator.

Upon being notified of a crime in progress, the patrol officer goes directly to the crime scene and takes care of any emergency situations, including injuries. If the suspect is still at the crime scene, the patrol officer should make an arrest. The longer the police take to arrive, the greater the possibility that evidence will be destroyed or contaminated. Delay may also mean witnesses will leave the scene or discuss the incident with each other, distorting their accounts of the crime. Once the patrol officer is notified to proceed to a crime scene, he or she should:

1. find out what has happened (be observant even while responding to the scene and departing from the patrol vehicle),
2. locate witnesses (including juveniles) and sources of evidence that will help determine what has happened,
3. figure out what further investigative steps should be taken (by either the officer, a technician, or another officer or investigator),
4. attempt to understand the motivations of the witnesses and evaluate the accuracy of their testimony (deciding whether to act on the testimony and whether some other officer might be successful with a particular witness), and
5. record what has been done, what has been learned, and what

is left to be done. (Block and Weidman, 1975, pp. 24–25)

The patrol officer complements the investigators. The more investigative functions the officer is allowed to perform, the more time detectives will have to work on specialized cases. Criminal investigations should be considered the responsibility of the entire department, and what better way to incorporate this premise than to increase the patrol's responsibility for investigations?

Patrol officers can and do solve crimes. For example, a study conducted by the Stanford Research Institute for the Oakland police department revealed that the patrol force had a better record of clearing cases than the detective unit. It also found that unless relevant information is discovered at the crime scene or a suspect identified, the detectives have little chance of solving the case. (Greenberg, 1975, pp. xvi, xx)

The Modern Investigator

Criminal investigation is a thinking and reasoning process. The modern investigator's primary objective is to gather facts about a criminal situation. This objective is accomplished by collecting all the accurate information pertaining to a specific act or crime. The initial steps are descriptive in nature. In this stage the investigator describes things and persons present without making any inferences among them or even to the crime. The investigator assembles documents and evidence and reviews the facts, evaluating every detail of the crime scene carefully and systematically.

Then the facts gathered must be linked to the crime. To bring an investigation to a successful conclusion, the investigator "creates hypotheses which link one fact to another and then, by linking the hypotheses, constructs a theory that explains the crime as a whole. In part, this is a process of determining which 'apparent' facts are 'real' facts, which factors are not relevant to the crime, and how the facts are interrelated." (Fitzgerald and Cox, 1987, pp. 8–9) For example, a man running out of a grocery store may lead an investigator to infer that the man committed a crime. However, the man may just be late for a bus. Information must be gathered to determine the facts.

The investigator must observe the crime scene very carefully, observing both what is present and what is missing. The investigator must put the puzzle together and establish the facts that link all the information and evidence to an individual responsible for the crime. The linkage can be delineated as follows:

The crime scene must be observed very closely. Detailing the nature and physical relationships of the evidence helps the investigator begin piecing the crime puzzle together.

- **Theory of crime**. The more facts can be shown to be consistent with theory and the tighter (i.e., the fewer the gaps in) the evidence, the more confidence the investigator has in the theory of crime he or she has formulated.
- **Inductive logic** moves from a number of particular and separate observations to a generalization. For example, from the bloodstains and the wounds, together with the laboratory reports, the investigator induces that the knife was the weapon used in the crime.
- **Deductive logic**, on the other hand, moves from the general to the particular. For example, from the observations that violent assaults are typically committed by a person with whom the victim has at least some social acquaintances, and that the last person the victim was seen with was one of the victim's relatives, the investigator might deduce that the victim was assaulted by this particular relative. (Fitzgerald and Cox, 1987, pp. 9–10)

Any conclusions must be based on reasoning, factual information, and evidence. To maintain the integrity of the investigative process, the investigator must remain objective and control any preconceptions or prejudices. As early as 1900 Inspector John D. Shea recognized the importance of the reasoning process for successful investigators. He stated, "The successful detective is called upon without time for much deliberation, to unravel these plots, to remove the obstacles placed in his way, and to get at the truth." (Dilworth, 1969, p. 52)

Detective Work, a study of criminal investigations by William B. Saunders, divides working an investigative case into five parts.

1. Establish a case of a reported incident as an instance of a specific crime or as otherwise warranting investigation.
2. Identify a suspect.
3. Locate the suspect.
4. Learn that the suspect can show irrefutable evidence of innocence, in which case the detective will have to start all over again trying to identify a more likely culprit.
5. Dispose of the case in one of several ways. (Saunders, 1977, p. 79)

During the 1970s, a number of studies reviewed the investigative process in larger municipal law enforcement departments and the federal government. They also examined different types of investigative activities, dividing the work of criminal investigators into six categories. Detectives solve crimes reported to them. Undercover agents infiltrate crime rings. Intelligence analysts conduct operations designed to obtain information about specific illegal groups. Neighborhood criminal investigators work in precinct or neighborhood stations and investigate routine crimes. Headquarters specialists are organized into specialized squads and concentrate on major crimes, such as robbery or homicide. Administrative personnel engage in anticrime patrol or case preparation. Their work is essentially clerical and may be used to boost morale. (Reppetto, 1978, p. 7)

Duties and Responsibilities

The responsibility of investigators is to gather facts to solve crimes. They seek the truth about a specific event. Their goal of breaking a case should be based on ethics, legal guidelines, accuracy, and a sincere search for the truth. To be successful, investigators must develop cooperation with the patrol force and crime lab personnel and be able to communicate with people in all socioeconomic classes and professions. Activities that investigators may be required to perform include the following:

- Determine that a crime was committed.
- Search the crime scene.
- Photograph and sketch the crime scene.
- Collect and process physical evidence.
- Interview victims and witnesses.
- Interrogate suspects.

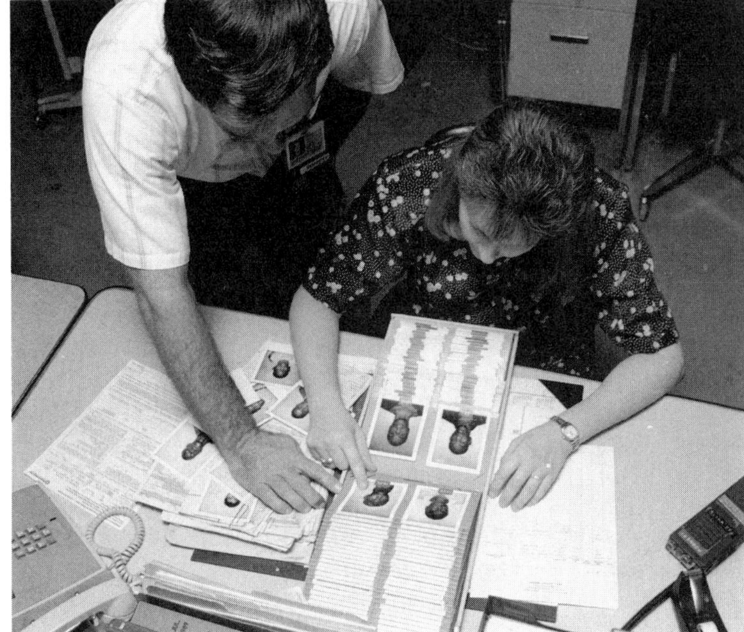

Police administration personnel assist in case preparation by searching photo lineups for likely suspects.

- Maintain field notes and write preliminary, follow-up, supplementary, and arrest reports.
- Maintain surveillance over suspects and known criminals.
- Recover stolen property.
- Arrest suspects.
- Prepare the case for court.
- Testify in court.

Criminal investigators must be familiar with investigative techniques and sources of information. They should also be familiar with departmental policy and legal guidelines established by the courts. A knowledge of criminal law and criminal procedures is expected of all investigators, regardless of their specialization.

Types of Investigations

Law enforcement personnel conduct several types of investigation. First, there are investigations of violations of laws and ordinances. Examples are crime and traffic accident investigations.

Second are investigations into the character, background, and suitability of individuals to determine their eligibility for positions of public trust. Third are investigations of conditions or circumstances that if left unchecked would result in an increase in traditional crimes. Examples are vice and organized crime investigations and studies to evaluate the effect of community facilities and programs upon juvenile delinquency. (International Association of Chiefs of Police, 1975, p. 2)

Summary

Criminal investigation has evolved slowly. The investigative process is usually associated with the establishment of public law enforcement agencies. American criminal investigation as a specialization has its roots in Europe, primarily in England. American police departments began appointing detectives during the mid-1880s.

In a contemporary American police department, the patrol officer has a vital role to play, such as conducting the initial investigation. The modern investigator's primary objective is to gather facts about a criminal situation. The investigator must link the facts to the crime. An investigator's duties and responsibilities include determining if a crime was committed and interviewing victims and witnesses. A criminal investigator needs broad knowledge of such topics as criminal law, criminal procedures, and investigative techniques.

Key Terms

Bow Street Runners
Thomas Byrnes
deductive logic
Henry Fielding
inductive logic
kin policing
Laws of Hammurabi
messenger
operative
Allan Pinkerton
Revenue Cutter Service
Star Chamber
Sûreté
theory of crime
Thief Taker
trial by combat
trial by ordeal
Twelve Tables
Francis Tukey
François-Eugenè Vidocq

Review Questions

1. Describe the various methods used to obtain information from individuals.
2. Describe Allan Pinkerton's contribution to the field of investigation.
3. What role do patrol officers play in the investigative process?
4. What are the duties and responsibilities of a modern criminal investigator?

References

Block P, Weidman D: *Managing Criminal Investigations.* Washington, DC: U.S. Government Printing Office, 1975.

Costello A: *Our Police Protectors: A History of the New York Police.* Montclair, NJ: Patterson, 1972.

Dilworth R: *The Blue and the Brass 1890–1900.* Gaithersburg, MD: International Association of Chiefs of Police, 1969.

Fitzgerald J, Cox S: *Research Methods in Criminal Justice: An Introduction.* Chicago, IL: Nelson-Hall, 1987.

Greenberg B, et al: *Felony Investigation Decision Model: An Analysis of Investigative Elements of Information.* Menlo Park, CA: Stanford Research Institute, 1975.

Horan J: *The Pinkertons: The Detective Dynasty that Made History.* New York, NY: Crown Publishers, 1967.

International Association of Chiefs of Police: *Criminal Investigation: Basic Procedures,* Vol. 1. Gaithersburg, MD: IACP, 1975.

Lane R: *Policing the City: Boston 1822–1885.* Cambridge, MA: Harvard University Press, 1967.

Pringle P: *The Thief-Taker.* London, England: Museum Press, 1958.

Reppetto T: The Detective Task: State of the Art. *Police Studies* 1:3, 1978.

Saunders WB: *Detective Work.* New York, NY: Free Press, 1977.

Thorwald J: *The Century of the Detective.* New York, NY: Harcourt, Brace, and World, 1964.

CHAPTER 2

Current Investigative Practices

Historically, police administrators have created a public impression that all crimes reported to the police are investigated. But the Uniform Crime Reports for the United States show that law enforcement agencies cleared only 21 percent of crime index offenses in 1988. A 46-percent clearance rate was reported for violent crimes. (p. 157)

In 1967, the President's Commission on Law Enforcement and Administration of Justice noted that only 25 percent of major crimes reported were cleared by arrest. The commission found that "if the suspect is neither known to the victim nor arrested at the scene of the crime, the chances of ever arresting him are slim." The problem was compounded by the fact that conviction after arrests was only 35 percent.

The Rand Study

In order to upgrade criminal investigative performance, one must first determine what criminal investigators actually do. The National Institute of Law Enforcement and Criminal Justice commissioned the Rand Corporation to study the police investigative role. The objects of the research were (1) to describe, on a national scale, current investigative organization and practices, (2) to assess the contribution that police investigation makes to the achievement of criminal justice goals, (3) to ascertain the effectiveness of new technology and systems being adopted to enhance investigative performance, and (4) to reveal how investigative effectiveness relates to differences in organizational form, staffing, and procedures. (Greenwood and Petersillia, 1975, p. 1)

Findings

The Rand study was limited to the felony offenses of homicide, rape, assault, robbery, burglary, and theft. The Rand analysis of criminal investigators' performance was based upon a questionnaire completed by 153 police agencies and a detailed review of investigative operations in twenty-five police departments. From a two-year study of the criminal investigative process, Rand concluded:

- Differences in investigative training, staffing, work load, and procedures appear to have no appreciable effect on crime, arrest, or clearance rate.
- The method by which police investigators are organized (e.g., team policing, specialist vs. generalist, patrol officers, or investigators) is related to variations in crime, arrest, and clearance rate.
- Substantially more than half of all serious reported crimes receive only superficial attention from investigators.
- Investigators' time is largely consumed in reviewing reports, documenting files, and attempting to locate and interview people in cases that experience shows will not be solved. For cases that are solved (i.e., a suspect is identified), investigators spend more time in post-clearance processing than in identifying the perpetrator.
- The single most important determinant of whether or not a case will be solved is the information the victim supplies to the immediate responding patrol officer. If information that uniquely identifies the perpetrator is not presented when the crime is reported, the perpetrator will probably not be subsequently identified.
- Most police departments collect more physical evidence than can productively be processed. Allocating resources to increasing the department's processing capabilities can lead to more identifications than some other investigative actions.
- Latent fingerprints rarely provide the only basis for identifying a suspect.
- In relatively few departments do investigators consistently and thoroughly document the key evidentiary facts that reasonably assure that the prosecutor can obtain a conviction on the most serious applicable charges.
- Police failure to document a case's investigation thoroughly may have contributed to a higher case-dismissed rate and a weakening of the prosecutor's plea-bargaining position.

- Most crime victims strongly desire to be notified officially as to whether or not the police have "solved" their case and what progress has been made toward convicting the suspect.
- Investigative strike forces have a significant potential to increase arrest rates for a few difficult target offenses, provided they remain concentrated on activities for which they are uniquely qualified. In practice, however, they are frequently diverted elsewhere. (Greenwood and Petersillia, 1975, pp. 2–5)

The Rand study destroys some of the mystique of investigative work and brings into focus a realistic concept of criminal investigation. One perception that may not be correct is that criminal investigators dig up evidence all by themselves, spending hours identifying criminals and tracking them down. This study and others suggest that most information leading to a decision to officially take action and to a solution is provided by the victim. (Black, 1970, pp. 733–48) Information from the victim is important in deciding whether an official report will be taken. As the Rand study demonstrated and as most experienced investigators know, many perpetrators are either arrested at the crime scene, identified by the victim or a witness, or identified by evidence observed at the crime scene.

Another perception is that crime solution is strongly related to the number of officers assigned to the investigative unit. This perception is analogous to the belief that increased patrols will decrease the crime rate in an area. In addition to the Rand study, several other reports (for example, the Kansas City study and the works of James Q. Wilson) and current crime statistics raise doubts as to whether "more" always means "better."

A third perception brought into question by the Rand study is that all serious crime receives considerable investigative attention. The study showed that while homicide, rape, and suicide were thoroughly investigated, other serious offenses received little or no attention.

Another interesting finding was the importance of routine patrol in clearing cases when the offender's identity was not known at the time of the crime. As has been reported in numerous works on investigation, a patrol officer's proper observation, securing, and protection of the crime scene is critical in improving the recovery of trace evidence, tracks, and latent prints. The recovery of such evidence is further increased when evidence technicians are called to the crime scene. This evidence may eventually lead to the identity of the suspect, but it rarely provides the basis for initial identification.

Another important finding was the need to keep the victim

informed. Numerous victimization studies have stressed that victims want to be kept abreast of the progress of their case and any dispositions being considered. Lastly, the report points out the importance of stringent case screening and investigative thoroughness.

Recommendations

The Rand study proposed nine recommendations to make the investigative process more effective and efficient. (Of course, police should evaluate the recommendations to determine their application to their departments.)

1. Reduce follow-up investigation on all cases except those involving the most serious offenses.
2. Assign a generalist-investigator (who would handle the obvious leads in routine cases) to the local operations commander.
3. Establish a **Major Offender Unit** to investigate serious crimes.
4. Assign teams of serious-offense investigators.
5. Strengthen evidence-processing capabilities.
6. Increase the use of the information-processing system in lieu of investigators.
7. Employ strike forces selectively and judiciously.
8. Place post-arrest (suspect in custody) investigations under the authority of the prosecutor.
9. Initiate programs designed to impress on citizens the crucial role they play in crime solutions. (Greenwood and Petersillia, 1975, pp. x–xiii)

Despite the universality of investigative work in all jurisdictions, presently there exist diverse investigative practices, procedures, and organizational structures. The Rand study recommendations can introduce several administrative adjustments to improve the information-gathering process, unify investigative unit structure, and enhance cooperative efforts with other investigative support units. Victim/investigator communication educational programs should be initiated for both the general public and all members of the investigative unit. These programs should emphasize the importance of victims' cooperation and how their information is used in the investigative process.

Administrative adjustments in investigative unit structure may lead to improved case management. Assigning cases based on a priority system (as discussed later in this chapter) can balance control of personnel assignments and work loads. Less serious cases and those requiring limited follow-up should be handled by a generalist-investigator. In smaller departments, this investigator may be a patrol officer. The generalist-investigator should be under the control of a district or shift commander to improve communication and cooperation between the investigator and other patrol personnel.

Serious crimes should be assigned to a Major Offender Unit with a well-trained, skilled investigative staff. Several small departments could consolidate their personnel resources to create such a unit. Whichever investigative unit structure is decided upon, a team approach provides additional insight on the case being investigated and lets the investigation continue when one investigator is off duty.

Investigative support unit cooperation may be improved by care in departmental assignments and early involvement of such units in the investigation. To strengthen evidence-processing capabilities, the evidence technician should be called to the scene as soon as possible to direct the collection of evidence.

The importance of timely legal assistance in an investigation cannot be stressed enough. Cooperation between the investigator and prosecution staff members is imperative. In serious cases, prosecution assistance should be requested at the crime scene. This reduces the potential for technical error and gives the prosecution staff member immediate knowledge of the particulars of the case. Prosecution assistance in a post-arrest investigation will ensure a complete and thorough investigation.

Team Policing (Rochester System)

The Rand Corporation study on criminal investigations evaluated the managing of criminal investigations by police departments. The theme of the report was that the entire police department contributes to the investigation process. Patrol officers, supervisors, and administrators all improve the productivity of the investigation process with **team policing**. Historically, police managers have often allowed criminal investigative units to operate with more independence than other units. As one police chief describes the detective unit:

> In few endeavors does there appear to be a greater area of mysticism than in the field of police investigation. Not commonly present during the preliminary investigation phase performed by patrolmen, the investigative mystique of the detective's job is uniquely traditional in

Rochester's team approach, which encourages close working relationships between patrol officers and detectives, has been successfully implemented in several cities.

> police history. The almost conspiratorial vagueness that surrounds investigative effectiveness can be a serious impairment to an administrator's ability to measure and control this criminal function of the agency. (Tielsch, 1970)

The city of Rochester, New York, under the administration of Chief Thomas F. Hastings, developed a management of criminal investigation concept for its police department. In developing the program, the city took into consideration the rising crime rate, a poor clearance rate, and the apathy and unwillingness of the investigative division to improve its effectiveness. To address the structural problems of the Rochester Police Department, the following concepts became the basis for innovation.

- Responsibility for preliminary and follow-up investigations should focus on a unit commander to provide for better management and utilization of resources.
- Patrol officers should work closely with detectives to improve preliminary investigations. Both groups should be placed under the same unit commander, work out of the same quarters, and service the same designated area of the city. The patrol officers should be encouraged to expand their role as crime solvers.

- The patrol and investigation functions should be operationally and structurally placed together to provide for information exchange and address the problem of apathy in the central detective division.
- Patrol officers and detectives should be responsible for manageable-sized areas of the city to become more familiar with the neighborhood aspects of the crime problem.
- Unit commanders should be responsible for developing innovative techniques to be used in their areas of the city to improve the patrol and investigative functions.
- While concentrating on improving investigative effectiveness, the department must continue to provide other types of police services. (*MCT Supervisors Manual,* pp. 31–34)

To place these concepts into operation, the Rochester Police Department was divided into seven districts, each with a captain as unit head. Each district had eight investigators and thirty-two officers assigned to it, in addition to supervisory personnel. The detective division was decentralized, with investigators being transferred to the seven neighborhood police sections. The centralized detective unit maintains the **Physical Crimes Unit**, which handles serious crimes such as homicide and rape. It has kept responsibility for the **Persons Unit**, which handles juveniles, and the **Property Crimes Unit**, which processes licenses, the service of warrants, and the Checks and Fraud Squad.

As Chief Hastings of the Rochester Police Department said, "In effect, we have been decentralizing detectives in the belief that patrol officers and detectives operating as a unit can be more efficient in the solution of crimes." (*Crime Control Digest,* 1975, p. 9) The Police Foundation in an audit report prepared by the Urban Institute supports Chief Hastings's assumption. The report confirms that patrol officers and detectives working in teams are more successful in solving crimes than detectives functioning in traditional ways.

Case Screening

An important tool in the management of criminal investigations is **case screening**, which facilitates "making a decision concerning the continuation of an investigation based upon the existence of sufficient solvability factors obtained at the initial investigation." (Crawley, 1977, p. 37) Those elements of information pertaining to a crime that are important in determining the likelihood of solving it are known as **solvability factors**.

The purpose of case screening is to determine whether an investigation should be suspended or a follow-up investigation of the reported crime is needed. Case screening offers the investigator a more effective method for determining case direction than the traditional informal basis used by detectives. It reviews actual investigative work loads.

There are two approaches to case screening—a list of unweighted criteria and a list of weighted criteria. Either method is acceptable depending on the police department. The Rochester Police Department developed an unweighted case-screening system that begins with the preliminary investigation. The patrol officer decides if there are enough solvability factors to continue with a follow-up investigation. There are twelve solvability questions.

1. Was there a witness to the crime?
2. Can a suspect be named?
3. Can a suspect be located?
4. Can a suspect be described?
5. Can a suspect be identified?
6. Can the suspect vehicle be identified?
7. Is the stolen property traceable?
8. Is a significant modus operandi (MO) present?
9. Is there physical evidence present?
10. Is there a positive evidence technician's report?
11. Is there a significant reason to believe that the crime may be solved with a reasonable amount of investigative effort?
12. Was there a definite limited opportunity for anyone except the suspect to commit the crime? (Crawley, 1977, p. 41)

Weighted case screening may be either statistically or nonstatistically derived. The Multnomah County, Oregon, police department lists cases in order of priority. In establishing this approach to investigative priorities, "officers consider the seriousness of the crime, the amount of readily available information about suspects, the availability of agency resources, and community attitudes." (Crawley, p. 37) Four major aspects of the crime are considered by the officers and rated numerically.

A. *Gravity of Offense*
   Felony = 4 points
   Misdemeanor = 3 points

Victimless crime = 2 points
Violations/status = 1 point

B. *Probability of Solution*
Suspects
Witnesses
Physical evidence
Undeveloped leads
(Score one point for each factor present.)

C. *Urgency for Action*
Danger to the other = 4 points
Immediate action required = 3 points
Impact on victims = 2 points
Pattern/frequency of crime = 1 point

D. *Supervisory Judgment*
Department policy
Totality of circumstances
Investigator's caseload
(The supervisor can add up to 4 points in this category.)

Priority	Points	Report Investigative Process Within
1	16–22	1–5 days
2	10–15	6–15 days
3	4–9	16–30 days
4	Less than 4	Suspended (form letter to victim)

Source: Team Policing, *Police Chief*, 1976, pp. 65–67

In the case-screening approach, the patrol officer collects complete and factual crime information. The officer determines the sufficiency of crime information collected and decides whether a follow-up investigation is necessary. A supervisor reviews the officer's decision.

The reality that case screening addresses is that the police cannot investigate all crimes. The case screening of reporting crimes can eliminate wasted effort and energy by, for example, minimizing or eliminating paperwork.

Investigative Function

Criminal investigations usually are divided into two areas, preliminary and follow-up, but a third area may be added—the special-subject investigation.

Preliminary Investigations

A **preliminary investigation** is initiated when a police officer answers a citizen's complaint of a reported crime. The preliminary investigation provides the foundation for the criminal case. It is aimed at identifying the offender, determining what occurred, locating witnesses if available, and obtaining physical evidence. During the preliminary investigation, the investigator accumulates specific information pertaining to the crime. He or she searches for evidence; questions suspects, victims, and witnesses; records all statements; identifies, examines, collects, and processes physical evidence; and photographs, measures, and sketches the scene. It is during this phase of the investigative process that solvability factors are identified. The quality of this initial investigative effort and report usually determines whether the crime will be solved.

The objectives of the preliminary investigation are to determine that a crime actually occurred, discover who committed the crime, and apprehend the offender. The investigator, usually a patrol officer, must collect data about the crime with the anticipation of court action when an arrest is made. The importance of the preliminary investigator's role cannot be overemphasized. He or she is far more than a note-taker. The contents of the investigative report must be accurate and factual.

After determining that a crime has occurred, the preliminary investigator must define the crime and identify the leads or solvability factors. Based upon solvability factors, the preliminary investigator determines whether the case can be closed early. Solvability factor information such as witness information, vehicle description, property details, and suspect data are important in determining the solvability of the case. The solvability factor search determines who the offender is and where he or she can be found. The initial investigation must be competently conducted and reported, and follow-up investigations should be continued only when success is possible.

The preliminary investigator should communicate the case status to victims and to important witnesses when possible. If the victim receives a copy of the investigative report, he or she can assume responsibility to provide additional information that may be useful to the police. The report also gives the victim a statement of the police action taken. The initial investigator should leave a business card with all persons interviewed, requesting that they get in touch if any additional information becomes available.

The preliminary investigation is the most important part of the criminal investigation process. In smaller police departments, it

This investigator is pursuing a lead by searching for bullet casings.

may be the entire investigation. In larger police departments, it eliminates duplication of effort.

Follow-Up Investigations

The **follow-up investigation** indicates the existence of sufficient solvability factors or leads for a detective to continue the case. The detective usually has freedom of movement and special skills to continue the investigation. The follow-up investigation extends beyond the crime scene and into the community. During this process, the detective thoroughly reviews the preliminary investigation to make sure valuable leads were not overlooked. The detective may have to duplicate some of the preliminary investigation if he or she finds weaknesses.

The investigator has specific tasks to perform, including "collecting evidence, recording the information, interviewing witnesses, and the like." (*Criminal Investigator: Basic Procedures*, 1973, p. 11) The purpose is to identify leads and follow them as far as possible toward apprehending the criminal. When a lead has been followed as far as possible without solving the case, the detective must determine whether the case status should be changed to inactive.

Investigators answer the questions who, what, when, how, and why as they pertain to each specific case. They also compare the case under investigation with similar cases in hopes of linking similar crimes together. Detectives determine how much time and effort to devote to the various phases of the investigative process.

The objectives of solving each case depend upon the case and the individual investigator. The investigator may use crime analysis (discussed in the next section) to determine any crime patterns and trend analysis helpful in proving linkages. The detective has the final responsibility for preparing the case for prosecution. The investigator's effort will directly affect the success record of the detective unit in obtaining convictions.

Special-Subject Investigations

Special-subject investigations concentrate on sensitive areas such as organized crime, vice, and narcotics. As with other forms of investigation, the special investigation's goal is the apprehension of offenders. It also focuses on developing informants to identify crime patterns that can lead to apprehension. Intelligence gathering is an important objective of the special investigative process.

Crime Analysis

Crime Analysis uses information collected from reported crimes and criminal offenders to prevent crimes and apprehend and suppress criminal offenders. Police operations are supported by crime analysis through strategic planning, manpower development, and investigative assistance. Crime analysis has always been conducted informally by police officers and investigators, but in the last decade, some bigger departments have established formal crime analysis units to assist investigators in crime solving.

The crime analysis unit receives information from the patrol, detective, records, communications, administration, and special units. It also collects information from outside agencies such as corrections, probation, state records, private organizations, and other law enforcement agencies. The information collected internally within the police department consists of preliminary investigative reports, supplementary reports, arrest reports, field contact reports, offense reports, statistical data, and various other department reports. Information collected from external agencies includes status and records of known offenders and crime problems in other law enforcement agencies.

Crime analysis units are most appropriate for crimes with a high probability of apprehension or suppression. They review all information obtained to determine its reliability and validity. The storage system may be either computerized or mechanical. Records are usually divided into criminal history files, property files, suspect vehicle files, crime description files, and known offender files. The crime analysis unit develops universal information factors such as suspect, vehicle, property, loss, and victim descriptors as well as geographic and chronological factors. Beyond universal factors, there are specific elements for each specific crime committed. These specific elements are analyzed to determine connecting links and patterns with similar crimes.

Crimes that are analyzed include robbery, burglary, theft, fraud, forgery, rape, other sex crimes, assault, and murder. A police department may not have the capabilities or the need to perform in-depth analyses of all crimes. For example, the Rochester Police Department analyzes only burglary, and rape and other sex offenses—the crimes with the greatest possibility of being solved.

The crime analysis unit disseminates its findings to the operational divisions either formally or informally. The unit may disseminate information as needed or on a monthly, weekly, or even daily basis. The unit develops lead reports for investigators and crime pattern information bulletins. Information can also be transferred to investigators through informal verbal communication.

The crime analysis unit correlates information, analyzes it, and gives it back to the investigator. This process aids in control and coordination of information. The purpose of the crime analysis unit is to assist the criminal investigator in solving, preventing, and suppressing crime. (Buck, 1973, pp. xv–xviii)

Specialized Units

Specialization of certain types of investigations has advantages over generalization. Obviously, specialized investigative units should only be established when a need exists. For example, before establishing a homicide unit a department should justify the need for it based on the number of killings occurring in its jurisdiction.

The *Task Force on Police* (1975, p. 235) recommends that police agencies with fewer than 75 people should assign criminal investigative specialists on the basis of need, defined as a heavy caseload and extensive follow-up. The *Task Force* further suggests specialization

Members of a specialized crime analysis unit use computer-generated information to help refine a city's beat structure.

for specific crimes when it increases effective use of investigative resources.

A study of the criminal investigative process sponsored by the Law Enforcement Assistance Administration recommended that a Major Offenders Unit be established in police agencies to investigate serious crimes. (Greenwood and Petersilia, 1975, p. x) Homicide, rape, assault, and robbery warrant special investigative efforts. In a Major Offenders Unit, trained and experienced investigators with access to modern information systems can concentrate their efforts on solving serious crimes.

Specialization has the potential (Eastman and Eastman, 1971, p. 19) for:

- a more precise placing of responsibility,
- more intensive training,
- a concentration of experience to develop and maintain skills,
- development of a high level of esprit de corps in the specialized unit, and
- general public or special-interest support.

Although specialization of investigative functions has its advantages, law enforcement agencies should recognize that it does have shortcomings. Police departments should establish specialized criminal investigative units only when they are needed.

Coordination

Criminal investigative activities should be coordinated with other operations in the police department. Good communications make for efficiency and effectiveness. Police departments should define procedures for sharing information among the various investigative specialists and patrol personnel. For example, homicide investigators should inform patrol officers on how to protect the crime scene when conducting a preliminary investigation. Investigators, crime personnel, and patrol officers all have a responsibility for successful completion of an investigation.

The *Task Force on Police* states, "Every police agency should coordinate criminal investigations with all other agency operations." (p. 236) It further advocates that this coordination should be supported by 1) clearly defined procedures for the exchange of information between investigative specialists and between those specialists and uniformed patrol officers, 2) systematic rotation of generalists into investigative specialties, and 3) equitable publicity regarding the efforts of all agency elements.

The police department of New York City and the Federal Bureau of Investigation (FBI) illustrated how two law enforcement agencies can investigate activities to solve a crime problem. In the late 1970s there was a rash of armed bank robberies in New York. Through a joint effort, the police and the FBI were able to clear 85 percent of the offenses in 1980 (compared to 52 percent in 1979). During the late 1970s and early 1980s the FBI and the NYPD were also responsible, through coordination of effort, for the arrest of Croatian terrorists. (Walton and Murphy, 1981).

Serial murders are another example of an investigative activity that provides a positive view of coordination. During the mid-1980s, ten women in three jurisdictions in the Tampa Bay area were abducted, raped, and murdered. This investigation involved personnel from the Hillsborough County Sheriff's Office, the FBI, the Pasco County Sheriff's Office, and the Florida Department of Law Enforcement. The coordination of this homicide investigation led to an arrest and conviction. (Terry and Malone, 1987)

Relationship with the News Media

The news media play an important role in presenting information about crime to the public. To work effectively police agencies need an understanding of the news media and their cooperation. The goal of the media is to keep the public informed. Crime news is of interest to the community. Some news media personnel hold the philosophy, "If it bleeds, it leads." But many follow an unwritten code of not interfering with a criminal investigation.

There is specific information that cannot be announced. For example, in Georgia the names and addresses of rape victims and juveniles cannot be announced. Also, the electronic news media must follow federal communication guidelines. For example, all information presented over the airwaves must be substantiated. Television and radio cannot broadcast conversations without the consent of the parties.

Both broadcast and print media have various means of obtaining information about crimes, among them secondhand accounts and radio scanners. To keep specific incidents in perspective and make sure the public receives an accurate account, it is wise to release certain information. The department may want to limit the information to the following facts. (*The News Media . . . and You*, 1990, p. 6)

- The type of incident (homicide, robbery, etc.).
- The location of the incident.
- The time and date of the incident (if available).
- A description of the suspect.
- Whether weapons were used.
- The extent of injuries, if any.

The news media have the right to disseminate any information they can obtain, but police investigators can restrict access to information. They can bar the media from crime scenes or from areas where they could interfere with or jeopardize an investigation. "Police may lawfully cordon such areas, restricting all persons (press and public) from entering until such time as the police operation is completed or access poses no risk to law enforcement interests." (Higginbotham, 1989, p. 28)

Figure 2–1 shows the news media policy of the City of Savannah, Georgia. Figure 2–2 is a media code of ethics created by the National Organization for Victim Assistance.

Summary

The Rand study destroys some of the mystique of investigative work and brings into focus a realistic concept of criminal investigative tasks. The nine recommendations of the Rand study for improving criminal investigations can help the police department.

FIGURE 2–1: News Media Policy of Savannah, Georgia

I. SUBJECT: NEWS MEDIA POLICY

II. PURPOSE: The Savannah Police Department recognizes the need for an informed public. Maintaining a relationship of mutual trust, cooperation and respect with the news media is essential to obtaining the support of the public this agency services. The purpose of this policy is to establish a cooperative climate in which media representatives may obtain information on matters of public interest. However, on occasion, certain information must be withheld from the news media to protect the constitutional rights of an accused, to avoid interfering with a department investigation, or because the information is legally privileged.

III. APPLICABILITY: This policy applies to all members (sworn and civilian) of the Savannah Police Department. It is designed to regulate the release of any information, whether case related or administrative, to the media.

IV. PROCEDURES:

A. PERSONNEL AUTHORIZED TO RELEASE INFORMATION

1. Public Information Officer:

(a) It is the responsibility of the designated Public Information Officer (PIO) to gather the facts of an incident and release the information to the news media. The Public Information Officer is to be regarded as the point of control for information dissemination to the media and as such shall be provided with information concerning ongoing investigations on a current basis.

(b) The PIO will be responsible for assisting news media personnel in gathering information and arranging interviews for daily news stories, and at the scenes of incidents.

(c) The PIO will be responsible for drafting written press releases to be distributed to all news media. These written press releases will be equally available to all news media as necessitated by specific occurrences within this agency's jurisdiction.

(d) The PIO will be responsible for arranging and assisting at the department news conferences.

(e) The PIO will be available for on-call responses to the scenes of major police activity to release information to the news media.

(f) The PIO will assist with crisis situations within the agency. The PIO's involvement will be consistent with duties described in this section.

(g) The PIO will coordinate and authorize, at the chief's direction, the release of information concerning confidential agency investigations and operations.

2. AT THE CRIME SCENE

(a) The highest ranking officer at the scene of an incident can release pertinent information to the news media. However, only verified, preliminary information on the incident is to be released at the scene. For more detailed information, the news media is to be referred to the Public Information Officer.

3. AT POLICE HEADQUARTERS

(a) The Information Officer on the front desk is to provide news media representatives with the department press board which contains copies of officers incident reports. Media representatives also are entitled to review continuation reports; however, continuation and supplemental reports are not to be posted on the press board. Rape and juvenile reports will not be posted either. News media representatives *are not* entitled to review supplemental reports.

(b) For information on major case investigations (i.e., homicide, suicide, rape, etc.), the Information Officer on the front desk will refer news media representatives to the Public Information Officer or detective supervisor for more detailed information. If neither the PIO nor the detective supervisor is available, the Watch Commander may release pertinent information.

(c) In the absence of the Public Informa-

FIGURE 2-1: *(Continued)*

tion Officer, the detective supervisor on duty will be responsible for gathering and releasing follow-up information on incidents to the news media.

B. INFORMATION GATHERING

1. Preliminary Information: The Watch Commander will ensure that preliminary reports are delivered to the Information Desk periodically during the shift. The Information Officer at the front desk will ensure that reports are promptly placed on the press after hours, or filed in the PIO's box during regular duty hours.

2. FOLLOW-UP INFORMATION

(a) During regular duty hours, the PIO will maintain close contact with the detective office for updated information on cases or incidents under investigation. After reguar duty hours, the detective supervisor can supply updated information to the news media. The detective officer is responsible for releasing information only on immediately occurring incidents, such as an arrest on an old case or a recently received major case. For routine updates on cases under investigation, media representatives will be referred to the PIO.

(b) The existence of the Public Information Officer does not imply any prohibition on other department personnel with regard to speaking to members of the news media. Indeed, the very nature of news gathering necessitates the immediate retrieval of accurate, factual information and often the best source of such information is the patrol officer or investigator. Department personnel may respond to media inquiries relating to police matters in which they are personally involved or about which they are sufficiently informed. If not personally knowledgeable about the subject of the inquiry, department personnel are to refer the person making the inquiry to someone capable of providing the information:
(1) Public Information Officer
(2) Detective Supervisor
(3) Bureau Commander

C. INFORMATION RELEASED

1. Each incident must be considered in light of its particular circumstances. Generally, this department is concerned with whether the release of information will hamper or interfere with an investigation, unnecessarily embarrass or jeopardize an innocent person, or promote pre-trial prejudice to the extent that a fair trial becomes difficult or impossible. For that reason, no statement or information will be released which is potentially prejudicial to the rights of the accused or which could compromise the prosecution's case. Specifically, information not to be released to the media includes:
(a) Names of juveniles or rape victims
(b) Statements made by the accused following arrest
(c) Details of suspect's previous arrest record
(d) Specific details of an incident identified as confidential by the District Attorney's office or the detective office.
2. The news media will be provided with the names of all persons (except juveniles) and the charges against the person after booking. Such information will not be released if the premature disclosure of the information would interfere with an ongoing investigation.
3. When contacted by a media representative, department personnel may request proper credentials prior to releasing any information or allowing media representatives access to any restricted area.
4. If a media representative requests information by telephone and the person is not known to the department employee receiving the telephone call, the PIO is not available to receive the call, the department employee may establish the identity of the caller by telephoning his or her agency.
5. Information on police policies, procedures, or announcements of general interest to the public, will be released only by the Chief of Police or at his direction.

(continued on next page)

FIGURE 2-1: *(Continued)*

D. RELEASE OF STATISTICAL INFORMATION

1. Release of Part I crime statistical information, not already included in regularly published crime reports, will be cleared in writing by the statistical analyst. The senior management analyst will approve such releases. Such approvals will be recorded in writing and filed together with the information released.
2. Any commissioned officer may release Part I crime statistics that have already been prepared by the Staff Services Bureau. However, the interpretation or analysis of all Part I statistical information will be done by either the Staff Services Bureau, the PIO or the Chief of Police.
3. All other statistical information, peculiar to individual bureaus, may be released by Bureau Commanders. It is noted that analysts of the Staff Services Bureau may be consulted to ensure consistency, accuracy and reliability of the information released to the news media. The analyst also will ensure that sound methods were used to gather the data.
4. All individuals authorized to release statistical data should consult analysts of the Staff Services Bureau to ensure the consistency, accuracy and reliability of the data. When interpretation or analysis of the data is required, it should be cleared with the Staff Services Bureau and the clearance recorded in writing and filed together with the data released.

E. INTERACTION WITH THE NEWS MEDIA

1. It is the policy of the Savannah Police Department to assist all accredited representatives of newspaper, radio, television and other news media gather information pertaining to the activities of the department.
2. Members of this department are urged to be as courteous as possible to accredited representatives of the news media.
3. The Savannah Police Department issues news media identification cards to authorized representatives of the news media. Media representatives are required to identify themselves by wearing the card on an outer garment while on police department property or while at crime scenes. The news media identification cards will be renewed annually to ensure that only legitimate cards are in circulation. News media identification cards remain the property of the Savannah Police Department and may be revoked for refusal to cooperate with police or for any interference with police activity.
4. It is often necessary to establish police lines to limit access to the scene of a crime or other serious incident. Police lines will be established if:
   (a) access to the scene would jeopardize the life of an officer or citizen.
   (b) access to the scene would limit quick police response to a rapidly changing situation.
   (c) access to the scene would destroy the integrity of the crime scene.
   (d) access behind established police lines for the news media is prohibited.
5. When feasible, all news media will be invited to offer input into the development of changes in policies and procedures relating to the news media. News media participation, when possible, in the process of developing said policies and procedures is encouraged as a means of establishing a cooperative climate between this agency and the news media.

F. MULTI-AGENCY INFORMATION RELEASE

1. When the Savannah Police Department is involved in a mutual effort with other service agencies (i.e., Fire Department, FBI, etc.) the agency with primary jurisdiction over the incident will be responsible for the release of information, or coordinating the release of information to the news media.

____________________ Date

____________________ Chief of Police

Source: Courtesy of the Savannah Police Department, 1988.

FIGURE 2-2: Media Code of Ethics

Proposed by the National Organization for Victim Assistance

In recognition that crime and trauma victims who are most of interest to the media deserve to be treated as *innocent* victims; are likely to be in a state of crisis; are likely to say and do things in that vulnerable state which they later consider undignified and embarrassing; are not likely to have had any experience in working with the media; are therefore vulnerable to "second injuries" by inaccurate, intrusive, or unfair press coverage; and may, in later times, re-experience their trauma if their stories are republicized without warning,

I shall:

Give the public factual, objective crime reports, including:

- the type of crime that has occurred;
- the community where the crime occurred;
- the name and description of a suspected or convicted offender if permitted by law; and
- significant facts that may prevent other crimes;

Present a balanced view of crime by ensuring that the victim and the criminal perspectives are given equal coverage whenever possible and appropriate;

When requesting to speak with victims, explain what experienced news sources already know—that they may be interviewed on or off the record, or on limited topics of their choosing, if they desire to give an interview; and further advise them that they have a right not to be interviewed at all;

Quote victims, family members, and friends fairly and in context, appreciating that their most dramatic statements may be misunderstood if not tempered by other statements also made by these sources;

Notify and ask permission of victims and their families before using "file-copy" videotapes or photographs for documentaries, news updates, or features;

In writing longer feature articles on victimization subjects, or in hosting radio and television talk shows, use the media as a public education service, with reliable information about the patterns of behavior and reactions being discussed, and always offer readers, listeners, and viewers the name and number of a qualified crisis line for victims and former victims for whom the show or article is a crisis-inducing event.

I shall not:

Photograph, film, or videotape detailed shots of crime scenes, remains of bodies, or visual evidence of brutality, instruments of torture, or the disposal of bodies; and never print or televise even general pictures of such scenes until assured that all relevant loved ones have been notified of the crime.

Print or broadcast unverified or ambiguous facts about the victim, his or her demeanor, background, or relationship to the offender.

Print or broadcast facts about the victim or the criminal act that might embarrass, humiliate, or hurt the victim unless there is a compelling need, such as an interest in the public's safety, to publish such facts.

Engage in any form of sensationalism in reporting crimes, their investigation, or prosecution, especially erring on the side of restraint with any victim or witness who was not previously a "public figure" or who has evidenced a desire not to become one as a result of the crime.

Source: Reprinted with permission of the National Organization for Victim Assistance.

The Rochester system is an example of successful team policing. The Rochester concept requires decentralization of the detective force and a good working relationship between detectives and patrol officers.

Another important tool in the management of criminal investigation is case screening, which helps determine whether to continue the investigation. In this process, solvability factors are calculated.

The three classifications of criminal investigation are preliminary, follow-up, and special-subject investigations. A preliminary investigation is initiated when a police officer answers a citizen's report of a crime. The follow-up investigation indicates the existence of sufficient solvability factors or leads for a detective to continue the case. In a special-subject investigation, effort concentrates on a selective area such as organized crime, vice, or narcotics.

A crime analysis unit correlates information, analyzes it, and gives it back to the investigator. This process allows for better control and coordination of information. The purposes of the crime analysis unit are to assist the criminal investigator in solving crime, preventing crime, and suppressing crime.

Specialization of certain types of investigations has advantages over generalization. Specialized investigative activities should be coordinated with other operations in the police department. Good communications enhance efficiency and effectiveness.

The news media play an important role in presenting information about crime to the public. Police agencies need to understand the news media and know how to gain their cooperation.

Key Terms

case screening
crime analysis
follow-up investigation
Major Offender Unit
Persons Unit
Physical Crimes Unit investigation
preliminary investigation
Property Crimes Unit
solvability factors
team policing
Special-Subject investigation

Review Questions

1. What are the major findings of the Rand study?
2. Discuss the recommendations of the Rand study.
3. Explain the Rochester team policing concept.
4. Explain case screening and solvability factors.
5. Explain the three classifications of criminal investigations.

References

Black D: Production of Crime Rate. *American Sociological Review*, 35:733–48, 1970.

Buck G: *Police Crime Analysis Unit Handbook*. Washington, DC: National Institute of Law Enforcement and Criminal Justice, 1973.

Crawley D: *Managing Criminal Investigators Manual*. Washington, DC: U.S. Government Printing Office, 1977.

Crime Control Digest vol. 9, 5:9, 1975.

Criminal Investigator: Basic Procedures, vol. 1. Gaithersburg, MD: International Association of Chiefs of Police, 1973.

Eastman G, Eastman E: *Municipal Police Administration*, Washington, DC: International Association of Chiefs of Police, 1971.

Greenwood P, Petersillia J: *The Criminal Investigative Process I: Summary and Police Implications*. Santa Monica, CA: Rand Corporation, 1975.

Higginbotham J: Legal Issues in Media Relations. *FBI Law Enforcement Bulletin* 57:8, 1989.

MCT Supervisors Manual. Rochester, NY: City of Rochester, 1970.

Task Force on Police. National Advisory Commission on Criminal Justice Standards and Goals, 1975.

The President's Commission on Law Enforcement and Administration of Justice: *The Challenge of Crime in a Free Society*. Washington, DC: Government Printing Office, 1967.

The President's Commission on Law Enforcement and Administration of Justice: *Task Force Report: The Police*. Washington, DC: Government Printing Office, 1976.

Team Policing: Management of Criminal Investigation. *Police Chief* 9:65–67, 1976.

Terry G, Malone M: "The Bobby Joe Long Serial Murder Case: A Study in Cooperation (Part I). *FBI Law Enforcement Bulletin* 56:11, 1987.

Terry G, Malone, M: U.S. Naval Investigative Service Command: *The News Media . . . and You*. Washington, DC: Washington Naval Yard, 1990.

Tielsch G: Unpublished Thesis: A Research Design for the Investigative Process in the Medium-sized Police Department. California State College at Long Beach, 1970.

Walton K, Murphy P: "Joint FBI/NYPD Task Forces: A study in cooperation." *FBI Law Enforcement Bulletin* 50:11, 1981.

CHAPTER 3

Legal Issues

An investigator has the responsibility of solving crimes and identifying offenders. The investigative process begins with the initial investigation to determine if a crime has been committed and continues until the case has been cleared or closed. Unless an investigation is discontinued because of insufficient solvability factors or information, the investigator's responsibility continues until the court process is completed.

A criminal investigator needs to know criminal laws and criminal procedures to bring a criminal offender through the criminal justice process. An investigator should develop good prosecutor relationships by conducting investigations along legal guidelines and collecting evidence and testimony within acceptable legal guidelines. Prosecutors need admissible evidence to present their case.

The investigator solves criminal cases by putting the **crime puzzle** together—that is, by obtaining witness descriptions and physical and circumstantial evidence. A good investigator is familiar with the legal aspects of a successful investigation. These include laws of arrest, search and seizure, search warrants, electronic surveillance, rules of evidence, admissions and confessions, and line-ups and identifications.

Arrest

The power to arrest is an awesome power. The authority to deprive a person of his or her freedom is unique to law enforcement officers. Because of the detrimental effect abuse of arrest powers can have on individuals and society, legal restrictions are placed on investigations and law enforcement officers in general. These include statutory and constitutional restrictions on both the federal and the state level.

The **Fourth Amendment** of the United States Constitution protects citizens from illegal arrests, or illegal seizure of their person. The Fourth Amendment states:

> The right of the people to be secure in their persons, houses, papers, and effects, against unreasonable searches and seizures, shall not be violated, and no warrants shall issue, but upon probable cause, supported by oath or affirmation, and particularly describing the place to be searched and the persons or things to be seized.

In 1980, the U.S. Supreme Court stated in *Payton v. New York* that "the simple language of the amendment applies equally to seizure of persons and to seizure of property." In 1963 in *Ker v. California,* the Supreme Court held that arrests by state and local law enforcement officers must meet the same standards that apply to federal law enforcement officers. "The Fourth Amendment applies to all seizures of the person," the Supreme Court has said, "including seizures that involve only a brief detention short of traditional arrest." (*United States v. Brignoni-Ponce,* 422 U. A. 873, 878, 95 S. Ct. 2574–2579 1975) The Georgia Supreme Court said: "A person is under arrest whenever his

A suspect trying to flee a crime scene can be arrested on probable cause.

liberty to come and go as he pleases is restrained no matter how slight such restraint may be."

An investigator or law enforcement officer must have **probable cause** before making a lawful arrest. The arresting officer needs probable cause, also known as reasonable grounds, to determine that a crime was committed. Probable cause means much more than intuition. It considers investigative experience, reasoning, and decision-making rationales. In *Brinegar v. United States* in 1949, the Supreme Court explained that "Probable cause exists where the facts and circumstances within the officers' knowledge and of which they had reasonable, trustworthy information, are sufficient in themselves to warrant a man of reasonable caution in the belief that an offense has been or is being committed."

Law enforcement officers can make lawful arrests upon probable cause either with or without arrest warrants. Modern statutes usually allow officers to make arrests without warrants when a crime has been committed in their presence, the offender is escaping, or the crime may be a felony and probable cause exists to make the arrest.

Whenever possible, however, investigators should obtain an **arrest warrant**, which gives the judiciary jurisdiction over the suspect to respond to criminal charges. An arrest warrant must usually meet the following requirements.

- It is supported by "probable cause."
- The affidavit for the warrant is supported by oath or affirmation.
- The person to be seized is particularly described.
- The warrant states the nature of the offense.
- The warrant designates the officer or class of officers who are directed to comply with the order of the court.
- The warrant is issued in the name of the state or the United States.
- The warrant is issued and signed by a neutral and detached judicial officer.

Specific states may have additional requirements. (Klotter and Kanovitz, 1981, pp. 121–128)

Search and Seizure

Investigators must keep abreast of recent court decisions relating to the Fourth Amendment. Failure to do so may hamper the investigative process. Although the Fourth Amendment generally requires that a valid search warrant be obtained for either a search or a seizure, there are exceptions to this general rule. The exceptions include search incident to arrest, consent searches, items in plain view, vehicles and containers, open fields, abandoned property, and stop and frisk.

When an officer takes an arrested person into custody, referred to as a **custodial arrest**, he or she can justify a search of that person. The Supreme Court permits a search of the person arrested and the area within the control of the arrestee. In 1973, in *United States v. Robinson*, the Supreme Court wrote:

> It is the fact of the lawful arrest which establishes the authority to search and we hold that in the case of a lawful custodial arrest a full search of the person is not only an exception to the warrant requirement of the Fourth Amendment but is also a "reasonable search" under that Amendment.

In *Chimel v. California*, the Supreme Court clarified that a search could be made of the area within an arrestee's immediate control. For example, a purse on a couch next to a woman arrested may be searched because it's within her immediate control. If the purse happens to be in another room, it cannot be searched.

A **consent search** occurs when a person voluntarily gives approval for an investigator to search the person or his or her premises or belongings. The investigator has the responsibility of obtaining a knowing and voluntary waiver. Threats, intimidation, deception, or the use of duress are not accepted by the courts. In a 1988 decision of the Eleventh Circuit Court of Appeals, *United States v. Bates*, a defendant's consent to search his automobile was determined to be voluntary, based on the fact that he was educated enough to understand the proceedings and had been informed of his right to refuse consent.

Plain view is a seizure doctrine, not a search doctrine. Investigators have the authority to seize contraband and criminal evidence lying in plain view. In *United States v. McDaniel*, the Supreme Court stated, "the police are not required to close their eyes and need not walk out and leave the article where they saw it," provided they were lawfully on the premises.

The Carrol doctrine, established in 1925 by the Supreme Court, held that because of the mobility of motor vehicles there are situations in which searches without warrant are justified. The courts have recognized four factors as important for warrantless searches of automobiles.

- Motor vehicles are highly mobile.
- An individual's expectation of privacy is less in an automobile than at home.
- Automobiles are frequently subject to government regulations.
- The contents of impounded vehicles are routinely inventoried to protect the property of the owner, protect the officers against claims for lost or stolen property, and protect the police from potential danger.

(*Georgia Law Enforcement Handbook*, 1984, pp. 81–82)

In *New York v. Belton*, the Supreme Court held that an arrestee and other occupants in a car are subject to having all articles and containers in the passenger compartment searched incident to an arrest.

In 1925 the Supreme Court held that the Fourth Amendment protection "is not extended to the open fields." Investigators can search an open field, orchard, beach, or some other area without a search warrant for items the investigator can see in plain view.

Warrantless searches can also be conducted on abandoned property. In the Abel case in 1960, upon the vacancy of a hotel room, a hotel manager gave approval for the room to be searched by an FBI agent. The Supreme Court held that when the room was vacated, possession returned to the hotel, which had authority to give consent to the search.

In **stop and frisk**, or field interrogation, law enforcement personnel have stopped and questioned suspicious individuals about their conduct. Stop and frisk is a police practice involving the temporary detention, questioning, and limited search of a person suspected of criminal activity. (Ferdico, 1979, p. 283)

Search Warrants

A valid **search warrant** makes a search legal and protects the investigator from civil and criminal liability. A search warrant is similar to an arrest warrant. It is an order in writing issued by a proper judicial authority in the name of the people, directed to a law enforcement officer, commanding the officer to search for certain personal property and bring it before the judicial authority named in the warrant. (Ferdico, 1979, p. 111)

Procedures for search warrants differ among the states and can be found in statutes, rules, and court decisions. It is the investigators' responsibility to learn the requirements of their state. An investigator obtains a search warrant from an authorized judge by swear-

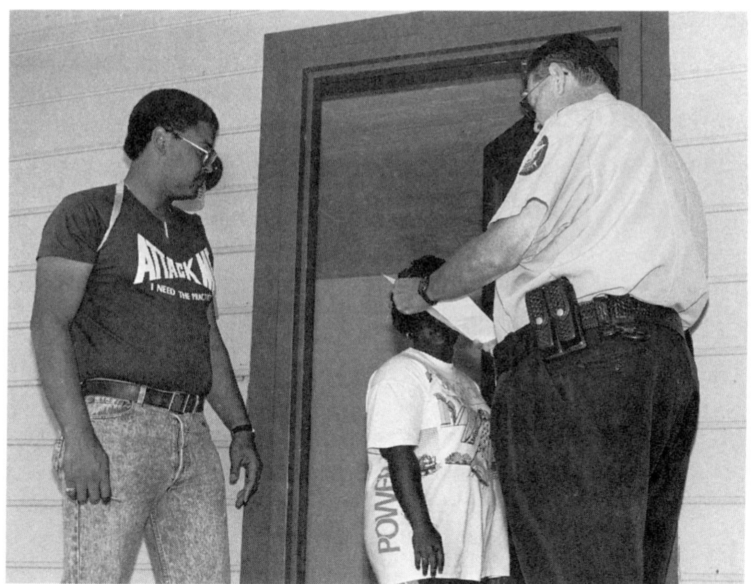

Serving a search warrant

ing an oath to an affidavit that the information presented and items to be seized are in the place described.

Most states require certain major characteristics for search warrants. The warrant specifically identifies and describes the property to be searched. The search warrant designates an investigator to perform the search and may specify time of day or no-knock search. The warrant is dated, signed by a judge, and returned to the judge with an inventory of items seized.

Generally, searches and seizures are considered unreasonable and in violation of the Fourth Amendment when done without a search warrant. Although there are exceptions, search warrants are more credible and preferred by the judiciary. Searches and seizures that are not valid are excluded as evidence. In *Weeks v. United States* in 1914, the Supreme Court held that evidence obtained illegally was inadmissable in federal courts. This is known as the federal exclusionary rule. In 1961, *Mapp v. Ohio* expanded the exclusionary rule to the states when the Supreme Court decided that evidence obtained illegally was inadmissable.

Electronic Surveillance

All forms of electronic surveillance must be conducted under regulations established by the Omnibus Crime Control and Safe Streets

Act (Title III) of 1968 and the statutes of individual states. The statutes usually consider serious offenses such as murder, kidnapping, and bribery of government officials to be valid causes for obtaining electronic warrants where permitted. Electronic surveillance for lesser reasons falls under the purview of "unreasonable searches and seizures" of the Fourth Amendment. Generally, **videotape surveillance** has been given court approval. Videotape surveillance has been used to record such events as Abscam investigators speaking with known gamblers and law enforcement officers talking to known criminals.

Rules of Evidence

An investigator usually needs evidence to make a case against an offender. Items or articles of evidence developed during an investigation can include latent prints, a plaster cast of tire tracks, blood-

Photographic surveillance of a crack house

stains found at a crime scene, or a weapon found on a suspect. Depending on the types of evidence discovered, it may be sent to a crime laboratory for analysis or to the police department's evidence room for safekeeping. A law enforcement officer must evaluate what will be considered legal evidence.

Rules of evidence may be defined as "a set of regulations which act as guidelines for judges, attorneys, and law enforcement officers who may be involved in the trials of cases." (Stuckey, 1980, p. 30) The rules were established to determine what happened during commission of a crime. Many law enforcement officers perceive rules of evidence as interference in their investigatory process.

One of the responsibilities of the investigator is to maintain the integrity of the evidence. He or she must know who has possession of the evidence at all times. The **chain of custody** traces the possession of the evidence from the moment the investigator gains control of it until its submission into court.

The investigator must first collect evidence that a crime was committed. The **corpus delicti**, meaning "the body of the crime" or "the element of the crime," must be proven by the prosecutor. For example, a jimmied kitchen door and a ransacked house with silverware missing are the corpus delicti of a burglary.

After it has been determined that a crime was committed and a chain of custody for evidence has been maintained, the next important question is the admissibility of the evidence. The rules of evidence determine what will be admitted in court and what must pass a series of tests. To be admissible, evidence must have been obtained legally and must meet federal and state constitutional restrictions. Any evidence obtained illegally will be inadmissible. For example, if an officer searches the trunk of a car without the owner's consent, finds cocaine, and then arrests the owner, the cocaine will be inadmissible because it was illegally obtained.

To be admissible, evidence must be considered material, relevant, and competent. **Material evidence** is important. For example, a handgun used in a murder would have great weight in assisting the jury to evaluate the facts of the case. **Relevant evidence** explains or provides additional information on the case. Relevant evidence helps to prove or disprove the case. For example, if burglary tools are found in the possession of a man leaving the scene of a reported burglary, they are relevant. Judges can use their discretion in admitting relevant evidence and often choose to screen out evidence that causes confusion or may prejudice the jury.

Competent evidence does not violate the exclusionary rule. For example, if an offender voluntarily confesses to a crime without being asked any question, his comments are admitted. The investigator must collect evidence in a legally acceptable way. Evidence must also be important to a case to be admissible. Any evidence the judge considers not of sufficient value will not be admitted. Judges attempt to keep judicial proceeding on track, and one avenue open to them is to find unimportant evidence inadmissible.

Additional evidence may be referred to as either corroborative or cumulative. "Corroborative evidence is that evidence which supports and confirms evidence already given. It is additional evidence of a different character about the same point. It has a tendency to strengthen other evidence presented." (Stuckey, p. 34) On the other hand, cumulative evidence is merely a repetition of evidence given before, usually by a different witness.

Types of Evidence

Evidence falls into the five general categories of direct evidence, indirect evidence, testimonial evidence, documentary evidence, and real evidence. *Direct evidence* is eyewitness evidence. For example, a witness saw the offender take the package from the front seat of the automobile. *Indirect*, or *circumstantial, evidence* implies that the offender committed the act. For example, the witness saw the offender walking away from the automobile with a package in his hand. *Testimonial evidence* is given orally by a witness. It does not have to be accompanied by real evidence. *Documentary* or *written evidence* includes everything from photographs to handwritten and printed materials. *Real evidence* consists of physical objects—for example, handguns, or fingerprints. All real evidence must be accompanied by testimonial evidence. It may consist of original objects, facsimile representations such as crime-scene sketches or photographs, tire tracks, bloodstains, wood particles, body fluids, hair, skin, and other items.

Investigators are expected to be familiar with the law and rules of evidence. They need to know what evidence will be acceptable. The burden of proof rests on the prosecutor while the investigator collects and develops the evidence that the prosecutor will present before the trier of the fact. Depending on where the case is in the judicial process, the **trier of the fact** may be either a judge or a jury. Evidence must be legally significant to be admissible. Evidence is not always factual. It may be open to interpretation, exaggeration, or even misunderstanding. The trier of the fact has the responsibility to evaluate the evidence.

Two terms that play a role in investigations are presumptions and inferences. A *presumption* is the drawing of a particular inference from a related fact. An *inference* is a deduction, logical conclusion, or assumption. For example, a witness who hears a gunshot

Plaster casts of tire tracks provide useful evidence for identifying a vehicle.

and sees a person walk out of a room with a gun may infer that the person lying on the floor was shot by the one who just walked out.

Importance of Evidence

Evidence possesses different degrees of importance from case to case and at various stages of a case (for example, whether it is being presented to a grand jury or at a trial). Another factor bearing on evidence is state procedural laws. Measures of importance in a criminal case include the following:

- *Proof beyond a reasonable doubt.* The burden of proof is on the state to produce enough evidence to convince the trier of the fact that, within a degree of sufficient certainty, the defendant is guilty. This does not mean, however, that the evidence must prove the defendant absolutely guilty, or guilty beyond question at all.

- *Preponderance of evidence.* A trier of the fact must be made to feel that the existence of that fact is more probable than not. If it were possible to weigh the evidence in a case on a scale, at least 51 percent of it—a preponderance—would have to be convincing.
- *Clear and convincing evidence.* Substantially more certainty may be required than a preponderance of evidence. Clear and convincing evidence would be about 80 percent convincing.
- *Prima facie evidence.* "First appearance" or "first impression" evidence is sufficient to raise a presumption of fact or establish some fact in question that hasn't already been rebutted or refuted. This kind of evidence may stand on its own merits without explanation if it isn't contradicted.
- *Reasonable suspicion.* The courts have consistently held that there's nothing unreasonable about an officer stopping a person and questioning him, or seeking an interview with possible suspects or witnesses, or calling on people in their homes where there seems to be good reason for doing so. (Kenney and More, 1979, pp. 43–46)

Admissions and Confessions

The due process clauses of the Fifth and Fourteenth Amendments require that admissions and confessions to crimes be made voluntarily. A confession may be defined as a statement implicating oneself in a crime. An admission is a confession, concession, or voluntary acknowledgment made by a party of the existence of certain facts. Admissions "are statements by a party, or someone identified with him in legal interest, of the existence of a fact which is relevant to the cause of his adversary." (Black, 1979, p. 45)

Confessions coercively obtained either through psychological or physical means are inadmissable since they violate due process. In addition to violence and brutality, the following police misconduct will violate due process and make any confession obtained inadmissable.

- Threats of violence.
- Confinement in a small space until the suspect confesses.
- Deprivation of food or sleep.

- Extended periods of incommunicado interrogation.
- Promises of leniency.
- Trickery or deception.
- Obtaining a statement during a period of unnecessary delay between arrest and arraignment. (Ferdico, p. 310)

To determine if the admission or confession was made voluntarily, the courts will review the characteristics of the defendant, including age, education, mental capacity, physical impairment, and prior dealing with the police. The 1964 decision *Escobedo v. Illinois* focused on a single circumstance. The Supreme Court emphasized the accusatory focus of investigators to elicit a confession.

In 1966, the Supreme Court again emphasized the single focus of the investigation and shifted the area of inquiry to the **Fifth Amendment** in *Miranda v. Arizona.* The Court said, "the prosecution may not use statements, whether exculpatory or inculpatory, stemming from custodian interrogation of the defendant unless it demonstrates the use of procedural safeguards against self-incrimination." (*Miranda v. Arizona* 384 U.S. 444 86 S.C., 1612)

Trial courts evaluate the circumstances surrounding a confession to determine if it was voluntary and free from duress. The Supreme Court requires a warning at the time of interrogation to overcome its pressures and to make sure the individual knows he or she is free to remain silent at all times. Since the **Miranda decision**, law enforcement officers have been reading suspects their constitutional rights.

> You have the right to remain silent. Anything you say can and will be used against you in a court of law. You have the right to talk to a lawyer and have him present while you are being questioned. If you cannot afford to hire a lawyer, one will be appointed to represent you before any questioning, if you wish.

Suspects should also be asked whether they understand their rights and understand that they are free to talk if they want to or refuse to answer any questions.

Line-Ups and Identification

There are a variety of ways to identify suspects. Perhaps the most important are eyewitness and photographic identification. Identification testimony in court comes from having a witness point out the defendant, asking the eyewitness if he or she identified the defendant earlier, or having a third person testify that the witness identified the defendant on an earlier occasion. (*Georgia Law Enforcement Handbook*, p. 115)

Photos of suspects may be used as evidence provided that a sense of fairness prevails and guidelines are established. Pictures should be shown to only one witness at a time and the investigator should not make any influencing comments (such as, "That individual has an arrest record."). Whenever possible, photos should be of the same kind, size, and appearance. Several photographs of individuals with similar appearances and clothes should be shown to the witnesses. Investigators must be careful not to violate the due process of potential defendants. Some police agencies use a composite drawing or a photocomposition process to develop a likeness of the perpetrator based on information supplied by witnesses. The technician making the composite should receive training in the proper techniques and be able to explain the process in court.

A **line-up** requires eyewitnesses to identify a suspected offender from a number of persons lined up along a wall. Again, the investigator must make sure the suspect's right to due process is not violated. In 1967, the Supreme Court decided in *United States*

In 1990, members of New York's Guardian Angels posted a composite drawing of the Zodiac gunman in an effort to help police track down the serial killer.

v. Wade that a suspected offender had the right to have an attorney during the line-up to make sure the procedure was conducted fairly. Guidelines for conducting line-ups follow.

- All persons in the line-up should be of the same age and race, have similar characteristics, and wear similar clothing.
- There should be at least six persons in the line-up.
- Any movements or statements should be made by each person in the line-up, one at a time. A person in a line-up may not be forced to speak any words or perform any acts. No statement should be requested unless a witness requests it.
- A color photograph of the line-up should be taken and developed as soon as possible.
- Witnesses should not see defendants in custody or be shown their photos before the line-up.
- Witnesses should view the line-up one at a time, out of each other's presence.
- No action should be taken or statement made to a witness to suggest that a suspect is standing in any particular place.
- As few persons as possible should be allowed in the room when the line-up is conducted.
- Before entering the room, the witness should be given a form on which the identification can be marked and signed.
- If counsel is present, he or she should be allowed to make suggestions.
- Prior to the line-up, the witness should give a detailed description of the perpetrator, which should be reduced to writing.
- If possible, law enforcement officers should not be used in the line-ups.
- Some authorities advocate blank line-ups (held in the absence of the suspect). Blank line-ups could prevent a witness from picking out the wrong person.
- The names and addresses of all persons participating in the line-up should be preserved. (*Georgia Law Enforcement Handbook*, p. 121)

A suspect does not have the right to refuse to participate in a line-up. Investigators should know the specific state rules, which may be more restrictive than those established by the U.S. Supreme Court. Law enforcement officers are required to conduct all line-ups and show-ups in a fair and impartial manner.

A **show-up** presents a single suspect to an eyewitness or victim of a crime. The investigator has to be concerned with suggestibility. A show-up after five or six hours may not be admissible. Usually a show-up occurs only at or near the crime scene, when the suspect is arrested or apprehended and immediately brought before eyewitnesses or victims for identification.

Generally, the same legal rules that apply to eyewitness identification apply to voice identification. Spectrograph or voice identification or voiceprints are gaining acceptance in the scientific community, although some states have rejected voiceprints as unreliable.

Summary

Law enforcement officers' right to arrest must be based upon probable cause. Arrest is a seizure of a person under the Fourth Amendment. Illegal arrests are unlawful and citizens are protected from unlawful arrests. Whenever possible, law enforcement officers should obtain an arrest warrant.

Generally, a search warrant is required for a room or premise to be searched and articles, materials, or items to be seized. Exceptions include search incident to arrest, consent searches, plain view searches, search of automobiles, open field searches, abandoned property searches, and stop and frisk searches. All searches, with or without warrants, must abide by the guidelines of the Fourth Amendment.

An investigator needs to know the rules of evidence to evaluate what evidence will be admissible. The investigator assists the prosecutor in case preparation by collecting lawfully obtained evidence. Electronic surveillance is often admissible in court.

Admissions and confessions must be free from physical and psychological duress. Suspects must be made aware of their right to either respond or refuse to answer questions. When defendants' identity is uncertain or vague, investigators often use eyewitnesses to identify them through photographs, line-ups, or show-ups. Specific rules should be followed when these identification methods are used in order to meet federal and state requirements.

Key Terms

arrest warrant
consent search
corpus delicti
crime puzzle
custodial arrest
federal exclusionary rule
Fifth Amendment
Fourth Amendment
line-up
material evidence
Miranda decision
plain view
probable cause
rules of evidence
search warrant
show-up
stop and frisk
trier of the fact
videotape surveillance

Review Questions

1. What constitutes a lawful arrest?
2. When should an investigator obtain a search warrant?
3. What are the exceptions to the general rules for obtaining a search warrant?
4. Why are the rules of evidence important to investigators?
5. What is the difference between a line-up and a show-up?

References

Black HC: *Black's Law Dictionary*, ed 5. St. Paul, MN: West Publishing Co., 1979.

Ferdico JN: *Criminal Procedure for the Criminal Justice Professional, ed.* 3, St. Paul, MN: West Publishing Co., 1979.

Georgia Law Enforcement Handbook. Norcross, GA: The Harrison Co., 1984.

Kenney JP, More HW Jr: *Principles of Investigation*, St. Paul, MN: West Publishing Co., 1979.

Klotter J, Kanovitz J: *Constitutional Law*, ed 4. Cincinnati, OH: Anderson Publishing Co., 1981.

Miranda v. Arizona, 384 U.S. 444 86 S.Ct. 1612.

Stuckey G: *Evidence for the Law Enforcement Officer*, ed. 2. New York, NY: McGraw-Hill, 1980.

United States v. Brignoni-Ponce (1975), 422 U.A. 873, 878, 95 S.Ct. 2574-2579.

CHAPTER 4

Sources of Information

Investigators cannot solve crimes without accurate information. Sources of information are innumerable. Criminal investigators must become familiar with those that will be most beneficial in the specific type of offense they are investigating. What is a burglary investigator's best source of information? What are the best sources for investigating a missing child? What sources does a drug investigator use to make a case? A good investigator must develop the skills for obtaining information. Law enforcement agencies should train their investigators in developing sources of information and preparing information documents for their agencies.

In November 1957, Sergeant Edgar Crosswell of the New York State Police observed an unusual number of limousines and motel reservations for the tiny community of Apalachin, New York. The license plates were not only from various points of New York State but from Ohio and other states. Upon checking the license plates, Sergeant Crosswell found that the automobiles were registered to men with criminal records. Crosswell suspected the host of the affair to be a bootlegger having a conference. On November 14 Sergeant Crosswell, with two U.S. Treasury agents and another New York state trooper, raided the premises and found many organized crime figures known to law enforcement. This raid verified for the first time that an underworld organization, the Mafia, existed.

By using sources of information—motel registrations, license plate checks, and rapport with the Treasury Department—Crosswell provided law enforcement and the American people with proof that a criminal conspiracy existed in America. According to today's standards the Apalachin raid may have been uneventful, but it was effective. Sergeant Crosswell was observant, showed initiative, and used the sources of information available to him to solve a crime.

Since investigators cannot know everything, they need to know the various sources of information that can assist investigations. They also need to appreciate their sources of information. Investigators who develop many sources of investigation will make their own jobs easier and increase their value to the law enforcement agency.

"A source of information is any record, custodian of records, directory, publication, public official, or business person, or any other person or object which might be of assistance to an investigator." (Federal Law Enforcement Training Center, Treasury Dept.) Investigators acquire information by communicating with people, studying various publications, and researching private and public records.

Computers

Computers are of extreme value to investigators because they can provide vast quantities of information quickly. Descriptions and background information on subjects and items can readily be obtained from computer crime or information systems. All information must be evaluated, verified, and compared with information in the investigator's possession. The information stored in computers is critically important to the decision-making process of investigators. Quality studies of record-keeping on the state level reflected that from 12 percent to as high as 49 percent of records were incomplete and inaccurate. (Palmiotto, 1988, p. 19)

In September 1965, the Federal Bureau of Investigation was given the responsibility of creating the first computerized information center for missing and wanted persons as well as stolen items in the United States. This system, known as the National Crime Information Center (NCIC), has over six million active records completely automated by computers that process over 270,000 inquiries every 24 hours, seven days a week. In 1970 the **NCIC Computerized Criminal History** file (NCIC-CCH) became an additional source of information. The criminal history files have data on a subject's prior offenses, arrests, and dispositions. Upon entering a subject's name, date of birth, race, and sex into the computer, an investigator will receive the person's FBI number, full name, height, weight, eye color, hair color, fingerprint classification, aliases, total number of arrests, charges, convictions, and dispositions.

The El Paso Intelligence Center (EPIC), located in El Paso, Texas, was designed to exchange worldwide narcotics information.

These magnetic tape drives contain the more than 6 million active records kept by the FBI's National Crime Information Center (NCIC).

The Drug Enforcement Administration (DEA) manages EPIC with the participation of other agencies, including the U.S. Customs Service, U.S. Coast Guard, Immigration and Naturalization Service (INS), and the Bureau of Alcohol, Tobacco, and Firearms. EPIC answers investigators' queries in support of ongoing investigations. Data on subjects, vehicles, vessels, and aircraft are kept in the EPIC system.

EPIC also maintains the **Integrated Combined System** (ICS), which keeps information on subjects involved in smuggling, the landing of private aircraft in the United States, and fraudulent claims of U.S. citizenship. Any federal, state, county, or city law enforcement agency may obtain information. The inquiring agency must provide a case number, subject's name, date of birth, and social security number. EPIC provides feedback to querying agencies on weapons, narcotics activity, alien pilots, vehicles, aircraft, vessels, and traffickers.

The **National Law Enforcement Telecommunications System** (NLETS) is a computer-switched communications network linking all law enforcement agencies in the United States. Information available through NLETS includes driver's license, motor vehicle registration, and criminal information records. Under this system, federal investigators can query a state law enforcement agency for the criminal history of a subject under investigation. An investigation on the East Coast could be solved with the aid of data from another state.

People as Sources

Law enforcement officers have contacts with a variety of law enforcement personnel from other agencies. Investigators should be familiar with other municipal, state, and federal law enforcement agencies in their geographic area. Fellow law enforcement investigators are an important source of information. Good investigators know other law enforcement investigators on a personal basis and develop a trusting relationship in the exchange of information. They know what is happening in their area and where to go and who to go to in order to cut through the bureaucratic maze to obtain information. Investigators should also develop working relations with law enforcement personnel in their own agency. Personnel in the investigator's own agency can often provide useful information and are too often overlooked.

Witnesses and victims are valuable sources of information. Of course, witnesses have rights that are protected by the Constitution and statutes. Investigators should interview witnesses and victims immediately after an incident to find out who, what, how, when, where, and why. Whenever possible, they should obtain written statements from witnesses and victims.

Informants are another source of valuable information. They can provide pieces of information or give detailed information regarding specific crimes. Informants voluntarily provide information that would not ordinarily come to the attention of law enforcement. Any citizen other than a witness or victim who provides information to law enforcement officials may be considered an informant. **Confidential informants** desire privacy and do not want their identity known. They may be concerned about their safety and may even be paid.

State and Local Sources

Often, information for a clandestine or fugitive investigation can best be obtained from sources other than people to avoid compromising the investigation. Many local sources are available to law enforcement officers by request or by administrative or court-ordered **subpoena**. An administrative subpoena is made up by the law enforcement agency requesting the information. This document cites such statutes as the Right to Privacy Act and states that the information requested is for official use only in conducting a criminal investigation.

Most businesses and public utilities will accept the administrative subpoena, since their primary concern is protecting themselves. If the business establishment refuses to recognize the administrative subpoena, the police must obtain a court-ordered subpoena.

Local sources of information such as utility companies will often establish a code number for the law enforcement agency. This code number allows the agency free access to information. Another method of developing a source of information is simply by establishing a personal contact in the business establishment. Initially the investigator will have to show identification to obtain information, but after personal contact has been made and rapport established a telephone call will usually suffice. Among the sources of information that have been successfully used by many investigators are telephone companies, credit bureaus, state computer systems, utilities, motor vehicle departments, the post office, beeper companies, the Social Security Administration, unemployment offices, professional licensing bureaus, and state license departments.

Telephone Companies

With one telephone call to the security department of the telephone company an investigator can retrieve all of the subscriber information on any listed phone number. If the number is unlisted a subpoena must be submitted. The telephone company can provide the subscriber's place of employment and its telephone number and the subscriber's name and address of the phone location.

These are useful when an investigator gets an undercover telephone conversation going with a fugitive and the investigator knows the telephone number and the telephone company knows the exact location of the telephone. Once this information has been obtained, the investigator can force his or her way into the house based on very good probable cause that the suspect is there. After all, the fugitive is on the phone and the phone is in the house.

The phone company can also provide the subscriber's social security number, which can open doors to other sources of information. The subscriber's home telephone number and the date it was installed are helpful if the investigator knows the address but not the number. If the person being looked for has moved, personal references he or she used to obtain phone service and their telephone numbers (which can also lead to their addresses) can put the investigator back on the trail. The subscriber's mailing address for billing—if different from the telephone location—can also be useful, as can the address of the last billing after he or she moved out.

All the investigator needs is one piece of information in order to complete the puzzle. The telephone company can use any of the preceding points to locate a suspect's whole record. It can also give long-distance information—the date, time, and city to which the call was going (or coming from, if collect), as well as the area code, the duration and cost of the call, and the number called from (if collect).

Most of the large telephone companies will arrange for subscriber information to be given out over the phone once a letter of request has been placed on file. The only exception is unpublished numbers. Many small telephone companies have the same policy, but some are more strict. To obtain toll-call information the investigator must submit a subpoena; usually an administrative subpoena suffices. The subscriber information sheet will also show directions to the house, which can be extremely helpful in rural areas.

As a last resort, an investigator can obtain a court-ordered subpoena to establish **pen registers,** devices that can instantaneously record the time, date, and number the suspect is dialing. Pen registers can also give the investigator the exact time and date the suspect receives a telephone call, though not the number of the person doing the calling. Finally, a **Title III** (wire taps) court order allows the investigator to put recorders and listening devices into the pen registers and monitor telephone conversations.

Mobile or cellular telephone service has recently become popular. This method cannot currently be monitored, but an investigator can subpoena the cellular telephone company serving a specific telephone and get subscriber information and tolls of every telephone call made. The tolls show the number of the cellular telephone, the number called, when the call was made, when it ended, and the duration in hours, minutes, and seconds.

Credit Bureau Information Machines

A national company known as Credit Bureau Information, Inc., has thousands of members: banks, car dealerships, credit card companies, and anyone who deals in credit. It reports all persons to whom it gives credit and who use the network to check on people's credit ratings. It has a phenomenal database—George Orwell's *1984* comes true—but it is a great tool to track someone down or investigate a person's activities as far as money that may be involved in crimes.

Most fugitives are careful about using their name, birthdate, and social security number and do not attempt to get credit at first since it requires a history of use. But generally after a year or two the fugitive will become lax and attempt to use his or her real credit record to purchase something. Some fugitives have been apprehended because they used their real social security numbers to get cable TV. They also, of course, gave the address where the cable service was being installed.

Information comes in various ways. For instance, you can enter a person's social security number and the credit computer will search all over the United States for it instantaneously. Or the search may require the suspect's name, current or previous address, birthdate, or type of employment. A spouse's name and social security number, if known, can be searched for a joint account. The more information the investigator can provide, the better the chances of a hit. The credit bureau can provide a great deal of information about a subject or fugitive, and the web of knowledge keeps expanding.

A search by social security number will give the investigator the person's name, current address, former address, date it was reported, and age or date of birth. If more than one name has been used with this social security number, all the names will be listed, coded "M1 of 3," then "M2 of 3," and so on and giving similar information on each person. This shows up for women who have been married and persons who have stolen another person's number.

Searches using demographic data will reveal the same as a social security number search but also give all social security numbers the person used. The printout will also show any inquiries a company has made as a result of the person's effort to buy something on credit. An investigator can put the company's number in the **Credit Bureau Information** (CBI) machine and receive the full name, location, and telephone number of the company. The printout will also give the subjects' credit history: companies they have credit with, their code number, the last date the company made a report on them to the credit bureau, the date their account opened, their credit limit, their balance, their credit status, whether it is a joint or an individual account, their account number at that company, and the date of last activity.

Any one of these pieces of information can be of unlimited help, especially if the subjects are using credit cards while they are fleeing. A telephone call to the credit card company can track their location

or direction of travel. The investigator can find out what type of automobile a fleeing suspect has, whether the suspect has filed for bankruptcy, or whether his or her salary has been garnisheed.
The uses of the CBI machine are unlimited.

Computer Information Systems

Every state has a computer system similar to the National Crime Information Center. For example, the state of Georgia has the Georgia Crime Information Center (GCIC), which maintains a computerized repository of criminal history information. GCIC operates a statewide communications network used by law enforcement agencies and interfaces with NCIC. All criminal investigations in Georgia are reported to GCIC.

Law enforcement agencies can obtain from it criminal reports on suspects and checks on stolen items (such as guns, equipment, motor vehicles, and so forth). GCIC can also transmit lookouts and messages between agencies. It assists law enforcement agencies in ongoing criminal investigations by developing lists of suspects through criminal justice data. GCIC will soon have an **Automated Fingerprint Identification System** (AFIS) that will compare latent fingerprints found at crime scenes against a master file that contains all fingerprint and criminal history information for known offenders in Georgia. (*Georgia Criminal Justice Data 1987*, p. 112.)

Investigators must become familiar with their state's computer information system. Modern technology allows law enforcement officers to have at their disposal the computer banks of all 50 states and the FBI'S computer bank at NCIC, which all federal agencies contribute to. The following information can be obtained from computers:

1. Automobile registrations and license numbers. A license plate number or **vehicle identification number** (VIN) will give the owner of the vehicle and, if different, the person who registered it, as well as the owner's address, the prior owner, and description including make, model, type of vehicle, and number of doors.
2. Driver's license information. This can be queried two ways, by the driver's license number or name, date of birth, and sex. The printout will give the investigator the name, date of birth, social security number, height, weight, sex, date of driver's examination and issuance of license, date of expiration, and whether the license has been suspended.
3. Criminal histories. They give all reported arrests, dispositions,

and locations of arrests. Sometimes the reported addresses of the defendant will be given. Information also includes scars, aliases, and all birthdates and social security numbers used.

4. Local police records. Such records are usually kept on computer files. For example, the Savannah Police Department (Georgia) keeps all of its arrest and traffic accident reports and all calls received and written reports. The department can retrieve information by entering any single name, address, license plate number, driver's license number, or any other identifier. All reports pertaining to that identifier can be obtained.

Utilities

Utility companies include gas, electric, and water. The best source of information for the investigator is the electric company, since everyone needs electricity. Its records can be searched by the subject's name or address. The electric company has subscriber information identical to the telephone company, including the address of the person who has the power.

When an investigator has a subscriber's address, such demographic information as employer, credit references, social security numbers, date of birth, and apartment number can be obtained. When conflicting information has been given in a low-income area, the investigator should check the emergency power service that operates during the winter and who pays the electric bill. Utility companies can divulge when service was initiated and their employees can be questioned about noticing the occupants in the house when they made service calls or took readings. Alternative mailing addresses for billings can also be obtained.

Mail Covers

With a court order, an investigator can have the United States Postal Service make copies of the fronts of all letters that a person mails or receives. This can be beneficial for analyzing a fugitive's relatives' mail, for mail being received from or mailed to the suspect. The postmark of the city where the letter was mailed will also be obtained.

Beepers

An investigator can get subscriber information from beeper companies by either name or beeper telephone number and have records made of all telephone numbers received.

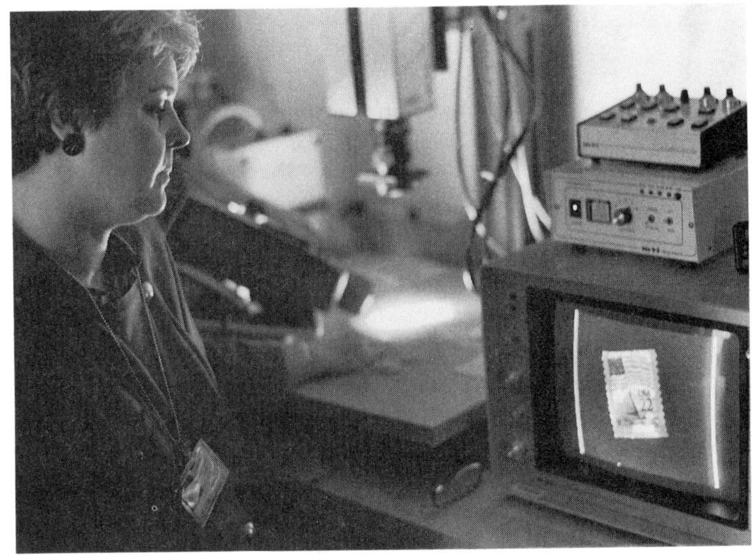

A forensic document analyst scrutinizes postage for evidence of cancellation marks. The United States Post Office can be very helpful to investigators attempting to analyze or track mail.

Social Security Administration

Although the Social Security Administration (SSA) does not give out any information on individuals or their social security numbers, it will confirm for the investigator that the social security number matches the right person. It will also confirm the birthdate. Of course, having a personal contact in the Social Security Administration would be most beneficial.

Unemployment Offices

Every state has an unemployment office. Investigators will have to develop personal contacts with unemployment personnel in their respective states. Investigators must be self-starters in this regard. The Georgia Unemployment Office, for example, will search its state computers via name and/or social security number. It will inform the investigator where the suspect is working and where he or she is having state taxes withdrawn from pay. The Georgia Unemployment Office will also advise the investigator if the person inquired about has applied for unemployment payments and if so, where and when the subject's next appointment will be for unemployment payment.

Department of Motor Vehicles

In addition to motor vehicle registrations, state departments of motor vehicles keep a record on microfiche of all car owners, the vehicles that are registered to them, and their license plate numbers. The microfiche shows the person's name, the type and year of the car, the city it was registered in, license plate number, and the registration number.

The investigator can also request a photostat of the subject's driver's license and the license photo.

Professional Licensing Bureaus

When a suspect's job specialty requires a license from a state regulatory agency (such as doctors, nurses, teachers, or hairstylists), information can be obtained from a state licensing bureau. Trade specialists like electricians, painters, and boilermakers can be checked with licensing bureaus. When the possibility exists that the suspect was a union member, union records should be checked.

State Licensing Bureaus

Most states license certain activities and equipment—for example, hunting, fishing, shrimping, and boats and trailers. When a suspect indicates interest in an activity that requires a state license, this source should be checked by the investigator. Most licensing records can be accessed by computers.

Federal Agencies as Sources of Information

Most federal agencies perform some investigative functions. They are a good source of information, but because there are many federal agencies the investigator must become familiar with the various agencies and the kinds of information available. An investigator who routinely solicits sources of information should obtain the *Chart of the Organization of Federal Executive Departments and Agencies,* prepared by the U.S. Senate Committee on Government Operations. This chart contains the name of each office, division, or bureau and its place in the organizational chart of the agency.

Drug Enforcement Administration

The Drug Enforcement Administration enforces federal laws pertaining to narcotics, marijuana, depressants, stimulants, and hallucinogenic drugs. It also keeps records of users, pushers, and suppliers of narcotics, as well as licensed narcotics dealers.

Federal Bureau of Investigation

The FBI is a unit of the Justice Department and has the responsibility of investigating many specific crimes. It can also be a valuable source of information pertaining to criminal records and fingerprints. The FBI also maintains a national stolen property index on property stolen from the government, a national fraudulent check index, and an anonymous letter index. Be aware that the FBI has a reputation of getting more information from other law enforcement agencies than it gives out.

Immigration and Naturalization Service

The INS is an agency within the Justice Department. It maintains records on naturalization—names of witnesses to naturalization proceedings, accounts of deportation proceedings, financial statements of aliens, and details on persons sponsoring their entry. Also maintained are lists of passengers and crews on ships from foreign ports, passenger manifests, and declarations such as information pertaining to the ship, date, and point of entry into the United States.

Bureau of Alcohol, Tobacco, and Firearms

The Bureau of Alcohol, Tobacco, and Firearms (ATF) is a unit of the Treasury Department. The ATF can trace any firearm from

In pursuing its mission of curbing the illegal traffic and criminal use of firearms, the Bureau of Alcohol, Tobacco and Firearms seizes thousands of weapons each year.

manufacturer or importer to retailer if the weapon was manufactured or imported after 1968. It maintains complete lists of all federal firearms license holders and federal explosive license holders, including manufacturers, importers, and dealers. ATF also keeps records of distillers, brewers, and persons or firms who manufacture or handle alcohol, as well as inventories of retail liquor dealers, names of suppliers, and names and records of bootleggers.

U.S. Customs Service

The Customs Service is another agency of the Treasury Department. It maintains records of importers and exporters, custom house brokers, and custom house truckers, as well as lists of suspects.

U.S. Secret Service

The Secret Service falls under the Treasury Department's umbrella and is best known for protecting the President. However, it does have other responsibilities relating to counterfeiting, forgery, and U.S. security violations. The Secret Service maintains records on individuals who threaten the President, Vice President, former Presidents, or their families. It also has handwriting specimens of known forgers and can compare questioned handwriting with the specimens on file for identification purposes.

Other Federal Agencies

There are numerous federal departments and agencies that can be sources of information. A good investigator will work on obtaining information through the various avenues open to him or her. The following federal agencies are some potential sources of information.

Department of Agriculture—The Office of the Inspector General is the investigative arm.

U.S. Forest Service—Maintains records on forest, mining, and pasture leases.

Food and Nutritional Service Agency—Maintains records of food-stamp recipients.

Department of Defense—keeps records on pay, dependents, allotment accounts, soldiers' deposits, and withholding statements of service personnel.

Department of the Air Force—The Office of Special Investigations (OSI) maintains investigative files.

Department of the Army—Investigative records are maintained by the U.S. Army Counterintelligence Record Facility at Fort Holabird, Maryland.

Department of the Navy—Investigations of naval personnel and civilians employed by the Navy are conducted by the Office of Naval Intelligence.

Department of Commerce—Information about individuals can be obtained from the Security Office in Washington, D.C.

Department of the Interior

National Park Service—Maintains records of mining, pasture, and concessionaires' permits. The files contain names, addresses, and background information.

Fish and Wildlife Service—Maintains records on a national level of violations against it.

Bureau of Indian Affairs—Maintains names, degree of Indian blood, tribe, family background, and addresses of Indians based on census records.

Department of State—Maintains foreign information, data on import and export licenses, and records on the date and place of birth of individuals applying for passports.

Federal Agencies and Commissions

Federal agencies and commissions are required by law to maintain records on their investigations or findings on specific situations or violations of laws. These agencies usually have a single responsibility or mission delegated to them by federal law. The security officer of the specific agency or commission usually is the contact person for the criminal investigator soliciting information.

- Agency for International Development
- Central Intelligence Agency
- Civil Aeronautics Board
- Civil Service Commission
- Energy Department
- Federal Aviation Agency
- Federal Communications Commission
- Federal Maritime Commission
- Federal Power Commission
- Federal Records Center
- Federal Reserve System
- Federal Trade Commission

- General Service Administration
- Interstate Commerce Commission
- National Aeronautics and Space Administration
- National Labor Relations Board
- National Science Foundation
- Securities and Exchange Commission
- Small Business Administration
- Veterans Administration

Businesses as Sources

Business records can be a valuable source of information to the criminal investigator. Banks, stockbrokers, insurance companies, travel agents, automobile companies, and even private investigative agencies can be sources. Obviously, different types of business can provide different sources of information.

Banks are monetary institutions that deal with loans and the exchange of money and facilitate the transmission of funds by checks, drafts, and the exchange of bills. The services banks provide include storing valuables, administering estates, providing tax services, purchasing and selling securities, selling insurance, and furnishing credit references, among others. Bank records—such as signature cards, bank deposit tickets, checking accounts, savings accounts, loan records, safe deposit records, and records of checks cashed—can be accessible to criminal investigators.

Securities brokers are another source of information. They buy and sell bonds and stocks. Records that can be obtained from them include buying and selling records, records of all transactions, customers' ledger accounts, cash transactions, margin requirements, position ledgers, dividend records, and credit information.

Real estate agencies can provide information on property transactions, loan applications, financial statements, and payment received. Abstract and title companies can also provide information on the purchasers and sellers of real estate. They maintain escrow files and files on the transfers of properties, locations of properties transferred, amounts of mortgages, and releases of mortgages.

Automobile companies can provide information on franchise agreements, financial statements of dealers, new car sales, used car sales, and trade-ins. Bonding companies can give information on the address of the person on bond and his or her collateral file and financial statement. Retail department stores keep records on charge accounts and credit files.

Private investigative agencies are good sources of information.

They have files on civil, criminal, commercial, and industrial matters. Records are kept on character checks, fraud investigations, blackmail investigations, and divorce proceedings. Depending on the nature of their work, investigative agencies will have records on security guards, undercover agents, polygraph examinations, and missing person checks.

Drug stores can provide the patient's name and address, the date, and the physician issuing the prescription. Other sources of information include hospital records, hotel records, insurance company records, and laundry and dry-cleaning records. Additional sources are newspaper records or morgues, photograph records such as school yearbooks, church groups, and police files.

The range of information sources available to investigators is so wide that it would be impossible to provide a complete list in this brief chapter. An investigator's sources of information are determined by his or her ingenuity, initiative, personal network, and willingness to work hard to solve a case.

The Freedom of Information and Privacy Acts

Investigators should be familiar with the Freedom of Information and Privacy Acts. The Freedom of Information Act (FOIA) applies to documents relating to the administrative agencies of the executive branch of government. The Privacy Act pertains to information about individuals.

Summary

Criminal investigators must become familiar with the sources of information that will be most beneficial in the specialized offense they are investigating. A source of information is any record, directory, publication, public official, business person, or any other person or object that might be of assistance to an investigator. Investigators acquire information by communicating with people, studying various publications, and researching private and public records.

Computers are of great value to investigators because they can provide information quickly. Descriptions and background information on subjects and items can readily be obtained from computer crime or information systems. Computer systems that assist law enforcement are the National Crime Information Center, operated by the FBI, and the El Paso Intelligence Center, which exchanges narcotics information worldwide.

People are a valuable source of information. Investigators have contacts with a variety of law enforcement personnel from various agencies who are a great source of information. Witnesses and victims are another valuable source of information, as are informants.

State and local sources of information, such as utility and telephone companies, can assist criminal investigators in solving crimes or apprehending fugitives. Federal agencies and business establishments such as banks and insurance companies can also be tapped as sources of information.

Key Terms

Automated Fingerprint Identification System
Credit Bureau Information
confidential informant
El Paso Intelligence Center
Integrated Combined System
National Crime Information Center Computerized Criminal History
National Law Enforcement Telecommunications System
pen register
subpoena
Title III
vehicle identification number

Review Questions

1. How are computers useful as sources of information?
2. Why are people valuable sources of information?
3. Describe some local sources of information used by law enforcement investigators.
4. How are federal agencies valuable as sources of information?
5. How are businesses valuable as sources of information?

References

Chart of the Organization of Federal Executive Departments and Agencies. Washington, DC: United States Senate Committee on Government Operations.

Federal Law Enforcement Training Center, Treasury Dept.

Georgia Criminal Justice Data 1987, Georgia Bureau of Investigation.

Palmiotto MJ: *Critical Issues in Criminal Investigation,* ed 2. Cincinnati, OH: Anderson Publishing Co., 1988.

CHAPTER 5

Interviewing and Interrogation

The key to crime-solving lies with people. Investigators must be able to communicate with witnesses, victims, informants, and suspects. Without information, the investigative process cannot be continued and the crime may never be solved. Although physical evidence (such as weapons, blood, or fingerprints) will be collected, the verbal evidence collected from witnesses, victims, and suspects will make up the bulk of evidence obtained. Gathering information from people depends upon their willingness to cooperate.

Although the terms *interviewing* and *interrogation* are often used interchangeably, they have different meanings. In its procedural manual *Criminal Investigation,* the International Association of Chiefs of Police (IACP) defines *interviewing* as "the process by which an officer seeks, obtains and evaluates information given to him by persons having personal knowledge of events or circumstances of a crime." (IACP, 1971, p. 112) An **interview** is a purposeful and planned conversation between an interviewer and interviewee to collect data pertaining to an investigation or to substantiate physical evidence. The interviewer's objective is to ascertain the details of a specific criminal incident. The interviewer should obtain as much information as possible in order to determine the truth about a specific situation. Through the interviewing process, the investigator relates physical evidence to a specific criminal act.

An **interrogation** is an adversarial situation. An interrogation may be defined as "a systematic questioning in a formal situation where the subject is resistant or unwilling to participate." (Kenney and More, 1979, p. 145) The person being interrogated wants to hide information from the investigator.

The communication process has a greater chance of being successful if the investigator conducting the interview or interrogation is sensitive to the needs of the interviewee or person interrogated. The interviewer should use simple, clear language and the interview should be conducted face-to-face to avoid misunderstandings. The interviewer should be familiar with jargon and the symbolic meaning of specific words. The heart of any interview is communication, both verbal conversation and body language such as facial expressions, gestures, and body positioning of the interviewee. Another effective communications tool is intonation, or raising and lowering the voice, slowing down or speeding up, and using various inflections.

Listening

An important communications skill is **active listening,** which requires training and experience. In a society where most people want to talk and few want to listen, it takes effort and concentration to develop this skill.

Investigative authorities estimate that approximately 95 percent of crimes are cleared through interviews and interrogations. The FBI has incorporated listening skills as part of interview and interrogation training for new agents. New agents role-play interviewing a witness. They must listen attentively, since the script includes only partial or unclear information. Indications are that the best listeners are the best interviewers. (Miner, 1984, p. 12)

Good listening requires concentration and understanding. Listening becomes difficult when emotions, personality traits, bias, and other distractions interfere with the process. Good communication requires an interest in the conversation, the withholding of judgment until the interview has been completed, and an ability to distinguish between facts and ideas. According to Robert L. Montgomery (1981, p. 13), ten characteristics distinguish good listeners.

1. Look at me while I'm speaking.
2. Question me to clarify what I'm saying.
3. Show concern by asking questions about my feelings.
4. Repeat some of the things I say.
5. Don't rush me.
6. Be poised and emotionally controlled.
7. React responsively with a nod of the head, a smile, or a frown.
8. Pay close attention.
9. Don't interrupt me.
10. Keep on the subject until I've finished my thoughts.

Body language is nonverbal, mostly unconscious, communication, which can reveal much about a person's emotional state.

Adjusting a watch band or bracelet is a sign of nervousness. The arm-cross gesture forms a momentary barrier and provides needed security.

Rubbing an eye is a sign that the person is lying. The gesture is an attempt to block out the deceit or to avoid looking in the face of the individual being lied to.

Placing fingers in the mouth indicates the person is feeling pressured. The gesture signals a need for reassurance, which, when supplied, puts the person more at ease.

Active listening is projected by the interviewers' actions. Their body movements, hand gestures, facial expressions, tone of voice, and eye contact convey attentiveness to what is being said. Their responses show that they comprehend the interviewee's comments, which helps build rapport and obtain information.

Active listening gives the interviewee the opportunity to express his or her ideas, attitudes, and emotions. The interviewer feels empathy toward the interviewee, who in turn develops a feeling of trust and confidence in the interviewer. "Active listening requires that you put yourself in the other person's shoes. Only if you can understand the message sender's own frame of reference and his words of reality can you really grasp the real meaning of his or her message." (Sayles and Strauss, 1981, p. 119)

Interviewing

In law enforcement investigations, the purpose of an interview is to ascertain crucial facts to solve a crime. Through verbal and nonverbal interaction, the interviewer obtains information about a specific crime situation or corroborative evidence to institute criminal charges against a suspect. Interviewing is an art and a science; it requires creativity. The art of interviewing requires experience and continuous practice to determine whether people are telling the truth, holding back information, or simply lying. The interviewer reads people and knows intuitively when they are speaking truthfully.

The interview should be directed in such a way that the interviewee will provide information willingly. First, the officer is concerned with simply accumulating any information that relates to a crime or an incident. He or she will seek to learn from the subject anything at all that will assist in painting a clear picture of what happened or corroborate information already known.

Second, the officer will attempt to identify or locate evidence or contraband. He or she will try to learn from the subject whether evidence or loot in fact exists and, if so, where it can be found.

Finally, the officer will use the interview to discover victims, witnesses, or suspects. Many cases are cleared because of information obtained during an interview. It provides the officer with an opportunity to identify the existence of additional victims, determine the identities of any other persons who might also be witnesses, and maybe even apprehend a suspect. (Kenney and More, 1979, p. 136)

Preparing for the Interview

The interviewing process requires preparation—knowledge of the case, knowledge of the subject, knowledge of yourself, the proper location, and the proper time. (Sometimes, during an emergency situation, there is no time to prepare.) The interviewer should know the who, what, where, how, and why of the case. What happened, what was the date, what was the time, who were the people involved? The amount of background information needed may depend on the seriousness of the case. The interviewer, who usually is the investigator assigned to the case, will normally become thoroughly familiar with evidence and case reports. This means knowledge of the crime scene and statements made earlier.

The more facts the investigator has acquired before an interview, the more he or she can control the conversation. Usually random questions are unsuccessful. These fishing expeditions have

A patrol officer interviews a near-hysterical victim at the scene of a crime, while a friend tries to calm her.

the interviewer groping for facts. The well-prepared interviewer has a better knowledge base to assimilate information and to evaluate and analyze comments or statements made during the interview. Ideally, subjects should be interviewed in the following order:

1. Victims or complainants.
2. Witnesses who observed the crime.
3. Witnesses who did not observe the actual crime but who have important information about anything that either preceded or followed the crime.
4. Suspects.

Establishing Rapport

Most people interviewed by law enforcement personnel are either victims or complainants. A **victim** may be defined as someone harmed by a criminal act. A **complainant** requests that law enforcement personnel investigate a possible illegal action. All interviews should be centered on the interviewee, who deserves to be treated with importance since he or she will be the source of information.

The interviewer must immediately establish a harmonious relationship with a genuine interest in the interviewee. Many people in American society need to feel important, and the interviewee who has been given this sense of self-importance will cooperate much faster. Threats, intimidations, or abuse will not work. The hard-line approach is a thing of the past.

The interviewer must get to know the interviewee. What kind of person is he? What kind of position does he have? How much education does he have? Does he have a family? What are his interests? If he's uncooperative, what will motivate him? What are his fears? The interviewer must uncover the reason for the subject's unwillingness and persuade him to cooperate. Appeals to his sense of justice, love of family, patriotism, or other emotional symbols may be effective. The human relations approach, combined with knowledge of the interviewee and a genuine interest in him or her, is probably the best formula for obtaining information.

The interviewer also needs to know himself or herself. Most interviewers have two or three skills that work best for them—for example, showing interest in the subject throughout the interviewing process or being able to read body language. Interviewers should know what skills are successful for them. What are their weaknesses? Do they have any prejudices or biases? Can they interview a child molester? Usually the interviewee's perception of the interviewer is important to a successful interview. The interviewer must have credibility and integrity and function as a professional. Interviewees provide information if they believe the interviewer:

- is motivated solely by the search for truth.
- will treat them as he or she would like to be treated.
- will be considerate, courteous, and understanding.
- will not judge, condemn, censure, ridicule, or belittle them.
- will deal fairly with the information they give.
- will not misquote or misrepresent them.
- is a sincere, dependable person, worthy of their trust.

Surroundings

The location or setting of the interview deserves attention. For example, a large crowd hampers interviews. Witnesses to a crime may not want to speak about the crime when other people are present. Also, their account of what they saw may influence or be influenced by other witnesses.

An interview should be conducted in private, one on one, not in the presence of family, friends, or curiosity seekers. In fact, other investigators or officers should not be present. The interviewee may possess a secret he or she will divulge only in private. For example, a married man who has witnessed a crime may not want his wife to know he's spending his free time in a bar.

Interviews should not be conducted in noisy areas where telephones are ringing constantly or conversations can be over-

In an office interview, the interviewer can establish initial rapport with the individual by conducting the session in comfortable, private surroundings without physical barriers.

heard. Constant interruptions interfere with a person's train of thought. People need to concentrate on questions and responses. Both the interviewer and subject should give their full attention to the interview.

The one exception occurs with the first officer at the scene of the crime, who immediately obtains a description of the suspect, property taken, and method of flight. The officer gives the dispatcher this information to alert other patrol units. For the follow-up interview, the investigator may ask the subject where he or she would like to be interviewed—home, police headquarters, or a neutral setting.

Another factor that facilitates communication is eliminating physical barriers, which separate people psychologically and make them feel uncomfortable. Interviewers should not sit too far away from their subjects. Familiar surroundings may be the most psychologically comforting for the subject. Physical discomfort such as heat, cold, or standing for long periods of time may make the interviewee unwilling to provide information.

Timing is important for an interview to be successful. Witnesses to a crime should be interviewed as soon as possible after the crime, when the events are still clear in their minds. Yet interviews should not be rushed. A cooperative witness unable to give sufficient time for an interview should be allowed to select a more convenient time when he or she will be free from interruptions. Hysterical or upset people should not be interviewed until they have calmed down. It may also be better to interview witnesses when they are alert, not too early in the morning. Interviews should be conducted at a time convenient to both interviewer and interviewee.

Developing Questions

In order for interviews to be productive, the interviewer and the subject should speak the same language in terms of both verbal and nonverbal communications. A few general questions will put the interviewee at ease and project that everything said has importance. After a few basic questions are asked and rapport appears to be established the interviewer should ask, "What happened?" The witness or subject should be allowed to tell the story as he or she perceives it. The narrative approach should be listened to attentively without interruption.

When the full story has been told, the interviewer should ask specific questions that he or she planned beforehand. Since questions are the principal tools of interviewing, skill in developing and asking them will have a bearing on the amount and value of information obtained from witnesses and suspects.

Questions to which the subject can reply simply yes or no should be avoided. Instead, "Tell me why you did that" requires an explanation of an individual's actions and leads to more information. Quick or rapid-fire questions should be avoided also. They lead to confusion and lack of cooperation. People should have an opportunity to think about the questions and their responses. Quick questioning may cause subjects to forget or withhold information. Suggestive or leading questions should be avoided too, because they may influence the answer or even suggest a desired answer, leading to incorrect information. In addition, complex and double negative questions should be avoided.

When used properly, questions are an important tool for the investigator. When a subject has completed his or her narrative, direct questions can clarify comments made during the narrative. Art Buckwalter lists twelve rules in the art of direct questioning. (Buckwalter, 1983, pp. 84–85)

1. Ask only one question at a time.
2. Word each question so that only one answer is required.
3. Keep your questions short and simple.
4. Ask straightforward, frank questions.
5. Make sure all questions are clear and easily understood.
6. Clear each answer before asking another question.
7. Do not rush the subject's answer.
8. Ask important questions in the same manner you ask unimportant ones.
9. Always give the subject an opportunity to qualify the answer.
10. Ask open-ended questions when soliciting expanded replies.
11. Ask precise questions when you want precise answers.
12. When an answer calls for another question, ask it at once.

Memory

Investigators should never give more information than they obtain. Whether a case will be solved depends to a great extent on the accuracy and completeness of information gathered from eyewitnesses. According to Elizabeth Loftus, a psychologist who has researched memory, a person's memory of an event can change drastically between the time he or she first witnesses it and the time the person recounts it to someone else.

Loftus believes that many factors can influence the accuracy of a report, including which questions are asked and even which words are used. For example, an investigator of the identification techniques used to charge Nicola Sacco and Bartolomeo Vanzetti—anarchists convicted of murder and robbery in Massachusetts in 1921—discovered that witnesses were subject to suggestions by the police. Loftus believes eyewitnesses are often inaccurate in estimating speed, time, and distance. Her conclusion? "When you question an eyewitness, what he saw may not be what you get." (Loftus, 1974, pp. 117–119)

An examination of identification procedures as they relate to recognition memory was done by D. M. Thompson, who writes that perceptual characteristics depend on knowledge of the objects in question. The matching of perceptual characteristics can seldom be made beyond a reasonable doubt in a witness's identification of an offender. Most witnesses can accurately identify offenders they are familiar with and those who were apprehended while committing the crime. On the other hand, witnesses can seldom positively identify offenders who are unfamiliar to them or who are not apprehended at the scene of the crime. In addition, identification of offenders solely on the basis of perceptual features should be accepted cautiously. (Thompson, 1982, pp. 151–157) Since victim and eyewitness reports of crimes are often incomplete, unreliable, or only partially correct, their quality is suspect. Yet such accounts play a crucial role in the solving of criminal cases.

Cognitive Interviews

A new interview technique increases the amount of information investigators can obtain from eyewitnesses. Criminal events can traumatize witnesses and victims, causing them to forget valuable information. Although faster, the traditional question-and-answer interview loses effectiveness with emotional witnesses and victims. By contrast, the **cognitive interview** focuses on helping eyewitnesses recollect as much as possible of what they saw or heard. The first two methods of cognitive interviews attempt to increase the overlap of elements between stored memory and retrieval paths. (Geiselman and Fischer, 1985, p. 2) The four methods are:

1. Reconstruct the circumstances. In this method the investigator instructs the witness to reconstruct the incident in general.
2. Report everything. The investigator explains that some people hold back information because they are not quite sure it is important. The witness is asked not to edit anything, even things that may not seem important.
3. Recall the events in different order. The instruction may be,

"It is natural to go through the incident from beginning to end. However, also try to go through the events in reverse order. Or try starting with the thing that impressed you the most in the incident and proceed from there, going both forward and backward in time."

4. Change perspective. Witnesses try to recall the incident from the perspectives of others who were present during the incident. Witnesses may be instructed to place themselves in the role of a prominent character in the incident and think about what he or she must have seen.

The cognitive interview also has five specific techniques to help an investigator obtain information following the narrative phase of an interview. The interviewer might suggest the following.

1. Physical appearance. Did the suspect remind you of anyone? If you were reminded of someone, try to think of why. Was there anything unusual about the suspect's physical appearance or clothing?
2. Names. If you think that a name was spoken but you cannot remember what it was, try to think of the first letter of the name by going through the alphabet. Then try to think of the number of syllables.
3. Numbers. Was a number involved, perhaps a license plate? Was it high or low? How many digits were in the number? Were there any letters in the sequence?
4. Speech characteristics. Did the voice remind you of someone else's voice? If so, try to figure out why. Were any unusual words or phrases used?
5. Conversation. Think about your reactions and the reactions of others to what was said. Were any unusual words or phrases used?

Interviewing Children

When questioning children and adolescents, the interviewer must take their age into consideration. Determining the credibility of children may be difficult, especially young children who have vivid imaginations and lack life experiences. A study conducted by researchers for Loyola University of Chicago found that children were less likely to make inaccurate statements than were their adult counterparts. The researchers discovered that while children often describe events incompletely (especially when they do not understand them), they are usually successful when asked specific questions about events. Even five-year-olds in the Loyola study answered the questions as accurately as adults. (Goodman and Michelli, 1981, p.84)

Recently, children have been receiving a great deal of attention as victims of crimes. Crimes against children, such as incest and sexual assault, get a lot of publicity. The interviewer needs to develop techniques to elicit what actually happened to the child. A relationship must be established, and language appropriate to the child's age should be used. Only simple, open-ended direct questions should be asked of a child. The interviewer needs to recognize the trauma the child went through and detach his or her own emotions from the event, no matter how difficult that is. An emotional interview is an ineffective interview.

Adolescents are physically and mentally more mature than young children, but they may be overly concerned with their own problems and thus may make poor observers. When a juvenile is a victim of or witness to a crime, the interviewer should operate with the usual interviewing techniques, keeping in mind the adolescent's age and experiences.

An adolescent who may be a suspect is provided legal safeguards by the U.S. Supreme Court. Investigators who question juvenile suspects should be familiar with these safeguards. The U.S. Supreme Court in *In re Gault* (1967) guarantees that a juvenile has the right to be notified of the charges and time to prepare for the case; the right to counsel; the right to be confronted and cross-examined by witnesses; and the right to remain silent in court.

Behavior-Oriented Interviews

Another time when the interviewer's emotions must be kept under control is during the **behavior-oriented interview** of crime victims. Behavior-oriented interviewing allows the interviewer to devote attention to the offender's behavior. For example, the reason behind an assault could be made clearer. It could provide the investigator with psychological and social insight into the offender. (Hazelwood, 1983, p. 8) The interviewer must perceive the crime through both the victim's and the criminal's eyes. A lack of objectivity will cloud the overall view of the crime. The interviewer assists the victim in overcoming emotions created by the crime, such as fear or guilt. The interviewer has to empathize with the victim in order to obtain valuable information from crime analysis. Interviewing the victim is the most crucial step in the process. The information obtained from the victim will be used in profiling the offender. In profiling a rapist, three steps are essential.

1. Careful interview of the victim regarding the rapist's behavior.
2. Analysis of that behavior in an attempt to ascertain the motivation underlying the assault.
3. Compiling of a profile of the individual likely to have committed the crime in the manner reported and having the assumed motivation. (Hazelwood, 1983, p. 9)

Reluctant Witnesses

During the initial stages of an interview, its tone should be established. A witness who is motivated to cooperate and confident that investigators can apprehend the offender will be cooperative. When a witness appears reluctant to provide information, the interviewer should attempt to determine why.

Witnesses may be uncooperative in order to protect themselves, their family, their relatives, or their friends. They may fear becoming involved, personal retaliation, or harm to themselves, their loved ones, or their business.

They may be reluctant to give any information because they are directly or indirectly involved in the crime and do not wish to jeopardize themselves. Or perhaps they just find the subject too sensitive, too risky, too unpleasant, too repulsive, too frightening, or a personal taboo.

Many witnesses do not want to become involved, to be inconvenienced, or to in any way place themselves in a position that may incur risk.

Sometimes an incompetent interviewer fails to ask for information, and the witness withholds it unintentionally. Some witnesses experience personality conflicts with the interviewer. Some do not realize the importance of their information to a case.

Through conversation, the interviewer attempts to motivate the witness into cooperating. Asking positive leading questions can help to establish a cooperative attitude—for example, "I appreciate your cooperation, especially since you don't particularly feel like cooperating. But I am sure you want the true facts to be known, don't you?" or "I need your help. You are in a position to help me get at the truth of the matter. You are going to help me, aren't you?" (Buckwalter, pp. 105–106)

Interrogation

Interrogation is an adversarial situation between the interviewer and the interviewee. Because the term has a negative connotation, "custodian interview" may be used in its place. (Attorneys and juries may think of interrogation as a browbeating technique to obtain a confession of guilt.)

Basically, an interrogator questions a suspect about a criminal offense to obtain information. The objectives of an interrogation are to gather facts and discover the truth. The interrogator has a responsibility to protect the innocent and obtain admissions from the guilty. Other goals are to find evidence and specifics related to the crime to corroborate information, and to locate stolen merchandise.

Interrogation requires specially trained people. Interrogators become proficient by doing, and maintain effectiveness by conducting interrogations. They should attend workshops and training sessions, be intelligent and well-rounded, and possess "street smarts." They need patience and the ability to get along with people. They must be professional and keep abreast of legal issues.

Persuasion

The aphorism "You catch more flies with honey than with vinegar" applies to the concept of interrogation. The interrogator should be good at **persuasion,** convincing suspects to cooperate and provide whatever knowledge they have about a specific incident. The interrogator uses persuasion to obtain the truth. Interviewees must be motivated to give assistance. "Motivation is the process of arousing, sustaining or altering behavior. This process includes both unconscious and conscious forces." (Anderson, 1978, p. 47)

There are three sources of motivation: emotion, reason, and rationalization. Emotions involve belief, desire, and feelings. Reason includes understanding a situation, interpreting the consequences of one's actions, and considering how to solve one's problems. Rationalization implies a reasoning ability that justifies one's actions. As Buckwalter states, "Emotion involves our hopes, likes, and feelings; reason: our thoughts, experiments, and knowledge; and rationalization: our justifications, explanations, and suppositions." (Buckwalter, 1983, p. 216) The interrogator can use emotion, reason, and rationalization to persuade an interviewee.

For persuasion to succeed, the credibility of the interrogator must be beyond reproach. Usually the interrogator's official position lends credibility. Of course, the interrogator should have rehearsed the facts of the case and the subject's background. The projection of courtesy and respect toward the subject are important in persuading the subject to cooperate.

Trigger words (such as *kill, rape, molest*) should be avoided. Milder, more persuasive terms should be used to reduce the apparent severity of the crime. For instance, the word *fight* may be less intimidating than *kill*. The interrogator must persuade the subject that he or she is not unique or even strange. For example, a child molester may believe he's the only person who has ever committed this act. The interrogator must be sensitive to this and permit the subject self-respect.

Confessions

One purpose of the interrogation is to obtain an admission or confession. The subject should have been reminded of the Miranda warning or constitutional rights as they relate to questioning. The interrogator must be patient, since the majority of people run out of things to say within 15 minutes. The interrogator must possess humanistic qualities and skills to keep the communication going. The suspect's admission or confession should be a natural outcome of the interrogation.

There are a variety of reasons that suspects admit or confess to an offense. They may believe that cooperation is the best course of action. The same attitudes, values, and beliefs that led them to commit the offense may also be the reason why they confess. Once a suspect confesses orally, he or she should be persuaded to put the confession in writing.

The confession should contain all the evidence pertaining to the specific crime to which the subject has confessed. It can be either handwritten or typed. The suspect can dictate the confession while the interrogator writes it out. The suspect then signs the confession. The interrogation can be recorded. Video and oral recordings may help clear up uncertainties, after the suspect gives permission for them. The recordings can be used to verify that the subject was not coerced to confess.

Recording Information

The interview process requires that notes be taken. "The objectives of note-taking are to get all the facts and to record them accurately, clearly, briefly, legibly and rapidly." (Buckwalter, p.54) Not only the spoken words but, when needed, the tone of voice, facial inflections, and emotions expressed should be recorded. Describing nonverbal behavior can increase the completeness and accuracy of the interview.

The interviewer must be skillful in taking legible notes accurately without creating disorganization or forgetting to listen during the interviewing process. The notes are meant to protect both the interviewer and the interviewee. At the conclusion of the interview, the notes should be reviewed with the interviewee. The interviewer will lose credibility if statements in them are inaccurate. The notes should be saved for further investigation or for possible use in court.

Lie-Detection Methods

Throughout history, a variety of lie-detecting methods have been used to determine criminal acts. Among the methods used today are polygraphs, drugs, hypnosis, and tests.

Polygraph

A **polygraph** is a mechanical instrument that records physiological responses to questioning. It records blood pressure, pulse, respiration, galvanic skin response (GSR), and chest and abnormal breathing patterns. The polygraph is only a machine. It cannot detect whether a person is lying or telling the truth. Only a skillful polygraph operator can determine that someone has been lying. Individuals using the polygraph should be trained in interview techniques, psychology, and psychophysiology. The polygraph is used during criminal investigation procedures and in screening individuals for employment.

The polygraph is used during criminal investigation procedures and in screening individuals for employment. Only a skillful polygraph operator can determine that someone has been lying.

The purpose of a polygraph examination is to determine whether the examinee has been involved in or has knowledge of an offense. The polygraph may also be used on victims and witnesses when an investigator doubts the credibility of their information. The polygraph is not foolproof. It may register that individuals who have no conception of guilt or wrongdoing are telling the truth, or it may indicate erroneously that extremely nervous individuals are lying.

Drugs

In the 1920s Dr. Robert House, an American anesthesiologist, developed the drug scopolamine for securing true statements from subjects. Other forms of truth serums have since been used to obtain the truth and confessions from suspects, among them sodium pentothal and sodium amytal. Dr. Robert L. Sadoff, a psychiatrist, has reached certain conclusions with regard to the use of **narcoanalysis.**

- "Normal" patients under the influence of sodium amytal are very likely to confess to wrongdoing.
- Neurotics are not only likely to confess to wrong behavior, but even tend to substitute fantasy for truth.
- Persons with strong unconscious self-punitive tendencies, such as moral masochists, not only confess more easily but also confess to crimes never actually committed.
- Narcoanalysis is occasionally effective in persons who would have disclosed the truth even without narcoanalysis. (Sadoff, 1966, p. 254)

Clinical studies indicate that individuals who have either a conscious or an unconscious reason to confess tend to give in to interrogations under drug influence. Drugs break down people's inhibition to verbalize and make them more open to suggestion. Psychiatrists may use narcoanalysis to probe into other aspects of the subject's character.

Hypnosis

In recent years hypnosis has received much attention. It can be most useful in the investigative and preparatory phases of investigation. It can refresh the memory of witnesses to a crime, victims, arresting officers, and investigators who may have forgotten minor details.

Hypnosis may also be used to recall license plate numbers, names, places, and details of an event, or even to overcome amnesia in a victim or witness. It may explore and explain motives and determine the truth or falseness of statements. Successful hypnosis requires the subjects to cooperate with the hypnotist. They must have a state of mind conducive to suggestion. **Hypnosis** may be defined as "a subjective state of mind in which a person is more prone to accept suggestions." (Arons, 1967, p. 15) When information has been recorded in the subconscious, it can be retrieved under hypnosis when the individual cooperates.

Primarily because of the suggestive nature of hypnosis and judicial scrutiny, its use as an investigative tool has come under criticism. Standards have been developed for how and when to use it. The California Attorneys for Criminal Justice suggest that:

- the hypnotist be a mental health professional with special training in the use of hypnosis, preferably a psychiatrist or psychologist,
- this person not be informed about the case orally but only in writing subject to scrutiny,
- the hypnotist be independent and not responsible to the parties,
- all contact between the hypnotist and the subject be videotaped from beginning to end,
- nobody representing either party be present with the hypnotist and subject during the session,
- prior to the session the hypnotist examine with the subject to exclude the possibility of physical or mental illness and to establish sufficient intelligence, judgment, and comprehension of what is happening,
- the hypnotist elicit all facts from the subject prior to the hypnosis,
- the hypnotist strive to avoid adding any new elements to the subject's description, including any explicit or implicit cue, before, during or after the session, and
- corroboration be sought for any information elicited during the session. (Margolin, 1981, p. 45)

Interviews and Tests

Criminal interviewing or interrogation may create anxiety, tension, and aggravation in the suspect. Suspects may indicate attempts at deception by a variety of physical, emotional, and mental symptoms.

Physical symptoms include excessive perspiration, flushing or paleness of the skin, an increase or decrease in pulse rate, dry mouth and tongue, excessive swallowing, and licking of the lips. They may also include such involuntary movements as muscle spasms and muscle tension, darting eye movement, facial tics, excessive craving for a cigarette, thickened and blurred speech, and stuttering.

Emotional symptoms include tension, nervousness, and anxiety.

Mental symptoms include confusion, faulty memory, hesitation, and long pauses. (Aubry and Caputo, 1965, pp. 123–124)

An interviewing technique that has recently helped investigators to better identify suspects is the behavioral analysis interview (BAI). The BAI lasts approximately 10 to 15 minutes and places suspects in a face-to-face, nonaccusatory situation. The interviewer asks a series of questions that are thought-provoking and designed to reveal guilt or innocence by what the suspects say or how they look when they respond. (Wicklander, 1980, p. 40)

Summary

Interviews and interrogations are methods used by law enforcement officers to obtain information to solve crimes. Victims and witnesses are usually cooperative during the interviewing process. The interrogation indicates an adversary situation in which a suspect or witness is unwilling to cooperate. Both interviewing and interrogations are important to the investigative process. Most investigators can easily become skillful interviewers, but interrogation requires special training and skills.

A skill important to interviewing and interrogation is listening. Good listening requires concentration and understanding. Listening becomes difficult when emotions, personality traits, bias, and other distractions interfere with this communication process.

In cognitive interviews, the interviewer jogs the memory of a victim or witness to a crime. Eyewitnesses often forget valuable information. Although the traditional question-and-answer interview is faster, it loses effectiveness with emotionally upset witnesses and victims.

Interviewers must give special consideration to children and adolescents. They must determine the credibility of children. When interviewing adolescents for offenses, interviewers should be aware of the special legal status of adolescents and make certain the correct procedures are followed.

Lie-detection methods are often used to detect criminal acts. Methods include polygraphs, drugs, and hypnosis.

Key Terms

active listening
behavior-oriented interview
cognitive interview
complainant
hypnosis
interrogation
interview
narcoanalysis
persuasion
polygraph
victim

Review Questions

1. What is the difference between interviewing and interrogating?
2. Why are listening skills important for interviewing?
3. Explain the concept of the cognitive interview.
4. What is meant by the behavior-oriented interview?
5. Describe three methods of lie detection.

References

Andersen KE: *Persuasion,* ed. 2. Boston, MA: Allyn and Bacon, 1978.

Arons H: *Hypnosis in Criminal Investigation.* Springfield, IL: Charles C. Thomas, 1967.

Aubry AS, Caputo RR: *Criminal Interrogation.* Springfield, IL: Charles C. Thomas, 1965.

Buckwalter A: *Interviews and Interrogations.* Boston, MA: Butterworth Publishers, 1983.

Geiselman RE, Fischer RP: "Interviewing Victims and Witnesses of Crimes." U.S. Justice Dept. *Research in Brief,* 12:2, 1985.

Goodman GS, Michelli, JA: "Would You Believe a Child Witness?" *Psychology Today,* 11:84, 1981.

Grau JG, ed: *Criminal and Civil Investigative Handbook.* New York, NY: McGraw-Hill, 1981.

Hazelwood RR: "The Behavior-Oriented Interview of Rape Victims: The Key to Profiling." *FBI Law Enforcement Bulletin* 9: 8–9, 1983.

International Association of Chiefs of Police: *Criminal Investigation.* Gaithersburg, MD: IACP, 1971.

Kenney JP, More HW Jr: *Principles of Investigation.* St. Paul, MN: West Publishing Co., 1979.

Loftus E: "Incredible Eyewitnesses." *Psychology Today* 12:117–119, 1974.

Margolin E: *Hypnosis-Enhanced Testimony: Valid Evidence or Prosecutor Tool?" Trial* 10:45, 1981.

Miner EM: "The Importance of Listening in the Interview and Interrogation Process." *FBI Law Enforcement Bulletin* 6:12, 1984.

Montgomery RL: *Listening Made Easy.* New York, NY: AMACOM, 1981.

Sadoff RL: "Psychiatric Involvement in Search for Truth." *American Bar Association Journal* 52, 1966.

Sayles LR, Strauss G: *Managing Human Resources.* Englewood Cliffs, NJ: Prentice-Hall, 1981.

Thompson DM: "The Realities of Eyewitness Identification." *The Australian Journal of Forensic Science* 6:151–157, 1982.

Wicklander DE: "Behavioral Analysis." *Security World* 3, 1980.

CHAPTER 6

Informants

The success of investigations depends upon information, and informants are an important source of information. Broadly defined, an **informant** is anyone who provides information relating to a crime to law enforcement officials.

Developing informants is essential to successful investigation and detection of many violent and financial crimes. These include fraud, organized crime, illicit drug operations, and property crimes such as burglaries and thefts. Informants are extremely important for any criminal activity that is covert. Apprehending drug dealers, for example, usually requires an insider who has knowledge of the operation.

In local policing, patrol officers and investigators may develop sources of information to provide them with a better understanding of the community they are policing. These sources can include friends, associates, and people who just like talking to police officers. Often federal and local law enforcement officials will look to the local police for information or solicit their input to initiate an investigation. Even county officials in some areas respect the contacts local police officers have in the community and draw upon them.

Classifying Informants

For our purposes, informants as sources of information are divided into concerned and annoyed citizens, demented persons, law enforcement officers, defendant/law violators, and juvenile informants.

A *concerned citizen* will often approach a patrol officer or detective with information about general criminal activity in his or her community. Often a routine conversation about a domestic dispute or burglary the person is reporting or even about a simple noise ordinance violation may be developed into a fruitful source of data about something totally unrelated. The citizen may be quite willing to provide such information as routine activities of people. The key to informants of this type is rapport.

Usually an *annoyed citizen* is angry over a crime issue. We all know of some criminal activity, no matter how small or removed we are from it. The investigator needs to focus on the crime activity annoying the citizen. Is the problem a general one ("Drugs in my son's school") or a more specific one ("John Jones is dealing crack to my son's friends.")?

A *demented person* may provide useful information. An experienced investigator will be able to determine if the information was obtained from the news media or community gossip or if the individual suffers from hallucinations. Investigators should be careful not to disregard information from a mentally disturbed person. Often individuals may perform a criminal activity or even say something incriminating in the presence of a demented person simply because he or she is not perceived as a threat. Of course, all information obtained should be verified with independent sources.

Usually *law enforcement officers* exchange information with one another. They may also be a source of referral for informants. For example, patrol officers may not be interested in developing informants but may know street people or individuals who are willing to provide information to law enforcement officers. Developing a friendly relationship with other law enforcement personnel along with a reputation for working with informants leads to developing new informants. Informants may also switch allegiance to an investigator who is known to be willing to cultivate and work with them if they have personality conflicts or differences with the original investigator. Not all law enforcement personnel have the inclination or temperament to work with informants.

The *defendant/law violator* is the prime informer in investigations and apprehensions. Because this person wants help in having criminal charges against him or her dropped or lowered to a less severe charge, the defendant will share or willingly obtain information. Charges do not necessarily have to be dropped to develop an efficient relationship. Usually any criminal action or arrest involves multiple violations, and an informant can be developed from a routine arrest if the officer applies basic human relations skills. The patrol officer or investigator must be aware of these opportunities and pursue them aggressively.

As an informant, a juvenile may possess a wealth of information.

Juveniles are often most helpful in crimes involving their peers and may possess a wealth of information. It may be difficult to work with them, as juveniles (defined in most states as people under age 18) are protected in our society under the *parens patriae* concept, which holds that children are to be protected by the state as if it were a substitute parent. Although the investigator must be sensitive to the special status of juveniles, information can be obtained from them depending on local law enforcement practices and conditions. Investigators have used juveniles as informants to obtain information for conducting surveillance, obtaining search and seizure warrants, and introducing police personnel to law violators.

In one case, a store owner was selling amyl nitrate (a popper also known as Rush) to youngsters. The store owner was also selling pornography to minors. But even though a church group, the mayor and city council, and other community citizens were upset, no one would come forward to testify. Few parents want their child to testify in court on such activities. Because it was a small town, it would be difficult to conduct a surveillance; another store owner or the suspect would probably spot a stakeout. An informant was needed, specifically a minor.

The local police department sponsors a scouting group. The juvenile officer solicited three boys from the group—ages 14, 15, and 16—to enter the store and make the buys. Their parents consented based upon the juvenile officer's reputation. The boys were given basic instructions and taken through a dry run of the buy. When they made the buy, the juvenile officer arrested the store owner, who was ultimately convicted of selling Rush to minors.

The juvenile officer sent three boys for several reasons. First, credibility: the boys could corroborate each others' testimony. Second, it quieted their parents' fears. Third, it made all the boys safer in actuality. (They also used assumed names.)

Law enforcement agencies may make distinctions among informants, confidential informants, and special employees. An *informant* openly provides information and has no reservation about being identified as a source of information.

A *confidential informant* provides information about criminal activity but does not want to be identified. Investigators receive a great deal of information from confidential informants, whose mode of living, habits, and personal relations put them in contact with violators of the law. One informant interviewed by the author stated it was not uncommon in his neighborhood to discuss crimes openly and admitted to providing information about his friends. Since this informant lived in the neighborhood, he had freedom of movement and was trusted. The identity of confidential informants must be kept secret, both for their personal welfare and also to maintain their usefulness. Once his or her identity becomes known, an informant becomes useless to the police.

A *special employee* provides information for pay, works undercover under the supervision of an investigator, and may actually participate in a crime. Investigators should never use derogatory terms such as squealer, stoolie, snitch, or fink for informants. Some agencies have adopted the term "cooperative individual," or CI.

Evaluating Informants

An informant's value to an investigator must be continuously evaluated. The informant should provide specific and vital information that is essential to solving a case or making an arrest. An informant should:

- supply meaningful information relevant to the direction of inquiry,
- supply descriptive *data vita* to the furtherance of the investigation,
- supply direct contact with the subject of the inquiry, and/or

- offer photographs, personal documents, and layouts of apartments, business establishments, and locations frequented by subjects of the investigation. (Grau, 1981, pp. 4–64)

The initial screening of a potential informant includes a criminal history record check, a life-style check that includes habits, and a determination of motives. According to expert James Farris, most informants furnish information for the following reasons:

- Financial gain
- Hope that police activity based upon the information will eliminate their competition
- Revenge
- To mitigate or avoid punishment for their criminal activities
- Vanity
- Civic-mindedness.

Failure to furnish information is generally due to fear of retaliation, social chastisement, and rejection by peer groups.

A number of factors impede law enforcement officers' efforts to recruit informants. These factors should be taken seriously by officers who desire to cultivate and maintain informants.

Disrespect, Contempt, or Dislike for the Police

This negativity is difficult to overcome, yet a positive relationship can be established on a one-to-one basis in which friendship, trust, and rapport are established by the investigator as an *individual*, rather than primarily as a police officer. Essentially, the investigator and the source establish a social relationship aside from and in addition to their "professional" relationship.

Contemptuous Behavior, Feelings of Superiority, or Arrogance by the Police

Labeling informants as snitches, stoolies, or other derogatory names, and the subsequent body language and attitudes directed toward the source can breed the contempt, dislike, and disrespect of the police, described above. An investigator may personally find an informant's behavior despicable or personality aberrant, yet this must not be reflected in one's behavior toward the informant. Any disapproval expressed must be directed toward specific actions of the individual, not his or her personality—and these actions must be tolerated.

Failure by the Police to Keep Appointments, Keep Promises, or Provide Adequate Security for the Meeting

There is no excuse for shoddy management of informants. Informants are vital to any total information collection effort and must be handled with care. Failure to be courteous, provide security, or keep promises will probably result in the loss of important resources, thus diminishing the informant network. Generally, protection of the informant's identity is paramount. All efforts to ensure this protection must be employed, even to the point of losing a case.

Failure to Provide Feedback

Positive reinforcement to keep the informant interested and productive can rest upon his or her perceptions of whether or not the information given was used productively or produced tangible results. Often, the mere sharing of how the information helped and what is being done in a positive vein serves as a source of continued motivation. This is particularly important for high-level sources who are motivated by social concern and furnish information hoping that something will be done to alleviate certain types of crime, misconduct, or antisocial behavior.

Fear of Reprisal

Generally, the agency must establish and maintain a reputation of protecting sources at all costs. Sources must feel absolutely confident that they will be protected, their identity will not be disclosed without permission, and information will not be released that could subject them or their families to physical or psychological harm or unwarranted lawsuits. If it becomes necessary to choose between case completion and source protection, the agency must decide in favor of the source, except in extremely rare and critical situations.

The federal Freedom of Information Act and similar state laws designed to protect individuals from incorrect, slanderous, or malicious and unnecessary collection of information do present some severe operational problems. Unless identities can be protected from those criminals who use these laws to discover the identity of informants, the creation of a viable source program is unlikely. The federal law has provisions that preclude disclosure of police sources. State laws must also balance the protection of individuals from harm due to malicious information, incorrect information, and the like with the recognition that some matters must be kept confidential. Some form of autonomous, impartial judicial review seems in order regarding requests for files that contain sensitive criminal intelligence information.

Failure to Develop Policies and Programs to Enhance a Free Flow of Information Between Police and the Public They Serve

Organizational arrangements, such as decentralization and team policing can facilitate police/citizen contacts. By increased contacts with the citizens of the community, informants are initially identified. Through conversation and interaction with a variety of people from all walks of life, the police learn personalities, backgrounds, individual access to information, and individual willingness to share or obtain that information. Then, contingent upon identifiable, prioritized crime problems, potential confidential informants can be approached and recruited. Ultimately, free flow of information and crime control becomes a collective effort between police and public rather than unilaterally by the police. (Palmiotto, 1984, pp.31–33)

Developing and Managing Informants

It is important to remember that the informant in one form or another is volunteering, and a certain degree of ego fulfillment may be necessary. First the investigator must motivate the informant by developing *rapport,* or a harmonious relationship, with the subject. The informant must be confident and believe in what he or she is doing. One investigator interviewed uses a **mission orientation,** defining the goals and taking whatever lawful actions are required to accomplish the goal. The investigator must be a good reader of character to develop an informant properly. While the informant must trust the investigator, the investigator needn't trust the informant. Investigators must assess the degree of control that will be needed to accomplish their mission. One major problem investigators may have is that informants want to do it their way, which may contradict the law enforcement position. Maintaining control over informants is an ongoing, ever-changing situation that requires a perceptive investigator.

The next step is establishing a mechanism to reinforce that control—for example, requiring the informant to make a telephone call at a specific time. This control mechanism may be the only controllable variable in the case and should be rigidly enforced, although a contingent backup call time should be designated. If the informant proves unreliable in making the telephone call, the investigator has an unreliable informant. This is a rather neutral issue to establish the reliability factor and tighten up with. Informants can be told that reliability counts for at least half of the work they are doing for the investigator.

Long-term management of an informant requires interaction between the investigator and the informant. Generally, informants should stick with one investigator to guarantee maximum performance.

Cultural Issues

Basic sociological and psychological concepts apply to informant management. The informant's value to a great extent is determined by loyalty, motivation, and direction supplied by the investigator. All of these elements depend on rapport. In the case of a person from a different culture there usually exists an **ethnocentric** bias. These cultural values define one's relationship with other people. Issues of intimacy, trust, betrayal, revenge, and loyalty must be understood in the context of the environment the informant comes from.

There are two separate issues. First, the investigator needs to define his or her relationship with the informant. Second, the cultural differences will determine the operational obstacles.

The investigator may want to discuss the ethnic and cultural aspects with a law enforcement officer from the culture in question. For instance, an investigator may usually function as an excellent undercover operative when relating to Italians but have little tolerance for the ways of Latin Americans. It would be wise to ask a Hispanic colleague for periodic reality checks when using Hispanic informants.

Working relationships between people from different cultures are often complicated by ethnocentric feelings and dynamics. In cases of ethnocentric reactions, a little help in understanding the other person's culture will curtail confrontations. The key in dealing with informants from other cultures is the investigator's realization that he or she must attempt to understand specific incidents from the informant's value system in order to develop rapport and achieve success. Gender and class differences can also lead to misunderstandings unless the investigator makes an effort to see both sides.

Legal Issues

Law enforcement agencies in democratic societies operate under the code of law and are accountable for their actions in a legal context. Informants raise questions of criminal and civil liability for the agency involved. All supervisors are concerned that proper operational procedures, such as simple documentation of informants, be followed. Informants work for a law enforcement agency; they do not function as free-lancers. Since they work for the government, they must follow specific legal guidelines, which are discussed further in the section on the formal-managerial model.

The Formal-Managerial Model

The **formal-managerial model** requires that an informant management officer be appointed to supervise the program. The department must select targets, set priorities, and define systems. Managerial personnel should be rated on the quality of the program, but informant recruitment should be left to individual officers. The manager should maintain formal records on each informant, and investigators should share access to their informants with the rest of the department.

The informant program consists of three elements: the informant, the handling investigator and alternate, and management. Some agencies assign a supervisory investigator on a full-time basis to manage the informant program. In others, this is an additional assignment for the manager of the investigative function. Essentially, the handling investigator recruits and controls informants exclusively. However, this control is closely monitored by the informant manager for compliance with agency policy and rules.

The informant manager develops policy and procedural guidelines and coordinates them with police management. Investigators are given guidelines and restrictions on what the informant is allowed to do and how, as well as general instruction formalizing the relationship between the investigator and the informant.

Informants cannot be placed in a position to act as or appear to be acting as sworn officers. Informants are instructed regarding specific information desired. Informants are not allowed to participate in felonious activities. And source meetings are documented and a brief report submitted to the person performing the informant management.

Additional procedures are formulated for meetings with and the protection of high-risk informants at all times, both during and following completion of the case, until they are no longer threatened.

Specific guidance for the use and approval of departmental funds must be clearly delineated in order to protect the investigator and the agency from allegations of improper, fraudulent, or negligent expenditures of public funds. The informant manager is the focal point for management of confidential funds for the department.

An additional responsibility for the informant manager is as a coordinating member of the intelligence unit, if one exists. In this capacity, the informant manager can advise the intelligence unit commander or the analysis unit about available informants, potential targets, and areas needing further source developments. He or she can provide necessary information regarding risk to, access to, and protection of, sensitive sources. The manager is responsible for the management, protection, movement, and assistance of high-risk sources, including case control of subsequent investigations regarding intimidation, assault, or other crimes directed against informants.

Periodic reviews of the files of all informants are conducted by the informant manager and handling investigators in order to evaluate the overall productivity of each informant and the quality, quantity, reliability, and veracity of information provided. These reviews also preclude the probability that the same informant is furnishing information to several investigators who then claim that the information is from several different, reliable informants and therefore more credible. They also reduce the chances of undue or unnecessary duplication of information coverage on specified targets.

The informant manager is the expert on informants in terms of techniques or recruitment, control, legal issues, and administration. He or she advises the chief of the agency in these matters and is also responsible for training departmental personnel in informant management.

The control of specific crime problems becomes a system's goal; means, methods, or tactics must be identified that will lead the agency toward goal accomplishment. The use of confidential informants is but one of several proactive tactics. (Others include surveillance, undercover operations, and stings.) The agency determines tactics contingent upon the threat of any given crime problem to the community by defining the problem as a target, prioritizing targets by immediacy of threat, and allocating departmental resources, such as assigning investigators for specific areas. Targeted areas for source coverage are identified and line units are directed to recruit informants who have access, if appropriate. Hence, if a problem area is best controlled by the use of confidential informants, it will be the responsibility of patrol as well as detectives to recruit informants having information germane to that area.

Managerial personnel should be rated on the quality of the informant program. This forces line managers to be concerned with a viable informant program in order to be retained or promoted.

The specific decision of whom to approach and recruit is left to the individual officers. However, strict guidelines from management exist regarding responsibilities of the officer and control and management of the informant.

All informants are checked to ascertain criminal history, prior use as an informant, and whether they are currently acting as informants for another law enforcement agency. This initial screening becomes the basis for a file on each informant. Files and documentation are maintained on all informants to evaluate their effectiveness, provide written documentation of information previously received, and establish their reliability and veracity for any further legal needs (for example, testimony in court, probable cause for search warrants, or court-ordered eavesdropping).

At a minimum, files will be kept on times, dates, places of meets, and persons present; information received; instructions or guidelines given; and disbursement of funds, if any. This documentation is necessary for future appraisal of the operation, the worth of the source, reliability and veracity of information, instructions given in case of future legal dispute, and a possible audit trail for expenditures of departmental funds.

Access to the files is limited to the informant manager, handling agent, and alternate for each departmental informant. All department informants are known by the informant manager, but investigators know the identity of their informants only. Assigning an alternative handling investigator or officer ensures continuity of informant handlings. Consequently, each informant is known by a maximum of only three people in the department.

Investigative reports with information furnished by sensitive informants are screened by the informant management officer to make sure the identity of the informant cannot be deduced from the facts presented and to record information received from each informant that assists in case development. This ensures proper management of all informants, and provides for cost effective analysis of the overall informant program.

Informants are considered *departmental resources,* not just the resources of each individual officer. Information requested or derived from informants is shared, though the handling of the informant remains with a specific investigator or alternate. For example, Investigator Jones may need information regarding a specific crime problem or investigation on which he is working. However, his current informants do not have access to the information. The informant manager may suggest that one of Investigator Smith's informants has access to such information. If Smith's informant has the information, the information is passed on to Jones via the informant manager, without disclosure of Smith's informant's identity to Jones.

Working an Informant

The investigator should size up the informant before trying to develop a strategy or approach to a specific case. During this process, rapport is built and the investigator learns about likes, dislikes, prejudices, and preferences that help establish the tone for situations he or she will be involved in with the informant. The investigator talks about circumstances of immediate concern to determine if any needs exist. Often the informant is in a position, perhaps under arrest or injured, that may provide the investigator with an opportunity to help. Nothing builds rapport better than being helpful.

Generally, an investigator attempting to control a situation is not helpful, since individuals under arrest or duress tend to be especially tuned in to the reality factor of their situation. If they perceive that the investigator is manipulating them, then the informants will also practice manipulation. As a rule, investigators should help informants if possible, but there are times when a general understanding of the informants' personal values and life situation serves just as well.

The investigator must get the informant talking. Most law enforcement officers first size up the person they are talking to. The next step consists of applying basic sociological analysis—for instance, obtaining the age, religion, and political orientation of the informant. Knowing the informant's socioeconomic status will reveal many aspects of his or her value system relating to money, time, and sophistication of operations. It may be helpful to determine the informant's attitude toward what the investigator may be requesting. Resourcefulness should also be determined: Does the informant think and act quickly, or is he or she generally confused when confronted by a new situation? The informant must be adaptable to make a successful transition to his or her new role.

The investigator should know what he or she will be looking

for. Suppose the investigator wants a drug buy to take place in a certain store. He or she must evaluate whether the informant can maneuver a dealer or not. If not, the investigator must provide a rationale that will make the buy happen at the right place. An informant who is wearing a body mike must be resourceful enough to keep from being searched. Always, the human variable rules. Everyone has limitations, and the investigator must know the informant's. It may help to test the informant by having him or her work on a small aspect of a case. The major considerations are time and the chances of discovery.

Investigators develop rapport when they listen to their informants and fit their operations into the informants' basic operating pattern. A common mistake is the failure to spend enough time developing rapport with an informant. It may take as little as one half-hour session or as much as several longer ones. The investigator must sense when rapport has become strong enough to accomplish the objective involved. Often, good informants have been lost because the officer didn't evaluate them accurately. Recently an officer lost a good informant because he tried to establish authority and control quickly, assuming he had the power to do so. The potential informant gave attractive but phony information because he was insulted and not as needy as the officer thought.

Remember that rapport means connection and ultimately dependence on both parties, investigator and informant. Communicating is often a cultural issue, and what may appear to be rapport may be only a testing ground, with the premise, "I'll trust you a little and let's see what happens." Both investigator and informant are going through this testing, usually on a subconscious level, and the psychological factor needs to be considered. Only when both feel truly safe with the relationship will they do business. At the same time, the officer should not appear indecisive and drag out the rapport-building process. The informant may perceive a delay as jerking him around and respond in kind to the officer.

True rapport comes from a combined personal human experience in personal interaction and an understanding of the cultural setting. Deepening of rapport will come as the investigator shows ability to empathize with the informant's obstacles. An example of how human experiences help in developing rapport comes out in a story told to the author. A friend told an investigator that she was annoyed because her 29-year-old fiancé had received a letter from a 17-year-old girl. The girl was a Guatemalan while the woman and her fiancé were Irish American. She thought the letter was romantic when it was actually just friendly. The investigator explained to her that the Latin style involved open demonstrations of affection and a Hispanic reader would have considered anything less a sign of indifference. The investigator showed the Irish woman a Latin-style love letter by way of contrast, and she realized that her first reaction had been ethnocentric.

The "present setting" is the facts and circumstances that bring the investigator and informant together. Some people will spy on others solely based upon their need, but most must have other motivation. They need to rationalize what they are doing as right or good. The setting and circumstances may dictate the investigator's style. "A nice guy" approach may be fine—if the subject considers it an appropriate attitude for an investigator. Draw out the informant. One investigator told the author that he never reads informants their constitutional rights because, given his personality, it would make him appear too tough. Instead, he operated on perceived and implied power.

Every investigator must determine what method works best for him or her. Is the investigator easygoing? Or abrasive and tough? The informant is calculating an accumulation of responses, so the investigator's goal should be to establish control and authority, but most of all cooperation.

If the investigator gets angry too often, the informant may be turned off and refuse to cooperate. However, anger may be appropriate at times as long as the investigator manages his or her feelings. Nonproductive dialogue can be made productive if the informant is aroused, scared, or threatened in some way. The key question is whether the investigator can soothe the informant and carry on business.

Once rapport has been established, the investigator needs to control the informant, making sure he or she follows directions as to when to report in and how to proceed properly. For example, a controlled drug buy usually requires that the informant not be in possession of any contraband at the time of the buy, so the investigator will want to search the informant before the buy. Or suppose a conspiracy investigation is under way. The informant may be required to avoid entrapping the defendant. The informant must obey the rules of the game—instructions as to law and criminal procedure. **Control** means the informant realizes and accepts that procedures, directions, and times of meeting with police personnel must be followed to the letter. The out-of-control or wild informant should be considered dangerous and problematic to the case.

After control has been established, the ongoing relationship must be maintained. Don't shift details to other investigators; an informant requires personal attention. In fact, any investigator who cannot handle such details well should not handle an informant.

The supervisor should evaluate this at the initial stages in case the informant needs to be taken over. Improper handling cannot be undone easily, if at all.

Recognizing Soft Intelligence

Law enforcement officers constantly learn basic information about criminal activity from various sources. Usually general data of possible criminals are of no particular interest, but data pertaining to marital status, physical health, and a potential defendant's family and friends are of value to investigators. Secondary interests of potential defendants all provide basic information that may be useful at some future date.

These kinds of **soft intelligence** may be developed through three methods. The first is an arrest situation. Interviews with contemporary investigators reveal that fewer than five percent of law enforcement personnel bother to note information found in a person's wallet during an arrest. The officers check the arrestee's car insurance card, motor vehicle registration, and driver's license expiration date. However, they fail to notice pictures of friends, phone

An arrestee's automobile may hold evidence of immediate or future value.

numbers and addresses of associates, and business cards of people the arrestee does business with.

Anything found in the arrestee's car may be very important, immediately or at a later date. All calls made by the arrested person should be logged while he or she is in custody. This information may prove valuable if the arrestee fails to appear for a court hearing. After all, the arrested individual is in trouble and presumably is phoning people who can help.

The second source of information is all the connections the investigator makes with people in the community or geographic area. Generally, community people provide the raw data the investigator uses to assess them all as potential informants. One avenue open to patrol officers is to develop rapport with convenience-store managers and workers. Sometimes providing little favors, such as checking on workers' safety, will lead to a worker becoming an informant. Helping rather than harassing people often leads them to provide information. Officers who develop rapport with people are usually successful in developing informants. They can relate to the individual's culture and value system and see him or her as an individual. Successful officers do not see people as simply good guys or bad guys. Patrol officers who develop informants this way will keep them after entering the investigative unit.

The third source of data is fellow law enforcement officers. Traditionally in law enforcement, information is covert, but there is also a tradition of trade-offs with fellow officers. So the better you get at developing information, the better information you will get from colleagues. Often a patrol officer who has no desire to work with informants will refer them to an investigator who has a reputation for working well with informants.

Soft intelligence doesn't make a case per se, but it may trigger a response or encourage someone to cooperate or provide closure on an issue. It can be compared to a jigsaw puzzle: Even the smallest piece can be important to one's understanding of a case.

Procedural Safeguards and the Need to Know

Informal operations require a high degree of sensitivity to the release of information that can affect the performance and integrity of an informant. The dilemma has been created by the conflicting need for secrecy and need to know the data.

In the federal agencies, a case concerning informants or their information is safeguarded within the agency on a "need to know" basis only. **Need to know** assumes that only what is needed will be shared and then only with people who have a reputation for being able to retain such information confidentially. Competent police operations respect the balance between the two needs. Secrecy carried too far means others who could assist an investigation are ignorant, while knowledge easily shared threatens the informant, the case, and possibly law enforcement officers working undercover now or in the future.

Agencies' approach to sharing information differ. Law enforcement agencies should take operational procedures into consideration when sharing data. A supervisor needs to know information provided by an informant and needs to know when information has been shared. Most sophisticated informant operations require formal identification, including photographing and fingerprinting the informant, to protect both the informant and the agency. The supervisor also should be in a position to evaluate the officer's handling of the informant. Such evaluations can curtail any criticism that the investigator operates too much on his or her own.

The secrecy of the case may be an issue. A drug enforcement unit, for example, is a confidential environment. Each operating unit works without knowledge of what the others may be doing. Coordination of operations occurs only at the higher levels to protect the case.

Since informants can be a source of leaks and security compromises, investigators should share information with them only when necessary. All informants can be expected to use any information they observe or are told about. At times the "need to know" rule is enforced fiercely within the agency but too casually with informants.

Crime-Specific Informants

Most informants have certain characteristics in common, but there are personality traits that tend to be seen among informants within certain specialties. There are also specific techniques that may be most effective in approaching informants within these areas. The three types of criminal activity most investigators will be working on are burglary, drug dealing, and sex offenses.

Burglary

Informants can be developed from a variety of sources once the investigator determines who has committed a burglary. A detective bureau can usually accomplish this through crime patterns and soft intelligence. The arrest of crime offenders from the burglary group may yield the investigator an informant—for example, a violator on the state motor vehicle department's revoked driving list or a defendant in need of bail at a reasonable rate. Offenders in trouble are often willing to provide information for assistance. One investigator said he might overlook a revoked driver's license if the offender would provide information, or he might make the arrest and speak to the district attorney on the defendant's behalf.

Another method of developing informants is a crime-stopper program, which has worked well in several areas of the country. This method is based on a payment of money for anonymous information. As a commercial crime, burglary tends to breed a commercial attitude among its participants. Often a holder of stolen property is willing to cooperate in exchange for leniency. The holder of a minor piece of stolen property will often divulge who it was bought from.

Controlled Substances/Drugs

The narcotics investigator must develop informants to deal with illicit drug activities. The investigator needs to obtain strong evidence and informants who can assist in establishing an undercover operation. In most cases, drug informants have been arrested and want to obtain leniency for their criminal offenses. Unfortunately, the most cooperative informants either are useless or require such a commitment of an investigator's time that they are ineffective. Underworld drug informants can provide valuable information, since they belong to or know members of a drug-trafficking operation. Although total reliance on underworld informants should be avoided, they can be used to:

- Obtain information on drug dealers, how and where they operate, and where they conceal the illicit drug supplies commonly referred to as stashes.
- Introduce an undercover agent to drug dealers and, if possible, to middle- and upper-echelon suppliers. This is sometimes referred to as "duking" the agent into the operation.
- Make drug buys and conduct negotiations with dealers that will lead to the purchase of drugs by undercover agents.
- Conduct surveillance in locales where unknown persons would not be able to operate, or obtain neighborhood acceptance of and establish covers for agents by being seen hanging around with them.

- Develop intelligence information for use in future narcotics investigations.
- Serve as prosecution witnesses (but only if their courtroom testimony is absolutely vital in bringing about the conviction of a narcotics dealer). (Katz, 1978, p. 6)

Narcotics informants provide information for a variety of reasons. They may want to eliminate competition and increase their own profits. They may be out for revenge, to sell information for money, or to obtain consideration for an offense they are charged with.

The informant charged with a crime needs assistance. He or she may want to have the charges dropped, the number of charges reduced, or the type of charges reduced to less serious ones. The potential informant may be amenable to plea bargaining. Usually the most reliable drug informants are the ones who want to avoid arrest or reduce their punishment for having committed an offense. Regardless of who makes the initial offer to provide information, ground rules should be established.

- Charges for which the informant was arrested must be filed and judicial proceedings carried forth.
- The officer cannot make any promises other than to contact the district attorney on the informant's behalf. Any promise must be made by a member of the district attorney's staff.
- If the informant is still in jail and cannot make bail, the district attorney must contact a judge and arrange for a reduction of bail.
- Reduction of bail and release from jail must be arranged in such a way that other inmates will not suspect the informant.
- Before any deal is made, the officer and the staff member from the district attorney's office must advise the informant of what is expected and what will happen if he or she does not produce or double-crosses the officer.
- It must be made perfectly clear that the informant will not receive immunity from arrest and prosecution for any crimes committed during the time he or she serves as an informant. (Katz, 1978, pp. 6–7)

Once an agreement is made, the investigator should work to maintain a harmonious relationship with the informant. An atmosphere of mutual trust is needed to work in drug operations successfully.

Sex Offenses

Informants in the sex offense areas are difficult to develop because of the intimacy of the sex act. In our culture, like most others, providing information about sex-related offenses may mean exposure of the informant's personal sexual preference and behavior.

In homosexual crimes against children, an informant may serve very well. On the other hand, rape cases are usually solved by conventional investigative methods. In cases of **pedophilia,** when children are the sex objects, it is important to respect the informant's personal dignity.

Pedophiles prey upon children through a process of seduction, which leads to three immediate problems. First, they are usually physically involved with the child. Second, they have established an emotional connection with the child. Third, the child doesn't want his or her parents or the public to know about the involvement. However, when the juvenile has been convinced that the investigator knows of the participation and realizes that a seduction has occurred, the youngster may open up. The investigator needs to reinforce the idea that because of the child's age it was wrong of the adult to become involved under any circumstances. Although this is a delicate process, it has worked for many investigators.

To assist in the investigation of rape cases, an investigator can develop an alliance with feminist groups. Only a small percentage of rape cases ever get reported. A contact in the National Organization for Women may provide names of victims or even be willing to act as an intermediary to gather factual information that could lead to an arrest. Experienced investigators know that obtaining a piece of information from one case and another piece from another may ultimately solve the crime.

In a typical tough case, the mother of a 16-year-old male told a juvenile investigator her son had been approached by a 53-year-old male at her son's place of employment, a local gas station. The man said he wanted to photograph the boy for a commercial advertisement and would pay up to $35.00 for photos. The boy was of course interested and told his mother about the offer. The youngster was willing to cooperate, according to his mother, because he was not going to do anything wrong.

The investigator asked to speak to the son, who said he wanted the money. The investigator suggested that the man was homosexual. The boy at first ignored this fact. Since the investigator was an experienced sex investigator he knew the boy did not understand seduction; in fact, he didn't know the definition of the word. The first step was to educate the boy without unduly jading him. Second, the investigator had to build the boy's self-esteem so he would see that it was the adult who was behaving inappropriately. Once the investigator convinced the boy that seducing a youngster was wrong, he obtained his cooperation.

A motivated informant who believes in what he is doing is the key to a successful investigation. In a sex case, the belief must be specific: It is wrong for an older man to approach a teenager. The emotional development of 14- to 16-year-olds makes sexuality a difficult area to judge. The victim may not want to discuss sexual feelings with the police. He may just want to forget the situation or be concerned that the man will retaliate. Teenagers often have a negative attitude toward authority—another reason the boy hesitated to go to the police.

In this case, the offender approached the juvenile for three months before he asked to take pictures. The man knew the youngster's basic attitude toward parents and authority. Basically, he psychologically profiled the boy.

Summary

Informants are essential to the successful investigation and detection of many violent and financial crimes. As sources of information, informants are classified as concerned or annoyed citizens, demented persons, law enforcement officers, law violators, or juvenile informants.

Law enforcement agencies distinguish among informants, confidential informants, and special employees. An informant openly provides information and has no reservations about being identified as a source of information. A confidential informant provides information about criminal activity but does not want to be identified. A special employee provides information for pay and works under the supervision of an investigator. There are also informants who provide information for specific types of crimes such as drugs, burglaries, and sex offenses.

Motives for informants providing information include financial gain, revenge, and civic-mindedness. A potential informant may refuse to provide information because of disrespect for the police, arrogance on the part of the police, fear of reprisal, or failure of the police to provide feedback. Investigators need to develop the skills that will persuade informants to volunteer information.

Investigators should recognize soft intelligence and be familiar with legal procedures, and know how to work informants. Law enforcement agencies should follow the characteristics of the formal-managerial model as it relates to informants.

Key Terms

control
ethnocentric
formal-managerial model
informant
mission orientation
need to know
pedophile
rapport
soft intelligence

Review Questions

1. How are informants classified?
2. How does an investigator ascertain the value of an informant?
3. What motivates an informant to provide police with information?
4. What are some of the factors that contribute to failure to recruit informants?
5. How does an investigator develop an informant?
6. What is soft intelligence?
7. What are some of the cultural issues that pertain to informant development and management?
8. Describe the characteristics of the formal-managerial model.

References

Grau JJ: *Criminal and Civil Investigation Handbook*. New York, NY: McGraw-Hill, 1981.

Katz HA: "Narcotics Investigations: Developing and Using Informants." *Police Law Quarterly* 7:6, 1978.

Palmiotto MJ: *Critical Issues in Criminal Investigation*. Cincinnati, OH Anderson Publishing Co., 1984.

CHAPTER 7

Writing Reports and Field Notes

Without effective communications, police officers and criminal investigators could not obtain the vital information needed to control and solve crimes. Writing skills, like report writing and note-taking, are as important as oral communications skills. Law enforcement officers must write reports for everything from a simple dog complaint to murder.

Effective reports are an essential element of a criminal investigation. An investigator usually compiles notes from interviews, organizes and evaluates them, and prepares a report. Information is obtained through interviews and interrogation. The laws of all states require written reports of all criminal offenses, and most law enforcement agencies require reports for all citizen contacts with the police. A law enforcement report is a legal document of an event or a criminal or citizen complaint, based upon factual information. This report should be retained for future use. Writing an effective report requires three basic steps.

- conducting a proper inquiry, thoroughly examining all relevant information, and taking accurate, complete notes,
- analyzing and organizing the findings of the inquiry, and
- communicating all relevant findings in a clear, concise, and coherent report.

Field Notes

The purpose of a criminal investigation is to gather all information pertaining to a specific case. The investigator should keep track of all factual data and details during the investigative process by making notes in a personal **field notebook**.

Because of the nature of police work, reports are usually prepared from field notes. The law enforcement officer's notebook serves as a permanent record and a memory bank. Few officers could remember every specific detail of a crime weeks, months, or years afterward, but with field notes they can recollect a crime scene for court testimony. Efficient investigators record details because they realize their memory may fail them. Investigators should take notes of observations of crime scenes, sources of information, and interviews. Notebooks can also help in preparing for interviews. For example, an arresting officer can give an interviewer background information that may play a role in the questioning of a suspect.

In a criminal investigation, the following essential information should be recorded in a notebook.

- the time the officer received the call or complaint and the means by which it was made,
- identity of the investigating officer or officers,
- exact identification of the offense, the location, the time, and the method,
- exact identification and description of each item of evidence the officer observes or obtains,
- all other officials who were notified,
- the marking and disposition of each item of evidence,
- what photos and drawings were made and measurements taken,
- all facts, with details, that the officer obtains,
- all statements, with details, that the officer obtains,
- complete identifying information on each person who makes statements or gives information,
- complete identification and description of the offender or offenders,
- details of the follow-up on each separate lead and of the search for leads,
- details of any arrests made,
- details of the route by which the offender entered and left,
- present location of the offender, if known, and
- further action indicated. (Levie and Ballard, 1978, pp. 27–28)

The information recorded in the notes becomes the content of the report. Efficient note-taking can lead to better reports. Also, notes taken during one investigation may be of help in another investigation.

Even information that seems unimportant should be recorded in detail. For example, a knife found at the scene of a crime should be accurately detailed and the exact location where it was found should be recorded. Efficient note-taking can assist the investigator in courtroom testimony. Law enforcement officers prepare for cases by reviewing their notes.

Notes should be taken as the information is received—for instance, during an interview, not twenty minutes later. They should be legible and understandable. All notebook entries should be in waterproof ink to remove any possibility of tampering. Personal information should not be written in the notebook; phone numbers, shopping lists, and friends' addresses can only cause embarrassment and project an unprofessional image if the notebook is used in court and the defense attorney reads its contents to the jury. The entries should be plainly written, since misinterpreted notes can create false leads and possible ridicule in the hands of a defense attorney. Each incident or interview should be on a new page. The officer's name and police department should appear.

Like any tool, some notebooks work better than others and some people prefer one type over another. The two basic types of notebook are the looseleaf and the binder. With the looseleaf, the officer can remove pages of a specific case without taking the whole book to the witness stand. However, the defense could accuse the officer of removing pertinent pages. With a bound book, the defense attorney cannot complain that pages beneficial to the defense have been removed. Its big disadvantage is that when an officer brings his or her notebook to the witness stand as a memory aid, the defense attorney may obtain permission to examine it, thus gaining access to information pertaining to other cases and of a confidential nature.

Reports

When a crime is reported to the police, preliminary investigation is usually conducted by a patrol officer, who obtains as much detail about the crime as possible. The **preliminary report** should contain names of the victims, location of the offense, type of offense, date and time the crime was reported, date and time the offense occurred, method of operation, identification of suspect if known, any eyewitnesses, and any other detailed information useful in solving the crime. For example, in a burglary the police officer should obtain a list of items missing, determine the point of entry, and canvass the neighborhood to find out whether the neighbors heard

FIGURE 7–1: Example of Armed Robbery Police Report

SAVANNAH POLICE DEPARTMENT — PRELIMINARY INVESTIGATION

PERSON ______ PROPERTY __X__ MISCELLANEOUS ______ JUVENILE ______

1 CTS	2 UCC	3 UCC	4 X-Y
1	1201		

5 INCIDENT	6 LOCATION OF OCCURENCE	7 CRN
ARMED ROBBERY	607 STEVENS LANE	921064397

8 COMPLAINANT LAST	FIRST	MIDDLE	9 ADDRESS OF COMPLAINANT	10 PHONE # (RES/BUS)
GREENBERG	MARCUS	L.	1012 INDIANA ST.	/

TIME

11 DISPATCHED TO BEAT #	12 DATE (OCC/DIS)	13 DAY OF WEEK	14 TIME (OCC/DIS)	15 DATE (LAST KNOWN SECURE) FROM	16 TIME (L/K SECURE)	17 BEAT THAT OFFICER IS ASSIGNED TO:
207	10-29-92	THURS	0943			207

CLR

18 CLEARED BY: A B C D E — CHG ___ SER ___ ADMIN ___ EX CLR ___ UNF ___

19 DATE CLEARED:

20 THEFT [X] REC [ ] — (1 CITY) 3 STATE 2 COUNTY 4 OTHER

21 TOTAL NUMBER ARRESTED — ADULT 0 JUVENILE 0

22 WAS SUSPECT ARMED? YES X NO ___

SUSPECT # 1

23 WAS SUSPECT SEEN? YES X NO ___

24 VICTIM TO SUSPECT RELATIONSHIP: STRANGER (1) Y — UNKNOWN (2) U X — ACQUAINT/FRIEND (3) N — RELATIVE (4) N — SPOUSE (5) N

25 NUMBER OF SUSPECTS ___

26 SPONTANEOUS STATEMENT MADE? YES ___ NO ___

27 SUSPECT ARRESTED? YES ___ NO X

28 NAME: LAST FIRST MIDDLE — UNKNOWN

29 ADDRESS AND RES. PHONE # — UNKNOWN

30 ALIAS/NICKNAME	31 RACE	32 SEX	33 AGE/DOB	34 HGT	35 WGT	36 HAIR (COLOR, LENGTH, STYLE)	37 FACE HAIR	38 EYES	39 INTOXICATED?
	ASIAN	M	20(S)	5'7	150	BRN - SHORT		BRN	YES ___ NO ___

40 SKIN TONE, COMPLEXION	41 HAT	42 GLASSES N P S	43 COAT	44 SHIRT	45 PANTS	46 SHOES	47 SCARS, MARKS, TATOOS, DEFORMITIES, TEETH
MED			RED		BLUE		

48 DRUGS YES ___ NO ___
[ ] 1 - AMPHETAMINE [ ] 2 - BARBITURATE [ ] 3 - COCAINE [ ] 10 - U - UNKNOWN
[ ] 4 - HALLUCINOGEN [ ] 5 - HEROIN [ ] 6 - MARIJUANA [ ] 11 - INHALANT
[ ] 7 - METHAMPHETAMINE [ ] 8 - OPIUM [ ] 9 - SYNTHETIC NARCOTIC [ ] 12 - ALCOHOL

PREMISE

1 HIGHWAY — 2 SERVICE STATION 49 — 3 CHAIN STORE — 4 BANK — 5 (COMMERCIAL) — 6 RESIDENCE — 7 ___

50		51 TV, RADIO, ETC.	52 HOUSEHOLD GOODS	53 VEHICLES	54 CURRENCY	55 JEWELRY	56 LIVESTOCK
STOLEN	[X]	$ .00	$ .00	$ .00	$ .00	$ 80 .00	$ .00
		57 CLOTHING, FURS	58 OFFICE EQUIP.	59 VEHICLE ACC.	60 FIREARMS	61 CONSUMER GOODS	62 OTHER
RECOVERED	[ ]						
LOST	[ ]	$ .00	$ .00	$ .00	$ .00	$ .00	$ .00

TARGET

63 ~~VICTIM~~ NAME OF BUSINESS/ STORE # — RICHARDSON JEWELERS

64 ~~VICTIM~~/BUSINESS ADDRESS — 607 STEVENS LANE

65 PHONE #

VICTIM I.D. — 66 DOB 11-21-16 — 67 AGE 74 — 68 SEX M — 69 HGT 5'4 — 70 WGT 115 — 71 RACE WHT — 72 HAIR GREY — 73 Y CITY RESIDENT? Y/N — 74 INTOXICATED? YES ___ NO X

75 POINT OF ENTRY/EXIT: (1) DOOR (2) WINDOW (3) ROOF (4) WALL (5) GARAGE (6) FENCE/GATE (7) TRUNK (8) OTHER

76 LOCATION ENTRY/EXIT: (1) FRONT (2) SIDE (3) REAR — (A) VISIBLE FROM STREET (B) HIDDEN FROM STREET

77 WILL VICTIM PROSECUTE? YES ___ NO ___

78 ITEM DAMAGED ENTRY: (1) LOCK/HASP (2) HINGE (3) GLASS (4) SCREEN (5) WOOD (6) BURG BARS (7) NONE (8) OTHER

79 INSTRUMENT FOR ENTRY: (1) BAR (2) BRICK (3) BODY/HAND/FOOT (4) SAW/CUTTER/KNIFE (5) KEYS (6) UNK (7) NOT LOCKED (8) OTHER

80 METHOD OF ENTRY: (1) SMASHED (2) PRIED (3) PUSHED IN (4) CUT (5) FORCED LOCK (6) NOT LOCKED (7) KICKED (8) REMOVED (9) OTHER

81 SUSPECT ACTION: (1) NOTHING TAKEN (2) SELECTIVE IN LOOT (3) MONEY ONLY (4) RANSACKED (5) ATE/DRANK (6) SMOKED

82 WEAPON YES ___ NO ___: REVOLVER (1A) — AUTO PISTOL (1B) — UNK PISTOL (1C) — RIFLE (1D) — SHOTGUN (1E) — KNIFE (2F) — HAND (3G) — OTHER (4H) — BLUE/BLACK — N.P./CHROME

VEHICLE

83 NONE X — SUSPECT'S ___ — VICTIM'S ___ — 84 YEAR — 85 MANUFACTURER — 86 MODEL — 87 STYLE — 88 COLOR — 89 TAG # — 90 STATE/YR.

91 DOOR LOCKED? YES ___ NO ___ UNK ___ — 92 KEYS LEFT IN CAR? YES ___ NO ___ UNK ___ — 93 STEERING COLUMN DAMAGED? YES ___ NO ___ — 94 VIN.

95 FINANCED BY (COMPANY) NONE ___ UNK ___ — 96 LOCATION IMPOUNDED — 97 OWNER NOTIFIED YES ___ NO ___ — 98 CHECKED 10-28 YES ___ NO ___ AVAILABLE YES ___ NO ___ — 99 CHECKED 10-29 YES ___ NO ___ AVAILABLE YES ___ NO ___

100 LIST 10-28 INFO.(MANUFACTURER, MODEL, COLOR, YR.) — 101 INSURANCE CO. OR AGENT — 102 SUPPORTS WITNESSES VEHICLE ID.

103 WITNESS L.F.M.	104 ADDRESS OF WITNESS	105 PHONE (WITNESS)
LOUISE MEADE	127 HARRISON	966-2798

106 NARRATIVE (USE BLOCK #, LIST ALL SERIAL #, INCLUDE: WHO, WHAT, WHEN, WHERE, HOW, AND WHY. EXPLAIN WHAT YOU DID OR DID NOT DO AND WHY.

ITEM NO #55 1 GOLD RING YELLOW IN COLOR VALUED AT $80.00

SIR: THE VICTIM ALSO BEING THE COMP; STATED THAT THE SUSPECT HAD BEEN COMING TO THE STORE FOR ABOUT THREE DAYS TRYING TO LEAVE A FIVE DOLLAR DEPOSIT ON A RING – TODAY 10-29-93 SUSPECT RETURNED WITH A PISTOL AND DEMANDED THE RING. SUSPECT GRABBED THE RING AND FLED WEST ON STEVENS LANE. LOOK OUT WAS POSTED ON SUSPECT

107 SERIAL NUMBER: X (1) N/A — (2) NO RECORD KEPT — (3) SEE ABOVE — (4) CALL LATER

108 WAS I.D. REQUESTED? YES ___ NO ___

109 SUPPORTING OFFICER — PR #

110 DATE AND TIME COMPLETED — 10-29-92 1003

111 SUBMITTED BY — Lauren Pruzan — PR# 8093

112 SUPERVISOR — Sgt C.D. Brown — PR# 5825

113 ADD REPORT ___ YES ___ NO — 114 REVIEW

SDP FORM 1-58 (JAN 91)

ORIGINAL

Source: Courtesy of the Savannah, Georgia Police Department.

or saw anything unusual. Figure 7–1 is a sample preliminary investigation report on an armed robbery.

When the preliminary investigation has been completed, the assigned investigator does the follow-up/supplementary, progress, and closing reports. **Supplementary reports** are used by investigators to add any additional information to a criminal case. A case is closed when new information has ceased or an arrest has been made. Most law enforcement agencies have a deadline, perhaps 30 days, after which **progress reports** are submitted and cases evaluated to determine whether they are to stay active or be closed.

Principles of Report Writing

Reports should be accurate, clear, complete, concise, and brief. Accuracy means that reports are exact, precise, truthful, relevant, and objective. Investigative reports must be free from bias and personal opinions. They deal with facts and details and do not include hearsay or personal judgments. A complete report includes all the details of an investigation but only those details related specifically to a case. Concise reports do not have unnecessary verbiage.

Investigative reports are concerned with information for a specific crime. Law enforcement officers must be able to distinguish among statements of fact, inference, and opinion. An objective expression of what an investigator hears or sees is a statement of fact (for example, Mr. Jones stated, "I was robbed"). Hunches, assumptions, and guesses are statements of inference (for example, "The man appeared to be drunk."). Judgments about people, acts, or situations are statements of opinions, even if they begin with a factual statement (for example, "Mr. Jones is a thief."). (Johnson and Pease, 1982, pp. 89–91)

Law Enforcement Reports

Law enforcement reports can be classified into two major areas, administrative and operational. **Administrative reports** deal with such daily activities as staffing, policy, procedures, and facility maintenance.

Operational reports deal with law enforcement activities. They include arrest reports, investigative reports (preliminary follow-up/supplementary, and progress), evidence reports, and crime reports. Law enforcement officers investigating crimes are primarily con-

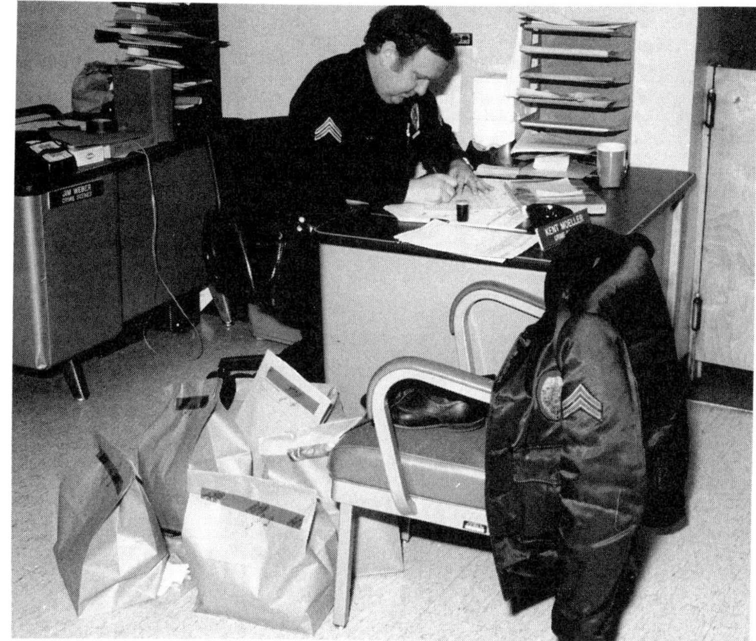

This investigator is in the lab writing up a report of a shooting scene. On the floor is the collected evidence, including clothes and gunshot-residue test samples, sealed in protective bags.

cerned with investigative reports. The only exception is **crime reports**, which provide statistical data to state and federal agencies. Evidence reports pertain to the finding, marking, examination, and disposition of evidence.

Investigative reports are used, not simply filed. They are needed for the efficient operation of criminal investigations. Reports can be used to keep other investigators informed of the progress and status of investigations. They can also be used to prepare court cases and provide the court with pertinent facts.

Investigators must realize that they are writing for people not familiar with the crime, people who have not seen the crime scene or interviewed witnesses and victims. Investigative reports may be read by other investigators, prosecutors, defense attorneys, judges, jurors, federal and state investigatory agencies, media personnel, and heads of various governmental agencies. The writer must relate the report to the offense and clarify how he or she reached conclusions.

Each report should attempt to answer six basic questions relating to a crime: who, what, where, when, how, and why? According to Hess and Wrobleski (1978, pp. 22–24), most reports need to answer the following questions.

When:
- did the incident happen?
- was it discovered?
- was it reported?
- did the police arrive at the scene?
- were the suspects arrested?
- will the case be heard in court?

Where:
- did the incident happen?
- was evidence found? stored?
- do victims, witnesses, and suspects live?
- do suspects spend most of their time?

Who:
- are suspects? accomplices? Include the following information.
  - sex
  - race, coloring
  - age
  - height
  - weight
  - hair color, size, condition
  - eye color, size, glasses
  - nose size, shape
  - ears: close to head or protruding?
  - distinctive features: birthmarks, scars, beard, etc.
  - clothing
  - voice: high or low, accent?
  - other distinctive characteristics, such as walk
- were the victims? associates?
- was talked to?
- were witnesses? saw or heard something of importance?
- discovered the crime?
- reported the incident? made the complaint?
- investigated the incident? worked on the case?
- marked and received the evidence?
- was notified?
- had a motive?

What:
- type of crime was committed?
- was the amount of damage or value of property involved?
- happened? (Narrate the actions of suspects, victims, and witnesses; combine with the information under How.)
- weapons, vehicles, and/or tools were used? (also under How)
- evidence was found?
- preventive measures (safe, locks, alarms, etc.) have been taken?

knowledge, skill, or strength was needed to commit the crime?
was said?
did the police officers do?
further information is needed?

How:
was the crime discovered?
does this crime relate to other crimes?
did the incident/crime occur?
was evidence found?
was information obtained?

Why:
was the crime committed? Was there intent? consent? motive?
was certain property stolen?
was a particular time selected?

Who, what, when, and where should be answered by factual statements, while how and why may be inferences. Inference statements should be identified. All possible motives should be reported.

Modus Operandi

While investigating a crime the investigator tries to determine the method of operation, or **modus operandi** (MO), used to commit it. The MO differs from crime to crime and from offender to offender. Criminals, like most people, are creatures of habit. For instance, a burglar successful in committing one burglary may intentionally or unintentionally use the same method in another burglary. The investigator needs to add the modus operandi to the MO file and check the MO file to determine if a known burglar committed the burglary under investigation. The investigator must record all the specific details of an offense in a written report and modus operandi file.

Property Description

The investigator should describe property accurately and in detail in notes and reports. Property that has been recovered, lost, or stolen should be assigned a monetary value. If the exact value is unknown, an estimated value should be given.

When describing lost or stolen items, the investigator should include as much information as possible to aid in identifying the objects. In reports about checks, bonds, or stocks, each item should be separately noted and whether it is negotiable or nonnegotiable should be indicated. When determining the value of property, investigators take depreciation into consideration. The source of the information should be identified. The investigator may have to consult an expert on unique or rare items. Property should be described according to the characteristics which follow. (Johnson and Pease, 1982, p. 21).

Narrative

Most reports involve writing a narration—that is, simply telling what happened. Narrative is objective writing that describes the

Describing Property

Jewelry

Type of article—e.g., bracelet, pendant, cufflinks, earrings, wedding band?
Quantity—pair or set?
Type of metal—18k white gold or 22k gold?
Stones—e.g., diamonds, emeralds, or zircons?
  Quality of stones?
  Color—e.g., white, green, blue?
  Cut—e.g., baguette, marquise, emerald?
  Weight in carats?
Inscriptions—e.g., a monogram, "Love"?
Additional characteristics
  Necklaces—length, number of strands, stones or beads, type of chain, type of clasp.
  Pendants—size; chain, ribbon or cord; type of clasp.
  Brooches, bar pins, or stickpins—size, shape, type of clasp, plain or engraved? filigree?
  Bracelets—width, type and number of stones, Link, solid, flexible, or filigree? engraved?
  Earrings—style, length, material, number and type of stones, screw, clasp, pierced, or slip?
  Rings—shape, size, material, type and number of stones, fraternal or other affiliation?

Watches

Quantity, case material, and color—(e.g., "1 man's gold wristwatch").
Brand—Bulova, Cartier, Timex, Omega, Rolex?
Type—digital, wristwatch, Roman numerals, closed-covered pocket watch?
Serial number—unique to each watch.
Model number—identifies the type and style of a particular brand.
Number, type, and color of stones.
Inscriptions—e.g., "From the Boys."
Band—color, material, length.
Number of jewels.
Miscellaneous characteristics, unique features.

Firearms

Quantity—e.g., "2 Remington .22 pump rifles."
Serial number—unique to each firearm.
Model number—identifies a particular type of weapon.
Type of article—revolver, automatic pistol, pump gun, rifle?
Make (manufacturer)—e.g., Remington or Smith or Wesson?
Type of grips—e.g., pearl, ivory, wood?
Type of finish—e.g., blue steel, nickel-plated, chrome?

details of an incident in the sequence of their occurrence. When writing reports, law enforcement officers should organize, evaluate, and verify their findings. Written reports should contain only relevant, specific, exact, clear, and objective information.

Good narrative writing is simple in vocabulary and construction. The organization of the report should show logic and thought. The principles of clear writing require correct sentence structure, good grammar and punctuation, and an acceptable writing style. A good report writer links correct English with the technical informa-

---

Inscriptions—e.g., "Rampo," "FAE"?
Miscellaneous characteristics, unique features.

Business Machines

Quantity—identify and describes each machine.
Serial number—unique to each machine.
Model number—identifies all machines of the same type.
Type of machine—e.g., cash register, adding machine, typewriter?
Brand name—e.g., IBM, Olivetti, Xerox?
Color—list predominant color first.
Size—dimensions, carriage width.
Inscriptions—company name.
Carrying case—list with machine if stolen.
Miscellaneous characteristics—damage to machines?

Visual and Sound Devices

Quantity—group together identical speakers, list sound devices separately.
Serial number—unique to each device.
Model number—identifies all like devices.
Type of Article
  Tape Recorder—8-track, cassette, or reel to reel.
  Videorecorder—Betamax or VHS.
  Receivers—note if item is a combined amplifier-tuner.
  Turntables—stereo receiver or separate unit.
Brand Name—Sony.
Model—Betamax 1402 cassette recorder.
Color—predominant color listed first.
Size—television screen size; for other devices overall dimensions.
Type of finish—wood and plastic.
Inscriptions—initials or writings.
Container—the item container should be described together with the device.
Miscellaneous characteristics—style of cabinet, power output, damaged areas and the like.

Money or Other Negotiable Property

Money—Obtain serial numbers if known and enter as a separate item.
List bills and coins by denomination.
Enter total amount as "property value."
Other negotiable items—e.g., checks, credit cards, airline tickets.
Name and address of owner if imprinted on the item.
Name and brand number of the bank on which check is drawn; issuer of credit card, money order, or other item.
Any signature or other entry written on the item.

tion needed by law enforcement agencies. Reports should be proofread and edited. The writer should be able to answer yes to the following questions.

1. Have I included all relevant information?
2. Have I omitted all irrelevant information?
3. Have I presented all relevant information in each section and under each heading?
4. Have I presented all details exactly, precisely, and objectively?
5. Have I phrased sentences clearly, precisely, and objectively?
6. Have I used proper paragraph form?
7. Have I used proper mechanics?
8. Have I communicated to the reader an accurate, complete, clear understanding of the case as a whole and in its parts? (Levie and Ballard, 1978, p. 80)

Summary

Communication helps law enforcement officers to perform their job effectively. Written reports of all criminal offenses must be filed by all law enforcement agencies, so the investigator must develop the skills of a good report writer.

Since the purpose of a criminal investigation is to gather all information pertaining to a specific case, the investigator should write down all the essential information in a notebook. Efficient notetaking can assist investigators in courtroom testimony.

The information contained in field notebooks is transferred into written reports. Reports should be accurate, clear, complete, concise, and brief. Investigative reports must be free from bias and prejudice.

Investigative reports can be used to keep other investigators informed of the progress of a case and to provide the court with pertinent facts. Written reports should include the modus operandi and the description of property when warranted. Most reports involve writing a narrative, linking correct English usage with technical investigative information to solve a criminal case. Good report writers remember that they are writing for readers unfamiliar with the facts of a case.

Key Terms

administrative report
crime report
field notebook
modus operandi
operational report
preliminary report
progress report
supplementary report

Review Questions

1. Why are field notes important?
2. What are the three basic steps in writing an effective report?
3. Describe the two major areas of law enforcement reports.
4. Explain the value of modus operandi and property description in reports.
5. Why is narrative writing important for an investigative report?

References

Hess KM, Wrobleski HM: *For the Record: Report Writing in Law Enforcement.* New York, NY: John Wiley & Sons, 1978.

Johnson RA, Pease RW: *Police Reports Writing.* New York, NY: Harcourt Brace Jovanovich, 1982.

Levie RC, Ballard LE: *Writing Effective Reports on Police Investigations.* Boston, MA: Holbrook, 1978.

CHAPTER 8

Surveillance and Undercover Operations

Surveillance and undercover operations can curtail the initiative of offenders. They can assist investigators in determining who the offenders are and what they are planning.

Surveillance

In his classic text on criminal investigation, Charles O'Hara (1973, p. 188) states, "**Surveillance** is the covert observation of places, persons and vehicles for the purpose of obtaining information concerning the identities or activities of subjects." The **surveillant** is the person who performs the observation. The subject is the person or place being watched.

Surveillance can take place for the purpose of preventing a crime from being committed, arresting offenders who are in the process of violating the law, or obtaining probable cause to obtain a search warrant. Surveillance can be time-consuming, expensive, and sometimes unproductive. However, there are situations in which it is the only investigative technique that can obtain the needed information. A surveillance is usually conducted to determine or verify (1) the nature or sequence of events in time; (2) the identity of persons; (3) the identity of vehicles; (4) the behavior, route, companions, or destination of persons; and (5) the route, destination, and intermittent stops of vehicles. (Walsh and Healey, 1988, pp. 16–74)

According to Bennett and Hess (1987, p. 240), "the objective of surveillance is to obtain information about people, their associates, and activities that may help solve a criminal case or protect witnesses." Surveillance can be designed to:

- gather information to build a criminal complaint,
- determine an informant's loyalty,
- verify the statement of a witness to a crime,
- seek information required to obtain a search or arrest warrant,
- identify a suspect's associates,
- observe members of terrorist organizations,
- find a person wanted for a crime,
- observe criminal activities in progress,
- make a legal arrest,
- apprehend a criminal in the act of committing a crime,
- prevent a crime from being committed,
- recover stolen property, or
- protect witnesses.

Preparation

A surveillance of any type must be a carefully planned operation. The purpose of the surveillance, the specific case to which it pertains, and any information available should be evaluated. Alternative methods of obtaining information should be explored. When the need to conduct a surveillance has been established, the method of surveillance has to be determined, the personnel chosen, and the equipment selected.

The surveillant must be briefed on all facts, suspects, descriptions of vehicles, and license numbers. The habits and hangouts, associates, and known addresses of the suspect should be provided. Also the surveillant should be familiar with the terrain and the culture of the area where the surveillance will take place. The method of communication between the surveillant and his or her supervisors has to be decided upon. The surveillant must be aware of the purpose of the surveillance (for example, to obtain probable cause in order to get a search warrant). All surveillants should have small change and cash for emergencies. Provisions must be made for emergency expenditures and relief shifts.

Surveillance officers should project an ordinary appearance. It is best if they do not possess any unusual physical characteristics, such as being exceptionally short, tall, or obese. They must have acting ability and blend into the surroundings. They should be alert and resourceful, with a good memory and powers of observation, since they will often be unable to take notes. Also, they must possess patience and endurance.

Before initiating the surveillance, the officer must become familiar with the suspect—aliases, a detailed description, any identifiable mannerisms and characteristics. A photograph should be obtained if possible. A good surveillant gets to know the suspect's habits and routines and all of his or her criminal activities. For example, a narcotics dealer may also be involved in stolen goods. The more information investigators have, the better prepared they will be for the surveillance.

Equipment

Equipment used by surveillance investigators depends upon availability and their ingenuity. For example, an investigator may use utility equipment to disguise the surveillance of a building. Cars, trucks, and vans should be inconspicuous. Bright colors and noisy equipment don't easily blend into a neighborhood.

The type of surveillance determines the type and amount of equipment needed. Equipment required for a surveillance may include:

- a 35-millimeter camera with telephoto lens,
- a movie camera with zoom lens,
- binoculars (with seven or eight times magnification),
- radio communication equipment for cars,
- a telescope,
- night-viewing equipment, and
- audiotape recorders. (Buckwalter, 1983, p. 15)

Typical surveillance equipment: portable radios, video camera, night vision scope, 35-mm camera, binoculars, and tape recorders.

Special Techniques

There are numerous methods that can be used in conducting a surveillance. Different techniques apply to such different types of crimes as gambling, burglary, and narcotics. Developing the skills of a good surveillant requires training, hard work, and patience.

A **stakeout** (fixed or stationary surveillance) involves surreptitious observation of premises and places. The fixed post may be either indoors or outdoors. The key to this operation is secrecy. This type of surveillance may be of either short or long duration. A stakeout can involve simply sitting in an automobile watching a residence or setting up an elaborate operation with sophisticated equipment.

One-Person Surveillance

In a one-person operation, a single investigator has total responsibility for the surveillance. The suspect must be kept in view at all times, and there is no room for mistakes.

The success of a one-person operation depends on vehicular and pedestrian traffic. A major problem is that it doesn't provide for officer changes.

Two-Person Surveillance

The two-person operation offers greater protection from detection. This method provides a number of surveillance options. For example, surveillants may periodically change their positions in relation to the suspect. "The exchange of positions between the lead and backup surveillants is an effective counterdetection technique. The usual procedure is for the lead to follow reasonably close to the subject, and the backup to follow the lead some distance behind, all the while being alert for possible confederates of the subject, as well as keeping the lead surveillant constantly in view." (Buckwalter, p. 29)

A variation is the leapfrog method, which puts the subject between two investigators. The officers remain at a fixed point until the suspect disappears from view. When a suspect uses the same route every day, a fixed post can be set up where the suspect disappeared the previous day. This technique has been valuable in locating hideouts and meeting places when the risk of tailing is great.

Three-Person Surveillance

Also known as the **ABC method**, three-person surveillance is complex but more effective than the other methods. When a suspect is being observed by three different people who change positions, it becomes more difficult to detect the surveillance.

With the ABC method, the investigators have more maneuverability. The lead surveillant (A) follows closely behind the subject. The backup surveillant (B) follows A. The rover (C) walks on the opposite side of the street, almost opposite but slightly behind or ahead of the subject.

Risks

Risks of surveillance include being "made" (recognized) by a suspect and getting lost. Surveillants must blend in with their environment. They should not meet the eyes of the subject, which tends to fix them in the mind of the subject. If the subject turns and it seems a face-to-face encounter will result, the surveillant should look anywhere except at the subject's face.

Don't adopt a slinking, sleuthing, creeping, peeking, "Hawk-

Night surveillance usually requires special photographic equipment, as well as adoption of an appropriate life-style and appearance for the surveillance environment. This photo was taken with a Kodak TMAX 400 camera.

shaw" manner. Don't slink in and out of doorways, sleuth behind the subject, creep from around parked cars, or peek from around corners. This is unnecessary and ineffectual. Above all, it attracts attention. A shadower who adopts these techniques may as well wear a sign proclaiming his or her activity.

Don't wear storybook disguises. False whiskers, artificial noses, simulated deformities, and the like are never convincing when worn by an amateur and seldom convincing for any length of time even when worn by a professional actor or applied by a professional makeup artist. These disguises are good for the theater but not for the street.

Shadowers will want to alter their general appearance occasionally to reduce the chance of being made. A snap-brim hat, a crushable hat, a reversible topcoat, and tinted sunglasses are practical. The topcoat and glasses protect against weather changes. Shadow work is hard on the eyes and glasses will provide relief. The surveillance may last long hours and weather changes are likely to occur. Changing the brim tilt or the crease of the hat or changing from one type of hat to another will alter the wearer's appearance.

Don't carry briefcases, notebooks, papers, or other noticeable objects. Don't make notes ostentatiously.

Don't greet fellow officers or allow them to greet you. Many otherwise successful surveillances have come to a premature conclusion because a greeting to or from a fellow officer has tipped off the subject that he or she was being tailed. (Dienstein, 1974, pp. 90–91)

Types of Surveillance

Automobile Surveillance

If a suspect uses a car, the surveillant must use an automobile. As with surveillance on foot, there are one-, two- and three-car types of surveillance. Automobile surveillance requires preparation, precautions, and skill. A car whose color, condition, and make don't draw attention is of utmost importance. In one-car surveillance, the investigator gets behind the suspect's automobile. Two-car surveillance may operate on parallel routes or both cars may follow the suspect. In three-car surveillance, parallel routes can easily be used and drivers can trade positions to avoid detection.

Helicopter Surveillance

Helicopter surveillance can aid automobile surveillance. Excellent ground-to-air communications are essential for the helicopter surveillance to be effective.

Audio Surveillance

The primary forms of **audio surveillance** are wiretapping and electronic eavesdropping. These devices include wiring a person who will be speaking with a subject, bugging a vehicle or room, and tapping a suspect's telephone. Detecting telephone surveillance is difficult because the wiring can be concealed. Bugging occurs when either a room or a person is wired for sound. A properly installed bug is extremely difficult to detect.

The U.S. Supreme Court considers audio surveillance a search, so a search warrant based upon probable cause must be obtained. The standards outlined under the exclusionary rule as it pertains to the Fourth Amendment must be followed. In 1967, in *Katz v. United States*, the Supreme Court decided that electronic surveillance and wiretapping are permitted under court order when probable cause exists.

Contact Surveillance

Weston and Wells (1986, pp. 153–154) write, "**Contact surveillance** techniques are based on the capacity of certain fluorescent preparations to stain a person's hands or clothing upon contact and thus to offer observable proof of a connection between the stained person and the object under surveillance." A suspect with fluorescent stains on his hands will have difficulty denying a connection with the offense.

Contact surveillance can be used either alone or as an aid in surveillance. For objects exposed to the weather, such as automobiles, a tracer paste is available. For objects like wallets or jewelry, a marking powder is used that becomes visible when wet or under ultraviolet light.

Notes

Activities observed during a surveillance should be recorded. Although note-taking should not draw attention, it is extremely important. Notes can be of assistance in further interviewing of witnesses or suspects. They can provide information needed to make an arrest or data that may be needed at trial.

Notes should be kept chronologically and give information pertaining to activities of both the subject and the surveillant. Accurate knowledge of the subject's activities may prove valuable for interviewing purposes. Surveillants may establish a pattern of the subject's behavior by reviewing their notes. The time and place of the subject's every action, a description of all persons contacted by the subject, license plate numbers, addresses, and phone numbers should all be included in surveillance notes.

Undercover Operations

Undercover investigators obtain information about criminal activities by associating with criminals or working within a criminal organization. An undercover operation can be considered another form of surveillance. It requires similar preparation and similar skills. An **undercover operative** can be defined as "a law enforcement agent who attempts to develop the confidence of an individual or to infiltrate a group or operation for the purpose of developing information concerning criminal activity." (Ward, 1975, p. 205)

Undercover assignments can be designed to:

- obtain evidence for prosecution,
- obtain leads into criminal activities,
- check the reliability of witnesses or informants,
- gain information about premises to conduct a later raid or arrest,
- check the security of a person in a highly sensitive position, or
- obtain information on or evidence against subversive groups. (Bennett and Hess, p. 246)

The Undercover Operative

An undercover investigator should be assigned to fit the specific case under investigation. This work requires an investigator with acting ability, self-confidence, and resourcefulness. Undercover operatives must remain calm in dangerous situations. They must be intelligent and have a good memory, since the opportunity to take notes won't always exist. Good judgment, adaptability, and communication skills are essential for undercover operatives, who must interact with a wide variety of people.

Factors to consider when selecting an undercover investigator include age, race, gender, ethnic origin, socioeconomic background, life-style, personality, and previous work experience. For example, it would be unwise to select a white man to work a narcotics case in a black neighborhood. Officers with field experience should be assigned the most dangerous cases. Young officers may be most effective for alcohol control and narcotics buys. If a journeyman bricklayer is required for the assignment, the investigator should have enough skill at laying bricks to convince co-workers.

The ability of undercover investigators is judged by how successfully they play their assigned role. How well does the operative blend into the environment and interact with the people? Does the undercover role reflect the investigator's life-style? Do the investigator's characteristics conform to the role played? The undercover operator must become part of his or her environment and be accepted as one of the gang.

Preparation

Undercover assignments require careful planning and a complete understanding of what they are intended to accomplish. Investigators need to study the subject, learn the geographic area, and rehearse their cover story. If the investigation involves a criminal or subversive organization, they should research the group.

Studying the Subject

The first step is to draw up a checklist of the subject's character and history.

1. Full name, aliases, and nicknames. If the subject holds public office, the title and the name of the department.
2. Addresses—past and present, residential and business.
3. Description.
4. Family and relatives. An acquaintance with members of the family may suggest another source of information.
5. Associates. This knowledge is essential to an understanding of the subject's activities.
6. Character and temperament. The strengths and weaknesses of the adversary should be known. Likes, dislikes, and prejudices are particularly helpful.
7. Vices—drug addiction, alcohol, gambling.
8. Hobbies. Suggest a simple way of developing acquaintance. A common interest of this nature creates a strong bond of sympathy.
9. Education. Suggests the limitations of the subject and indicates the investigator's desired level of education.
10. Occupation and specialty. These suggest a possible meeting ground and indicate the subject's character.

Learning the Area

Investigators should make a thorough study of the area in which they are to operate. If the role involves pretending previous residence there, the operative should possess an intimate knowledge of neighborhood details.

The general layout and features of the area can be learned from a street map. Bordering areas should be included in the study. The operative should also learn about the neighborhood's national and religious background. Transportation facilities and public utilities should also be mastered.

Rehearsing the Cover Story

A fictitious background and history for the new character of the investigator should be prepared, including the names, addresses, and descriptions of the assumed places of education, employment, associates, neighborhoods, trades, and travels. The investigator's background story should seldom be wholly fictitious. It is imperative for the successful undercover investigator to possess all of the requisites for the assignment, such as appropriate personality, ability, background story, and attention to details.

Provision should be made in the cover story for some of the following:

1. Frequent contact with the subject.
2. Freedom of movement and justification for actions.
3. Background that will permit the investigator to maintain a financial and social status equivalent to the subject's.
4. Mutual points of interest between agent and subject.
5. Means of communication with agent's superiors.
6. Alternate cover story (Plan B) in case the original cover is compromised.

Researching Criminal and Subversive Organizations

An investigator who must penetrate a criminal or subversive organization should develop knowledge of its history and background, biographies of the officials, and identities and backgrounds of members and former members. The operative should also study the methods of identification employed by the members, the nature, location, and accessibility of files and records, and the schedules and locations of meetings.

Terminating the Undercover Operation

There are two types of termination possible, planned or unplanned. If the termination is planned, the following questions should be considered:

- Will the fact of the investigation ever be disclosed?
- How will the agent be withdrawn without raising questions?
- How can the results be utilized without exposing the fact of investigation, if desired? (Walsh and Healey, 1988, pp. 16–93)

The undercover operation should be terminated as gracefully as possible with some believable excuse—for example, relocating for employment purposes. The investigator may not want the subject or others to realize that an investigation has taken place.

Summary

Surveillance can curtail the initiative of offenders and it can assist investigators in determining who the offenders are and what they are planning. A surveillance purpose can be to prevent a crime from being committed, to arrest offenders while in the process of violating the law, or to obtain probable cause to obtain a search warrant. The objective of surveillance is to obtain information about people, their associates, and activities that may help solve a criminal case or protect witnesses.

A surveillance of any type must be carefully planned. The purpose of the surveillance, the specific case to which it pertains, and any information available should be evaluated. The surveillant must be briefed on facts, suspects, descriptions of vehicles, and license numbers.

Numerous methods can be used in conducting a surveillance. These include fixed, one-person, two-person, and three-person operations. There are also automobile, helicopter, audio, and contact surveillances. Activities observed during a surveillance should be discreetly recorded.

Undercover investigators obtain information about criminal activities by associating with criminals or working within a criminal organization. An undercover investigator should be assigned to fit the specific case. This work requires an investigator with acting ability, self-confidence, and resourcefulness. He or she should blend into the environment and interact convincingly with the people there. When the time comes to terminate the investigation, the operative must do so as gracefully as possible.

Key Terms

ABC method
audio surveillance
contact surveillance
stakeout
surveillance
surveillant
undercover operative

Review Questions

1. What is the purpose of a surveillance?
2. Define the difference between surveillant and subject.
3. Describe the value of undercover work.
4. Why is preparation important for surveillance and undercover work?
5. How should an investigator prepare for an undercover assignment?
6. What should be considered when an undercover investigation is terminated?

References

Bennett WW, Hess KM: *Criminal Investigation*, ed 2. St. Paul, MN: West Publishing Co., 1987.

Buckwalter A: *Surveillance and Undercover Operations*. Boston, MA: Butterworth Publications, 1983.

Dienstein W: *Technics for the Crime Investigator*, ed 2. Springfield, IL: Charles C. Thomas, 1974.

O'Hara CE: *Fundamentals of Criminal Investigation*, ed 3. Springfield, IL: Charles C. Thomas, 1973.

Walsh TJ, Healey RJ, eds: *Protection of Assets*, vol 2. Santa Monica, CA: The Merritt Co., 1988.

Ward RH: *Introduction to Criminal Investigation*. Reading, MA: Addison-Wesley Publishing Co., 1975.

Weston PB, Wells KM: *Criminal Investigation*, ed 4. Englewood Cliffs, NJ: Prentice-Hall Inc., 1986.

CHAPTER 9

Analytical Investigation

Analysis is a basic function of criminal investigation. An investigator accumulates information and reviews it according to the logical steps in reconstructing a crime. The investigator never considers **analysis**—a logical thought pattern—as a separate function. An investigator assigned to a case begins by establishing what information is needed and planning how to obtain it. At the same time, the investigator constantly develops ideas about who committed the crime and how and discards those that do not fit the facts as they are accumulated. These ideas, or **hypotheses,** are the basic tools of intelligence analysis as well, as Figure 9–1 shows.

Without the explicit performance of the analysis function, the intelligence unit operates as little more than a file unit. Although the intelligence unit may have a great deal of information that can assist investigators, it must be given meaning and direction. This task is not always easy. For example, new criminals or criminal activities may not fit known or normal crime patterns.

Relationship to Data Collection

Distinctions between analysis and other phases of the intelligence process are not absolute. For example, there may appear to be a one-way relationship between the products of investigative activities and the intelligence report, since the report is the direct result of collecting a particular body of information. However, the same report can also indicate a need for information that leads to collection operation. Collection and analysis are often performed simultaneously as well.

FIGURE 9–1: The Analysis Process

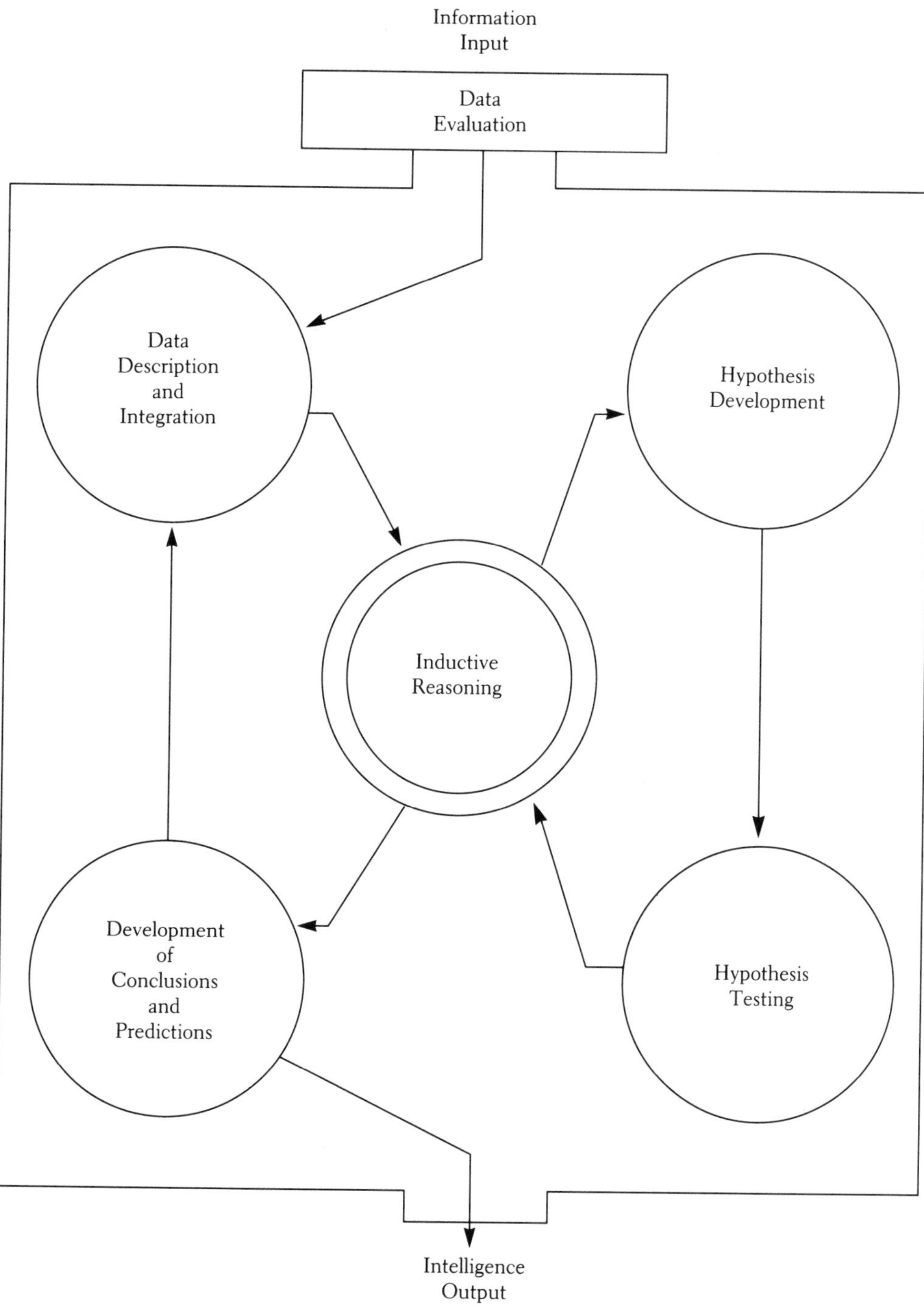

Source: Reprinted with permission of Sheldon I. Arenberg.

Generally, investigators provide **intelligence analysts** with raw information, while analysts process and relate the raw information to existing data and develop suggested avenues of approach for the investigator. Using information supplied by investigators, analysts make judgments concerning the short- and long-term implications of criminal activity in terms of tactical operations and strategic assessment. Investigators use intelligence information to make decisions regarding particular enforcement operations. Their activities are highly interdependent, but the overall responsibilities are necessarily distinct, allowing analysts to maintain a broad view of criminal activity while investigators focus on specific enforcement problems.

Properly used, analysis can facilitate a more thorough understanding of the apparently complex and often vague phenomenon of organized crime and increase the likelihood that appropriate policies and strategies can be developed. Without such insight, law enforcement administrators are operating in a vacuum, responding daily to crises in an ad hoc, disorganized, and nonsystematic manner. Law enforcement as an institutional power must develop workable, rational, and just policies. The intelligence process can play a significant role in achieving this goal.

Most law enforcement agencies do not have the luxury of full-time intelligence analysts. Typically, the intelligence officer is expected to be knowledgeable in tactical and strategic analysis of data that have been collected. Some agencies can afford full-time analysts. Even so, an understanding of basic and analytical techniques on the part of field officers leads to a better tactical intelligence product and an appreciation of the agency's strategic goals. Thus, whether a full-time analyst is available or not, contemporary intelligence officers are well advised to be operationally cognizant of basic intelligence analysis techniques.

Many analytical techniques are useful within the field of both tactical and strategic criminal intelligence. However, four analytical processes have been shown to be virtually essential in understanding the structures, operations, and trends of organized crime, economic crimes, terrorism, and corruption. These are link diagramming, hierarchical analysis, flow structuring, and net-worth estimating. This chapter will focus on link diagramming.

Link Diagramming and Organized Crime

There are several definitions of **organized crime,** but three characteristics always prevail.

- Organized crime is the integration of divisions of labor, involving numerous people and organizations, operating over long periods of time, to acquire profit and power through illegal activities.
- The participants in an organized crime operation make considerable effort to hide their activities.
- Boundaries, which may be jurisdictional, state, and national, are exploited by organized crime.

Special procedures that facilitate the investigation, case structuring, and prosecution of organized crime activities have been devised. One problem identified as requiring a special procedure was the integration and presentation of information collected from many sources, at various locations, over a period of time. Conventionally, this myriad information was organized in the investigator's memory. This works for criminal investigations that are limited in time span, number of individuals included, and number and type of criminal activities involved.

Such is not the case in investigations of organized crime. Data are collected and activities exist over a long period of time. Many people and organizations are involved, and often different investigators are brought in during an investigation. The result has been that law enforcement's conventional techniques of integrating data have often been ineffective. Some principal members of an organized crime activity are overlooked; the time required to build substantive cases operates to the detriment of the criminal justice system; or prosecutors find it difficult to explain complex relationships to a jury.

One effective tool for integrating large amounts of organized crime data is known as **link diagramming,** a graphic method for integrating large amounts of data related to an organized crime or other criminal conspiracy. Link diagramming facilitates criminal analysis and investigation, provides an excellent summary or overview of a complex situation for law enforcement management and criminal prosecutors, and has been used effectively in court to present complex cases to juries.

The technique consists of two basic, sequential steps. The first step is the conversion of the written material of a report or set of reports to a graphic summary form called an association matrix. The second is the conversion of the matrix to a diagram that illustrates the relationships contained in the matrix. Since the final diagram depicts relationships among people, organizations, and activities, it is called a link diagram.

The Association Matrix

A *matrix* is a structured set of boxes, with an equal number of boxes horizontally and vertically. A **row** is a horizontal set of boxes, and a **column** is a vertical set of boxes. A **cell** is the specific box in which a particular row and column intersect.

In essence, the **association matrix** is a simple device for putting a sizable amount of data (say, from a number of law enforcement reports) on one sheet of paper to provide analysts or investigators with the big picture. Furthermore, the matrix relieves users of remembering what preceded the piece of information that has just come in. All of the data, in terms of association, are in front of them. A simple example will illustrate this concept.

Suppose that you are driving through the state of California and want to know the distances between the cities that you wished to visit: San Francisco, Oakland, Sacramento, Los Angeles, and San Diego. With the aid of various maps, you determine that the distance between San Francisco and Oakland is 13 miles, Sacramento to Oakland is 84 miles, Los Angeles to San Diego is 137 miles, Oakland to Los Angeles is 336 miles. Sacramento to San Francisco is 97 miles, Los Angeles to San Francisco is 441 miles, Oakland to San Diego is 573 miles, Sacramento to San Diego is 539 miles, San Francisco to San Diego is 578 miles, and Los Angeles to Sacramento is 402 miles.

These data in this form are too clumsy to use for planning and are not worth memorizing. So you opt to construct a matrix. The five cities you wish to visit and the mileage between them—the *definable relationship*—will be entered in their appropriate cells.

The first step is to count the number of cities involved and construct a matrix accordingly. The second step is to label each row with each city and then label each column in precisely the same order as the rows. Thus, you will begin with a five-by-five matrix.

Next, you sequentially enter each pertinent element of information in its appropriate cell. For example, the first piece of data is that the distance from San Francisco to Oakland is 13 miles. Figure 9–2 shows that information entered in its appropriate cells. It goes in two cells because the distance from Oakland to San Francisco is the same as that from San Francisco to Oakland.

The next piece of information is that the distance between Sacramento and Oakland is 84 miles. After you have entered this and all other data you collected, the matrix will look like Figure 9–3.

Upon examination, you note that no data have been entered on the upper left to lower right diagonal. That's not surprising, since

FIGURE 9–2: Beginning the Matrix

	S.F.	Oak.	Sac.	L.A.	S.D.
San Francisco		13			
Oakland	13				
Sacramento					
Los Angeles					
San Diego					

Source: Reprinted with permission of Sheldon I. Arenberg.

you realize that you never collected the data for those cells and had you collected them, each would have been zero. In your mind's eye, draw a dotted line down the zero diagonal. If you were to fold the matrix along the dotted line, you would find that the information contained in the lower triangular matrix is a mirror image of that in the upper triangle.

Since all data are duplicated, only half the matrix as heretofore constructed is actually needed. Hence, the effective form of the final matrix is as shown in Figure 9–4.

The Link Diagram

The association matrix is essentially an interim step in producing graphic material to assist investigations and prosecutions. The goal is the development of pictorial data that will clearly show the relations among people, organizations, and activities. To understand the construction of a link diagram, work through an example.

Assume that you, as an investigator, have been looking into a potential narcotics operation involving a labor union and a local hotel. As part of the investigation, you have collected bits and pieces of information (shown in Figure 9–5). You wish to organize this

FIGURE 9-3: Completing the Grid

S.F.		13	97	441	578
Oak.	13		84	336	573
Sac.	97	84		402	539
L.A.	441	336	402		137
S.D.	578	573	539	137	
	S.F.	Oak.	Sac.	L.A.	S.D.

Source: Reprinted with permission of Sheldon I. Arenberg.

information so as to clearly present your current status to either your supervisor, a prosecutor, or yourself.

Obviously there is too much data in Figure 9-5 to present as is, and it is not integrated into any pattern. An association matrix can facilitate your understanding of the relationships that exist among the people, the organizations involved, and the potential crimes. Begin with the people. Reviewing your data, you determine that five people are mentioned who could be involved in a criminal activity or activities. Therefore, the first step is to construct and label a five-by-five matrix.

Using your data, complete the matrix. The first report in Figure 9-5 that indicates a relationship between two people is Report 4. Since this information is *certain* in structure (there is no doubt that B and D were together), enter a solid dot in the cell where row D and column B intersect. Add the report number to the cell to facilitate your recall of the source document should the need arise.

The next report dealing with people is Report 5. However, doubt exists about whether D and C actually discussed narcotics; the character of the data is *uncertain*. Therefore, enter an open dot in the cell where row D intersects with column C. Completing

FIGURE 9-4: The Final Matrix

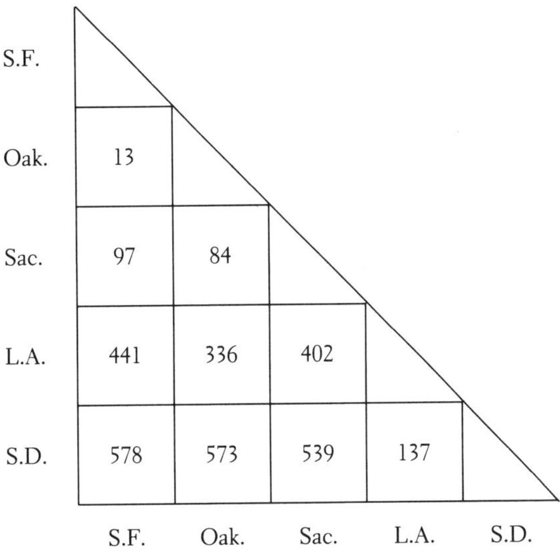

S.F.					
Oak.	13				
Sac.	97	84			
L.A.	441	336	402		
S.D.	578	573	539	137	
	S.F.	Oak.	Sac.	L.A.	S.D.

Source: Reprinted with permission of Sheldon I. Arenberg.

FIGURE 9-5: Raw Data

Report No.	Item of Information
1	D heads labor union M
2	D personally owns stock in hotel P
3	Hotel P employs A, B, and C
4	D is observed dining with B
5	D may have talked to C about narcotics
6	A has record for narcotics dealings
7	B and C observed in car
8	A lives with flight attendant E
9	Waiter at hotel reported that he thought D spoke to A about a personal loan using union monies
10	B and C are suspected narcotics dealers
11	Union M lends money to hotel P
12	Flight attendant E has flown South American routes for past two years as an employee of airline L

Source: Reprinted with permission of Sheldon I. Arenberg.

FIGURE 9–6: Sample Narcotics Association Matrix

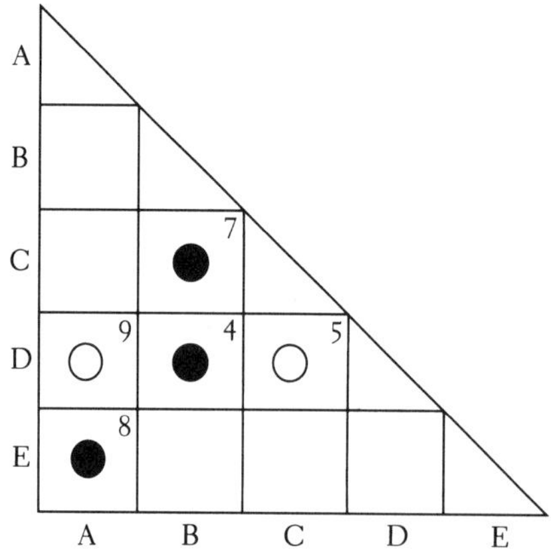

Source: Reprinted with permission of Sheldon I. Arenberg.

your study of the data from Figure 9–5 yields a matrix correlating individual relationships as shown in Figure 9–6.

After completing the matrix, you are in a position to develop a pictorial representation of these associations. Such link diagrams have been used:

- to give investigators insights into their own case and suggestions on how to proceed.
- as an aid in briefing both law enforcement management and prosecution.
- as an aid in court, when investigators testify in complex cases such as conspiracies.

To begin turning the association matrix into a link diagram, draw one circle for each individual in the matter under study and label them. You may place them in any order at the outset.

Using the matrix, connect the people as follows. Where the association is known with certainty, connect the appropriate circles (individuals) with solid lines. Where the association is only suspected, use dotted lines. Thus, Figure 9–7 is the link diagram equivalent of the matrix in Figure 9–6. The numbers in parentheses are the reports from which the links derive.

But Figure 9–7 is a mess. Because some lines cross and some are curved, it is difficult to interpret and will be little use to someone who has never been exposed to the details of the problem. The ideal drawing keeps all lines straight and noncrossing. Figure 9-8 is a cleaned-up version of the link diagram in Figure 9-7.

Although Figure 9-8 meets the graphic criteria, it is not overly informative because we have not employed all of the information from Figure 9-5. The next step is to relate the individuals to the organizations that they are connected with. To do this, first expand the matrix in Figure 9-6. Then connect the individuals with the criminal activities they are or may be involved in. The completed matrix is shown in Figure 9-9.

To reflect these additional associations in the link diagram, enclose all the individuals in the same organization with a rectangle and label it. When an individual belongs to two or more organizations, overlap the rectangles. The rule is one circle to an individual, one rectangle to an organization. To indicate actual or suspected criminal activities in a link diagram, use a color or shading code. In Figure 9-10, horizontal stripes across a person's circle represent possible narcotics violations and vertical stripes indicate potential fraudulent labor practices.

The link diagram from the data in Figure 9-5 is now complete. It leads to the following hypothesis of criminal activity.

FIGURE 9-7: Sample Narcotics Link Diagram, Unstructured

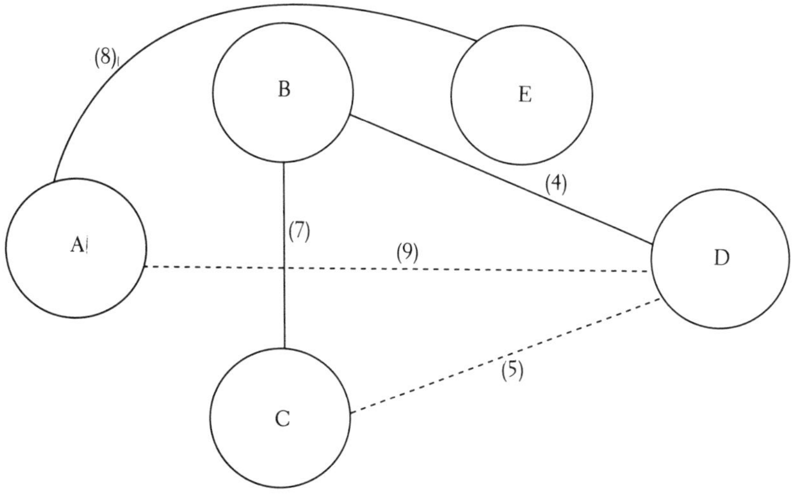

Source: Reprinted with permission of Sheldon I. Arenberg.

FIGURE 9–8: Sample Narcotics Link Diagram, Structured

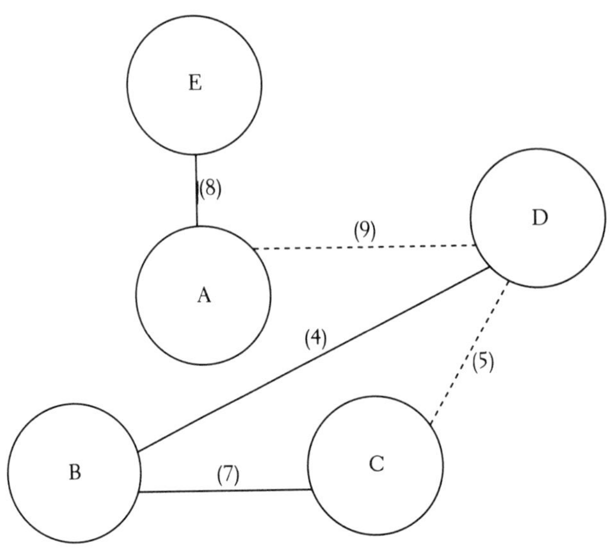

Source: Reprinted with permission of Sheldon I. Arenberg.

D, the head of Union M, may also be the leader of a narcotic group consisting of A, B, C, and E. Funds are supplied by fraudulent union loans to Hotel P. The narcotics may be delivered locally by flight attendant E, who may be smuggling them into the United States on Airline L planes arriving from South America.

The following steps are recommended.

- Establish a surveillance on E.
- Verify the relationships between A and D and C and D.
- Suggest that the U.S. Department of Labor audit Union M's loan portfolio.
- Suggest that the Internal Revenue Service and the local state taxing authority audit D's personal financial transactions.

Advantages of Analytical Analysis

Analytical analysis has as a major advantage the use of pictures or charts to describe criminal activities and to geographically link the sequence of events as they have occurred. A visual analysis can indicate exact locations of details and reveal to investigators where to put forth efforts to fill missing gaps. The use of charts in courts can speed the legal process because investigators using charts are usually better organized and often better informed. (Morris, 1982, p.2)

Disadvantages of Analytical Analysis

There appear to be no major disadvantages to analytical analysis other than that some investigators and their supervisors may be unsophisticated in the use of charts to make a case.

FIGURE 9–9: Detailed Association Matrix

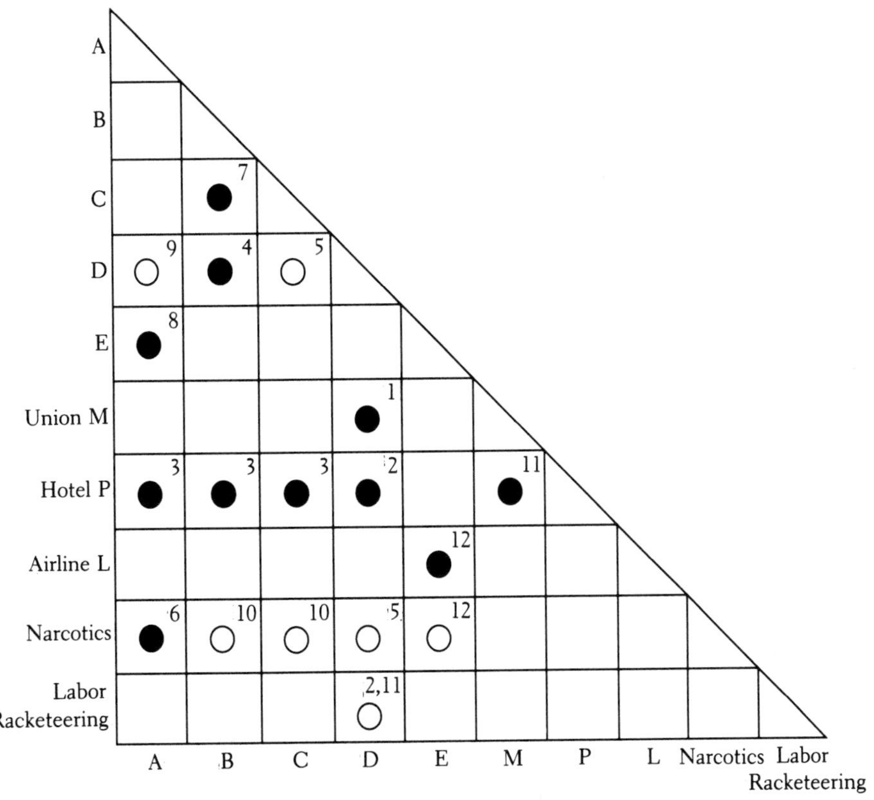

Source: Reprinted with permission of Sheldon I. Arenberg.

FIGURE 9–10: Detailed Link Diagram

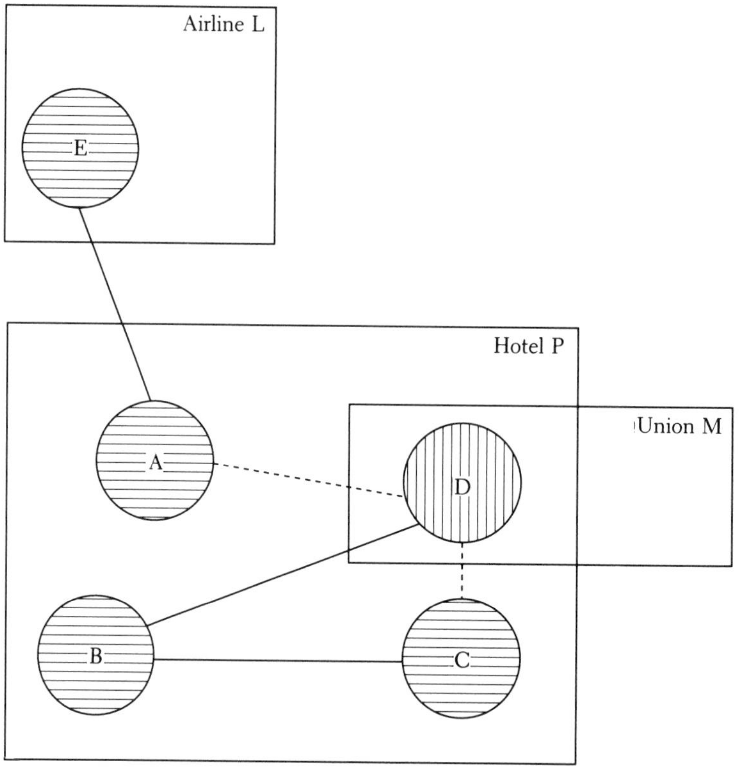

Source: Reprinted with permission of Sheldon I. Arenberg.

Summary

Analysis is a normal function of the police investigator. The investigator accumulates information and reviews it according to the logical steps in reconstructing a crime. Properly used, analysis can facilitate a more thorough understanding of the complex and often vague phenomenon of organized crime. Analysis also increases the likelihood that appropriate policies and strategies can be adopted.

Investigation, case structuring, and prosecution of organized crime activities require the collection of large amounts of data. One effective tool is link diagramming, a graphic method for integrating large amounts of data related to an organized crime or other criminal conspiracy.

The goal of link diagramming is the development of pictorial data that clearly show the relationship among people, organizations, and activities. The purpose of analysis techniques is to use collected information and to transfer data from one investigator to another. It should assist the prosecutor's case.

Key Terms

analysis
association matrix
cell
column
hypothesis
intelligence analyst
link diagramming
organized crime
row

Review Questions

1. Describe analysis as it relates to criminal investigations.
2. Name the four analytical processes that are considered essential to the understanding of organized crime.
3. Explain link diagramming.
4. What is the association matrix?

References

Link diagramming models courtesy of Sheldon I. Arenberg, Santa Monica, CA. Used with permission.

Morris, J: *Crime Analysis Charting*, Orangevale, CA: Palmer Enterprises, 1982.

CHAPTER 10

Crime Scene Investigation

The scene of any crime must be construed as possessing evidence, and the collection of evidence and the testimony of police officers and criminal investigators are extremely important to the successful clearance of a case. The crime scene is proof that a crime has been committed. It serves as the initial point of a criminal investigation and contains evidence connecting suspects with the crime.

Usually, when a crime is reported to the police, a beat officer responds. The first law enforcement officer who arrives at the scene is usually the most important person in the investigation. This officer must protect any evidence at the crime scene and protect the scene from contamination. The duties of the first police officer who arrives at the scene of a crime fall into several general categories. (Moreau, n.d., p. 20) These include protecting oneself, caring for the injured, securing and protecting the scene, identifying witnesses and suspects, maintaining control of the scene, establishing contact with headquarters, and preparing notes to document actions and observations for later reference.

Although it is difficult to set rigid rules that apply to all crime scenes, pertinent information must be obtained—the time the crime was reported, the time the officer arrived at the scene, and who telephoned the police. Initially, the officer must proceed cautiously for his or her own safety, in case the suspect is still at the scene. Also, the officer does not want to damage any possible evidence that could be found on the floor, light switches, lamps, or other items. The officer should be extremely observant and make written notes on the following points when evaluating the scene of the crime. (Svensson, Wendel, and Fisher, 1981, p. 20)

1. Doors. Open, closed, or locked? On which side was the key?
2. Windows. Open or closed? Locked?
3. Lights. On or off? Which lights were on?
4. Shades or shutters. Open or closed?
5. Odors. Cigarette smoke, gas, perfume, etc.?
6. Signs of activity. Was the house clean or dirty? Meal preparation, dishes in sink?

Protecting the Crime Scene

No objects or bodies should be moved unless absolutely necessary. The scene of the crime needs to be as it was during the commission of the crime. If anything is moved, the officer should make a written notation of the specific item and the reason for tampering with it. The officer should not contaminate the crime scene by smoking, eating, drinking, using the toilet facilities, or tampering with the utilities.

The importance of the crime scene lies in the chance that physical and chemical evidence can be collected and analyzed in order to connect a specific individual with the crime. Figure 10–1 is a model policy for safeguarding evidence. Since the crime scene contains valuable evidence, it needs to be properly protected from contamination, loss, or unnecessary moving of items or objects that can be used for evidence. Any tampering with evidence may interfere with establishing a corpus delicti.

The crime scene should be closed to all persons who lack a legitimate investigative interest in the case. Too many individuals at the scene of the crime may lead to evidence being removed or even destroyed. Many people and factors, including the following, can, singly or in combination, do serious harm to a crime scene. (Kenney and More, 1979, pp. 163–164)

- The weather. Especially when a crime scene is located outdoors, evidence may be changed or erased by wind, rain, snow, harsh sunlight, or extreme temperatures.
- Persons who committed the crime or are connected with the suspect. They may attempt to remove or destroy incriminating evidence.
- Newspaper and television reporters and photographers. Since their main concern is gathering news, their goals can conflict with those of the investigation.
- Curious citizens, souvenir collectors, and thieves. They can introduce confusing fingerprints and alter the condition of

important evidence. In some instances, they may steal it.

- Other members of police agencies who aren't assigned to the scene but come along to "help." They may contaminate or destroy valuable evidence because they don't know what they're doing. They can also get in the way.
- Victims or other persons who have been affected by the crime. They may be so sickened by the sight and condition of the

FIGURE 10–1: Model Policy for Evidence Control

	Effective Date May 1, 1990	*Number*
Subject *Evidence Control Policy*		
Reference	*Special Instructions*	
Distribution	*Reevaluation Date* April 30, 1991	*No. Pages* 2

I. PURPOSE
The purpose of this policy is to establish guidelines for maintaining the integrity of the evidentiary chain of custody.

II. POLICY
It is the policy of this law enforcement agency to ensure that evidence in its custody can be properly secured and stored, readily retrieved, and that any changes in its custody have been properly and fully documented.

III. DEFINITIONS
A. Chain of Evidence: The continuity of the custody of physical evidence—from time of original collection to final disposal—which may be introduced in a judicial proceeding.
B. Impounding Officer: The member of this law enforcement agency who initially receives the evidence and initiates the chain of custody.
C. Physical Evidence: Any substance or material found or recovered in connection with a criminal investigation.
D. Evidence Custodian: Agency member accountable for control and maintenance of all evidence accepted by or stored in the agency's evidence room.
E. Evidence Room: Facilities utilized by this law enforcement agency to store evidence.

IV. PROCEDURES
A. Processing Evidence:
1. Any member of this agency who has evidence to be placed in the evidence room shall make an inventory of that evidence at the location it was found or recovered. The inventory shall be witnessed and confirmed by a supervisor and shall include the following information for all items of evidence:
a. Description of the item (including make, model number, and serial number, if any);

crime scene that they try to clean it up or put it back the way it was before the crime occurred.

Dimensions of the Crime Scene

There are no established rules for defining the dimensions of a crime scene. Technically, a crime scene begins where the criminal

FIGURE 10–1: *(Continued)*

b. Source (from whom or location obtained); and
c. Name of person primarily responsible for collecting the item or items.

2. The impounding officer shall properly handle, mark, and package all evidence, and transport all physical evidence to the evidence room, or other authorized secure location as soon as practical.
3. Evidence of a hazardous nature shall be appropriately packaged and stored in accordance with established agency policy. Such substances include but are not limited to items which may have been exposed to or contaminated by communicable diseases, hazardous chemicals or waste products, or explosives or highly combustible products. Where appropriate, the evidence custodian will make arrangements and assume responsibility for storage and control of such substances outside the evidence room.

B. Impounding Evidence

1. The evidence custodian shall be responsible for receiving, storing, maintaining, releasing, and accounting for all evidence in compliance with established agency policy.
2. When evidence is deposited with the evidence custodian or in an approved holding facility, an evidence receipt shall be completed by the impounding officer. The evidence receipt shall include all information necessary to both document and ensure the integrity of the chain of custody. All drugs should be weighed and monies counted by the evidence custodian and recorded on the evidence receipt.
3. The evidence custodian shall be responsible for developing and maintaining a master file of all evidence invoices and evidence tags completed. This file may be either manual or automated and shall be cross-indexed with the chain of evidence custody file.

C. Storage of Evidence

1. The evidence custodian shall assign a storage location to each item of evidence and record this information on the evidence receipt and evidence tag.
2. Evidence requiring added security, to include money, precious metals, jewelry, gemstones, weapons, narcotics, and dangerous drugs shall be stored in a separate secured area.
3. Perishable items shall be stored in a refrigerator or other suitable container.

D. Access to the Evidence Room

1. Only members of this agency authorized by

5. Any wheelchairs, crutches, prosthetic devices, and medication should be transported with, but not in the possession of, the prisoner.
6. Prisoners shall not be left unattended during transport. Any escape shall be immediately reported to the communications center.

BY ORDER OF

____

CHIEF OF POLICE

Source: The International Association of Chiefs of Police.

New York City police cordoned off this entrance to St. Patrick's Cathedral after a bizarre 1988 incident. The clothes on the sidewalk being guarded by the officer were left by a man who stripped naked, entered the cathedral, and killed an usher with a prayer book stand.

initiated the action of the crime. It follows through to the escape route and places where the criminal may have gotten rid of any evidence. Usually the best evidence is found at or near the site of the crime. For example, in a forced entry at a store, the area surrounding the cash register may contain the most evidence. The first officer who arrives at the scene is responsible for defining the dimensions of the crime scene.

Conducting the Preliminary Investigation

The **scene investigator** conducts the preliminary investigation and then decides whether to continue the investigation. If witnesses are uncooperative or if there is insufficient evidence the investigation will be closed. Of course, for capital cases or serious felonies, or if there is a public outcry, the case will continue.

The scene investigator is the key person involved in the preliminary examination of the crime scene. He or she finds out all possible information about the crime and the scene of the crime from all witnesses and victims. The scene investigator also collects all pertinent information from the initial officer at the scene. The initial phases of the preliminary investigation consist of thinking and planning. The scene investigator examines the crime scene closely without disturbing any evidence or the scene itself. The scene investigator must satisfy legal requirements concerning physical evidence that has been found at the crime scene and be able to:

- identify each piece of evidence, even months after collecting it.
- describe the exact location of the item at the time it was collected.
- prove that from the moment of collection until it was presented in court, the evidence was continuously in proper custody.
- describe changes that may have occurred in the evidence between the time of collection and its introduction as evidence in court.

The purposes of a preliminary investigation are to reconstruct events and analyze methods of operation, motive, items stolen, and any actions performed by the perpetrator. Criminals usually leave some kind of clue, and it is the responsibility of the crime scene investigator to reconstruct the crime and make a case against the criminal. All items at the scene should be considered important in reconstructing the crime; nothing should be overlooked or considered too small.

The investigator has to formulate a plan before beginning the investigation of a crime scene. A systematic plan includes the geometry of search, possible sources of clues, and the location of photographs. Procedures are outlined to suit the specific conditions of the crime scene investigation. (Svensson, Wendel, and Fisher, 1981, pp. 24–31)

Searching the Crime Scene

The crime scene is searched in order to find, collect, and preserve physical evidence for obtaining a conviction in court and to solve the crime. Fox and Cunningham (1985, pp. 18–19) recommend the following general rules in conducting a crime scene search.

1. Any evidence that is being significantly deteriorated by time or the elements has first priority.
2. All of the major evidence items are examined, photographed, recorded, and collected, in the order that is most logical, considering the requirements to conserve movement. Casts are made and latent prints lifted from objects to be moved from the scene.

Items should not be moved until they have been examined for trace evidence. Fingerprints should be taken, or at least developed and covered with tape, before the object is moved.
3. When an (obviously) deceased person is involved, the evidence items lying between the point of entry to the scene and the body are processed. Then the detailed search of the deceased is conducted. After the search, the body should be removed and the processing of obvious evidence continued.
4. After the more obvious evidence is processed, the search for and collection of additional trace material begins. Trace evidence should be sought before any fingerprint dusting.
5. After the trace materials have been collected, other latent prints are lifted.
6. When sweeping or vacuuming, investigators should segment surface areas, package the sweepings from each area separately, and note the location of each point of recovery.
7. Normally, elimination fingerprints and physical evidence standards are collected after the above actions.

Generally, the method of searching an outdoor scene is similar to that used for an indoor scene. However, the crime scene cannot be as clearly defined. Outdoor surfaces are usually rough and fingerprints may be difficult to find. Weather conditions such as rain and snow can create problems. An outdoor search should take place during daylight for greater visibility.

Vehicle Searches

There are numerous reasons for conducting vehicle searches: to locate contraband, or to find evidence that the vehicle was used in the commission of a crime or involved in a hit-and-run.

The search of an automobile begins with the exterior, with careful attention given to the hood and grill areas. The exterior of a vehicle is searched for automobile damage, cloth imprints or road grime on the finish, or fibers or hair on the car. Any evidence should be noted, sketched, and photographed. After the exterior has been searched, the vehicle should be examined for fingerprints.

The interior of the automobile is searched in five segments—right front, left front, right rear, left rear, and the deck above the back seat. (See Figure 10–2.)

The investigator vacuums the floor from all passenger areas and places the contents in separate containers, marked to indicate which part of the vehicle the contents came from. The car is vacu-

FIGURE 10–2: Segmented Vehicle Search

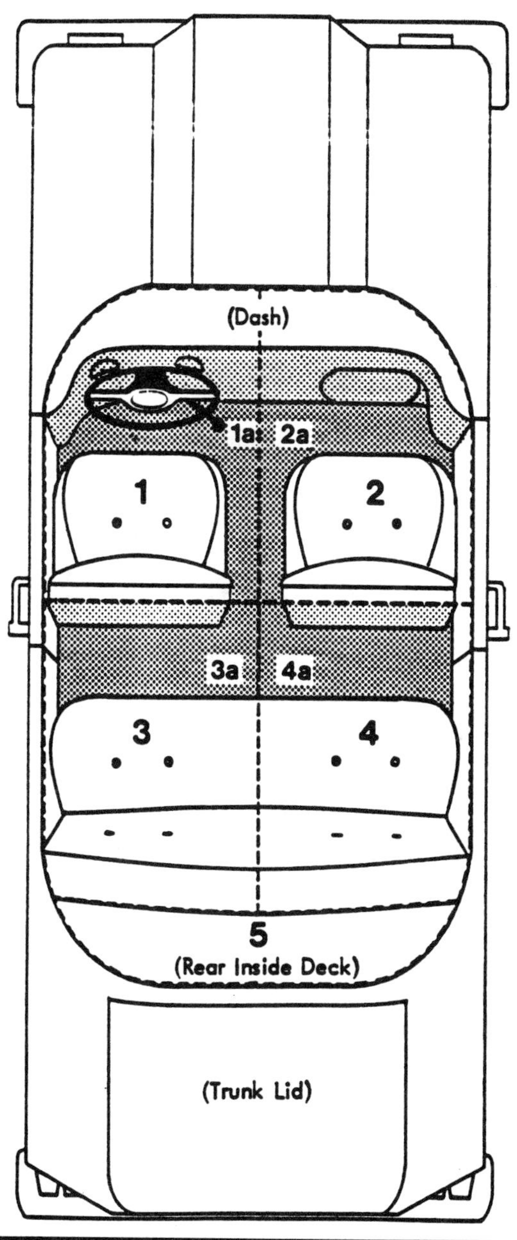

Source: Richard H. Fox and Carl Cunningham, *Crime Scene Search and Physical Evidence Handbook* (U.S. Government Printing Office, 1985).

umed before fingerprints are taken to avoid mixing investigators' hair and fibers with recovered material.

After fingerprinting, the car is searched for drugs, weapons, and stolen goods. If any stains are observed in or on the vehicle, they should be photographed and the specific location noted. The trunk and the area under the hood are searched. If the automobile may have been involved in a hit-and-run, the undercarriage is searched for hair, blood, fibers, and human tissue. The investigator collects any pieces of broken glass or metal. (Fox and Cunningham, 1985, pp. 24–27)

The goals of searching a person, living or dead, are similar. A victim's clothing is examined for trace evidence. The clothes are vacuumed in order to compare any transferred evidence on the victim with that of the perpetrator. If the victim struggled with an assailant, fingerprint scrapings should be taken. With a dead victim, a body search is conducted in the same way as a scene search. Normally, the medical examiner searches the interior of the victim's clothes. (Kenney and More, 1979, p. 214)

Mechanics of the Search

Several methods have been developed to search a crime scene. There are advantages and disadvantages to each technique. The method of indoor crime-scene searches is dictated by the size of the room and its contents. (O'Hara, 1973, pp. 50–55)

Spiral Method

The searchers initiate the search at the beginning of a spiral, starting on the outside and moving toward the center.

Radial Method

In the radial, or wheel, method, the area is considered to be circular. The searchers begin at the center of the wheel and proceed outward. The procedure should be repeated several times to double-check the area.

Grid Method

In the grid, or double strip, method, the search is repeated from side to side. The rectangle parallels the base and then parallels the side, as Figure 10–3 illustrates.

Zone Method

The search area is divided into quadrants, with one searcher assigned to each. Depending on the size of the search area, the quadrants can be expanded.

To determine whether the search has been thorough, it is helpful for investigators to complete the following checklist for securing and searching the crime scene. (Joseph and Allison, 1980, pp. 27–28)

1. Were any injured cared for?
2. Was the crime scene roped off and marked?
3. What time did you arrive at the scene?
4. What was the condition of the weather?
5. Names of persons at scene upon arrival.
6. What time was act first reported to police?
7. Who put in first call?
8. Name of photographer of crime scene.

FIGURE 10-3: Grid Method of Search

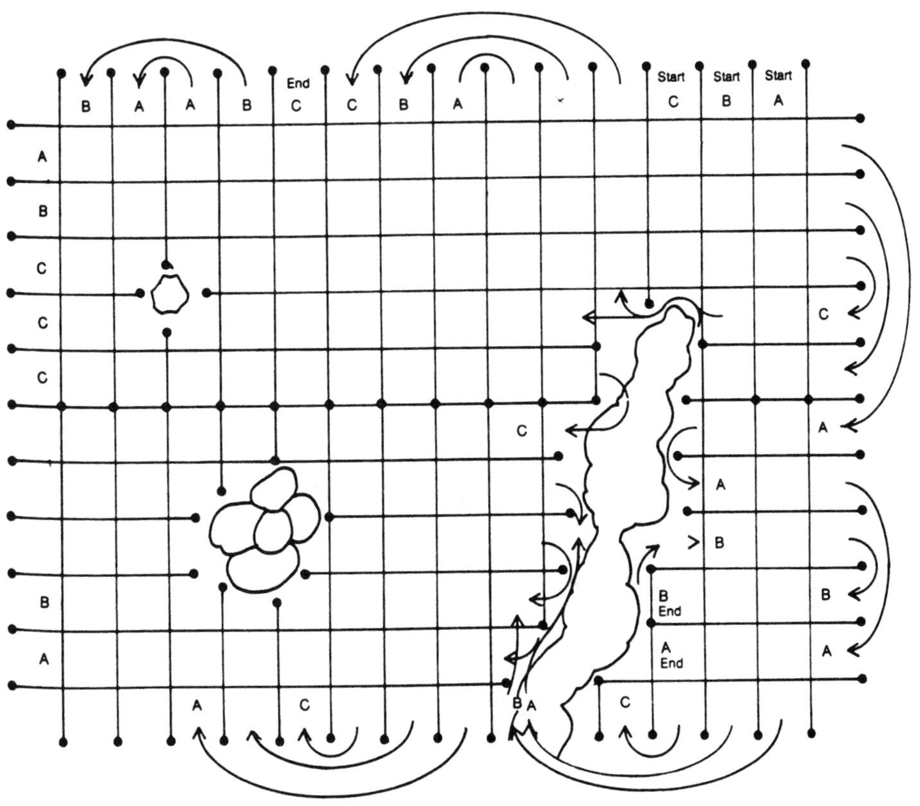

Source: Reprinted by permission from page 153 of *Criminal Investigation*, 3d ed., by Wayne W. Bennett and Kären M. Hess;

9. Name of person making crime scene sketch.
10. At what time was search started?
11. How did weather affect evidence?
12. Geographic location or address of nearest house.
13. Address of dwelling or building in village or town.
14. Conditions of windows, closets, doors, bathrooms, and all other rooms, plus basement and attic.
15. Evidence that body was moved, if homicide.
16. Report on clothing and contents of pockets.
17. Fingernail parings and transferred fibers and hair.
18. All recovered evidence noted on evidence recovery sheet.
19. Any problems encountered in dealing with excess traffic in area of scene?
20. What, if any, evidence had to be moved during search?
21. Was any firearms evidence neutralized, and by what officer?
22. Complete data on witnesses: names, addresses, etc.
23. Were neighbors able to provide any positive information?
24. In outdoor search, what method was employed?
25. Was path of entry and exit established?
26. Were castings of tire tracks and footprints made? Tool marks? Medium?
27. Was evidence marked and packaged according to agency practice?

Recording the Crime Scene

Accurate records of the crime scene are valuable during the follow-up, or latent, investigation. Crime scene records help the investigator to reconstruct the scene of the crime. Records are kept by the investigator from his or her initial assignment to the case and maintained until the case has been completed. Written records of the case are supplemented by sketches, drawings, and photographs. Written records of the case should be kept in the order of observations made. The following items, among others, should be included in the investigator's notes. (Fox and Cunningham, 1985, pp. 33–34)

1. Dates, times, and locations. The date and time of the investigator's assignment to the case should be noted, as well as from whom and by what means the assignment was received. The exact time of arrival, exact location of the crime scene, light and weather conditions, the names of officers contacted, and names of other persons on the crime scene at the time of the investigators's arrival should be noted.

2. Detailed description of the victim. The name, age, height, weight, complexion, color of hair and eyes, and, when possible, the social security number and birthdate of the individual are included. The type and color of outer garments should be described.
3. Wounds. Information should include the exact location of a wound or injury, its type, size, and in the case of a bruise, color. For example, an entry describing a gunshot wound to the forehead might read: "Gunshot wounds 1/4 inch in diameter in line with the center of the nose and 1 inch above the eyebrow line. A dark-gray circle 1/2 inch wide appears around the wound's outside edge."
4. General description of the crime scene. The investigator should note any damage to items, any apparent disturbance of the normal arrangement of furniture or other objects, and the presence of objects that seem unusual in the context of the scene.
5. Type of camera and film used to photograph the crime scene. As each photo is taken, the f-stop, shutter speed, distance focused, direction in which the camera faced, use of flash, object or area photographed, and time should be noted. A sample entry might be: "#1—f22, 1/100, 15 ft., N.E., flash: showing hallway from back door to bedroom, where victim was found. 0902 hrs."
6. The discovery of each significant item of evidence. The entry should include the description of the item, when it was discovered, by whom, the exact place, how the container was sealed and marked, and the disposition of the item after it was collected. For example: ".38 Cal. S & W Chief, revolver, blue-steel frame and barrel with wood grips, 2" barrel, Ser. #23653, 36" from N.E. corner of bedroom, 43" W. of N. edge of E. door. Marked JD on inside of cylinder hinge, placed in a small evidence bag, sealed with tape, marked #6 JD 6/6/71 at 0923 hrs. Released to Officer John Brown, lab firearms examiner, 1400 hrs. 6/6/91 JD."
7. The failure to locate items. This entry includes the absence of items that would normally be associated with the crime being investigated, with the area of the crime scene, or with any deceased victims. An example would be an item of clothing missing from the victim's body that could not be found at the scene.

Notes are valuable in writing the reports for the case and recalling events and information about it.

Sketching the Crime Scene

An accurate and objective description must be made before any items or objects are moved, altered, or destroyed. Since the crime scene plays an important part in collecting evidence, a sketch can provide an outline of evidentiary facts and circumstances for a jury and court. Sketches are also useful in questioning persons and writing the investigative report. The sketch provides information about distances; the photograph emphasizes details.

All measurements of a sketch should be accurate to prevent distortion. Common mistakes include accurately measuring the room but estimating the placement of the furniture. Another error includes pacing distances while putting feet and inches into the sketch. It is extremely important to decide what should be sketched before beginning the process. Usually a rough graph is made before witnesses and victims are interviewed. The following rules for sketching, given by Hans Gross, a world-renowned investigator of the early twentieth century, are still valid today.

- Determine the direction of the compass and draw it on the sketch.
- Control measurements. Don't rely on others to give them.
- Do not draw things that are clearly irrelevant to the case. The advantage of a sketch over a photo is that it contains only the essentials.
- Never rely on memory to make corrections at the station house or at home.
- Draw the scale on the sketch. If a camera has been used, mark its position on the sketch.

Police use of sketching falls into three types: the sketch of locality, of grounds, and of details.

The sketch of *locality* gives a picture of the scene of the crime and its environs, including such items as neighboring buildings and roads leading to the location or house. In arson cases, the sketch of locality is of great value in determining whether the fire was caused by nearby inflammable property.

The sketch of *grounds* pictures the scene of the crime with its nearest physical surroundings—for example, a house with garden or the plan of one or more floors in a house.

The sketch of *details* describes the immediate scene only; for instance, the room in which the crime was committed and the details thereof. Nowadays the sketch of details of a room is generally carried out by **cross-projection,** in which walls and ceiling are pictured as if on the same plane as the floor.

Cross-projection sketches are drawn to scale with measurements. The distances are measured by projecting lines from the corners of the room that meet at the object on the floor or the evidence. The same line projections can be used to locate evidence on the walls, as well as windows and doors. Figure 10–4 is a sample cross-projection sketch.

The **triangulation** method of sketching is particularly useful outdoors. Distance can be measured from trees, fences, and so forth. This method, shown in Figure 10–5, has two reference points with an apex on the object or evidence.

The **baseline,** or coordinate, method is used in a large indoor area or outdoors. Coordinate sketches are used to pinpoint the location of objects or evidence. One method uses a baseline drawn between two known points, as in Figure 10–6. The baseline could also be a wall or the mathematical center of a room.

A crime scene sketch should include the following information. (Fox and Cunningham, 1985, pp. 35–36)

1. The investigator's full name and police rank.
2. The date, time, crime classification, and case number.
3. The full name of any person assisting in taking measurements.
4. Address of the crime scene, its position in a building, landmarks, and compass direction.
5. The scale of the drawing, if a scale drawing has been made.
6. The major discernible item of physical evidence and the critical features of the crime scene. The location of such items is indicated by accurate measurements from at least two fixed points.
7. A legend or key to the symbols used to identify objects or points of interest on the sketch. Color may be used to distinguish objects or features; however, the use of several colors can become confusing and may complicate reproduction of the sketch.

The next three figures are crime sketches for a particular case, the Doe/Blow homicides. Figure 10–7 shows the crime scene close up. Figure 10–8 is a sketch of locality. Figure 10–9 shows the injuries of one victim, full figure and in profile.

There are two types of sketches, a rough sketch drawn by the investigator at the scene of the crime and the finished sketch, which should be accurately drawn to scale. The tools for measuring include one 8-foot and one 12-foot tape for short distances, one steel

FIGURE 10-4: The Cross-Projection Sketch Method

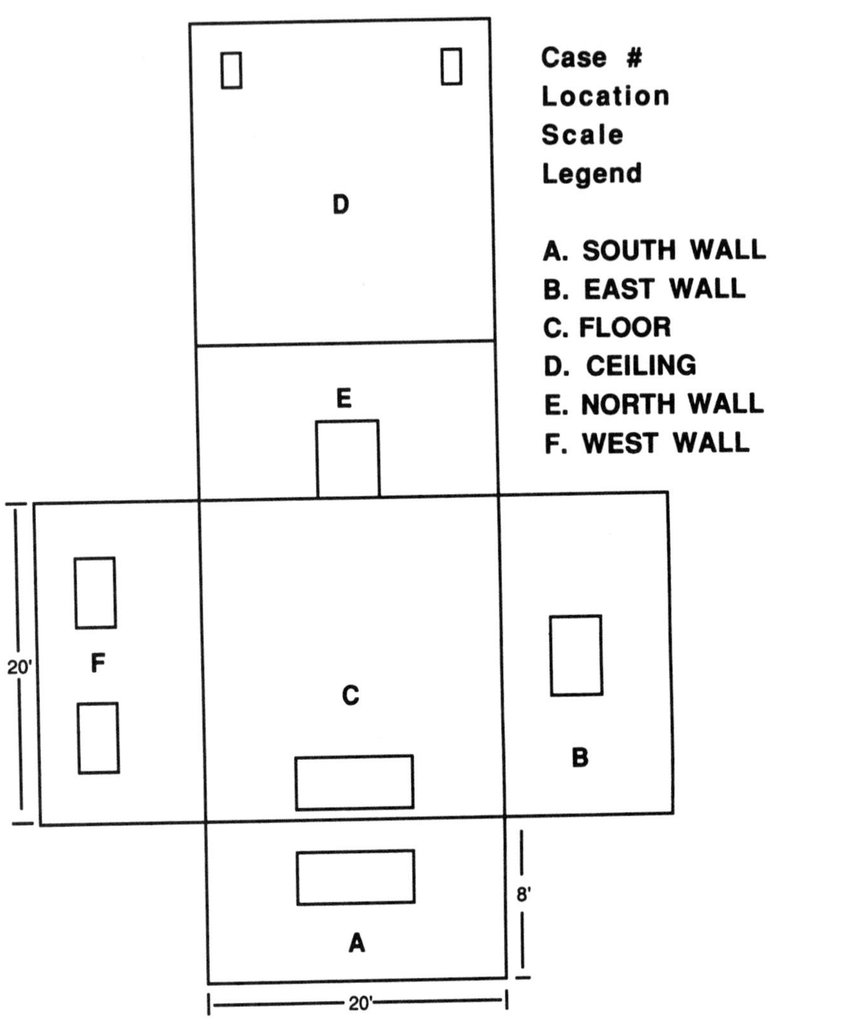

50-foot tape for long distances and car accidents, one straightedge, a magnetic compass for obtaining directions outdoors, and thumbtacks to hold the tape in place when the scene investigator is alone.

Sketching should be combined with photographs for all serious crimes—homicides, felonious assaults, fatal automobile accidents, burglaries, arson, and other violent felonies. The crime scene investigator should be prepared to explain crime-scene sketching in court. (DeAngelis, 1980, pp. 18–19)

FIGURE 10–5: The Triangulation Sketch Method

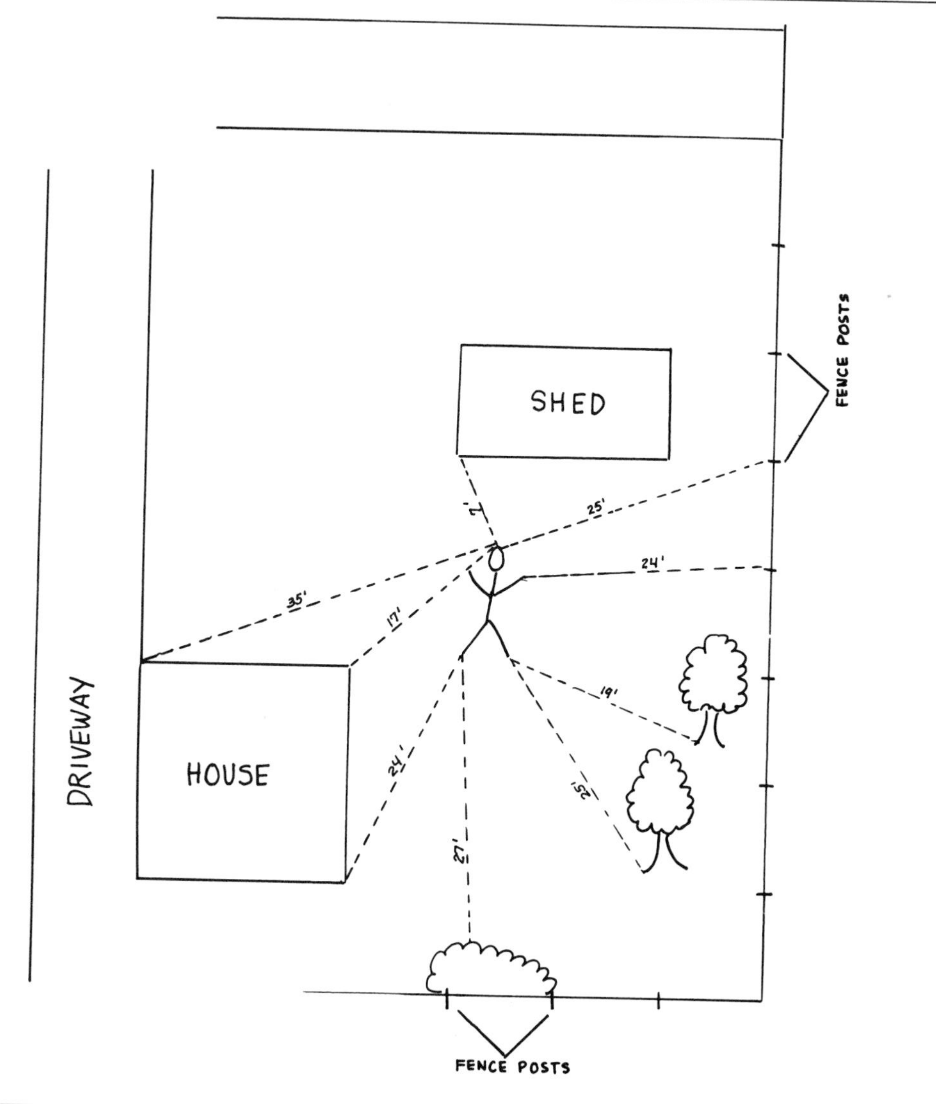

Source: Copyright © 1992 by Matthew Bender & Co., Inc. Reprinted with permission from *Police Investigation Handbook* by Barton L. Ingraham and Thomas P. Mauriello. All rights reserved.

FIGURE 10–6: Baseline Sketch Method

The baseline is anchored on the window edge and the doorjamb because the near (west) wall is not straight.

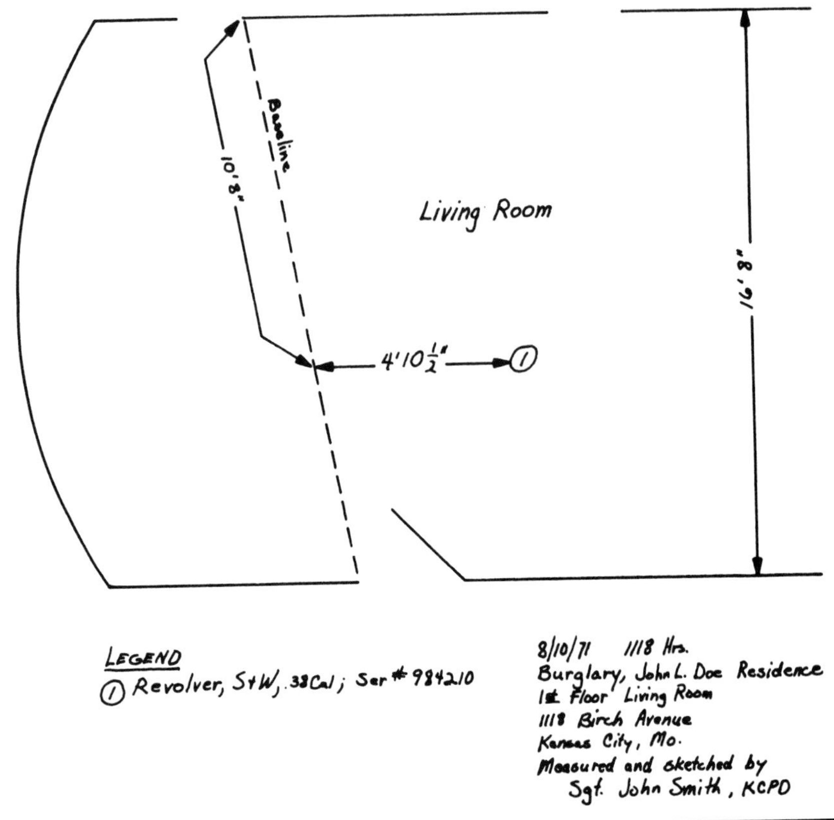

Source: R. H. Fox and C. Cunningham, *Crime Scene Search and Physical Evidence Handbook* (U.S. Government Printing Office, 1985).

- Officers should practice measuring and converting items on the sketch so that they can accomplish this without difficulty when they are called as witnesses.
- Officers should be prepared to define a scale drawing with its application. For example, "The scale drawing is used to accurately represent the crime scene. It is not possible to prepare a sketch the exact size of the crime scene, so all measurements are reduced proportionately. For example, if there are a 24-foot wall and an 8-foot couch, then whatever scale is used, the wall will be three times larger than the couch. If the scale is one inch equals four feet, the wall will be six inches wide and the couch two inches wide."

FIGURE 10–7: Sample Grounds Sketch

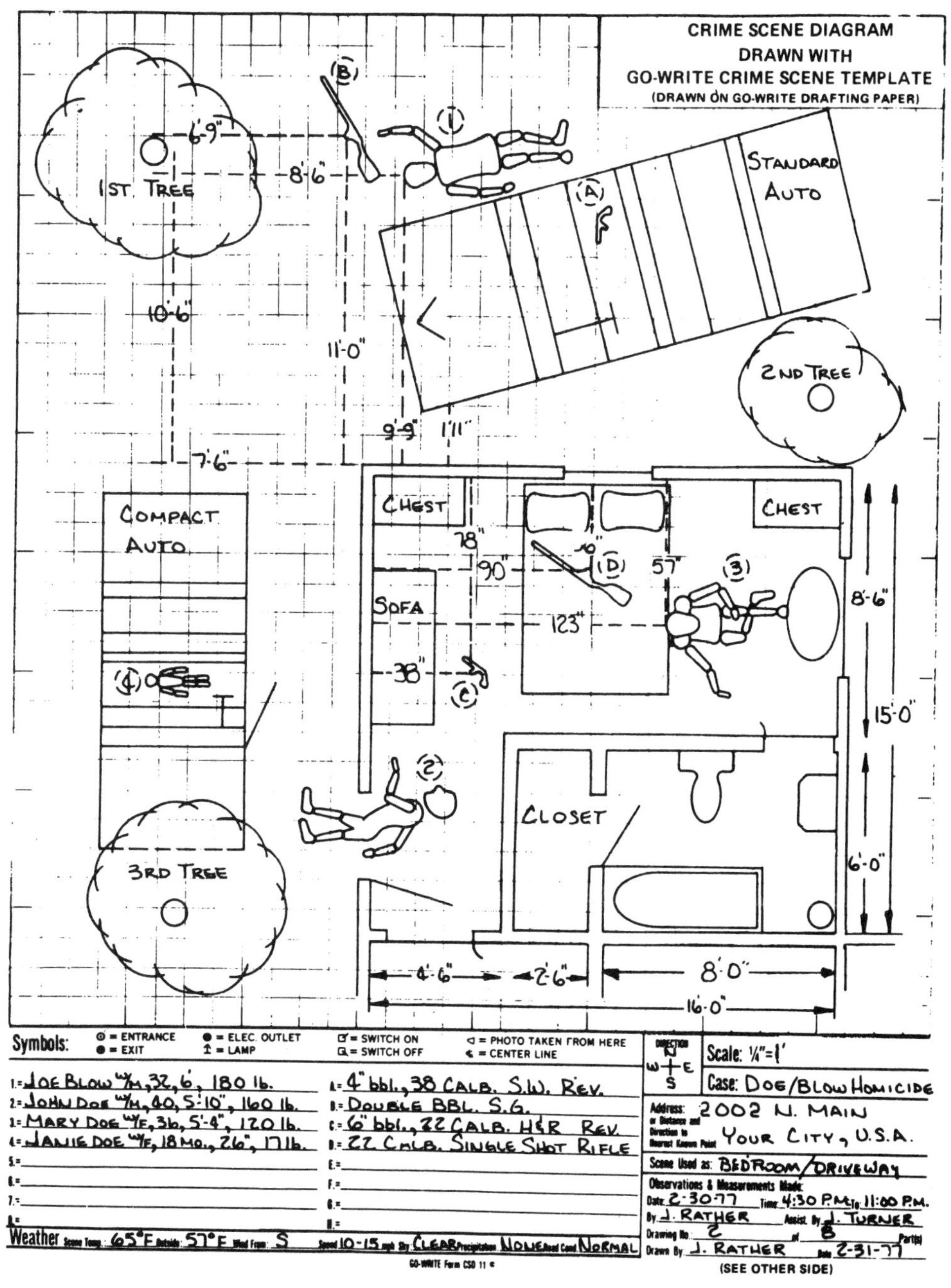

Source: A. Joseph and H. C. Allison, *Handbook of Crime Scene Investigation,* Boston, MA: Allyn & Bacon, 1980), p. 54.

FIGURE 10–8: Sample Locality Sketch

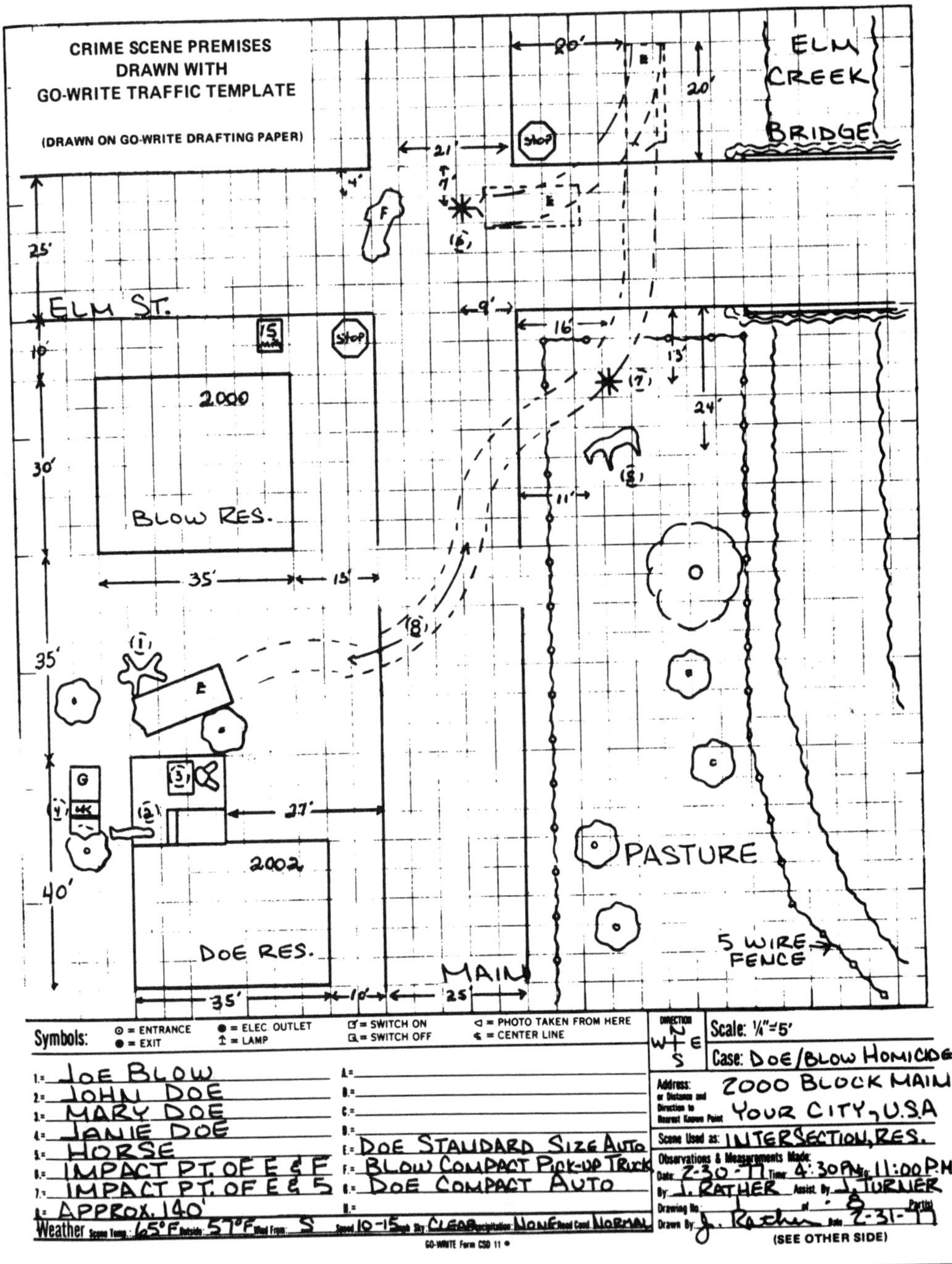

Source: A. Joseph and H. C. Allison, *Handbook of Crime Scene Investigation,* (Boston, MA: Allyn & Bacon, 1980), p. 53.

FIGURE 10–9: Sketch of Victim's Injuries

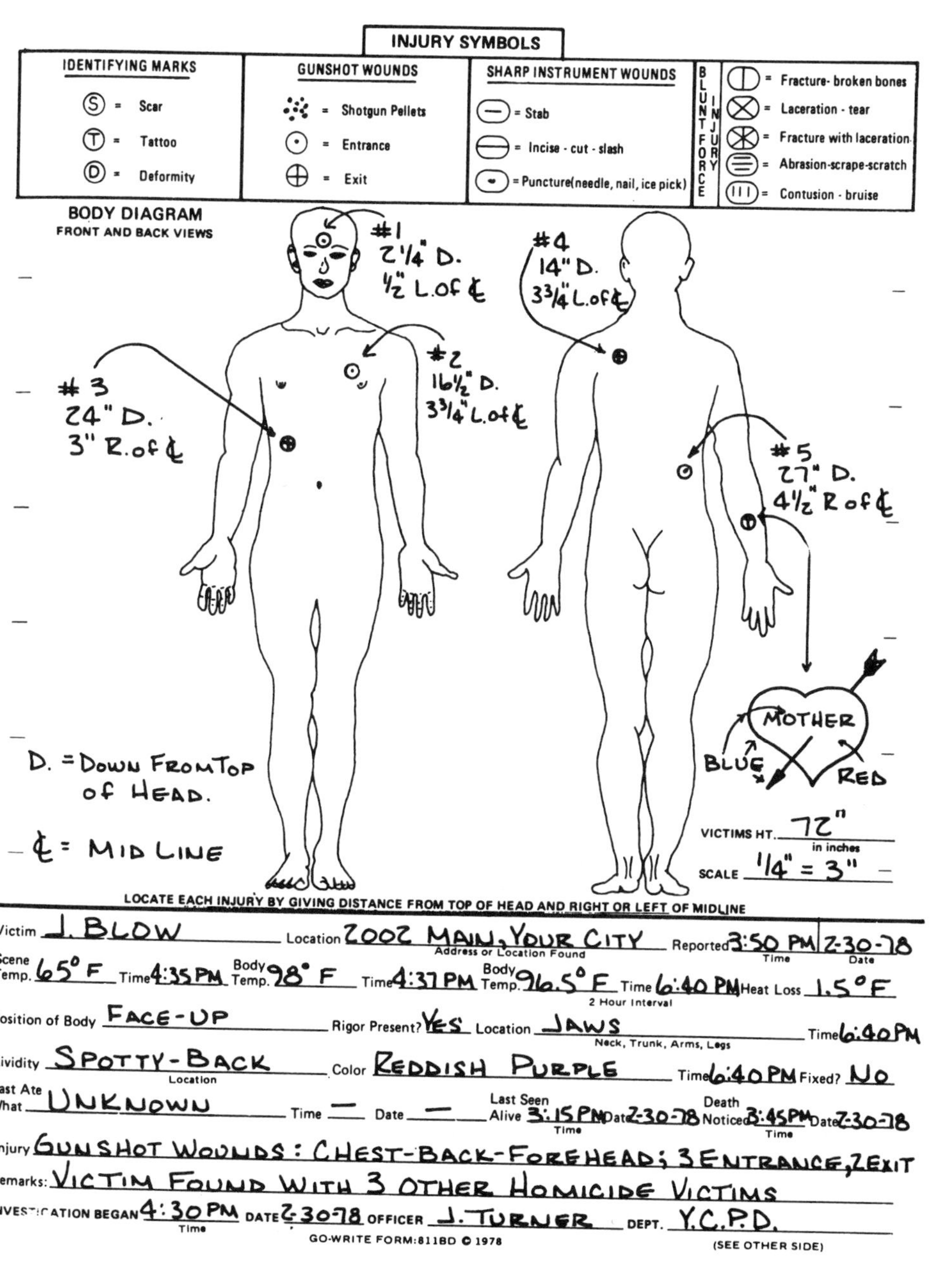

INJURY SYMBOLS

IDENTIFYING MARKS	GUNSHOT WOUNDS	SHARP INSTRUMENT WOUNDS	BLUNT FORCE INJURY
Ⓢ = Scar	= Shotgun Pellets	= Stab	= Fracture- broken bones
Ⓣ = Tattoo	= Entrance	= Incise - cut - slash	= Laceration - tear
Ⓓ = Deformity	= Exit	= Puncture(needle, nail, ice pick)	= Fracture with laceration
			= Abrasion-scrape-scratch
			= Contusion - bruise

BODY DIAGRAM
FRONT AND BACK VIEWS

#1 2 1/4" D. 1/2" L. of ℄

#2 16 1/2" D. 3 3/4" L. of ℄

#3 24" D. 3" R. of ℄

#4 14" D. 3 3/4" L. of ℄

#5 27" D. 4 1/2" R of ℄

MOTHER
BLUE
RED

D. = DOWN FROM TOP OF HEAD.

℄ = MID LINE

VICTIMS HT. 72" (in inches)

SCALE 1/4" = 3"

LOCATE EACH INJURY BY GIVING DISTANCE FROM TOP OF HEAD AND RIGHT OR LEFT OF MIDLINE

Victim J. BLOW Location 2002 MAIN, YOUR CITY (Address or Location Found) Reported 3:50 PM (Time) 2-30-78 (Date)

Scene Temp. 65° F Time 4:35 PM Body Temp. 98° F Time 4:37 PM Body Temp. 96.5° F Time 6:40 PM (2 Hour Interval) Heat Loss 1.5° F

Position of Body FACE-UP Rigor Present? YES Location JAWS (Neck, Trunk, Arms, Legs) Time 6:40 PM

Lividity SPOTTY-BACK (Location) Color REDDISH PURPLE Time 6:40 PM Fixed? NO

Last Ate What UNKNOWN Time — Date — Last Seen Alive 3:15 PM (Time) Date 2-30-78 Death Noticed 3:45 PM (Time) Date 2-30-78

Injury GUNSHOT WOUNDS: CHEST-BACK-FOREHEAD; 3 ENTRANCE, 2 EXIT

Remarks: VICTIM FOUND WITH 3 OTHER HOMICIDE VICTIMS

INVESTIGATION BEGAN 4:30 PM (Time) DATE 2-30-78 OFFICER J. TURNER DEPT. Y.C.P.D.

GO-WRITE FORM:811BD © 1978 (SEE OTHER SIDE)

FIGURE 10-9: *(Continued)*

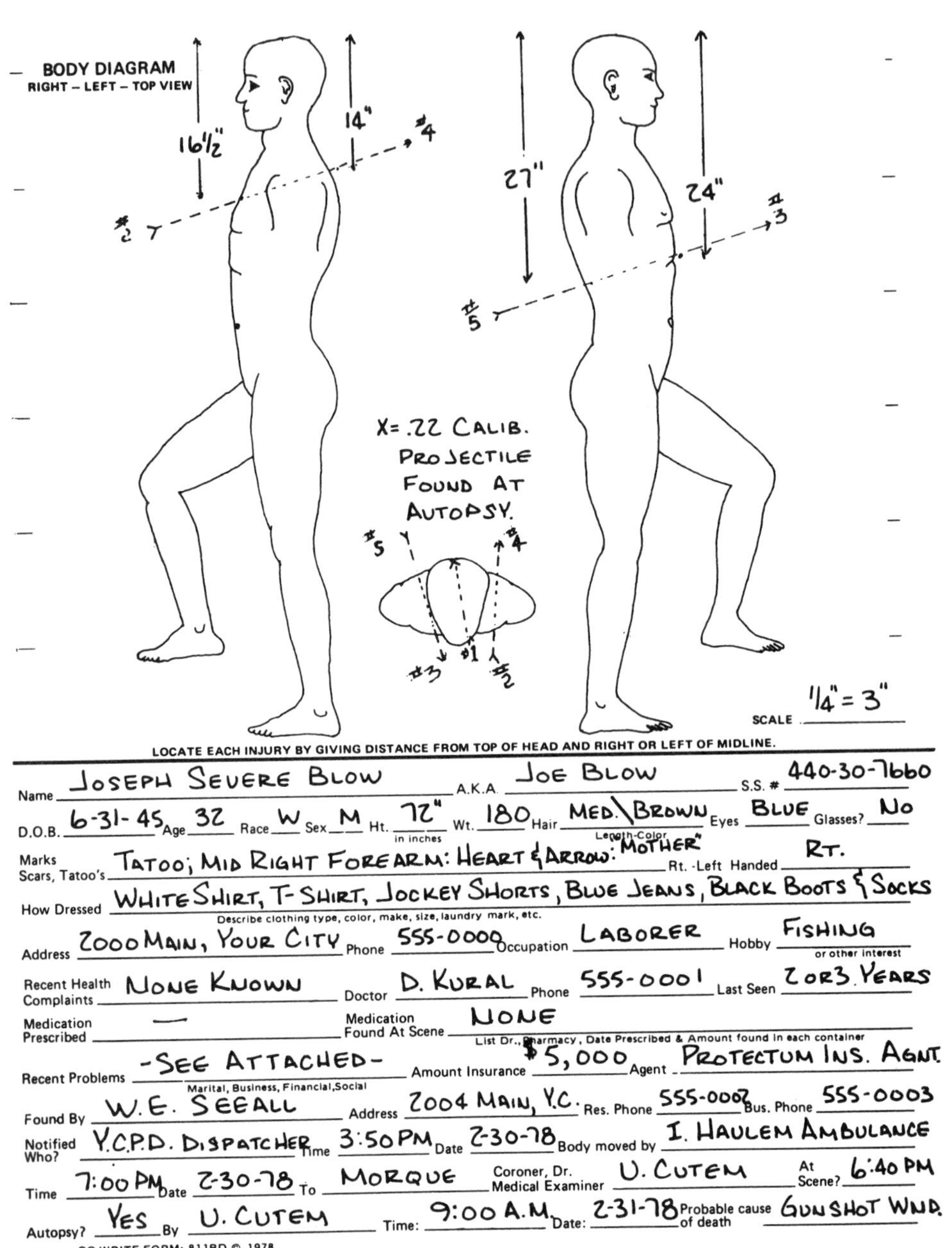
BODY DIAGRAM
RIGHT – LEFT – TOP VIEW

16½"
14"
#4
#2
27"
24"
#3
#5
X= .22 CALIB. PROJECTILE FOUND AT AUTOPSY.
#5
#4
#3
#1
#2

SCALE ¼" = 3"

LOCATE EACH INJURY BY GIVING DISTANCE FROM TOP OF HEAD AND RIGHT OR LEFT OF MIDLINE.

Name JOSEPH SEVERE BLOW A.K.A. JOE BLOW S.S. # 440-30-7660

D.O.B. 6-31-45 Age 32 Race W Sex M Ht. 72" (in inches) Wt. 180 Hair MED.\BROWN (Length-Color) Eyes BLUE Glasses? NO

Marks Scars, Tatoo's TATOO; MID RIGHT FOREARM: HEART & ARROW: "MOTHER" Rt. -Left Handed RT.

How Dressed WHITE SHIRT, T-SHIRT, JOCKEY SHORTS, BLUE JEANS, BLACK BOOTS & SOCKS (Describe clothing type, color, make, size, laundry mark, etc.)

Address 2000 MAIN, YOUR CITY Phone 555-0000 Occupation LABORER Hobby FISHING (or other interest)

Recent Health Complaints NONE KNOWN Doctor D. KURAL Phone 555-0001 Last Seen 2 OR 3 YEARS

Medication Prescribed — Medication Found At Scene NONE (List Dr., Pharmacy, Date Prescribed & Amount found in each container)

Recent Problems -SEE ATTACHED- (Marital, Business, Financial, Social) Amount Insurance $5,000 Agent PROTECTUM INS. AGNT.

Found By W. E. SEEALL Address 2004 MAIN, Y.C. Res. Phone 555-0002 Bus. Phone 555-0003

Notified Who? Y.C.P.D. DISPATCHER Time 3:50 PM Date 2-30-78 Body moved by I. HAULEM AMBULANCE

Time 7:00 PM Date 2-30-78 To MORGUE Coroner, Dr. Medical Examiner U. CUTEM At Scene? 6:40 PM

Autopsy? YES By U. CUTEM Time: 9:00 A.M. Date: 2-31-78 Probable cause of death GUNSHOT WND.

GO-WRITE FORM: 811BD © 1978

Source: A. Joseph and H. C. Allison, *Handbook of Crime Scene Investigation,* (Boston, MA: Allyn & Bacon, 1980), p. 55.

- Officers should be aware that the measurements of scale drawing need only be as accurate as the instruments allow—that is, "reasonably accurate."
- Officers should be able to explain the divisions of an inch on an ordinary twelve-inch ruler.
- If there were any changes made on the rough sketch. Officers should state that the change was made to clarify the rough sketch.
- Officers should be prepared to explain why items shown in a photograph are not included in the sketch.
- Officers should be prepared to explain each item on the rough sketch and the finished drawing, including directional arrow, scale, and legend.
- The exhibit, when presented in court, should be readable and in permanent form. This may include being mounted so that it does not bend.

Photos and Videotapes

Since photos do a better job of explaining a crime scene than any investigator could possibly do, the scene should be photographed before any items are touched. Explicit photos should be taken to show how the physical evidence was found prior to its removal.

Various types of cameras can be used for crime scene photography. Usually a large-format camera, perhaps 120 or four-by-five, is used so that when the pictures are enlarged for court they have greater resolution and small objects can easily be seen. Instant cameras can be used for specific purposes, and some police departments use 35-millimeter cameras.

There is no firm rule on how many photographs should be taken. The crime scene photographer decides based on experience. Photographs have several purposes. They can reveal relationships of evidence items at the crime scene. They can refresh memories. They can convey the crime scene in its original state to the jury. Location, witness, close-up, and evidence photos should be taken of most crime scenes. (Svensson, Wendel, and Fisher, 1981, pp. 61–63)

Location Photos

Photos of the location of the crime scene should be made. In the case of a residence, for example, the exterior of the dwelling should be photographed, showing the locations of doors and windows. Surrounding areas of the house should be photographed, such as the front and back yards and the view in each direction (looking north, south, east, and west). In some cases, an aerial photo is useful to depict the location of the residence and other areas of interest in proximity to the primary crime scene.

Witness Photos

Witness photos are overall pictures, showing the crime scene as observed by a witness. In the case of a murder in a house, witness photos might depict the victim lying on the floor as viewed from several locations in the room. These photos are designed to tell a story, to relate to someone who was not present what the location looked like. To accomplish this task, several overlapping photos should be made. In addition, long-range and intermediate-range photographs should be taken to show both perspective and the relative positions of different items found at the crime scene.

Close-up Photos

To further clarify the scene, close-up pictures should be taken. Two photos should be routinely taken: one as the item actually appears, and the same photo with a scale (such as a 6-inch ruler) included. It is important that the film plane be parallel to the plane of the object. The scale and the parallel film plane ensure that good-quality enlargements or 1:1 photos of the evidence can be produced later.

Evidence Photos

All items of evidence should be photographed before they are removed or changed in any way. Photos should be made of shoe imprints, fingerprints, bloodstains, weapons, defense wounds, and so on. Additional photos should be taken during the crime scene search when new evidence may be discovered as a result of moving items at the scene.

Investigators should keep a **photo log** that includes date, photographer's name, type of camera, lens, film, case number, and a list of every photograph taken. The list might also include the shutter speed, f-stop, and a short description of the evidence location. Photos are admissible in court only when the crime scene investigator can testify that they accurately depict the scene of the crime. Photos should reveal the relationships and distances between objects. The crime scene photographer should save all negatives.

Specific requirements should be taken into consideration when crime scenes are photographed. The National Institute of Justice publication *Crime Scene Search and Physical Evidence Handbook* (Fox and Cunningham, 1985, pp. 43–46) makes suggestions for pho-

In photographing an arson scene, it may be helpful to have someone point out specific areas that provide clues to the fire's origin.

tographing arson scenes, burglary scenes, vehicle accidents, deceased persons, live victims and suspects, and fingerprints.

The handbook recommends that complete coverage be taken of an arson scene. Close-ups are needed of the area or areas where the fire began. Other areas that should be photographed are the exteriors of all structures involved in the fire and interior views that give a complete representation of the damaged areas and any adjacent undamaged areas.

In photographing a burglary scene, the handbook suggests that particular attention be paid to:

- the interior and exterior of the building,
- damaged areas, particularly those around the points of entry and exit used by the criminal,
- close-ups of damaged containers that were the targets of the burglar (safes, jewelry boxes, strongboxes, etc.),
- tool marks, both close-up and from a perspective that shows the position of the mark with respect to the general scene, and
- fingerprints, which are of particular value in a burglary investigation.

For photographing a car accident scene, lenses are usually at normal focus length to eliminate distortion pertaining to the width of the road, distance between points, and so forth. Photos should be taken as soon as possible after the accident. Critical aspects to be photographed include:

- the overall scene of the accident, from both approaches to the point of impact,
- the exact positions of the vehicles, injured persons, and objects directly connected to the accident,
- all points of impact, marks of impact, and damage to real property,
- all pavement obstructions and defects in the roadways,
- close-ups of damage to vehicles (one photo should show the front and one side, and another should show the rear and other side of the vehicle),
- tire tracks, glass, and associated debris, and
- skid marks. If possible, photos should be taken before the vehicle is removed and again after it has been moved.

The handbook states, "The evidentiary value of a photograph of a deceased person is often considerably reduced by the inclusion of views that can be later alleged to be deliberately inflammatory. The unnecessary exposure of the sexual organs is a frequent case in point." (Fox and Cunningham, p. 45)

Dead bodies should be photographed in a horizontal position, with the camera placed over the victim's head at a height of at least

Photographing a burglary scene includes taking close-ups of all burglarized objects; in this case, a file cabinet. (See p. 450.)

five feet. Close-ups of injured parts of the body are more effective in color than in black and white. A lens filter may create lifelike tones when wounds, blood, or other discolorations on the corpse affect identification.

With live persons, either victims or suspects, areas of the body normally not visible should be photographed under the supervision of a physician who will provide testimony on them. Usually this type of photo is not taken at crime scenes.

The handbook suggests, "Before photographing any part of the female body normally covered by clothing, written consent of the subject must be obtained. If the subject is a minor, the written consent of the parent is needed and the photography must be done with witnesses present." (Fox and Cunningham, p. 45)

All the uses that can be made of photography in preparing and presenting of fingerprint evidence should be considered. Fingerprints that can be seen without dusting powder should be photographed first, since they could be damaged during the dusting process.

Videotapes

Videotaping the crime scene is another way to record evidence and information pertinent to the case. The videotape should not be erased or edited, since the whole tape has to be submitted as evidence. The individual recording the crime scene narrates the audio portion. The name of the individual recording the videotape, the date, time, case number, and any other important information should be recorded.

A videotape can capture the environment of a crime scene much better than photographs. Videotaping can record physical evidence such as fingerprints, footprints, bloodstains, and any weapons found at the crime scene. The admissibility of videotape as evidence usually is determined by the standards used in allowing photographs, so investigators should study the admissibility requirements in their local judicial districts.

Specialized Scientific Methods

Technology today provides ways to extract more information than ever before from certain types of evidence. They include fingerprints, body fluids and blood, footprints and tire treads, ID etchings, firearms, human hair, fibers and fabric, paint, glass, tool marks and metals, soil and dust, and documents.

Fingerprints

Fingerprints are a valuable form of physical evidence often found at the scene of a crime. Prints of the palm of the hand and the sole of the foot are made under the same conditions as fingerprints and preserved in the same way. "Generally prints are formed from the friction ridges, which deposit grease and perspiration on the object touched. It may also happen that the fingers are contaminated with foreign matter, e.g., dust, blood, and so on, or they may press against some plastic material and produce a negative impression of the pattern of the friction ridges." (Svensson, Wendel, and Fisher, 1981, p. 74)

A crime-scene investigator has to know where to look for fingerprints. This will depend on the crime committed. For example, the motives are different for a homicide and a burglary. If a burglar broke into a dwelling during the night, the investigator will search for fingerprints on the entrance area. For a homicide with robbery as the motive, the investigator will look for prints on the victim's wallet. Fingerprints are divided into three main groups: plastic, contaminated with foreign matter, and latent.

- Plastic fingerprints occur when the finger touches or presses against a plastic material in such a way that a negative impression of the friction ridge is produced. Such a print may be found in paint on a newly painted object, in the gum on envelopes and stamps, on substances that melt easily or soften when they are held in the hand (e.g., chocolate), on adhesive tape, in thick layers of dust, plastic explosives, putty that has not hardened, wax that has run from a candle, sealing wax, edible fats, flour, soap, thick and sticky oil films, grease, pitch, tar, resin, and clay, among other materials.
- Prints of fingers contaminated with foreign matter usually contain dust. When a finger is pressed in a thin layer of dust, some of the dust sticks on the friction ridges. When the finger is subsequently placed against a clean surface, a fingerprint results that may be fully identifiable. Similarly, a print can be left when the finger is contaminated with other substances—for example, pigments, ink, soot, flour, face powder, oils, or certain types of safe insulation. Fingerprints in blood are often indistinct.
- Latent fingerprints results from small amounts of grease, sweat, and dirt being deposited on the object touched from every detail in the friction ridge pattern on the tip of the finger. The palms of the hands and soles of the feet have no oil glands.

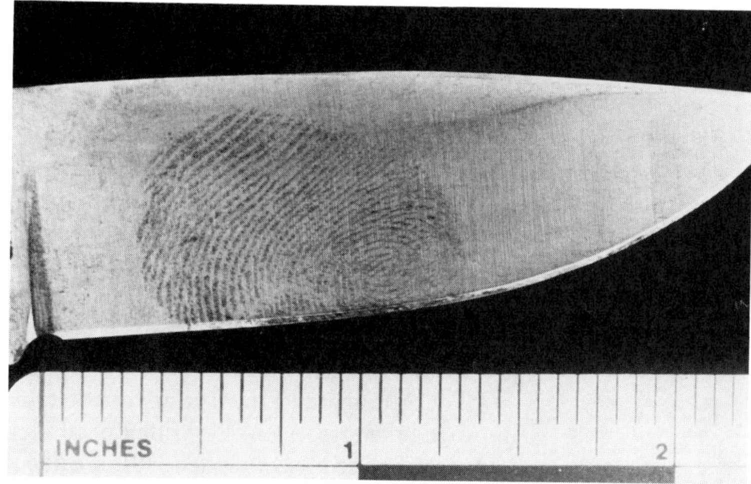

A latent fingerprint on a knife blade.

> Grease found on the inside of the fingers comes mostly from other parts of the body that are continually touched by the hands. The secretion from the friction skin contains 98.5 percent to 99.5 percent water and 0.5 percent to 1.5 percent organic and inorganic components. If the hands are cold, practically no liquid is secreted; when they become warm, this secretion returns to normal.

There are limitations on what information can be obtained from latent prints. The age of the prints, and the sex, age, and ethnic background of an individual cannot be determined. Unless a person does manual labor (say, a stonemason or gardener), it would be difficult to identify an occupation from fingerprints.

The crime scene investigator has the responsibility of collecting latent fingerprints. Careful attention should be paid to objects and surfaces that may not be obvious—toilet seats, dresser drawers, filing cabinets, tabletops, backs of chairs, rear-view mirrors, and telephones. Objects that are used often, such as doorknobs, may not provide good prints, but they should be processed anyway. The investigator needs to perceive the scene of the crime as the offender did, taking into account such factors as the time of day and the physical layout of the premises. (Fox and Cunningham, 1985, pp. 51–52)

There are a variety of ways to develop fingerprints. Powders can be brushed over a latent print. Another method is the development of a latent print with iodine, because iodine discolors and attacks objects exposed to it. Substances found on the skin discolor very easily. A silver nitrate solution can also be used to develop latent prints. Another method is cyanoacrylate fuming, where the item to be printed has been placed in contact with a cyanoacrylate substance that makes the ridges of the prints appear white. Lasers (light amplification by stimulated emission of radiation) are used to obtain latent prints from nonporous surfaces such as concrete walls, clothing, and metals. Some forensic crime labs use image processing, in which latent prints are examined by a video camera and a signal is fed into a computer, which processes the image. (Svensson, Wendel, and Fisher, 1981, pp. 66–72)

The Automated Fingerprint Identification System (AFIS) has improved the effectiveness of fingerprint identification. The Rand Corporation's study concluded, "Where adequate processing capabilities exist, cold searches of latent fingerprints are far more effective in increasing the apprehension rate than are follow-up investigations." (Greenwood, Chaiken, and Petersillia, 1975, pp. 40–41)

The California Identification System (CAL-ID) is the first statewide automated identification network, providing law enforcement agencies throughout California with remote terminals for conducting computerized fingerprint searches and retrieving fingerprint images for hardcopy printout or screen display. The FBI's identification division uses the **latent descriptor index** to search the division's automated files based on latent fingerprint pattern types, physical description information, and case information. (Neudorfer, 1986, p. 4)

Since approximately 40 percent of all crime scenes have fingerprints, it appears latent prints can have an impact on solving crime. Although the average homicide suspect kills only one person, a burglar in San Francisco steals more than 100 times in a year. If 100 burglars could be identified, it would make a significant impact on the crime rate. Clearly, routine crime scenes like burglary, not just the dramatic ones like murder, should be searched for prints. These facts have led the San Francisco Police Department to implement its own automated latent print system.

There are many reasons for a municipal police agency to have an AFIS system. (Moses, 1987, p. 55) For the first time, a single latent fingerprint left at the scene of a crime could be searched against the entire fingerprint base in a matter of minutes. This would lead to rapid identification of the perpetrator and to his or her timely arrest. Rapid identification and arrest would greatly increase the probability of recovering stolen property and preventing further criminal activity by that person.

If no identification were made, the latent print would be stored in the unsolved latent database. Thereafter, the fingerprints of every newly arrested suspect could be routinely compared against the latent fingerprints from every unsolved crime to date. Multiple fingerprint identifications would result in multiple counts filed against a defendant and increase the bargaining power of the district attorney. Rapid fingerprint identifications would significantly reduce the criminal's chances of success in committing an offense and would thereby serve as a powerful deterrent to crime.

Full utilization of fingerprint evidence would increase police effectiveness and stimulate greater public confidence in the law enforcement agency. Greater efficiency would result in more crimes being investigated and would allow more time to be spent on the more difficult cases.

Automated fingerprint search would lead to greater protection of civil liberties. Rapid fingerprint identification would lead directly to the criminal, minimizing the number of negative police contacts with innocent persons that often result from bad leads, "hunches," or investigative inexperience.

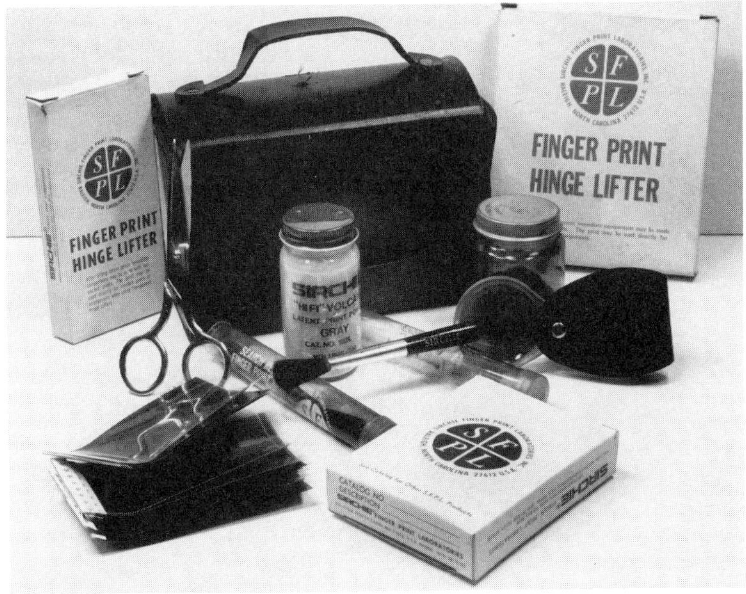

A crime scene fingerprint kit.

Body Fluids and Blood

Body fluids and blood are often important as evidence. Their remains at the scene of a crime appear as stains or as a liquid. **Body fluids** include, besides bloodstains, semen, vaginal fluids, saliva, urine, perspiration, pus, and human milk. Biological success of the body fluid as evidence depends on the purity of the sample. About 80 percent of people are **secretors,** who have in their other body fluids detectable amounts of the same ABO group characteristics as are found in their blood. Nonsecretors, the other 20 percent of the population, do not have such characteristics.

Where bloodstains and blood splatters are present, the events leading up to them should be reconstructed. The appearance and shape of bloodstains can provide useful information about the offense. MacDonell (1971, pp. 27–28) provides several rules concerning bloodstain evidence.

- Spots of blood may be used to determine the directionality of the falling drop that produced them. Their shape frequently permits an estimate of their velocity and/or impact angle and/or the distance to final resting place.
- The diameter of a blood spot is of little or no value in estimating the distance it has fallen after the first five or six feet. Beyond this distance, the change is too slight to be reliable.
- The edge characteristics of blood spots have absolutely no meaning or value unless the effect of the target surface is well known. This is especially true when attempts are made to estimate distance from scallops around the edge.
- The degree of spatter of a single drop depends far more on the smoothness of the target surface than the distance the drop falls. The coarser the surface, the more likely the drop will be ruptured and spatter. A blotter, for example, will cause a drop to spatter to a considerable extent at a distance of 18 inches, whereas a drop falling more than 100 feet will not spatter all if it lands on a smooth surface like glass.
- No conclusion as to the cause of a very small bloodstain should ever be drawn from a limited number of stains. Very fine specks of blood may result from a castoff satellite from a larger drop. In the absence of the larger drop, however, and when hundreds of drops smaller than 1/8 inch are present (often as small as 1/1,000 inch in diameter), it may be concluded that they were produced by an impact. The smaller the diameter of the drops, the higher the velocity of the impact. The difference between a medium-velocity impact, such as an ax or hammer blow, and

a high-velocity impact, such as a gunshot, is sufficient for differentiating the two.

- Directionality of a small bloodstain is easily determined if the investigator recognizes the difference between an independent spatter and a castoff satellite thrown from a large drop. Small independent stains have a uniform taper resembling a teardrop and always point toward the direction of travel. Castoff droplets produce a tadpole-like, long, narrow stain with a well-defined "head." The sharper end always points back toward the origin. Since these satellite spatters travel a very short distance, the larger drop can almost always be traced.
- The character of a bloodstain, either made by drops or by larger quantities of blood up to several ounces, may reveal movements both at the time of initial staining and later if a body or other stained surface is moved from its original position.
- Depending on the target and impact angle, considerable back spatter may result from a gunshot wound. The range of back spatter, however, is considerably less than that occurring in the direction of the projectile. This is especially true with exit wounds when expanding-type slugs are used.
- Blood is aerodynamically a very uniform material. Its ability to reproduce specific patterns is not affected to any significant degree by age or sex. Likewise, since blood is shed from a body at constant temperature and is normally exposed to an external environment for such a very short time, atmospheric temperature, pressure, and humidity have no measurable effect on its behavior.

Footprints and Tire Treads

Footprints and tire treads found at the scene of a crime can provide evidence to assist in solving the case and obtaining a conviction. Where appropriate, photographs and casts should be made. Footprints, indoors or out, may be used to establish the entry and exit of the perpetrator. They can provide information such as size, number, and physical condition of the offenders. Floors, broken glass, desktops, paper, chairs, and other surfaces may retain dust impressions of footprints or tire treads.

When footprint and tire-tread evidence is present, the investigator should search the suspect areas with a flashlight and darken the area if possible, directing the beam of light parallel to the suspect surfaces. Photos should be taken, with the light source as close to the floor as possible for a sidelighting effect.

The investigator should retain the original evidence, if possible, to send to the lab and protect the impressions so they will not rub off in handling. If the original evidence cannot be retained, the impression should be lifted with large pieces of fingerprint-lifting tape. *Do not dust or otherwise treat the impression.* Start the tape at one edge and roll over the impression, attempting to keep out air

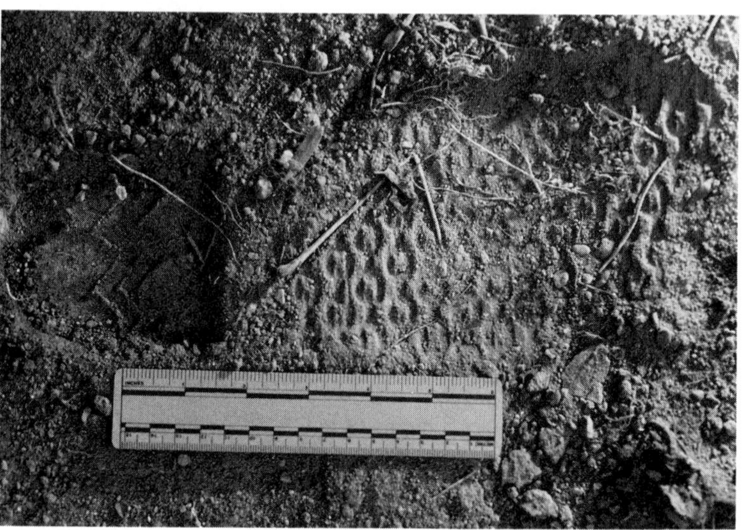

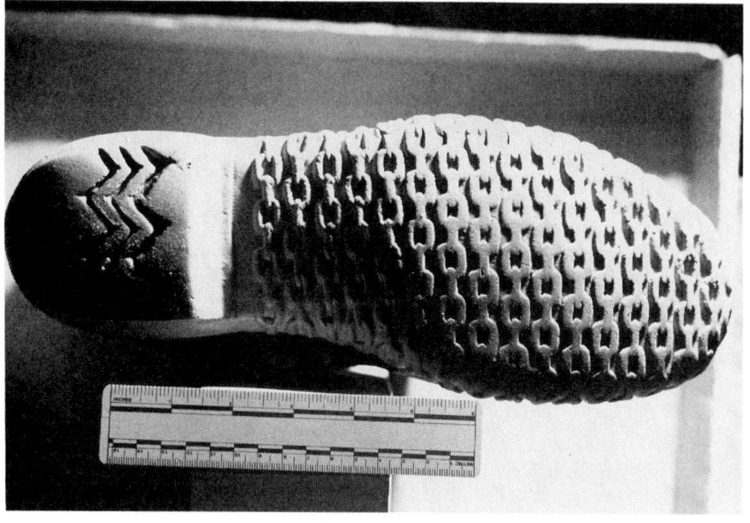

These photographs led to conviction by matching the imprint with the suspect's shoe.

FIGURE 10–10: Sample Gait Pattern

(A) direction line, (B) gait line, (C) foot line, (D) foot angle, (E) principal angle, (F) length of step, (G) width of step.

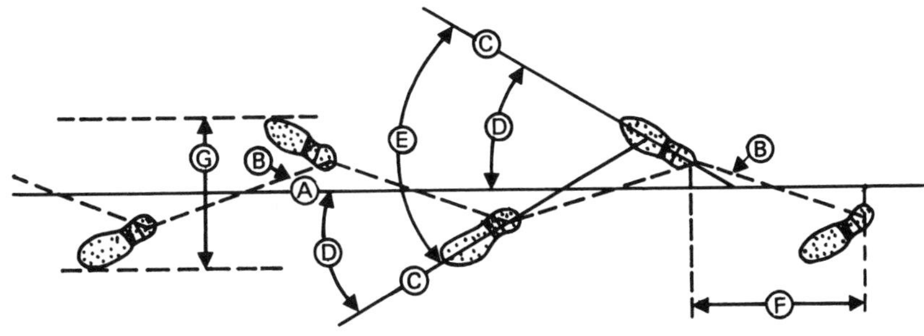

Source: Reprinted with permission from Fischer, Svensson, Wendel, *Techniques of Crime Scene Investigation*, 1987, 4th edition. Copyright CRC Press, Inc., Boca Raton, FL.

bubbles. Moistened photographic film-gelatin forms an excellent surface for lifting impressions. Clear film is made by fixing and washing. The film should be placed in water, wiped off, and dried until tacky. The tacky film should be applied to the impression with a squeegee (scraper or roller) from one edge, using care to avoid air bubbles. Protect the lifted impressions so they will not be destroyed or erased during handling or shipping.

A person running or walking has a particular gait. A **gait pattern** comprises the "directional line, gait line, foot line, foot angle, principal angle, length of step, and width of step." (Svensson, Wendel, and Fisher, 1981, p. 214)

The directional line is the direction taken by the individual. The gait line usually coincides with the directional line. It often zigzags if the person walks with the legs wide apart. The foot line goes through the longitudinal axis of the foot marks and may be different for the right and left foot. The foot angle is the angle between the foot lines of the two feet. Thus, it is the sum of the two foot angles. The length of step is the distance between the center points in two successive heelprints. As the gait line zigzags, the length of step is between the points of the directional line opposite the centers of the heelprint. The width of step is calculated between the outer contours of the two feet. Figure 10–10 illustrates a sample gait pattern.

The most valuable details of the footprint are those that show signs of wear, characteristic fittings or marks of fittings that have

A serial-number etching—identifying property ownership

worn off, marks of nails, pegs, repair marks, and injuries. An accumulation of characteristics can form decisive evidence. Footprints are preserved when they show details.

In moldable material like earth, sand, clay, or snow, a foot impression occurs. Footprints can also form on a hard base if the sole of the shoe carries a foreign substance such as dirt, dust, flour, or moisture.

Etching

Identification marks, symbols, and serial numbers can be used to determine ownership of such property as handguns, rifles, shotguns, paper and coin money, and deeds to cars or houses. Sometimes criminals eradicate ID marks to obtain ownership of property that rightfully belongs to someone else. They may attempt to completely alter the imprinted number of a motor block or the serial number of a bicycle or rifle and replace it with another number.

If the number cannot be changed, they completely obliterate it to prevent the item from being traced back to its original owner. There are three methods of obliterating serial numbers in metals: override them, grind them down, or grind them down and replace them. (O'Brien and Sullivan, 1980, p. 188)

When a criminal attempts to override the original serial number by pressing another serial number over it, the goal is to confuse the reading of the numbers. The grind or file method completely removes the serial number from the surface, but numbers when originally compressed onto the metal may remain below the surface when filed off. With the aid of various restoring methods, the original serial number may be read. If the perpetrator inserts a new serial number, a trained forensic technician can notice that the numbers are not straight, not the same size, not aligned with one another, at different depths, or unevenly spaced.

Firearms

Since firearms play an important role in many crimes, ammunition components left at the scene can assist in establishing the criminal's identity. Cartridge cases left at the crime scene can be connected directly to a specific firearm. When firearms are found at the scene, precautions must be taken to prevent accidental discharges.

It is important to measure the location of shell casings, bullet holes, bullets and bullet fragments, and shotgun shot patterns. This information can help reconstruct the crime scene and verify witnesses' and suspects' statements. Weapons found at the crime scene should not be moved until they have been photographed, sketched, and measured.

The crime scene investigator should check for depressions on the floor beneath the weapon, which would reveal that the weapon was dropped from some height. The weapon should be checked for traces of blood, hair, paint, fiber, or wood. When a dead person is holding the weapon, the grip and position of the weapon in the hand should be noted. (Svensson, Wendel, and Fisher, 1981, pp. 246–247)

Firearms tests can assist the investigator in deciding how far from the impact the weapon was fired and whether the suspect or victim in question fired a weapon. Tests include: observing the wound, observing the powder residue, determining the firing distance, finding gunshot residue, and determining whether a person has fired a gun. DeAngelis (1980, pp. 86–87) outlines courtroom presentation of firearms evidence.

- Police officers must be able to identify a firearm as the one found at the scene. They must be able to point out their initials, placed on the firearm earlier.
- A common error is a lack of or ambiguous markings placed on firearms evidence.
- The crime scene investigator and the firearms examiner must clearly demonstrate their positions in the chain of custody and control. It is the pathologist's responsibility to recover

the projectile(s) from a body, but both the pathologist and the investigator are responsible for seeing that the projectile is marked correctly.

- A common error is an inaccurate description of firearm evidence. (In one case, for example, a .45 semiautomatic weapon was called "automatic.")
- Frequently peripheral evidence is forgotten in the courtroom because of a lack of communication. Often the firearms examiner is prepared to discuss the individual characteristics of the known and the test-fired projectiles; the pathologist brings a medical report and X-rays; and the identification officers are prepared to identify the gun and ammunition found on the scene. But they may forget the victim's clothing or pieces of wood paneling from a wall where the projectile was found. This peripheral evidence is of great corroborative value.
- A common deficiency in the presentation of firearms evidence is a lack of pretrial discussion among the firearms examiner, pathologist, investigator, and prosecuting attorney. Often this is because the firearms examiner is from a state or federal lab some distance away.

Human Hair

Human hair grows from a root embedded in a follicle located in the skin. It grows about one-half inch a month, although this varies among individuals. The external human hair consists of the surface cuticle, composed of transparent, pigment-free overlapping scales pointing toward the tip end of the hair; the cortex, or cornified shaft, surrounding the medulla and containing some color pigment granules of melanin; and the medulla, or core, which contains cellular debris and some pigments. (Moenssens, Inbau, and Starrs, 1986, pp. 477–479)

Human hair retains its structural features for a long period. It resists putrefaction, making hair an important identification source for disaster victims and mutilated corpses. Currently there is no way of positively identifying that hair has come from a specific person. But hair evidence can still be useful in criminal cases.

- If an intruder is attacked by a dog, hairs from the animal may be deposited on his or her clothing. Identification and comparison of these hairs may contribute to placing a suspect at the crime scene. Of course, the circumstantial proof may lose much of its value if the suspect has a dog or can prove contact with another dog, since not as much can be learned from studying animal hairs as from human hair.

- In sexual assaults and rape cases, pubic hairs from the victim on the suspect's body or clothing or those of the suspect on the victim help to substantiate that an assault occurred. Head hairs present on the clothing or body of the victim may establish the color of the suspect's hair.
- Damaged hair from the victim of a crime may furnish a clue as to the type of weapon used. Fragments of the weapon or paint from it may be present on the hair.
- Hair recovered from a suspect's vehicle and compared with hair from the victim of a hit-and-run accident may establish that the vehicle was involved in the incident.

Human hair can originate from many parts of the body—head, eyelashes, legs, genital area, beard, arms, and chest. Sometimes it can be determined that a particular hair came from a specific part of the body. Hair from the head is usually uniform in diameter, while hair from the eyelids or eyebrows is short and stubby. The hair from a beard is coarse and curved. Back hair and chest hair vary in thickness along the shaft and have fine, gradual tip ends. Leg and arm hairs are short and contain little pigment. Hair found in the pubic area is wiry, with a broad medulla.

Hair can be used to determine the sex and race of an individual. The lab determines gender through the *Y* and *X* chromosomes by straining the follicular cells from the hair root. Hair can establish whether a person was Caucasian, Negroid, Mongoloid, or of mixed race, primarily by pigment distribution and other characteristics. (Moenssens, Inbau, and Starrs, 1986, pp. 482–483)

Specific procedures must be followed when hair is collected as evidence. Hair found at the crime scene should be removed with tweezers. All hair samples should be placed in a piece of clean folded paper or in a clean container like a pillbox. It is important to collect hair from both the victim and suspect for comparison. With a deceased victim, samples of hair should be obtained from the legs, arm, underarm, chest, and pubic areas. The collection should contain approximately 40 hairs from each area, packaged by area. Hair surrounding any wounds is placed in a container.

When hair is collected from a living person, the pubic and head areas have to be combed before any hair samples are collected. Any cutting required should be made as close to the skin as possible. At least 20 hairs should be obtained for a sample. When getting hair samples the investigator needs to be careful, since using tweezers can damage the hair. The tweezers should be cleaned before another area is sampled to avoid contaminating the evidence. (Fox and Cunningham, 1985, p. 77)

Fibers and Fabrics

Clothing, ropes, rugs, blankets, and other objects are composed of yarns made of textile fibers. These fibers can be classified into four categories. Animal fiber includes wool from sheep, cashmere hairs from the Kashmir goat, and silk fibers, to mention a few. The most common vegetable fiber is cotton. Other vegetable fibers include jute and sisal, which are used for industrial purposes. Asbestos is a mineral fiber. The majority of fabrics used in the United States are synthetic—for example, rayon, nylon, and polyester.

There are a number of reasons why the crime scene investigator should look for and carefully preserve fiber materials. (Moenssens, Inbau, and Starrs, 1986, pp. 495-496)

- Fibers present on a weapon may help to establish that it was used in the particular crime.
- Fibers present on a fired bullet may establish that the bullet penetrated a certain garment or garments.

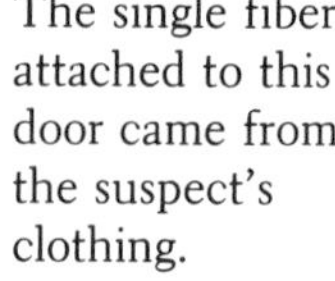

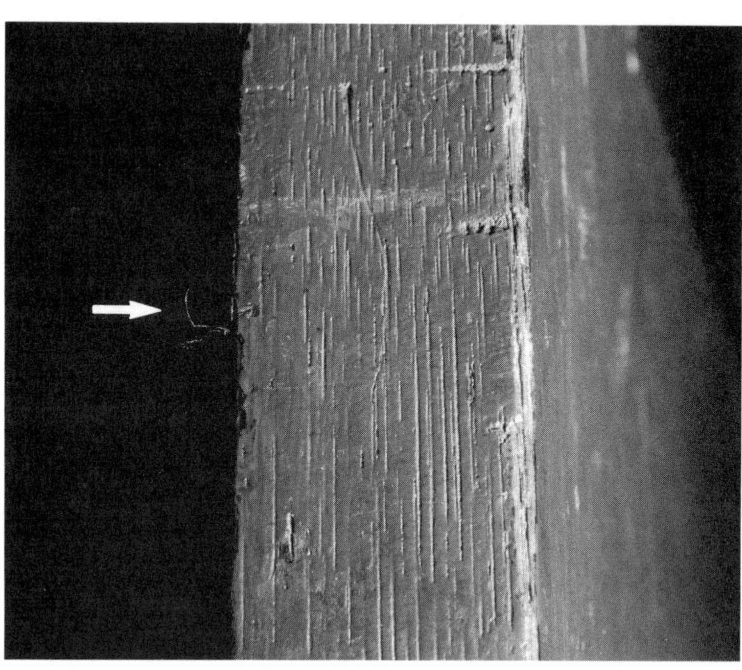

The single fiber attached to this door came from the suspect's clothing.

- Fibers present on a vehicle may establish that it was involved in a hit-and-run or other crime.
- The presence of trace materials on fibers may indicate the offender's environment or occupation and lead to his or her apprehension.
- Fibers present on the body or clothing of the victim of an assault, rape, or homicide may help identify the assailant.
- The interchange of fibers between two individuals may tend to establish physical contact between them.
- Deposits of blood or semen may be present on fibers, which may result in determining the blood group or isolating spermatozoa.
- The condition of damaged fibers may reveal information as to the type of instrument that caused damage to the fiber as a wound was inflicted.
- Fibers from stolen furs may be present on the clothing of the suspect, helping to establish his or her connection with the incident.

The absence of fibers in a close contact situation is not necessarily proof of no contact. Some fabrics, especially synthetic ones, have very few loose fibers.

Cloth fragments are frequently collected as evidence at the scene of a crime. Nails, splinters, sharp edges, or tree branches may have picked up cloth fragments from the perpetrator. Fragments of cloth can often be found in the undercarriage of an automobile involved in a hit-and-run. Cloths can be used to initiate fires. Impressions of cloth are found in wet paint, wax, putty, and other soft materials.

When cloth fragments are found, their color, pattern, shape, size, and kind of material should be recorded, as well as where the cloth was discovered. The investigator has to be careful not to flatten or damage the cloth when handling it. Fibers should be collected in paper envelopes, not placed directly in plastic or glass containers.

Glass

Glass can be valuable in a criminal investigation because of the variations in its physical properties. The breaking of glass may occur by accident or be intentional in the commission of a crime—for example, breaking the side window of a car to steal the tape deck. In this situation, glass fragments may be embedded in the perpetrator's clothing. In a hit-and-run, a headlight is frequently broken.

A piece of broken glass may provide valuable evidence about the entrance to or exit from the crime scene, or may provide other evidence—hair, fibers, bodily fluids, fingerprints—that adhered to it.

Glass fragments can be compared with those found at the crime scene and on the offender.

In examining glass fragments, the crime scene investigator should consider the various ways glass can be subject to force. A glass plate's strength lies primarily in its surface. When the surface is damaged, the remainder of the glass can be cracked or fragmented easily.

Glass has elasticity and can bend slightly, so with continuing force, radiating cracks can occur. A BB shot into the glass may not penetrate, but it may cause a cone-shaped fragment on the other side of the glass. When sufficient force is used, the glass cracks will radiate in a star shape from the cone. Secondary fractures will also occur, with fragments torn in the direction of the force.

"Radial fractures in a pane of glass and the spiral concentric features tend to create pie-shaped fragments, the narrow end of the fragment being the one closest to the point at which the force was applied." (Fox and Cunningham, 1985, p. 152) See Figure 10–11 for several common patterns of glass fragmentation.

FIGURE 10–11: Typical Glass Fragmentation Patterns

TYPICAL GLASS FRAGMENTATION PATTERNS

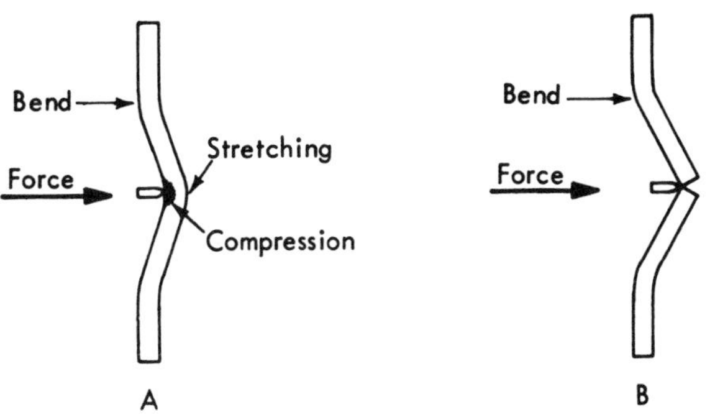

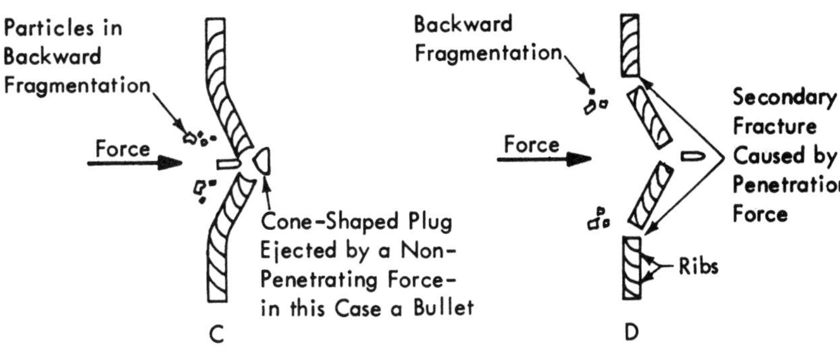

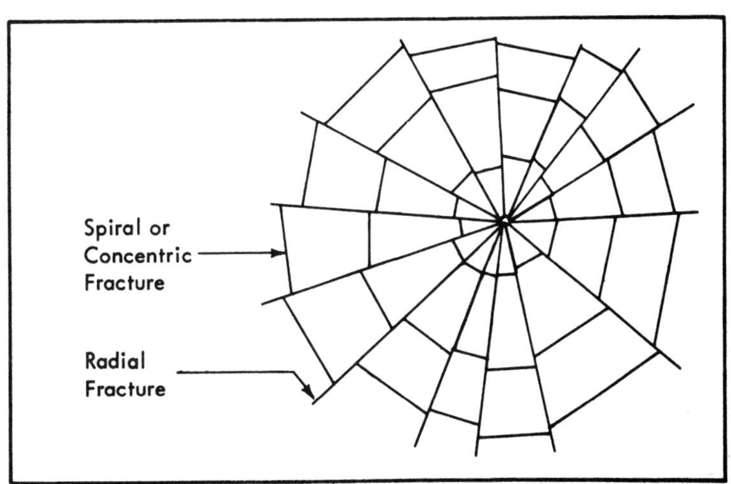

Source: R. H. Fox and C. Cunningham, *Crime Scene Search and Physical Evidence Handbook* (U.S. Government Printing Office, 1985).

Paint

A fresh paint smear or a chip from a dried surface can be evidence in a criminal investigation. As physical evidence, paint is most often used in cases involving a hit-and-run or a burglary. When a burglar uses an instrument for a forced entry, paint chips often cling to the instrument or paint chips from the instrument may be left on the door or window seal.

Paint should be collected as small flakes or chips, traces of oxidized ("chalking") paint, smears from fresh paint, or an intact painted surface or item. (Fox and Cunningham, 1985, p. 151)

When burglary tools have paint on them, it is microanalyzed for paint that matches paint at the crime scene. In the hit-and-run investigation, the crime scene should be thoroughly searched for paint particles thrown off by the collision between two automobiles or between a person and a car. The clothing of the pedestrian/victim should also be checked for paint particles from the hit-and-run vehicle. (Moenssens, Inbau, and Starr, 1986, p. 505)

Tool Marks and Metals

Tools used to commit crimes often leave marks at the scene. Marks can be left in metal, putty, paint, and wood by screwdrivers, axes, knives, pliers, cutters, drill bits, and chisels, among others. Tool marks are of two types: "those in which only the general form and size of the tool are apparent, and those in which injuries, irregularities, and other particular characteristics of the tool are produced in the form of striation or indentation." (Svensson, Wendel, and Fisher, 1987, p. 236)

A hammer striking soft metal or wood leaves an impression of the hammer's head. A glancing blow leaves striations caused by the irregularities of its edges. When tools such as crowbars, jimmies, and screwdrivers are used to pry wooden surfaces, a series of striations or impressions remains on the face of the tool. Frequently crowbar marks have the characteristics of an individual tool. Often the depth of the tool mark allows a good cast to be made.

Scissors, shears, cutting pliers, bolt cutters, pieces of wire, padlocks, and hasps usually leave cuts that have identifiable characteristics on the cut edge. Knives, hatchets, axes, razors, wood chisels, and paint scrapers often have slight nicks in their blades because of improper use or sharpening. Hatchets will leave wear marks on the cut branches of a tree or the skull of a homicide victim. Marks left in wood by either a plane or an ax are often identifiable. Pliers used to loosen a nut or a piece of metal often leave identifiable characteristics. When wrenches are used, however, the continuous adjustment of the grip can prevent a good impression. (Joseph and Allison, 1980, pp. 98–99)

The investigator might find broken metals at almost any crime. For example, pieces of metal are frequently broken from the headlight ring or other parts of a car in a hit-and-run. Stolen items are often broken from their mounts. In these cases, the mount is important in proving the item was stolen. An antenna broken from a walkie-talkie used during a burglary helped lead to a conviction in a Kansas City case. (Fox and Cunningham, 1985, p. 106)

The most important aspect of metal comparison is the shape of the broken metal. Broken metal items discovered on the suspect

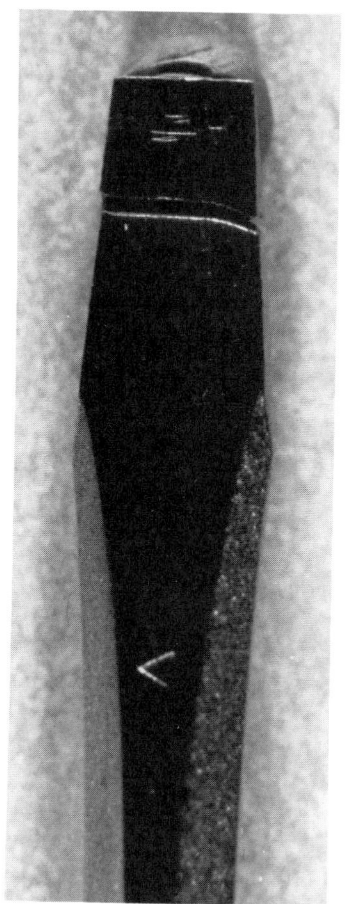

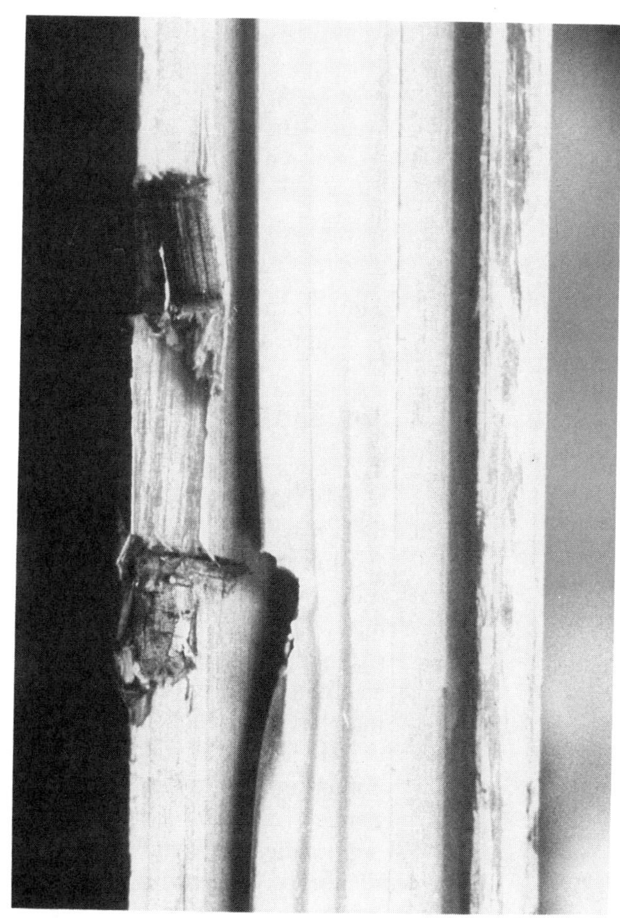

The screwdriver matched to this tool mark supplied incriminating evidence in a burglary case.

Soil and dust evidence

should be marked and sent to the lab for comparison. Items should be wrapped in clean paper, sealed, and placed in a film container.

Soil and Dust

In one way or another, soil is present at every crime scene. It can be recovered as a heterogeneous mixture that may include sand, rock, clay, black dirt, plant material, and other debris.

In outdoor crimes, soil is often taken from a crime scene or left there by the offender. Tools and weapons put down momentarily may collect soil. They can be analyzed for soil in order to place the suspect at the scene. Soil can be recovered from the scene of a car accident or the undercarriage of the vehicle, or the victim's clothes may have soil deposits.

It may be difficult to obtain an accurate scientific analysis when comparing soil samples. "Because of the wide variety of trace evidence of soil and dust, as well as the limitless scientific analytical approaches that might be selected, it is impossible to suggest the degree of certainty with which an opinion of a soil comparison might be expressed. There are undoubtedly cases where two soil samples might be positively identified as having come from a common source, but those cases would be rather rare. In most instances, the opinion would be couched in terms of probable, possible, or consistent with." (Moenssens, Inbau, and Starr, 1986, p. 515)

Documents

The examination of documents consists of comparing handwriting, typewriting, and other written and printed material to establish an identification. Documents can also be checked for latent fingerprints after they have been examined and photographed.

Documentary evidence should be in the same condition during the examination process as when it was found. It should not be marked, soiled, torn, or folded unnecessarily by the police. Each document has to be placed in a separate container. *The Handbook of Forensic Science* (1984, pp. 78–80) lists the various types of documents examined.

1. Handwriting (script)
2. Hand printing or lettering
3. Forgeries
   a. If traced, try to locate the pattern or master signature from which traced.
   b. If simulated or copied, include sampling of genuine signature to determine the accuracy of simulation.
   c. If freehand, the forger has no knowledge of how the genuine signature looks.
4. Typewriting
   a. New machines are usually difficult to identify with questioned material.
   b. An examination of questioned typewriting specimens can determine a possible make and model of typewriter used.
   c. Questioned and known typewriting specimens of the same size and typestyle cannot be identified unless they exhibit individual defects or wear characteristics.
5. Paper
   a. Definite identification is seldom possible.
   b. Consideration should be given to indented writing, watermarks, tool or knife marks along the edges, whether the paper was torn in a manner to leave stubs in a tablet, and whether torn edges can be compared with torn edges on a source item.
6. Writing instruments (pencils, pens, crayons, markers, etc.)
7. Checkwriters
   a. Examination of checkwriter impressions assists in determining the manufacturer of the machine.

   b. Positive identification of questioned and known samples is difficult, because the construction of checkwriting machines inhibits the development of unique identifying defects and wear characteristics.
8. Printing and other duplication or photocopying processes.
9. Indented writing
   a. Sidelight indentations and photograph the results.
   b. Process document on the Electrostatic Detection Apparatus (ESDA), which raises indented writing not visible by sidelighting.
   c. Document should not be folded, creased, or excessively handled.
   d. To avoid making accidental indented writings on a document in evidence, do not write on paper that is on top of document.
   e. Do not attempt to bring up indented writing by rubbing a pencil across it.
10. Obliterated or eradicated writing
   a. Nondestructive methods include photography and video, using ultraviolet and infrared techniques.
   b. Staining methods may produce minor stains. The lab should be advised whether minor staining may be applied.
11. Used carbon paper
   a. Carbon paper should not be folded or creased.
   b. Examination may disclose the context of handwritten or typed material pertinent to an investigation.
12. Burned or charred paper
   a. Questioned entries on charred or burned paper may be disclosed with appropriate examination.
   b. The material should be shipped between layers of cotton in a strong container.

It is difficult to determine the age of a document, but watermarks, letterhead or other printing, and typewriting can provide clues.

Summary

The scene of any crime possesses evidence. The collection of evidence and the testimony of police officers and criminal investigators are extremely important to the successful clearance of a case. The first law enforcement officer who arrives at the scene must protect any evidence from contamination, loss, or unnecessary moving. The crime scene should be closed to all persons who lack a legitimate investigative interest in the case.

The scene investigator is the key person involved in the preliminary examination of the crime scene. The purposes of a preliminary investigation are to reconstruct events and analyze methods of operation, motive, items stolen, and any actions performed by the perpetrator.

The crime scene is searched to find, collect, and preserve physical evidence for obtaining a conviction in court and to solve the crime. The methods of searching a crime scene include the spiral, radial, grid, and zone methods. Indoor searches are dictated by the size of the room and its contents.

Accurate records of the crime scene are valuable during the follow-up, or latent, investigation. They help the investigator reconstruct the crime. Records are kept by the investigator until the case is completed. An accurate, objective description must be made before any items or objects are moved, altered, or destroyed. A crime scene sketch can provide an outline of evidentiary facts and circumstances for a jury and court.

Sketching and photographing should be done for all serious crimes such as homicides, felonious assaults, fatal automobile accidents, burglaries, arson, and other violent felonies. The crime scene should be photographed before items are moved or touched to show, accurately and clearly, the crime scene as it was found. The photo log should include date, photographer's name, type of camera, lens, film, case number, and a list of every photograph taken.

Fingerprints are a valuable form of physical evidence often found at the scene of a crime. Fingerprints include all types of prints of friction ridges, including those on the palm of the hand and the sole of the foot. Where the investigator looks for fingerprints will depend on the crime committed.

Body fluids and blood are often important as evidence. Their remains at the scene of a crime appear as stains or liquids. Other types of evidence include footprints and tire treads found at the scene of a crime. Identification marks, symbols, and serial numbers help to determine ownership of property. Guns, money, and deeds to cars and houses are marked to determine ownership. Criminals may eradicate identification markings to obtain ownership of property.

Since firearms play an important part in many crimes, ammunition components left at the scene can assist in establishing identification. Cartridge cases can be connected to a specific firearm. Hair, fibers, glass, paint, and tool marks are also found at crime scenes, and the investigator must be careful to collect and preserve them as evidence to help solve the crime.

Key Terms

baseline
body fluids
cross-projection
gait pattern
latent descriptor index
latent fingerprints
photo log
scene investigator
secretors
triangulation
witness photos

Review Questions

1. What are the duties of the first officer who arrives at the scene of a crime?
2. Describe some of the people and factors that can seriously harm a crime scene.
3. What are the mechanics of a crime scene search?
4. What information should be contained in a sketch?
5. Explain the value of photographing a crime scene.
6. What are the three main categories of fingerprints?
7. Explain the value of the Automated Fingerprint Identification System (AFIS).
8. What are the rules concerning bloodstain evidence?
9. Why should the crime scene investigator look for footprints and tire treads?
10. Outline the courtroom presentation of firearm evidence.
11. Describe the use of hair in criminal cases.
12. Explain the importance of fibers, paint, and glass as evidence.

References

DeAngelis FJ: *Criminalistics for the Investigator.* Encoe, CA: Glencoe, 1980.

Fox RH, Cunningham CC: *Crime Scene Search and Physical Evidence Handbook.* Washington, DC: U.S. Government Printing Office, 1985.

Greenwood PW, Chaiken A, Petersillia J: *The Criminal Investigative Process.* The Rand Corporation, 1975.

Handbook of Forensic Science. Washington, DC: U.S. Dept. of Justice, 1984.

Joseph A, Allison HC: *Handbook of Crime Scene Investigation.* Boston, MA: Allyn & Bacon, 1980.

Ingraham BL, Mauriello TP: *Police Investigation Handbook.* New York, NY: Matthew Bender & Co., 1992.

Kenney JP, More HW Jr: *Principles of Investigation.* St. Paul, MN: West Publishing Co., 1979.

MacDonell HL: *Flight Characteristics and Stain Patterns of Human Blood.* Washington, DC: U.S. Dept. of Justice, 1971.

Moenssens AA, Inbau FE, Starrs JE: *Scientific Evidence in Criminal Cases,* ed.3. New York, NY: Foundation Press, 1986.

Moreau D: "An Investigative Perspective on the Collection, Packaging and Preservation of Questioned Document Evidence." Quantico, VA: n.d.

Moses K: "The Promise Fulfilled: Making a Local AFIS System." *The Police Chief,* 10: 50-57, 1987.

Neudorfer CD: "Fingerprint Automation:

Progress in the FBI's Identification Division." *FBI Law Enforcement Bulletin* 55(3):3-8, 1986.

O'Brien KP, Sullivan RC: *Criminalistics: Theory and Practice.* Boston, MA: Allyn & Bacon, 1980.

O'Hara CE: *Fundamentals of Criminal Investigation,* ed. 3. Springfield, IL: Charles C. Thomas, 1973.

Svensson A, Wendel O, Fisher B: *Techniques of Crime Scene Investigation.* New York, NY: Elsevier, 1981.

CHAPTER 11

The Crime Laboratory

The crime laboratory serves as an effective tool for analyzing physical evidence. It can assist in determining if a crime was committed and in answering the investigative questions of who, what, when, why, and how.

The crime lab is staffed by forensic scientists. The interchangeable terms **forensic science** and **criminalistics** refer to the natural sciences such as biology, chemistry, and physics. The principles of these disciplines are applied to the investigative and legal process to determine the guilt or innocence of a suspect. Forensic science is the application of science to those criminal and civil laws that are enforced by police agencies in a criminal justice system. (Saferstein, 1987, p. 2)

Traditionally, criminalistics has been restricted to physical evidence, such as trace evidence and firearms. The crime lab analyzes evidence collected at a crime scene by an investigator. A law enforcement investigator needs a basic understanding of criminalistics principles. How can the crime lab assist in an investigation?

The use of crime labs has increased since 1966, when the *Miranda* decision moved to protect the accused's right to remain silent when being questioned about a crime and the right to have an attorney present while being interrogated. *Miranda* resulted in a decreased reliance on confessions for convictions. Instead, a relationship must be established between the suspect and the evidence found at the crime scene. The physical evidence must be thoroughly examined and attested to before an accused can be found guilty of a crime. The criminalist must be ethical, impartial, and professional in evaluating all evidence.

The President's Crime Commission in 1967 (p. 51) stated, "More and more, the solution of major crime will hinge upon the discovery at crime scenes and subsequent scientific laboratory analysis of latent fingerprints, weapons, footprints, weapons, hairs, fibers, blood and similar traces."

Criminal investigators and other law enforcement personnel initiate the process of criminalist inquiry. Laboratory personnel only respond to the evidence submitted to them. Investigative personnel need to familiarize themselves with what evaluation the crime lab can and cannot perform.

Purpose of a Crime Lab

A crime laboratory plays an important role in the investigative process. "It provides this aid by answering, or helping to answer, the vital questions of whether a crime has been committed; how and when it was committed; who committed it and, just as important, who could have committed it." (Fox and Cunningham, 1985, p. 1) The primary goal of a crime lab is to eliminate or at least reduce uncertainty in evaluating evidence by providing factual data based on scientific examinations.

The first crime laboratory in the United States was established in 1923 by the Los Angeles Police Department. In 1932, the FBI organized a national crime lab whose services could be used by all law enforcement agencies across the country. Today there are about 320 crime labs in the United States. Of course, the capabilities of all crime labs are not identical. Some offer more services than others, and some develop expertise in specific areas.

Approximately 50 percent of the labs operating today were established during the 1970s. Scientific personnel and budgets for them increased, and the labs acquired new scientific instrumentation. Labs are usually under the control of police agencies, with services restricted to law enforcement clients. Approximately two-thirds of laboratories' caseloads are in the area of drugs and driving while intoxicated. The rest are in the areas of personal and property crimes.

The traditional evidence categories of fingerprints, firearms, and bloodstains/body fluids analysis are the most important forms of physical evidence in deciding cases. Lab directors believe forensic science evidence is most valuable in the crimes of homicide, rape, and hit-and-run accidents. Such evidence has its greatest impact at trial, in corroborating suspect guilt, and in verifying the statements of suspects, victims, and witnesses. Also, directors believe that jurors and police administrators have the poorest understanding of evidence, while police investigators and prosecutors

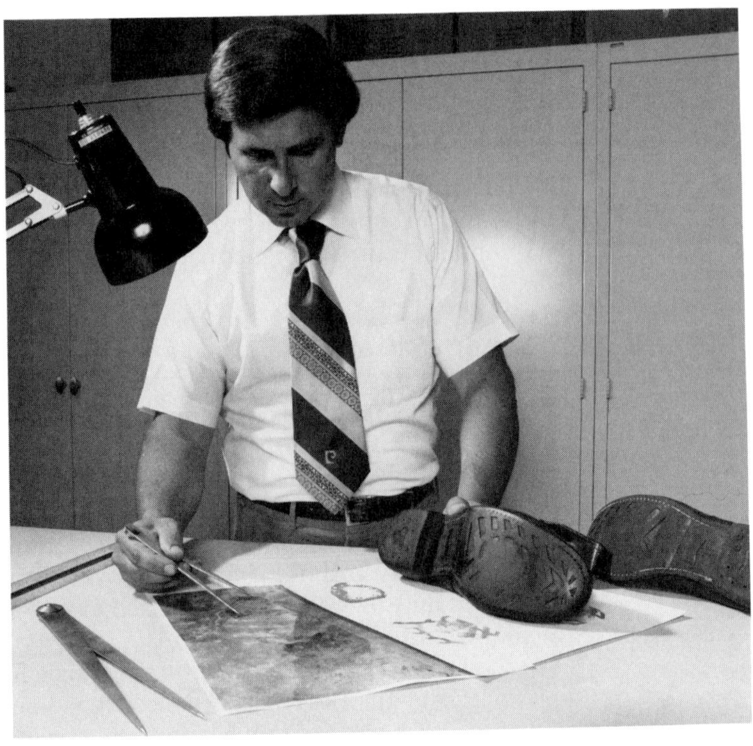

An FBI lab analyst matching up shoeprints

have the best understanding. Defense attorneys and judges fall between the two groups. (Peterson, Mihajlovic, and Bedrosian, 1985, p. 22)

Criminal investigators should become familiar with the lab in their jurisdiction. Forwarding evidence to the facility that has the capabilities to evaluate it can save valuable time.

"Recent studies of the use of crime laboratory support have repeatedly shown the importance of police training in crime scene search to both the volume of use of a crime laboratory, and the involvement of the laboratory in the more serious crime cases. The proper means of processing a crime scene, marking and packaging physical evidence and transporting it to a crime laboratory requires specialized training, however, of a nature that is within every police officer's ability to acquire. Scientific knowledge is not a prerequisite. What is required, in addition to procedural knowledge, is an appreciation of what could potentially be evidence, and what type of information the crime laboratory examiner might obtain from different physical clue material." (Fox and Cunningham, 1985, p. 1)

Since the *Miranda* decision, it is imperative that criminal investigators utilize the skills and scientific examinations of criminalistics. Factual scientific evidence is now considered more concrete and valuable than eyewitness evidence. Yet some criminal investigators still refuse to use the facilities of the crime lab. This may be attributed to the following reasons.

- Lack of knowledge as to how the laboratory can aid them.
- Unfamiliarity with the more esoteric varieties of clue behavior, which may result in some crime scene evidence not being preserved for examination.
- Failure to collect physical evidence, perhaps due to a fear of cross-examination on some technicality. This lack of confidence is the result of inadequate training and experience. Many detectives, especially in important cases, become cautious and decide to let an expert handle the matter, but before the expert arrives at the crime scene, evidence may be lost forever.
- Overpresentation of lab capabilities by misinformed instructors. When the lab cannot deliver the results detectives have been led to expect, many of them become disillusioned and abandon it altogether except for token use in hopeless cases where "it looks good in the report."
- Inconvenience. This arises when there is no local lab to which a detective may deliver physical evidence rapidly and easily or when a lab result cannot be obtained quickly. (Ostenburg, 1982, pp. 3–4)

To be effective, criminalistics technicians must rely on informed investigators who understand what physical evidence is, how to collect and preserve it, how to obtain the information it carries, and how to interpret the information. The lab depends on investigators to collect, preserve, and transmit clues found during the course of an investigation. The lab cannot analyze anything that it does not receive or that has been contaminated through improper handling. The scientist or technician must be advised about the circumstances and conditions in which evidence was found.

The criminalistics technician complements the investigator. What the investigator collects and preserves as evidence becomes valuable to the criminalistics technician, who knows how to analyze its meaning for a case. When possible, both parties should work together at the scene of a crime. The investigator knows how to find the important physical evidence, while the criminalistics technician knows how to handle it with care and skill.

Criminalistics technicians come to the crime scene prepared with all the tools of their profession—evidence bags, identification tags, and the proper forms for labeling. They know how to handle blood samples, semen, and fabric remnants until they can be taken to the lab for analysis. The investigator and criminalistics technician can make an effective team when they work together. (Califana and Levkiv, 1978, p. 4)

Fundamentals of a Crime Lab

A crime lab must: discover, collect, and preserve physical evidence; maintain and establish a chain of evidence possession; provide complete security of evidence at all times; ensure that all evidence is subjected to all useful examinations; interpret all of the revealed facts consistently and as completely as possible; provide accurate, clear, objective, and understandable court presentations of findings, their meaning, and their interpretation; and furnish counsel and assistance on all technical matters to the officials responsible for enforcing the law. (Kirk and Bradford, 1965, p. 85)

The discovery and collection of physical evidence are extremely important in the evaluation process. These tasks can be performed by law enforcement personnel, evidence technicians, or laboratory personnel. Procedures must exist to maintain the integrity of the evidence. A chain of evidence procedure should eliminate improper handling of evidence, which could cause contamination, damage, or loss.

Everyone who has had possession of the evidence must be recorded. Normally the person who collects the evidence places an ID tag or mark on it and records the collection. Each transferring of evidence, from the time it is collected to its submission in court, is recorded in order to maintain the chain of custody.

Evidence must be secured from contamination, damage, or unintentional alteration, as well as theft, removal, or loss. To maintain the security of evidence, as few people as possible should handle it. Evidence should be handled only by skilled technicians who wear protective clothing and expose only one item at a time whenever possible. Procedures are required to avoid accidental removal of microscopic evidence, which is often the most valuable and the hardest to retrieve.

Usually the first person who examines the evidence has the best chance to determine its potential value. The investigator should inform the criminalistics technician of the case's facts, what he or she observed, and findings from interviews and interrogations. The lab interprets the findings from physical evidence. Since criminalistics technicians present the physical facts of the evidence to the court, they should be familiar with legal procedures. They must substantiate the facts of the case in terms that laypeople can understand. Finally, the criminalistics technician cooperates with the prosecutor by providing factual information pertaining to the physical evidence analyzed. The criminalistics technician presents only factual findings, even if they conflict with the investigator's findings or do not substantiate the prosecutor's case.

Evidence

Collecting, preserving, and evaluating criminal evidence is crucial to a criminal investigation. The FBI defines evidence as "Anything which a suspect leaves at a crime scene or takes from the scene or which may be otherwise connected with the crime." (FBI, 1984, p. 1) The FBI also describes evidence as physical, real, tangible, laboratory, and latent.

Types of Evidence

Evidence may be either direct or indirect. **Direct evidence** is eyewitness testimony. The facts are explicit and prove that the crime occurred. For example, Robert saw Harry punch Joey, causing him to bleed. **Indirect evidence** may be either physical or circumstantial evidence. For example, a cast made of an automobile tire has specific characteristics that match the tire on the suspect's car. The cast and tire are physical evidence, but they are not proof that the suspect is guilty. If Robert saw Harry running from a room with blood on his clothes, then entered the room and found Joey flat on his back and bleeding profusely, this too would be circumstantial evidence.

Evidence may also be testimonial or documentary. **Testimonial evidence** is given orally by a witness in an attempt to persuade the trier of fact that a specific proposition is either true or false. **Documentary evidence** is a written or other permanent record. It may be typed, handwritten, printed, photostatted, photographed, audiotaped, or videotaped.

According to the International Association of Chiefs of Police, "**physical evidence** is generally defined as any unspoken evidence, a thing, an object, a substance, a visible or invisible gas which has some connection with a crime under investigation." (IACP, 1975, p. 79). Physical evidence can aid in solving the case because it can: develop MOs or show similar MOs, develop or identify suspects, prove or disprove an alibi, connect or eliminate suspects, identify stolen goods, or provide leads.

Physical evidence can prove an element of the offense. For example: Safe insulation, glass, or building materials on a suspect's clothing may prove entry; stomach contents, bullets, residue at the scene of a fire, semen, blood, tool marks may all prove elements of certain offenses; and safe insulation on tools may be sufficient to prove illegal possession of burglary tools.

Physical evidence can prove the theory of a case. For example: Footprints may show how many people were at the scene; and auto paint on clothing may show that a person was hit by a car instead of otherwise injured. (FBI, 1984, pp. 1–2)

Physical evidence falls into two classifications, evidence with individual identifying characteristics and evidence with class characteristics only. The former is evidence that can be identified as coming from specific sources or people because it contains enough identification characteristics, markings, or microscopic evidence. Examples are handwriting, fingerprints, tool marks, pieces of glass, and broken pieces of wood.

Evidence with class characteristics only can never be definitely identified, since there is more than one possible source of it. Examples are blood, soil, hairs, fibers, glass fragments, shoe prints, or tool marks when there are not enough markings for positive identification.

Categories of Evidence

Physical evidence found at crime scenes can be divided into 23 categories, according to one study. (Peterson, 1974, p. 42)

1. Tool marks. Includes all physical conditions where one object, serving as the tool, acted on another object, creating impressions, friction, marks, or other striations. A screwdriver, pry bar, automobile fender, and gun barrel might all produce tool marks.
2. Fingerprints and palm prints. All such prints, latent or visible, including footprints and prints from gloves or other fabric.
3. Organic, botanical, and zoological material. Excreta, residues from botanical sources, and food stains are typical.
4. Glass and plastic fragments. Broken, chipped, or splintered glass or plastic discovered in locations suggesting that it was the

result of an offender's actions or was transferred to such a person.

5. Tracks and impressions. Skid and scuff markings, shoe prints, depressions in soft soil or vegetation, and all other forms of tracking. (Tool marks are not included in this category.)
6. Paint, liquid, or dried paint in positions where it could have been transferred to individuals passing by. Freshly painted areas, cracked and peeling surfaces on windowsills, and automobile collisions are examples.
7. Clothing. Items of clothing that were left, carried, removed, or discarded by offenders. Individual fiber characteristics are included in this category.
8. Wood fragments. The fragmenting and splintering of wood, with prying, kicking, and chopping actions at the entry point, are the most frequent examples.
9. Dust. Instances where "dust" (all forms of surface contamination) was disturbed by an offender in the criminal act.
10. Cigarettes, matches, and ashes. Discovery of any of these combustible materials, or their remains, in positions that suggest their relationship to offenders.
11. Paper. Cases where the paper itself may be traced to its original position and where latent prints or other contaminating substances may be present on its surface.
12. Soil. The presence of soil or soil-like material in locations where identification or individualization seems possible.
13. Fibers. Includes both natural and synthetic fibers discovered primarily on sharp corners or edges or on surfaces where electrostatic or mechanical forces caused a transfer.
14. Tools and weapons. Instances where tools and weapons were found at crime scenes or in cars and there was a strong possibility that they were involved in a criminal act.
15. Grease and oil. Any lubricant or fatty substance, sometimes possessing environmental contamination, found in a position suggesting its relevance to a crime.
16. Construction and packing material. All those substances found in work areas and not belonging in any other category.
17. Documents. Written or printed paper capable of being traced to a particular person or instrument. Suicide and robbery notes—as well as cases involving the theft of equipment such as check protectors—where a document could be traced back to that instrument.
18. Containers. All bottles, boxes, cans, and other containers that held substances or residues of an informative nature.
19. Metal fragments. Materials found near industrial machinery

and scenes of collisions and other scrapings likely to be transferred to offenders.

20. Hair. Any suspected animal or human hair found in an environment, with reasonable probability of being traced to an offender.
21. Blood. Any suspected blood, liquid or dried, animal or human, present in a form suggesting a relationship to the offense or the individual involved.
22. Inorganic and mineralogical material. Inorganic substances not falling in any other categories.
23. Miscellaneous. All other physical phenomena.

Crime Lab Services

The quality and diversity of crime labs in the United States vary due to budgetary and staff limitations and the criminalistics needs in different geographic areas. A crime lab may offer some or all of the following services.

Crime laboratories in the United States provide a wide variety of services. This lab in Dade County, Florida, conducts DNA testing.

Physical Science Unit

Principles of chemistry, physics, and geology are applied to the identification and comparison of crime-scene evidence. The physical science unit is staffed by criminalistics technicians who have the expertise to use chemical tests and modern analytical instrumentation to examine items as diverse as drugs, glass, paint, explosives, and soil. In a lab that has a staff large enough to permit specialization, the responsibilities of this unit may be further subdivided into sections devoted to drug identification, soil and mineral analyses, and the examination of a variety of trace physical evidence.

Biology Unit

Biologists and serologists apply their knowledge to identifying and grouping dried bloodstains and other body fluids, comparing hairs and fibers, and identifying and comparing botanical materials such as wood and plants.

Firearms Unit

The examination of firearms, discharged bullets, cartridge cases, shotgun shells, and ammunition of all types is conducted by the firearms unit. Garments and other objects are also examined in order to detect firearm discharge residues and to approximate the distance from a target at which a weapon was fired. This unit also applies the basic principles of firearms examination to tool marks.

Document Examination Unit

The handwriting and typing on questioned documents are studied by the documentation unit to ascertain authenticity and/or source. Related responsibilities include analysis of paper and ink and examination of indented writings (the partially visible depressions on a sheet of paper under the one on which the visible writing appears), obliterations, erasures, and burned documents.

Photography Unit

A complete photographic lab is maintained to examine and record physical evidence. Its procedures may require the use of highly specialized photographic techniques, such as infrared, ultraviolet, and X-ray photography, to make invisible information visible to the

Gunshot residue (GSR) analysis quantifies the amount of chemical residues (specifically barium and antimony) found on a person's hands after firing a weapon. By identifying the manufacturer from the headstamp of an expended shell, the crime scene investigator can determine whether or not to have swabs taken for gunshot residue. A GSR collection kit consists of a solution of 5 percent nitric acid ($HN0_3$) and several swabs. Swabs are analyzed in the lab with atomic absorption spectrophotometry.

naked eye. This unit also aids in preparing photographic exhibits for courtroom presentation.

Toxicology Unit

Body fluids and organs are examined by the toxicology group to determine the presence or absence of drugs and poisons. Frequently, such functions are shared with or may be the sole responsibility of a separate lab facility under the direction of the medical examiner's or coroner's office.

In most jurisdictions, field instruments such as Breathalyzers are used to determine the amount of a person's alcohol consumption. Often the toxicology section trains operators, as well as maintaining and servicing these instruments.

Latent Fingerprint Unit

The responsibility for processing and examining evidence for latent fingerprints, when submitted in conjunction with other examinations, belongs to the latent fingerprint unit.

Polygraph Unit

The polygraph, or lie detector, has come to be recognized as an essential tool of the criminal investigator rather than the forensic scientist. However, during the formative years of polygraph technology many police agencies incorporated this unit into the lab's administrative structure, where it sometimes remains today. In any case, its functions are handled by people trained in the techniques of criminal investigation and interrogation.

Voiceprint Analysis Unit

In cases involving telephone threats or tape-recorded messages, investigators may require the skills of the voice print analysis unit to tie the voice to a particular suspect. A good deal of casework has been performed by the sound spectrograph, an instrument that transforms speech into a visual graphic display called a **voiceprint**. The sound patterns produced in speech are unique to each individual, and the voiceprint displays this uniqueness.

Evidence Collection Unit

The concept of incorporating crime-scene evidence collection into the total forensic science service is slowly gaining recognition in the United States. This unit dispatches specially trained personnel (civilian and/or police) to the crime scene to collect and preserve physical evidence that will later be processed at the crime laboratory.

Equipment

An important issue in the operation of a crime lab is the type of equipment needed. A list of every conceivable type of equipment used by a crime lab would fill a book. The specific equipment needed depends on the lab's mission. This section describes the minimum equipment needed for all crime laboratories. Definitions are from *Criminalistics* (Saferstein, 1987).

Comparison Microscopy

Forensic microscopy often requires a side-by-side comparison of specimens. Basically, the comparison microscope is two compound microscopes combined into one unit. It uses a bridge incorporating a series of mirrors and lenses to join two independent objective lenses into a single binocular unit. A viewer who looks through the eyepiece lenses of the comparison microscope sees a circular field divided into two equal parts by a fine line. The specimen mounted under the left-hand objective is seen in the left half of the field and the specimen under the right-hand objective is observed in the right half of the field. The optical characteristics of the objective lenses are closely matched to assure that each specimen is seen at equal magnification and with minimal but identical distortions.

Modern firearms examination began with the comparison microscope, with its ability to give the firearms examiner a side-by-side magnified view of bullets. Bullets that are fired through the same rifle barrel display comparable rifling markings on their surfaces. Matching the majority of striations present on each bullet indicates that the bullets traveled through the same barrel.

Stereoscopic Microscopy

The waves that make up a beam of light can be pictured as vibrating in all directions perpendicular to the direction in which the light is traveling. However, when a beam of light passes through certain types of specially fabricated crystalline substances, it emerges vibrating in only one plane. Light that is confined to a single plane of vibration is said to be plane-polarized. A common example of this phenomenon is the passage of sunlight through polarized sunglasses. By transmitting light vibrating in the vertical plane only, these sunglasses eliminate or reduce light glare. Most glare consists of partially polarized light that has been reflected off horizontal surfaces and thus is vibrating in a horizontal plane.

Because polarized light appears no different to the eye from ordinary light, special means must be devised for detecting it. A second polarized crystal, called an analyzer, is placed in the path of the polarized beam. If the polarizer and analyzer are set perpendicular to one another, or crossed, no light will penetrate.

A stereoscopic microscope can be outfitted with a polarizer

and analyzer to allow the viewer to detect polarized light. Such a microscope is known as a polarized microscope.

The most obvious and important applications of this microscope relate to studying materials that polarize light. The stereoscopic microscope is used for locating trace evidence that could be found in debris, garments, on weapons, or on tools.

Thin-Layer Chromatography

The technique of thin-layer chromatography incorporates a solid stationary phase and a moving liquid phase to separate the constituents of the mixture. A glass plate is coated with a thin film of glandular material (commonly, silica gel or aluminum oxide). This glandular material serves as the solid stationary phase and is usually held in place with a binding agent such as plaster of paris. If the sample to be analyzed is a solid, it first must be dissolved in a suitable solvent. A few microliters of the solution are spotted with a capillary tube onto the glandular surface near the lower edge of the plate. The plate is then placed upright in a closed chamber that contains a selected liquid with care that the liquid does not touch the same spot.

The techniques of thin-layer and gas chromatography are especially well suited to the needs of the drug analyst because they separate drugs from their diluents while providing for their tentative identification.

The analyst must have some clue as to the identity of the illicit material before using these techniques. Hence, in a typical drug analysis, chromatography accompanies color and crystal tests.

Spectrophotometry

The selective absorption of light by drugs in the ultraviolet and infrared regions of the electromagnetic spectrum provides a valuable technique for characterizing drugs. UV spectrophotometry is often a useful tool for establishing the probable identity of a drug. For example, if an unknown substance yields a UV spectrum that resembles amphetamine, thousands of substances are immediately eliminated from consideration, and efforts can now begin to identify the material from a relatively small number of possibilities.

Mass Spectrometry

As a sample emerges from the gas chromatograph, it immediately enters the mass spectrometer, where it is exposed to high-energy electrons that cause the sample molecules to break apart. With few exceptions, no two substances fragment in the same fashion. Hence, this fragmentation pattern serves as a "fingerprint" of a chemical substance.

A forensic analyst can with one instrument separate the components of a complex drug mixture and then unequivocally identify each substance present in the mixture.

Electrophoresis

An electrical potential is placed across a stationary medium (usually a starch or agar gel coated onto a glass plate). Only substances that possess an electrical charge will migrate across the stationary phase. The technique is particularly useful for separating and identifying complex biochemical mixtures such as dried blood.

Because many of the substances in blood carry an electrical charge, they can be separated and identified. Forensic serologists have developed several electrophoretic procedures for characterizing dried blood. Many enzymes present in blood are actually composed of distinct proteins that can be separated by electrophoresis on starch gel. These proteins will migrate on the plate at speeds that vary according to their electrical charge and size. After the electrophoresis run, the separated proteins are stained with a developing agent for visual observation. Characteristic band patterns are obtained that are related to the enzyme type present in the blood.

Low-Tech Equipment

The following definitions for equipment recommended for a crime laboratory were provided by Roger Parian, director of the Georgia Bureau of Investigation Crime Laboratory in Savannah.

- *Shoot tank.* A bullet recovery system, usually a water tank, to shoot into to recover a bullet without marking or damaging the bullet's surface.
- *Trigger pull determination instrument.* Usually a spring scale mechanism to measure the amount of force required to pull a trigger and cause a weapon to discharge in a normal manner.
- *Bore light.* Device to illuminate the interior of the barrel or cylinders of a weapon.
- *Vacuum sweeper.* Attachment for a standard vacuum cleaner that allows debris to be captured for trace evidence examination.
- *Balances.* A scale to weigh evidence such as marijuana or a projectile. The balances must be certified and calibrated. The

balances are also used to weigh reagents for preparation of chemical solutions or qualitative standards.

- *Assorted tools.* An assortment of tools is needed for lab repairs or for evaluating evidence. Tools include hammers, drills, saws, wrenches for taking apart various instruments, gun-cleaning tools for different calibers, and pin punches for dismantling weapons.

New Technologies

Science continues to develop technologies that help investigators solve crimes. Two of the most important advances in recent years are DNA profiling and laser technology.

DNA Profiling

In the 1980s, a breakthrough in DNA technology provided a powerful tool to assist in solving difficult cases. Deoxyribonucleic acid

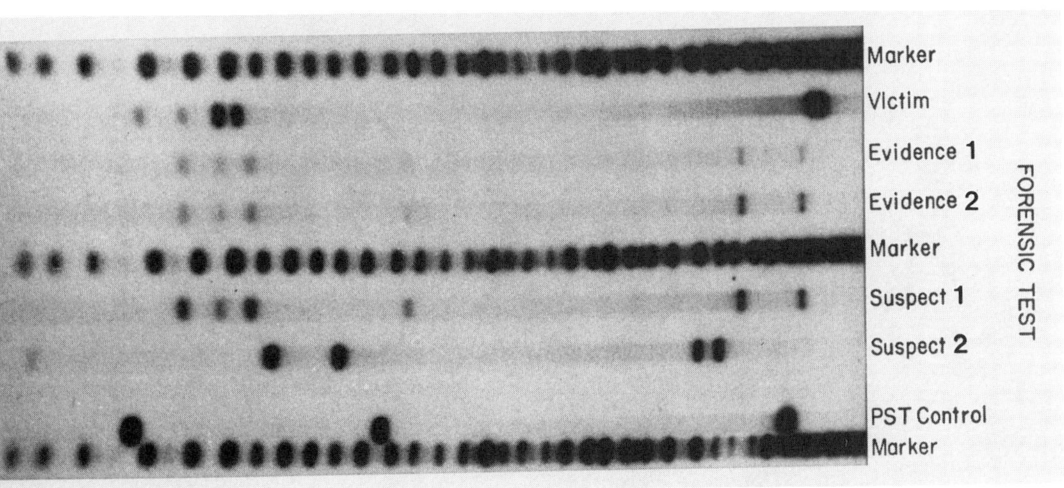

Identifying a rape suspect through DNA profiling. In this autoradiograph, DNA was isolated from blood samples of a rape victim (Victim, and two suspects—Suspect 1 and Suspect 2). DNA was also isolated from a semen stain from the victim's underwear (Evidence 1), and a vaginal swab taken from the victim (Evidence 2). The lanes labeled Marker contain known-sized fragments that act like a ruler to measure the size of the DNA fragments in the samples. The lane labeled PST Control contains a known human DNA for reference. The pattern seen in Evidence 1 and 2 indicates that Suspect 2 is excluded as the source of the biological material while Suspect 1 matches and is included.

(DNA) is found in the nucleus of living cells. It is part of chromosomes within the nucleus and provides the genetic code that determines an individual's characteristics. Four basic building blocks—nucleotides—make up the genetic code. The nucleotides are adenine, cytosine, guanine, and thymine. They have an enormous array of different sequences.

Restriction fragment length polymorphism (RFLP) is one technique used to analyze body fluids and tissue specimens. Special proteins are used to cut the DNA being analyzed. These proteins, called restriction enzymes, recognize sequences of four to eight nucelotides that are referred to as restriction sites. Polymorphic restriction sites are of great value to forensic scientists. DNA is cut into fragments of various lengths. Criminalistics technicians separate the fragments via electrophoresis.

Using probes—other pieces of DNA of known sequences—the locations on the plate can be analyzed. This results in a pattern of bands that may be transferred to photographic film the analyst can interpret. Forensic analysis can reveal the semen from a DNA identification profile. Blood, hair, and even tissues can be used to identify a decomposed body with DNA profiling.

Lasers

In 1976 a laser laboratory of Xerox Corporation discovered fluorescing fingerprints. That same year a Japanese detective discovered its advantages for forensic cases. In 1978 the FBI started the **Laser Latent Print Detection System**.

Dr. E. R. Menzel, an authority on the laser's use in forensic science, holds that the sensitivity of a laser depends on its environment and the electrical power available. A larger laser unit permanently housed in a crime lab can examine a substance in greater detail than a small portable unit. Lasers can detect body fluids, verify blood, locate gunshot residue, and establish gunshot patterns. They can also detect fingerprints on human skin. (Goodroe, 1987, pp. 85–86) Laser applications in forensic science include the following. (Poulsen, 1988, p. 4)

- Latent prints: inherent luminescence.
- Chemically enhanced prints.
- Trace evidence.
- Serology.
- Document examinations: inks and prints.
- Ink analysis.
- Vehicle processing (interior and exterior).

Using a portable Omnichrome Argon Ion Laser, Detective Sergeant Jeff Thompson of Ocean County, New Jersey, processes latent fingerprints in a sexual assault case.

- Paint comparison and location.
- Glass chip analysis.
- Drug analysis (drug residue location).
- Blood location and enhancements.
- Shoe prints: oblique lighting and photography.
- Bodies: prints, fibers, serology, floaters, and arson victims.
- Arson investigations: prints in soot and hydrocarbon detection.
- Number restoration.
- Gunshot residue: barium and antimony/nitrates and nicrocellulose.

This list continues to grow as new applications are discovered.

Forensic Science Libraries

In 1985 the **Forensic Science Information Resource System** (FSIRS) was established to provide information services to personnel in the FBI laboratory division and to state and local crime lab personnel throughout the United States. This information facilitates evidentiary examinations and research and development of forensic science knowledge, techniques, and instrumentation.

FSIRS is now the center for the distribution of forensic science information in the United States. It provides literature search services and delivers documents (on written request) to crime labs. FSIRS houses about 10,000 scientific and technical reference books. (Wade, 1988, pp. 15–18)

Forensic science has numerous databases. These include the criminal justice periodical index (CJPI), a reference guide to forensic science, criminology, criminal law, security systems, corrections, and police science. The legal resource index (LRI) specifically indexes forensic science information. The National Criminal Justice Reference Service (NCJRS) has an extensive document collection. Scisearch is an interdisciplinary index to the literature of science, organized by the Institute for Scientific Information. Forensic science information can also be retrieved from such database categories as biology, biography, business, chemistry, computers, defense,

State and local crime laboratory examiners receive practical hands-on training on serology at the FSIRS Center.

education, geology, humanities, languages, marine services, and pharmacology.

The Forensic Science Research and Training Center (FSRTS) conducts research to develop new information, techniques, and instrumentation. It also provides instruction to federal, state, and local crime lab personnel.

Central and Regional Labs

There are two systems of crime labs operating in the United States, central and regional labs. A central laboratory concentrates its services in a specific location convenient to the majority of its users. It's a good system for small geographic areas with large populations. Regional labs usually serve areas that are geographically large and have small populations.

The state of Georgia has had a unified system since 1952, with a centralized lab located in Atlanta and five regional crime labs throughout the state. Two major federal forensic crime labs—the Bureau of Alcohol, Tobacco and Firearms and the main U.S. Army lab—are also in Georgia. The army lab, in Fort Gordon, trains forensic science personnel for assignment as examiners in other army labs. It performs all services except blood and breath alcohol tests, toxicology, and mechanical printing.

The Drug Enforcement Administration has a specialized laboratory in McLean, Virginia, and seven regional labs throughout the United States. The main lab functions as a special testing and research facility and also advises the regional labs. The regional crime laboratories do drug analysis and perform the "signature program," in which microscopic sampling can trace the geographic location of illegal drugs. Special agents and forensic chemists work closely together. The chemists determine where the drug originated. Special agents locate the clandestine drug laboratory and maintain contact with the chemist to establish a time for seizure. Forensic chemists accompany special agents to the site to: ensure safety of personnel in the investigation of materials present, assist in evaluating the evidence, assist in debriefing subjects, and conduct a preliminary examination of evidentiary material. The DEA crime lab analyzes drugs for the FBI and for other law enforcement agencies, if requested. (Anthony, 1980, p. 29)

The U.S. Postal Service has a main crime laboratory in Washington, D.C., and four regional labs, in Memphis, New York City, Chicago, and San Francisco. The postal service labs analyze hand-

At the U.S. Postal Inspection Service Crime Lab, a latent fingerprint expert examines prints developed on rifled mail.

writing, fingerprints, drugs, tool marks, and bombs (especially letter bombs).

The FBI crime lab is available to all federal, state, county, and municipal law enforcement agencies. It offers a wide variety of technical services, including document examination, scientific analysis, radio engineering, and electronics. It can also provide technical assistance for kidnapping cases, airline disasters, and photographic problems. In addition, the FBI lab has files of questioned material: the national fraudulent check file, bank robbery note file, anonymous letter file, national motor vehicle certification of title file, and photographic material file. The FBI maintains a standard reference file and collection for typewriter standards, watermarks standards, safety paper standards, check writer standards, office copier standards, automotive paint, firearms, hair and fibers, blood serums, safe insulation, shoe prints, and tire treads.

Accreditation

Criminalistics as a profession is a relatively new field. Academic prerequisites include chemistry and biology. Few colleges offer academic programs in forensic science. Currently, criminalistic training is obtained through workshops, seminars, and on-the-job training. The American Society of Crime Laboratory Directors has an accreditation board that has accredited approximately 20 percent of the nation's crime labs since 1981. The objectives of the accreditation program are:

- to improve the quality of laboratory services provided to the criminal justice system,
- to offer the general public and users of lab services a means of identifying facilities that meet accreditation criteria,
- to develop and maintain criteria that labs can use to assess their level of performance and strengthen their operation, and
- to provide an independent, objective system by which lab facilities can benefit from a total organizational review. (Bashinski, 1988, p. 16)

The accreditation process requires an on-site inspection conducted by trained inspectors who examine the laboratory's facilities, equipment, and operating procedures. The staff is interviewed and case records are reviewed. If granted, accreditation runs for five years, after which the lab is reaccredited upon the successful completion of another on-site inspection. If the crime lab has any deficiencies, it has a year to remedy them before the final decision of the board. Crime labs are under no mandate to seek accreditation, but laboratory standards provide a guide by which practitioners can measure their overall performance.

Summary

The crime lab analyzes physical evidence and assists in determining whether a crime has been committed. The crime lab is serviced by forensic scientists, trained in such natural sciences as biology, chemistry, and physics. Traditionally, criminalistics has been restricted to physical evidence, such as trace evidence and firearms. Science can substantiate evidence collected at a crime scene by an investigator.

Since the *Miranda* decision in 1966, the use of the crime laboratory has increased. Criminal investigators and other law enforcement personnel initiate the process of criminalist inquiry. Lab personnel only respond to the evidence submitted to them.

The number of crime lab facilities doubled during the 1970s. Budgets increased, as did the number of employees and the amount of new scientific instrumentation.

Fingerprints, firearms, and bloodstains/body fluids analysis are the most important forms of physical evidence in deciding cases. Because of the different capabilities of crime labs, it is important that criminal investigators become familiar with the lab in their jurisdiction. They can save valuable time by forwarding evidence to a facility that has the capabilities of evaluating the evidence submitted.

Since the *Miranda* decision, it's imperative that criminal investigators utilize the skills and scientific examinations of the criminalistics technicians. Judges and juries tend to consider factual scientific evidence more concrete and valuable than eyewitness evidence. The laboratory depends on investigators for the collection, preservation, and transmission of clues found during the course of an investigation. A crime lab cannot examine evidence that has been contaminated through improper handling, preservation, or transmission.

Evidence must be secured from contamination, damage, unintentional alteration, theft, removal, or loss. To maintain the security of evidence, as few people as possible should handle it. Usually the first person who examines the evidence has the best chance to determine its potential value. The investigator should inform the criminalistics technician of the case's facts.

Collecting, preserving, and evaluating criminal evidence is crucial to a criminal investigation. Evidence may be either direct (eyewitness testimony) or indirect (physical or circumstantial evidence). Testimonial evidence is given orally, and documentary evidence is a written or other permanent record. Physical evidence with individual identifying characteristics has been identified as coming from specific sources or people because it contains enough identification characteristics, markings, or microscopic evidence. Physical evidence with class characteristics only cannot be definitely identified.

Physical evidence from a crime scene can be classified into as many as 23 categories. These range from tool marks and fingerprints to organic and inorganic substances such as hair and metal objects.

Crime labs are often divided into units that perform various services. Such units cover physical science and biology, firearms, document examination, photographs, toxicology, latent fingerprints, polygraph tests, voiceprint analysis, and evidence collection. Basic equipment in crime labs includes various microscopes, equipment for thin-layer chromatography and spectrophotometry, and facilities for mass spectrometry and electrophoresis. Most crime labs also employ numerous pieces of low-tech equipment such as shoot tanks and balances.

Breakthroughs in DNA technology provide a powerful tool to

assist in solving difficult cases. DNA, found in the nucleus of living cells, makes up chromosomes within the nucleus and provides the genetic code that determines an individual's characteristics. Another new technology is lasers, which can be used to develop latent prints and to discover gunshot residue fluorescing under basic illumination. New applications are being found daily.

Two systems of crime labs, central and regional, operate in the United States. A central laboratory concentrates its services in a specific location convenient to the majority of its users. It's a good system for small geographic areas with a large population. Regional laboratories usually serve areas that are geographically large and have small populations.

The Forensic Science Information Resource System was started in 1985 to offer information services to personnel in the FBI laboratory division and to state and local crime lab personnel throughout the United States. This information facilitates evidentiary examinations and research and development of forensic science knowledge, techniques, and instrumentation. Another movement that began in the 1980s was the accreditation of crime laboratories. Approximately 20 percent of the nation's crime labs have been accredited by the American Society of Crime Laboratory Directors. The primary objectives of the accreditation process are to maintain quality crime laboratories and make certain they are staffed by competent personnel.

Key Terms

criminalistics
direct evidence
DNA
documentary evidence
forensic science
Forensic Science Information Resource System
indirect evidence
laser
latent print detection system
physical evidence
testimonial evidence
voiceprint

Review Questions

1. What is the purpose of a crime laboratory?
2. What effect did the *Miranda* decision have on crime labs?
3. Are the capabilities of different crime laboratories similar? Explain.
4. Who do criminalists rely on to be effective?
5. Explain the different types and categories of evidence?
6. Describe the different types of equipment crime labs have.
7. What are the two laboratory systems?
8. What is DNA profiling?
9. Describe the value of lasers in criminal investigation.

References

Anthony R: "Analytical Laboratory Network: A Key to DEA Anti-Drug Effort." *Law and Order*. 28:3, 1980.

Bashinski JS: "Laboratory Standards: Accreditation, Training and Certification of Staff in the Forensic Sciences." Unpublished paper, 1988.

Califana AL, Levkiv JS: *Criminalistics for the Law Enforcement Officer*. New York, NY: McGraw-Hill, 1978.

Dienstein W: *Technics for the Crime Investigator*, ed. 2. Springfield, IL: Charles C. Thomas, 1974.

Federal Bureau of Investigation: *Handbook of Forensic Science*. Washington, DC: U.S. Government Printing Office, 1984.

Fox RH, Cunningham CL: *Crime Scene Search and Physical Evidence Handbook*. Washington, DC: U.S. Government Printing Office, 1985.

Goodroe C: "Laser-Based Evidence Collection and Analysis." *Law and Order*, 9:85, 1987.

International Association of Chiefs of Police. *Criminal Investigation: Basic Procedures*. Gaithersburg, MD: IACP, 1975.

Kenney JP, More HW Jr: *Principles of Investigation*. St. Paul, MN: West Publishing Co., 1979.

Kirk PL: *Crime Investigation*, ed. 2. New York, NY: John Wiley & Sons, 1974.

Kirk PL, Bradford LW: *The Crime Laboratory*. Springfield, IL: Charles C. Thomas, 1965.

Ostenburg JW: *The Crime Laboratory*, ed. 2. New York, NY: Clark Boardman Co., 1982.

Peterson JL: *The Utilization of Criminalistics Services by the Police*. Washington, DC: U.S. Government Printing Office, 1974.

Peterson JL, Mihajlovic S, Bedrosian JL: The Capabilities, Uses, and Effects of the Nation's Criminalistics Laboratories." *Journal of Forensic Science*, vol. 30, 1:22, 1985.

Poulsen TW: "Lasers in Court—A Current Report on Laser Applications to Forensic Investigations." Unpublished paper, 1988.

President's Commission on Law Enforcement and Administration of Justice: *Task Force Report: The Police*. Washington, DC: U.S. Government Printing Office, 1967.

Saferstein R: *Criminalistics: An Introduction to Forensic Science*, ed. 3. Englewood Cliffs, NJ: Prentice-Hall, 1987.

Wade C: "Forensic Science Information Resource System": *FBI Law Enforcement Bulletin*, 6:15–18, 1988.

CHAPTER 12

Sex Offenses

LYLE L. SHOOK

Sex is a pervasive factor in human behavior. Because of the mission of law enforcement, it is inevitable that the police will become involved in a wide variety of sexual investigations. Sexuality encompasses such an array of acts that the law cannot cover all possibilities. In fact, some sexual behavior bears no obvious relation to what most people would call sex.

Sex is like fire. Controlled, it provides many benefits and high levels of pleasure. Out of control it causes shame, fear, guilt, injury, and death. Nowhere else in the law do we see such an incredible effort to censor human behavior. "Our own culture is often criticized for being obsessed with sex. Whether or not that criticism is justified, it is certainly true that a very large part of our value system, our shared heritage of moral codes, and our legal system is devoted to the control of sexual activity." (Stone and Deluca, 1980, p.186)

Matters of sexuality may cause a greater variety of problems and challenges than any other aspect of law enforcement. Few acts result in more community concern, fear, anger, or confusion than variant (and usually illegal) sexual conduct.

What people should or should not do sexually is a value judgment. Such values are in a constant state of change. What is acceptable today may have been illegal in the past, while what is illegal today may be legalized in the future.

Sexual values in the United States reflect the current interpretation of our Judeo-Christian history. That interpretation has become justification for laws on masturbation, fornication, nudity, adultery, homosexuality, prostitution, pornography, and other forms of sexual behavior.

Today, the police officer is faced with a diversity of public opinion on almost every aspect of sexual behavior. At a time when society appears to be obsessed with sex, there are many who attempt to exploit it. Advertising uses sex to sell everything. Sex is a main theme in music, motion pictures, television, magazines, books, and art. Americans talk about it, joke about it, think about it, and dream about it. We dress for sex, work for sex, and play for sex. Yet at the same time, we pass laws against it, fight sex education, censor nudity and sexual slang, march against erotic literature, and suffer from homophobia.

The law in some states makes it illegal to have sex before marriage, or **cohabit**. At one time it was a felony to engage in oral or anal sex anywhere in the United States; it is still a felony in some states. As a nation we are very homophobic, but homosexuals perform no sex acts that heterosexuals don't. We have laws that determine at what age sex is acceptable. Pornography is a major concern, but it's well over a billion-dollar-per-year business. Free sex is OK but the purchase of sex is not. Somewhere in America there is a law against almost every form of sex outside of marriage and many sexual acts within marriage. Most Americans are not aware of many of these laws and disregard them if they are. It is little wonder that there is so much sexual confusion and violation of the law.

Society is composed of individuals who form a variety of groups. In a democracy, we like to think that majority opinion is a major consideration in creating law. In reality, that is seldom the case. Experience has also taught that the majority is not always right, especially concerning moral and ethical issues. The moral majority may be neither.

The basic question that our society struggles with is government control of sex versus free choice. Some states have adopted consenting sexual laws for adults, while others continue to regulate a wide variety of sexual behavior. Police officers are often caught between the law and what citizens are doing. If the police equally enforced all sex laws, to all people, all the time, the majority of Americans would be in jail.

American law clearly attempts to repress many acts of sexuality. But people will tolerate only so much control. One might equate sex to a bobber floating in a pail of water. Free and on the surface, it will float back and forth, but if pushed to the bottom, it will fight to get free. When it does break loose, it not only returns to the surface but violently erupts through the surface. The more we repress sex, the greater the danger that it will erupt into violence and criminal behavior. There is evidence that those who labor to repress the sexual lives of others may be contributing to the American sex crimes problem. Repression, censorship, and double standards promulgate ignorance, which in turn contributes to sexual confusion, dysfunction, crime, violence, and death.

Aspects of Illicit Sexual Behavior

Researchers have identified certain elements common to sex offenders. Knowledge of these traits, which include motives, escalation, addiction, and impulse, can help investigators solve sex crimes.

Motives

One of the most important elements in the investigation of sex crimes is motive, which may be difficult to discover and near impossible to grasp. Some sex offenses are so bizarre that motive is beyond one's ability to perceive.

The following six motives for sexual behavior are offered as a guide for the investigator to better understand why some people get into trouble with the criminal justice system.

First, the act may be a replacement for another sexual experience. A person may have had a normal or acceptable sexual life until something disrupted that pattern. A partner may have passed away, been lost to divorce or illness, been called for military duty, or sent to prison. A normal outlet may be lost because of obesity, venereal disease, or a lack of desire. In an effort to find a replacement, the individual may encounter the law.

Second, the individual desires something sexually different. At first, one's partner is new and exciting. But with the passage of time, routine sex with the same partner, in the same house, same bed, in the missionary position on Friday night, after the news, with the lights off, can become boring. Another difficulty arises when one partner refuses to permit a sexual technique that the other wants. The partner who has the desire often seeks an outlet elsewhere. When it comes to sex, it seems that variety is the spice of life.

Third, the behavior is an arousal without which normal sex cannot be performed. Examples include erotic literature or pictures and fetish items such as a person's feet, hair, or a pair of panties. Cross-dressing, dressing like a baby, being urinated or defecated upon, dressing in black leather, exposing the genitals, window peeping, inserting objects into body cavities, and giving or receiving pain are but a few requirements of foreplay and sexual arousal for some. Such sexual scenarios can result in police intervention.

Fourth, the practice increases the pleasure of the sexual behavior. Some people set the mood by using soft background music, silk sheets, erotic films, and sexual toys, liquor, or drugs. Others seek sex in locations where they risk being caught, get involved in group sex, or cross-dress. Still others increase their pleasure by giving or receiving pain, hanging themselves, or setting indiscriminate fires.

Fifth, the activity is *autoerotic* and no additional person is needed for sexual gratification. Examples include masturbation, intense fantasy, and hanging.

Sixth, the sexual behavior is a rebellion against conventional codes of conduct. Many people find stimulation in doing what is prohibited. When the legal age to drink alcohol is 21, a beer always seems to taste better when you are 19. The illegal obtaining and consumption seem to enhance the taste. Sexual examples of this rebellion include adultery, oral or anal sex, the purchase of sex, obscenity, public or group sex, sex with a child or much older person, gallows partners, rectal insertion of rodents or a fist, and enemas.

Escalation

A second concept that is important to the investigator is escalation. Recent research, especially that conducted at the behavioral sciences unit of the FBI Academy at Quantico, Virginia, has produced strong evidence that many sex offenders escalate their behaviors. Some people who engage in variant sex styles never go beyond that point. But others begin with a seemingly harmless activity and gradually escalate to the level of community threat. This condition is also referred to as **progressive degeneracy**.

At some point as an individual escalates, he or she crosses the line into criminal sexual behavior. A few escalate to such abominable crimes that even they are horrified at what they have done.

Sexual Addiction

It seems clear that sex, like other behaviors that lead to high levels of pleasure, is addictive. Once a behavior pattern is established that results in a desirable outcome, an individual will repeat it time after time, often to the exclusion of all other sex acts. A person who becomes addicted to an illegal sexual activity will often risk anything to keep engaging in it. Because of the tendency to repeat, it is crucial that investigators keep accurate, up-to-date records on sex offenders. M.O. files and photo files are especially important. Many states require known sex offenders to register with and report to the sheriff of the county in which they reside.

Dr. Stephen B. Levine, a psychiatrist at University Hospitals of Cleveland, states that "Sexual compulsiveness covers a wide range of behavior, including perversion, obscene phone calls, exhibitionism, voyeurism, pedophilia, sadism, cruelty, rape and masochism. A typical sexual addict is a man who feels socially deficient, views himself as a loner who feels he was socially isolated as a child and teen and who has a history of being abused psychologically, physically and sexually." (McKnight, 1989, p. A-2)

Investigators who work on sex-related cases may find it productive to network with any of the four nationwide sex-addict support groups. Together, these groups currently have about 20,000 members.

Impulse

Police investigators are aware that some human behavior results from **impulse**, a sudden desire to engage in an unplanned activity. While all people have impulses, some may not be able to control their desires or resist acting upon them. In some states, an irresistible impulse is a legal defense against criminal behavior.

Irresistible impulse explains why an individual who leads a highly respected life may suddenly commit a variant sex act without the faintest idea why. Police files are full of such cases. They are sometimes more tragic to the offender than to the victim.

"Under the conditions of an all-important movement even an average man may be driven to commit an act which he will regret for the rest of his life." (Reinhart, 1957, p. 10) If that impulse is irresistible and involves the deepest of sexual drives, the individual may lose sight of everything but the desired object. Under such conditions, anyone may engage in an activity he or she would otherwise consider bizarre or even repulsive. Investigators should never eliminate a suspect in a sexual crime just because he is a "nice guy." Someone who looks too good to be true often is.

Classifying Sexual Behavior

In broad perspective, sexual behavior may be classified into three general categories: consensual, annoyance, and threatening. Police intervention and investigation may be required in all three. Glossary definitions in this section are taken from *Investigation of Variant Sex Styles* (Shook, 1990, p. 111).

Consenting Sex

Police involvement in consenting sex may be the result of many things. Stories abound of sexual encounters in cars where the individual on top throws out his or her back and the partner on the bottom can't get free. They blow the car horn until help comes—often in the form of a law enforcement officer.

Acts as common as masturbation and intercourse may bring on a fatal heart attack or stroke. When someone dies, there is a good chance investigators will be called.

If a partner providing cunnilingus decides to blow air into the vagina, the recipient may develop an embolism and die suddenly. During fellatio, the recipient may block the giver's airway, resulting in death by suffocation. In a case of autoerotic hanging, a safety device may not work and the person accidentally strangles to death. An individual or couple using electrical probes for sexual stimulation may be electrocuted.

Prostitutes are injured or killed by their pimps and sometimes by customers, or johns. The customer may be mugged by the pimp or the prostitute. Serious injury or death can result from the discovery of adultery by a significant other. There are numerous examples of sexual activity that is consensual but involves police investigation.

The number of people who are injured or die each year while engaged in consenting sexual activity is unknown. Many such deaths are classified falsely or in error, making research difficult, but the number of cases is likely higher than reported. Sometimes the police spend countless hours of investigation, only to discover that there was no violation of the law.

Law enforcement agencies in general assign low priority to investigating sex violations that involve mutually consenting partners, unless the case generates public complaints or it is politically advantageous to act. It is not uncommon for a mayor to order the police to sweep the streets of prostitutes three weeks before the election. Consenting sexual acts are often offensive only to an outsider.

Annoyance Sex

Annoyance Sex covers a wide range of sexual activities that offer little threat to individuals or the community. The behavior may cause fear but is more of an irritation or nuisance than a threat. The greatest danger occurs when the individual is discovered and confronted by an irate friend, spouse, parent, or crowd, any of whom may injure or kill the offender.

The participant also runs the risk of being attacked by the victim. Take, for example, a male who enters a bar and picks up a transvestite whom he truly believes is female. As the drama of seduction unfolds, the man suddenly realizes that "she" is a he. Many window peepers are injured accidentally after being discovered. They may make a backyard escape and encounter a wire fence, hole in the ground, clothesline, birdbath, or mean Doberman.

Annoyance sex is a common police problem. Few agencies have the time or personnel to assign a high priority to such complaints.

Exceptions are based on the level of threat, pressure from the public, or the socioeconomic status of the victims or neighborhood.

Threatening Sex

In sexual behavior that is threatening, injury or death is always a possibility. In **threatening sex**, the victim may be beaten, strangled,

Glossary

Consenting Sex

Adultery: Sexual intercourse between a married person and an individual other than his or her legal spouse.

Anilingus: Licking or pushing the tongue into the anus of another.

Bigamy: Marrying someone while still legally married to another.

Cunnilingus: Application of the mouth to the vagina, vulva, or clitoris (oral sex with a female).

Fellatio: Application of the mouth to the penis (oral sex with a male).

Fetish: Sexual interest in an object or a nonsexual part of a body (feet, hair, etc.).

Flagellation: Sexual stimulation or gratification from whipping or being whipped.

Fornication: Sexual intercourse outside of marriage.

Gerontophilia: The choice of an older person for sexual intercourse.

Heterosexuality: Sexual interest in persons of the opposite sex.

Homosexuality: Sexual interest in persons of the same sex.

Masochism: Inflicting mental or physical pain on oneself for sexual stimulation or gratification.

Masturbation: Manual manipulation of the genital organs (male or female) commonly resulting in orgasm, exclusive of sexual intercourse.

Nudity: Wearing no clothing over sexual areas of the body.

Osphresiophilia: Being sexually excited by odors.

Pornography: Sexually arousing books, movies, etc.

Sodomy: Varies from state to state. Involves sexual relations with an animal, rectal intercourse, and in some cases oral sex.

Transsexual: A person who undergoes surgery to become a member of the opposite sex.

Transvestite: One who plays the role of the opposite sex by cross-dressing.

Tribadist: A woman who practices coitus by wearing a dildo.

Triolist: An individual who performs sex with several partners in the presence of others.

Urolagnia: Sexual excitement or gratification by the feel, smell, or taste of urine.

Annoyance Sex

Bestiality: Sex with an animal or bird.

Coprolalia: Using language about feces and urine for sexual stimulation.

Coprolagnia: Sexual stimulation or gratification by the feel, smell, or taste of urine and/or feces.

cut, shot, tortured, burned, electrocuted, bitten, or subjected to various items being inserted into the body. Often victims suffer not only physical injury but psychological damage as well.

Serious sexual cases resulting in injury or death receive high investigative priority because most offenders will repeat their crimes until caught. An old police saying is, "Once a sex offender, always a sex offender."

Coprophilia: Sexual stimulation and gratification associated with defecation. Feces may be spread on body or at location.

Coprophagia: Sexual gratification from eating feces.

Exhibitionism: The exposure of sex organs to another for sexual stimulation or gratification.

Frotteur: A person who rubs, bumps, or presses against another in a crowd for sexual stimulation or gratification.

Kleptomania: One who is sexually stimulated or gratified by stealing. Items may be of little or no value.

Prostitution: Promiscuous sexual intercourse for money.

Pygmalionism: Sexual excitement associated with female statues, inflatable life-size dolls, and mannequins.

Voyeurism: Sexual excitement or gratification by watching others who are engaged in sexual activity or nude.

Zoophilia: Sexual excitement or gratification caused by stroking and fondling of animals. (Coined by Krafft-Ebing, the term does not refer to sexual intercourse with animals, which he called *zooerasty*.)

Threatening Sex

Anthropophgy: A form of cannibalism where the individual derives sexual pleasure from eating human flesh.

Castration: Removal of the testicles.

Incest: Sexual relations between family members.

Infanticide: Murder of an infant.

Infibulation: Piercing the body, especially sexual areas, or mutilating genitalia for sexual stimulation or gratification.

Lust murder: A brutal sexual murder where the body is usually mutilated; the breasts and genitalia may be removed.

Necrophilia: The desire to have sex with a corpse.

Pederasty: Insertion of the penis into the anus of a child for sexual gratification. (Commonly referred to as sodomy.)

Pedophilia: Sexually desiring a child or adolescent.

Piqurer: One who derives sexual stimulation or gratification from stabbing someone (usually a female in a crowd) with a sharp instrument.

Pyromania: The desire to set fires for sexual excitement or gratification.

Rape: Sexual intercourse forced on another person.

Sadism: Sexual excitement or gratification from inflicting physical or mental pain on another person.

A Superior Court judge charges a jury in deliberating on the facts of a rape case. Understanding the legal definition of what constitutes a rape is crucial to jurors in reaching a just verdict.

Rape

Rape involves forcing a sexual act against one's will. A variety of laws apply, depending on the state involved, type of sexual behavior, degree of force, age of the victim, presence of a weapon, and extent of injury.

At one time, all states used the limited common-law definition of rape. Some now use a criminal sexual conduct law that offers considerable flexibility in charging a suspect.

Under common law, **rape** is committed when a male engages in sexual intercourse with a female (1) by forcible compulsion, (2) who is incapable of consent by reason of being physically helpless or mentally incapacitated, or (3) who is less than 12 years old. In the latter case, the male must be at least 16, but different states may use different ages.

In common law, two basic elements are required to establish rape. First, the sexual intercourse must be without the female's consent. There is no valid consent if she acts under duress, force, or threat or if she is under age, mentally incapacitated, intoxicated, or unconscious. Consent is not valid if she was tricked into believing the male was her husband. Until recently, the law required reasonable resistance from the victim. It is now understood that resistance may place her in greater danger.

Second, there must be **carnal knowledge** of the female—that is, the penis penetrates the vagina. The penetration can be ever so slight and emission is not necessary.

States that have modernized their criminal codes use a criminal sexual conduct statute that covers both men and women and a wide range of sexual assault. Depending on the act and the degree of force, a suspect can be charged on up to four levels.

Rape is the only sex offense in the Uniform Crime Report (UCR) list of index crimes, which the FBI collects from local law enforcement agencies and publishes once a year. Unfortunately, the FBI still uses the common-law definition of rape. Data submitted to the UCR always appear under the most severe criminal charge, so if a victim is raped and murdered, the crime will appear only as a murder. Reporting is not mandatory, and a few agencies do not participate in the UCR. For local political reasons, some police agencies do not report honestly.

The largest problem may be that many victims do not report rape to the police. Date rape and rape of the elderly are seldom reported. When these are included, the actual number of rapes must be at least twice as high as the statistics indicate.

Rape Investigation

The investigation begins at the moment of awareness, when the call comes in. The important work performed by the police dispatcher is often overlooked. It is the dispatcher who elicits basic information on who, what, where, and when. Where is the victim? Is she injured? Is the assailant still there? Did he have a weapon, and if so, what? The victim should be told to stay on the line and informed that the police are on the way. The victim should be instructed to do nothing until the officers arrive. Most rape victims want to douche, take a bath, put on clean clothing, and pick up the mess, but that would destroy much evidence. Initial contact is critical.

Patrol officers are almost always the first to arrive at the scene. What happens within the first few minutes often determines the outcome of the case. Upon arrival, the officer should clearly announce that he or she is a police officer, since the victim may fear that the assailant has returned.

Saving a life and offering aid to the victim is always the highest priority. But while giving first aid, the officer can make plans for preserving evidence. If an ambulance is summoned and there is time, a path to and from the victim can reduce the amount of crime scene destruction.

Within minutes the patrol officer must determine what happened, what additional help is needed, and where the crime took place, then secure that area. If the victim can speak, the officer must try to determine how recently the attack occurred. Did the victim know the assailant? Try to obtain a description. Determine how he fled the scene and in which direction. This information must be dispatched as soon as possible if the assailant is to be apprehended.

The victim should be offered as much privacy as possible. If her clothing is torn away or missing, cover her with something. Keep onlookers and other police officers away from her, and talk to her in private.

At the same time, the patrol officer must determine the victim's mental condition and try not to add to her stress. A victim's fear may be reduced through a victim-oriented attitude of compassion and understanding. It is unprofessional to blame the victim or ask if she enjoyed the sex or had a climax. Questions such as these have no relationship to the crime investigation.

Rape is motivated not by sex but by hate, anger, and violence. Sex is used as a weapon to inflict humiliation, pain, or death. The hate and anger may be directed against women as a group or society in general. The victim is only a substitute target.

Rape is both an emotional and a physical assault, and greater harm may result from the emotional assault. Rape victims may show fear, anxiety, anger, and shock, both physically and verbally. They may laugh, cry, have fearful flashbacks, shake, or vomit while discussing the crime. They may be incoherent or may appear controlled and calm, masking their inner feelings. The officer should not interpret composure to mean that the assault did not occur.

While mental confusion, physical shock, exhaustion, or even self-discipline may cause the victim to be calm and composed, fear is always present. This fear may last for days, years, or a lifetime, depending on the trauma experienced. The victim may have been threatened or have come close to death. There is always the fear that the rapist knows her, knows where she works and lives, and will return to rape or otherwise harm her in the future. Such fear can suddenly reappear years later, especially when the victim learns that the rapist has been released from prison.

Some argue that it is better to have a female officer work with the victim of sexual assault, although the officers' gender is less important than their training and professional attitude. Many small police departments have no female officers. Some larger departments send a male/female team.

It is important to let the victim tell the story in her own words. She may have a total memory loss and be confused about the incident. Under extreme stress, the body has a tendency to shut out the trauma it is going through. This explains how a victim can be in direct contact with an assailant for some time yet be unable to describe anything about him, the scene, or what occurred. An inexperienced officer may confuse this condition with dishonesty. Hypnosis may be helpful in restoring blocked memory. The victim may not be able to make an identification because it was dark, the assailant was wearing a mask, he sprayed her with tear gas, or he blindfolded her.

It is important to comfort her, reassure her of her safety, let her know that you believe her, and offer support. She should be informed of everything that is happening and is going to happen. The victim has the right to determine her care and participation.

The initial interview should be brief. The victim's physical and emotional condition is always a consideration. The officer should establish rapport as soon as possible and reduce the victim's fear with calm reassurance. The officer's behavior during the initial contact sets the stage for the recovery of the victim and the success of the investigation. A victim treated in a callous, indifferent, disbelieving manner becomes a victim again, this time of the judicial system. Such treatment is unprofessional and may contribute to a difficult, lengthy recovery period.

The initial interview attempts to gather enough information to begin the investigation. The victim should be asked to describe exactly what happened. Does she know the offender, can she describe him, does she know where he can be located? Only one person should be present at the initial interview, and it should be conducted in a private location. The officer should convey tact, compassion, and patience, and should not appear embarrassed by the sexual nature of the interview.

The victim should be encouraged to seek medical treatment and undergo a thorough examination. She should be offered transportation to the hospital. The officer should advise her to take fresh clothing because her clothing will be needed for evidence if she chooses to prosecute.

Rape Crime Scene

Preliminary investigation procedures were described in Chapter 10. All standard requirements of crime scene preservation, search, fingerprints, measurements, photography, sketches, notes, reports, and collection and preservation of evidence apply to sexual cases. But some aspects of sexual evidence are noteworthy.

If the case is fresh, the victim is usually the best source of evidence. There may be semen on her body. Officers should be alert for used condoms, wipe rags, or deposits of semen on bedding or other locations. In rare cases, the assailant may have urinated or defecated on the victim or at the scene. If the victim bit or scratched the assailant, his blood, flesh, or hair may be found under her fingernails. Hair from the assailant may have transferred to her, especially in the pubic area. These sources of evidence take on special importance because a very small sample of flesh or body fluid is often sufficient for a DNA match, which will stand in court as positive identification.

The transfer of blood, hair, semen, urine, and feces is reciprocal. If caught reasonably soon, the assailant may have samples from the victim's body on himself. The assailant may have taken a souvenir from the rape scene, such as the victim's panties, bra, or a lock of hair. Like other sex offenders, rapists often maintain a collection to remind them of their conquests.

If the rape scene is indoors, the bathroom may be a major source of evidence. After the rape, the assailant may have cleaned himself up and, without thinking, deposited the cleanup materials in the wastebasket. Many times after a rape, the assailant is nervous and must urinate. Always check the toilet seat for fingerprints if the assailant used the bathroom.

If a sex crime occurs outdoors, special attention must be given to soil and vegetation tracing.

Sexual investigations can have multiple crime scenes. The victim may have been accosted at one location, transported to another, and raped there. There are cases where the victim was transported to several locations, raped in each, then driven back to the area where she was picked up. The vehicle in which she was transported is another scene that demands careful investigation.

If the attack was fatal and the body is still present at the crime scene, carefully document every aspect of the area. Pay special attention to damage on the body, recording bite marks, hickies, cuts, punctures, and blows to areas of sexual stimulation (the vagina, buttocks, breasts, neck, and face). The hands are also of special interest. Before moving the body, place each hand in a clean paper bag and bind the top of the bag at the wrists with rubber bands or string. In cases of violence, the hands reach out in defense—and often collect evidence. If the evidence should work loose while the body is in transit to the morgue, the material remains in the bag.

The crime scene must be investigated as soon as possible, with special attention given to unique elements of the offense such as a struggle or sexual activity. If the crime scene is outdoors, special attention must be given to tire and shoe impressions as well as soil and vegetation tracing. Weather can destroy such evidence very quickly.

Medical Examination

If a rape case goes to court, a medical examination of the victim is virtually mandatory. The victim has the right to refuse such an examination. She also has the right to be examined by her own physician. While the importance of the medical examination is explained to the victim, gentle persuasion by the officer, relatives, or friends may be necessary. The victim must understand that consent to a medical examination does not mean that she is compelled to testify in court.

The clothing worn by the victim during the attack will probably contain evidence. If the victim is physically capable of standing, place a large piece of clean paper on the floor and request that she stand on the paper when she undresses and allow her clothing to fall onto the paper. The paper may then be examined for evidence freed during the process of undressing. Each item of clothing will be individually prepared for transport to the crime laboratory.

Male police officers should not be present in the examination room during the medical procedure. Hospitals are equipped with rape kits that provide containers for those samples required. The physician will visually examine the victim's body, with special atten-

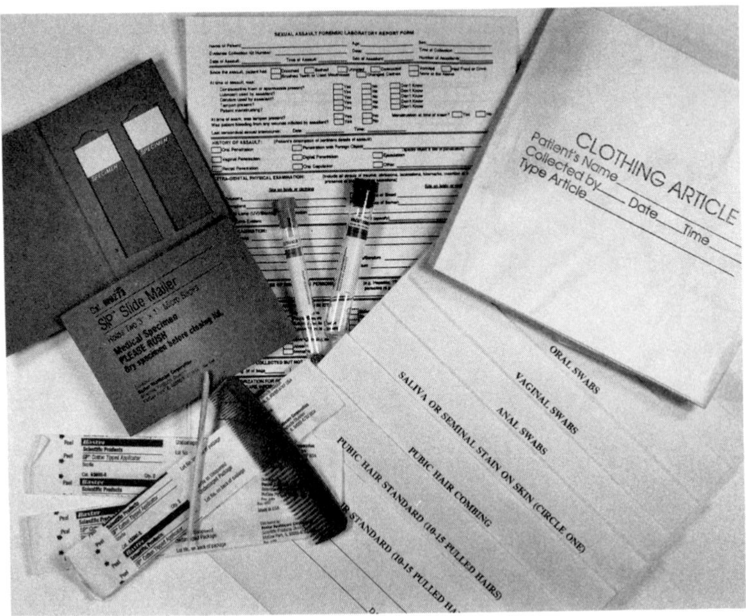

A rape evidence collection kit includes instructions and devices for collecting various samples of hairs, scrapings, and bodily fluids.

tion to sexual areas. Scrapings should be taken from beneath fingernails. Exterior trauma such as cuts, bruises, and bite marks will be photographed, as will the victim's overall appearance. The vagina, anus, mouth, and throat are examined and smears collected.

Rape is not a medical determination. The presence of semen and/or sperm in the vagina means only that the victim had sexual intercourse within the past 48 hours, not that she was raped. Similarly, the absence of semen and sperm does not mean rape did not occur. Some rapists use condoms. With the spread of AIDS and other sexually transmitted diseases, the use of condoms during rape may increase.

Medical evidence from the rape examination is submitted to the investigator, who transports it to the crime laboratory for examination. Many large cities have laboratories that conduct these tests. It is of paramount importance that chain of custody be documented at every step of the process.

Interview

The police are responsible for providing the court with a logical, accurate, and legally responsible case. There is nothing better than physical evidence, but most cases are resolved by testimony from the victim or witnesses. Interviewing techniques are discussed in Chapter 5, but sexual cases can be different.

Many police officers, victims, and witnesses are embarrassed to speak about sexual matters. An informal approach will help to put people at ease. Language will vary based on the person's age, education, and socioeconomic standing. The officer should not assume that the person being interviewed understands proper sexual terminology. If slang or colloquialisms are used that the officer does not understand, he or she may need to ask for clarification. If a small child says, "The man put his thing in my wee-wee," the interviewer should not convert it to read, "The male assailant penetrated my vagina with his penis." It would be difficult for a judge and jury to believe that a child used such formal language.

Topics associated with rape are personal and embarrassing for many people to talk about. The interviewer must know the terminology and not be bothered by it. If the victim or witnesses detect uneasiness in the officer, they will become uneasy, inhibited, and more restrained. On the other hand, the officer must be careful not to seem indifferent, detached, or calloused, for that will quickly alienate the victim.

Because the interview is sexual in nature, a witness should always be present, especially if the victim is a child. The officer's statements may be misunderstood or misinterpreted, especially by a victim who has recently undergone a traumatic sexual experience. A female witness usually makes the victim feel less nervous. Some officers like to employ a female nurse because of her education, experience, and position. The association with the medical profession adds credibility.

A careful interview is a major contribution to the relatively new tool of criminal investigation called the criminal personality profile.

Profiling the Rapist

Given enough information, it is possible to determine a great deal about an unknown assailant and put together a personality profile. The FBI's behavioral science unit started profiling criminals informally in 1972. By 1981 it had trained 55 special agents to profile in their respective geographic areas of the United States. Rape and lust murders lend themselves well to profiles.

In building a suspect's profile, it is equally important to know what the suspect said. Some rapists reveal considerable information about themselves through their speech. The three case studies in this chapter are from the author's files.

In profiling, information about the crime scene is important. The FBI's behavioral science unit requests a detailed map of the area, preferably a commercially produced map. The map should show the location of the crime scene from first contact to where the victim was left, as well as everything significant about the case. Information about the neighborhood is also helpful.

Failure to Report Rape

Every rape victim will decide whether to report the assault based on her individual feelings, needs, and desires, and how she interprets them. Victimization studies show that far more rapes occur than are reported, especially when date rape and rape of the elderly are included. The following list covers only some of the most common reasons for not reporting a rape. The sad fact is that many of these reasons are valid.

Case Study #1

A 22-year-old criminal justice major was studying alone in her apartment at about 9:30 p.m. The doors were locked. Because her radio was on, she did not hear a male slide a window open in another room. He grabbed her from behind and held a hand over her mouth, then tied a cloth over her eyes so she could not see. He told her he wanted to have sex with her and that if she did not scream and would do as he said, he would not hurt her. He told her that she was too pretty to hurt.

He sat on her chest and forced her to perform oral sex. She choked when he ejaculated, and he asked if she was all right. She assured him that she was and asked for a cigarette. He agreed and stated that he needed a rest before they had intercourse. As she smoked, he asked her if he was too heavy. He said he had been much heavier but had recently cut back to 200 pounds because his coach was after him to do so. She said that she was trying to lose a little weight and asked how he did it. He said that he worked out at the gym and cut back on his mother's food. As she smoked, he lectured her about how bad smoking was for her health. He mentioned that his father was a minister in the community and never allowed smoking at home.

After she finished her cigarette, he gently removed her jeans and panties, fondled her breasts and vagina, and assured her that he would not do it to her until she was ready. He asked her if she had VD. She said no. He said that he was going to use a condom anyway and that she would not want to become pregnant by him. He then proceeded to have sexual intercourse with her, being careful not to hurt her physically. He told her several times that she was much better than the other girls he had raped. He asked if he was good for her and said that he liked to do it with pretty girls. He then added that this was the only way he could get them into the mood.

When finished, he asked if she was OK

- The victim fears reprisal. She is often told by the offender not to report the crime and warned of dire consequences if she does.
- The victim feels she did something wrong or stupid that contributed to the crime. She will be embarrassed if her actions become known.
- She is embarrassed by the sexual activity that took place and does not want the information publicly known.
- She was doing something or was in a location she does not want her husband, boyfriend, parents, or others to know about.
- She is aware of how other victims have been treated by police, prosecutors, judges, husbands, boyfriends, and significant others. She knows that the victim is often made a victim repeatedly.
- The victim seriously questions the competency of the criminal justice system to arrest and prosecute the rapist.

---

and apologized for his behavior and the mess. She informed him that it was all right to leave it and she would clean it up. During the rape, she felt his shirt and pants and was sure he was wearing a sweatsuit. He placed his hand on her breast, kissed her, and told her to lie on the floor with the blindfold in place for five minutes. As he departed, he thanked her and told her that she was beautiful.

What the suspect said and did in this case helped bring the case to a close. Analyzing this information indicated to the investigator that the suspect, as he said, had raped before. He was careful not to let the victim see him. The suspect had tried to calm her fears, had not attempted to punish or degrade her, and was careful not to hurt her. His reference toward making it with pretty women, and his kissing and fondling her indicated that he was acting out a fantasy.

Rapists are often more aggressive, angry, and hostile. This suspect was polite, showed concern for his victim and her health, apologized, and thanked her. Several of his statements, for example, that this was the only way he could get pretty girls—indicate low self-esteem.

After arrest, it was determined that the suspect was 200 pounds but had been heavier at one time and that his father was a minister in that community. Smoking was not allowed in his home. He was a student and played basketball at a cross-town college. He had been in an accident that had left his face scarred. His self-esteem was low.

The victim deserves considerable credit because she did not panic, talked with the suspect, and remembered details of their conversation. She convinced him to leave the mess, which included the used condom with a complete sample of semen and pubic hair. (A positive DNA match was later made from the sample.) The victim called the police immediately, and the suspect was stopped just two blocks from her apartment. He was wearing a sweatsuit.

Case Study #2

A middle-aged, unmarried female who played the church organ gradually became very friendly with a deacon of the church who was married, had a family, and sang in the church choir. One night after choir practice, she invited him to her mobile home. They had drinks, went to bed, and enjoyed sex together. During intercourse, she heard a noise by the window. After the man had left, she began to wonder if someone had observed her in bed with this married man. The more she thought about the entire affair, the more concerned she became about her reputation.

The next morning she went to her minister and told him the entire story. He told her that she had been raped and insisted that she report the incident. They both came in to make the report. During her private interview, she quickly confirmed that the entire affair was consensual. She also reported that the deacon had recently voted to remove the minister due to his incompetence. The rape report was an attempt at reprisal by the minister.

- The victim knows the suspect and does not want him sent to prison. She may have had a long-standing relationship with him and/or desire a future relationship.
- She may not know that she has been raped. She may think that rough sex is the way it is supposed to be done or that men have a right to take what they want.
- She may be given bad advice by someone who does not have all the facts.

False Reporting

The Uniform Crime Report indicates about 15 percent of all reported rapes are unfounded. Law enforcement agencies must be very careful with rape cases until the merit of the charge is established. Their obligation to a man who is falsely accused is as strong as their obligation to a woman who is truly a victim of rape.

Prostitution

Sex in exchange for money is **prostitution**. Throughout history, societies have attempted to eradicate prostitution, but none has been successful. Prostitution is completely illegal in 48 states. It has been decriminalized in Alabama, although soliciting is still illegal and local communities may pass a city ordinance against prostitution. Nevada has legalized prostitution by county option.

In states where prostitution is illegal, the law is seldom enforced unless there are complaints or an election looms. Enforcement is usually directed toward streetwalkers, seldom toward the dating services that cater to clients in higher socioeconomic brackets.

Sex for hire takes many forms. It may be heterosexual or homosexual. It involves adults, teenagers, and children. It may be for sexual intercourse, masturbation, cunnilingus, fellatio, or other sex acts. The prostitute may walk the streets, work bars or truck stops, be a call girl, work in a brothel or for an escort service, be kept by a wealthy individual, be a political hooker, or work for a major corporation as a "public relations specialist" to please important customers who can grant huge government contracts. The prostitute may work full-time or part-time. He or she may be selective or indiscriminate. Some work independently and some with a pimp, while others are part of organized crime. Prostitutes have their own union. It is common for the police to have a working relationship with prostitutes, because they can be good sources of information about other crimes.

Persons against prostitution feel that it is wrong to sell sex and that sex outside of marriage is not blessed by the church. They point out that there is no love involved and that the act is nothing more than intervaginal masturbation. They feel that prostitution dehumanizes those individuals involved.

Those in favor of prostitution feel that eradication is impossible. As many as ten million acts of prostitution may take place each week in the United States, so there is an obvious need for the service. It is argued that we buy and sell every other kind of human service, why not sex? If the act is consensual, it is like any other business contract. Love has never been a requirement for sex; millions of married couples are not in love with each other but continue to have sex. And what is wrong with intervaginal masturbation?

The investigation of prostitution consumes considerable police time in some communities—time that many feel could be better spent on serious crimes.

Sexual Misadventure Deaths

In sexual misadventure, death may result from a number of variant sexual behaviors. Because of their infrequency, deliberate attempts to alter the death scene, the shock to relatives and acquaintances, and strong social taboos, the investigator is presented with challenges not encountered in other cases.

Many sexual misadventure cases have strong overtones of violence, even though criminal liability cannot be established. Any investigative error may have devastating ramifications because of insurance, as well as socioeconomic and religious considerations. Improper or careless investigation could lead to an erroneous conclusion of suicide or murder, which could result in needless and destructive prosecution.

Sexual asphyxia is an embellishment of masturbation. The origins of such behavior are unknown, but ancient historical evidence of it exists. "Of all the currently recognized forms of erotic risk-taking, none results in death more frequently than asphyxia." (Hazelwood, Dielz, and Burgess, 1983, p. 6)

Sexual gratification is achieved by masturbation while inducing oxygen starvation to the tissues of the body, especially the brain. This condition is known as hypoxia. The conscious state of hypoxia tends to produce a euphoric condition not unlike that of a mild alcoholic or drug intoxication. "A disruption of the arterial blood supply resulting in a diminished oxygenation of the brain . . . will heighten sensations through diminished ego controls that will be subjectively perceived as giddiness, light-headedness, and exhiliaration. This reinforces masturbatory sensations." (Resnick, 1972, p.10) A more common example of accidental hypoxia is found in private pilots who fly too high for too long without supplementary oxygen.

The most common method of self-induced asphyxiation is neck compression by hanging. Some people use chest compression, airway restraint, or breathing in a gas or chemical vapor. The first stage of hypoxia gives an extreme feeling of euphoria, the second stage is unconsciousness, and the third stage is death. The goal of the individual is to masturbate during the first stage. A fail-safe method of escape is required, in case the person goes too far and slips into the unconscious stage. When death takes place, it is usually because the escape failed to work. No one knows how many people practice autoerotic asphyxia, but Hazelwood, Dielz and Burgess have estimated that 500 to 1,000 deaths result each year. The overwhelming majority of victims are male.

Autoerotic asphyxia almost always takes place in an isolated location. Fantasies play an important role. The victim may be nude or partially nude, have fetish items or erotic literature present, record the scene on automatic camera or video recorder, be cross-dressed, show evidence of bondage, or use a variety of other paraphernalia. Documentation of one's own sexual exploits allows the victim to relive the event again and again.

In hanging, the most popular method, some kind of padding is often found under the neck restraint. Padding is intended to prevent visible damage to the neck that would be hard to explain to

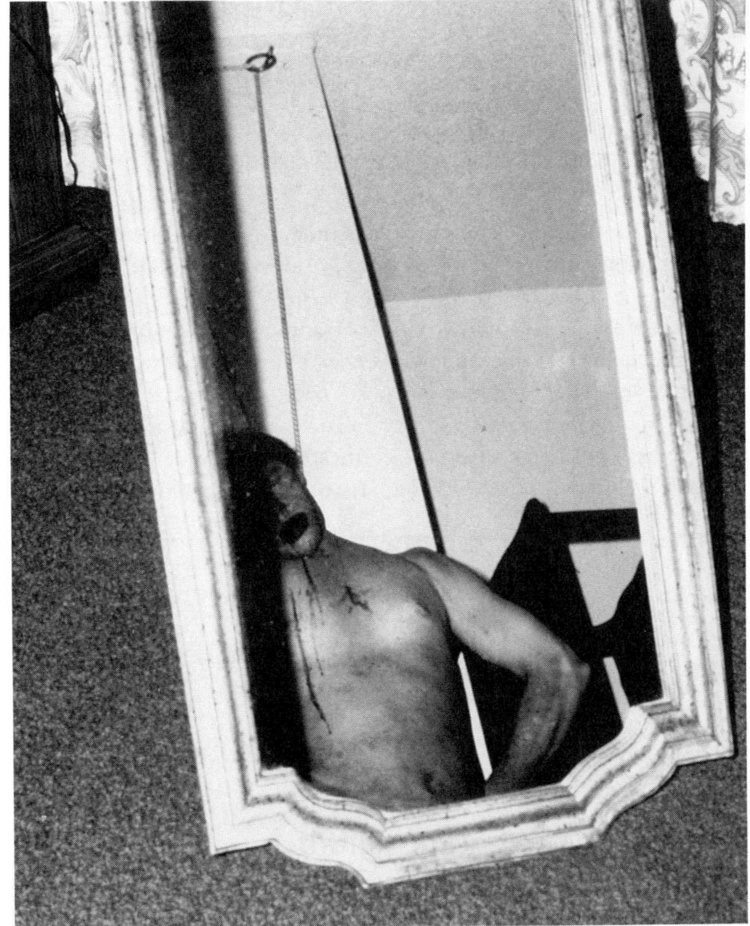

In this self-induced asphyxiation case, which ended in death, the victim set up a mirror to watch himself.

friends and family. The padding, along with much of the rest of the scene, is evidence that the individual intended to live. Such evidence indicates death by accident, not suicide or murder.

Autoerotic death can be difficult to investigate. Many friends or loved ones refuse to believe that such a death is sexual. In some cases, they rearrange the scene before calling the police.

"Death in these cases most often comes as a surprise to those who knew the victim because ordinarily there has been no evidence to establish history of related behavior, such as personality disorders." (Swanson, Chamelin, and Territo, 1988, p. 249) Significant others often are totally unaware of this aspect of the victim's life-style.

Autoerotic asphyxia can happen to very young victims. Children may be involved in sexual behavior long before adults suspect.

Case Study #3

A 52-year-old male was found in a small apartment. He was nude except for nylon stockings. His body lay on the bed with his head and upper torso extended beyond the edge. He had secured a dog chain near the ceiling, placed a dog collar around his neck, and attached the other end of the chain to the collar. His arms extended to the floor and he could control the pressure on his neck by raising or lowering his upper body. He padded his neck with a woman's nightgown.

He had attached a snap-type clothespin to each of his nipples. Attached to each clothespin were a pair of women's panties and an orange. These items were intended to cause pain, which was part of his scenario. He had several dog collars around his arms, each locked in place with a padlock. The locks, chain, and collars were part of his bondage fantasy. The victim had been finger-painting in feces on a TV tray nearby. During the autopsy, two oranges were found inside his rectum. Each was intact and measured approximately six centimeters in diameter. The man was a semiprofessional and was well respected in his community.

Female autoerotic deaths appear to be very rare. In 1975, special agent Frank Sass of the FBI, writing in the *Journal of Forensic Sciences*, reported what appears to have been the first documented case in the United States.

Case study #3 is but one example of the wide variety of sexual asphyxia deaths.

Sexual Exploitation of Children

"Throughout history, sexual exploitation and abuse of children has been a fact of life. Until recently, there were few arrests, prosecution was rare, and rehabilitation was all but nonexistent." (Shook, 1988, p.197) Child sexual abuse is sex between a child and an adult. Sexual exploitation of children is an all-inclusive term intended to cover many activities, such as child pornography and prostitution.

For most of American history, sex with children has been such a taboo subject that it was seldom discussed or prosecuted. All states have laws against having sex with a minor. A common violation is statutory rape, in which the victim is almost always female and the act is commonly consensual. Force is not involved. The only consideration is age of consent, which has been established by each stage legislature. Given existing age limits, statutory rape is a common crime in America. Considerable sex takes place before the law allows it.

Incest is a sexual relationship with a near relative. Some states include first and second cousins. Most incest that is reported is between a parent and child, although brother and sister incest is common. The prohibition covers stepchildren.

Pedophilia is the condition in which a child or adolescent is chosen as the preferred sexual object. The pedophile may be any adult—male or female, heterosexual, homosexual or bisexual, married or single. Reported cases usually involve young males, but the crime is so underreported that it is difficult to make judgments.

Some general characteristics of pedophiles can be determined from reported cases. First, they have multiple victims. Many count their victims by the hundreds and some have had sex with well over a thousand children. Second, they show excessive interest in children. Third, they tend to lock into an age range and gender. One who molests young boys may show no interest in girls. Some pedophiles are bisexual, but most prefer one sex. It was thought for a long time that girls were the most frequent victims, but recent research shows boys to be at equal or greater risk.

Fourth, the pedophile has access to children, especially within the preferred age range. Access is gained through marriage, employment, or religion. It is common to arrest a pedophile who is a teacher, coach, youth director at church, YMCA or Boy Scout leader, day-care worker, babysitter, child psychologist, child photographer, or in some other way in daily contact with children. Unsuspected access in a trusted position provides cover for the molester's sexual activity.

A fifth general characteristic of the pedophile is an active association with religion. Religious people tend to assume that because good people go to church, all people who go to church are good. The pedophile works to establish just such a trust level. Once he is established as Mr. Nice Guy, the door is open. Society thinks of the child molester as a dirty old man in a trenchcoat hanging around a schoolyard, but in reality most are professionals who are looked upon as community leaders and outstanding citizens.

Sixth, pedophiles are collectors. The collection is used to stimulate themselves and the child. It also helps to lower the child's inhibitions and shows that others have sex, especially children with adults. The collection often is a large assortment of things such as erotic literature and pictures, sexual aids, tape recordings, books on child psychology and human sexuality, diaries, lists of victims and their preference, photographic equipment and darkrooms, videotapes or music that kids in the desired age bracket like, letters from other pedophiles, and many other things of youthful interest.

The collection is very important and will be hidden in a place that allows the pedophile easy access when he needs it. Almost anything will be done to protect the collection. Destruction takes place only if the pedophile knows that he is about to be caught and there is no other alternative.

The best physical evidence in pedophile cases is usually the collection. When seeking a search warrant, the officer must list all those things that may be found. Many items, taken by themselves, would appear to have no bearing on the crime, but in total they show intent. Much evidence is overlooked because officers miss the connection between the materials and the pedophile's intent. Take, for example, detective magazines. Many people have a stack of detective magazines lying around the house. But every copy in the pedophile's collection may have a story about a child. Those articles may be marked in some special way.

Pedophile investigations often generate a surprising response. Victims do not want the offender to be prosecuted or punished. Victims, friends, and associates will testify that the offender is a nice person, a fine Christian gentleman, and a good friend. Victims see the investigator as a threat to their friend and often lie to protect him. They may try to hinder the investigation and even assist the offender in his defense. Some are too embarrassed to tell what happened. Few boys or men want to testify in open court that they had a same-sex experience with the pedophile, for fear they will be labeled homosexuals.

It is important to understand the the pedophile is often a master of the art of seduction. A strong offender/victim bond takes place. Many children are lonely. Not all kids are good-looking, intelligent, happy, healthy, or wealthy. Numerous children have low self-esteem and self-confidence. They do not find what they need at home, school, or church. The pedophile picks up on this and provides friendship, help, a pat on the back, and an ego boost. He offers what the child desperately needs in exchange for sex. The seduction bond between a pedophile and his victim may be as strong as the seduction bond between adults.

The pedophile knows how to listen to children and will take as much time as needed to seduce the child. It is the rare pedophile who falls back on threats or intimidation.

Seduction bonding that results in cooperative victims should not be misinterpreted as consent, complicity, or guilt. The investigator must be aware of what is happening and take the time to build a bond with the victim that will replace the pedophile's bond.

Prevention is the key to ending child sexual abuse. Children must learn that it is all right to talk about sex with their parents. They must understand the difference between acceptable and unacceptable touching. Parents must speak to a variety of safety concerns and be selective about babysitters. Through proper education, children can be taught to reduce their risk of molestation and reduce their danger if they find themselves in a bad situation. Criminal sexual behavior directed at children offers the police many opportunities for proactive prevention efforts.

Summary

Sex is a basic motivator in human behavior. There are many laws that attempt to control what people do sexually. Most of these laws are violated by large numbers of people, thus requiring selective intervention by the police. Many forms of behavior that do not appear to be sexual are in fact motivated by the sexual drive. Investigation and enforcement usually depend on complaints or political pressure.

Motive is important but often difficult for the investigator to understand. Some sex offenses are so bizarre that comprehension is all but impossible. It is important for the investigator and the public to be aware that behavior that is sexually criminal is addictive and does escalate. If the offender is not apprehended, the behavior will eventually degenerate. Sex crimes committed by a given offender will get worse. Impulse plays an important role for some sex offenders, and it may be irresistible. At such a moment, everyone is capable of doing something they may regret for the rest of their life.

Sexual behavior may be classified as consensual, annoyance, or threatening. Investigators get involved in all three categories because injury or death may result from almost any type of sex.

Rape, although severely underreported, is a common form of threatening sex. The investigator must be careful to reduce the victim's stress and not add to her trauma. The investigator needs to understand that rape is motivated by violence and anger, not by sex.

Rape investigation requires many special techniques not found in other crimes. The development of positive identification based on DNA has placed considerable importance on the collection of body fluids. The development of criminal profiling by the FBI is another major contribution to criminal investigation of rape and serial violence.

The failure of victims to report rape is a major problem. If the police are unaware of the crime, nothing can be done. The fact that some rapes are falsely reported places a burden on the investigator to avoid making an innocent man a second victim.

Prostitution is a crime in all states except Alabama, where it has been decriminalized, and Nevada, where it has been legalized by county option. Laws against prostitution are seldom effective and are enforced only on complaint or for political reasons.

Death by sexual misadventure can be one of the most challenging areas of criminal investigation. Death may result from any sexual behavior. Many autoerotic deaths look like murder or suicide but in fact are accidental.

The sexual exploitation of children is a major concern and is underreported. The investigation of pedophilia is especially challenging because the offender is often a trusted person in the community. The pedophile is a master at the art of seduction and it is difficult to find a witness who will testify against him.

Key Terms

annoyance sex
carnal knowledge
cohabit
impulse
pedophilia
progressive degeneracy
prostitution
rape
sexual asphyxia
threatening sex

Review Questions

1. A basic question in our society is government control of sexual behavior versus people's freedom to choose their actions. Why is this issue important to the investigator?
2. Explain the importance of motive in criminal sexual investigation and give examples of different motives.
3. What is escalation?
4. Why should the investigator be aware of impulse and how may it affect a case?
5. Why might the police become involved when consenting sex takes place without violation of the law?
6. What is annoyance sex, and why do the police get involved?
7. Give examples of threatening sex and explain why the police give such cases high priority.
8. Explain the necessary elements in a rape case and the limitations of the common law.
9. Why is rape investigation different from other investigations?
10. Describe a medical examination of a rape victim, explain the type of evidence that can be developed, and show its importance to the case.
11. What is a criminal sexual profile and what is it based on? Why is it important?
12. Discuss prostitution in America and give reasons why the police should or should not investigate such behavior.
13. What is a sexual misadventure death?
14. The pedophile is often a master of seduction. Explain the importance of this statement to investigators who work on child sexual exploitation cases.

References

Hazelwood RR, Dielz PE, Burgess AW: *Autoerotic Fatalities*. Lexington, MA: Lexington Books, 1983.

Hazelwood RR, Rassler RL, DePue RL, Douglas JE: "Criminal Personality Profiling: An Overview," In *Practical Aspects of Rape Investigation: A Multidisciplinary Approach*. New York, NY: Elsevier, 1987.

McKnight, JJ: "Sex Addicts Prone to Other Addictions." *The Montgomery Advertiser and Alabama Journal*. Montgomery,AL: April 22, 1989.

Reinhart, JM: *Sex Perversions and Sex Crimes*. Springfield, IL: Charles C. Thomas, 1957.

Resnick, HLP: "Eroticized Repetitive Hangings: A Form of Self-Destructive Behavior." *American Journal of Psychotherapy*, Jan. 1972.

Sass FA: "Sexual Asphyxia in the Female." *Journal of Forensic Sciences*, pp.181–185, 1:1975.

Shook LL: "The Investigation of Pedophilia." In *Critical Issues in Criminal Investigation*, Palmiotto MJ, Ed. Pilgrimage, Cincinnati, OH: Anderson Publishing Co., 1988.

Shook LL: "Sexual Glossary." In *Investigation of Variant Sex Styles*. Montgomery, AL: Auburn University of Montgomery, 1990.

Stone AR, DeLuca SM: *Investigating Crimes: An Introduction*. Boston, MA: Houghton Mifflin Co., 1980.

Swanson CR Jr., Chamelin NC, Territo L: *Criminal Investigation*, ed.4 New York, NY: Random House, 1988.

CHAPTER 13

Death Through Violence

Death can result from various reasons. It can be due to natural causes such as heart attacks, strokes, or old age. It can result from accidents such as drowning, falling, or accidentally overdosing on drugs. The final two causes of death are suicide and homicide.

The investigation of an unexpected death is normally a medical problem before it can become an investigation problem. The investigation is terminated if death was due to natural causes, accident, or suicide. There are three phases of an investigation. (Snyder, 1967, pp. 7–8)

First, why did the person die? This question is answered by the physician, the autopsy surgeon, and the medical laboratory. Was death caused by infection, poisoning, asphyxia, electricity, or any of a host of other conditions?

Second, by what means and in what manner did death take place? For example, if asphyxia was the cause of death, was it produced by choking, strangulation, drowning, or smothering? If the person died from an infection, was it caused by pneumonia, meningitis, a stab wound, or the bite of a rabid animal?

The answer to this problem may involve both medical examination and investigative efforts by the coroner and the police. If investigation indicates that death was a result of criminal or negligent conduct by another person, the final phase presents itself.

Third, who was responsible? This problem will be resolved almost entirely by the investigative acumen and zeal of the coroner and the police. However, it is important that a logical sequence be maintained and that investigative activities be kept in orderly progression.

An investigator must cover three areas adequately. First, before

It is imperative to take photographs of a dead body before it is moved.

a dead body is moved it is imperative that photographs be taken, measurements made, fingerprints searched for, and a variety of other tasks done. Once the body is removed, the death scene can never be replicated exactly.

Second, once a body is embalmed an important substance cannot be evaluated. Embalming involves removing the blood from the body and replacing it with a substance that supposedly produces a lifelike appearance. The blood is one of the most important substances for determining cause of death.

Third, when a body has been buried it is difficult and very expensive to disinter. Time increases the difficulty of a scientific examination and diminishes the chances of a successful conclusion as to the cause or instrument of death. Of course, cremation destroys any possibility of further scientific work on the body.

Suicide

A **suicide** is the act of intentionally killing oneself. This could be accomplished by drowning, hanging, taking drugs, or a number of other methods. An investigator needs to reconstruct the death to determine if it was a suicide. Could the person have killed himself or herself?

When reconstructing the death scene, the investigator places persons and articles in their exact positions at the time of death. "As a general rule, self-inflicted injuries occur in a predictable manner, and certain inferences can be drawn from the location of the injury and its physical features. Although the location and manner of inflicting the injury are not conclusive indicators, they do establish a degree of probability relating to the apparent suicide." (IACP, 1975, vol.2, pp. 15–16) The investigator should be aware of the following:

1. The location of the injury, the extent of the injury, and the direction from which it was delivered are revealing.
2. People who commit suicide usually select a method that is not thought to be painful.
3. Mentally ill persons may inflict extreme pain on themselves.
4. The person may push aside clothing to allow the death instrument to have direct contact with the body.
5. Before slashing his or her wrists, a person will normally roll up long sleeves.
6. In hanging, the rope is placed next to the skin.
7. Women committing suicide usually don't disfigure their faces.
8. The medical report and crime lab report should conclude that the death was a suicide.

A person may commit suicide for a variety of reasons, among them ill health, old age, marital problems, financial problems, an unhappy love affair, loss of a loved one, and revenge (often used by teenagers to get even with their parents or a sweetheart). Of course, some suicides appear to be completely senseless. The investigator attempts to gain factual information to explain the suicide. The investigator needs to search for diaries, notebooks, or any writings that may indicate that the dead person was contemplating suicide.

Family, friends, and acquaintances must be questioned to determine if the dead person made any statements or comments about the possibility of taking his or her own life. Many people who commit suicide give warning signs—for example, "I'm going to kill myself if I get fired." The investigator should verify all statements made by the deceased.

Suicide Notes

Some people leave suicide notes explaining why they killed themselves. The investigator must prove the wound was self-inflicted and determine the validity of the suicide note. The investigator must have various elements of the suicide note evaluated for consistency.

- *Writing instrument* (pen, pencil, typewriter). An effort should be made to locate the writing instrument used to produce the note.
- *Paper* (formal stationery, notepad, torn fragment). Attempt to locate a supply of the paper used for the note. For instance, an investigator of a suicide in which the note was written on yellow

A suicide note should be photographed, placed in a transparent envelope, and analyzed by a document examiner.

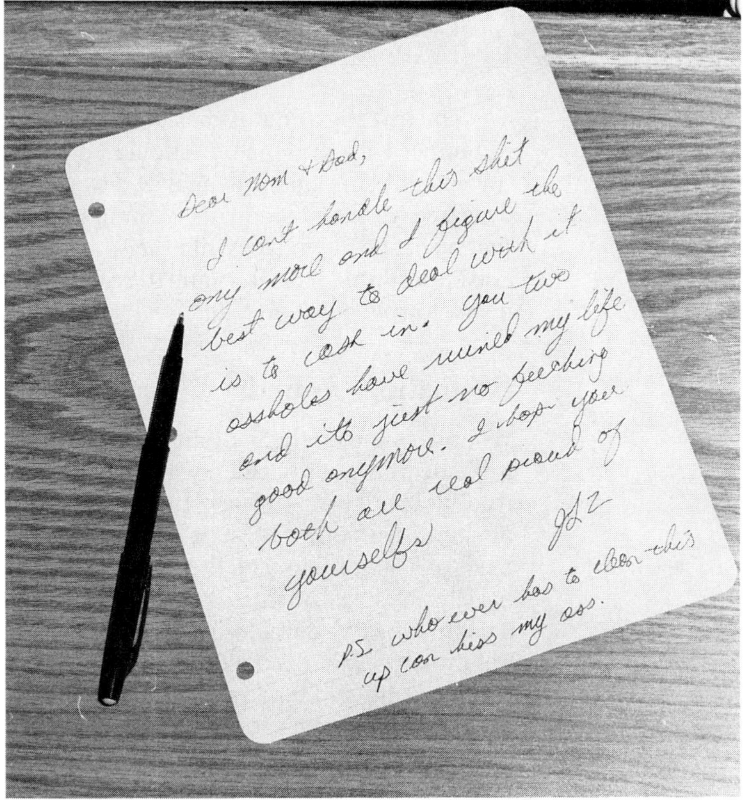

paper should search the individual's home or place of business to locate similar paper.

- *Place of composition.* If the officer can determine where the note was written, additional evidence may become available. For instance, when the paper was detached from a notepad or written on a soft desk blotter, impressions made by the writing may either support the authenticity of the note or raise questions about it.
- *Type of composition.* The suicide note may have been written weeks before the actual occurrence. When it is possible to determine the time of writing, the whereabouts of other individuals at that time should be verified.
- *Form of note.* Attention should be given to how the note is addressed, the type of signature (formal or informal), length of note, and legibility of writing.
- *Content of note.* The content usually indicates a motive for the act. The note may be a confession, a plea for understanding, or a means of punishing a survivor with a burden of guilt. The tone may range from anguish to serene resignation. All references to specific events or individuals should be checked. (IACP, 1975, vol.2, p. 17)

The investigator must be careful, when handling the note, not to tamper with evidence. It should be photographed, placed in a transparent envelope, and analyzed by a document examiner. The deceased person's handwriting should be evaluated to determine that he or she did in fact write the suicide note. An autopsy should also be performed to determine the cause of death. The investigator needs to rule out homicide.

Evaluating Wounds

Wounds found on the body are important elements in determining if the death was an accident, suicide, or homicide. Photographs of wounds should show clearly the location of the body, the location of the instrument that may have caused the death, and specific kinds of wounds found on the body. Wounds found on suicides may have been caused by shooting, hanging, automobile crashes, or cuts. The investigator should learn how the various types of wounds are self-inflicted. For example, a person committing suicide in a car may leave no skid marks when he hits a stone wall at 80 miles per hour. Or, how much force was used to inflict a stab wound? For instance, a stab wound combines a stabbing and cutting and the wound is usually larger than the width of the knife. A knife wound that has been forced through the skin parallel to the cleavage planes and then withdrawn will leave a wound that is closed, or nearly closed. If inserted across the cleavage planes, it will leave a skin wound that is gaping wide. (Snyder, 1967, p. 190)

Reporting Suicides

There is an inconsistency in the reporting of suicide in the United States. It may be reported as an accidental death in one locale and as a suicide in another. This makes it difficult to interpret the statistics pertaining to suicides. *Guide to the Investigation and Reporting of Drug Abuse Deaths* (Shneidman, 1977, pp. 52–53) poses a number of questions about the accuracy of suicide reporting.

1. What percentage of all deaths are autopsied?
2. Who, at present, are the certifying officials, officers, or agencies? Are these medical examiners, physicians in the community, sheriffs, coroners? How are they selected? How trained?
3. What are the present official criteria given to certifying officials in various jurisdictions to guide them in reporting a death as suicide?
4. What are the present actual practices of certifying officials in reporting suicidal deaths? To what extent are practices consistent with or different from the official criteria?
5. By what actual processes do the certifying officials arrive at the decision to list a death as suicide?
6. How are autopsies performed? Who determines when an autopsy is to be performed? Are the services of a toxicologist and a biochemist available?
7. What percentage of deaths are seen as equivocal or undetermined or as a combination of two or more modes (for example, accident-suicide, undetermined)?
8. What are the criteria for special procedures in an equivocal death?
9. How much of the total investigation of a death is dependent upon the police reports? What is the relationship of the coroner's investigation to the local police department's?
10. When, if ever, are behavioral or social scientists involved in the total investigatory procedure of a death?
11. What percentage of certifying officials in the United States are medically trained? Does medical training significantly influence the way in which deaths are reported?

Homicide

Homicide is the killing of one person by another. Homicide investigation is a specialized field that requires education, training, and practical experience. The success of a homicide investigation often depends on the initial activities of the first officer at the scene. The following data should be recorded.

- Date and exact time of receiving information.
- Method of transmission of the information.
- Name and other data identifying the person giving the information.
- Complete details of the information.

The homicide scene is the most important crime scene an investigator will analyze. Intelligent and careful examination allows for the collection of bits and pieces of evidence that may eventually lead to solving the crime. There are three basic principles involved in initiating an effective investigation. (Geberth, 1983, p. 2)

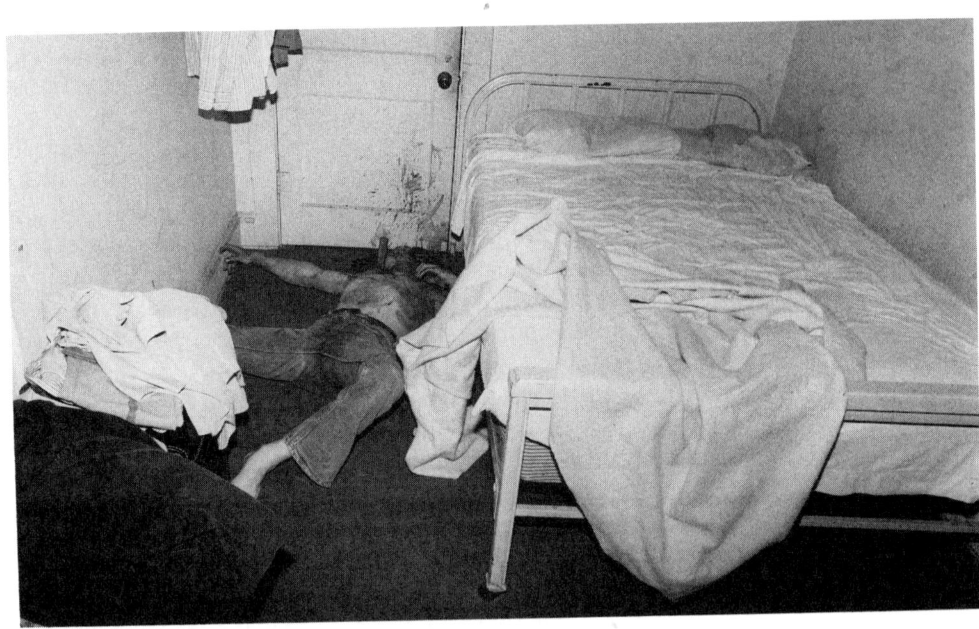

The success of a homicide investigation often depends on the initial activities at the scene. Various types of data need to be compiled including physical evidence and immediate eyewitness information.

1. Patrol officers must respond rapidly to the homicide crime scene in order to protect evidentiary materials before they are destroyed, altered, or lost.
2. Anything and everything should be considered evidence. Whether this evidence is physical or testimonial, it must be preserved, noted, and brought to the attention of the investigators. The only testimonial evidence collected at this point is eyewitness accounts or spontaneous statements of a suspect at the scene.
3. After the scene is secured, the homicide investigators must be notified immediately.

A homicide investigation begins with the crime scene because the police are usually called to the scene; they are usually the first to find the body and locate witnesses. The dead body and the surrounding area provide significant information, including perhaps the identity of the dead person, the approximate time of death, and clues to the circumstances of the death.

The homicide crime scene is initiated at the location where the body was found, the **primary crime scene**. Areas to be included in the primary crime scene include point of entry, escape route, and where the suspect lives. There may be **multiple crime scenes** when the body has been moved, at any location where physical or trace evidence has been discovered, or in a vehicle that may have been used to transport the body.

Responding officers and investigators must realize at all times that any object or item could be evidence. Nothing can be removed or even touched until the crime scene has been thoroughly searched. All items and objects need to remain in their original position in order to obtain an accurate account of the crime scene. Figure 13–1 is a checklist of information the officers should compile at the scene. The New York City Police Department recommends the following procedures for first officers arriving at crime scenes.

- Determine the entire area of the crime scene, including the paths of entry and exit and areas that may contain evidence.
- Isolate the area and seek assistance if necessary. Notify superiors, investigating officers, or specialized units.
- Refrain from entering the scene and disturbing, touching, or using any items found there. (Never use the crime scene itself as a command post or a telephone communications center.)
- Exclude all unauthorized persons from the crime scene until the forensic technicians arrive. An assigned detective or supe-

FIGURE 13-1: Death-Scene Checklist

(This form is to be used as a supplementary source sheet for readily available information and is not intended to replace conventional reports. Copies should be distributed to investigating officers and medical examiners.)

Name of Deceased:

First Middle Last

Address:

Age: **Race:** White Black Hispanic Asian American Indian Unknown

Sex: Male Female

Telephone number:

Marital status: S M W D Separated Unknown

Next-of-kin:

Name:

Address:

Telephone Number:

Police Notified by:

Date: Time:

Name:

Address:

Telephone number:

Relationship to deceased:

Deceased found:

Date: Time:

Address: (if different from above)

Location: Apartment House Townhouse Other (describe)

Entrance by: Key Cutting chain Forcing door Other (describe)

Type of lock on door:

Condition of other doors and windows: Open Closed Locked Unlocked

Body found:

Living Room Dining Room Bedroom Kitchen Attic Basement Other (describe)

Location in room:

Position of body: On back Face down Other:

Condition of body:

Fully clothed Partially clothed Unclothed

Preservation: Well preserved Decomposed

Estimated Rigor: Complete Head Arms Legs

Livor: Front Back Localized

Color:

FIGURE 13-1: *(Continued)*

Blood: Absent Present Location
Ligatures: Yes No

Apparent wounds: None Gunshot Stab Blunt force
Number:
Location: Head Neck Chest Abdomen Extremities
Hanging: Yes No Means:

Weapon(s) present: Gun (estimate caliber)
Type:
Knife:
Other (describe)

Condition of surroundings: Orderly Untidy Disarray
Odors: Decomposition Other

Evidence of last food preparation:
Where:
Type:

Dated material:
Mail:
Newspapers:
TV Guide:
Liquor Bottles:

Last contact with deceased:
Date:
Type of Contact:
Name of Contact:

Evidence of robbery: Yes No Not determined

Identification of deceased: Yes No
If yes, how accomplished:
If no, how is it to be accomplished:

Evidence of drug use: (prescription and nonprescription) Yes No
If drugs are present, collect them and send with body.

Evidence of drug paraphernalia: Yes No
Type:

Evidence of sexual deviate practices: Yes No
Type: (collect and send with body)
Name and phone number of investigating officer.

Source: *FBI Law Enforcement Bulletin,* August 1981.

rior may be allowed entry to the scene for evaluation purposes, when absolutely necessary. Other unavoidable exceptions include a doctor or medical examiner.
- Keep a chronological log containing the name, shield number, command, title, office, and address of each police officer, investigator, ambulance driver, medical examiner, and so forth entering the crime scene.

The first officer to arrive at the homicide crime scene may eventually be a key witness at a trial. To be an effective witness, the primary investigating officer must keep a record of pertinent facts, noting his or her time of arrival, witnesses present at the crime scene, what was observed upon arrival, and any evidence found at the scene. In the preliminary investigation, the first officer should:

- proceed to the scene promptly and safely,
- render assistance to the injured,
- effect the arrest of the criminal,
- locate and identify witnesses,
- interview,
- maintain the crime scene and protect evidence,
- interrogate the suspect,
- note conditions, events, and remarks,
- arrange for the collection of evidence (or collect it),
- report the incident fully and accurately, and
- yield responsibility to the follow-up investigator.

Investigating a homicide is an exacting task. A competent inquiry must take place for physical evidence to be uncovered. The investigation begins with an efficient search, with the investigator collecting and preserving evidence according to procedures established by laboratory personnel.

"Processing a scene refers to the methods used by investigators to recognize, identify, preserve, and collect, as far as possible, all facts and items of evidentiary value that may assist in reconstructing what actually happened." (Lipskin and Field, 1984, p. 8) The investigator must be able to recognize and collect pertinent facts and evidentiary items important to the successful completion of the homicide investigation. During this process the investigator needs to be thorough, painstaking, and systematic.

Many items require special handling and/or collection techniques—for example, gunshot residue, blood, and biological fluids. Investigators of death scenes should be familiar with collection methods required by crime labs and be properly equipped to collect and handle specimens.

In *Practical Homicide Investigation* (1983, pp. 7–8), Geberth writes "There is a principle in homicide investigation that refers to a theoretical exchange between two objects that have been in contact with one another." The theory of exchange (or transfer) is based on three facts: The perpetrator will take away traces of the victim and the scene; the victim will retain traces of the perpetrator and may leave traces on the perpetrator; and the perpetrator will leave behind traces at the scene.

Objects, body materials, and impressions may all constitute physical evidence when an investigator processes a death scene. *Objects* include, among other things, weapons, tools, firearms, displaced furniture, notes, letters, or papers, bullets, vehicles, and cigarette butts. *Body materials* include blood, semen, hair, tissue, spittle, urine, feces, and vomit. *Impressions* include fingerprints, tire tracks, footprints, palm prints, tool marks, bullet holes, newly damaged areas, and dents and breaks.

Recording the Homicide Scene

Detailed notes, sketches, and photographs must be developed during the course of the investigation. Once the crime scene has been protected and the basic inquiry completed, the homicide investigator begins to describe the crime scene. Comprehensive notes provide a repository for specific details and can supplement photos and sketches. The investigator's notes are documentary evidence. The courts also accept audiotapes and videotapes as documentation.

Note-taking begins with a description of the dead body and the surrounding area. The investigator does not move the body or touch anything at the scene. The description of the victim should include sex, age, appearance, body build, hair color, clothing and any sign of injury. When blood is visible, the notes should include where it was found and whether it was fresh or dried. The investigator needs to describe any tears in clothing, stab wounds, or gunshot wounds. The hands should be inspected for cuts, bruises, or torn fingernails, as well as for any signs of weapons. The notes should state whether there were any watches, rings, or jewelry on or near the deceased person.

The body must be described accurately in reference to all articles in the room, including furniture, doors, and windows. All weapons should be carefully described, including caliber and type, without being handled. When a weapon is found, walls, floors, ceilings, and furniture must be searched carefully for bullet holes or shells. There is no such thing as taking too many notes.

There are two reasons why descriptions of the dead body and the surroundings are important. First, officers are likely to see many things that otherwise would be overlooked. Writing it down while looking at it assures greater accuracy and makes the investigator's testimony more effective.

Second, at this stage of the investigation officers have no preconceived ideas who the murderer might be or how the crime was accomplished. If they wait until later to write up their notes, they may have a theory as to what happened and may overemphasize those observations that fit into their theory of the case while minimizing those that are incompatible. They may try to make the observation fit their theory rather than constructing a theory to conform with unbiased fact.

Sketching

Usually a death-scene sketch is done after the preliminary search of the scene and before removal of physical evidence. The exact location of all items should be recorded in the sketch. Lipskin and Field (1984, pp. 13–14) recommend the following techniques.

- Decide what key features are to be sketched.
- Indicate north on the sketch.
- Control all measurements by using measuring tape or a rule.
- Have another officer verify all measurements.
- Take two separate sets of measurements when noting the position of the body, one set from the head and another from the feet.
- Locate all objects accurately and identify them by numbers or letters. Draw stick figures to represent bodies.
- Include all essential items in the drawing.
- Make all sketch corrections at the death scene.
- Record date, time, sketcher, case number, and persons who assisted with measurements.
- Use a legend (drawing and charting symbols).
- Take indoor measurements from fixed objects (walls, room corners, door and window frames, or bathroom fixtures).
- Take outdoor measurements from corners of buildings (record address) and light poles (record pole number).

The finished drawing (formal drawing or plat) is usually prepared for the courtroom presentation and is based on the information recorded in the rough sketch. Unlike the rough sketch, it is drawn to scale and embodies all the fine points of accepted drafting techniques. The finished drawing can be as simple or complex as required. Items pertaining to the investigation may be added to the drawing by means of transparent plastic overlays.

Crime Scene Photos

Crime scene photographs are a permanent visual record, an attempt to recreate the homicide scene to provide details about specific aspects of the investigation. Photos must be complete and accurate and cover all aspects of the homicide scene before any items of evidence are disturbed or removed. Photos should be taken in sufficient numbers to show the overall death scene from various perspectives. Video recordings of the death scene should be taken whenever possible. Photos should be submitted in evidence with a vertical reference to the scene and a north-south orientation. All close-ups of the death scene must indicate direction. The New York City Police Department requires the following photos of a homicide scene.

- The front entrance of the building.
- The entrance to the apartment or room in which the deceased was discovered.
- Two full body views, one from each side. (If deceased has been removed, the original body location.)
- Two photos relating the body location to its general surroundings, from opposite and diagonal directions.

This slit screen provided the entrance to a homicide scene.

- Possible entrance and/or escape routes of the perpetrator(s).
- Area photo of evidence in situ and close-ups of specific evidence.
- Plastic bags or sheeting if they are the apparent cause of death.
- Identification photos of the deceased, which are normally taken at the morgue.

Identifying Bodies

Identification of dead persons is difficult because changes occur in the body due to **putrefaction**, or decomposition. The process begins with a green discoloration of the face and abdomen, while other parts of the body reveal a brownish discoloration. Usually the body becomes black a few days after death, and it becomes difficult to determine the victim's race.

Identifying bodies usually requires the expertise of medical examiners. Fingerprints are the best means of identification, followed by dental charts. Medical records of injuries or operations, as well as tattoos and scars, can be helpful.

Occasionally, identification must be based on portions of the body. The amount of accurate information that can be derived appears to be in proportion to the number of body parts that can be evaluated. When a skeleton is the only thing available for examination, an anthropologist has to be called in. Experts can determine the victim's gender and height from bones. Investigators should not attempt to make solo identifications without the medical examiner or expert in the specified field, but the following paragraphs provide some guidelines. (Snyder, 1967, pp. 69–72)

In general, male skeletons are larger and the surface of the bones rougher than those of females. On a complete skeleton, a trained person can determine sex accurately in practically all cases. Given the pelvis alone, accuracy is 95 percent; skull alone, 92 percent; both pelvis and skull, 98 percent; and the long bones alone, about 80 percent.

Perhaps the most common portion of a skeleton available for examination is the skull. Relatively speaking, male skulls are larger and the forehead tends to slope more. The bony ridges above the eyes are prominent, whereas in the female skull they are relatively small or absent entirely. The eye sockets tend to be square in the male skull and round in the female, and the male chin tends to be flat while the female chin is more pointed. In the male skull, the mastoid process is larger and all the points of attachment of the neck muscles are larger and rougher.

The pelvis reveals more accurate information about the sex of the individual than any other portion of the skeleton. It may be a reliable index of sex even in a prepubescent child.

The female pelvis is designed for child-bearing and in general its shape is broader and flatter than the male's. One of the most characteristic differences is in the angle made by the undersurface of the pubic bones, which join together at the front of the pelvis. In the male pelvis this angle is less than 70 degrees, while in the female it is greater than 70 degrees and often more than 90 degrees. The cavity of the pelvis is relatively narrow and deep in the male; in the female, it is wide and shallow. The socket joint in the male pelvis averages about 52 millimeters in diameter and faces directly sideways. In the female, the diameter averages about 46 millimeters and faces somewhat forward as well as outward. As with the skull, all places on the pelvis for muscle attachments are larger and more prominent in the male.

The long bones of the arms and legs offer less reliable information than the skull and pelvis. However, in general, a male's long bones are about 8 percent longer, heavier, and stronger than a female's. The joint surfaces tend to be larger, and various ridges and prominences for muscle attachments are rougher and more sharply defined.

Estimating the Time of Death

A body should not be removed from a homicide crime scene until it has been examined by a medical examiner or coroner, because once it has been moved it can never be placed in the exact same manner as it was found. Medical examiners often assist in reconstructing the homicide scene and determining what occurred before and during the homicide. Their inquiry is geared to determining the circumstances leading to the cause of death and verifying that the condition of the body is consistent with the cause of death. The homicide investigator and the medical examiner/coroner should function as a team and exchange information to conclude what actually occurred at the homicide scene.

In murder cases, time is an important factor. The murderer must be placed at the crime scene at the time of death. If the time of the murder cannot be estimated, it will be difficult to obtain a conviction.

It is difficult to estimate the time of death from the physical changes in the body. However, the following information can help the investigator make a closer approximation. (Lipskin and Field, 1984, p. 40)

- When was the individual last seen alive?
- What was the individual wearing at that time? Is it the same clothing he or she is wearing now?
- Is the clothing consistent with the activity of the individual? (Example: The person was found dead in a bank parking lot dressed in a red negligee.)
- When last seen, did the individual have any medical complaints?
- Indoors, were lights/TV/radio on? Was the furnace/air conditioner operating? What was the date of the most recent newspaper found inside? If mail was found in the mailbox, what was the date of the last postmark? Was the dwelling secure? Were there any signs of forced entry?
- Outdoors, determine the precipitation and temperatures (highs and lows) for period between the last time the subject was seen alive and the body's discovery. The local branch of the National Weather Service can provide monthly weather summary reports and the U.S. Coast Guard can give tide reports.

It is impossible to fix the exact time of death, but there are four ways a medical examiner/coroner determines the approximate time of death. (Geberth, 1979, pp. 28–29)

1. *Livor mortis* (lividity). The blood settles to the lowest point of the body due to gravity. Lividity begins about 30 minutes after death and takes 8 to 12 hours to "fix." The intensity of color (bright to dark red at completion) indicates the time factor. It also can reveal whether or not the body has been moved. This is the most reliable factor.
2. *Stomach contents.* The autopsy can identify and measure the contents of the stomach to determine when the person last ate. It takes two or three hours for digestion to occur.
3. *Body heat.* The human body gives off heat when it is the same temperature as the environment. This is affected by clothing, body build, age, and the surface on which the body lies. Placing one's hand on a protected portion of the body (usually under the arms) gives a rough determination of time. It is warm if the body has been dead only a few hours. If the area is cold and clammy, under ordinary conditions the victim has been dead 18 to 36 hours. The medical examiner usually uses a thermometer placed in the body.
4. *Rigor mortis.* The temporary rigidity of muscles after death, known as **rigor mortis**, is the poorest of the gauges because of the many variables involved: Obese people do not always

develop rigor, skinny people develop it fast, a fight or body shock usually accelerates it, heat speeds it up, and cold maintains it. Also, contrary to popular belief, rigor mortis starts at the same time throughout the entire body. It is present within 8 to 12 hours of death.

Evidence from Cause of Death

The cause of death often provides valuable evidence for solving a homicide and successfully prosecuting the offender. There are many causes of death, but this chapter will examine only the most common causes other than illness—firearms, asphyxiation, sharp instruments, blunt force, fire, and poisons.

Firearms

Accidental deaths, suicides, and homicides are often caused by a firearm, which usually leaves trace evidence on the body. This evidence helps prove what weapon caused the death. Residue from the firearm on the victim's hand should be collected whenever possible before the body is removed. The firearm wounds in a body can reveal the type of ammunition and the range, angle, and direction of fire.

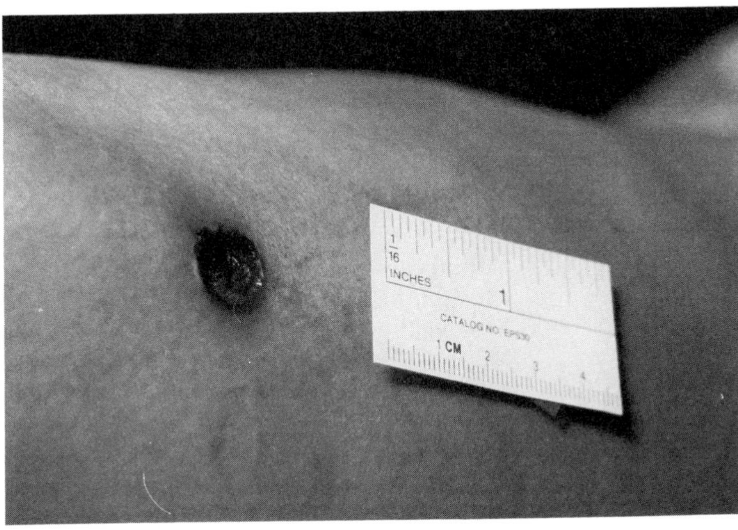

A bullet entrance wound

The entry and exit wound of a bullet can usually be identified. Ragged punctures and uneven surfaces are caused by ricocheting bullets with a tumbling action. Gashes that may look like knife wounds can be caused by bullets passing across a body. A high-speed bullet causes shock waves that destroy tissues in the body. Often, bone damage can indicate the bullet's path of travel. Round regular holes with minor bleeding indicate entrance wounds. There may be grayish soiling from carbon and oils on the bullet and a reddish-brown abrasion collar caused by the bullet's impact. Some entry wounds of small caliber are inconspicuous. They may be behind closed eyelids, under hair, in body openings, or under clothing.

Often exit wounds show more damage than entrance wounds. These wounds are rough and ragged in shape and larger than the bullet itself. Compressed tissues in front of the bullet burst when the bullet breaks through and exits the body. The bullet may be fragmented, deformed, or tumbled by its impact. Because of this, exit wounds may bleed more than entrance wounds, and pieces of internal tissue may protrude from the wound.

A contact wound has an abrasive collar, with its edges and the bullet track burned. Surrounding fabric that the bullet passes through is also burned. A sooty, grimy halo around the wound may be caused by the smoke and flame. When the muzzle of a firearm touches human skin, firing it causes the gases and the gun's residue to be blown into the bullet track within the body. A gun muzzle held 1 to 48 inches from a person leaves wounds that are round but whose edges show minor splitting. Muzzles over 48 inches away make rounder holes with circular abrasive collars. However, small-caliber contact wounds may look like long-range wounds.

Asphyxiation

Death involving asphyxiation may be caused by strangling, hanging, drowning, or electrical shock. When the body is deprived of oxygen, asphyxia occurs. Death by asphyxia is often due to accident or to natural causes. For example, food or bones can be trapped in the windpipe or throat. Chemicals causing asphyxia include carbon monoxide, carbon dioxide, ammonia, and chloroform. Suicides and homicides are seldom caused by asphyxia.

Asphyxiation by strangulation results from compression on the neck, usually by some instrument such as a rope or necktie. If strangulation was caused manually, it must be homicide, because human beings cannot strangle themselves with their own hands. (When the person loses consciousness, his or her hands relax and breathing resumes.) In manual strangulation, fingernail impressions are left on the victim and hemorrhaging occurs in the throat area.

Strangulation by hanging is asphyxiation by the use of a cord, rope, or some similar material that works against the weight of the body. Hanging is often suicidal and sometimes accidental. Except for lynchings, it is seldom homicidal.

Asphyxiation by drowning is caused by water or liquid being inhaled into the airways, blocking the passage of air to the lungs. When water is inhaled into the windpipe, it causes choking. The choking leads mucus membranes to form. Mixed with water, they agitate breathing, causing a sticky foam to fill the windpipe. Drowning occurs when the victim is submerged in water.

Electrical shock death by asphyxiation occurs when oxygen ceases, causing the heart and brain to stop. The effects of electrical shock depend on an individual's health, whether he or she is wet or dry, the amount of voltage received, the length of time in contact with the voltage, and aftereffects of the shock.

Often, electric shocks leave marks and grey or white puckered entrance and exit wounds on the body. Joule burns (severe burns from high voltage) are brown and reflect the shape of the item that caused the contact. Lightning deaths leave marks that look like ferns. High-voltage shocks often leave metal marks where the object melted into the person and may cause bone fractures. Electrical shock deaths are usually accidental.

Sharp Instruments

Deaths involving sharp-edged instruments include stabbings, cuttings, and choppings. The type of wound, along with the victim's personal history, can assist in determining whether the death was accidental, suicidal, or homicidal.

Stab wounds result from sharp, pointed objects like knives, scissors, ice picks, hat pins, stilettos, screwdrivers, and triangular files. The cut occurs when the weapon is pushed in and drawn out. The wound's shape depends on the direction from which the weapon penetrates, the shape of the weapon, and the movement of the weapon while in the wound. For example, if the weapon is slightly turned there will be a notch on one side of the wound. Accidental stab wounds are caused by falling through glass doors or on sharp pointed objects, but stab wounds that lead to death are usually homicidal.

A cut is caused when a sharp edge is pressed to and drawn over the surface of the body, leaving an incised wound. Razors and knives account for most incised wounds, which may cause infections and hemorrhages. The head, neck, and arms are the usual surfaces where cuts occur. When there are many cuts on the outer surface of the forearms and the palms they often indicate self-defense. Homicidal cuttings are brutal; they leave deep, clean cuts.

A chopping wound leaves a mangling, tearing cut and is usually made with a heavy object like a machete, hatchet, ax, or cleaver. Death may occur because of shock, hemorrhage, or serious damage to vital organs. Chop wounds are usually homicidal and are made on the organs or the arms, shoulders, neck, and head. There may be multiple injuries because the victim is attempting to defend him- or herself. Accidental chop wounds can occur from propeller blades of boats, fans, or planes, but there are few suicidal chop wounds.

Blunt Force

Deaths involving blunt force include beatings, explosions, falls, and crushings. Death could be caused by a fist, foot, or weapon. This type of force causes injuries to the skin and tissues—abrasions, bruises, and lacerations.

Abrasions are surface injuries to the exterior skin surface. Examples are bite and fingernail marks. Contusions or bruises happen when blood escapes within tissues from small ruptured blood vessels. The color is red-blue and the area may be swollen. The bruise size may reveal the extent of the physical violence causing it. Lacerations are caused by depressions to the skin that tear tissues. They may result from blows from sticks, hammers, or fists, from being hit by a car, or from falls.

A beating involves blunt force and leaves bruises on the body. Weapons leave an injury pattern that can help determine the type of weapon used. For example, if a person is kicked, a distinct impression is left on the clothes and body.

Normally, deaths from explosives are accidents during construction, a training exercise, or a military maneuver. Explosives are more often used to hide the cause of death than to kill. Generally, deaths by falls are accidental. The blood alcohol of the victim should be examined. A person may be crushed to death by a motor vehicle in a construction or industrial accident. This type of death may also occur in panic situations, such as rock concerts or fires in restaurants.

Fire

Deaths by fire are usually accidental. It can be difficult to establish the victim's identity and to connect the cause of the fire with the cause of death. If a fire appears intentional, an arson investigation should take place. At times a murderer sets a fire to conceal evidence of, say, shooting the victim. The investigation of a death by fire will depend on the pathologist's conclusion as to the cause of death. If the victim was alive at the time of burning, the autopsy will indicate carbon monoxide in the blood. Burned bodies can usually be autopsied and pathologists can identify wounds on burn victims.

Poisons

Deaths from toxic substances occur when substances intended for external use only are taken internally. This type of death may be accidental, suicidal, or homicidal. Industrial, home, or food poisoning often results in accidental death. Poisoning can occur from bad liquor. Homicide by poisoning is rare but should not be ruled out. Often murder by poison may be made to look like a suicide.

Due to America's drug problem, many people die from overdosing. The crime scene and victim's life-style may indicate death from an overdose of drugs. Usually in a suicide there are tablets or capsules near the body. Drug abusers have higher suicide rates than nonusers.

If death appears accidental, all evidence supporting the investigator's deduction should be recorded. All causes other than natural must be ruled out. The investigator should determine that no motive for murder exists and that there were no threats against the victim.

Collecting and Preserving Evidence

How evidence is collected and preserved often determines the outcome of scientific examination. When collecting evidence, investigators must make certain that each item is protected from destruction and contamination. There should be no doubt as to what the item is, where it was located in the death scene, and from whom it was collected. The homicide-scene investigator should develop an itemized list of all evidence collected at the scene and put the evidence in the homicide-scene sketch. (Lipskin and Field, 1984, pp.18–19)

The following guidelines describe how evidence should be collected and disposed of. (Geberth, 1979, p. 33)

- Each item should be described exactly and completely with the corresponding case numbers, date, and time affixed.

- Each item should be packaged in a separate, clean container of the proper size to prevent cross-contamination and damage.
- Each package should be sealed to retain evidence and prevent unauthorized handling.
- Each piece should be marked to show its original location and position, and this information should appear in the investigator's notebook.
- Each piece should be marked distinctly by the searching officer to show identification.
- Each piece of evidence should be properly disposed of to the laboratory, property clerk, or FBI lab.
- Proper records should be kept regarding the evidence for proper presentation in court.

Medicolegal Investigation

"The ultimate purpose for a medicolegal investigation of death is to arrive as close as possible to a determination of the complete circumstances surrounding a death and the true manner and direct cause of death." (Lipskin and Field, 1984, p. 93) A medicolegal investigation emphasizes identifying the victim by photographs, fingerprints, dental and medical reports, and relatives or friends. The medicolegal investigation reviews toxicologic and autopsy tests to determine the cause and manner of death.

An **autopsy**, or postmortem examination, is usually performed by a forensic pathologist. Pathologists are trained to examine abnormal changes in the body functions or tissues that may be caused by poisons or diseases. They possess the skills to determine how, when, and where the victim died.

Sudden, unexpected, or unattended deaths are of special interest. National, state, and regional crime labs have available toxicology, pathology, and serology experts who can provide consultation. State laws and regional customs usually influence the procedures for performing an autopsy. For example, the state of New York requires an autopsy for all accidental deaths. Autopsy procedures should be complete and systematic. The order of examining a dead body is as follows: externals, head and brain, incision of body, thorax, abdomen, pelvis, extremities, and various internal regions. (McClay, 1979, p. 22)

The microscopic examination of various parts of the body supplements visual examinations. All examinations of dead bodies must follow guidelines established by state laws where the autopsy is being performed.

Medical Examiner as Expert Witness

The medical examiner who will testify in the case should know the legal problems that may arise and be prepared to assist the prosecutor or defendant on an equal basis. Certain mechanical steps may assist the medical examiner to become a better expert witness. (Gottschalk et al., 1984, p. 72).

- Arrange the case file in logical groupings so that data may be reviewed quickly.
- Bring together the other witnesses from the same medical examiner's office, toxicologists, and investigators, and decide who should interpret what evidence. Otherwise, there may be confusion over records. Worse, a physician's opinion may be misconstrued as that of a chemist or vice versa. Make sure all participants are fully apprised of the issues and can review pertinent scientific data and similar local experience.
- At pretrial depositions where the advocates may desire copies of the entire file, arrange for the court reporter to make the copies and return the original to the medical examiner. Large firms of attorneys have been known to lose subpoenaed records, but court reporters are rarely lax in this regard.
- Bring appropriate true copies of work records and photos to court along with the file, to be introduced in lieu of the originals. (Otherwise, the medical examiner may never see the original again.)

The Psychological Autopsy

The **psychological autopsy** focuses on the psychological aspects of death and deals with procedures to clarify the nature of death. Its main function is to accurately determine whether the death was natural, accidental, suicide, or homicide.

The psychological autopsy attempts to recreate the decedent's intentions by interviewing individuals who knew the decedent's behavior, actions, and character well enough to provide accurate information. Rapport must be established with the respondent and questions should be detailed.

All details of the interviewing procedures are reviewed with the medical examiner or coroner. Psychological data should be included in the medical examiner's or coroner's report. Behavioral scientists have skills that should be used like those of chemists or physical scientists. Behavioral scientists may also advise the homicide investigator on clues that can be used to assess the suspect's intent.

The psychological autopsy may have therapeutic value to survivors. Therapeutic work with the survivors/victims is called **postvention**. The interviewer should be aware of the emotional difficulties of bereaved persons and be concerned for their mental health. (Gottschalk et al., 1984)

The following categories are often included in psychological autopsies. (Shneidman, 1969).

- Information identifying the victim (name, age, address, marital status, religious practices, occupation, and other details).
- Details of the death (including the cause or method and other pertinent details).
- A brief outline of the victim's history (siblings, marriage, illnesses, medical treatment, psychotherapy, suicide attempts).
- Death history of the victim's family (suicides, cancer, other fatal illnesses, ages at death, and other details).
- The personality and life-style of the victim.
- The victim's typical patterns of reaction to stress, emotional upsets, and periods of disequilibrium.
- Any recent (from last few days to past year) upsets, pressures, tensions, or anticipations of trouble.
- The role of alcohol or drugs in the victim's overall life-style and death.
- Nature of the victim's interpersonal relationships (including those with physicians).
- Fantasies, dreams, thoughts, premonitions, or fears of the victim relating to death or accident.
- Changes in the victim before death (of habits, hobbies, eating, sexual patterns, and other life routines).
- Information relating to the "life side" of the victim (upswings, successes, plans).
- Assessment of the victim's intention.
- Rating of lethality.
- Reaction of informants to the victim's death.
- Comments, special features, etc.

Helping the Survivors

Father Kenneth Czaillinger of Cincinnati, Ohio, recommends forming support groups for parents who have lost children through death. His suggestions can help victim advocates assist homicide survivors in understanding some of their reactions to their tragedy.

1. Generally it takes 18 to 24 months just to stabilize after the death of a family member. It can take much longer when the death was a violent one. Recognize the length of the mourning process and don't have unrealistic expectations of yourself.
2. Your worst times usually are not at the moment a tragic event takes place. Then you're in a state of shock or numbness. Often, you slide into the pits four to seven months after the event. Strangely, when you're tempted to despair may be the time most people expect you to be over your loss.
3. When people ask you how you're doing, don't always say "fine." Let them know how terrible you feel.
4. Talking with a true friend or with others who've been there and survived can be helpful. Those who've been there speak your language. Only they can really say, "I know; I understand." You are not alone.
5. Often, depression is a cover for anger because what you're going through seems so unfair and unjust. Find appropriate ways to release your bottled-up anger.
6. Take time to lament, to experience being a victim. It may be necessary to spend some time feeling sorry for yourself. "Pity parties" can be therapeutic.
7. It's all right to cry, to question, to be weak. Don't let people put you on a pedestal and tell you what an inspiration you are because of your strength and your ability to cope so well. If they only knew!
8. Remember, you may be a rookie at the experience you're going through. This is probably the first violent death you've coped with. You're new at this, and you don't know what to do or how to act. You need help.
9. Reach out and and try to help others in some small ways. This little step forward may help prevent you from dwelling on yourself.
10. Many times of crisis can ultimately become times of opportunity. Mysteriously, your faith in yourself, in others, and in God can be deepened through crisis. Seek out people who can serve as symbols of hope to you.

Infanticide

Deaths of infants are usually the result of asphyxia, which can be due to accidental or natural causes. If a death occurs from strangulation or through a violent act, **infanticide** may have taken place.

When investigating an infant's death, the key questions are: Could the baby have lived with proper care? Was the baby breathing after birth? Medical records must be checked if a baby dies from injuries to determine if the child received treatment. What was the mother's mental condition after the baby was born? Was she depressed? What is the father's mental condition? Neighbors and friends can provide information about the parents' temperaments.

Battered Children

Often battering parents were abused as children. They use the techniques of child-rearing they learned from their parents. In the **battered child syndrome**, children are abused during emotional outbursts when parents feel frustrated. Many times parents feel guilty, after injuring their children.

Battered children often receive injuries of the head and stomach, which may be internal and show no outward signs. Children may be dropped to the floor, or held by their ankles and swung against a wall, or beaten repeatedly on the head. These actions may cause hemorrhaging under the skull.

An investigator must carefully examine the child's body, especially the parts normally covered by clothing, like the insides of the thighs and the armpits. The feet should be checked for burns. The general cleanliness and the nutritional state of the child should be observed. Most children have scars from falls, but excessive scars are suspicious.

Mass Murder

Killing four or more people in a single incident within a short span of time is **mass murder**. An example is the McDonald's massacre on July 18, 1984, in San Ysidro, California. A deranged security worker shot and killed 20 people. "Victims of a murder spree typically are selected by chance; they tend to come into contact with their killer purely by accident and their death may come solely as a result of the killer's reaction or mood state at the moment." (Holmes and De Burger, 1988, p. 18).

Serial Murder

The definition of **serial murder** is killing several victims at intervals ranging from two days to several months or several years. Exam-

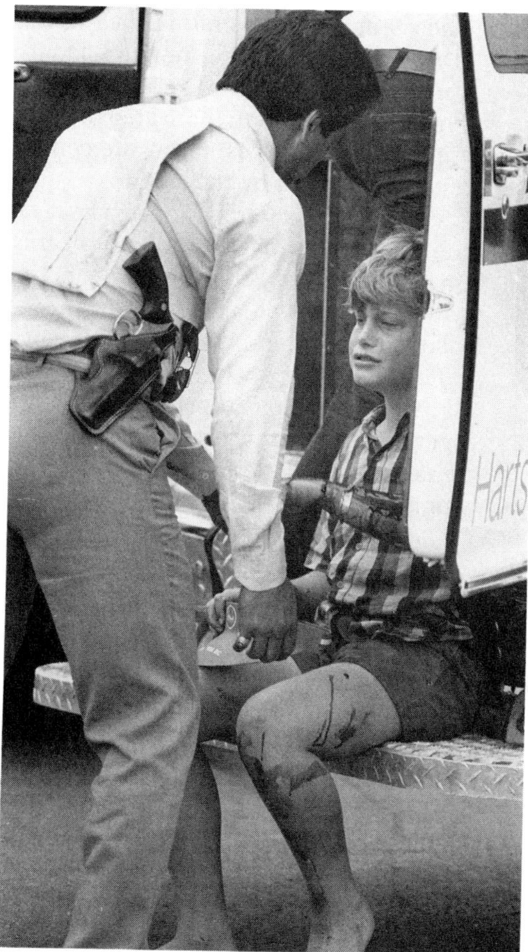

A young boy wounded in the 1984 McDonald's massacre tells his story to police as he receives aid.

ples of serial murders are the Hillside Strangler case in California, the homicides committed by Ted Bundy as he traveled throughout the United States, and the killings and dismemberment of young males by Jeffrey Dahmer in Milwaukee. In *Serial Murder* (1988, pp. 18–19), Holmes and De Burger outline elements of this type of homicide.

- The central element is repetitive homicide. The serial murderer kills again and again and will continue to kill if not prevented. The time span may involve many months or years.
- With rare exceptions, serial murders are one-on-one.

- The victim and perpetrator usually are strangers or know each other only slightly. Serial murder seldom occurs among strongly affiliated persons.
- The serial murderer is motivated to kill for killing's sake. These are not crimes of passion in the conventional sense, nor are they precipitated by the victim.
- Clear-cut motives are lacking in many serial murders due to the frequent stranger-perpetrator of this crime. But there are *intrinsic* motive systems, typically nonrational, that originate within the individual. They govern and structure the serial killer's homicidal behavior. These motive systems ordinarily reflect neither passion nor personal gain. A killer such as "Pittsburgh Phil" Strauss (hit man for Murder, Inc.), who operated from an *extrinsic* source of action, is not labeled a serial murderer, despite his attributed record of nearly 100 homicides.

This billboard was displayed in Leeds in Yorkshire, England, to ask for public assistance in the apprehension of the Yorkshire Ripper. The billboard includes a sample of the man's handwriting and a telephone number to call to hear his voice.

FIGURE 13–2: Basic Elements in Victim Profiling

Physical Traits	Marital Aspects	Personal Life-Style
Age	Martial status	Alcohol and drug use
Sex	Marital adjustment	Daily activities
Race	Children	Recent changes?
Height/weight	Marital reputation	Sports interests
Dress at time	Past divorce?	Hobbies
Hair color	Friends and enemies	Demeanor
Occupation	**Education**	**Personal Demographics**
Present position	Number of years	Residence
Past positions	Schools attended	Past residences
Special training	Intelligence	Neighborhood complexity
Medical History	**Psychosexual History**	**Court History**
Physical	Personal fears	Arrest record
Mental history	Sex history	Past court record
Dental records	Personality history	Pending cases

Psychological profiling assists the homicide investigator in locating serial murderers. Profiling takes theories from the fields of psychology, sociology, psychiatry, and criminology. Profiles are useful in solving at least seven types of crime (Geberth, 1981, pp. 46–49): sadistic torture in sexual assaults, evisceration, postmortem slashing and cutting, motiveless fire-setting, lust and mutilation murders, ritualistic crimes, and rape.

The profile analyzes behavioral patterns and personality characteristics of the criminal. The goal of profiling is to develop categories that can be applied toward solving a specific crime. "First of all, the profiler must examine and analyze all pertinent reports. Second, by studying these reports and formulating appropriate motives for such behavior, the profiler offers the police a 'reasonable guess.' And third, the profiler must be prepared to assist the law enforcement professional." (Holmes and De Burger, 1988, p. 84)

A number of items need to be reviewed for an accurate profile. They include crime scene information, neighborhood composition, the victim's last activities, the medical autopsy, the crime investigation, and a profile of the victim. From police information, the profiler can develop a psychological profile that will provide valuable information and investigative direction. Profiling may include such information as sibling position, religious preference, and sexual orientation. The purpose of the profile is to narrow the field, not to name a specific individual. The basic elements of offender profiling are as follows. (Holmes and De Burger, 1988, p. 93)

- offender's age group,
- race,
- employment history,
- arrest record,
- likelihood of striking again,
- sex,
- marital status,
- type of employment,
- sexual history, and
- interrogation strategy.

A profile of the victim can also be developed. Information on victimology has been growing. People who behave in specific ways appear more likely to become victims. Some people are very vulnerable, while others are not. The profiler has to determine if there are any characteristics that all the victims have in common. This information is forwarded to the investigator to assist in solving the case. Figure 13–2 shows the basic elements of victim profiling.

Lust Murder

Although uncommon, lust murders are among the most heinous crimes committed. The lust murder is sexually motivated and involves torture, violent sexual trauma, mutilation, or dismemberment. There are basically two kinds of men who commit lust murder. Both are asocial, but the police distinguish between the organized and the disorganized asocial personalities.

The organized asocial murderer is completely indifferent to society's welfare and projects a self-centered, irresponsible behavior. Generally, he dislikes people but displays an amiable facade in order to manipulate them for his personal use. He is also cunning and methodical and fully aware that his behavior is criminal. He searches out the victim, who usually lives a distance away from the crime scene.

The disorganized asocial murder is a loner who lacks interpersonal communication skills. This individual commits the lust mur-

FIGURE 13–3: Profiles of Organized and Disorganized Murderers

Organized	Disorganized
Average to above-average intelligence	Below-average intelligence
Socially competent	Socially inadequate
Skilled work preferred	Unskilled work
Sexually competent	Sexually incompetent
High birth-order status	Low birth-order status
Father's work stable	Father's work unstable
Inconsistent childhood discipline	Harsh discipline as child
Controlled mood during crime	Anxious mood during crime
Use of alcohol with crime	Minimal use of alcohol
Precipitating situational stress	Minimal situational stress
Living with partner	Living alone
Mobility, with car in good condition	Lives/works near crime scene
Follows crime in news media	Minimal interest in news media
May change jobs or leave town	Significant behavior change (drug/ alcohol abuse, religiosity, etc.)

Source: *FBI Law Enforcement Bulletin,* August 1985.

der near his place of employment or residence. (Hazelwood and Douglas, 1980, p. 19) Figure 13–3 shows other profile differences between organized and disorganized murderers.

The crime scenes of organized and disorganized lust murderers are different in four areas: the murderer's action during the offense, victim characteristics, use of vehicles in the crime, and types of evidence left at the scene. (Reesler and Burgess, 1985, p. 19).

The disorganized crime scene indicates that the criminal did not have a plan of action but acted on the spur of the moment. The offender may select a victim randomly and normally tries to catch the person off guard. He overpowers his victim and kills suddenly. He may use excessive force to dehumanize the victim. Sexual acts or mutilations, if any, are usually performed after the death. Urine, feces, and semen may be found on the victim. The face, genitals, and breasts may be mutilated or there may be disembowelment or amputation. The disorganized lust murderer may even keep the corpse.

The organized lust murder often selects a stranger who may be a victim of opportunity, selected because of location. He may select his victim based on age, appearance, occupation, life-style, or hairstyle. The organized murderer is personable and can talk to strangers without attracting suspicion. The offender wants to control his victim, and rape as well as murder could be part of his plan. Restraints such as belts, rope, chains, handcuffs, and blindfolds may

FIGURE 13-4: Crime Scene Differences Between Organized and Disorganized Murderers

Organized	Disorganized
Planned offense	Spontaneous offense
Victim a targeted stranger	Victim/location known
Personalizes victim	Depersonalizes victim
Controlled conversation	Minimal conversation
Crime scene reflects overall control	Crime scene random and sloppy
Demands submissive victim	Sudden violence to victim
Restraints used	Minimal use of restraints
Aggressive acts prior to death	Sexual acts after death
Body hidden	Body left in view
Weapon/evidence absent	Evidence/weapon often present
Transports victim or body	Leaves body at death scene

Source: *FBI Law Enforcement Bulletin,* August 1985.

be used. The victim is murdered in a slow, deliberate manner. The organized offender has obsessive and compulsive traits that the crime scene may reveal. (Reesler and Burgess, 1985, pp. 20–24) Figure 13–4 shows the crime scene differences between organized and disorganized murderers.

Family Homicide

Next to the highway, the home is the primary place of slaughter in America. Killings of and by children and spouses are receiving the attention of law enforcement personnel and behavioral scientists. Domestic violence is a serious problem, and it can lead to a homicide in the family. Seventeen family and situational factors are associated with cases of family homicide. (Hagman et al., 1987, pp. 22–24)

1. Objective evidence that the family member who committed the homicides, and who subsequently committed or attempted to commit suicide, was using an identified drug at the time of the incident.
2. Clear evidence that, at the time of the homicide, the perpetrator was under the influence of a significant amount of alcohol.
3. Objective evidence—from the police record, court records, the family, or neighbors—that the perpetrator had committed acts of violence against one or more members of the family who were eventually victimized.
4. Any evidence that the perpetrator was previously confronted

by officers of the law regarding family conflict, whether an arrest was made or not.

5. Objective evidence that the perpetrator had illegally used either prescription or illicit drugs in the past.
6. Objective evidence that the perpetrator had received diagnosis of or treatment for a mental disorder in the past.
7. Objective evidence that the perpetrator had been an abused child.
8. Objective evidence that the perpetrator belonged to a social or cultural group where he or she would be required to save face or maintain "honor" in any kind of degrading family situation. This could include being "faced down" by a mate or having a mate demonstrate infidelity in some manner.
9. Well-known suicidal threats made by the perpetrator within six months of the homicide.
10. Any message, tape, note, or other communication indicating that the perpetrator intended to destroy himself or others.
11. Clear evidence given by agency records, neighbors, or family members that the perpetrator had recently suffered significant periods of depression.
12. Evidence from objective sources (neighbors, agencies, or rela-

Virginia police investigate a shoot-out between a husband and wife that left them both dead and two officers wounded. The wife died in the street; the husband died from shots exchanged with the officers who arrived in response to calls by neighbors.

tives) that the perpetrator had suffered a recently failed love relationship, usually involving another family member.
13. Evidence that the perpetrator had recently separated from or been rejected by the family unit. This rejection could be physical or social.
14. Evidence that the perpetrator had made threats of vengeance against family members, usually in relation to the failed love relationship.
15. Objective evidence of any sort that the victims of the family homicide were using drugs or alcohol at the time of the event.
16. Any objective evidence that the victims in some way instigated, baited, or encouraged the perpetrator toward violence.
17. Objective indications that the neighborhood where the family homicide occurred had a higher-than-average incidence of violent behavior.

Family violence is a serious social and police problem in American society. Approximately 13 percent of murders are family-related, so investigators need to be familiar with the investigative techniques for this type of homicide.

Summary

Death can result from many things, including such accidents as drowning, falling, or accidentally overdosing on drugs. An unexpected death normally requires medical investigation to determine whether it was due to natural causes, accident, suicide, or homicide.

Suicide is the act of intentionally killing oneself. The investigator has to determine whether the dead person could have killed him- or herself. A person may commit suicide for a variety of reasons, including ill health, old age, marital problems, financial problems, an unhappy love affair, loss of a loved one, and revenge on a loved one. Many people who commit suicide give warning signs first. The investigator should verify all statements made by the deceased and be familiar with how various types of wounds are self-inflicted.

Homicide investigation is a specialized field requiring education, training, and practical experience. It begins with the crime scene, because the police are usually called to the scene and the surrounding area provides significant information. The initial investigation is usually conducted by the first officer at the homicide scene, who must note his or her time of arrival, witnesses present at the scene, what was observed upon arrival, and any evidence found at the scene.

Detailed notes, sketches, and photographs should be developed during the course of an investigation. The homicide investigator describes the dead body and the surrounding area, without moving the body or touching anything at the scene. A death-scene sketch is done for all violent death investigations. The exact location of all objects should be recorded in the sketch. Crime scene photos are a permanent visual record.

The body should not be removed from a homicide scene until examined by a medical examiner or coroner. Medical examiners often assist in reconstructing the homicide scene and determining what occurred before and during the homicide.

How evidence is collected and preserved can determine the outcome of scientific examination. The investigator must make certain that each item of evidence is protected from destruction and contamination. A medicolegal investigation identifies the victim by photos, fingerprints, dental and medical records, and relatives or friends. The medicolegal investigation reviews toxicology and autopsy tests to determine the cause and manner of death.

The psychological autopsy determines whether death was natural, accidental, suicide, or homicide. The psychological autopsy recreates the decedent's intentions.

Deaths of infants are usually due to asphyxia, which could be the result of accidental or natural causes. If a death occurs from strangulation or a violent act, infanticide may have taken place. The battered-child syndrome describes children who have been physically abused and have received external or internal physical injuries. Mass murderers are individuals who have killed four or more people in a single incident. Serial murderers kill several people at intervals ranging from two days to several months. Lust murder is sexually motivated and involves torture, violent sexual trauma, mutilation, or dismemberment. Family homicides account for approximately 13 percent of the murders in America.

Key Terms

autopsy
battered child syndrome
homicide
infanticide
lust murder
mass murder
multiple crime scene
postvention
primary crime scene
psychological autopsy
putrefaction
rigor mortis
serial murder
suicide

Review Questions

1. What are the three phases of an investigation?
2. When investigating a suicide, what elements should the investigator be aware of?
3. What action should be taken by the first officer responding to a crime scene?
4. What is the theory of transfer, or exchange?
5. What are the uses of a homicide-scene sketch?
6. What kinds of information are useful in estimating the time of death?
7. Explain the following terms: body heat, rigor mortis, livor mortis, and stomach contents.
8. How should trace physical evidence be collected?
9. What is a psychological autopsy?
10. Explain infanticide and the battered child syndrome.
11. What are the differences among mass murder, serial murder, and lust murder?
12. Discuss the situational factors associated with family homicides.

References

Crime Scene Manual, New York City Police Department, 1977.

Geberth VJ: "The Homicide Crime Scene—Parts 1 and 2." *Law and Order*, July/Aug 1979.

Geberth VJ: "Mass, Serial, and Sensational Homicides." *Law and Order*, October 1986.

Geberth VJ: *Practical Homicide Investigation*, New York, NY: Elsevier, 1983.

Geberth VJ: "Psychological Profiling." *Law and Order*, October 1981.

Gottschalk LA et al: *Guide to the Investigation and Reporting of Drug Abuse*, Rockville, MD: National Institute of Drug Abuse, 1984.

Hagman JC et al: "Psychological Profile of Family Homicide." *The Police Chief*, December 1987.

Hazelwood RA, Douglas JE: "The Lust Murderer." *FBI Law Enforcement Bulletin*, April 1980.

Holmes RM, De Burger J: *Serial Murder*, Beverly Hills, CA: Sage, 1988.

International Association of Chiefs of Police. IACP, *Criminal Investigation*, ed.2 (vols. 1, 2). Gaithersburg, MD: 1975.

Lipskin BA, Field KS: *Death Investigation and Examination*. Colorado Springs, CO: The Forensic Sciences Foundation Press, 1984.

McClay J: "Postmortem Procedures and their Application to Criminal Investigation." *Law and Order*, July 1979.

O'Hara CE: *Fundamentals of Criminal Investigations*, ed.3. Springfield, IL: Charles C. Thomas, 1973.

Reesler RK, Burgess A: "Crime Scene and Profile Characteristics of Organized and Disorganized Murderers." *FBI Law Enforcement Bulletin*, August 1985.

Shneidman E: *Guide to the Investigation and Reporting of Drug Abuse Deaths*, LA Gottschalk et al., eds. Washington, DC: Government Printing Office, 1977.

Shneidman E: "Suicide, Lethality, and the Psychological Autopsy." In Shneidman and Ortago, eds., *Aspects of Depression*. Boston, MA: Little, Brown, 1969.

Snyder LM: *Homicide Investigation*, Springfield, IL: Charles C. Thomas, 1967.

CHAPTER 14

Assault and Robbery

Assault and robbery are two sides of the same coin. Both involve violence or the threat of violence. Robbery evokes a strong reaction of fear because it implies force or the actual use of force takes place. Assault is a violent act committed against individuals. The assaulted individual could be a friend, a family member, or a stranger. An assault can lead to no visible injuries or to a near death. Because an assault could result in serious physical injury, it causes fear for many individuals.

Assault

Assault is an intentional, unlawful act that threatens to harm or actually does harm another person by the use of force. The key element is harm; merely insulting someone is not assault. An assault can be a threat of violence, a physical beating, or a stabbing. Many assaults occur between family members—for example, a husband beating his wife or a mother physically abusing her children.

Assault can be classified as either simple or aggravated. A **simple assault** is an attempt to commit a violent injury to another person or to commit an act that places the other person in reasonable apprehension of immediately receiving a violent injury. An **aggravated assault** occurs when one person intends to murder, rape, or rob another. It also includes assaults with deadly weapons or with any object, device, or instrument that is likely to result in serious bodily injury.

Usually, simple assault is classified as a misdemeanor while aggravated assault is a felony. Because of their violent nature, assaults cannot be treated lightly. Cases of assault have to be investigated and arrests made where appropriate. The decision to arrest should be based on the nature of the assault, the seriousness of the injury, and the prior arrest record of the assailant. (IACP, 1975, p. 53)

In the vast majority of assault cases the victim knows the assailant. A study of 241 aggravated assault cases in St. Louis, Missouri, found the clearance rate to be generally high at 77 percent. (Pittman and Handy, 1964, p. 469) However, the more time elapsed following the assault, the less chance the police had of arresting the offender. The success rate was highest when the offender was apprehended within one hour of committing the assault. In 193 of the 241 aggravated assault cases, the identity of the offender was known to the victim, witnesses, or the police. In only seven cases was the offender not apprehended.

When investigating an assault, the investigator should determine what type of weapon was used and whether the offender knew the assailant. What was the assailant's motive? The investigator must conduct a thorough interview with the victim. If the victim is being transported to the hospital, a police officer should accompany him or her.

The scene of the crime is searched as soon as possible after the assault. This search can be conducted in the presence of the victim. Items to look for include footprints, fingerprints, scuff marks, and any other indications that there may have been a struggle. A piece of cloth or a button could be valuable evidence. If the victim is not present during the initial search, it may be a good idea to bring him or her back to the scene to shed new light on the event.

All witnesses to the assault should be interviewed and statements taken of what they witnessed. The area should be canvassed to locate any witnesses no longer present at the crime scene. Investigators may want to interview the victim and witnesses after the assault scene has been searched. Evidence found at the scene may lead to additional questions. The investigator may be looking for a motive and opportunity. Interviews are based on information developed during the investigation.

A suspect should be placed in the vicinity of the assault. Did he or she have a motive and the opportunity to commit the assault? Did the suspect have possession of the weapon used in the assault? Physical evidence found at the crime scene may relate the suspect to the assault. The suspect's criminal record should be reviewed for prior assault arrests.

When an investigation has failed to identify the assailant, the victim's background, friends, and activities should be checked. Relatives, acquaintances, and neighbors should all be interviewed. Department records should be reviewed to find if the victim has been involved in similar incidents in the past. If the victim has received medical treatment, the doctor should be questioned. The doctor may know what kind of weapon was used and the approximate time of the assault, as well as whether the victim is on drugs or has a medical disability that interferes with memory. (IACP, 1975, p. 56)

According to the Uniform Crime Report, aggravated assault (one of the eight index crimes) had a 60 percent clearance rate by law enforcement agencies nationwide during the 1980s. Weapons of assault can include hands, fists, and feet, in addition to knives, blunt instruments, and firearms.

A type of assault that has recently become common on the West Coast and in Florida is the **drive-by shooting**, which relates to street drug activity. An individual drives down the street shooting at someone with whom he has a conflict. Usually the problem involves a bladerunner ripping off a dealer, disputes over territory, or an individual's failure to pay for the dope.

These assaults are committed by males in their late teens or early twenties. The car offers concealment and makes it easy to escape. These crimes are not difficult to solve, since the victim can identify the suspect. In the state of Georgia, drive-by shootings are treated as aggravated assaults with intent to murder. A twenty-year maximum sentence is attached to conviction.

Robbery

Since robbery involves not just the loss of property but threatened or actual violence, it's considered a very serious crime. It creates fear for many people. The Uniform Crime Report defines robbery as "the taking or attempting to take anything of value from the care, custody, or control of a person or persons by force or threat of force or violence and/or by putting the victim in fear." According to the Uniform Crime Report, the crime of robbery accounted for approximately 36 percent of violent crimes nationwide during the 1980s. Cities of one million or more people have the highest robbery rate, while rural communities have the lowest. Law enforcement solves approximately 25 percent of robberies nationwide.

A study sponsored by the National Criminal Justice Information and Statistical Services in 1974 (pp. 1–5) found the following.

- The combined rate for robbery and attempted robbery without injury was two to three times greater than that for robbery and

attempted robbery with injury.
- The proportion of robberies committed by strangers was greater than the proportion of assaults committed by strangers.
- Person under 35 were more likely to have been victims of robbery without contact than those 35 and over.
- Persons with annual incomes of less than $10,000 were more apt to be victims of robbery than those with incomes over $10,000.
- In general, crimes against individuals were least well reported, although crimes of violence were more frequently brought to police attention than crimes of personal theft.
- Attempted commercial robberies were fairly well reported.
- The most commonly cited reasons for not reporting personal and commercial victimizations to the police were a belief that because of lack of proof nothing could be accomplished, and a feeling that the experience was not sufficiently important to merit police attention.

A special report published by the Bureau of Justice Statistics found that between 1973 and 1984, "Two-thirds of the victims of these robberies had property stolen, and a third were injured; nearly a fourth suffered both injury and property loss." (1987, p. 1) The survey also found that robbery occurs in conjunction with other crimes. For instance, approximately 11 percent of homicides were committed with robbery as a motive. Other robbery victims were raped or had their cars stolen.

In almost half of the robberies, weapons were displayed. Guns were used 20 percent of the time. Victims were predominantly white males, and older people were less likely to be victims. Factors affecting the likelihood that a robbery would be reported to police included whether anything was stolen, the monetary value of the stolen property, whether the victim was injured, the seriousness of the injury, and whether a weapon was used.

Categories of Robbery

The *Police Robbery Control Manual* (U.S. Department of Justice, 1975) categorizes robberies into four types: street, residential, vehicle, and commercial robbery.

Street Robbery

Street robberies may be classified as visible or nonvisible, depending on their locale. Visible robberies are those that take place on a public street or thoroughfare, unobstructed from public view.

Nonvisible robberies take place in public places, facilities, or buildings not categorized as streets or thoroughfares. The place or structure shields the perpetrator from view. One example would be a robbery in a public transportation facility.

Visible street robberies occur in open areas, frequently on side streets or in parking garages. The characteristics of visible street robberies can include surprise, the use of physical force, and speed. These robberies usually are spur-of-the-moment decisions requiring no planning. Since street robberies happen quickly, victims usually are unable to provide a good physical description. Street robberies are classified as armed, unarmed, and the purse snatch. The most common type of visible street robbery are muggings and the purse snatch. Force can be used, and the victim may be beaten or knocked to the ground. Young people—sometimes two or more—are often involved in a mugging or purse snatch.

There are similarities and differences between visible and nonvisible street robberies. Nonvisible robberies usually are committed by youths. They take place off the street in commercial or residential buildings, or in public transportation facilities. Knives are the principal weapon used.

Residential Robbery

In residential robberies, an assailant enters a person's dwelling—apartment, house, or mobile home—with the intent of taking that person's valuables. The offender gets in simply by knocking on the front door and forcing entrance. There may have been a relationship between the victim and the suspect. If there is no victim/suspect acquaintanceship, the residence was selected because valuables and money are thought to be there. Residential robbers are professionals who are usually armed with a handgun or a knife. The residential robbery is rare.

Vehicle Robbery

Vehicle robberies usually are committed against commercial drivers. The most frequent targets are delivery vans, buses, and taxicabs. The robbery of taxicabs and buses usually takes place at night, while delivery vans are most often robbed during the day.

Generally, the vehicle robber is in his late teens or early twenties and armed. This robber plans an escape and is not concerned with the safety of the victim. An assailant in a taxicab often gives an address in a secluded area and robs the taxicab driver after arriving there. This robber is capable of causing injury and even death. The robbery of delivery vans can occur on the spur of the moment.

Commercial Robbery

Small businesses and stores such as chain stores and gas stations open at night are the victims of most commercial robberies, which usually involve some planning and the use of a gun. Stores in out-of-the-way places and/or operated by elderly persons are prone to robbery. Violence may be used against victims who resist. They could be seriously injured or murdered. (Ward et al., 1975, pp. 5–8) Although commercial robberies cannot be eliminated, police officers can suggest robbery deterrents. (IACP, 1975, p. 69)

- Keep the interior and front and rear entrances well lit.
- Keep the rear and side doors locked at all times.
- Maintain a clear view into the building from the street.
- Record, by serial number and series, some bait money to be kept in the cash register and given to a robber.
- Keep as little cash on the premises as possible.
- Keeps checks separate from cash.
- Be sure alarms are in working order at all times; if the business does not have an alarm, simple and inexpensive signaling devices can be connected between neighboring stores.

Savannah, Georgia, had a rash of armed robberies of convenience stores in the late 1980s. The police were able to curtail the number of armed robberies by convincing the convenience stores to establish a camera program. A 35-mm camera would be placed in the store facing the counter to obtain an accurate picture of the offender. The camera would be activated by taking money from a specific location in the cash register, and would take 18 pictures of the offender. The police department would maintain the cameras. After the cameras were installed, the robbery rate decreased substantially due to increasing arrests of robbers identified through the program.

Trends in Robbery

Between 1962 and 1980, the per capita robbery rate for both Canada and the United States increased four-fold. Since the early 1980s the robbery rate has declined in both countries. However, it has not fallen to the levels of the 1960s, and it does not appear it will return to that level in the 1990s.

What has caused the increase in robbery? Reasons given include increasing urbanization and modernization; robbery is an

An armed robbery suspect photographed by a hidden camera in a retail store

urban crime. Another reason for the robbery increase is demographic change. More young people tend to commit crimes such as robbery. A third reason may be the pervasive use of drugs. (Gabor and Normandeu, 1989, pp. 273–74)

Contemporary robbers lack sophistication. They do not plan; often they use drugs or alcohol when they commit the offense; and they usually are unconcerned with the consequences of their actions. In a study of robberies in the 1980s, Gabor and Normandeu found that although robbery may be considered a violent crime, only 30 percent involved physical force. They also found that "robberies varied in their sophistication, violence, and profits, according to the nature of the target." The bank robber was the most sophisticated, obtained the greatest profits, and was the least violent. Approximately half of the robbers did no planning at all, and if they did it consisted of less than an hour. The major motive for armed robbery was that it "constitutes the fastest and most direct way of getting money." (1989, pp. 276–77)

The study found that the greatest fear most robbers had was the possibility that they would have to use violence. Upon completion of the robbery the offenders reacted in a variety of ways. Some had feelings of relief and satisfaction, while others were nervous.

Approximately 20 percent of the robberies were solved, with about one-third of the arrests taking place on the day of the crime.

Types of Robbers

To apprehend robbery offenders, their motivations, techniques, and perceptions must be taken into consideration. Why did the offender commit the offense? Conklin (1972, pp. 63–77) describes four distinct types of robbers: professional, opportunist, addict, and alcoholic. The classifications are based on motivation for the theft, techniques used, and the degree of commitment to crime as a life-style.

Professional Robbers

The professional robber has been portrayed by the news and entertainment media as an offender who carefully plans his crime, executes the robbery with accomplices, and lives the good life. Conklin defines professionals as "those who manifest a long term commitment to crime as a source of livelihood, who plan and organize their crimes prior to committing them, and who seek money to support a particular life-style that may be called hedonistic." (1972, p. 64) There are two types of professional robbers; one commits robberies exclusively. Other professionals commit robberies occasionally and are committed to other forms of crime. The first type of professional robber is committed to robbery because it is profitable and carried out quickly. This robber exhibits skill and plans the crime. Generally, he or she robs commercial businesses known to have large sums of money. Usually the robbery is committed with accomplices assigned various tasks. For example, one member may have to steal a car, another may drive the car to and from the crime scene, another may be assigned the task of preventing customers or workers from notifying the police, and one may commit the actual act. The professional often carries a weapon and may be skilled in its use. Money obtained from the robbery may be spent quickly for personal pleasures. Some professional robbers may accumulate enough money for bail or to employ an attorney in case of apprehension.

Opportunist Robbers

The second category of robber, known as the opportunist robber, may be the most common. The opportunist robber is not committed to the crime of robbery and commits other crimes such as shoplifting and larceny. Targets are chosen because of accessibility and vulnerability. Usually, small amounts of money are obtained from the robbery. Opportunist robbers are usually lower class and young—either teenagers or in their early twenties. The opportunist robber does not plan the crime, and individuals involved in the robbery are not assigned individual tasks. This type of robber wants a little extra cash either for spending money or for clothes. Generally, weapons are not used.

Addict Robbers

The addict robber has a weak commitment to the crime of robbery. Addicts view robbery as dangerous and use it only as a last resort to obtain money. Robberies committed by addicts are usually not planned, and they have a better chance of being cleared than professional robberies.

Alcoholic Robbers

The alcoholic robber usually attributes the crime to being intoxicated, often robbing to get money for alcohol. The alcoholic should be considered an opportunist and not a professional. There exists little or no planning; these robbers take few precautions and have a good chance of being apprehended.

Investigating Robbery

Like other crimes, a robbery calls for both a preliminary and a follow-up investigation. Figure 14–1 analyzes the elements likely to be called on to solve armed robbery cases, including aspects of the investigation.

The Police Executive Research Forum (PERF) report on robbery (Eck, 1983, pp. xxiv–xxviii) suggests a number of improvements for conducting and managing investigations. The two sections that follow examine these suggestions.

Preliminary Investigation

Greater emphasis should be put on collecting physical evidence when such evidence can be used. Physical evidence is seldom used to identify an unknown suspect, but it is valuable in corroborating identifications made through other means. Few agencies have the resources to send trained evidence technicians to all crime scenes. But policies defining when technicians should or should not be sent can avoid the overuse of technicians, a subsequent decline in the quality of their work, and the collection of more evidence than can be used.

Guidelines should be developed for the use of evidence technicians in routine cases such as robberies and burglaries without seri-

FIGURE 14–1: Elements Useful in Solving Armed Robberies

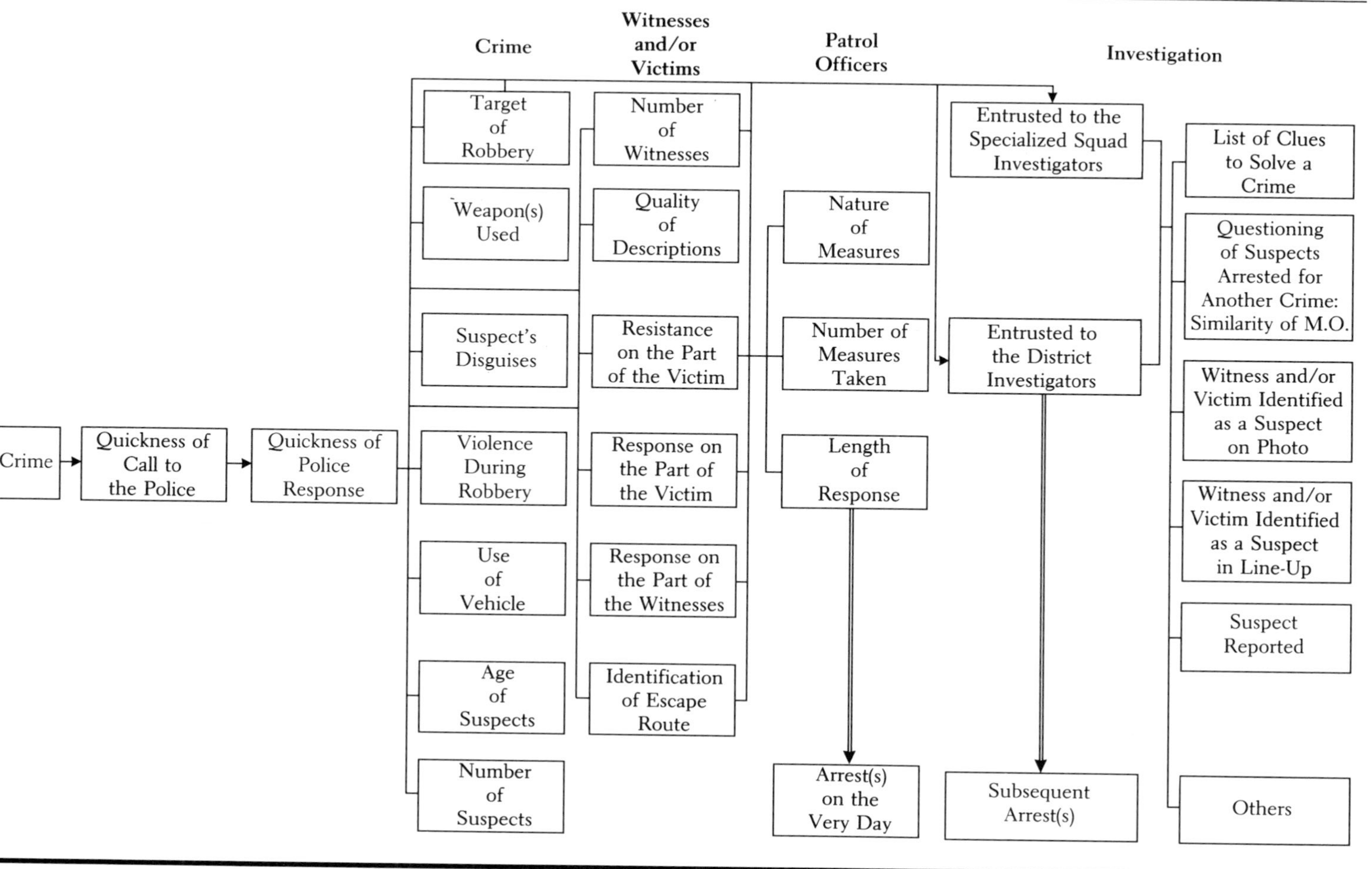

Source: Adapted from Gagnon & LeBlanc, "Response in Armed Robbery Cases" *Canadian Police College Journal,* Vol. 7, No. 4, 1983. Reprinted with permission of Canadian Police College Journal.

ous injuries or extremely high losses. The criteria should take into account the fact that physical evidence is not likely to be useful unless the suspect is identified by other means.

Evidence technicians are needed in the following situations.

- A suspect is arrested at or near the crime scene, and physical evidence from the scene will be useful in the prosecution.
- A suspect has been identified but not arrested, and physical evidence can corroborate the identification.
- There are enough leads that the suspect may be identified, and physical evidence should be collected to corroborate any further identification.
- There are peculiar circumstances to the crime, indicating that it may be part of a pattern, and physical evidence may corroborate the identification of a suspect traced through other crimes in the series.

Greater effort should be devoted to canvassing neighborhoods for witnesses. Considerable evidence establishes the importance of witnesses in identifying suspects and leading to arrests and convictions. Yet patrol officers often fail to canvass neighborhoods near crime scenes for witnesses. Relying solely on victims and those witnesses immediately available at the crime scene reduces the effectiveness of further investigative efforts. It is crucial that patrol officers conducting preliminary investigations routinely search for potential witnesses who were no longer at the crime scene when officers arrived.

Patrol officers should use departments more extensively. Checking department records was found to be an especially productive activity for patrol officers, but they do so with varying frequency in the agency studies. Officers may believe that they are tied to their vehicles and that records are difficult and time-consuming to locate. Police managers should design record systems that enhance radio and telephone accessibility for patrol officers.

Patrol officers should make greater use of informants, who are particularly useful in identifying suspects and bringing about arrests. Patrol officers rarely use them, perhaps because they are untrained in the skills of cultivating informants. Patrol managers should provide the training and encouragement to help patrol officers develop informants.

Follow-Up Investigation

Law enforcement agency records should be used more effectively. The effective use of records is as important in follow-up investigation as in preliminary work. Good organization is the key.

Fingerprint files should be organized so that a large number of prints can be searched rapidly. The success of single-print files for identifying suspects demonstrates how this can be accomplished. Mug-shot files should be indexed by facial and other characteristics as well as by race and sex.

Files of stolen property and information obtained from dealers in used merchandise should be more wisely used. Some success has resulted from matching automated stolen property files to automated repair and warranty records maintained by private firms.

Detectives should make more extensive use of informants, and agencies should have policies defining how to handle them. Though informants are traditionally an important source of information, they are not extensively used in robbery and burglary investigations. This must be changed. At the same time, police agencies must implement policies governing the use of informants to forestall an array of legal and constitutional problems. The policies should define how and when informants are compensated, the types of bargains that can be made with them, which officers have the authority to bargain, control over informant activities, the agency response to any criminal acts by informants, the confidentiality of files and the protection of informants' identity.

The PERF study also makes a number of suggestions on how to improve management of the follow-up investigation. The report recommends three techniques. First, formal *case screening* will minimize wasting time on cases that cannot be solved. This process will provide forecasts of investigative results for managers.

Second, there should be a policy on the *length of time investigations will continue* before their status is reported to supervisors. This would focus more attention on cases that require supervisors' involvement in long investigations, leading to sharing of information and more accurate data about investigators' caseloads.

Third, the *monitoring* of both robbery and burglary investigations is important to ensure that investigative resources are used effectively. The study by PERF recommends three forms of monitoring. In investigator assignment monitoring the supervisor is responsible for assigning cases to investigators, who conduct them as they see fit. The cases are monitored by the supervisor. In unit assignment monitoring, cases are assigned to the entire unit instead of an individual investigator. The supervisor continually monitors cases. Triage assignment monitoring combines the first two types. Cases are divided into three categories: those that cannot be solved and are screened out, those that require little time and effort, and those that require a great deal of time and effort. (Eck, 1983, p. xxix).

Crime Pattern Analysis

Crime analysis is primarily concerned with identifying short-term patterns of criminal behavior or events and associated characteristics. (*Issues in Crime Analysis in Support of Patrol,* 1975) Some form of crime pattern analysis exists in most police agencies, but it is often conducted by an investigator or officer in an informal manner. A formal unit should be established to collect, analyze, and disseminate crime information.

Crime pattern analysis is most effective when applied to offenses that have a high probability of recurrence. These include auto theft, burglary, and robbery. For example, the central crime analysis unit of Rochester, New York, analyzes burglaries and robberies. It divides robberies into those where a weapon is used versus strong-armed muggings. Rochester also has investigative coordinators in all seven police sectors. Their job is to detect crime patterns in a sector and relay any patterns detected to the patrol and investigative forces. The investigative coordinators meet weekly with the head of the crime analysis unit to exchange information. These meetings are also open to other police agencies. (Palmiotto, 1988, p. 62)

Similarly, the crime analysis unit of the Stockton, California, police department studies burglary and robbery. Its crime series analysis matrix graphically displays a large volume of crime data in a format susceptible to case comparison of modus operandi factors. The matrix is an investigative tool that aids both crime analysts and investigators by allowing them to comprehend and manage data generated during a crime series. Also, the matrix can permit early identification of similar offenses. (Yamida and Spice, 1979, pp. 58–59)

Robbery Analysis for Investigative Links

Robbery Analysis for Investigative Links (RAIL) offers robbery investigators a computerized link analysis system to assist them in solving robbery, which receives media attention and is usually considered a violent crime. Since robberies are often committed against strangers, little information exists to assist in crime-solving. With a computerized link analysis system, even small amounts of information can be collected and collated to give the investigator a larger data field to work with.

Eugene Hunyadi, a robbery investigator trainer for the Ohio Peace Officer Training Academy, developed the robbery analysis for investigative links. RAIL instantaneously provides criminal investigators with valuable information about similar cases. Investigators are concerned with interdepartmental and intradepartmental communication problems. In the traditional method of storing reports, investigators must retrieve them manually to search for similar M.O.s. With a central database storage facility, investigators can input information for a case under investigation, which can later be accessed by them or other investigators.

The investigation of robbery should become systematic and cases should be solved much sooner with the use of RAIL. But first law enforcement personnel must become computer literate. Knowledge of behavioral sciences would be helpful in understanding why many items are asked. The RAIL program has been designed to meet the needs of investigators on a small scale, with capabilities to expand to a larger database. It uses an IBM-compatible microcomputer with a 20MB hard drive, a minimum of 640 KB RAM, and one 5¼" floppy disk drive. The software program is dbase Plus. Figure 14–2 is the RAIL manual.

Employees' Behavior During a Robbery

The primary goal of employee and customer behavior during a robbery is to reduce the possibility of injury. All individuals present during a robbery should follow these guidelines. (O'Hara, 1973, pp. 410–411)

- The persons present should follow the robbers' instructions. Since the criminals are extremely nervous, an unexpected action on the part of an employee or customer may precipitate gunfire.
- Employees instructed to hand over money should endeavor to keep the loss at a minimum. In other words, while obeying an order to hand over money, they should not volunteer to reach for money not visible to the robbers.
- Employees should observe the robbers carefully. Physical descriptions, peculiarities of behavior, method of operation, voice, and exact words are invaluable aids to the investigators. An employee who has a view of the street should note any accomplices outside and try to remember details of the getaway car.
- When the robbers are leaving, employees should remain until the danger is removed.
- Employees should be aware of the presence of physical evidence and avoid obliterating such evidence as fingerprints.

FIGURE 14–2: Robbery Analysis for Investigative Links

Developed by
Eugene R. Hunyadi
Instructor
Ohio Peace Officer Training Academy
P.O. Box 309
London, Ohio 43140
(614) 466-7771

Preface

The following will serve as a reference manual for the proper completion of the Robbery Analysis for Investigative Links (RAIL). Most of the questions herein are self-explanatory, however, some may be confusing and when this occurs please refer to this manual. Before beginning the assessment form, please note the following guidelines:

1. *Dates:* write all dates by first using the month, day and year respectively, i.e., 08/02/89.
2. *Times:* write all times with reference to military designation, i.e., 10:15 p.m. will read as 2215 hours.
3. When inputting data, use either all upper case or all lower case designations.
4. Type in a single letter for the correct response to each question unless otherwise stated.
5. Memo fields contain 4,096 characters. To access memo fields, use control home. To save and return to record, use control W.
6. If you face difficulty in any area of this program feel free to contact its originator.

I. Administration

1. ORI Number:
2. Investigator's Name:
3. Best Contact Number:
   ( ) -
4. Case Status:
   [A] Open
   [B] Inactive
   [C] Cleared by Arrest
   [D] Exceptionally Cleared
   [E] Arrest Warrant Issued
5. This RAIL Report Pertains to the Following Type Case:
   [A] Aggravated Robbery
   [B] Robbery
   [C] Attempted Robbery
6. Based on the Information of This Case, Do You Believe This Offender Has Committed Similar Offenses Before:
   [A] Yes [B] No
7. Today's Date / /
8. Date of Occurrence: / /
9. Estimated Time of Offense:

II. Victim Information

10. Last Name:
11. First Name:
12. Middle Name:
13. Alias(es):
14. Date of Birth: / /
15. Name of Business:
16. Type of Business:
17. Address:
18. City:
19. State:
20. Zip:
21. County:
22. Property Taken:

III. Offender Information

23. This is Offender in This Incident. (If more Than one Offender, Complete Offender Supplemental Form.)
24. The Offender is:
    [A] Unknown–Not Seen (Go To #49)
    [B] Unknown–Seen (Go To #36)
    [C] Identified–Not in Custody
    [D] In Custody
    [E] Deceased

FIGURE 14–2: *(Continued)*

25. Last Name:
26. First Name:
27. Middle Name:
28. Alias(es):
29. Address:
30. City:
31. State:
32. Zip:
33. County:
34. Date of Birth: / /
35. Social Security Number:
36. Sex:
    [A] Male
    [B] Female
37. Race:
    [A] Black
    [B] Caucasian
    [C] Hispanic
    [D] Oriental/Asian
    [E] Other
38. Age (or best estimate) at Time of Incident:
39. Height:
40. Weight:
41. Hair Length:
    [A] Long
    [B] Short
    [C] Shaved
42. Predominant Hair Color:
    [A] Gray/White
    [B] Blond
    [C] Brown
    [D] Black
    [E] Red
    [F] Other
43. Was Wearing Glasses:
    [A] Yes
    [B] No
    [C] Unknown
44. Facial Hair:
    [A] None
    [B] Mustache
    [C] Beard
    [D] Other
45. Clothing of Offender at Time of Incident
    [A] Business Suit
    [B] Casual
    [C] Gaudy or Garish
    [D] Sport or Athletic
    [E] Western Wear
    [F] Work Clothes
    [G] Uniform
    [H] Other
46. Offender Wore a Disguise or Mask:
    [A] Yes (Describe in Narrative)
    [B] No
47. Noticeable Scars, Tattoos, or Birthmarks:
    [A] Yes (Describe in Narrative)
    [B] No
48. Other Outstanding Physical Features of the Offender Not Reported Above (crossed eyes, noticeable limp, physical deformity, etc.):
    [A] Yes (Describe in Narrative)
    [B] No

IV. Vehicle Information

49. Is a Vehicle Known to Have Been Used in This Incident:
    [A] Yes
    [B] No (Go to #58)
    [C] Unknown (Go to #58)
50. License Number:
51. License State:
52. Vehicle Year:
53. Make:
54. Model:
55. Color:
    [A] Passenger Car
    [B] Van
    [C] Pick-up Truck
    [D] Jeep Type
    [E] Tractor–Trailer
    [F] Motorcycle
    [G] Other

V. Offense M.O.

58. If the Offender Initiated Contact by Means of Deception, Indicate Type Used:
59. If the Offender Initiated Contact by Means of Surprise, Indicate Type Used:
60. If the Offender Initiated Contact by Direct and Immediate Physical Assault, Indicate Type Used:

FIGURE 14-2: *(Continued)*

61. Were There Potential Witnesses at the Scene Capable of Providing Added Information:
    [A] Yes (Specify in Narrative)
    [B] No
62. Description of the General Area of Offender-Victim Contact:
    [A] Rural
    [B] Suburban
    [C] Urban
    [D] Other
63. Is There Evidence That the Offender Disabled the Telephone, Security Devices, or Other Utilities:
    [A] Yes (Describe in Narrative)
    [B] No
64. Are There Indications That the Offender Took Steps to Obliterate or Destroy Evidence at the Scene:
    [A] Yes (Specify in Narrative)
    [B] No
65. Was There Any Communication From the Offender Before, During, or After the Crime:
    [A] Yes (Specify in Narrative)
    [B] No
66. Was the Victim(s) Bound:
    [A] Yes
    [B] No
67. Article Used to Bind or Restrain the Victim(s):
    [A] Article of Clothing
    [B] Tape
    [C] Cordage
    [D] Chain
    [E] Handcuffs
    [F] Gag(s)
    [G] Other
    [H] Two or More
68. The Evidence Suggests the Restraining Device(s) Was:
    [A] Brought to the Scene
    [B] Found at the Scene
    [C] Both A & B
    [D] Other

VI. Forensic Evidence

69. Weapon(s) Used by Offender in This Incident:
    [A] None (Go to #75)
    [B] Firearm
    [D] Ligature
    [C] Cutting Instrument
    [E] Hands/Feet
    [F] Other
70. Recovery of Weapon:
    [A] Recovered
    [B] Not Recovered But Information Known
    [C] Not Recovered, No Information Known (Go To #75)
71. Type of Firearm Used:
    [A] Handgun
    [B] Rifle
    [C] Shotgun
72. Caliber or Gauge of Firearm Used (if known):
73. Number of Grooves and Direction of Twist:
74. Size of Shotgun Shell Used:
75. Were Identifiable Fingerprints Obtained From the Scene:
    [A] Yes
    [B] No
76. Is a Photo or Composite of Offender Available:
    [A] Yes
    [B] No

VII. Narrative Summary

77. Please Answer Questions Where You Were Asked to Specify, Describe, or Explain by Listing the Question Number First:

Source: Reprinted with permission of Eugene Hunyadi.

Summary

Assault is an intentional, unlawful act that involves the threat or use of force against another person. A simple assault is an attempt to commit a violent injury to another person or to commit an act that places the person in reasonable apprehension of immediately receiving a violent injury. An aggravated assault occurs when one person intends to murder, rape, or rob another.

The investigator should determine what type of weapon was used and whether the offender knew the assailant. The scene of the crime is searched as soon as possible after the assault. This search can be conducted in the presence of the victim.

Since robbery involves not just property loss but threatened or actual violence, it's considered a very serious crime. The categories of robbery include street, residential, vehicle, and commercial robbery.

Small businesses such as convenience stores and gas stations open at night are the victims of most commercial robberies. Commercial robberies usually involve some planning and the use of a gun. Stores that are in out-of-the-way places and operated by elderly persons are especially prone to robbery. Violence is sometimes used against victims who resist.

Police officers responding to a robbery in progress are responding to a dangerous situation. Handling this call improperly can cause harm to the officer, victims, or witnesses. The safety of citizens must be the primary consideration.

Generally, robberies are committed rapidly, and police seldom stumble upon them. Police response to alarms can be helpful in reducing this crime. Of course, a rash of false alarms will make officers skeptical, but they should always assume a robber is there unless told otherwise.

The preliminary investigation requires that a neighborhood canvass be conducted in the immediate vicinity of the robbery and the possible escape route. When the preliminary investigation does not result in an arrest, a detective usually performs a detailed follow-up investigation. Additional information must be obtained and analyzed. Investigators review criminal history files and attempt to narrow the suspects down.

The Police Executive Research Forum (PERF) report on robbery suggested a number of improvements for conducting and managing both preliminary and follow-up investigations. The preliminary investigation can be improved by placing greater emphasis on collecting physical evidence and canvassing neighborhoods for witnesses. Also, patrol officers should be more devoted to canvassing neighborhoods for witnesses and using department records and informants more extensively. In the follow-up investigation, PERF recommended that law enforcement agency records should be used more effectively, that detectives should make more extensive use of informants, and that agencies should have policies on the use of informants.

Crime pattern analysis is concerned with criminal behavior and associated characteristics. Some form of crime pattern analysis exists in most police agencies, but often it is conducted by an investigative officer in an informal manner. A formal unit should be established to collect, analyze, and disseminate crime information.

Robbery Analysis for Investigative Links (RAIL) offers robbery investigators a computerized link analysis system to assist them in solving robbery. RAIL instantaneously provides criminal investigators with valuable information about similar cases. The investigation of robbery should become systematic, and cases should be solved much sooner with the use of RAIL.

The primary goal of employee and customer behavior during a robbery should be to reduce the possibility of injury. Employees should follow established guidelines that have been successfully used to curtail injuries.

Key Terms

aggravated assault
drive-by shooting
Robbery Analysis for Investigative Links
simple assault

Review Questions

1. Describe assault, simple assault, and aggravated assault.
2. Describe the activities that are performed in investigation of an assault.
3. Explain the four categories of robbery described in the *Police Robbery Control Manual.*
4. What can police officers tell business owners to deter robbery?
5. Describe the four types of robbers.
6. What activities should the police perform while conducting a robbery investigation?
7. What are the recommendations made by PERF regarding the preliminary investigation? The follow-up investigation?

References

Bennet WW, Hess KM: *Criminal Investigation*, ed.2. New York, NY: West Publishing Co., 1987.

Bureau of Justice Statistics: *Robbery Victims*, Washington, DC: U.S. Dept. of Justice, 1987.

Conklin JE: *Robbery and the Criminal Justice System*. New York, NY: New York Police Dept., 1972.

Deladurantey J and Sullivan D: *Criminal Investigation Standards*. New York, NY: Harper and Row, 1980.

Eck JE: *Solving Crimes: The Investigation of Burglary and Robbery*. Washington, DC: Police Executive Research Forum, 1983.

Gabor T, and Normandeau A: "Armed Robbery: Highlights of a Canadian Study." *Canadian Police College Journal*, vol. 13, no.4, 1989.

Gagnon R, LeBlan M: "Police Response in Armed Robbery" *Canadian Police College Journal*, vol.7, no.4, 1983.

Hunyadi E: "Computerized Link Analysis for the Crimes of Homicide, Sexual Assault, and Robbery." Unpublished master's thesis, University of Cincinnati, 1989.

International Association of Chiefs of Police. *Criminal Investigations*, ed.2. Gaithersburg, MD: IACP, 1975.

Issues in Crime Analysis in Support of Patrol: A Review and Assessment of the Literature. Bloomington, IN: Recent Developments in Law Enforcement and Criminal Justice, Inc., 1975.

National Criminal Justice Information and Statistical Services: *Crime in Eight American Cities*. Washington, DC: U.S. Dept. of Justice, 1974.

New York Police Dept.: *Investigator's Guide*, New York, NY, n.d.

O'Hara C: *Fundamentals of Criminal Investigations*, ed.3. Springfield, IL: Charles C. Thomas, 1973.

Palmiotto MJ, Ed.: *Critical Issues in Criminal Investigation*, ed.2. Cincinnati, OH: Anderson Publishing Co., 1988.

Pittman J and Handy W: "Patterns in Criminal Aggravated Assault." *Journal of Criminal Law, Criminology, and Police Science*, 55: 462–470, 1964.

Police Robbery Control Manual. Washington, DC: U.S. Dept. of Justice, 1975.

Sanders W: *Detective Work*. New York, NY: The Free Press, 1977.

Ward RH: *Introduction to Criminal Investigation*. Menlo Park, CA: Addison-Wesley Publishing, 1975.

Yamida DC, Spice HA: "Crime Series Analysis Matrix: An Investigative Tool." *The Police Chief*, June 1979.

CHAPTER 15

Burglary

A review of crime in the United States during the 1980s reveals that burglary accounted for approximately 28 percent of all property crimes. Two of every three burglaries are residential. Approximately 70 percent of all burglaries involve forcible entry, 22 percent are unlawful entries without the use of force, and the other 8 percent attempt forcible entry. The police were able to solve approximately 14 percent of all burglaries committed during the 1980s. Approximately 80 percent of the burglaries cleared involved perpetrators over 18 years of age.

The Uniform Crime Report defines **burglary** as "the unlawful entry of a structure to commit a felony or theft." The crime of burglary can be traced to common law, when it was classified as a crime against occupancy and habitation. In the modern era, burglary is a statutory offense. Many people in our society call a burglary a "robbery," when in fact the threat or use of force must take place to properly define the crime as a robbery.

The Model Penal Code recommends a burglary statute that has been adopted by most states, often with minor changes: when a person "enters a building or occupied structure, or separately secured or occupied portion thereof, with purpose to commit a crime therein, unless the premises are at the time open to the public or the actor is licensed or privileged to enter. It is an affirmative defense to prosecution for burglary that the building or structure was abandoned."

Crime did not increase in the 1980s, but the fear of crime did. When people fear crime they want politicians and the police to do something about it. The offense of burglary creates fear for many Americans. When the security of their home is invaded by strangers, are they safe anywhere? The President's Commission on Law Enforcement recognized the general public's fear of burglaries:

> Because burglary is so frequent, so costly, so upsetting and so difficult to control, it makes great demands on the criminal justice system. Preventing burglary demands imaginative methods of police patrol, and solving burglaries calls for great investigative patience and resourcefulness. . . . Burglars are probably the most numerous class of serious offenders in the correctional system. It is a plausible assumption that the prevalence of the two crimes of burglary and robbery is a significant, if not a major, reason for America's alarm about crime, and that finding effective ways of protecting the community from those two crimes would do much to make 'crime' as a whole less frightening and to bring it within manageable bounds.

The Nature of Burglary

The nature of burglary, coupled with the public's lack of knowledge of how to control it, leads to minimal control of and arrests for this offense. Burglary is the most common felony crime but has the lowest clearance rate for property crimes, including auto theft and larceny. A study conducted by the Stanford Research Institute (SRI) in the early 1970s found that the patrol unit accounted for an overwhelming majority of burglary arrests compared to the detective unit. Since patrol forces are required to be on the street, they are readily available to respond to criminal complaints. The SRI study also pointed out that "the largest number of burglary arrests is for those individuals who have had prior encounters with the police. Heavy narcotics and juvenile involvement is also evident." (Greenberg et al., 1973, pp. 14–15)

The number of cases solved for a particular crime can be evaluated in two ways. The first is arrest clearance and the second is **exceptional clearance,** when the police know who committed the crime but due to mitigating circumstances (for example, the death of the offender) they are unable to make an arrest. The vast majority of burglaries cleared by arrest are solved within 48 hours after they are reported. The clearance rate decreases over a 30-day period. The police should respond quickly to a reported burglary in order to protect the crime scene from being contaminated by victims.

Witnesses are an important source of police information. They can often provide descriptions of suspects and their vehicle. SRI findings indicate that victims' reports are not usually effective sources for solving burglaries. Victims primarily provide information about what items are missing. Witnesses and casual informants are more effective in suspect identification than victims.

Most contemporary burglars probably should not be considered professionals, since they actively commit other crimes such as robbery, auto theft, shoplifting, and forgery. This makes it difficult to determine their modus operandi, as they do not have any readily identifiable trademarks or habits.

Patterns of Burglary

The analysis of burglary patterns can be traced to a study sponsored by the defunct Law Enforcement Assistance Administration and published in the early 1970s by Harry Scarr. The three jurisdictions that provided the study sites were Washington, D.C., police department, the Fairfax County (Virginia) police department, and the Prince Georges County (Maryland) police department. Fairfax County and Prince Georges County border Washington, D.C. Scarr found the following patterns to be characteristic of burglaries.

- *Offenders,* by taking advantage of existing opportunities and/or creating their own, commit crimes.
- *Citizens,* by their behavior, increase or decrease the probability that they will become victims of a particular crime.
- The *political jurisdiction*—largely via its major law enforcement component, the police—attempts to counter the moves of offenders and abet the moves of citizens, in the never-ending interaction among these three elements.

Burglary is a crime of opportunity. The act of burglary is a *behavior.* As a behavior, it involves "needs to be met, opportunities to meet them, perceptions of these opportunities, means to take advantage of such opportunities, satisfactions when needs are met, decisions about alternative routes to need-meeting, and the existence of outside interference in the process." (Scarr, 1973, pp. 3–15)

Committing the crime of burglary may satisfy the criminal's need for money. Many drug addicts commit burglary to obtain money to indulge their addiction. Other motives for committing burglary are a desire to "live the good life," a craving for excitement, and peer pressure.

Specific skills may be required to commit a burglary. A burglar may use brute force—say, breaking a door—or sophisticated methods—disconnecting a burglar alarm or picking a lock.

The burglar looks for an opportunity to commit the act. For example, are doors and windows left open? Any police officer responsible for checking commercial establishments knows that many doors and windows are left unlocked, sometimes on purpose. Can a door be opened with a credit card? Burglars read obituaries and society pages to determine when residences will be unoccupied for funerals and weddings. They watch to see if mail and newspapers accumulate at a residence.

Some individuals in American society consider committing burglary an appropriate way to meet their monetary needs. It appears to offer a good chance of success with a minimum of risk. It has been considered a passive act, since the burglar usually wants to avoid all contact with people during the crime. Entering an unoccupied building minimizes the possibility of being identified and getting caught. Some burglars are committed to burglary as a profession. For example, cat burglars commit the crime only at night and some burglars specialize in certain types of buildings (motels, hotels, apartments, residential homes, or commercial establishments).

Once merchandise has been obtained illegally, the burglar must get rid of it. Often it is sold to acquaintances and friends. Some merchandise can be sold at construction sites, at pawnshops, in specific neighborhoods, or to fences—people who deal in stolen goods.

General Traits

The Law Enforcement Assistance Administration drew a number of generalizations concerning the nature, patterning, and victims of burglary.

Nature of the Offense

Residential burglaries occur more frequently than nonresidential burglaries and their number is increasing faster than that of nonresidential burglaries. However, when the number of potential targets is considered, businesses have a greater probability of being burglarized. Goods that are portable and easily convertible into money are the preponderance of stolen items. Cash and home entertainment equipment are the most popular targets.

Most burglaries involve a theft of moderate value. In suburban jurisdictions studied, two-thirds of all burglaries involved the theft of items worth less than $500.

Both residences and businesses are usually entered via a door or window. Urban burglaries involved forced entry relatively more often than suburban burglaries. Most burglaries involve some degree of forcible entry, usually breaking glass or forcing a lock. A substantial proportion of entries are effected through unlocked windows and doors.

Burglary frequencies do not vary systematically by month or by season. Residential burglaries are mostly weekday phenomena, but nonresidential burglaries are likely to occur on Friday and Saturday nights.

Most burglaries, reported or unreported, are completed. Attempted burglaries generally account for only about a fifth of all burglaries reported to the police.

In structures with some type of alarm system, a high percentage of alarms failed to function or were defeated. Surprisingly, establishments that used an alarm system were more likely to be burglarized than those that did not.

Pattern of the Offense

Residential burglary rates tend to be geographically stable in urban areas but unstable in suburban areas undergoing rapid population growth. Nonresidential burglary frequencies tend to be geographically stable in both urban and suburban areas. Frequencies of residential and nonresidential burglaries are more highly correlated geographically in suburban than in urban areas.

Victims of the Offense

Victims are more likely than nonvictims to perceive a general crime problem in their neighborhood. Victims of burglary are more likely to be victims of other crimes than are nonvictims. Nonvictims are more likely to have taken simple precautions against burglary than victims.

If someone sees or hears a residential burglary in progress, the observer is more likely to be a neighbor of the victim than a stranger. Structures on corner lots are more likely to be burglarized than noncorner locations.

Burglar Profiles

During the early 1970s, Thomas Reppetto conducted a study of burglars in the metropolitan Boston area. He found that age, race, and drug-use classification overlapped extensively. In developing burglar profiles, he used direct quotations to convey representative attitudes for each of the specific types of burglars. (Reppetto, 1974, pp. 23–26)

The *juvenile offender* in this study was arrested numerous times and placed on probation. Since he lacked education and experience, he was unable to perform many conventional jobs. The juvenile burglar tends to work with friends and usually works his neighborhood since he walks to his burglaries. Comments: "I'm just walking down the street and a couple of friends say, 'Hey, do you want to break into a house with us?' I say 'OK, if it's a good hit.' " Reppetto found that juvenile burglars are not deterred by burglar alarms, police patrols, or unfamiliar neighborhoods. Also, their lack of skill leads them to hit easy targets. They dispose of stolen goods in a haphazard manner and consider their crime a game.

The *18- to 25-year-old offender,* according to the Reppetto study, has been in and out of jail for years. This group prefers burglary to other types of crime because they believe it to be more profitable. Comments: "I purse-snatched when I was 15. I grew out of that into something bigger." "I changed as I learned more... from low-class neighborhood to high-rise apartments. . . . it's another step." One young man worked affluent single-family suburban homes. "When gains don't outweigh the other, you don't take the chance." This group of burglars made fewer but more profitable hits than the juvenile offenders. Occupants or a dog were greater deterrents than a burglar alarm.

Reppetto found *white burglars* similar to blacks in skill and methods used, but they were more likely to be married and have a job. White burglars preferred to burglarize single-family homes and worked predominantly white neighborhoods. One burglar commented, "If you get caught in a Puerto Rican neighborhood, you might be killed." The study found that white burglars preferred not to burglarize housing projects, to travel from home to commit burglaries, and to be cautious about hitting the same neighborhoods twice.

Black burglars preferred to burglarize residences owned by whites because they felt they were more affluent. One comment: "If it was a black guy, I'd know that there wasn't too much money. If it was a white guy, I'd know there was." Black burglars lacked the mobility of white burglars. They were often confined to black neighborhoods because they felt conspicuous in affluent white neighborhoods. They were also more likely to be deterred by police patrols than white burglars.

Drug users were usually under 25 and had been doing drugs for several years. They needed money to support their habits and preferred burglarizing single-family dwellings. They did little planning and could be deterred by sophisticated security devices.

Nondrug users were concerned with avoiding confrontations

and would be deterred by police patrols, dogs, security devices, and occupants at home. However, they were not deterred by locks or other mechanical devices.

Types of Burglars

In *The Fence,* Marilyn Walsh characterizes the pecking order of burglars, based upon detectives' information. She identifies six types of burglars: good, known, young, juvenile, booster, and junkie. (Walsh, 1977, pp. 61–62)

Good Burglars

The professional thief is considered a good burglar. A member of the elite circle of thieves, he has the following hallmarks: He is nearly always a specialist, is generally an older thief but may be in his mid-twenties, works less often than other thieves, selects only targets of high value, and rarely carries a weapon. There is a subset of good burglars the police designate as "safe men." This group—the most skilled of thieves—is small and getting smaller.

Known Burglars

The less skilled but highly active thief whose consistency the police have noted over several years is the known burglar. His hallmarks are generally a less than subtle style of entry, volume rather than quality thefts, a substantial arrest record, a low to minimal planning capacity, a high activity level, and the frequent possession of weapons. This thief tends not to stay in the trade as long as the good burglar due to extensive imprisonment, which causes a loss of affiliation with former cohorts, or due to a switch from burglary to robbery.

Young Burglars

Usually between 17 and 25 years old, the young burglar is in the process of becoming a thief. The police classify him as "young" until his behavior or known associations earn him membership in one of the previously discussed groups. The young burglar has few distinctive hallmarks (except youth), but generally he associates very obviously and constantly with other young thieves, steals a variety of merchandise as the opportunity arises, has an arrest record, has an extremely high activity level, and is often in possession of a weapon.

Juvenile Burglars

Since his behavior is monitored primarily by youth officers, the juvenile burglar is rarely encountered by the detective. He is distinguished, however, by the following: he is under the age of 16, usually is advised by older thieves or fences, is not addicted to drugs, steals low-volume merchandise in his neighborhood, and often associates with gangs. The juvenile burglar is another thief in the process of becoming, a situation that saddens and horrifies the seasoned detective.

Boosters

A burglar who depends primarily on quantity rather than quality merchandise thefts is a **booster.** He usually has an extensive record for both larcency and narcotics.

Junkies

The addict/thief, or **junkie,** is generally the least skilled and most active of thieves. The junkie thief has the longest arrest record of any. He steals the most available items, which are rarely valuable, and while very systematic, he exhibits almost no planning in his theft. He is the most hapless, least respected, and least rewarded of thieves.

Types of Burglaries

In *Criminal Investigation: Specific Offenses* (1975, pp. 90–91), the International Association of Chiefs of Police divides burglaries into two categories, residential and business. They can be further divided into the subgroups of apartment, house, store, and warehouse burglaries.

Apartment Burglaries

Some burglars obtain entry to apartments by posing as door-to-door salesmen, delivery men, or strangers seeking information. When the occupant does not answer, the burglar forces his way into the apartment by jimmying a door or window or picking a lock. In general, apartment burglars are selective as to the type of property they take. Some take only money or jewelry, while the opportunist takes anything he can carry away.

House Burglaries

Burglaries of houses may occur throughout a community, but high-income neighborhoods are more frequently attacked. The proceeds are usually money, clothing, electrical appliances, furs, and jewelry. The house burglar employs many methods to gain entry, but quite frequently the welcome mat is extended by occupants who fail to lock their doors or windows properly. Some common methods of entry are:

- prying open a door or window,
- using a glass cutter to cut a hole in a pane, enabling the burglar to unlock a door or window,
- "slipping" inadequate locks with a knife blade, thin piece of metal, or plastic strip,
- finding the house key hidden under the doormat or in the mailbox, and
- knocking on the door and posing as a salesman, delivery man, or stranger seeking information.

Store Burglaries

Retail stores are prime targets of burglars. Department stores, discount stores, taverns, restaurants, supermarkets, drugstores, and dry cleaners all sustain heavy losses.

Warehouse Burglaries

Professional burglars devote considerable planning to warehouse burglaries. Given an "order" by an illegitimate business operator for a certain type and quantity of merchandise, they locate a warehouse where such merchandise is stored, then put it under surveillance to determine delivery schedules and the security of the storage facilities. A warehouse employee may be solicited to inspect the interior and point out vulnerable spots, in return for a promised commission on the sale of the stolen goods.

The Preliminary Investigation

A patrol officer responding to a burglary should proceed to the scene quietly and cautiously. The officer should be observant and look for suspicious persons and vehicles. When responding to a burglary-in-progress call, the siren and red lights are not used. In fact, the officer should drive past the address to park the police

A crime scene investigator dusts a file cabinet for fingerprints in a burglary case—after photographing it.

cruiser. The first two officers at the burglary scene should be at diagonally opposed corners of the building in order to protect one another. The exterior and interior of the burglary premises must be searched thoroughly.

The investigator must obtain such information as the type of structure burglarized, means of entry, individuals recently on the premises, property taken, and modus operandi. The preliminary investigation asks who the occupants are, whether any doors or windows were left unlocked, and whether there are any repair people in the area. A complete inventory of stolen items and their purchase value should be taken. The following investigative outline can be of assistance to officers conducting a preliminary burglary investigation. (Pena, 1982, pp. 261–262)

1. *Type of burglary.*
   a. Residence (house, single family, apartment, mobile home, etc.).
   b. Business (store, office, factory, warehouse, gas station, etc.).
   c. Occupants. Any present at time of burglary?
2. *Location.* Complete address and nearest cross street. Descrip-

tion of the residence or building (size, number of stories, color, etc.). Complete identification of resident or occupant.
3. *Date, time, and day of week reported.* When did occupants last leave location? Were all doors and windows locked and by whom? Where were the keys?
4. *Visitors:* Were there any recent visitors to premises (relatives, business associates, salesmen, utility reps, poll takers, etc.)?
5. *Entry.* Means and point of entry: evidence of forcible entry on doors, windows, locks, possible tool marks. If no evidence of forcible entry, possibility of passkey or lock-trip device (plastic strip). Photography and sketching techniques are used, with emphasis on building, point of entry, and tool marks.
6. *Prints.* Fingerprints, footprints, and tire tracks inside and outside.
7. *Property taken.* A complete list of all property taken. Special attention is given to when the missing property was last seen by the victim. If it was not seen for some time before the break-in, it may have been misplaced or taken earlier by a relative or visitor. If property that would normally be attractive to a burglar was not taken, that could be a lead. Why would the burglar limit himself to one type of property only (drugs, fur, etc.)?
8. *Modus Operandi.*
   a. Type of property attacked.
   b. Point of entry (door, window, roof, or transom on front, side, or rear of building? First, second or other floor?)
   c. Means of attack. Tool (screwdriver, crowbar, key, lock pick, ladder, ropes, brace and bit, chisel, glass cutter, etc.). On a safe burglary, was an explosive used, burning torch, combination and lock punched out, box ripped open with a bar, or combination manipulated?
   d. Date, time, and day of the week property attacked.
   e. Object of attack (anything available, or selected items?)
   f. Trademark. Assaulted victim, committed nuisance (e.g., urinated or defecated), cut telephone wires, left obscene or other notes, poisoned pets, posed as peddler or handicapped person looking for employment, used moving van or truck. Did burglar hide inside until business closed? Is burglar a ransacker who leaves mess (e.g., drawers and doors open with property and clothing scattered) or is he methodical and neat? Did burglar help himself to food or drink? Is there evidence that he was familiar with the premises? Did he use matches or leave cigarette butts?
   g. Are there other burglaries in the area with the same modus operandi?

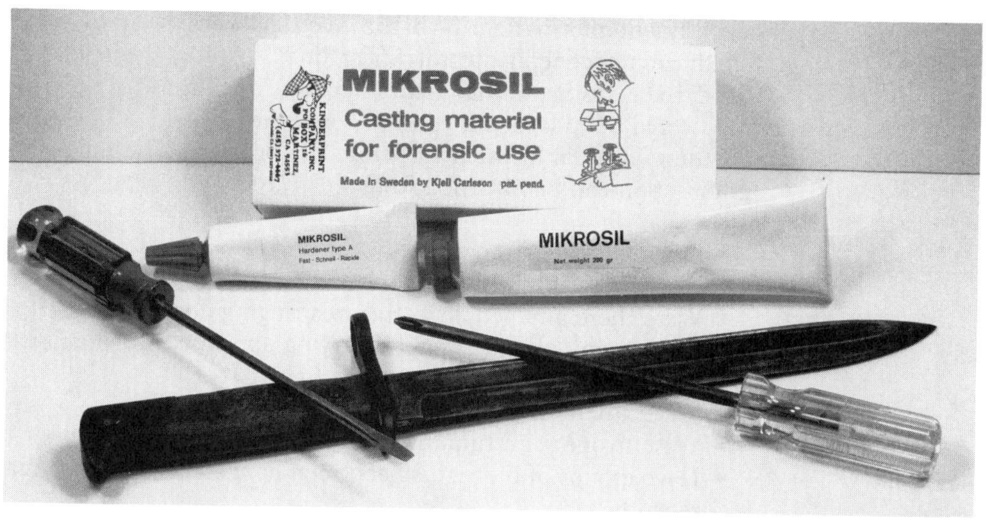

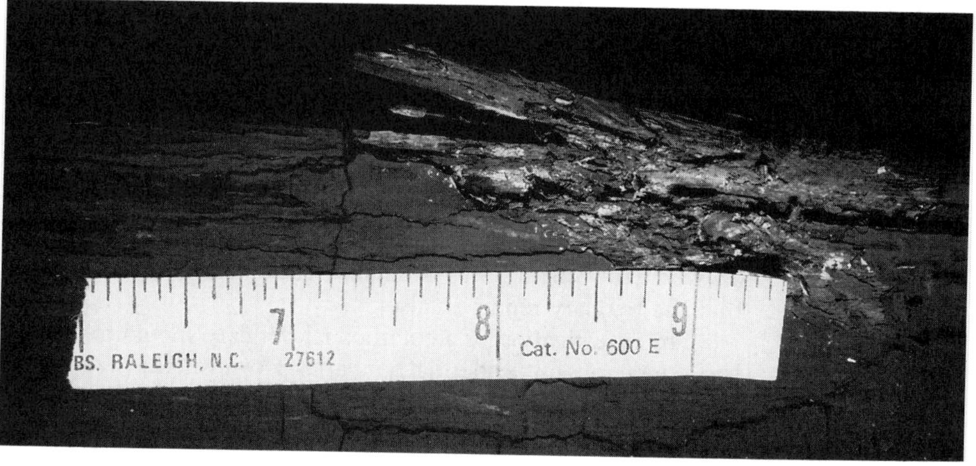

Impressions made with a casting kit aid the investigator in matching pry marks to the actual tools used in the burglary.

The Follow-Up Investigation

With residential burglaries, the follow-up investigator should first interview the officer who conducted the preliminary investigation. The interview can help the investigator better comprehend the circumstances surrounding the crime scene and provide insights about the victim.

Next, the investigator should interview the victim, recording all pertinent information. Then the investigator may want to examine the crime scene. If a patrol officer did not canvass the neighborhood, the investigator may want to do so. The purpose of the canvass would be to locate anyone who saw the break-in or observed anything unusual in the area before the burglary. The following information can be obtained from a canvass.

- Did anyone observe any strangers in the area?
- Were there any vehicles in the area that did not belong there?
- Were there any people in the area ringing doorbells?
- Did anyone observe people carrying appliances or suitcases, during or after the time of the crime?
- Were any unusual noises heard?
- Was anyone seen running from the scene?
- Have groups of teenagers been seen hanging around the area recently?
- Did anyone hear an alarm ringing?

The investigator must ascertain whether the victim owned all the property he or she claims has been stolen. A check with records or with the crime analysis unit can determine whether there has been a rash of burglaries in the area that might have inspired a false report. The investigator may also want to check the victim's insurance company to determine whether the amount of coverage was recently increased. The investigator may request receipts or ask where the property was purchased if he or she has any suspicions that the burglary report is false.

The investigation of a commercial burglary should follow the basic guidelines for residential burglaries. However, the investigator should keep in mind some major differences outlined in the NYPD's *Investigator's Guide* (Ch. 4, pp. 3–4).

Commercial establishments usually have more complicated alarm systems than residences. The bypassing of the alarm system or telltale signs that the offender had specific knowledge of how to circumvent it should be investigated. If necessary, bring in an expert to find out why the system did not function (or was not set to function).

Many businesses are in areas fairly desolate at night, so the investigator may have a problem locating witnesses. Check other commercial establishments in the area to see if they have a night shift or security personnel present during night hours. Check bus routes and any delivery personnel who may have been in the area.

Examine the scene thoroughly to see if it reveals anything about the offender. Is it possible that he stayed inside and broke out? Is there any unusual damage inside that suggests the burglary may have been a direct attack on the owner by a recently discharged or disgrunted employee? Obtain background information on problem employees.

The New York Police Department indicates that 15 to 20 percent of burglaries committed in its precincts are referred for further investigation. The NYPD trains its detectives to follow the procedures outlined in its *Investigator's Guide* (Ch. 4, pp. 5–6).

1. Gather all the information that applies to the case.
2. Analyze the data gathered and survey the crime scene.
   a. Did the crime occur the way it looks?
   b. Is the complainant covering something up?
   c. Is the value or amount of property taken excessive for the location?
3. Can you relate circumstances surrounding this burglary to other burglaries in the immediate area?
4. Can the victim or witnesses identify the offender?
5. Gather all evidence from the scene (latent prints, tool marks, cylinders from locks, etc.) and forward it to the proper unit for examination.
6. Notify the precinct sector if you have ascertained that this is part of a burglary pattern in a specific area of your precinct.
7. Check with the victim's insurance broker to find any inconsistencies in the amount of property removed from the premises.
   a. Was insurance coverage recently changed?
   b. Was an inordinate amount of property recently added to the policy?
   c. Has the victim made any recent claims?
8. If it is a commercial enterprise, find out how business has been lately. Check with:
   a. banks,
   b. insurance agency,
   c. accountant,
   d. creditors,
   e. employees, and
   f. insurance adjuster.

The top priority in burglary investigations is cases involving substantial financial and property losses. Next in line are those with good leads. Of course, cases where the victim complains that nothing is being done would receive some attention. Leads are rare in burglary cases, but when informants exist there's a good chance the case will be solved. It also increases the clearance rate when offenders plead guilty to multiple burglary charges. (Sanders, 1977, p. 151)

Safecracking

Safe burglaries are less common than expected due to the fact that, in most instances, it takes quite a lot of time to break in. Opening a safe is not an easy process. The possibility exists that employees, the victim, or the people who installed the safe are involved in the crime. Or perhaps the combination was left in an unsecured area and found by the burglar. In a safe burglary, the investigator must make certain the crime scene was properly processed. It is important to protect any tool marks found on the safe, in case suspects are later found with tools in their possession. Methods used to penetrate a safe include rip jobs, punch jobs, chop jobs, burning, and carryouts.

This safe was taken by a burglar into a hallway, where it was turned upside down and ripped open.

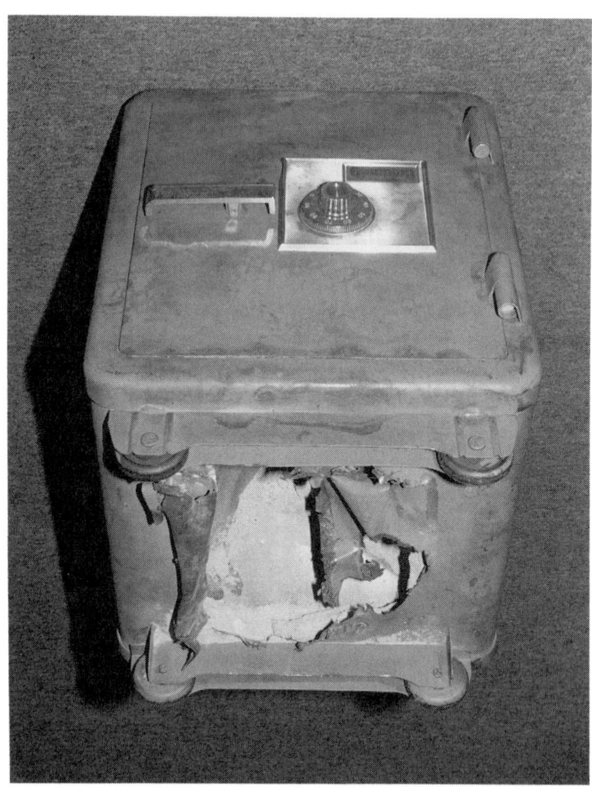

Rip Job

In a rip job, an electric drill or brace and bit are used to drill a hole in a corner of the safe. A sectional jimmy or crowbar is inserted into the hole and the corner of the safe is pried open until a point of the dial is exposed. In some cases, both upper and lower corners of the safe may be drilled and pried open.

Punch Job

Some experience and luck are required for a successful punch job. This procedure involves knocking off the dial with a sledgehammer, then holding a drift pin or center punch against the safe's spindle and striking it sharply with the hammer. This is successful only if the tumblers are on the end of the spindle; the force of the blows forces the spindle back and releases the lock. Some safes are punchproof because the tumblers are not affected by the spindle.

Chop Job

In a chop job, the thief turns the safe upside down and attacks the bottom, its weakest part. Though crude, this may be the easiest way in.

Burning

An acetylene torch is used in burning a safe, a dangerous business for the amateur. The torch is applied to the middle of the safe and a circle burned around the dial, which is then removed. This allows the safe door to be opened.

Carryout

When the safe is taken from the premises to another location where it is broken into, it is called the carryout method.

Inside Jobs and False Reports

It is not uncommon for a burglary complainant to falsify a report to collect an insurance claim. The investigator who is suspicious of the complainant can request a polygraph examination.

Preventing Burglaries

What can be done to curtail burglary? There are some precautions to take, but there is no foolproof method that will eliminate the crime. Many police departments have crime prevention officers who perform security surveys of residences and businesses. The following sections provide advice law enforcement officers can pass on to concerned citizens.

Residential Security

Residential security may be more difficult to achieve than business security. Some residents hope a barking dog will scare away intruders. Some keep dogs that will attack intruders on command. Of course, the attack dog may also be a problem for the newspaper carrier, the letter carrier, and other delivery people.

Many people believe that a gun offers them great protection against an intruder, but studies indicate that very few burglaries are prevented by homeowners' weapons. Guns at home are often used against another family member during a dispute or to commit suicide, and children often have accidents playing with them. Sometimes a home is burglarized because there are firearms on the premises and the offender wants to steal them.

The most effective precaution is secure doors and windows with locks that are not easily jimmied. Doors should have deadbolt locks and chains. Windows can be secured with key-operated locks. The use of burglar alarms may assist in preventing burglaries. One problem, however, is that citizens often misuse them. For instance, they open the front door before shutting the alarm off.

Another prevention technique that has had limited success is **operation identification,** which places ID numbers on items that might be stolen. One problem with operation identification is that different geographic areas of the country use different numbering systems. Some areas use the owner's social security number while others may use a driver's license number, making it difficult to trace items to other parts of the country. Even keeping a record of serial numbers is not always helpful, because some companies repeat serial numbers on similar items.

People who go away for a time on vacation or business can take precautions that minimize their chances of being burglarized. (IACP, 1975, pp. 107–108)

- Individuals should not publicize the fact that they are leaving on a trip. Announcements in newspapers are definitely unwise. People should also be cautious about where they discuss the trip and make sure important details are not overheard by strangers.
- Lock all doors, windows, and screens before leaving the house.

- Do not draw all blinds and shades. Leave windows partially uncovered to give the appearance of normal living.
- Do not leave lights burning continuously. This is deceptive only for a few hours each evening. The rest of the time, it advertises that the house is unoccupied. Use a timing device to turn lights on and off at appropriate intervals.
- Make arrangements to have the lawn cut regularly during the summer and snow shoveled during the winter.
- Halt all mail, newspapers, milk, and other routine delivery services during the absence.
- Request local police to check the house. Inform them of your whereabouts and tell them who locally possesses a key and has permission to enter the premises during your absence.

Business Security

Apprehending burglars is difficult. If a burglar is not arrested at the crime scene, he has an excellent chance of avoiding arrest and conviction. But since burglaries are crimes of opportunity, they can usually be prevented. Business establishments can implement various prevention techniques to reduce their chances of being burglarized.

For example, secure doors, windows, skylights, and all other possible points of entry. The premises should have adequate internal and external lighting. A police officer riding on patrol can visually check the interior of a business when it's lighted. Adequate lighting can discourage a burglar and cause him to move on to an unlighted business establishment.

Business owners should not allow large amounts of cash to remain on the premises overnight. They should be deposited in the bank. The cash register should be left open. Another important security feature business owners should consider is a burglar alarm. Depending on the establishment, the owner could place bar grills on the windows and doors.

The police might recommend that business owners have the security needs of their establishment surveyed. Figure 15-1 is a sample security survey for both businesses and residences.

Encountering a Burglar

What should people do when they encounter a burglar in their home or workplace? The following section describes three situations and explains how the police should advise citizens to respond.

In the first situation, you return home to find something that looks suspicious. Perhaps a window is opened that you know was left shut.

Do not enter the house. Go to a neighbor's house or some other nearby point and call the police. If possible, watch your house from a distance and obtain a description of anyone leaving it. Observe the burglar's vehicle and attempt to obtain a license number.

In the second situation, the burglary takes place at night while you are in the house.

Do not directly confront the burglar. Do not shout "Who's

FIGURE 15-1: Security Survey Guidelines

Business Establishment

- I. Possible Maximum Loss Through Criminal Attack (Assessment of Targets)
  - A. Personal safety
  - B. Cash
  - C. Merchandise
  - D. Damage factors
- II. Direct Protection of Targets
  - A. Safe
    1. Rating
    2. Anchored
    3. Lighted
    4. Visible from street or mall
  - B. Cash Registers
    1. Visible from street or mall
    2. Open at night
    3. Limited cash accumulation
    4. Locked when unattended
    5. Limited access
  - C. Merchandise
    1. Controlled storage room
    2. Removed from windows
    3. Controlled displays
    4. Inventory accountability
    5. Identifiable tags or marking system
  - D. Deposits
    1. Prepared in protected area
    2. Made daily
    3. Armored service
    4. Made by two or more employees
    5. Varied times and routes
- III. Employee Training
  - A. Shoplifting
  - B. Robbery
  - C. Checks and credit cards
  - D. Internal controls (opening and closing procedures, cash handling, purchasing and receiving, etc.)
- IV. Building Surfaces
  - A. Front, left side, right side, rear
    1. Construction
    2. Doors
    3. Windows
    4. Vents
    5. Lighting
  - B. Roof
    1. Doors
    2. Skylights
    3. Vents and ducts
    4. Lighting
  - C. Floor
    1. Construction
    2. Cellar
    3. Ongrade
    4. Post and lift
  - D. Key control
    1. Changes as necessary
    2. Accountability
- V. Outside and Perimeter
  - A. Trees and shrubs
  - B. Loading docks
  - C. Trash storage

there?" and rush out of the bedroom. Turn on a light in the bedroom. Move around, make noise, and pretend to talk to someone in order to scare the burglar off. Give him time to get away. Gradually move to other rooms, turning on lights and making noise. When you reach the telephone, call the police. Return to your bedroom or another room that can be locked and wait for the police.

You awaken during the night to find a burglar in the bedroom. This situation could be very dangerous. Do not scream or attempt to attack the burglar. Stay in bed and pretend to be asleep. When the burglar has left the room, proceed as in the second situation,

FIGURE 15-1: *(Continued)*

Business Establishment

- D. Roof access
- E. Fences and gates
- F. Police access

VI. Surveillance
- A. Lighting
- B. Visibility
- C. Cameras

VII. Intrusion Detection
- A. Sensors
- B. Control
- C. Announcement
- D. Response

Residence

I. Possible and Probable Maximum Losses Through Criminal Attack (Assessment of Targets)
- A. Personal safety
- B. Cash
- C. High-value personal possessions
- D. Damage factors

II. Direct Protection of Targets
- A. Cash storage

III. Family Member Training
- A. Telephone/door answering procedures
- B. Locking responsibilities
- C. Intruder-in-the-house procedures

IV. Building Surfaces
- A. Front, left side, right side, rear
  1. Construction
  2. Doors
  3. Windows
  4. Vents
  5. Lighting
- B. Roof
  1. Construction
  2. Doors
  3. Skylights
  4. Vents and ducts
  5. Lighting
- C. Floor
  1. Construction
  2. Cellar
  3. Ongrade
  4. Post and lift
- D. Key control
  1. Changed since occupancy
  2. Accountability

V. Outside and Perimeter
- A. Trees, shrubs, hedges
- B. Roof/garage/basement access
- C. Fences and gates
- D. Visibility

VI. Surveillance
- A. Lighting
- B. Visibility

VII. Intrusion Detection
- A. Sensors
- B. Controls
- C. Announcement
- D. Response

Source: Adapted from NCPI training handout. Courtesy of the National Crime Prevention Institute, University of Louisville.

gradually turning on lights and making noise. Give the burglar time to escape and call the police as soon as possible.

Burglary Investigation Decision Model

The concept of screening burglary cases before assigning them to investigators originated at the Stanford Research Institute in 1972. The SRI model was based on burglary case data from six police departments in Alameda County, California. SRI found that guidelines were needed to assist investigators in preliminary and follow-up investigations. Large police agencies, buried in crime reports, expressed an interest in an evaluation method such as case screening to determine which burglaries should receive follow-up investigations.

SRI developed a case screening model that is crime specific and statistically derived. The model contains 25 information elements. Using discriminate analysis, SRI found six elements that led to the arrest of a suspect. When the model was used in four police agencies for 500 burglary cases, it accurately predicted the case outcome between 67 and 92 percent of the time. Figure 15–2 is SRI's burglary decision model.

In the late 1970s, the Police Executive Research Forum replicated the SRI model and found it very accurate. The PERF study suggests that the SRI model can be adjusted to fit the specific needs of police agencies. The model conserves resources by allowing investigators to concentrate on cases that are solvable. PERF considers the SRI model a decision-making tool that gives police managers the information they need to allocate resources for the investigation of burglaries most effectively. PERF recommends that every police agency establish a case screening method for burglary investigations and develop (if it has the resources) its own statistically weighted screening model. (Eck, 1979, pp. 3–9)

Summary

Burglary can be traced to common law, when it was classified as a crime against occupancy and habitation. In the modern era, burglary is classified as a statutory offense. The Modern Penal Code defines burglary as when a person "enters a building or occupied structure, or separately secured or occupied portion thereof, with purpose to commit a crime there, unless the premises are at the time open to the public or the actor is licensed or privileged to

FIGURE 15-2: SRI Burglary Investigation Decision Model

Information Elements	Weights
Estimated Range of Time of Occurrence	
Less than one hour	5
One to twelve hours	1
Twelve to twenty-four hours	0.3
More than twenty-four hours	0
Witness's report of offense	7
On-view report of offense	1
Usable fingerprints	7
Suspect information developed (description or name)	9
Vehicle description	0.1
Other	0
Total Score	

Instructions
1. Circle the weights for each information element that is present in the incident report.
2. Add the circled weights.
3. If the sum is 10 or less, suspend the case. Otherwise, assign the case for follow-up investigation.

Source: Adapted from Eck, *Managing Case Assignment: The Burglary Investigation Model.* Police Executive Research Forum, 1979, p. 6. Reprinted with permission of Police Executive Research Forum.

enter. It is an affirmative defense to prosecution for burglary that the building or structure was abandoned."

Burglary is an act against property or a place. It is a crime of opportunity. As a behavior, the act of burglary involves "needs to be met, opportunities to meet them, perceptions of these opportunities, means to take advantage of such opportunities, satisfactions when needs are met, decisions about alternative routes to need-meeting, and the existence of outside interference in the process."

The nature of burglary, coupled with the public's lack of knowledge of how to control it, leads to minimal control and arrests for this offense. Burglary has the highest frequency of felony crimes and the lowest clearance rate for property crimes. In burglaries that are solved, the vast majority of arrests occur within 48 hours after the burglary is reported. The clearance rate decreases over a 30-day period.

During the 1970s, Thomas Reppetto conducted a study profiling burglars as: the juvenile offender, the 18- to 25-year-old offender, the white offender, the black offender, the drug user, and the nondrug user. Marilyn Walsh, with detective input, divided burglars into six types: the good, known, young, juvenile, booster, and junkie burglar.

Patrol officers should respond to burglary calls cautiously. Their preliminary investigation should determine a complete inventory of items taken, the type of structure burglarized, the means of entry, what individuals were recently on the premises, who the occupants are, whether any doors or windows were left unlocked, and what the burglar's modus operandi was. The follow-up investigator should interview the officer who conducted the preliminary investigation, interview the victim, examine the crime scene, and canvass the neighborhood for witnesses who have not yet come forward.

The International Association of Chiefs of Police divides burglary into two categories, residential and commercial. Residential protection from burglary may be more difficult to achieve than business security. Methods used to prevent burglaries include using effective door and window locks, installing alarms, and placing identification numbers on items that might be stolen. Although prevention is the first line of defense, police departments should advise concerned citizens of what to do if they encounter a burglar.

The Stanford Research Institute originated a screening method for determining which burglary cases are solvable enough to warrant a follow-up investigation. The Police Executive Research Forum replicated the SRI model, found it very accurate, and suggested that individual police agencies adjust the SRI model to fit their needs.

Key Terms

booster
burglary
exceptional clearance
junkie
operation identification

Review Questions

1. Define burglary.
2. Explain the patterns of burglary.
3. What is meant by burglary profiles?
4. What are the six types of burglars?
5. Explain the IACP's classification of burglaries.
6. What occurs during the preliminary investigation of a burglary? The follow-up investigation?
7. What is a rip job? A punch job? A chop job? A carryout job?
8. What are some of the procedures citizens can follow to protect themselves from burglary?
9. What advice can you give a citizen who encounters a burglar?
10. Explain the SRI burglary decision model.

References

Bennett WW, Hess K: *Criminal Investigation*, ed. 2. New York, NY: West Publishing Co., 1987.

Eck J: *Managing Case Assignment: The Burglary Investigation Decision Model Replication*. Washington, DC: Police Executive Research Forum, 1979.

Greenberg B, Yu O, Land K: *Enhancement of the Investigative Function*. Springfield, VA: National Technical Information Service, 1973.

International Association of Chiefs of Police: *Criminal Investigation: Specific Offenses*, ed. 2. Gaithersburg, MD: IACP, 1975.

New York Police Dept.: *Investigator's Guide*. New York, NY: NYPD, n.d.

Pena M: *Practical Criminal Investigation*. Casta Mesa, CA: Custom Publishing Co., 1982.

Pope C: *Crime Specific Analysis: The Characteristics of Burglary Incidents*. Washington, DC: U.S. Government Printing Office, 1975.

Reppetto TA: *Residential Crime*. Cambridge, MA: Billinger Publishing Co., 1974.

Sanders WB: *Detective Work*. New York, NY: The Free Press, 1977.

Scarr HA: *Patterns of Burglary*. Washington, DC: U.S. Government Printing Office, 1973.

Walsh ME: *The Fence*. Westport, CT: Greenwood Press, 1977.

CHAPTER 16

Larceny

The laws that govern property in the United States can be traced to medieval England. **Real property** has become synonymous with real estate, while **personal property** consists of money, items, and objects. Personal property can include pets, cars, televisions, and most other items. Most people in the United States own property. The concept of personal property includes "not only a physical or representative object, but also the right to own, use, sell, or dispose of it as regulated by law." (Grillot and Schuber, 1989, p. 46)

Larceny-theft is depriving another person of property without justification. It encompasses withholding property permanently or temporarily or disposing of it without any chance of the owner recovering it. According to the *Uniform Crime Report*, approximately 60 percent of larceny-theft offenses are property crimes. It is the most common of the eight major crime index offenses reported to the police. It accounts for approximately 55 percent of all arrests for crime index offenses. Almost half of the arrested persons are under 21 years of age and almost one-third under 18. Nationwide, about 24 percent of larceny-thefts are cleared. The *Uniform Crime Report* defines larceny-theft as "the unlawful taking, carrying, leading, or riding away of property from the possession or constructive possession of another. It includes crimes such as shoplifting, pocket-picking, purse-snatching, thefts from motor vehicles, thefts of motor vehicle parts and accessories, bicycle thefts, etc., in which no use of force, violence, or fraud occurs. In the Uniform Crime Reporting Program, this crime category does not include embezzlement, con games, forgery, and worthless checks."

Thieves steal money, automobiles, televisions, clothing, bicycles, and other property that belongs to other people. They may sell the stolen property or keep it for themselves. Larceny-theft is a crime based on cunning and skill and may require planning by the professional thief. It can also be a crime of opportunity, especially if committed by amateurs. Kleptomaniacs, who are compulsive thieves, are responsible for only a small number of offenses.

Most states divide larceny-theft into two categories based on the value of the property stolen. **Grand larceny** is a felony. In most states, stealing something worth more than $100 is grand larceny. **Petty larceny**, a misdemeanor, is usually the charge for property valued at $100 or less. In most states, the keeping or selling of found property is also a crime.

Investigating a Larceny-Theft

In the preliminary investigation of a larceny-theft, the investigating officer examines the crime scene, collects physical evidence, interviews the victim and witnesses, and attempts to develop suspects based on the modus operandi. What methods do the suspects use to commit their crimes? Computerized records can be scanned to identify the M.O.s of past crimes.

Stealing money and property usually requires some planning and skill. The offender must plan the theft and dispose of the property. The type of property stolen can be a major clue. Some thieves specialize in specific items such as money, jewelry, furs, televisions, or government bonds.

The follow-up investigation continues where the initial investigation leaves off. Leads are developed, suspects identified, and stolen property recovered. Figure 16–1 shows the steps to follow in investigating a theft.

The investigative techniques to be used in a specific larceny-theft case can be determined by the type of theft committed. Investigators should record the following data during the initial stages of the investigation. In minor or uncomplicated larceny-theft cases, not all of the information is necessary. (O'Hara, 1973, pp. 333–336)

- Date and hour of the theft. If this is unknown, establish when the stolen object was last seen and when the theft was discovered.
- A complete list and description of the missing property. If several witnesses can offer this information, obtain it independently from each to verify its accuracy.
- The location of the property immediately before the larceny, places the property was previously located, and places searched.
- Reasons for placing the property in the location described.

FIGURE 16-1: Investigation of Thefts

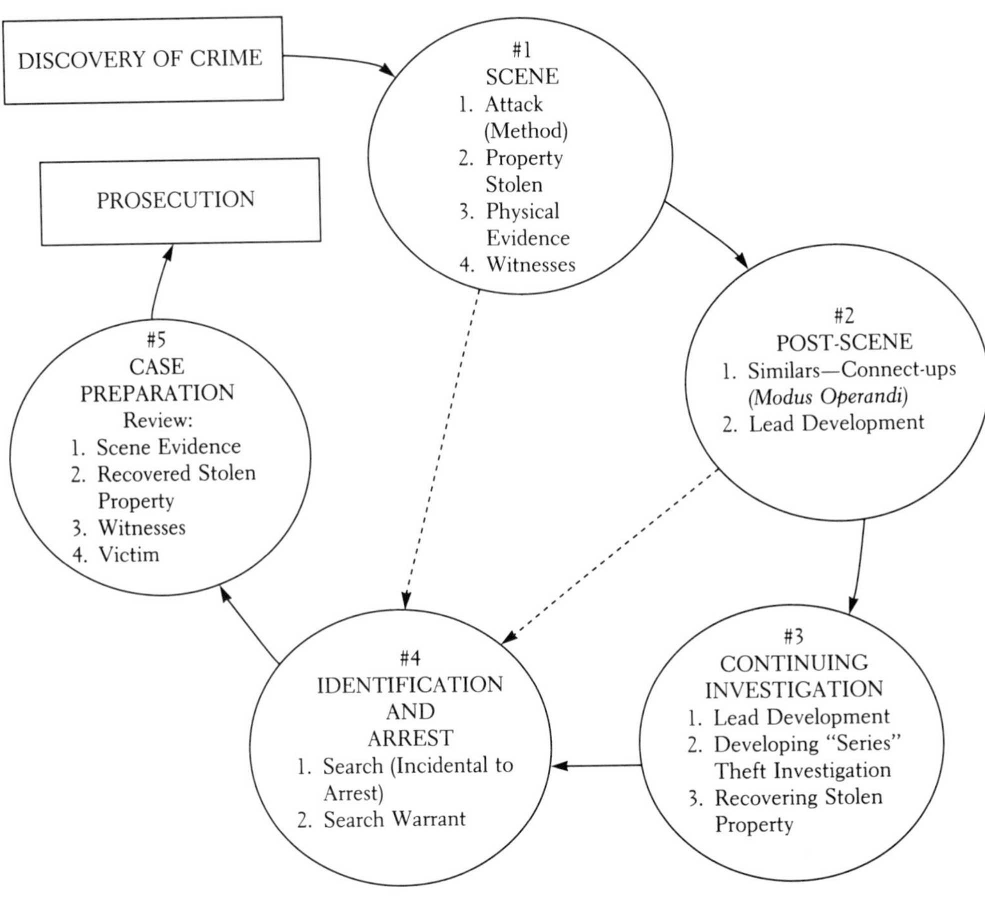

Source: International Association of Chiefs of Police, *Criminal Investigation: Basic Procedures,* 4th ed., 1975, p. 4.

The investigator should reflect on the logic of placing the property in this location and on the presence or absence of safeguards.

- Identity of the person who first discovered the loss. How did it come to his or her attention? Was this the logical person to make the discovery? If not, who was? Who witnessed the discovery?
- Persons who knew of the existence of the property.
- Persons who knew the location of the property.
- Persons who had access to the property.

- Movements of persons who had access shortly before and after the loss in cases where the time interval is reasonably short.
- In commercial establishments, persons absent from work.
- Ownership of the property: the true owner, the person who had possession at the time of theft, and the person responsible for the property.
- Proof of ownership, custody, or responsibility.
- Estimated value of the property. Bills of sale are best, but where documentary evidence is absent, the approximate date of purchase and the identity of the vendor.
- Suspects named by the owner or others. Reasons for their suspicions. Employees exhibiting unusual behavior within the last month.
- Reconstruction of the larceny: modus operandi, means of access, time, method of concealing the larceny. In larceny by false pretense, the conversations and transactions that took place between the perpetrator and the victim or other parties.
- Character of property, salability, uses, and convertibility.
- Possible markets for the property.
- Interrogation of each suspect: activities before and after the larceny; when they were last in the vicinity, persons who can verify their alibis, financial circumstances (present indebtedness and contemplated investments or purchases), and relations with the owner.
- Records: previous larceny complaints made by the victims, history of periodic or systematic thefts, employees with police records, and background of suspects.
- Interviews of building employees and others who may have observed persons approaching the area containing the property at unusual times or in a peculiar manner. Complete physical descriptions of any suspects they describe.
- Physical evidence such as latent fingerprints, shoe prints, articles of clothing, or similar traces at the scene.

Figure 16–2 shows which kinds of larceny occur most frequently.

Auto Theft

More than 1,600,000 motor vehicle thefts occur in the United States every year. The estimated value of motor vehicles stolen tops $8 billion annually and the average value of a stolen vehicle is about $5,000. About 80 percent of vehicles stolen are automobiles, 15 percent are buses or trucks, and 5 percent, motorcycles, motorscoot-

FIGURE 16–2: Larceny Analysis*

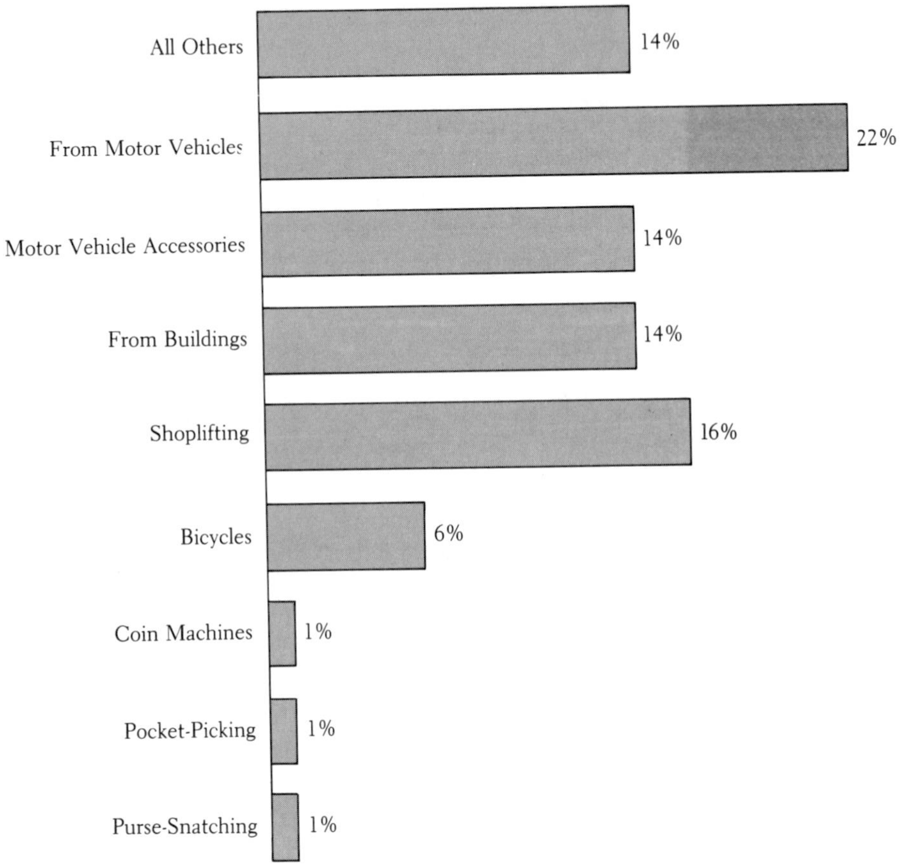

All Others 14%
From Motor Vehicles 22%
Motor Vehicle Accessories 14%
From Buildings 14%
Shoplifting 16%
Bicycles 6%
Coin Machines 1%
Pocket-Picking 1%
Purse-Snatching 1%

*1991 figures.

Source: *Uniform Crime Report,* 1991.

ers, and snowmobiles. According to the *Uniform Crime Report,* approximately 15 percent of motor vehicle thefts reported nationwide are cleared. More than 200,000 arrests are made each year. Sixty percent of those arrested for motor vehicle theft are under 21 years of age and 40 percent are under the age of eighteen. Motor vehicle thefts are up 29 percent since 1987. For this same period the rate per 100,000 inhabitants has increased 24 percent. (*Uniform Crime Report,* 1991)

The National Insurance Crime Bureau

In 1992 in an attempt by the insurance industry to control and eventually stop the increase in vehicle thefts and insurance claims, the Auto Theft Bureau and the Insurance Crime Prevention Institute were combined to create the **National Insurance Crime Bureau (NICB).** The NICB united the investigative, informational, data gathering, and educational operations of the two organizations to take action against vehicle theft and insurance theft. Further, the insurance industry pays an estimated $17 billion annually in exaggerated and fraudulent claims; 10 percent of property-casualty claims are either inflated or fabricated. NICB assists police agencies in targeting white collar professionals and career criminals who make a living from the insurance industry. Callers can receive rewards of up to $1,000 for anonymous tips leading to the arrest and indictment of individuals perpetrating insurance fraud and vehicle theft. Information also leading to the prevention of these criminal activities will be considered for a reward. (NICB, *Information*, 1992)

Vehicle Theft Trends

In a recent study, the National Insurance Crime Bureau compared data on stolen car models from 1985 to 1991. The data was obtained from insurance members that comprise 95 percent of the market. In 1991, more than 280,000 auto thefts were reported. The NICB found that the same models popular with thieves in 1986 were still popular in 1991. The 1989 Mitsubishi Starion was the most stolen model based on the number of thefts per thousand. The Chevrolet Camaro and Monte Carlo, Pontiac Firebird, Buick Regal and the Toyota MR2 were the most popular models. The NICB study reported that older vehicles actually were more popular with thieves than newer models. Since auto larceny is a crime of opportunity, the owner can remove much of the opportunity. The more time the thief must spend on committing the crime, the greater are his chances of getting caught.

Approximately 15 percent of reported motor vehicle thefts are fraudulent. Auto-related frauds are a principal form of white-collar crime. During the 1990s a new form of auto theft began to occur known as carjacking. Carjacking is the taking of a motor vehicle from a person by force, the threat of force, or intimidation. Another variation of this crime, the "bump and run" happens when thieves stage a minor rear-end collision. The surprised motorist gets out of the vehicle to inspect damages. One thief robs him while the second drives off with his automobile.

There could be several explanations for this. Vehicle manufacturers and law enforcement personnel estimate that it takes three years for auto thieves to solve a deterrence system. If this assumption is correct, then we can expect middle-aged cars are more likely to be stolen since auto thieves have solved anti-theft devices installed on these cars. Owners are less likely to install anti-theft devices as cars get older. The key point of the NICB study is that the top new stolen cars change little as the cars age. (*Crime Control Digest,* August 3, 1992, pp. 7–8)

The Savannah (Georgia) Police Department's Auto Theft Bureau reports that most automobiles stolen are late 1970s to late 1980s models. Thieves prefer big cars like an Oldsmobile 88, which have enough horsepower to allow the thieves to give the police a run for their money. The Chevrolet Caprice is the most popular car stolen in Savannah. Four-door cars are more popular than two-door cars simply because passengers in the back seat can quickly get out of the vehicle when running from the police. The Savannah police indicated that vehicles that were easy to jump start, such as General Motors products, were most likely to be stolen. The usual method of breaking into the vehicle was to smash a window with a screwdriver or a porcelain chip. Generally porcelain chips are broken from sparkplugs and attached to a handle of some sort, such as string or wire, and banged against the vehicle glass. This method reduces the time, noise and chance of detection. Another method of breaking into the vehicle is to use a flatiron to pry open the door lock.

Categories of Automotive Thefts

Automotive thefts can be divided by criminal motive into the following four categories (IACP, 1973, pp.134–135):

1. *Joy riding.* This category of theft accounts for the majority of reported stolen automobiles. Youthful offenders who steal for transportation or racing dominate the classification.
2. *Use in Crime.* Criminals steal automobiles to provide transportation to the scene of other crimes and to reduce the possibility of identification. Opportunity and type of automobile required determine the methods employed by the criminal to start the engine.

   To further reduce the elements of identification the criminal auto thief may alter the license plates. The interior dome light and license plate light may be removed or broken to prevent recognition. The trunk lock may also be broken. The rear

FIGURE 16-3: Top Fifty Stolen Cars

Rank	Year	Make	Model	NICB Thefts	Prod.	Thefts per 1,000
1	1989	Mitsubishi	Starion	13	159	81,761
2	1987	Pontiac	Firebird	1,858	80,414	23,105
3	1988	Mitsubishi	Starion	90	3,945	22,814
4	1988	Pontiac	Firebird	1,280	56,449	22,675
5	1987	Mitsubishi	Starion	144	6,845	21,037
6	1987	Chevy	Camaro	2,685	128,056	20,967
7	1988	Chevy	Camaro	1,857	90,484	20,523
8	1989	Chrysler	Conquest	100	4,953	20,190
9	1985	Pontiac	Firebird	1,691	86,221	19,612
10	1989	Plymouth	Horizon	81	4,164	19,452
11	1987	Chevy	Monte Carlo	1,434	74,738	19,187
12	1986	Chevy	Camaro	3,317	178,870	18,544
13	1986	Pontiac	Firebird	1,832	100,210	18,282
14	1988	Mitsubishi	Tredia	63	3,514	17,928
15	1986	Toyota	MR2	605	34,084	17,750
16	1986	Honda	Prelude	528	30,200	17,483
17	1988	Chrysler	Lebaron	447	26,346	16,967
18	1987	Toyota	MR2	335	19,782	16,935
19	1988	Chevy	Monte Carlo	466	28,603	16,292
20	1987	Buick	Regal	986	61,659	15,991
21	1988	Alfa Romeo	Milano	28	1,870	14,973
22	1985	Mazda	RX-7	864	58,848	14,682
23	1989	Volkswagen	Cabriolet	153	10,531	14,529
24	1987	Porsche	928	32	2,223	14,395
25	1989	Alfa Romeo	Milano	7	494	14,170
26	1988	Volkswagen	Cabriolet	153	10,931	13,997
27	1986	Chevy	Monte Carlo	1,569	113,394	13,837
28	1988	Chrysler	Conquest	126	9,581	13,151
29	1986	Buick	Regal	1,140	87,064	13,094
30	1988	Volkswagen	Scirocco	48	3,690	13,008
31	1985	Chevy	Camaro	2,072	167,309	12,384
32	1987	Volkswagen	Scirocco	108	8,815	12,252
33	1988	Porsche	911	80	6,532	12,247
34	1985	Pontiac	Grand Prix	728	59,790	12,176
35	1985	Buick	Regal	1,455	120,772	12,047
36	1988	Honda	Prelude	902	77,601	11,624
37	1989	Hyundai	Sonata	397	34,756	11,422
38	1987	Pontiac	Grand Prix	185	16,543	11,183
39	1985	Chevy	Monte Carlo	1,248	113,847	10,962
40	1987	Olds	Cutlass Supreme	1,246	114,013	10,929
41	1987	Mazda	626, MX6	932	85,385	10,915
42	1987	Chrysler	Conquest	163	15,014	10,857
43	1986	Mazda	626, MX6	1,012	94,126	10,752
44	1985	Toyota	Supra	285	27,442	10,386
45	1989	Honda	Prelude	681	65,737	10,359
46	1985	Olds	Cutlass Supreme	2,412	234,470	10,287
47	1987	Alfa Romeo	Milano	60	5,840	10,274
48	1985	Cadillac	Eldorado	735	75,215	9,772
49	1988	Pontiac	Fiero	246	25,371	9,696
50	1986	Mitsubishi	Starion	53	5,532	9,581

Source: Courtesy of the National Insurance Crime Bureau

seat cushions may be removed to allow room for the proceeds of the crime.

3. *Stripping.* Stripping is removing parts and accessories for personal use or for resale. Engines, "four on the floor" transmissions, radios, etc., find a ready market for the youthful car enthusiast or the unscrupulous auto parts dealer.
4. *Resale.* The recovery rate of stolen automobiles has been gradually decreasing over the past year. This is attributed to the increasing activity of organized car theft rings. Tens of thousands of cars stolen each year are never recovered by the police nor returned to their rightful owners. Professional car thieves have the organization, skill, equipment, and facilities not only to steal automobiles but to alter and sell them as well.

Joyriders are usually in their midteens to early twenties. They usually commit the offense with companions and depend upon an opportunity to steal; for example, an owner leaving keys in the vehicle. The joyrider looks for recreational pleasures and appears to be nonpractical.

The Savannah Police Department's Auto Theft Bureau reported to the author that young males are responsible for most of the stolen vehicles in Savannah. They usually range in age from fifteen to nineteen years old; the youngest offender was twelve. The youngster steals for high-speed thrills, entertainment, and for peer recognition and with no monetary gain in mind. McCaghy and Cernkovick claim that to the joyrider symbolism appears important—cars are stolen for what they mean and not for what they do. (McCaghy and Cernkovick, 1987, p.205)

Automobiles are often used to commit serious crimes such as robberies. They can also be used for rapes, kidnapping and burglaries. The Auto Theft Bureau of Savannah's police department reports that stolen vehicles are often used for robberies or muggings. Rarely are occupants of stolen vehicles apprehended before the crime has been committed unless an informant notifies the police. Normally, the criminal uses a stolen vehicle for only a short period of time since he does not want to be identified. An offender apprehended in a stolen automobile after the commission of another crime will usually be prosecuted only for the more serious crime and not for the stolen vehicle.

Chop shops are places where motor vehicles are stripped or disassembled for their parts. A car thief may get $500 to steal a car and the chop-shop operator may make $2,500 selling parts from the vehicle. Automobile parts can be cut with torches or the parts can be altered, so they cannot be specifically identified. Chop-shop

A New York police officer inspects the motor and front end of an expensive sports car after a raid on a chop shop. This particular criminal operation involved hundreds of new cars and taxicabs.

operators have minimal costs. All they need is an old garage or barn with sufficient work space. They often use the **long line,** a communications network that connects many salvage yards and body repair shops. Whenever a specific part is needed anyone connected to the long line can call another yard and place an order.

There are also **steal-to-order** businesses that will steal vehicles on order. These thieves maintain indexes of automobiles that have the highest black market value. The commercial thief logs the popular model vehicle and when he gets an order he knows where to go to deliver his order. Law enforcement authorities are recognizing that profits from professional vehicle theft rings and chop-shop operations can be a major source of revenue for financing other criminal enterprises. (NATP, 1987, p.24)

Auto repair shops and body shops intent on stealing a vehicle will duplicate the key to the ignition while the automobile is being repaired. This occurs not only in Savannah but throughout the country. Savannah recently uncovered a stolen car ring that operated this way. The auto-thief ring not only stole cars but committed robberies and burglaries using their stolen vehicles. In addition, the ring's leader had a contract with a local auto rental company to repair all vehicles that had broken windows or glass. At the same time a local glass repair shop was burglarized and had car window shields and auto glass stolen. This stolen car ring made a 100 percent profit on this deal, breaking the windows with the auto rental company they had a contract with and replacing the windows with stolen glass.

Automobiles stolen by professionals are rarely recovered. The thieves are very difficult to detect and prosecute. The professional knows how to steal cars and how to alter them, and he also knows what documents are needed to resell the vehicle. The professional auto thief employs others to perform the actual stealing. Alterations are made to the stolen vehicle such as changing seat covers and altering serial numbers. When the mechanical alterations and documents of the automobile are completed, then the vehicle is sold to an individual, a used car dealer, or at a public auction.

Auto Theft Reported to Police

When an automobile theft is reported, a police officer writes a report and tries to determine the circumstances surrounding the reported theft. After establishing that an automobile theft actually took place, all pertinent information about the automobile must be obtained. This includes year, make, model, color, any unusual features, or dents. A common error of inexperienced officers is to hurry the information-gathering process. The officer must maintain an accurate and complete report relating to the fundamentals of the automobile theft. When a description of the stolen vehicle has been obtained, it is called in to the dispatcher.

The Savannah Police Department Auto Theft Bureau reports that many vehicles are reported stolen when they are actually traded for illegal services. An individual visiting a prostitute may trade his vehicle for the services. Another individual may trade his vehicle for a $25 piece of crack cocaine. There are police reports of cases where a person will pick up a perfect stranger, go into a convenience store with the keys in the ignition and come out to find his vehicle gone. This suggests a trade; who would pick up a hitchhiker and go to the convenience store and leave keys in the ignition?

Another example of a reported stolen motor vehicle occurs when a vehicle owner with a bad debt who cannot make the payments on his or her vehicle sells it for $1,000 with the expectation that the new owner will take over the payments. The new owner fails to make payments and the original owner asks the police to get the vehicle. Or, if unable to make loan payments, an owner may steal his or her own vehicle, strip it for the parts, and sell them to a salvage company. They will then burn the vehicle, destroying all fingerprints and trace evidence. The Savannah Auto Theft Bureau reports they receive at least one report of this type of offense a month.

Theft-by-conversion constitutes another type of crime whereby the police are used as a collection agency. Small automobile rental companies report vehicles stolen when they are not returned to them. A question exists as to when the vehicle should be returned since the contract does not specify. In another type of offense, after the drivers no longer use the vehicle they arrange for it to be stolen and vandalized.

Searching for a Stolen Vehicle

When searching for a stolen vehicle, it is best to start at the scene of the crime and to work out in a circular pattern until a large portion of the neighborhood has been covered. (This method can be extremely useful when the driver has merely misplaced his vehicle.) Law enforcement officers have developed techniques for recognizing stolen vehicles. There are two kinds of abnormalities that attract attention to a stolen vehicle: "(1) The extremes in driver behavior and (2) the physical characteristics of the car resulting from damage sustained at the time of the theft or from attempts made to disguise its identity." (*Criminal Investigation*, 1973, p.147) The International Association of Chiefs of Police has developed a checklist to assist officers in locating stolen vehicles (IACP, pp.150–151):

1. When searching for a stolen vehicle, always be alert for the traffic violator, the reckless driver, and in some instances, the very cautious driver. Frequently, the cautious driver is driving a stolen vehicle and is attempting to avoid undue attention.
2. Be suspicious of the driver who answers questions that have not been asked. He may be trying to divert your attention from signs that indicate the vehicle is stolen.
3. Check the key in the ignition lock—it may be a dummy key with no cuttings.
4. Check the ignition lock. The cylinder may have been removed and the ignition turned on by the movement of the contact disc within the lock case.
5. Ask the suspect driver to turn off the motor and then try to restart it. There may be a jumper at the back of the ignition

lock or there may be a substitute lock connected to the wire loom. In either case, the operator will have to reach for the substitute lock, or jumper to restart the engine.

6. Check the operation of the ignition key in the door lock. (Some foreign cars and older models need only one key for ignition and door.)
7. Compare the name on the operator's license with the names on the various papers in the glove compartment or the vehicle registration card.
8. If a license check has been made, compare the names on the operator's license with that of the legal owner.
9. Examine the license plates to determine if they are affixed securely.
10. Be alert for signs of forced entry: broken vent glass, scratch marks along the door, and the like.
11. Examine the **vehicle identification number (VIN)** to determine if it has been changed or altered.
12. Keep in mind locations where stolen automobiles have been found in the past.
13. Stolen automobiles are not always recovered on the street; they are sometimes recovered in garages, parking lots, or shopping centers. Check these areas whenever possible.

Police Practices

During the last several years automobile thefts have increased substantially throughout the country. To curtail the automobile thefts, the city of Colorado Springs created the **Reduced Auto Theft Unit (RATU)**. To obtain a better understanding of the problem that faced the unit, they had the Crime Analysis Unit (CAU) conduct a detailed analysis of auto thefts. The CAU found that auto thefts were usually committed by juveniles or young adults.

With the information obtained from the Crime Analysis Unit the RATU developed a number of innovative investigative techniques. One technique resulted in working pattern cases "backwards." An individual or group of known auto thieves fitting a specific pattern would be identified and link analysis used on auto thieves and their associates and on auto gangs. A second technique involved special concentration on the most popular target vehicles because these cases usually involve the career criminal. The officers of the unit would work the hours when the most vehicles were stolen and would interrogate suspects immediately after their arrest. A third technique required close monitoring of likely distributors for stolen parts, accessories and vehicles. Tape decks, radios, cellular phones, and CD players are all popular stolen accessories.

In follow-up investigations by the RATU detectives track every reported auto theft case to insure that proper attention has been given. They inspect salvage yards for stolen vehicles, and an auto theft investigator attends all court proceedings involving either an attempted theft or stolen motor vehicle. The investigator is also available to testify to the facts of a specific case and to the auto theft problem and its impact on the community. (Ricks, pp. 20–23)

Other police agencies throughout the country utilize diverse methods to combat automotive theft. The Chicago Police Department's Auto Theft Unit uses computers to track every stolen vehicle to isolate geographical areas where the most vehicles are stolen. With this information, surveillance teams can be assigned to these locations. Computers are also an effective tool in Arizona where towing companies must report the vehicle identification number (VIN) of any vehicle towed. The VIN is put into the computer to ferret out stolen vehicles. If the computer check indicates a stolen vehicle, an investigation will be initiated.

In Florida, the Broward County Sheriff's Auto Theft Task Force follows up on all tips, searches body shops (which is legal in Florida without a warrant), and employs informants to pursue stolen motor vehicle rings. The New York City Auto Theft Squad inspects salvage yards since many cars are stolen for parts. (Stern, 1990, pp. 65–66)

Towing Company Schemes

Towing companies are sometimes involved in unscrupulous operations in which they gain control of vehicles legally and dispose of them illegally. A vehicle is brought to the storage area of a towing company and searched for title, bill of sale, or documentation, allowing the company to identify the owner or lien holder of the vehicle. If the lien cannot be satisfied or eradicated, the towing operator sells the vehicle for parts. If the identity of the owner cannot be established, the towing operator starts a lien process to auction the vehicle for costs incurred in storage. Generally, little effort is made to notify the owner of the vehicle. Like some other states, Florida permits a towing company to sell a vehicle at public auction and keep some money for reimbursement expenses. (The law requires that the remainder of the money be forwarded to the state.) However, unscrupulous towing operators record a lesser amount than the correct selling price of the vehicle, thereby retaining most of the money. Falsifying the sales price on motor vehicle department documents allows the towing operator to pay less sales tax.

Towing company operators can forge the signature of the lien holder or the owner and process the vehicle through the state's motor vehicle department without question. Records showing the vehicle did not sell at public auction can be submitted to the motor vehicle department. This allows the towing owner to keep the vehicle for towing and storage services or sell it and keep the money from the sale. Falsifying the extent of motor vehicle damages to insurance companies leaves the impression that the vehicle cannot economically be repaired. The towing company gets the title of the vehicle and sells it at its discretion. When a clear title cannot be obtained, the VIN of another auto with a similar year, make and model is used to obtain title. (Gillo, pp. 7–8)

Motor Vehicle Theft Enforcement Act

In 1984 the **Motor Vehicle Theft Enforcement Act** was signed by President Reagan. The purpose of the law is to provide for the identification of certain parts of motor vehicles and their replacement parts. The law also attempts to reduce the opportunities for exporting stolen motor vehicles. The act requires that permanent numbers be placed on fourteen specific parts of all lines of automobiles. The parts to be numbered include the engines, transmissions, all doors, hoods, bumpers, front fenders, deck lid and rear quarter

Police departments may sponsor a vehicle-theft deterrent program to educate the public on how to protect their vehicles in keeping with safeguards initiated by national legislation.

panels. These parts are the most desirable for a chop shop. The numbers and their labels self-destruct if they are removed. The law has a fine of $10,000, or five years imprisonment, or both for anyone who removes, obliterates or tampers with an identification number of a motor vehicle or motor vehicle part. (National Auto Theft Bureau, 1987, pp. 18–19)

Crime of Opportunity

Auto larceny is a crime of opportunity, and the car owner has the ability to remove much of the opportunity. The automobile thief must evaluate the vehicle to be stolen and must perform the act quickly to be successful. If the thief lacks the experience of overcoming anti-theft devices then he will pass the more secure car up and move on to easier targets. The New York City Police Department (*Investigator's Guide*, n.d., pp. 6–7) outlines suggestions that can be of value to the automobile owner.

1. Lock your car and remove the key.
2. Remove your registration from the glove compartment.
3. Install anti-thief devices.
4. Leave your steering wheel cut sharply to one side.
5. Avoid parking patterns.
6. Do not use a license plate key ring.
7. Never "drop keys in a slot if attendant is not present."
8. Never leave valuables visible.

Fraudulent Auto Theft Reports

The National Auto Theft Bureau estimates that approximately 15 percent of reported motor vehicle thefts are fraudulent, though it is impossible to determine the exact number of frauds in America. Former New York City Police Commissioner Benjamin Ward estimates that approximately 25 percent of reported automobile thefts are fraudulent. One method to defraud called **owner give ups** occurs when the owner of a vehicle conspires with a third person to have his insured vehicle disposed of so he can collect insurance money. Another method used by motor vehicle owners is dumping vehicles into water. The vehicle is dumped into water and since it's difficult to obtain evidence from a rusted and corroded vehicle, the owner cannot be prosecuted. In some states the insurance company pays a stolen vehicle claim within thirty days. The National Auto Theft Bureau (1987, pp. 8–29) developed a number of red flags that provide guidelines for identifying fraud. These include:

1. Car involved is a late model, expensive vehicle.
2. Date of coverage and date of claim closely related.
3. The insured furnishes the address or phone number of a bar, hotel, or motel as a place to be contacted by the claims adjuster.
4. The insured volunteers to visit the claims office for payment.
5. The insured returns proof of loss or other written communication in person (to avoid violation of mail fraud laws).
6. The claim or theft investigator discloses that:
   a. The insurance agent never viewed the insured vehicle.
   b. The insurance premium was paid in cash.
   c. The insurance agent has no previous other business in effect with the insured.
   d. Only comprehensive insurance coverage was purchased.
7. The insured wants to retain title and salvage on a total loss where salvage appears financially unfeasible.
8. The title or proof of ownership is a duplicate issue or is from a distant state.
9. The insured presents an assigned title, still in the name of the owner, as his proof of ownership.
10. The insured is unable to produce title, proof of ownership, or failed to report the theft to the police.
11. The vehicle has no lien noted and the owner does not appear to have the means to have made a cash purchase.
12. The vehicle is reported to be expensively customized or a show model.
13. The vehicle is rebuilt, a previously recovered theft, or the subject of a prior major collision claim.
14. The vehicle is alleged to have been stolen prior to titling and registration.
15. Expensive articles are reported to have been in the vehicle at time of theft.
16. The previous owner cannot be located or is unknown to the claimant.
17. The vehicle is reported stolen, and recovered a short time later, burned or stripped of its interior.
18. The insured is unable to produce a sales invoice or recovers his own vehicle.

Insurance Fraud Schemes

Auto-related frauds are a principal form of white collar crime. The effects of these organized rings can include property loss, personal injury or both. The automobile fraud rings can include medical doctors, attorneys, paralegals, and insurance company employees like claims adjusters. Attorneys and law firms that concentrate on personal injuries—"ambulance chasers"—often employ "runners" or "cappers" who drum up business by spreading the word that anyone involved in a motor vehicle accident should come to them for legal assistance. An example of a typical case involves a two-car collision with only the drivers as occupants. When the insurance claims are filed, it turns out that additional people were occupants of the vehicles. All individuals claim injuries that require treatment by doctors and other medical personnel who are all involved in the fraud. To obtain insurance money either property damage or personal injury must occur. (Rubin, 1991, p.21)

A multimillion dollar automobile scheme was discovered in the early 1980s by a multiagency task force including the New York City Police Auto Crime Division, the Postal Service, and the Federal Bureau of Investigation. The insurance scheme was successful since the participants controlled all aspects of the fraud process, from acquiring the insurance through processing accident claims by insurance carriers. The automobile insurance was obtained from a broker involved in the fraudulent scheme, who would then obtain insurance for the automobile with an alias or a variety of names. The insurance policy was steered to a specific company involved in the scheme, and once the insurance became active, a vandalism claim against the company was initiated to recoup registration, license, and insurance expenses. (Normally, the claims adjuster was part of the scheme too.) A short time after the vandalism claim, another claim was filed involving a collision, with the insured clearly liable for damages for both vehicles. Generally, the collision involved a parked vehicle that was owned by members of the scheme. The vehicle was towed to a body shop where photographs and paperwork were completed by the claims adjuster. The insurance company would pay the claim since nothing seemed out of order.

The body shop became the focus of the scheme due to a large number of high-priced wrecks, which became cars photographed for staged automobile accidents. The investigators understood the mechanics but absorbing the specific information received from body-shop owners, insurance carriers, and brokers required the use of a computer. Computer printouts allowed investigators to keep track of the more than three thousand claim files and to identify certain patterns that were used. Information included a list of claim files; VIN of automobiles used; lists of claimants and insured; listing of addresses; telephone number listings; license plate number listings; list of policies written by brokers; list of files obtained from insurance company; list of claims appraised by the same insurance adjuster; and list of body shops. (Beekman, *FBI Law Enforcement,* pp. 17–19). The multi-agency approach is illustrated in figure 16–4.

International Trends

Selling stolen vehicles overseas often doubles the original sales price of the motor vehicle. Exporting stolen vehicles may have a greater profit than selling stolen vehicles in the United States. With international trade increasing and the expansion of many of America's ports, stolen car rings will have greater access to motor vehicles. Proximity to shipping ports may contribute to a high auto theft rate. High theft rates are reported not only by New York City, Boston, and Philadelphia, but also by Houston, Tampa, Newark, and other cities with shipping terminals.

For a vehicle to be shipped overseas the assistance of individuals who know the shipping business must be obtained. These individuals—referred to as freight forwarders—make all the arrangements and prepare the mandatory shipping documents. Usually these individuals don't see the items to be shipped and, because of this, freight forwarders may unknowingly prepare documents with erroneous cargo information. One technique used by automobile thieves is to give incorrect vehicle identification numbers to freight forwarders who would enter these on the shipping documents, thus avoiding confiscation by custom agents. Another technique used by auto thieves is to list the stolen vehicles as some other item such as a household good. In another scheme, auto thieves ship legally purchased vehicles with legal certificates of title. When the vehicles arrive at the foreign port, the VIN plates are taken off and sent back to the United States with the certificate of title. The VIN plates are then placed on similar stolen vehicles and the stolen vehicles are shipped out of the country. (Beekman and Daly, pp. 15–16)

Carjacking

During the 1990s a new form of auto theft began to occur, known as **carjacking.** Carjacking (sometimes known as **carpirating**) is the taking of a motor vehicle from a person by force, the threat of force, or intimidation. Incidents of carjacking have increased since the early 1990s and carjacking is a growing phenomenon in American cities and suburbs. It has become a popular crime of violent sport in some geographical areas of our country with youths stealing the cars and taking them for joyrides. The crime of carjacking is technically a robbery and a person committing this crime would be charged with a robbery and the statistic would be counted as such

FIGURE 16–4: Report Number 2—List of Vehicle Numbers and Related Principles Sorted by VIN Number, Case Number: 195 75552 F(2)

File	Agency	VIN	License	Name	Incident Type	Location	Estimated Amount	Mileage	Check Amount	Claim Date
1358	AIC	2W87K9N1856283	997UDS	Jones			1,664	026720	199	
							1,664		199	
1762	USF	2W87K9N194327	537VDD	Brown			3,982	001317	3,782	05 21 80
							3,982		3,782	
2395	GAC	2W87TAN124179	656JDQ	Smith				12384	8,252	
									8,252	
308	BOC	2W87TAN124453	2663ABJ	Updown Corp			4,386	015385	4,368	06 11 81
							4,386		4,368	
82	BOC	2W87TAN127752	121VMC	White	PC	BN	6,400	065375	6,400	05 27 81
	BOC	2W87TAN127752	143TZY	Johnson	PC	BN	4,756	002986	4,756	05 27 81
1264	GAC	2W87TAN127752	121VMC	White			4,975	002059	4,975	10 08 80
84	BOC	2W87TAN127752	121VMC	White	PC	BN	5,452	11858	5,422	
							21,583		21,553	
1081	HAR	2W87TAN14464	218VNT	Black			4,203	021632	4,003	08 23 82
							4,203		4,003	
1326	USF	2W87V7N203089	642FVM	Regal			1,996	043619	1,996	06 19 81
2371	USF	2W87V7N203089	642FVM	Regal			1.996	043619	1,996	06 19 81
							3,992		3,992	
402	TRA	2W87WAN10382	1383AEV	P. Fiero			4,640	010997	4,776	04 30 81
							4,640		4,776	
27	GAC	2W87WAN103822	1383AEV	P. Fiero	PC	BN	4,907	010977	4,907	04 30 82
280	BOC	2W87WAN103822	1383AEV	P. Fiero			4,694	010997	4,426	06 12 81
1676	USF	2W87WAN103822	1383AEV	P. Fiero			4,840	008146		06 03 81
339	HOR	2W87WAN103822	1383AEV	P. Fiero			4,761	10997		05 22 81
33	WAU	2W87WAN103822	1383AEV	P. Fiero	PC	SI	3,901	008362	3,909	05 20 81
1305	GAC	2W87WAN103822	1383AEV	P. Fiero			4,907	010997	4,907	04 28 81
44	MEM	2W87WAN103822	1383AEV	P. Fiero	PC	SI	4,707	010497	4,707	04 24 81
268	BOC	2W87WAN103822	9383ADD	J. Rambo			4,771	010997	4,771	04 21 81
45	ANF	2W87WAN103822	1383AEV	P. Fiero	PC	SI	4,711	010997	4,711	04 17 81
292	AML	2W87WAN103822	1383AEV	P. Fiero			4,776	10997	4,776	04 17 81
38		2W87WAN103822	1383AEV	P. Fiero	PC		5,202		4,407	
763	WAV	2W87WAN103822	1383AEV	P. Fiero			3,909	008362	3,909	
1343	USF	2W87WAN103822	1383AAEV	P. Fiero					45,907	

Source: *FBI Bulletin*, Vol. 55, No. 3, March, 1986, p. 19.

for the FBI's *Uniform Crime Report*. The robbery unit of the detective division would investigate this crime and not the auto theft unit. In Savannah, Georgia the Violent Crime Unit investigates carjackings.

Carjacking thieves approach motorists on roadway ramps, stoplights, parking lots, garages, fast food outlets, and gas stations. The classic carjacking takes place with a lone gunman pulling a pistol on a surprised driver. Another variation of this crime, the **bump and run,** happens when thieves stage a minor rear-end collision. The surprised motorist gets out of his vehicle to inspect the damages, and one thief robs him while a second drives off with his automobile. In New York City and its suburbs thieves have used the bump and run to steal luxury automobiles such as Mercedes-Benzes, BMWs and Infinitys to ship to foreign countries. Thieves can then receive double the value of these vehicles. These luxury cars are shipped to developing countries like Ghana, Haiti, and the Dominican Republic. There are even cases where hijackers have stopped all traffic on a major New York City expressway to take a vehicle by gun point.

To combat the hijacking of luxury automobiles, the Auto Crime Division of the New York City Police Department cooperated with the National Insurance Crime Bureau in setting up a shipping company to recover carjacked automobiles. This sting operation led to the recovery of cars that were to be sent to Africa and the arrest of 112 men. (Hevesi, 1992, p.26)

In the Southwest many carjacked four-wheel-drive vehicles are shipped to Mexico or to Honduras, Costa Rica, and Guatemala where bad roadways create a big demand for these vehicles. In 1991 Los Angeles reported approximately four thousand hijackings with some of these involving assault and murder. It appears that car pirating takes place not only in lower socioeconomic areas but in affluent neighborhoods as well. Rock stars and Hollywood celebrities have been victims of this crime. (*U.S. News and World Report*, 1992, p.42)

Carjackings may be a result of the availability of guns, coupled with the sophistication of antitheft auto technology such as steering wheel locks and alarms. Unsophisticated thieves have difficulty breaking through the sophisticated deterrence systems of luxury automobiles. Taking a vehicle by gun point is easier and less time-consuming. The glut of self-service facilities from automatic teller machines to fast-food restaurants to self-filling gas stations leaves the average person a potential victim to predators.

To combat carjacking federal and local law enforcement agencies are coordinating an attack on the crime. This proactive stance includes the operation of a computer network and the expansion of a hotline to report carjackings is also being undertaken.

In the Washington, D.C. area the FBI became involved in undercover operations using decoy drivers and special weapons teams to combat carjacking. (Bowstein and York, 1992, pp. D1 and D3) Although the hijacking of motor vehicles is primarily a state crime, sometimes federal statutes are violated, allowing federal investigative agencies to become involved. Violation of federal laws include the altering or removing of motor vehicle numbers, interstate transportation of a stolen motor vehicle, trafficking in certain motor vehicles or motor vehicle parts, interstate transportation in aid to racketeering-violent crimes, and membership in racketeer influenced and corrupt organizations.

Shoplifting

According to the Small Business Administration, shoplifting accounts for approximately 28 percent of all retail losses. Shoplifters are almost equally divided between women and men. About half of all shoplifters are under the age of 18, and 82 percent are under 40. It is difficult to assess accurately the scope of shoplifting. Few shoplifters are apprehended, and not all those apprehended are prosecuted. Shoplifting can be conducted in numerous ways. It can be simple: The thief conceals an item in a shopping bag, handbag, or pocket. However, specialized methods are also used. (Fischer, 1987, pp. 283–284)

- Wearing large, baggy clothes like bloomers or pantyhose that can be filled like shopping bags.
- Using slit pockets in coats or jackets, or hiding merchandise inside a coat or up a sleeve.
- Entering the fitting room and putting on stolen clothes under the thief's own clothes.
- Hiding items in purses or umbrellas.
- Placing small items in the palm of the hand.
- Using shopping bags, sometimes even the store's own bags.
- Hiding items with other prepackaged items (for instance, placing jewelry in toothpaste boxes).
- Wearing the item in plain view.
- Grabbing the item and running.
- Using booster boxes, which have special spring lids where merchandise can be concealed, or cages women wear to make them appear to be pregnant.

- Hiding items in books, newspapers, or magazines.
- Hiding an item between the thighs, concealed by a skirt or dress.
- Switching or destroying tickets.

Types of Shoplifters

Shoplifters come from various economic and social classes and range in age from eight to 80. They often have the money to pay for the item they are stealing. Shoplifters can be divided into various categories, including the professional, the drug addict, the amateur, and the teenage shoplifter.

Professionals

The professional shoplifter steals goods to resell for a profit. "The professional shoplifter is identified by the fact that he steals in concert with others, uses such devices as a trick box or double bloomers, or takes large quantities of expensive merchandise." (Curtis, 1971, pp. 24–32)

Professionals are trained in shoplifting techniques and are clever, alert, and well-disguised. They work quickly and efficiently.

Often professionals shoplift expensive merchandise. They may work in gangs, have a network of fences and lawyers, and know police officers who help them out of a jam. Professional shoplifters can be dangerous and are very practical thieves who plan their crime well. They look like ordinary shoppers and blend into the environment.

Drug Addicts

Drug users shoplift to support their habits. They may shoplift food and groceries. Initially, addicts obtain money for drugs from parents, family, relatives, and friends. But when those sources of funds dry up, they turn to crimes like shoplifting.

Amateurs

Amateur shoplifters probably account for 95 percent of all shoplifting incidents. They come from all economic classes. "Probably 70 percent of the people caught shoplifting today represent the better-fed, better-clothed, and better-housed segment of the population." (Curtis, 1971, p. 28)

Teenagers

The teenage shoplifter often steals on impulse. Four, five, or six teenagers may be apprehended for the theft of a single item.

Generally, girls outnumber boys as teenage shoplifters. They steal makeup, jewelry, clothing, and recreational items. Young girls steal for themselves, and not to reap a profit. They lack sophistication and their shoplifting techniques are often clumsy. Teenagers may shoplift for thrills, as a gesture of defiance, or in response to peer pressure to do something daring.

Warning Signs

It is difficult to deter professional shoplifters, but the vast majority of amateur shoplifters can be stopped. A list of signs to look for was developed by a large midwestern store. (Fischer, 1987, pp. 286–287)

- *Packages.* A great many packages; empty or open paper bags; clumsy, crumpled, homemade, untidy, obviously used, poorly tied packages; unusual packages—freak boxes, knitting bags, hat boxes, zipper bags, newspapers, magazines, schoolbooks, folded tissue paper, briefcases, brown bags with no store name on them.
- *Clothing.* A coat or cape worn over the shoulder or arm; coat with slit pockets; ill-fitting, loose, bulging, unreasonable, or unseasonable clothing.
- *Actions.* Unusual actions of any kind; extreme nervousness; strained look; aimless walking up and down the aisles; leaving the store but returning in a few minutes; walking around holding merchandise; handling many articles in a short time; dropping articles on the floor; making rapid purchases; securing empty bags or boxes; entering elevators at the last moment or changing mind and letting the elevator go; excessive concealing of merchandise behind purse or package; placing packages, coat, or purse over merchandise; using stairways; loitering in vestibules.
- *Eyes.* Glancing without moving the head; looking from beneath a hat brim; studying customers instead of merchandise; looking in mirrors; quickly glancing up from merchandise from time to time; glancing from left to right in cross aisles.
- *Hands.* Closing hands completely over merchandise; palming; concealing or destroying ticket; folding merchandise; holding identical pieces for comparison; working merchandise up sleeve and lowering arm in pocket; placing merchandise in pocket; stuffing hands in pocket; concealing ticket while trying on merchandise; trying on jewelry and leaving it on; crumpling merchandise.
- *At counters.* Taking merchandise from counter but returning

repeatedly; taking merchandise to another counter or to a mirror; standing behind crowd and taking merchandise from counters; placing merchandise near the exit counter; starting to examine merchandise, then leaving the counter and returning to it; holding merchandise below counter level; handling a lot of merchandise at different counters; standing a long time at counter.

- *In fitting rooms.* Entering with merchandise but without salesperson; using room before it has been cleared; removing hangers before entering with packages; taking in identical items; taking in items of various sizes or obviously wrong sizes; gathering merchandise hastily, without examining it, and going into the fitting room.
- *In department.* Sending clerks away for more merchandise; standing too close to dress racks or cases; placing shopping bag on floor between racks; refusing a salesperson's help.
- *Miscellaneous.* Requesting questionable refund; acting in concert—separating and meeting, setting up lookouts, swapping packages, following companion into fitting room without salesperson.

Boat Theft

The theft of boats and marine equipment has become a serious problem. Two factors that contribute to an increase in marine thefts are jurisdictional disputes among law enforcement agencies and the lack of uniform state laws. There are no accurate statistical data to assist law enforcement officials in analyzing and studying marine theft. Because of the maze of conflicting jurisdictions, marine theft is difficult to solve. In 1977 the U.S. Coast Guard established guidelines for handling incidents of stolen vessels and marine equipment. The Coast Guard detailed five federal laws and explained how specific acts relate to marine thefts. Figure 16–5 illustrates to what agencies boat owners should report theft.

Law enforcement investigators can obtain statistical data from the National Crime Information Center (NCIC) boat file. The insurance industry can provide a panoramic view of thefts relating to boats and marine equipment. The NCIC defines a boat as "a vessel for transport by water, constructed to provide buoyancy by excluding water, and shaped to give stability and permit propulsion." (Lyford, 1985, p. 5)

When a boat is reported stolen, its registration number, document number, and/or permanently affixed hull serial number can

FIGURE 16–5: Reporting a Stolen Boat

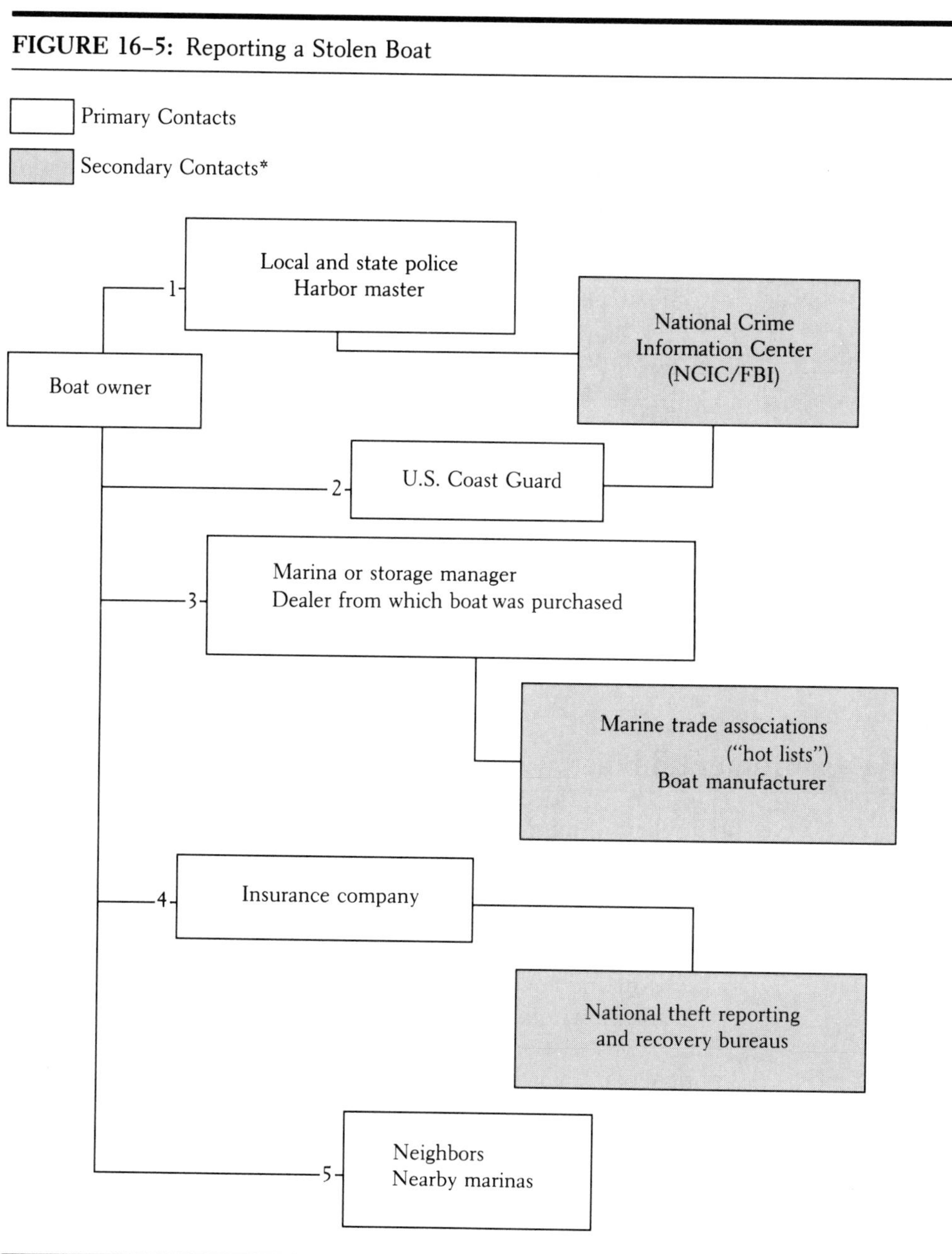

Source: *FBI Law Enforcement Bulletin,* May 1982.

*While boat owners cannot contact these agencies directly, they should strongly request that the primary contacts quickly do so.

be entered into the NCIC boat file. Data fields of the boat file facilitate entry of the following information.

- The identity of the agency holding the theft report,
- The registration or document number of the boat,
- The identity of the states of registry or United States, indicating whether the U.S. Coast Guard issued the registration number,
- The year the registration or document number expires,
- The type of material used to construct the outer hull (e.g., metal, plastic, wood),
- The hull serial number,
- The type of propulsion (e.g., inboard, outboard, sail),
- The type of boat (e.g., airboat, houseboat, hydrofoil, sailboat, yacht),
- The overall length of the boat,
- The color of the boat,
- The date the theft occurred,
- The case number of the agency receiving the theft report,
- The manufacturer's complete name and model name and/or number, and
- Any additional descriptive information that may help to identify the boat.

Heavy Equipment Theft

The theft of farm equipment and construction equipment means the loss of millions of dollars. Many thieves of heavy equipment steal by orders and strip the equipment for intrastate, interstate, or international sale. Well-organized professional criminals handle this type of movement.

Farm and construction equipment does not have permanent identification numbers, but each company has its own ID numbers. Heavy construction equipment may have several ID plates for component parts, which thieves often remove and replace with counterfeit plates. The lack of a registration or title requirement for heavy equipment makes locating stolen equipment difficult. There is often no accurate way to determine the serial number of stolen equipment.

Law enforcement officers may have difficulty dealing with farm and construction equipment because they are unfamiliar with the terminology. Often inaccurate information is used for entering the vehicle into the NCIC. Investigators have to depend on the owners' records and expertise when reporting heavy equipment thefts and identifying stolen equipment. Construction equipment is included in the NCIC under vehicle files and article files. For example, trailers, engines, and transmissions are entered into vehicle files. Article files include hay balers, cultivators, plows, and buckles for bulldozers and tractors. There are certain steps law enforcement officers can take to curtail heavy equipment thefts. (Lyford, 1982, pp. 2–5)

- Become familiar with off-road equipment by visiting dealerships and learning about the various numbering systems, where the serial plates are located, and where the component numbers, if any, can be found.
- Determine what type of documentation, if any, the dealer supplies to the purchaser of equipment and what record system the dealer maintains in order to verify ownership.
- Become familiar with the workings of the National Crime Information Center. Learn which equipment is entered in the vehicle file and which is entered in the article file.
- Don't stop with NCIC if there is reason to believe the machine was obtained under less than legitimate circumstances. Supply all identification numbers to the manufacturer and request that it furnish the name of the purchaser so ownership can be established.
- Make contact with operators of off-road equipment to obtain their help in tracking down stolen equipment.

Sneak Theft

Sneak thefts are usually committed by gangs who employ various distracting techniques to steal from financial institutions. Generally, the gang of sneak thieves consists of four or five members, including a female with a child. Their first step is to determine where the travelers' checks are stored. (Normally, checks are kept in a platform or customer service area.) Then a member of the gang begins to purchase a limited amount of travelers' checks. The other gang members, scattered throughout the bank, employ distraction techniques, such as dropping a can full of coins or starting loud arguments. While the clerk is distracted, the first gang member scoops up a quantity of blank checks.

Between 1983 and 1988, statistics from the New York FBI office revealed approximately 130 reported sneak theft incidents, with travelers' check losses amounting to $3.5 million. These sneak thefts account for about 10 percent of the bank larcenies reported to the FBI. (Keeley and Gannon, 1989, pp. 6–8)

Cargo Theft

The term **cargo** generally means anything that enters the country by the nation's transportation system. Cargo theft refers to both acts of theft (stealing the entire carton or container) and pilferage (stealing only some of the carton's contents). (*Cargo Theft and Organized Crime*, 1972, pp. 1–14) Cargo theft leads to both direct and indirect financial loss. Insurance premiums may become prohibitive and sales can be lost when goods are hijacked. Also, cargo theft can lead to loss of government revenue and freight rate increases to help cover losses. The federal government loses revenue since it is unable to collect duties on stolen cargo.

Sometimes cargo is checked into the terminals but cannot be found for delivery. Often there is collusion between truckers and cargo handlers in delivering merchandise to the warehouse dock. Generally, cargo thefts occur at the terminal where goods are being turned over, not at their point of origin.

The *Deskbook for Management and Law Enforcement* says the obvious characteristics of many cargo thefts should show even casual observers "(1) the extent to which collusion must be present and (2) the different sets of individuals who may be necessary to assure the success of such crimes." (1972, p. 15)

Computer Theft

The increasing use of computer systems to maintain records and conduct financial business provides an opportunity for theft. Among programs that can be manipulated by computers are payroll, accounts payable and receivable, inventory records, cash accounts, customer accounts, scrap and salvage records, and travel and entertainment records.

Computer crime is any statutorily proscribed behavior that is assisted by or requires the knowledge of computer technology. Forty-five states and the federal government have computer-related crime statutes. It is difficult to compile accurate computer crime statistics.

Types of Computer Theft

Twelve types of computer-related crimes are outlined by Conser et al. in *Critical Issues in Criminal Investigation.* (Palmiotto, 1988, pp. 38–40)

- *Data diddling.* Changing data before or during their entry into the computer. Examples are forging or counterfeiting documents, exchanging valid computer media with prepared replacements, violating source entries, and neutralizing or avoiding manual controls.
- *Trojan horse.* The covert placement of computer instructions into a computer program so that the computer will perform unauthorized functions while fulfilling its intended purpose. Examples are instructing the computer to ignore an overdrawn checking account, to ignore past-due billing dates, and to order an excess number of items from a particular vendor.
- *Salami technique.* An automatic means of stealing small amounts of assets from a large number of sources. An example is to automatically transfer small amounts of interest earned on back accounts to an account controlled by the perpetrator or an accomplice. These amounts may be only a few thousands of a cent, but they add up to a sizable sum of money over time. Because of rounding techniques (to the nearest penny), the accounts will continue to balance.
- *Superzapping.* A utility program (superzap) bypasses all controls in order to modify or disclose any of the contents of the computer. This allows the perpetrator to make changes in accounts or data files.
- *Trapdoors.* As the name implies, an avenue into a computer program known only to one or a few person(s). It allows a person to gain access to the program code to modify it or to bypass password protection routines.
- *Logic bomb.* A computer program routine that, when executed, usually causes a malicious act to occur, such as erasing a file (or files) or causing the entire system to crash. Such programs are usually entered into the computer with instructions not to be executed until certain conditions exist (e.g., a specific date or hour, three months after termination of employment).
- *Asynchronous attack.* A sophisticated method employed to confuse the operating system. Computer systems that run batch jobs do so on a priority basis and assign computer resources as jobs are being executed. An asynchronous attack can override the priority and assign too much or too little of the computer's resources to a particular job. This form of attack requires a high level of programming expertise.
- *Scavenging.* As one might search wastebaskets and trash containers for discarded information that may be of some value, so too can a knowledgeable user search the computer and its peripherals (e.g., buffer storage, temporary storage tapes). Both

types of scavenging may occur at computer facilities.

- *Data leakage*. Techniques employed to remove data or copies of data from a computer. Methods include hiding the data in innocuous reports and using miniature radio transmitters to broadcast the contents of a computer to remote areas.
- *Piggybacking* and *impersonation*. Physically or electronically gaining access to areas or data by following or posing as an authorized user.
- *Wiretapping*. Electronically tapping a computer facility or transmission wires going into and out of such a facility to obtain copies of data. However, since there are easier methods, this is not likely to be used.
- *Stimulation* and *modeling*. Using the computer's capability to supply information to the perpetrator of a planned crime. An example is the accountant who uses a computer to duplicate an accounting system targeted for embezzlement. The accountant uses the model to observe what the consequences of certain transactions are and determine the best means of manipulating the ledgers to escape detection.

Investigating and Preventing Computer Theft

The criminal investigator of computer-related crime should follow investigative procedures similar to those for investigating other types of crimes. For instance, the investigator must protect the crime scene, collect evidence, and interview victims and witnesses. The investigator must also be computer literate and understand computer technology and terms. Computer-related crime is a specialized area but one that investigators can develop the skills to investigate and prosecute successfully. See Chapter 18 for a more thorough coverage of computer crime. The National Crime Prevention Institute recommends a number of procedures to prevent computer theft. (1986, p. 102)

- Document all changes to computer programs before they are made, through a central supervisory function.
- Restrict access to the computer center.
- Separate responsibility for computer access according to functions (paying, receiving, accounting, and payroll). Also, the computer programming function should be separate from the operating function.
- Require that continuous records be maintained of data used.
- Record all errors, restarts, and running times.
- Maintain duplicate copies of important files in a separate location.

- Simulate a wide variety of possible embezzlement methods and develop countermeasures for each.

Fraud

Fraud is a statutory crime that involves pretense or misrepresentation. An individual defrauds another person out of money, labor, or property. Eldefonso and Coffey break the concept of fraud into eleven factors. (1981, p. 235)

1. There must be some form of pretense.
2. The pretense must be more than withholding facts.
3. There must be misrepresentation of something that exists or did exist other than a forecast, an intention, a promise, an opinion, or bragging.
4. The misrepresentation must be a lie.
5. The lie must be intended to deceive.
6. The liar must be aware that it is a lie told for the purpose of illegally gaining property.
7. The deception must be successful.
8. The deceived person may or may not be negligent.
9. The property may be taken away.
10. The victim must be injured.
11. The property must be defined in the written law of the jurisdiction.

People have developed thousands of schemes to defraud individuals or business establishments, and the government. The 1980s were inundated with fraud schemes. In one scandal, tanks that were sold to the Army could not function. In the Housing and Urban Development scandals, government money went to build golf courses instead of financing housing for lower- and middle-class families. In the savings and loan scandal, millions of small investors lost their life savings. It may take the entire decade of the 1990s to unravel that one. Discussing every fraud scheme in operation would require volumes. This chapter will look only at some typical examples, including credit card fraud, checking account fraud, and real estate fraud.

Credit Card Fraud

Credit cards are a way of life for many Americans. Banks, department stores, and oil companies all issue and honor them. Business establishments have to honor credit cards if they hope to remain in business. Small businesses, retail stores, and restaurants depend on customers using credit cards to purchase merchandise.

However, some people use stolen, forged, or fictitious credit cards. The use of unauthorized credit cards has developed into a huge underground economy that costs billions every year. Large credit card issuers like American Express have investigators assigned to the problem.

There are procedures businesses can follow to reduce their losses due to credit card fraud. (*National Crime Prevention Institute*, 1986, p. 104)

- Maintain current files of cancellations from credit card companies. Require that such files be checked each time a credit card is offered in payment.
- Call the credit card company for authorization if the signature on the card does not match that of the purchaser, the card appears mutilated or altered, the purchaser has no other identification, the amount of purchase is above an established limit, or there is any other reason to suspect the authenticity of the card.
- Train all members of the organization to follow established credit card procedures without exception.

Checking Account Fraud

Check forgery and bad check offenses are separate violations in most jurisdictions. A bad check is one that a person tries to cash with nonsufficient funds (NSF) in the bank. Check forgery means obtaining money by cashing worthless checks. Check forgery can range in sophistication from NSF to phony payroll checks. (McCaghy and Cernkovich, 1987, p. 308)

- *NSF checks* are personal checks written on the forger's account, which lacks the balance to cover the amounts. Hence the checks bounce back from the bank stamped "Nonsufficient Funds."
- *Stolen personal checks* are legitimate checks, obtained through burglary or robbery, on which the offender forges the owner's name.
- *Phony personal checks* are personal checks bearing a fictitious name, which the forger signs.
- *Phony payroll checks* are counterfeited company checks made out to a fictitious name, which the forger signs.

Over thirty million fraudulent checks are written annually. There are basically two types of check forgers, systematic and naive. Systematic forgers are sophisticated and organize their lives around their offenses. They normally work alone. Because they worry less about the crime, they eventually become careless, make an error, and get caught.

Naive forgers are unsophisticated and take few precautions when committing their crime. They cash checks when having financial difficulties or family problems.

Real Estate Fraud

Real estate fraud has become a national problem. We often read of real estate scams in Florida. They have been around for decades. This decade began with two top officials of the General Develop-

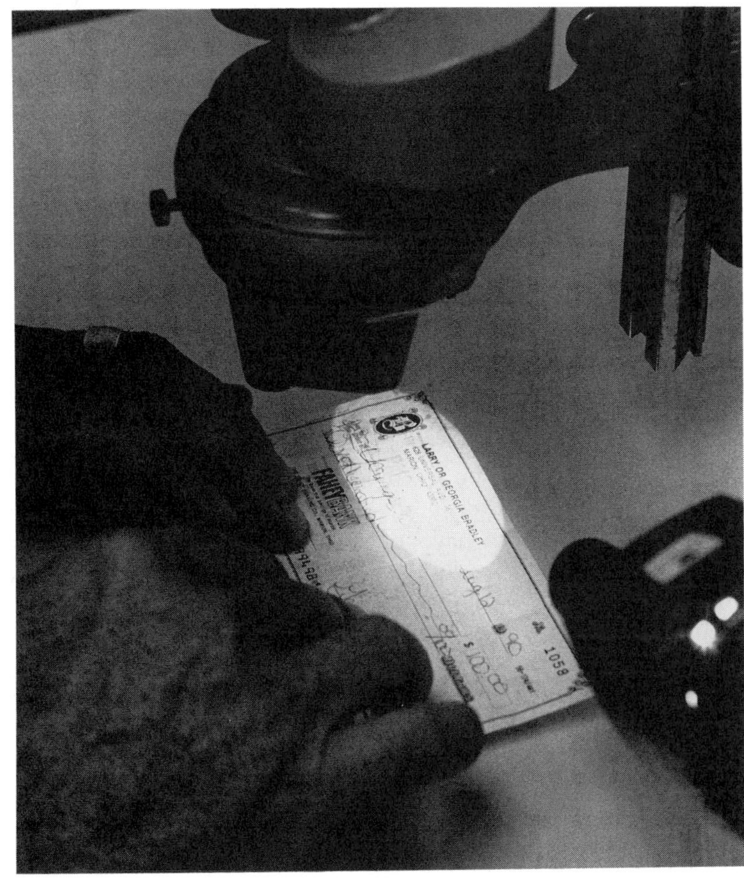

A handwriting analyst uses a microscope to inspect a check for forgery.

Jeff Ross—chief prosecutor for Harris County, Texas—began protecting his bank account from forgers in 1987 by having his photo and physical description printed on the checks. "Now," Ross says, "only a person with my looks and physical description can pass my checks. If all check owners would get this done to their checks, we would see a dramatic decrease in forgeries."

ment Corporation of Miami pleading guilty to working with house appraisers to inflate the value of homes. For example, one retired worker paid $158,000 for a home that was later valued at $95,000. When the owner sued and won the case, he still could not collect the difference since the company declared bankruptcy. In addition, the mayor of Hialeah and a councilman were indicted for accepting $1 million in bribes for favorable zoning. Along the same lines, the mayor of Miami Beach admitted to accepting $35,000 from the president of a savings and loan to build a private dock.

Other real estate frauds that have been discovered include building shopping centers in the desert, office buildings in the boondocks, and communities where no one will live. In another real estate scam called land flips, investors obtain land at very low prices and then sell it back and forth among themselves at higher prices with inflated appraisals in order to get loans from savings-and-loan companies.

In the early 1990s, federal and state authorities investigated dozens of real estate deals that involved mortgage and appraisal fraud in the area of Atlanta, Georgia. The real estate scam involved alleged kickbacks on down payments to inflate real estate prices. Gerrilyn Brill, chief of the fraud section of the U.S. attorney's office in Atlanta, says, "They make it appear as if the purchaser has made a down payment but there is a side agreement not revealed to the lending institution that the down payment be refunded after the closing. This agreement can involve the seller, the buyer, the real estate agent or broker and even the closing attorney." The state of Georgia has no laws governing appraisers or mortgage companies.

Good candidates for the real estate scam are professionals who recently moved to Atlanta and do not know the market and those who have large disposable incomes but little savings or bad credit. Many will not realize they are the victims of a scam until they try to sell their home and find out it isn't worth what they thought. (Curriden, 1990, pp. E1 and 12) Figure 16–6 illustrates the way this particular fraud works.

Fencing

The estimated value of stolen property is at least $3 billion annually. To be valuable to thieves, stolen property must make them a profit. An individual who deals in stolen goods as a business is called a **fence**. He or she buys stolen goods from the thief and sells it to a customer for a profit. Of course, the cost of goods to the consumer is considerably lower than at a legitimate retail establishment.

Fencing operations can be either simple or complex. A fence can buy items from a thief and sell them directly to consumers at a construction site or a bar. The modern fence typically owns a legitimate business, perhaps an antique dealership, and is a white male between 35 and 55 years of age. Although the fence does not actively participate in theft, he does motivate and support thieves by purchasing their wares. If a fencing operation can be put out of business, it will be more difficult for thieves to dispose of their stolen goods, and theft will seem like a less appealing way of earning money.

Summary

The laws that govern property in the United States can be traced to medieval England. Larceny-theft is depriving another person of property without justification. It can mean withholding property

FIGURE 16-6: Sample Real Estate Scam

Here is one way, authorities say, that real estate scams are being carried out in metro Atlanta's soft real estate market:

"BUYER A" assumes a $200,000 construction loan to buy property from a distressed builder facing hard times.

"BUYER A" immediately sells to "BUYER B," known as the "straw man" in the scheme, seemingly for the $300,000 asking price.

"BUYER B" gets a $240,000 loan from a mortgage lender by having "BUYER A" vouch that he has made a standard 20 percent down payment of $60,000. (Down payments are usually paper transactions, involving checks or promissory notes that are destroyed after the mortgage loan is secured.)

"BUYER B" then offers the property for sale for $250,000, hiring an appraiser who supports the property's worth at $300,000.

A third, unsuspecting buyer pays a low down payment of $10,000 and assumes a $240,000 loan on property that is actually worth only $200,000.

"BUYERS A & B" split the $10,000 down payment and what's left of the $40,000 difference between the $200,000 construction loan they originally assumed and the unsuspecting buyer's $240,000 loan.

Source: *The Atlanta Journal/Constitution*, February 25, 1990. Reprinted with permission from The Atlanta Journal and The Atlanta Constitution. Reproduction does not imply endorsement.

permanently or temporarily or disposing of it without any chance of the owner recovering it.

Thieves steal money, automobiles, televisions, clothing, bicycles, and a variety of other property. Larceny-theft is a crime based on cunning, skill, and planning for the professional thief. It can be a crime of opportunity if committed by amateurs. In a preliminary investigation, the crime scene is examined and physical evidence collected. The investigator attempts to establish the thief's modus operandi.

Over 1,600,000 motor vehicle thefts occur in the United States every year. The estimated value of vehicles stolen yearly tops $8 billion dollars. The number of motor vehicle thefts that are known to the police have been increasing for the last several years. Cars popular with thieves when they are new remain popular targets.

Automobile thefts are committed for reasons such as joyriding, use in crime, stripping, and resale. Joyriding thefts, and vehicles stolen for the purpose of committing a crime are usually recovered; vehicles stolen by professional thieves are rarely recovered.

Because automobile thefts have increased substantially throughout the country a number of communities have established theft reduction programs.

According to the Small Business Administration, shoplifting accounts for approximately 28 percent of all retail losses. Few shoplifters are apprehended and even fewer are prosecuted. In many cases the thief simply puts an item in a shopping bag, handbag, or pocket. Shoplifters are of various economic and social classes and ages. They can be divided into professionals, drug addicts, amateurs, and teenagers.

The theft of boats and marine equipment has become a serious problem. Two factors that contribute to an increase in marine thefts are jurisdictional disputes among law enforcement agencies and the lack of uniform state laws. Thefts of farm equipment and construction equipment cause the loss of millions of dollars in equipment and manhours each year. Many professional thieves steal heavy equipment for sale either intrastate, interstate, or internationally. Law enforcement officers may have difficulty in dealing with farm and construction equipment because they are unfamiliar with the terminology.

The increased use of computer systems to maintain records and conduct financial business provides an opportunity for theft. Payroll, accounts payable and receivable, inventory records, cash accounts, customer accounts, scrap and salvage records, and travel and entertainment records can be manipulated by computers. Computer-related crime is a specialized area but one that an investigator can develop the skills to investigate and prosecute successfully.

Fraud is a statutory crime involving pretense or misrepresentation. An individual defrauds another person, a business, or the government out of money, labor, or property.

A fence deals in stolen property as a business. He or she buys stolen goods from a thief and sells them to consumers for a profit. Of course, the cost to the consumer is considerably lower than at a legitimate retail establishment.

Key Terms

bump and run
cargo
carjacking
car pirates
CAU
chop shop
fence
grand larceny
joyriding
long line
Motor Vehicle Theft Enforcement Act
National Insurance Crime Bureau (NICB)
owner give-up
personal property
petty larceny
RAT Unit
real property
spotters
steal to order
stripping
theft-by-conversion
VIN

Review Questions

1. What is the offense of larceny-theft?
2. How should a preliminary investigation of a larceny-theft be conducted?
3. What is the National Insurance Crime Bureau?
4. Describe the automobile theft trends.
5. What are the four categories of auto theft?
6. What is a chop shop?
7. Describe some of the fraud schemes relating to automobiles.
8. How do the police search for a stolen vehicle?
9. What is the 1984 Motor Vehicle Theft Enforcement Act?
10. What are the preventive techniques recommended by the New York City Police Department to make stealing automobiles difficult?
11. What is carjacking? Why has it become the crime of the 1990s?
12. What are some of the specialized shoplifting techniques used by professionals?
13. What are some of the signs a store employee should look for to deter shoplifting?
14. What are some of the problems relating to boat theft? Heavy equipment theft? Cargo theft?
15. What are sneak thefts?
16. Name the types of computer theft.
17. What are the eleven factors in the concept of fraud?
18. What role do fences play in the crime of theft?

References

Beekman M E: "Automobile Insurance Fraud Pays . . . and Pays Well." *FBI Law Enforcement Bulletin,* Vol. 55, No. 3.

Beekman M E, Daly M R: "Motor Vehicle Theft Investigations: Emerging International Trends." *FBI Law Enforcement Bulletin,* vol. 59, No. 9.

Bennett W, Hess K: *Criminal Investigation,* ed.

2. New York, NY: West Publishing Co., 1987.

Bowenstein A, York M: "Calling Carjacking Terrorism, Area Officials Coordinate Attack," *Washington Post,* September 17, 1992.

Cargo Theft and Organized Crime. Washington, DC: U.S. Government Printing Office, 1972.

Crime Control Digest, August 3, 1992.

Criminal Investigation: Specific Offenses, Gaithersburg, MD: International Association of Chiefs of Police, 1973.

Criminal Investigation, vol. 1 Washington, D.C.: International Association of Chiefs of Police, 1973.

Curriden M: "Alleged Scams Sour New-Home Purchases." *The Atlanta Journal/Constitution,* May 25, 1990.

Curtis B: *Security Control: External Control.* New York, NY: Chain Store Age Books, 1971.

Deskbook for Management and Law Enforcement. Washington, DC: U.S. Dept. of Justice, 1972.

Eldefonso E, Coffey A: *Criminal Law.* New York, NY: Harper and Row, 1981.

Fischer RJ: *Introduction to Security,* ed. 4. Boston, MA: Butterworth, 1987.

Gallati RR: *Introduction to Private Security.* Englewood Cliffs, NJ: Prentice-Hall, 1983.

Gillo C: "Towing Companies: Friends or Foe?" *FBI Law Enforcement Bulletin,* vol. 59, No. 6.

Grillot H, Schuber F: *Introduction to Law and Legal System,* ed. 4. Boston, MA: Houghton Mifflin Co., 1989.

Hevesi D: "Sting Operation," *New York Times,* January 18, 1992.

Information, Palos Hills, Ill: National Insurance Crime Bureau, 1992.

Investigator's Guide. New York, NY: New York City Police Department, n.d., chapter 22.

Lyford G: "Heavy Equipment Theft." *FBI Law Enforcement Bulletin,* vol.50, No. 3, 1982.

Lyford G: "Boat Theft: A High Profit/Low-Risk Business." *FBI Law Enforcement Bulletin.* vol. 51, No. 5, 1985.

Keeley M, Gannon J: "Sneak Thefts." *FBI Law Enforcement Bulletin,* vol. 58, No. 12, 1989.

McCaghy C H, Cernkovick S A.: *Crime in American Society.* New York, NY: Macmillan Publishing Co., 1987.

"Motor Vehicle Theft Enforcement Act" *National Auto Theft Bureau,* 1987.

National Auto Theft Bureau. *1987 Annual Report,* Palos Hills, IL: NATB, 1987.

National Crime Prevention Institute: *Understanding Crime Prevention.* Boston, MA: Butterworth, 1986.

New York Police Dept.: *Investigator's Guide,* New York, NY: NYPD, n.d.

O'Hara C: *Fundamentals of Criminal Investigation,* ed. 3. Springfield, IL: Charles C. Thomas, 1973.

Palmiotto MJ, Ed: *Critical Issues in Criminal Investigation,* ed. 2. Cincinnati, OH: Anderson Publishing Co., 1988.

Ricks P C: "The Rat Patrol." *F.B.I. Law Enforcement Bulletin,* vol. 60, No. 1.

Rubin, H: "Staged Auto Accidents: The Safest White Collar Crime." *Law and Order,* July 1991.

Stern G M: "Effective Strategies to Minimize Auto Thefts and Break Ins." *Law and Order,* July 1990.

Uniform Crime Reports. Washington, D.C.: U.S. Government Printing Office, 1991.

"Willing to Kill for a Car." *U.S. News and World Report,* September 21, 1992.

CHAPTER 17

Accident Investigation

The investigation of automobile accidents is an important aspect of police work. Statistics reveal that more people are killed and injured in vehicle accidents than in any other form of accident. Traffic accidents are responsible for millions of dollars in property losses. The National Safety Council defines an accident as "that occurrence in a sequence of events which usually produces unintended injury, death, or property damage."

An investigation is an inquiry or examination, with systematic attention paid to detail and relationships. The accident investigation is a matter of obtaining, recording, refining, and interpreting information. Investigations can lead to criminal charges which include felonies or misdemeanors, such as driving while intoxicated, vehicular homicide, reckless driving, and hit-and-run. In addition to criminal charges, civil actions can also be brought for millions of dollars and lawsuits may be brought against the municipality where the accident occurred. Because of the seriousness of these offenses, it is essential that the investigator obtain accurate and factual information in determining the causes of the traffic accident. Did there exist an obstruction on the highway, were there defects in the vehicle, or was the driver at fault? A traffic investigator should determine what type of accident occurred, where did the accident happen, when did the accident happen, why did the accident happen, who was involved, and how did the accident happen.

Commission on Accreditation

The Commission on Accreditation for Law Enforcement Agencies requires that police agencies develop written standards on traffic accident procedures, provide emergency assistance to the injured, protect the accident scene, conduct at-scene and follow-up investigations, prepare reports; and take proper enforcement action relative to the accident. The commission also recommends the following responsibilities for the first officer responding to the scene:

1. Administer emergency medical care and provide basic life support.
2. Summon ambulance and/or additional assistance.
3. Protect the accident scene.
4. Preserve short-lived evidence.
5. Establish a safe driving pattern around the scene.
6. Locate witnesses and record accident information.
7. Expedite the removal from the roadway of vehicles and debris. (*Standards for Law Enforcement Agencies*, 1989, p. 63–1)

Levels of Accident Investigation

Accident investigation can be a simple operation or a complex one. The process usually begins with collecting information about people, vehicles, and the highway. Most accidents are simple and require little investigation. If an accident investigation is required, the sequence begins with reporting and at-scene investigation, with technical follow-up, reconstruction, and causal analysis coming later. (Baker, 1986, pp. 10-5–10-8) In the reporting step basic data is collected and the investigator attempts to identify and classify the accident, property, people, and the reason for the accident. The result of the accident is recorded and information available at the scene must be obtained. This can be extremely valuable in cases with fatalities. Usually, a technical follow-up will be undertaken for legal purposes. Examples of technical follow-up include: disassembling a vehicle to discover equipment deficiencies, examining lamps, tires, and seatbelts, or measuring speed and acceleration of vehicles.

Reconstruction involves fitting the pieces together to determine how the accident occurred. Skills required for reconstruction include a working knowledge of arithmetic, algebra, an understanding of dynamics, and an idea of reaction time. Examples of skills required include: analyzing movements of vehicles and bodies in collisions, making momentum diagrams and calculations, and estimating driver or pedestrian delays. Cause analysis determines why the traffic accident occurred from the available information. It is an inferential process that is primarily speculation on the accident investigator's part. The investigator attempts to determine such

Driving while drunk is a criminal offense. Traffic investigators, therefore, must sometimes investigate crimes. The presence of beer cans in this wrecked car suggest that the crash was alcohol-related.

things as the contribution of driving conditions to the accident, factors that contributed to driving failures, or the possible influence of the road surface.

Accident Investigation Procedures

Traffic accident investigations are concerned with vehicles, drivers and pedestrians, witnesses, vehicle defects, road and weather conditions, and the collection of physical evidence. Proper police procedures require that a traffic investigator be at the accident scene to handle initial medical situations, request additional officers if needed, protect the scene, and collect and preserve evidence. Essential measurements, photographs, sketches, and written reports are done at this time. The traffic investigator may have to make an on-scene arrest or give a citation for violation of the motor vehicle law or city ordinance. The investigator who has been initially assigned to the traffic accident should follow the plan of action below to be effective.

1. *Evaluation.* Evaluate the assistance requirement necessary. Request assistance from the appropriate allied agencies: ambulance service, fire department, coroner's office, and possible assistance for traffic control. Request the necessary tow service trucks and any specialized equipment.
2. *First Aid.* Attend to the injured.
3. *Protect the scene.* Stabilize the scene as soon as possible. Place flares or cones to warn oncoming traffic of the emergency that exists ahead.
4. *Witnesses.* Locate the witnesses and have them stand by until such time as they may be interviewed.
5. *Evidence.* Take the appropriate measurements, collect evidence, note the debris, and photograph as appropriate.
6. *Vehicle removal.* Direct the tow services into and out of the scene, giving them as much assistance as possible to expedite their presence in the area in a minimum amount of time.
7. *Open the roadway.* Effect the sweep and wash-down of the scene as soon as possible following the vehicle removal, and restore the normal traffic flow.
8. *Statements.* Take statements from witnesses and then drivers.
9. *Arrests.* Make arrests as necessary.
10. *Reporting.* Complete the investigative report. (Clark, 1982, p. 28)

A traffic investigator must be a good observer, able to analyze situations and evaluate verbal and written statements with physical evidence and probability. The on-scene traffic investigator must maintain control of the traffic scene in order to conduct a logical, sequential, and thorough investigation. Unless this has been done, a factual account of the traffic accident will not be possible.

Traffic Knowledge Required

Accident investigations can involve death or injury, property damages, driver impairment due to drugs or alcohol, or the presence of hazardous materials. One purpose of a traffic accident investigation is to determine if there exists enough evidence to make an arrest. Insurance companies and individuals involved in an accident will want to determine negligence for claim purposes or possible law suits. Governmental officials will want specific information in order to prevent future traffic accidents and to be prepared for potential civil action. Sergeant C. D. Brown of the Savannah Police Department indicated that accident investigators needed to know nine principal items of information.

1. Roadway conditions
2. Roadway evidence—debris and tire marks
3. Tire mark evidence
4. Tire construction
5. Brakes
6. Light examination
7. Drag factor—test skids and drag sled
8. Minimum speed formula
9. Scale diagraming—coordinate offset method

Roadway Conditions

Various factors contribute to a traffic accident. One factor may be the conditions of the road at the time of the accident. Obstructions, weather and light, glare, slipperiness, and poor roadways in need of repair are often a contributing factor in accidents. For example, potholes could cause a driver to lose control of his vehicle. Obstructions such as parked cars, clusters of trees, billboards, big trucks, road signs, telephone poles, and pedestrians can hinder the view of a driver.

Weather and light are important to visibility. The inability to see ahead for a substantial distance can be a driving hazard; often darkness and fog can be factors in an accident. The driver may be driving too fast for conditions—faster than his ability to see an object in the road to safely stop his vehicle. Other potential causes of accidents could be pedestrians in dark clothes, extreme darkness, rain, ice, and snow.

Glare is another factor that could contribute to a traffic accident. However, it often goes undetected and is difficult to evaluate. Three types of glare contribute to accidents: headlight glare, glare from fixed lights or backlighting, and sunlight glare. (Baker, 1986, p. 170) Headlight glare occurs at night and has a high probability of being a factor in a vehicle hitting a fixed object, going off the road or hitting a pedestrian. Streetlights, floodlights, and advertising signs are considered fixed lights and create conditions that can blind a driver. Backlighting causes a glare on the traffic signal or traffic sign so that the driver may not see a red traffic signal and go through it. During the day a driver could be blinded by sun glare. Usually an hour and one-half before the sun sets or after it rises seems to be the most serious danger to the driver. Follow-up investigations should be done at the same time of day as that of the accident.

Another factor that should be considered is the road's surface condition. Is the road slippery? Is there any ice, snow, oil, or soft asphalt that interfered with the driver's ability to control his or her vehicle? Did the surface condition of the road contribute to the cause of the accident? The traffic accident investigator has to review and evaluate the conditions of the roadway at the time of the accident to determine if the roadway played any role in the traffic accident.

Roadway Evidence

Motor vehicle accidents usually leave some physical clue of what transpired. This can include pedestrian injuries, property damage,

Accident investigations often turn up information that is crucial to determining the cause of the mishap or whether criminal charges will be filed. Here, examination of a vehicle that went out of control shows it was caused by a broken tie rod. (indicated by arrow.)

or road marks. The traffic accident investigator has the responsibility of discovering and interpreting physical signs correctly. Physical evidence may not always provide a thorough explanation of the causes of the accident but it can supplement statements of witnesses. Roadway marks left at the accident scene may be visible but what do they mean? What do skid marks indicate? What does debris left at the scene indicate? Marks left by a traffic accident must be carefully examined by the traffic accident investigator. He will photograph and take accurate notes of what was at the traffic scene. Measurement will usually be taken to determine the length of skid marks and vehicle locations from fixed points.

Two types of roadway marks left at the accident scene are tire marks and debris. Debris is "the accumulation of broken parts of vehicles, rubbish, dust and other materials left at the accident scene by a collision." (Baker, 1986, p. 233) Debris can be vehicle parts, pieces of glass, metal, paint chips, and even liquids such as coolant from the radiator. When vehicles collide debris usually moves forward unless it is deflected. Scattered debris could assist in determining the point of impact and direction of travel at the time of the accident. Debris from the underside of the vehicle, such as rust and paint jarred loose, usually drops in a blown-out pattern from where it strikes the pavement. This path may not be the direction the vehicle was heading. An example of this is a sideswiped vehicle. Items such as clothes found at an accident scene may demonstrate where a pedestrian was hit by a vehicle. Blood may show where a person was located in the car. Damage to mailboxes and shrubs can show the path which the vehicle traveled or where the car went off the road.

Roadway evidence includes tire marks that need to be matched with vehicles involved in the accident. In order to recognize tire marks left on roadways the investigator has to have knowledge of tires and vehicle reaction when involved in collisions and evasive actions in order to decipher and explore their value as physical evidence, which can be of extreme value. Tire marks are classified as imprints of tires, skid marks, and scuff marks. Imprints can be defined as "any marks on the pavement or ground left without sliding by tires on rotating wheels." (Baker, 1986, p. 254) The Northwestern Traffic Institute describes five kinds of imprints:

1. *Prints* of tires on wet or sticky material left on the road surface in the tread pattern.
2. *Impressions* of tires in soft material.
3. *Deposits* from tires are loose or soft material picked up by tread grooves and left somewhere else in the same groove pattern.

4. *Deposits from underside debris* in tire tread grooves.
5. *Ruts* in soft surfaces.

The imprints of tires reveal a vehicle's position on or off the roadway. Imprints of tires usually disappear quickly unless they are an oily substance. Tire prints are made when an adhesive substance attached to the tire has been deposited on the roadway. Impressions made of mud or snow can easily be recognized. Deep, firm tracks in snow or the wet ground are ruts. They show the vehicle's direction and may even demonstrate the point of collision. Ruts are durable, conspicuous and easily photographed.

A skid mark that has been deposited on the surface of a roadway can be attributed to a vehicle's wheels and tires not rotating. Scuff marks and side skid marks are markings left on the roadway as a result of a force other than centrifugal force. Roadway shoulders or unpaved roads create furrow skid marks by the sliding tire similar to skid marks made in soft material such as mud, sand, and snow. Dry, hard roadway surfaces "erase" skid marks interspersed with murky smears when the friction of the sliding tire leaves distinctive deposits. Wet roadway surfaces have a "squeegee" mark. Whenever possible skid marks should be taken before the vehicle has been removed. The investigator wants to establish that skid marks at a traffic accident scene were made by vehicles involved in the accident. Direct questions should be asked of the driver—"Were you driving this car? How fast were you going when at the time you put on the brakes? Did you jam your brakes?" (Weston, 1968, pp. 188–90)

Tire Construction

The construction and condition of a tire play an important role in the safe operation of a motor vehicle. Because they will need to explain how tires can contribute to vehicle accidents, the investigators should be familiar with how tires are built. Basically tires are divided into bias, belted, and radial. The bias tire, the traditional tire used for years and still widely in use, is composed of a textile substance of either rayon, nylon, or polyester. The belted tire, which employs a fiberglass substance, has belts located below the tire tread as reinforcement. Steel belted tires use steel chords. Radial tires are constructed with various layers of plies laid archwise from bead to bead forming a belt. This allows the interior of the tire to work independently of the thread.

At the scene of a vehicle accident, tires can be checked for a variety of defects. Were there any cuts or glass, nails or other items embedded in the tire? Was there any deterioration of the tire rubber, or fabric? Did the stem of the valve break? The traffic accident investigator, depending upon the seriousness of the accident, may want to examine the tires to determine if tire wear was due to the owner's neglect or the manufacturer's workmanship. Tire wear can contribute to an accident. For example, an underinflated tire could cause the driver to lose control.

Brakes

Bad brakes are often blamed as a cause for accidents. For example, deficiency of brake fluid, worn brakes, or brakes in need of adjustment could all result in accidents. When skid marks are lacking at an accident scene involving a collision, this could be an indication that the brakes were malfunctioning. The traffic accident investigator may want to test the brakes to ascertain if they are functioning. If a technical examination is required of the braking system, the services of a qualified mechanic should be obtained.

Vehicle Light Examination

When vehicles traveling in opposite directions are involved in a fatality or when an automobile collides with a motorcycle, the investigator may want to examine either the headlights or the taillights. Often the car driver claims that the driver of the motorcycle did not have his headlights on. The brake lights and taillights should be checked in a rear-end collision, which could be caused by the rear vehicle trying to overtake the slower vehicle in front. The investigator should also check when a signal should have been given for turning, slowing, or any other circumstances involving the use of vehicle lights.

The traffic accident investigator at the scene of a accident should observe whether the lights were functioning or damaged. If the lights are considered to be a potential cause of the accident, then the investigator should consider obtaining approval in removing them. Bulbs and filaments should be thoroughly examined by a qualified examiner. Lights should not be tested at the scene. Collect the bulbs and have them checked by a qualified examiner.

Drag Factor

Friction on the roadway caused by sliding has been referred to as the **drag factor**. The technical term for drag factor—coefficient of friction—refers to "the ratio (retarding) force developed by a skidding wheel and the weight the wheel exerts on the pavement." (Clark, 1982, p. 129) The drag factor varies on any given stretch of roadway and it describes the relationship between the roadway and the tires of a vehicle. Various surface conditions can affect the drag factor such as dryness and type of pavement. Test skids used to be conducted to determine the drag factor using the vehicle involved in the accident under similar driving conditions. Now considered unsafe, test skids are no longer recommended. If test skids must be done, a vehicle of the same type as the one involved in the accident should be used. The skid marks are measured and compared to the drag factor tables. (Drag factor tables published by Goodyear, General Motors, and Northwestern Traffic Institute are accepted in court.) Usually a range is provided; for example, a vehicle was traveling between 20 and 30 miles per hour. (A range gives the benefit of doubt to both the officer and the defendant.) This range represents the minimum speed to create a skid mark with the existing road conditions under which the accident occurred.

If skid tests are to be conducted, then certain procedures should be followed. The skid tests should be conducted between 25 and 40 miles per hour for purposes of safety. These speeds are acceptable for vehicles exceeding the test speed limits. (Clark, 1982, pp. 129–30)

Scale Diagraming

Diagraming the scene of a traffic accident goes hand in hand with the accident report. Most states require that a diagram be drawn to show how the accident occurred. This diagram becomes a part of the accident report.

A scale diagram can be drawn on letter-size paper. Depending upon the type of accident it could show an intersection indicating the direction of travel of the vehicles, point of impact, and where vehicles were located after the point of impact. The diagram uses arrows to show direction of travel. A scale diagram reveals that traffic accidents fall into one of the following categories (Weston, 1968, p. 228):

1. Pedestrian versus vehicle.
2. Right-angle collisions of cars moving in the same direction.
3. Rear-end collisions of cars moving in the same direction.
4. Head-on left-turn collisions involving vehicles approaching each other from opposing directions.
5. Collisions with parked vehicles.

6. Side-swipe or turning collisions involving vehicles moving in the same direction.
7. Head-on.
8. Collisions with fixed objects.
9. Vehicles running off roadway at curves or restrictions in roadway.

Depending upon the seriousness of the traffic accident reports may also include photographs of the accident scene and statements from victims and witnesses. When accidents are of a serious nature, traffic investigators may want to obtain the services of a professional draftsman. A professional scale drawing would be much larger than the letter-size drawing, and would most likely be used for a serious offense such as a hit-and-run where a fatality or disabling injury took place.

Primary Causes of Accidents

A study prepared by the Department of Transportation found that more than 64 percent of traffic accidents are due to human errors and deficiencies. Environmental factors cause approximately 19 percent of traffic accidents, and vehicle causation factors comprise the rest. (J.R. Treet, 1979, p. 7)

Human factors causing traffic accidents are divided into five categories: recognition errors, decision errors, performance errors, critical nonperformance errors, and nonaccident involvements. These categories were further subdivided into a number of errors. For instance, "improper lookout" was identified as one leading cause of traffic accidents. Drivers would change traffic lanes, pass vehicles, and pull out from an intersection without carefully looking for oncoming traffic. Speeding as a cause of accidents appears to be primarily a problem with the young. Another human-factor cause of traffic accidents was found to be inattention. Drivers failed to observe road signs and traffic signals. Improper evasive action—when a driver overbrakes or oversteers—often causes traffic accidents. Alcohol impairment was found to be the most frequent human condition that causes accidents.

Environmental factors include roadway, visibility, and other nondriving or vehicle-related factors that could cause traffic accidents, as previously discussed. Divided highways and the elimination of at-grade intersections have contributed to fatality rates over the years. Major concerns identified with view obstructions include trees, shrubbery, and parked vehicles. Traffic accidents caused by view obstruction occur most frequently at road intersections. Slick roads are credited for causing many traffic accidents.

Vehicle factors involved in accident causation include the brake system, tire and wheels, communication systems, steering systems, doors, power train, suspension system, driver seating, and controls. The three leading vehicle accident causes are brake failure, inadequate tread depth of tires, and brake imbalance. Most vehicle problems that cause traffic accidents can be eliminated by preventive maintenance.

Criminal Activities Involving Vehicles and Traffic Accidents

There are a variety of specific activities that motorists are involved in that can lead to injuries and fatalities as well as being criminal violations of the law. Driving under the influence of an alcoholic or drug substance not only violates the law, but often leads to permanent injuries and death. There are thousands of recorded accidents where innocent people became disabled or lost their lives as a result of being struck by vehicles driven by drivers under the influence of some substance.

Three additional areas that need to be examined are leaving the scene of an accident, referred to as hit-and-run; vehicular homicide; and pursuit driving—refusing to stop for a police officer when signaled to do so. Depending on the seriousness of injury, long prison terms are sometimes given for certain types of offenses involving the use of a vehicle.

Driving Under the Influence of Alcohol and/or Controlled Substances

Driving under the influence of alcohol and drugs has been the cause of many serious traffic accidents. These substances affect emotions and attitudes, and can reduce a driver's ability to make the correct decisions. They can affect the ability of drivers to anticipate potentially dangerous situations or function carelessly. Drivers under the influence of a substance may lack muscular coordination and be uninhibited, confused or sleepy. Alcohol and drugs pass through the body and are absorbed in the bloodstream. Generally the effects of drugs on driving are similar to alcohol. Drivers under the influence feel they are doing a better than usual job and that no harm will come to them. The amount of alcohol in the body is termed blood alcohol concentration (BAC). There are a number of mental

Sun glare, often most dangerous at dusk, can cause accidents. This late-afternoon photo was taken within 15 minutes of a collision involving two trucks. Note how easily the poles on the truck blend into the sky.

or emotional stages that indicate BAC level in the body. (Schultz, *Police Traffic Enforcement*, 1975, p. 75)

1. *Sobriety*
   No apparent influence—person appears normal
2. *Euphoria*
   Sociable, talkative
   Increased self confidence, decreased inhibitions
   Loss of attention, judgment
3. *Excitement* (BAC of 0.09 percent to 0.25 percent)
   Loss of judgement and predictability
   Impaired memory
   Increased reaction time
   Some muscular incoordination
4. *Confusion*
   Mentally confused, dizzy
   Exaggerated emotions
   Disturbed vision
   Decreased sense of pain
   Poor balance, staggering gait, slurred speech
5. *Stupor* (BAC of 0.27 percent to 0.40 percent)
   Inability to stand, walk, or react to surroundings.
   Possible vomiting and falling asleep.

6. *Coma* (BAC of 0.35 percent to 0.50 percent)
   Unconsciousness, which if persisting for more than ten hours, generally becomes fatal.
7. *Death* (BAC of 0.45 percent)
   Respiratory paralysis occurs.

Since driving under the influence is an illegal act, the accident investigator who suspects that a driver involved in a vehicle accident is under the influence of alcohol or drugs should have the driver tested on the spot, with a roadside sobriety test. If the driver tests positive, then an arrest should be made. Within the last decade organizations such as Mothers Against Drunk Driving (MADD) and Remove Intoxicated Drivers (RID) have fought for strict enforcement of laws dealing with drivers under the influence of any substance. Most states have increased the drinking age to twenty-one and the President's Commission on Drunk Driving has recommended that states standardize the blood alcohol content (BAC) to 0.10%. (Presidential Commission on Drunk Driving, 1983, p. 17) Traffic accident investigators who fail to arrest drivers involved in accidents driving under the influence of a substance may find themselves the subject of not only criminal action but also of civil litigation.

Hit-and-Run

Leaving the scene of a traffic accident is typically referred to as a **hit-and-run**. A driver of a vehicle involved in a traffic accident who leaves the scene of an accident has committed a criminal offense and a hit-and-run investigation is considered a criminal investigation. This investigation requires that the driver who left the scene be found and arrested, and that the cause of the accident be determined. A hit-and-run offense can be either a misdemeanor or a felony. If only property is involved, the offense will likely be considered a misdemeanor but if injury or death is involved, the offense will be a felony. In most states, a hit-and-run crime has occurred if the driver did not stop immediately at the time of the accident, and failed to furnish identification by providing his name and address, driver's license, and ownership of vehicle. Drivers leave the scene of an accident for a number of reasons. These include: driving while under the influence of alcohol or a controlled substance; driving without a license or vehicle insurance; carrying a passenger who is not a spouse; driving a stolen vehicle or having stolen items in the vehicle; leaving the scene of another accident; fleeing a crime scene; or being wanted for a crime. (Weston, 1968, p. 207)

FIGURE 17–1: Example of Hit and Run Accident Report

GEORGIA UNIFORM MOTOR VEHICLE ACCIDENT REPORT

Accident No. 920805300 — Agency NCIC No. GA0250300
Date 8-9-92 — Day of Week: Sat — Time 2045 — Dept. Notified 2047 — Off. Notified 2047 — Off. Arrived 2050 — Total No. Vehicles 2 — Total No. Injured 1 — Total No. Fatalities 0
County CHATHAM — Inside City of SAVANNAH
Road of Occurrence CARGO DR. — At its Intersection With SAN ANTON DR.

Veh. No. 1 — Vehicle Type: passenger car — Vehicle Maneuver: straight — Year 89-90 — Make NISSAN — Model 300 ZX — Vehicle Color RED — Vehicle removed by DRIVER

Veh. No. 2 — BROWN, CHARLES D. — 206 CHATHAM AVE. — SAVANNAH, GA. 31419 — Drivers License No. 260889381 GA — D.O.B. 3-27-51 — Sex M — Race: White — Driver Condition: Not drinking
Year 1990 — Make PONTIAC — Model LEMANS — Odometer 16,122 — V.I.N. KL2TN1463LB322314 — License Plate No. CKF-502 — State GA. — Year 92 — Vehicle Color BLACK — Driver Phone Number 748-4607
Vehicle Type: passenger car — Vehicle Maneuver: stopped — Insurance Co. STATE FARM — Policy No. 411-4661-F12-11E — Vehicle removed by EVER READY GARAGE — Citations NONE

DPS-523 (1/88)
DPS MICRO FILM NUMBER (DO NOT WRITE IN THIS SPACE)
MAIL TO: ACCIDENT REPORTING SECTION, P.O. BOX 1456, ATLANTA, GA 30371

Vehicle # 1 — Speed Limit 25 — Estimated Speed 50 — Direction of Travel: N — Number of Lanes 2

Vehicle # 2 — Vision obscured by: not obscured — Speed Limit 25 — Estimated Speed 0 — Direction of Travel: N — Vehicle Condition: no known defects — Number of Lanes 2 — Vehicle Class: privately owned

Type Accident: rear end — Location at POI: on roadway — Light Condition: dark-lighted — Surface Condition: dry — Weather: clear
Road Character: curve and level — Road Composition: black top — Road Defects: no defects

Driver Veh. 2 — 4 / 1 / 1

Injured taken to MEMORIAL — By EMS — Photographs Taken: NO

EMS Notified Time 2047 — EMS Arrival Time 2050 — EMS Hospital Arrival Time 2105
Report by CPL. J. WILLIS — Department SPD — Report Date 8-9-92 — Checked By LT. M.C. BROWNE — Dated Checked 8-9-92 — page 2 of 4
DPS-523

920805300 — GA0250300 — 8-9-92 — Georgia Uniform Motor Vehicle Accident Report

Witness — Name	Address	Phone
SMITH, JAMES	620 WRIGHT DR.	925-1160
SMART, ADAM	220 Cole ST.	352-3011
LOFTON, CAROL	12 SPEAR ST.	354-2091
PATRICK, ANN	10410 CARGO DR.	925-7021

REMARKS

Vehicle #1 was traveling north on Cargo Dr. at a high rate of speed. Vehicle #2 was stopped facing north on Cargo ~~to~~ waiting to turn left onto San Anton Dr. Vehicle #1 ran into the rear of vehicle #2, after the collision vehicle #1 fled the accident scene traveling east on Colleen Dr.

Witnesses Smith and Smart stated that the suspect vehicle was an 89–90 red Nissan 300ZX. Witness Lofton stated the suspect vehicle was a red sports car. Witness Patrick was able to get the tag number of the suspect vehicle (CLD-921) and described the driver as a white female with long brown hair.

A GCIC check on the tag (CLD-921) supplied by the witness showed it displayed on a 1984 Jaguar owned by Linda Moot, 2109 Skidaway Rd.

Report by Cpl. J. Willis SPD — page 3 of 4
(1/88) DPS-523

920805300 — GA0250300 — 8-9-92 — Georgia Uniform Motor Vehicle Accident Report SUPPLEMENT

ADDITIONAL REMARKS

8-11-92 11:40 – Went to 2109 Skidaway Rd. viewed 1984 Jaguar bearing suspect tag number, CLD-921. Vehicle is Blue in color. Evidently CLD-921 is incorrect tag number. Ran numerous combinations of CLD-921, nothing close to Nissan 300ZX.

8-14-92 10:00 – While checking local repair shops located a red Nissan 300ZX with damage to the front end at Whites Body Shop. Mr. White gave me the name and address of the owner, Karen Giles, 108 Habersham St.

8-14-92 1200 – Went to Ms. Giles residence. Ms. Giles is a white female with long brown hair, had scratches and cuts on nose and forehead. Denied any knowledge of this accident stated she had fell asleep and struck

Report by Cpl. L. Rouse 8-19-92 — page 1 of 2
ATTACH TO DPS-523 — DPS-523

Source: Courtesy of David Dixon, Savannah Georgia Police Department.

Accident No. 920805300 | Agency NCIC No. GA0250300 | Accident Date 8-9-92 | Georgia Uniform Motor Vehicle Accident Report SUPPLEMENT

Injured Last Name	First	Address	City	State	Zip	Age	Sex	Veh No	Position	INJ Code	Taken from Scene	Eject Code	Safety Equip in use	Ped Man

Injured taken to: By

Witness Name	Address	Phone

ADDITIONAL REMARKS

8-14-92 1200 - a tree somewhere on Hwy 80.

8-14-92 1400 - Went back to White Body Shop to further inspect suspect vehicle. No evidence of bark or wood in area of damage. Damage is also not consistent with striking a tree. Located black paint transfer in area of damage. Photographed black paint transfer. Took samples of Black and red paint.

8-14-92 1500 - Went to Ever Ready Garage inspected Brown vehicle. Located red paint transfer in area of damage. Took samples of Red and black paint

8-14-92 1545 - Dropped paint samples at State Crime Lab for comparison

Report by Cpl. L. Rouse 8-14-92 page 2 of 3

ATTACH TO DPS-523 DPS-523

Accident No. 920805300 | Agency NCIC No. GA0250300 | Accident Date 8-9-92 | Georgia Uniform Motor Vehicle Accident Report SUPPLEMENT

Injured Last Name	First	Address	City	State	Zip	Age	Sex	Veh No	Position	INJ Code	Taken from Scene	Eject Code	Safety Equip in use	Ped Man

Injured taken to: By

Witness Name	Address	Phone

ADDITIONAL REMARKS

8-19-92 1000 - Received results of Crime Lab paint comparison. Positive for transfer

8-19-92 1200 - Due to Crime Lab results, and the fact that Ms Giles tag number is only one number different than tag number given by eye witness descriptions witness of suspect vehicle I charged Ms. Giles as follows:

1- Driving on Suspended license 40-5-121
2- No Liability Insurance 40-6-10
3- Failure to Report Accident 40-6-273

Court date - September 3, 1992 1030 AM

Report by Cpl. L. Rouse 8-19-92 page 3 of 3

ATTACH TO DPS-523 DPS-523

INDICATE ON THIS DIAGRAM WHAT HAPPENED

NOT TO SCALE

INDICATE NORTH

SAN ANTON

LARGO DR.

POI

1 2

Width of Road 30

VEHICLE DAMAGE CIRCLE POINT OF INITIAL IMPACT

TOWED VEHICLE OR TRAILER DAMAGE CIRCLE POINT OF INITIAL IMPACT

UNDERCARRIAGE DAMAGE none slight moderate extensive fire present

The traffic accident investigation has a number of procedures that must be put into effect when a hit-and-run occurs. At the accident scene, the investigator ascertains the extent of injuries and a description of the vehicle, driver and occupants of the fleeing vehicle, damage, if any, done to the vehicle, and the direction of travel. Once a description has been obtained the information is sent over the airwaves, enabling all nearby law enforcement agencies to search for the vehicle. The investigator must interview and take statements from victims and witnesses. Complete and accurate information should be obtained as to injuries and property damage. Was a plate number obtained? Who obtained it? Can victims or witnesses identify the driver of the fleeing vehicle? Does any one at the accident scene know the make, model, color, or damage to the fleeing vehicle? Who actually observed the accident? A careful examination of the accident scene may discover that broken glass or fragmented parts, such as fiberglass or paint chips, could later be matched with the suspect vehicle and establish probable cause that the vehicle was involved. Debris such as dirt, rust, door handles, glass from headlights and taillights, hubcaps, or personal items such as clothes thrown from the vehicle could provide valuable information as to the owner of the vehicle. Motor oil, radiator water or parts such as fan belts, fan blades, bolts and evidence of punctured tires could provide information on how far the vehicle could travel from the accident scene. Fixed objects damaged by the fleeing vehicle could be studied for traces of paint and damage to the vehicle. The vehicle could be traced by flowing water, oil, or tire tracings left behind. All physical evidence must be guarded and a chain of custody maintained.

The traffic accident investigator does a follow-up investigation and checks license plate numbers, including partial numbers with the motor vehicle department, auto-parts suppliers, auto repair shops, and towing companies. The investigator tries to figure out the reason behind the driver coming to the specific location of the hit-and-run. Does the driver of the hit-and-run vehicle travel the same route at the same time daily? A graphic illustration of the vehicle based on the description of witnesses could be prepared for canvassing purposes or for posting flyers in key locations near the vicinity of the accident. If no suspects are identified, the investigator should periodically check the accident scene of the hit-and-run. By doing this the investigator may come across a salesman or route person who might have observed something at the scene but left before the police arrived.

When the investigator identifies the vehicle involved in the hit-and-run accident he then has to connect the owner of the vehicle with the crime. If the owner was not the driver, then the driver of the vehicle has to be identified. The investigation of a hit-and-run is difficult because a motive may appear to be lacking. The driver may have panicked and left out of fear or he may have been under the influence of alcohol or an illegal substance. Since information can only be obtained from victims, witnesses, and physical evidence found at the scene, the identification and apprehension of a hit-and-run driver is difficult. Modus operandi are nonexistent and confidential informants are of no value.

Vehicular Homicide

Laws pertaining to vehicle deaths vary from state to state. Investigators must know their state laws and the elements of what constitutes a crime if they are to make a case. Vehicular homicide could be based upon negligence, which can vary from speeding in a residential neighborhood to driving the wrong way down a one-way street. It can also include reckless driving. An example of negligence occurs when a toddler runs out onto the street of a residential neighborhood and is struck by a vehicle exceeding the speed limit. The investigation of vehicular homicide requires that all the accident procedures applied to a traffic accident be applied to this type of offense. This includes measuring skid marks, collecting evidence, taking statements from witnesses or victims, and the driver of the vehicle. Photographs and a sketch of the accident scene should be taken. Medical reports of injuries or the medical examiner's report should be obtained. Accurate information must be obtained for prosecution and for any civil action that will come from this type of case.

Pursuit Driving

Each year hundreds of law enforcement officers are injured or killed when they are involved in vehicle pursuit. Not only are officers potential victims when they undertake a vehicle chase but so are pedestrians and other drivers on the highway. In addition, often the vehicle being chased ends up in an accident with the driver, passengers, and innocent people injured or killed. Most states require that before a police vehicle is considered to be acting in an emergency status it must have both lights and siren activated. In all emergency pursuits they must drive with due care and must consider the safety of pedestrians, passengers, and the driver of the pursued vehicle as well as their own safety. Pursuits are normally high-speed chases that are initiated when a traffic violator fails to stop for the police or when the police are attempting to apprehend a wanted person or a suspect of a recently committed crime.

Approximately 32 percent of pursuit driving ends up in a traffic accident and one percent in death. (Alpert and Fridell, 1992, p. 107) Because of the great potential of personal injury and death to officers, occupants of vehicle being pursued, and to innocent bystanders, law enforcement agencies are becoming more restrictive in approving pursuit driving. The primary reason for these restrictive policies is due to civil litigation against municipalities and officers.

Summary

The investigation of automobile accidents is an important aspect of police work. Statistics reveal that more people are killed and injured in vehicle accidents than in any other form of accident. The accident investigation is a matter of obtaining, recording, refining, and interpreting information. The accident investigator's primary concern lies in determining the causes of the traffic accident. The investigator of a traffic accident asks why the accident occurred and who was at fault.

The Commission on Accreditation for Law Enforcement Agencies requires that police agencies have written standards on traffic accidents. The process of accident investigation usually begins with collecting information about people, vehicles, and the highway. This basic data collection process intends to classify data and identify the property, people involved, and the reasons for the accident.

Traffic accident investigations are concerned with vehicles, drivers and pedestrians, witnesses, vehicle defects, road and weather conditions, and the collection of physical evidence. The on-scene traffic investigator must maintain control of the traffic scene in order to conduct a logical, sequential and thorough investigation. The traffic investigator needs to know nine basic items of information: roadway conditions, roadway evidence, tire mark evidence, tire construction, brakes, light examination, drag factor, minimum speed formula and scale diagraming.

There are a variety of specific activities that motorists are involved in that can lead to injuries and fatalities as well as being violations of the law. Driving under the influence of alcohol or drugs, hit-and-run, and vehicular homicide are criminal offenses that usually involve a traffic accident. Pursuit driving can also be dangerous and lead to traffic accidents. The traffic accident investigator needs to be familiar with criminal offenses that are accident related. All accident investigations should be conducted in a professional manner following proper legal and departmental policies and procedures.

Key Terms

at-scene investigation
debris
drag factor
hit-and-run
light examination
minimum speed formula
pursuit driving
reckless driving
roadway evidence
scale drawing
skid marks
tire construction
tire marks
vehicular homicide

Review Questions

1. Why are investigations of motor vehicle accidents an important aspect of police work?
2. Where does the traffic accident investigator's primary concern lie?
3. What are the responsibilities of the first officer responding to an accident?
4. What are the various levels of an accident investigation?
5. Describe the accident investigation procedures.
6. What are the nine basic items of information needed to investigate a traffic accident?
7. What are some criminal activities involving vehicle and traffic accidents?

References

Alpert GP, Fridell LA, *Police Vehicles and Firearms*, Prospects Heights, IL: Waveland Press, 1992.

Baker JS, Fricke LB: *The Traffic-Accident Investigation Manual*, Ninth Edition, Evanston, IL: The Northwestern University Traffic Institute, 1986.

Baker JS: *Traffic Accident Investigator's Manual for Police*, Second Edition, Evanston, IL: The Traffic Institute, Northwestern University, 1963.

Clark W: *Traffic Management and Collision Investigation*, Englewood Cliffs, N.J.: Prentice-Hall, 1982.

Geller WA: Ed., *Local Government Police Management*, Third edition, Washington, D.C.: International City Management Association, 1991.

Presidential Commission on Drunk Driving, *Final Report*, Washington, D.C.: Presidential Commission on Drunk Driving, 1983.

Standards for Law Enforcement Agencies, Fairfax, VA: Commission on Accreditation for Law Enforcement Agencies, 1989.

Schultz, DO: *Police Traffic Enforcement*, Dubuque, IA: Wm. C. Brown Company, 1975.

Treet, JR et al. *Tri-Level Study of The Causes of Traffic Accidents*, Executive Summary, Washington, D.C.: U.S. Department of Transportation, 1979.

Weston, P. *The Police Traffic Control Function*, Second Edition, Springfield, IL: Charles C. Thomas Publisher, 1968.

CHAPTER 18

Narcotics and Other Drugs

In recent decades, drug abuse has become a serious social problem in the United States. Not only has the use of narcotics and other dangerous drugs reached epidemic proportions, but it has also led to the commission of other crimes, such as murders, robberies, rapes, burglaries, frauds, shoplifting, arson, weapon violations, forgeries, and sex offenses.

The Controlled Substances Act

The Controlled Substances Act (CSA), Title II of the federal Comprehensive Drug Abuse Prevention Act of 1970, requires law enforcement agencies to control the abuse of drugs and other chemical substances. A consolidation of numerous laws that regulate the manufacture and distribution of narcotics, depressants, and hallucinogens, the CSA places chemical substances under five schedules. A drug's placement is based on its medical use, potential for abuse, and dependence liability. The Department of Health and Human Services and the Drug Enforcement Agency may add, delete, or change the schedule of a controlled substance. In addition, the manufacturer of a drug, a medical society, a pharmacy association, or an interest group can petition to add, delete, or change the schedule of a drug. When the DEA receives a petition, it initiates its own investigation of the drug. The key issue is whether the substance has the potential for abuse. The following elements indicate a potential for abuse. (*Drugs of Abuse*, 1988, pp. 4–5)

- There is evidence that individuals are taking the drug or drugs containing such a substance in amounts sufficient to create a hazard to their health or to the safety of other individuals or to the community.
- There is significant diversion of the drug(s) containing such a substance from legitimate drug channels.
- Individuals are taking the drug(s) containing such a substance on their own initiative rather than on the basis of medical advice from practitioners licensed by law to administer such drugs in the course of their professional practice.
- The drug(s) containing such a substance are new drugs so related in their action to a drug already listed to make it likely that they have the same potential for abuse. This makes it reasonable to assume that there may be significant diversions from legitimate channels, significant use contrary to or without medical advice, or substantial hazards to the health of the user or the safety of the community. Of course, evidence of actual abuse of a substance shows a potential for abuse.

After determining that a substance has the potential for abuse, the DEA determines on which schedule it will be placed. Figure 18–1 shows the regulatory requirements for controlled substances.

Schedule I

The drug or other substance has a high potential for abuse.

The substance has no currently accepted medical use in treatment in the United States.

There is a lack of accepted safety for use of the substance under medical supervision.

Schedule II

The substance has a high potential for abuse.

The substance has a currently accepted medical use in treatment in the United States or a currently accepted medical use with severe restrictions.

Abuse of the substance may lead to severe psychological or physical dependence.

Schedule III

The drug substance has a potential for abuse less than that of the substances in schedules I and II.

The substance has a currently accepted medical use in treatment in the United States.

Abuse of the substance may lead to moderate or low physical dependence or high psychological dependence.

FIGURE 18–1: Regulatory Requirements for Controlled Substances

Controlled Substances	Schedule I	Schedule II	Schedule III	Schedule IV	Schedule V
Registration	required	required	required	required	required
Recordkeeping	separate	separate	readily retrievable	readily retrievable	readily retrievable
Distribution Restrictions	order forms	order forms	records required	records required	records required
Dispensing Limits	research use only	Rx: written; no refills	Rx: written or oral; refills*	Rx: written or oral; refills*	OTC (Rx drugs limited to M.D.'s order)
Manufacturing Security	vault/safe	vault/safe	secure storage area	secure storage area	secure storage area
Manufacturing Quotas	yes	yes	NO but some drugs limited by Schedule II	NO but some drugs limited by Schedule II	NO but some drugs limited by Schedule II
Import/Export Narcotic	permit	permit	permit	permit	permit to import; declaration to export
Import/Export Non-Narcotic	permit	permit	**	declaration	declaration
Reports to DEA by Manufacturer/ Distributor Narcotic	yes only	yes only	yes	manufacturer	manufacturer
Reports to DEA by Manufacturer/ Distributor Non-Narcotic	yes	yes	***	***	no

*With medical authorization, refills up to 5 in 6 months
**Permit for some drugs, declaration for others
***Manufacturer reports required for specific drugs

Source: Adapted from *Drugs of Abuse*. Washington, DC: Government Printing Office, 1988.

Schedule IV

The substance has a low potential for abuse relative to the substances in schedule III.

The substance has a currently accepted medical use in treatment in the United States.

Abuse of the substance may lead to limited physical dependence or psychological dependence relative to the substances in schedule III.

Schedule V

The substance has a low potential for abuse relative to those in schedule IV.

The substance has a currently accepted medical use in treatment in the United States.

Abuse of the substance may lead to limited physical dependence or psychological dependence relative to the substances in schedule IV.

Types of Drugs

Narcotics are central in the field of medicine, used to relieve pain, suppress coughs, and control diarrhea. **Narcotics** refers to opium derivatives or their synthetic substitutes. They can be abused by smoking, sniffing, or intravenous injection. They can induce a short-lived euphoria.

Initially, narcotics may provoke unpleasant reactions. They tend to reduce vision and incur drowsiness, constipation, vomiting, nausea, and apathy. "Physical dependence refers to an alteration of the normal functions of the body that necessitates the continued presence of a drug in order to prevent the withdrawal or abstinence syndrome, which is characteristic of each class of addiction drugs." (*Drugs of Abuse*, 1988, p. 12) The physical symptoms experienced during withdrawal may depend on the amount of narcotics used.

The main source of narcotics is the poppy **Papaver somniferum**, which has been cultivated in Mexico, Laos, Lebanon, Pakistan, and Afghanistan. An **opium gum** is produced from the poppy plant. Usually the opium imported to the United States has been broken down into alkaloid constituents known as codeine and morphine.

Morphine

A drug effective in relieving pain, **morphine** is the principal constituent of opium. It is generally marketed in the form of white crystals, hypodermic tablets, and prepared for injection. Morphine can be recognized as darkening with age, tastes bitter, and is odorless. This substance can be administered intravenously, intramuscularly, and subcutaneously. The user develops tolerance and dependence rapidly. Only a small amount of morphine is used for medical purposes. Most morphine will be converted to codeine or to hydromorphone.

Cocaine and Crack

South American Indians have used **cocaine** for medical purposes for centuries by chewing the leaves of the coca plant. During the nineteenth century Americans and Europeans used cocaine as a painkiller or stimulant. It was also considered a cure for morphine addiction.

In its pure form, cocaine is a powerful stimulant. It causes in its user a great sense of power and a state of euphoria. A concentration of cocaine in the body can lead to psychotic outbursts, disorientation, and possibly death. Four South American countries supply most cocaine: Peru, Bolivia, Ecuador, and Columbia. Columbia processes the cocaine for export to America and other countries. Cocaine has often been the drug of choice of upwardly mobile and affluent users, among them attorneys, medical doctors, Wall Street brokers, and celebrities.

In the mid-1980s, drug dealers began to synthesize a deadly form of cocaine in labs and to concentrate the cocaine to a more powerful level. This form of cocaine became known as **crack**.

"Crack is cocaine hydrochloride powder converted to a base state which is suitable for smoking. It is made by mixing powdered cocaine with baking soda (or ammonia) and water." (*Controlling Drug Abuse*, 1988, p. 8) The mixture is dried until it hardens, then cut or broken into small chunks of rocks. When this process has been completed, it is ready to sell. A hit of crack can cost as little as $10, making it extremely attractive to low-income users. When smoked, crack becomes extremely addictive and may lead to increased consumption.

Crack can also be combined with other drugs. "Marijuana cigarettes have been sold sprinkled with crack. Crack is also 'laced' or combined with Valium or heroin, which are used to counterbalance crack's intense high." (*Drug Trafficking*, 1989, p. 8) Initially, crack was distributed by networks of local dealers who would buy traditional cocaine HCl from wholesalers and then convert it to crack. These local dealers have given way to large organizations that process, distribute, and sell crack. Competition for market share has led to violence in major distribution areas.

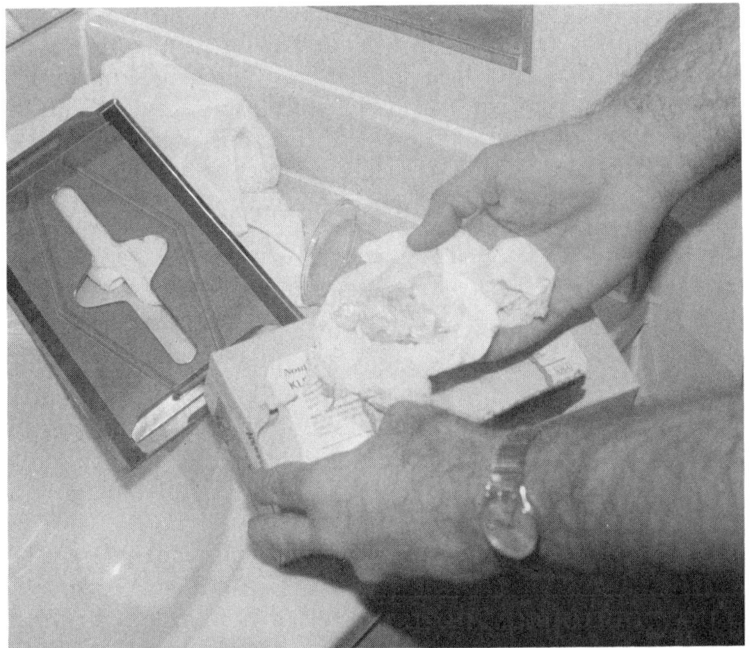

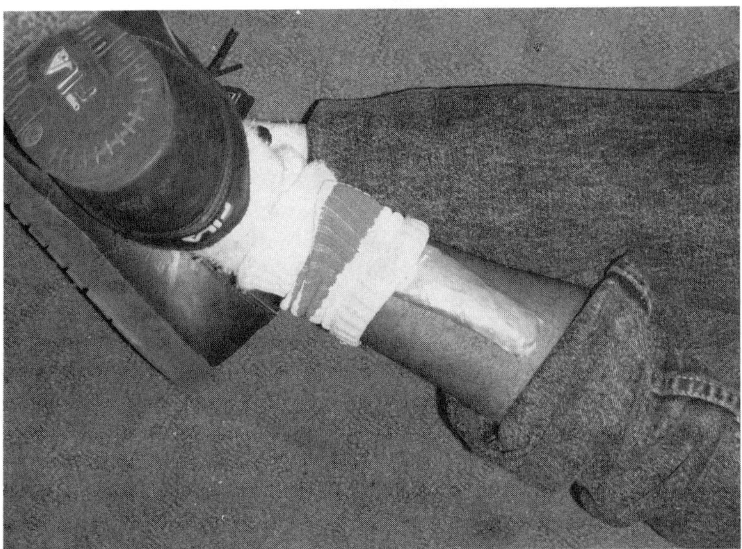

The experienced investigator knows where to search for concealed narcotics.

Heroin

Heroin was first synthesized in Germany in 1874. The Bayer Company sold heroin as a pain reliever in 1898. Its addiction potential was unknown at that time. Pure heroin has a bitter taste and is a white powder. It is usually not sold on the street.

Illegal heroin may vary in color. **Black tar** heroin, from Mexico, may be sticky like roofing tar. Its color can range from dark brown to black as coal.

A new synthetic form of heroin, **fentanyl**, may be an even more deadly problem to the United States. Fentanyl was originally developed as an anesthetic. It can be produced in forms thousands of times more potent than Mexican heroin. It can be packaged like heroin and diluted with the same substances.

Marijuana

In the United States, **marijuana** refers to the cannabis plant and any part or extract of it. Marijuana is a tobacco substance produced by drying leaves and flower tops of cannabis. It can vary in its potency and cause psychic change in humans. Marijuana is the most commonly used drug in the United States. Approximately 25 percent of the marijuana consumed is grown in this country. "Its effects can include a feeling of euphoria, disorientation, a sense of heightened awareness, and, in some cases, a mild hallucinatory effect." (*Drug Trafficking,* 1989, p. 11)

Marijuana proliferates in many areas of the United States. This healthy crop, grown by hydroponics, was discovered at an Ohio residence.

Marijuana appears to be most dangerous when it has been saturated or laced with more potent drugs like PCP, LSD, heroin, or crack. These mixtures are dangerous because they can lead to overdoses or a dependency on the adulterating drug.

Methamphetamine

A synthetic drug, **methamphetamine** has been in powder form since the 1960s. It can be taken orally, by pill, or by injection. Also referred to as crank or speed, the drug causes an intense upper and at times uncontrollable manic behavior in addicts. Methamphetamine is generally produced in illicit domestic laboratories.

During the 1980s, a smokable form of crystalline methamphetamine was introduced in Hawaii from Asia. Its effects are comparable to those of crack, but its high lasts 2 to 14 hours compared to crack's 10 minutes or so. Overdoses are often fatal. Some law enforcement authorities predict crystalline methamphetamine could become the crack problem of the 1990s. (*Drug Trafficking*, 1989, pp. 13–14)

LSD

Lysergic acid diethylamide (LSD) was first synthesized in 1938. Its psychotomimetic effects were discovered in 1943 when a chemist accidentally took LSD. The chemist "was aware of vertigo and an intensification of light. Closing his eyes, he saw a stream of fantastic images of extraordinary vividness accompanied by a kaleidoscopic play of colors. The condition lasted for about two hours." (*Drugs of Abuse*, 1988, p. 39)

LSD has high potency and is usually sold in the form of thin square tablets of impregnated gelatin or paper. Tolerance to LSD can develop rapidly.

PCP

Phencyclidine (PCP) was investigated in the 1950s as a human anesthetic, but its side effects were delirium and confusion. During the 1960s PCP became available for use in veterinary medicine, but it was taken off the market in 1978. PCP has been called angel dust, crystal, supergrass, killer weed, embalming fluid, and rocket fuel. It may be sold as a powder, liquid, or tablet. Often it is applied to a leafy material such as marijuana, mint, parsley, or oregano, and then smoked.

PCP varies in its effects and appearances. This drug can cause a sense of detachment, distance, numbness, loss of coordination, or slurred speech, as well as a false sense of invulnerability and strength. Involuntary eye movement, a blank stare, and an exaggerated gait are often observed when PCP has been taken. Repeated use of the drug can cause psychoses. Except for crack, PCP is the riskiest drug to abuse. (*Drugs of Abuse*, 1988, p. 50)

Designer Drugs

Chemical compounds that are specifically designed as analogues to controlled substances are called **designer drugs**. "An analogue, in this usage, is a substance that is sufficiently different from a controlled substance to legally differentiate it from a drug on the controlled substance list, but which is similar in chemical structure

A stash of narcotics paraphernalia found in a drug search

and in the pharmocological effects to its illicit analogue." (*Drug Trafficking*, 1989, p. 15)

Chemists are adept at creating substances that have the effects and the addictive qualities of controlled substances. Ecstasy, for example, a combination of synthetic mescaline and amphetamine, is a well-known designer drug that causes hallucinogenic effects. Unethical chemists are developing new designer drugs faster than they can be controlled.

A wide variety of drugs have pharmacological or mood-altering properties that make them attractive to potential users. These drugs include natural hallucinogens like peyote and mescaline, synthetic drugs like LSD and PCP, and even registered drugs used for legitimate medical purposes, such as Dilaudid. The latter are considered safer than street drugs, since their constituents and properties are known.

Drug-Trafficking Organizations

There are a number of drug-trafficking organizations that bring drugs into the United States. While these organizations vary in structure and in operations, they do affect each other. These organizations vary as to size, sophistication, clientele, area of operation, and product. They also differ in degree of vertical and horizontal integration, propensity for violence, and interaction with other organizations.

All drug-trafficking organizations have the common characteristic of engaging in illicit activities. Although the drug business does not subscribe to the normal procedures of legitimate business, it does believe in supply and demand. Thus, drug traffickers need to develop efficient operations and rules to operate their criminal businesses. Successful ones can adapt to changing conditions and alter sources of supply. Illicit drug organizations develop into large organizations when they are good at what they do.

A penchant for dealing in cash and a desire to get the cash into the legitimate economy pervade drug-trafficking organizations. This problem becomes more complex as the organization grows. Drug traffickers need to "launder" their illicit money into legitimate businesses. Since large amounts of cash are obtained from drug trafficking, tracking the proceeds can lead to successful criminal investigation. The attempt to launder cash obtained from drug trafficking may be used to identify the traffickers. (*Drug Trafficking*, 1989, pp. 16–40) The next section discusses money laundering in detail.

Colombian Drug Cartels

The Colombian drug cartels are the largest international drug organizations. Their organizational structure is like an onion. The leaders are at the center, insulated but directing the operations. The outer layers are involved in the direct selling of drugs, production, growing, and smuggling. Colombia has four principal cartels: the Medellin, the Cali, the Bogota, and the North Atlantic Coast. the Medellin and Cali cartels supply most of the cocaine coming into the United States.

La Cosa Nostra and the Sicilian Mafia

La Cosa Nostra (LCN) and the Sicilian Mafia have established a drug-trafficking partnership. They cooperate in a number of criminal areas of mutual interest. The Sicilian Mafia is involved primarily in heroin trafficking and works with LCN in several locales in the United States. Law enforcement authorities believe that LCN and the Sicilian Mafia are responsible for large quantities of heroin annually brought into the United States.

There are reports that the Sicilian Mafia has been exchanging heroin for cocaine. With LCN acting as middleman in cocaine distribution, they are developing ties with the Colombian cartels. LCN maintains working relationships with other organized crime groups in order to perform specific racketeering activities. LCN members work with other organized crime groups like the Asian gangs, outlaw motorcycle gangs, ethnic street gangs, and Hispanic crime groups.

Asian Organized Crime Groups

During the 1980s, Asian gangs became a major force in illicit drug trafficking in the United States. These gangs, primarily Chinese, operate on both coasts of the United States. Chinese organized crime leaders in America use their contacts with overseas criminal organizations to obtain a regular supply of commodities they wish to distribute here—heroin, prostitutes, and videocassettes.

The Asian population in the United States has grown substantially since the 1960s, due to the repeal of restrictions on Asian immigrants, the end of the Vietnam War, and the United Kingdom's agreement to return Hong Kong to China. Many new immigrants knew little English, and some quickly discovered a shortcut to economic advancement through criminal organizations. Law enforcement needs to infiltrate Asian organized crime groups, but there are currently not enough Asian law enforcement personnel.

Jamaican Posses

A number of Jamaican organized crime groups operate in the United States. Known as posses, these groups grew out of political affiliations and geographic locations in Jamaica. They are exclusively involved in drug trafficking and have been active in the United States since 1984. Because of the large Jamaican populations in New York and Miami, most posses have connections in these cities.

There are indications that Jamaican posses are developing working relationships with members of traditional organized crime, Colombian drug cartels, and West Coast street gangs. The posses direct violence against anyone interfering with their activities, and are even willing to engage law enforcers in shootouts.

Jamaican posses are unique in that they often launder their own money. They use Western Union to transfer money or purchase real estate or legitimate businesses such as auto repair shops and record stores. The posses are mobile, with large networks of couriers and distributors. They often use aliases, making it difficult to track them.

In investigating the Jamaican posses, law enforcement investigators should review wire transfers, analyze telephone calls, and trace firearms recovered from posse members. Because of the violent nature of the posses, the Federal Bureau of Prisons has established a computerized list of Jamaican criminals, which could be of assistance to law enforcement.

Outlaw Motorcycle Gangs

There are approximately 500 outlaw motorcycle gangs in the United States. Four are national in scope: the Hell's Angels, the Outlaws, the Pagans, and the Bandidos. These gangs specialize in specific aspects of drug trafficking. For example, the Pagans specialize in PCP and methamphetamine, the Bandidos handle methamphetamine manufacturing, distribution, and sales, and the Outlaws deal in cocaine.

Local and regional motorcycle gangs are also involved in drug trafficking. Law enforcement officials have difficulty infiltrating outlaw motorcycle gangs, but they have had limited success with gang members who thought their lives were threatened.

California Street Gangs

California has earned the honor of being the home of the most dangerous street gangs in the country. The two primary gangs are

Graffiti of a crack pipe (upper left) tipped police in Roselle, New Jersey, to the whereabouts of drug dealing in the area. Their investigation led to the arrest of 28 crack dealers ranging from juveniles to a 56-year-old.

the Crips and the Bloods, which have clandestine drug laboratories in the Los Angeles area. They use a number of techniques to distribute crack and PCP. They employ individuals who sell to drivers of passing vehicles or have street workers direct customers to the distribution point.

The Los Angeles street gangs are radiating from their point of origin to other locations, including Kansas City, Chicago, Seattle, and Vancouver. A terrifying aspect of street gangs is their use of violence against other gang members, the general public, and the police. The weapons used during these violent sprees are semiautomatic rifles, sawed-off shotguns, and large-caliber handguns. The police have a difficult time investigating street gangs because of their lack of a formal structure and the high mobility of drug dealers. One strategy for handling gangs is the use of federal drug statutes, which are more stringent than those of most states.

Other Domestic Trafficking Organizations

Traditional criminal organizations that specialize in drug trafficking can be found in metropolitan areas throughout the country—for example, Chicago, East St. Louis, and Detroit. Generally, urban organizations want to monopolize the drug trade in their area. Rural areas also have career criminals who are involved in drug trafficking. Young professionals with high-stress jobs sometimes become involved in drug trafficking after they develop a dependency on drugs. Occasionally, yuppies become full-time drug traffickers.

Other Foreign Nationals

An increased influx of immigrants to the United States has led to an increase of foreign nationals engaging in drug trafficking. For example, Dominican Republic nationals have engaged in cocaine trafficking in areas from Kansas to Rhode Island. Southern Delaware has been supplied by Haitian traffickers.

Money Laundering

Money laundering refers to activities that mask the existence, nature, and disposition of monies obtained from the sale of illicit drugs. Since drug sales are carried out primarily in cash, money laundering is indispensable to the drug-trafficking business. Both small and large drug-trafficking organizations need the assistance of money-laundering specialists. When large amounts of cash are involved, money laundering becomes an especially complex endeavor.

Government Regulations

The main obstacle to money laundering in the United States is the Bank Secrecy Act, which requires financial institutions to report all transactions of $10,000 or more. Financial institutions must report specific information about the customers' identities within 15 days of the transaction and maintain reports on file for five years.

Drug dealers use a method called smurfing to circumvent the $10,000 reporting law. Individuals known as **smurfs** make deposits below the required reporting amount at different banks. In response to smurfing, the Money Laundering Control Act of 1986 made reporting requirements more rigid and provided for transactions to be more assiduously monitored.

There are also money-laundering schemes where drug dealers take their money out of the country. Some traffickers hide their money by purchasing legitimate businesses or investing in personal property such as jewelry, bullion, gold coins, automobiles, and other items that can be converted into cash. The most sophisticated method and the hardest one to track is for the drug dealer to own a bank or control a financial institution. (*Drug Trafficking*, 1989, pp. 40–43)

Law enforcement officers consider money laundering one of the most difficult areas of drug trafficking to understand and to penetrate. This difficulty can lie in not comprehending the who, what, where, and how of money-laundering schemes. However, in the late 1980s, the Federal Bureau of Investigation, the Drug Enforcement Administration, and the U.S. Customs Service successfully concluded undercover operations that led to the seizure of drugs and money and the identification of organization members. Undercover agents penetrated the money-laundering organizations, observed people collecting illicit drug money, and discovered how, where, and to whom money was being sent.

There are numerous groups involved in money laundering and there is competition for the drug traffickers' business. This is reflected in the rates charged; for example, a wire transfer might cost 8 percent while cash smuggling might be 5 percent. The risk of exposure increases when money launderers use a legitimate bank, establishing a paper trail. However, it is a quick means of moving money with limited risks to the drug trafficker. Money launderers who have good contacts and a record of few seizures, money losses, and arrests will get the most business. A well-organized money-laundering group can handle $100 million or more annually.

Money laundering has three steps. "First, illicit money is generated from the distribution and sale of drugs. Second, the money is turned over to a money launderer for transfer out of the United States. Third, the money is moved out of the country into international channels by wire transfers, conversion, or smuggling." (Florez and Boyce, 1990, pp. 22–25)

Wire Transfers

The use of wire transfers depends on a U.S.-based financial institution willing to accept huge cash deposits. One way to accomplish this is simply to bribe key bank personnel.

Some launderers avoid bribery by making several deposits under $10,000 and only one large deposit. This generates only one currency transaction report (CTR), which usually does not flag federal investigators. These deposits can be in cash, converted money orders, cashier's checks, or other negotiable instruments. Launderers may also make single large deposits in rural banks throughout the United States, transfer the funds to a central domestic bank account, and then move the entire amount in a single transaction.

Conversion

The conversion method of money laundering is a lengthy process, but it is used by many launderers because of the relative ease of carrying paper documents out of the United States. This method starts when the money launderer receives a large amount of cash, usually in small-denomination bills, from the trafficker's distribution network.

The central money launderer then hires five to ten persons to go to different banks, post offices, or other places that sells cashier's checks, money orders, or traveler's checks. They purchase cashier's checks for under $10,000, to avoid the CTR reporting regulation, or money orders for $500, which are then used to purchase larger cashier's checks. The converted items are then moved out of the country by mail, through commercial shipping, or by someone hired to take a flight out of the country.

Converted items can also be deposited in a domestic bank and then wired to a foreign bank account. A good operation can easily convert $1 million in one day, using ten people with $100,000 each to complete 15 to 20 transactions.

Smuggling

The third method for transferring illicit cash is smuggling. This is not a preferred method because it increases the possibility of losses through accident, theft, or seizure by authorities. Any money launderer who accepts a consignment of cash is responsible for it from the time of pickup until it is delivered to the trafficker and must be prepared to make good any losses.

To smuggle money, the launderers usually hire *mules*, persons paid to physically transport the cash or converted items out of the country on their persons or in their luggage. Some launderers hide the cash in items for export, such as cars, televisions, or stereos.

Launderers also use private airplanes to smuggle cash out of the United States. In one investigation, customs agents seized a

Learjet in Texas as it was preparing to cross the border with $5 million in cash on board.

Drug Intelligence

Illicit drug use and drug trafficking cannot be contained without good intelligence. Regardless of their size, police agencies should gather, analyze, and disseminate drug intelligence. The *National Drug Control Strategy* (1989, p. 86) lists the following priorities for drug intelligence.

- Increased intelligence efforts to concentrate on the infrastructure of trafficking organizations and their allied enterprises, particularly money laundering.
- Improved drug automation and information systems to allow swifter, better, and more cost-effective drug law enforcement prosecutions, and interdictions.
- Sharing of intelligence developed in the course of investigations and intelligence operations, and dissemination of finished, analyzed intelligence to appropriate federal law enforcement and intelligence agencies.
- Establishment of an interagency working group chaired by the Office of National Drug Control Policy to develop plans for an intelligence center to unite U.S. drug-related analytical capabilities and improve intelligence capabilities. Results will be presented to the appropriate Cabinet Council.

All appropriate federal, state, and local information pertaining to drug trafficking and drug production should be shared with law enforcement agencies. The confidentiality of sources and the method of collection must be maintained. Legally sensitive data and information on criminal investigations have to be safeguarded. Careful planning and implementation are essential to collecting drug intelligence.

Information needed to control drug trafficking has to be acquired overseas, either unilaterally by U.S. agencies or through liaison with foreign governments. The Drug Enforcement Agency coordinates the collection of drug information from foreign governments. The National Drug Control Strategy recommends that law enforcement organizations should work closely with the Central Intelligence Agency, the Department of Defense, and the Department of State. In the process of collecting other intelligence, these federal agencies obtain drug-related intelligence that can be useful to law enforcement agencies.

Analysis

Domestic intelligence is important for controlling drug use at the local level. The Georgia Police Academy found that drug units do an excellent job of collecting drug intelligence, but the information is never processed because "the analysis was not written into a report detailing the important section of the data. Or the analysis was considered too sensitive for other officers or drug units to use." (*Introduction to Drug Investigation*, n.d., Section 10) Information that is not disseminated to drug investigators who could use it is useless. If it will not be used, it should not have been collected. The data and information collected should be put into some logical sequence and cross-indexed to make it easy to retrieve. This collation should allow for the removal of outdated and insignificant information.

Information assembled from various sources needs to be analyzed to determine if a pattern or method of operation can be established. The Georgia Police Academy trains its drug investigators to ask these questions: "What does this information tell us when viewed in this sequence? What does it latently tell us when viewed another way? What other sequences might be used to make sense out of it?"

To understand the nation's drug problem, law enforcement must understand the illegal multinational enterprises and financial networks that support it. The first steps are to coordinate foreign and domestic collection of information and produce drug intelligence against trafficking organizations. To strike out at international drug trafficking, law enforcement must obtain an accurate perception of drug organizations and disseminate this information. (*National Drug Control Strategy*, 1989, pp. 89–90)

Police and Drugs

Many of America's large and small communities are inundated with drugs, crime attributed to drugs, and even more fearful acts of violence attributed to illicit drugs. These acts of violence are associated with street-level drug dealing, especially of crack cocaine. Street gangs are responsible for much of the violence.

The threats of drug trafficking and drug use define the kinds of action that can be taken against users and dealers. (Moore and Kleiman, 1989, p. 2) The police goals are to:

- reduce the gang violence associated with drug trafficking and prevent the emergence of powerful organized criminal groups,
- control the street crimes committed by drug users,
- improve the health and economic and social well-being of drug users,
- restore the quality of life in urban communities by ending street-level drug dealing,
- help prevent children from experimenting with drugs, and
- protect the integrity of criminal justice institutions.

Offenders Who Use Drugs

Offenders who use drugs run the gamut from petty thieves to armed robbers. Drug sellers come in all types and ages. Stereotypes of drug users must be replaced with accurate pictures of users. Law enforcement officers should be aware of who drug users are, the types of crimes they commit, where they commit the crimes, and what kinds of police activities can prevent them from victimizing innocent people. Figure 18–2 analyzes the characteristics of drug-involved offenders. Obviously there are no simple solutions.

Adolescent Users

The use of illicit drugs by adolescents has increased dramatically during the last twenty years. These illicit drugs include marijuana and alcohol. Self-reporting studies reveal that 25 percent of people between the ages of 13 and 17 have used marijuana or some other illicit drug within the last year. It seems the use of chemical substances often begins in junior high school. Reasons youngsters use alcohol or illicit drugs include poor parental supervision, friends who use chemical substances, and a lack of school friends. Half of all teenagers use alcohol, another third consume both alcohol and marijuana, and some are polydrug users. Some young people who distribute drugs do not have delinquent life-styles and usually do not come to the attention of authorities. Other youngsters are deeply involved in drug dealing. They may act as lookouts, recruit customers, or protect drug sellers from being robbed. Drug-using adolescents are more likely to continue their illicit behavior as adults if:

- they come from poor families,
- there are other criminals in their families,
- they do poorly in school,

FIGURE 18–2: Types of Drug-Involved Offenders

Type of Offender	Typical Drug Use	Typical Problems	Contact with Justice System
Occasional Users			
Adolescents	Light to moderate or single-substance, such as alcohol, marijuana, or combination use.	Driving under influence; truancy; early sexual activity; smoking.	None to little.
Adults	Light to moderate use of single substances such as hallucinogens, tranquilizers, alcohol, marijuana, cocaine, or combination use.	Driving under influence; lowered work productivity.	None to little.
Persons Who Sell Small Amounts of Drugs			
Adolescents	Moderate use of alcohol and multiple types of drugs.	Same as adolescent occasional user; also, some poor school performance; some other minor illegal activity.	Minimal juvenile justice contact.
Adults	Moderate use of alcohol and multiple types of drugs including cocaine.	Same as adult occasional user.	None to little.
Top-Level Dealers			
Adults (only)	None to heavy use of multiple types of drugs.	Major distribution of drugs; some other white-collar crime such as money laundering.	Low to minimal.
Lesser Predatory Dealers			
Adolescents	Moderate to heavy drug use; some addiction; heroin and cocaine use.	Assaults; range of property crimes; poor school performance.	Low to moderate contact with juvenile or adult justice system.
Adult men	Moderate to heavy drug use; some addiction; heroin and cocaine use.	Burglary and other property crimes; many drug sales; irregular employment; moderate to high social instability.	Low to high contact with criminal justice system.
Adult women	Moderate to heavy drug use; some addiction; heroin and cocaine use.	Prostitution; theft; many drug sales; addicted babies, AIDS babies; high-risk children.	Low to moderate contact with criminal justice system.

FIGURE 18–2: *(Continued)*

Drug-Involved Violent Predatory Offenders			
The "Losers"			
Adolescents	Heavy use of multiple drugs; often addiction to heroin or cocaine.	Commit many crimes in periods of heaviest drug use including robberies; high rates of school drop-out; problems likely to continue as adults.	High contact with both juvenile and adult criminal justice system.
Adults	Heavy use of multiple drugs; often addiction to heroin or cocaine.	Commit many crimes in periods of heaviest drug use including robberies; major source of income from criminal activity; low-status roles in drug hierarchy.	High contact with criminal justice system; high incarceration.
The "Winners"			
Adolescents	Frequent use of multiple drugs; less frequent addiction to heroin and cocaine.	Commit many crimes; major source of income from criminal activity; take midlevel role in drug distribution to both adolescents and adults.	Minimal; low incarceration record.
Adults	Frequent use of multiple drugs; less frequent addiction to heroin and cocaine.	Commit many crimes; major source of income from criminal activity; take midlevel role in drug distribution to both adolescents and adults.	Minimal; low incarceration record.
Smugglers	None to high.	Provide pipelines of small to large quantities of drugs and money.	Variable contact.

Source: Adapted from M. R. Chaiken and B. D. Johnson, *Characteristics of Different Types of Drug-Involved Offenders.* Washington, D.C.: U.S. Department of Justice, 1988.

- they started using drugs and committing other delinquent and antisocial acts early in life,
- they use multiple types of drugs and commit crimes frequently, and
- they have few opportunities in late adolescence to participate in legitimate and rewarding adult activities.

Adult Users

Generally, adults who are drug users do not commit other crimes. Many middle-class and upper-class people like to experiment with the latest drug fad. They use drugs "to experience altered states of thinking, seeing, and feeling." (Chaiken and Johnson, 1988, pp. 9–15)

The daily user of cocaine or heroin is most likely to commit crimes. The typical adult offender gets involved in drug dealing, which may lead to shoplifting, using stolen credit cards, and forging checks. Drug dealers have also been known to burglarize homes and businesses. Some even commit violent crimes.

Two types of drug-selling offenders come to the attention of the police: "Offenders whose frequency of apprehension reflects their high rates of crime, and offenders who are basically unprofessional, inept, low-rate offenders." (Chaiken and Johnson, 1988, p. 24) The former are more likely to have:

- a prior conviction for robbery, burglary, arson, rape, child molesting, kidnapping, or murder,
- failure to complete a previous sentence (due to escaping), and
- pretrial release on bail or own recognizance when arrested for a new crime.

Information that is not routinely available but could significantly improve the law's ability to distinguish between high-rate and lower-rate drug-involved offenders includes convictions for robbery as a juvenile and indications of persistent and frequent use of drugs.

Drug Dependence

A clear understanding of the terms drug dependence and drug addiction is required for criminal investigators who work in the drug field. From a medicolegal viewpoint, **drug addiction** can be considered "a drug-induced change in the physical state of an individual, such that she/he required the continued presence of the drug to function normally. Further, upon abrupt termination of the drug, the addict would suffer through a physical crisis of varying degree known as a **withdrawal syndrome** (also termed abstinence syndrome). The withdrawal crisis could be ended at any time by readministering the drug." (Liska, 1990, pp. 7–9)

Drug dependency describes the way an addict's body changes physiologically until the drug is required for normal functioning. An addict develops a tolerance for the drug taken, so the dosages must be increased to obtain the desired effect. Narcotics addicts, barbiturate addicts, and alcoholics experience a physical dependence on their drug, develop tolerance, and go through withdrawal symptoms. A person can be deeply involved with a drug in three stages.

1. *Addiction.* Physical change, development of tolerance, withdrawal syndrome.
2. *Drug dependency.* May be physical or psychological. Withdrawal and tolerance are not necessarily seen. Applicable to any drug situation.
3. *Behavioral pattern of compulsive use.* The extreme on a continuum of a drug involvement. High tendency to relapse. Physical reliance and withdrawal not prerequisites.

Responding to Drug Abuse

There are two basic models for responding to the abuse of chemical substances. The first is the disease or public health model, which defines substance abuse as a disease to be prevented or treated, like any other health problem.

The second is the moral-legal model, which defines alcohol and other psychoactive drugs as either legal or illegal and attempts to control their availability through penalties. The moral-legal model uses three methods to control potentially dangerous drugs in the United States. (Abadinsky, 1989, pp. 9–10)

Regulation

Certain substances that may be harmful to their users can be sold, but with restrictions. These substances are heavily taxed (providing the government with an important source of revenue). Alcoholic beverages and tobacco products are subjected to disproportionate taxation, and their sale is permitted only to people above a certain age. Special licenses are usually required for the manufacture, distribution, and sale of regulated substances.

Medical Auspices

Certain potentially harmful substances may be used under medical supervision. The medical profession controls legal access to such substances as barbiturates, amphetamines, certain opiates (morphine and codeine), and heroin substitutes such as methadone.

Law Enforcement

Statutes make the manufacture or possession of certain dangerous substances a crime and empower specific public officials to enforce the statutes. Certain substances are permitted for medical use, but punishment is specified for persons possessing these substances outside of accepted medical practice. For example, heroin has no permissible use in the United States; it is absolutely prohibited. However, other psychoactive substances—for example, morphine and Seconal (secobarbital sodium)—are permissible for medical use but illegal under any other circumstances.

Conducting a Drug Investigation

Investigative techniques basic to all crimes should be used in addition to specialized techniques unique to drug investigations. These can include the use of informers, drug buys, undercover work, drug stings, and other miscellaneous investigative techniques.

For many law enforcement agencies, drug investigations are a specialty. The success of drug investigators is measured by their ability to interact with illicit drug dealers and users. Many pressures are placed on drug investigators, among them operational pressures, public hostility, concerns about bodily harm, unusual work hours, and lack of training.

Police organizations usually equate arrests with success. Drug investigators may be evaluated by number of arrests, amount of drugs confiscated, and amount of money confiscated. Members of the public may fear that drug investigators will stumble into illegal activities they are involved in. Drug investigations can be dangerous. Investigators must adjust their work schedules to accommodate the schedules of drug users and dealers. Often drug investigators are given little training before being assigned to drug work.

Case Screening

Case screening is a tool to help the drug investigator decide whether to continue an investigation based on its number of solvability factors. Designed to provide sufficient information about a drug case at the earliest possible time, case screening allows the drug investigator to discontinue unproductive cases.

Solvability factors are information items about a particular crime that indicate its likelihood of being solved. Through statistical analysis or successful experiences, each law enforcement agency can develop solvability factors. The following solvability factors are recommended in the *Introduction to Drug Investigation*. (n.d., Sec. 13)

1. How serious is the crime/violation?
2. Was there a witness to the crime/violation?
3. Can a suspect be named?
4. Can a suspect be described?
5. Can a suspect be identified?
6. Can the suspect's vehicle be identified?
7. Is sufficient physical evidence present?
8. Is a sufficient M.O. present?
9. Is there sufficient reason to believe that the crime/violation may be successfully solved with a reasonable amount of investigative effort?
10. What resources are available to pursue an investigation of the crime/violation?

Applying the solvability questions to the information known in the case-screening process can determine whether enough leads exist to warrant continuing the investigation. If insufficient information exists but with some effort a case can be developed, it may justify continuing the investigation. However, when insufficient information exists and there is little or no possibility of new leads, the investigation should be discontinued.

Generally, drug investigations concentrate their efforts on three investigative priorities: users on the street, street-level pushers, and major dealers/distributors.

A law enforcement agency or drug task force makes a detailed assessment of drug activity and identifies the problem, decides where the efforts will be directed, and selects a target. Target selection makes screening drug cases easier. For example, if street-level pushers are the target, the information available concerning them can assist in the decision to conduct a follow-up investigation.

Resources and Records

A drug case begins with the receipt and verification of information. The drug investigator learns who is involved in illegal drug activity. Information can be received from various sources, including the investigator's organization, other law enforcement agencies, and informants. Then the investigator has to verify the information's accuracy. This can be accomplished by surveillance, monitoring a suspect's activities, or checking information sources.

When the initial information has been corroborated, the investigator makes a thorough plan for the investigation. Usually the success of a drug investigation depends on small details. The target of the investigation determines the planning circumstances, the type of investigation, and the arrest strategy.

Departmental resources are important factors in the planning of a drug investigation. An investigator can work only with available tools. The following factors should be evaluated. (*Narcotics Investigator's Manual*, n.d., pp. 8–9)

- *Available personnel.* The type and duration of any surveillance, the type of buy undertaken, and other critical decisions cannot ignore a realistic appraisal of personnel needs.
- *Money.* Since the most common forms of narcotics arrests involve either purchasing narcotics or using a flashroll to encourage dealers, a realistic appraisal of available funds must be part of the planning process.
- *Time.* Strategies will vary in response to the learned intentions of the suspect and time considerations as they relate to the agency. For instance, in certain situations it may be advisable to postpone a planned action rather than risk failure because of new or unexpected developments. At other times, the consequences of inaction may outweigh uncertainties. The mobility of the suspect is critical to the amount of time that can be used for an investigation.
- *Equipment.* Particularly with reference to any planned surveillance, the investigator must know what equipment is available in the department and how much of it he or she can reasonably expect to use. Equipment includes items such as binoculars, cameras, body transmitters, night scopes, and special weapons. Field test equipment suitable for the specific drugs anticipated must also be inventoried.

A valuable part of any drug investigation is legal assistance. Since drug laws are complex, numerous legal technicalities could nullify months of investigations. Drug investigators must follow the investigative guidelines developed by the prosecutor's office. If any questions arise (either legal or on a specific tactic relating to a drug case) the prosecutor's office should be consulted.

A review of department records and reports should be conducted for all drug investigations. Numerous investigative leads can often be found within a police department's own records system. The following records and reports should be routinely checked during the progress of the investigation. (*Narcotics Investigator's Manual*, n.d., pp. 9–10)

- *Offense reports.* Filed in general records, these are initial reports filed by responding officers. They contain reports of minor incidents in addition to actual offenses.
- *Investigative follow-up records.* These contain all information recorded during any follow-up investigation based on offense or incident reports. They may contain a case summary if the investigation developed into a court case.
- *Arrest records.* Completed at time of arrest, these may contain details concerning residence, employment, or some other matter that can assist an investigation.
- *Field interrogation reports.* These relatively informal records contain information about minor or incidental activity of patrol officers, including name of person stopped and time and place of conversation.
- *Modus operandi files.* These are detailed descriptions of characteristic patterns of criminal activity associated with individuals.
- *Identification photos.* These provide details of personal appearance when they were taken; the person may look different now. Photos may be filed with limited criminal history and personal details.
- *Fingerprint files.* These provide a final identification check. They may include criminal history and personal details.
- *Wanted bulletins.* These contain details of personal appearance, type of known criminal activity, and personal habits.
- *Gun registration records.* These contain name of registered owner, residence, and type of permit. Depending on the size of the department, they may not be maintained by local police.
- *Warrant files.* These show the names of persons for whom warrants have been issued, date, offense, and subsequent action.
- *Juvenile records.* These list incidents involving juvenile offenders, as well as family information and personal details. They are maintained separately from general arrest records.
- *Traffic records.* These include type of violation cited, name of individual, time and place of violation, and vehicle involved. They are also maintained separately from general records.
- *Traffic accident reports.* These contain any information reported by persons involved in traffic accidents or recorded during any investigation of a traffic accident. They include names of witnesses, site investigation, and reports of interviews.
- *Dispatcher's records.* Since these are available chronologically,

they can be helpful in establishing a comprehensive view of police reaction to a particular incident. Responding officers and peripheral activity are included.

Investigators should also examine records and documents maintained by nonpolice agencies within their geographic area. Obviously the target and the nature of the investigation will determine the extent of the document search. Federal and state laws specify what kinds of information can be made available. Federal agencies, which possess considerable resources of personnel, equipment, and data, can also help drug investigators. (*Narcotic Investigator's Manual*, n.d., pp. 10–12)

- *State motor vehicle administration.* Information about operator's licenses, certificates of title, motor or serial numbers, license plates.
- *Court records.* Criminal, juvenile, civil, and probate proceedings.
- *Probation and parole officers.* Parole status of individual, record of employment, residence, comments of parole officer. Access to parole officers' records is regulated by local ordinances.
- *Public welfare and social service agencies.* Details concerning employment, residence history, and dependents. Access to reports varies; investigators should check local regulations.
- *Coroner's office.* Relatives of the deceased, next of kin, witnesses who testified at coroner's inquest.
- *Licensing bureaus.* Names of applicants for licenses, dates, disposition of requests, references cited by applicants.
- *Bureau of vital statistics.* Birth records, marriages, death records.
- *Board of education.* Personnel records, student records.
- *Board of elections.* Lists of registered voters, length of residence.
- *Attorney general's office.* Conflict with any investigation in progress, outcome of similar investigations, legal assistance.
- *Drug Enforcement Administration (Justice Department).* The most direct source of assistance for narcotics investigations, the DEA maintains records of narcotics law violators and other investigative files, maintains the EPIC/NADDIS computerized intelligence systems, performs lab analyses of drugs, provides legal assistance and expert testimony.
- *Federal Bureau of Investigation (Justice Department).* Comprehensive ID files, crime lab analyses, expert testimony, investigative files, NCIC, training programs, investigative advice and guidance.
- *Immigration and Naturalization Service (Justice Department).* Records of alien registration, immigration, naturalization; lists passengers and crew members of foreign vessels.

- *Alcohol, Tobacco, and Firearms Division (Treasury Department).* Information on gun sales and ammunition sales; lists of distillers, brewers, and firms engaged in handling and sale of alcoholic beverages.
- *Compliance and Investigations Branch (Department of Agriculture).* Results of inspections made under Pure Food and Drug Act; permits and applications for permits from meat packers, food canners, and other food handlers.
- *Bureau of Customs (Treasury Department).* Information concerning importers and exporters, international shippers; registry and licensing of vessels; information relating to smuggling.
- *Visa Division (State Department).* Responsible for alien visa control; oversees immigration quotas and departure of aliens from the United States.
- *Passport Division (State Department).* Determines eligibility of applicants for passports and of persons registered in American consulates for U.S. citizenship.
- *U.S. Postal Service.* Maintains route and rate data pertaining to domestic mail service.
- *Interstate Commerce Commission.* Maintains route and rate data pertaining to interstate shipments and common carriers engaged in commercial transport.
- *U.S. Coast Guard (Department of Transportation).* Keeps records of movements of ships in U.S. waters and background material on all U.S. merchant seamen; performs coastal patrol.
- *U.S. Maritime Commission.* Lists crew members of all U.S. vessels; lists common carriers by water engaged in foreign commerce and persons engaged in freight forwarding, docking, warehousing, and other freight terminal facilities.
- *Social Security Administration.* While many of its records are considered confidential, identification numbers can be traced to place of issuance.

A great deal of information can also be obtained from private businesses and organizations. Useful contacts for investigators include churches, transportation companies, phone companies and other utilities, laundries, banks, credit unions, labor unions, and insurance companies (see Chapter 4).

Informers

The use of an informer always raises safety issues. The drug investigator must also maintain the integrity of evidence and verify the authenticity of the information provided. Drug informers can be obtained from a variety of sources. (Pace and Styles, 1972, p. 40)

- The ranks of drug users.
- Other criminals such as burglars, petty thieves, and prostitutes.
- Casual street acquaintances of the field officer.
- Neighbors and friends of the suspected violators.
- School personnel, ministers, and businesspeople.

The management of drug informers is based on their involvement in the investigation. For instance, management procedures for contacting an occasional informer differ from those for a known associate of a street dealer. Legal considerations and informant reliability must be considered in the handling and use of informants.

Legal Considerations

Information provided to drug investigators by drug informants is hearsay. Hearsay evidence is always admissable to prove probable cause, but it will not support a conclusion that probable cause exists unless there is a reason to believe the information is reliable. Showing such reliability usually takes the form of listing past instances where information was provided, stating the type(s) of information given, and then showing how subsequent investigative activities proved the information to be reliable.

Reliability Factors

Drug information coming from *police officers* is, in and of itself, considered reliable, so it is not necessary to show a past history of informant reliability. Prosecutors must, however, show the basis for police information if those providing it are not going to witness in court (for example, investigators who want to continue working undercover).

Drug information coming from *good citizens* is usually considered reliable; it is generally not necessary to show a past history of reliability. *Victims* of and *witnesses* to crimes are presumed reliable when their identities are revealed and they are available to testify in court. Their identities can be kept confidential if subsequent searches reveal evidence of the crime.

Drug information coming from *criminal informants* is deemed reliable if information from a reliable source supports it or if the informant has a history of reliability.

Drug Buys

In drug-buy activities the investigator and/or the informant, working undercover, make contact with the drug suspect. An introduction that sets the stage for the buy is extremely important. Usually an informant makes the introduction after giving the investigator pertinent information about the drug seller that will lead to a successful meeting—for example, the informant's relationship with the drug seller, how deals are made, how the suspect works, and the amount of drugs that can be purchased.

Drug investigators need to know the type of people they will be dealing with. Are they violent? Drug-buy operations can be classified by either the general purpose of the buy or who acts as buyer, the informant or the investigator. (*Managing Drug Investigative Activities*, n.d. Section 10, pp. 76–95)

Informant Buys

The informant buy is a transaction where the informant is acting under your direction to purchase drugs. Variations on this type of operation include the direct informant buy, the search warrant buy, the unsupervised buy, and the indirect buy.

In the direct informant buy, the investigator controls all the elements of the transaction and plans on having the informant testify in court.

The search warrant buy is supervised. The informant has to be carefully monitored to and from the target location.

The unsupervised buy is a transaction that is authorized by the agency when no direct charges are going to be made. This type of buy is often used as a test to see if the informant can actually make buys. Sometimes several buys are needed to establish the informant with a dealer so that the informant can then introduce the undercover investigators to the dealer.

In the indirect buy, the drugs and/or money pass through the informant's hands, though the undercover investigator is present and part of the transaction. This establishes credibility between the dealer and the investigator, which is reinforced by the fact that the dealer is not arrested. It allows for the informant to be dropped out of future transactions. Normally, no charges are made on the indirect purchase, but the case should be documented the same as a case for prosecution, just in case the investigator decides later to charge the dealer.

Investigator Buys

Investigator buys, or direct undercover buys, center on the hand-to-hand transaction involving the undercover investigator and the suspect. The knowledge and skills are cumulative, like building blocks. Variations include the search warrant buy, the street buy, the direct buy, and the buy/bust operation.

Search warrant buys are very simple. The investigator buys directly and need only establish the cause. There is no need for the elaborate cover surveillance of the informant search warrant buy. However, most situations are usually handled by a buy/bust operation. Investigators should keep the search warrant buy in mind if they cannot set up a buy/bust and if they are trying to get large caches of dope or need to get records or other evidence. Even though an undercover officer is directly involved in the case, detailed planning is required for the actual raid.

Street buys involve buying drugs from street-level dealers. This can be done directly or via an informant, depending upon conditions. This type of operation usually does little to solve the overall drug problem, but because of the high visibility of street dealers, there is a lot of political/community pressure on police to take action. Drug investigators should try to motivate patrol officers to take action against these dealers.

The direct buy, or target buy, is an undercover investigator buy supported by intelligence information about the suspect. This is normally an ongoing case, with a significant organization and/or dealer being targeted for investigation. The most common method of penetration is the use of an informant for the introduction to the dealer.

In the **buy/bust** operation, the dealer will be arrested. This operation requires the application of intelligence, surveillance operations, and tactical planning.

Drug Stings

Local law enforcement is most effective in controlling drugs on the street level, which curtails other crimes that are a by-product of street drugs. The city of Miami, Florida, implemented a sting operation in the late 1980s. The Strategy to Inhibit Narcotics Growth (STING) has three overlapping phases, each targeting a specific problem—buyers, places, and sellers. (Dickerson, 1988, pp. 3–5)

Phase I: The Sting

Once specific hot spots were located, a videotape of conditions in each area was prepared to document the blatant nature of street sales. Photographic evidence showed passing motorists being flagged down in the street and besieged by entrepreneurs peddling illicit drugs.

Task force teams of uniformed patrol officers, traffic enforcers, undercover personnel, and SWAT members were assembled to clean the street of real dealers. Undercover officers then assumed the role of street dealers. Purchasers who had become accustomed to frequenting the same location would drive up and stop, either to buy or to do some comparison shopping.

Once stopped, the buyer was removed and taken to the arrest apartment, where a uniformed officer would search and flexcuff the prisoner. Walk-up sales were much simpler and reduced the chance of escape. As the sale was made, two other officers approached and walked the purchaser back to the arrest apartment.

Prior to the sting operations, the average buyer had little to fear from police or the courts. Arrests tended to be sporadic, as they were either the chance result of a buyer giving an officer probable cause during routine patrol or the result of a call-for-service dispatch. Small-time buyers knew the dealers were the targets.

Phase II: The Drug House

Following the success of the first phase, the department directed its energies to the derelict apartment houses where freebase operations were being conducted in ostensibly vacant quarters.

Phase III: Buy/Bust

Traditional buy/bust operations target a limited number of dealers and are hazardous, expensive, and time-consuming. The Miami police decided to attempt the mass arrests that had worked so well in sting operations.

The first buy/bust targeting street sellers began on August 26, 1986. To complement the usual force of plainclothes officers and uniformed patrol officers, four K-9 dogs trained to detect narcotics were added. The dogs were especially productive in the follow-up search of an area after the arrest teams completed their work.

Dealing with Crack Houses

As the smokable form of cocaine powder known as crack became readily available, drug dealers needed a location where the substance could be distributed and smoked, so the crack house came into existence. "A **crack house** can be defined as any building where crack and other illegal narcotics are sold, which has been fortified to delay entry by police officers armed with search warrants." (Brown, 1988, pp. 5–7) Most crack houses maintain a small amount of crack on hand.

The Houston Police Department developed several nontraditional strategies that have proved effective against crack houses.

- Maintain high visibility by placing a saturation of uniformed patrols in the immediate vicinity of the crack house.
- Park marked patrol cars in front of the crack house.
- Temporarily detain and briefly question persons in the vicinity of the crack house who are reasonably suspected to be engaged in criminal activity, in an effort to develop probable cause to arrest.
- Notify the property owner that the building is being used for narcotics trafficking and that continued violations may result in action against the property.

If the crack house is part of a drug organization under the purview of the narcotics division, traditional investigative strategies will be used. However, all raids will be coordinated with the patrol division where the crack house is located.

Nontraditional strategies are less effective against operators of multiple crack houses, who suffer only minimal monetary losses when one house is seized by the police. Since these drug dealers are not directly involved with buyers, specialized investigative techniques, such as surveillance, have to be initiated. Investigative efforts continue until crack house operators who insulated themselves are successfully prosecuted.

Saturation Operations

Another strategy local police use to keep street dealers and drug users on their toes is **saturation**, or inundating an area with police officers. For example, for a day or two the Savannah Police Department will saturate a 30- or 40-block area with police officers from the tactical, traffic, motorcycle, and horse patrol units.

Saturation operations are designed to clean up areas for several days and to show force in known drug areas. When police sweep through an area, drug dealers close up shop and take their sales elsewhere. A major purpose of a drug sweep is to show the community that the police care about them and support them in solving their drug problem.

In an operation that used some saturation concepts, the New York Police Department initiated Operation Pressure Point in 1984 to rid the city of all drug-prone enclaves. This comprehensive law enforcement effort to deal with the drug problem called for a two-pronged attack.

Phase I, the enforcement phase, consisted of proactive enforcement of highly visible, uniformed patrols in the most blatant, drug-prone segment of the target area. These patrols worked in tandem with narcotics division plainclothes teams. As each area became stabilized, the units moved on to the next designated area, leaving a small force behind to prevent a recurrence of drug activity.

Phase II, the neighborhood involvement program, was implemented when the entire target area was stabilized and the community had demonstrated confidence in the police effort. This phase was designed to stimulate the community to take an active role, in conjunction with the police department, in reclaiming its neighborhood from the drug dealers and users. It involved intensive police community interaction, education and training for the residents (especially the youth), and a unique referral process for the many resident drug addicts.

Before Operation Pressure Point could begin, extensive groundwork had to be done. First, cooperation had to be obtained from other criminal justice components. Their input was solicited and they were informed that the operation could affect their agencies. The second step was obtaining community support. Press releases and the media were used to inform the community of the police objectives for the operation and to solicit their support for the neighborhood involvement program. In the last stage, police personnel and training were provided. This stage also emphasized police sensitivity toward a community besieged by drug dealers and users. (Caroll, 1989, pp. 1–2)

Marijuana and Controlled Substance Excise Tax

In 1990 the state of Georgia imposed an excise tax on marijuana and controlled substances whether they are real or counterfeit, held, possessed, transferred, used, consumed, sold, or offered for sale in violation of state laws. Law enforcement and prosecuting offices refer cases to the Georgia Department of Revenue, which initiates procedures to collect all revenues due the state of Georgia for income, sales, and excise taxes. Collection procedures include seizure of bank accounts, jewelry, vehicles, and any other real or personal property owned by the nontaxpayer. This is in addition to any actions taken by law enforcement forfeiture seizure statutes. Figure 18–3 is a Department of Revenue report of arrest involving controlled substances.

Tampa: Drug Enforcement Strategies

In the summer of 1985, the crime rate of Tampa, Florida, began to soar when crack cocaine appeared on the scene. With crack came street dealing in the open and the deterioration of neighborhoods

FIGURE 18-3: Arrest/Seizure Involving Marijuana or Controlled Substances

Department of Revenue
Field Services Division
Task Force—803
Trinity-Washington Building
Atlanta, Georgia 30334
Telephone Number: (404) 656-4598
FAX (404) 656-6849

Marcus E. Collins, Sr.
Commissioner

Fred B. White
Director

Reporting Agency: ______________________ Date of Seizure: ______________________
Address: ______________________ Address: ______________________
Officer: ____________ Phone: (___)______ City: ____________ Zip ____________
County: ______________________

Quantity Seized:	Description:	Possession:
_____ Grams of Marijuana		
_____ Grams of Controlled Substance		
_____ Dosage Units—Controlled Substance Not Sold By Weight		
$ Cash Seized		
$ Cash Seized		

Please identify or briefly describe by whatever official name, common or usual name and designate of whom or where cash and/or drugs were found.

Identification of the Individual Arrested in Connection With Above Substances:				
1. Name	DOB	Social Security No.:		
Address		City	St.	Zip
2. Name	DOB	Social Security No.:		
Address		City	St.	Zip
3. Name	DOB	Social Security No.:		
Address		City	St.	Zip

Please identify or briefly describe any cash, personal or real property in possession of or belonging to the individual named above (if known). Place an asterisk by the items under condemnation by your agency:

____

____

When possible please attach copies of arresting officer's general report, summary reports, crime labs results, etc. for additional case support.

Note: The Georgia Revenue Department charges a tax for selling illegal drugs.

Source: Georgia Department of Revenue.

where crack was sold. From 2 to 20 drug dealers appeared in multiple locations throughout the City of Tampa. Users in their cars lined up on residential streets to purchase crack. To make a bad situation even worse, drug dealers had confrontations over locations. The quality of life in neighborhoods where crack was being marketed declined rapidly.

The Tampa Police Department used various strategies to deal with the drug problem. Traditionally, uniformed patrol officers are responsible for conditions in their assigned areas. But beat patrol officers did not have the intelligence information or time to deal effectively with street dealers. So four narcotics squad members were assigned to each of eight plainclothes officers, whose chief responsibility was to investigate complaints related to narcotics. These units received support from the selective enforcement bureau, a 24-member uniformed unit.

The Tampa Police Department developed a combination of strategies to combat its drug problem. (Smith et al., 1990, pp. 1–5)

- Reverse sting operations, where officers posed as drug dealers and arrested buyers.
- Buy/busts, in which the undercover officer purchased drugs from a seller and then immediately arrested him or her.
- Uniformed deterrence, in which marked vehicles and uniformed officers remained at a "drug hole" for extended periods of time.
- Search warrants for suspected drug houses.
- Wiretaps to identify major suppliers of street-level dealers.
- Civil condemnation procedures for drug houses.
- Infiltration of drug organizations by undercover officers to identify members and develop criminal cases.
- An airport interdiction team to apprehend couriers bringing drugs into the city.
- Task forces organized in cooperation with other police agencies at local, state, and federal levels.

Several neighborhood operations were undertaken using highly visible officers and citizens. One, Attack Crack Together (ACT), resulted in establishing roadblocks in certain drug-infested neighborhoods.

Although these strategies met with some success, they often just displaced the selling of drugs from one location to another. In the spring of 1988, the Mayor's Operation Crackdown demolished 50 structures that had been used for illicit drug activities. Tampa has repeated this operation several times.

The Tampa Police Department finally concluded that its street-level drug enforcement plan must include all of the following elements.

- The strategy must be citywide.
- There must be a long-term commitment to the plan.
- Adequate resources must be allocated.
- Citizen involvement must be solicited and maintained.
- There must be a method to communicate with individual citizens without exposing them to retaliation.
- There must be an immediate response to citizens' complaints.
- The strategy must involve officers from each division or bureau of the police department rather than just a specialized unit.
- There must be a system to assure constant monitoring of conditions prevailing throughout the city.
- There must be active media involvement to enhance public education and support.

The QUAD Unit

During the winter of 1989, the Tampa Police Department established the Quick Uniformed Attack On Drugs (QUAD) unit to suppress drug sales at the street level. The assumption was that suppressing street-level drug dealing required close supervision, specialized training, maturity, and good judgment. QUAD officers had to be willing to work flexible hours and perform traditional police work as well as their assigned special task of suppressing street drug dealing.

Tampa had approximately 60 locations where drug dealing was taking place. Forty officers and a drug-finding dog were assigned to the QUAD unit. This action was taken with the following issues in mind. (Smith et al., 1990, pp. 9–15)

- Tampa was experiencing a growing crime problem fueled by drug abuse.
- To reduce crime, the police must make the control of street drug sales their number one priority.
- Neighborhoods were suffering severely from the presence of street drug dealers and needed immediate relief.
- The city could not afford the hundreds of additional officers necessary for round-the-clock coverage at 60 locations.
- A new strategy was required to address the problem.

In order to encourage citizen involvement, high-ranking members of the Tampa Police Department and officers from the QUAD

Tampa, Florida's QUAD Squad in action

unit were involved in dozens of large and small neighborhood meetings. The purpose of the meetings was to locate crack houses and dope holes.

QUAD squad officers were paired with undercover narcotics officers and plainclothes officers. The narcotics detectives would help in drafting search warrants, filing federal charges, and processing assets seized. If the investigation looked to be very time-consuming, it would then be turned over to the narcotics division. The police communication section would provide the QUAD squad with daily printouts of drug-related complaints and the detective division would forward to it reports of drug-related crimes.

Other city departments were encouraged to develop liaisons with the police department. This cooperation led city zoning, fire, and code enforcement inspectors to accompany QUAD officers on their investigations. Whenever warrants were served by the QUAD officers, civil inspections became part of the routine. QUAD officers also provided drug recognition and training to city parks and recreation workers. The Tampa Public Housing Authority gave the QUAD officers approval to take police action on their property when they were not present, including keeping nontenant drug dealers from housing authority property.

To control the selling of drugs on open streets a city ordinance was passed to prohibit loitering. A nuisance abatement board was established and authorized to declare any residence or commercial establishment a public nuisance if drug activity was occurring there.

Asset Forfeiture

The passage of federal legislation gave drug investigators assistance to discontinue the operations of drug dealers when they were arrested. The Comprehensive Crime Control Act of 1984 revised civil and criminal forfeiture procedures to encompass all felony drug cases. The **asset forfeiture** provision of the law permits law enforcement investigators to seize any property constituting or derived from drug trafficking. Assets seized can be either tangible or intangible personal property.

Bank records are an important source of leads in locating assets that can be seized. Bank records can be obtained through search warrants, court subpoenas, civil summons, or other legal avenues. Banking transactions are of two types, those that flow through accounts and nonaccount transactions. Figure 18–4 details the types of transactions and the records banks maintain for them.

Before taking any legal action to obtain a subpoena or other legal document, the drug investigator should determine whether the felon has checking accounts, savings accounts, loan accounts, investment accounts, or a safe deposit box. Bank checks and currency exchanges are difficult to locate. The primary methods drug traffickers use are currency and cashier's checks. Once they have safely deposited their money in a bank, they may launder it by wire transfers to other banks abroad or in the United States.

The tracing of financial records is more than a paper chase. It can lead to assets that can be seized by using civil procedures, which are faster than criminal seizures. Bank records are the key to finding hidden assets and unknown principals, witnesses, and coconspirators. (Morley, 1989, pp. 15–47)

Preventing Drug Abuse

Under the sponsorship of the U.S. Department of Justice, the International Association of Chiefs of Police and the Drug Enforcement

FIGURE 18–4: Types of Banking Transactions and Records Maintained

- **I. Account Transactions**
  - A. Deposits
    1. Teller tape
    2. Deposit ticket
    3. Item deposited
    4. Cash-in ticket
    5. Credit memo
  - B. Withdrawals
    1. Teller tape
    2. Check
    3. Cash-out ticket
    4. Debit memo
- **II. Nonaccount transactions**
  - A. Loans
    1. Loan application
    2. Loan ledger
    3. Correspondence file
    4. Loan disbursement documents
       - a. Teller tape
       - b. Bank check
       - c. Credit memo
    5. Loan repayment documents
       - a. Teller tape
       - b. Copies of checks
       - c. Cash-in tickets
       - d. Debit memos
  - B. Securities (CDs, stocks, bonds, etc.)
    1. Bank copy of security (delivered)
    2. Security held in safekeeping
    3. Payment instrument
       - a. Teller tape
       - b. Copy of check
       - c. Cash-in ticket
       - d. Debit memo
    4. Disbursement instrument
       - a. Teller tape
       - b. Bank check
       - c. Credit memo
  - C. Bank checks (cashier's checks, treasurer's checks, money orders, traveler's checks)
    1. Copy of bank check
    2. Copy of application
    3. Purchase document
       - a. Teller tape
       - b. Copy of check used
       - c. Cash-in ticket
       - d. Debit memo
    4. Redemption document
       - a. Teller tape
       - b. New bank check issued
       - c. Credit memo
       - d. Cash-out ticket
  - D. Wire transfers
    1. Application for wire
    2. Federal Reserve wire memo
    3. Swift message memo
    4. Funds-out documentation
       - a. Teller tape
       - b. Copy of check used
       - c. Cash-in ticket
       - c. Debit memo
    5. Funds-in documentation
       - a. Teller tape
       - b. Bank check
       - c. Credit memo
  - E. Safe deposit box
    1. Signature card contract
    2. Entry record

Source: CH Morley, *Tracing Money Flows Through Financial Institutions.* Washington, D.C.: U.S. Department of Justice, February, 1989.

Administration developed a manual for police chiefs and sheriffs. *Reducing Crime by Reducing Drug Abuse* provides law enforcement with a prescription to prevent drug abuse. Its summary review of law enforcement, intervention, and treatment efforts shows that, while there are successes to celebrate, there are too many failures. (1988, p. 47)

Law Enforcement

While increasing the number of arrests is necessary and should not be abandoned, it is not resulting in a dramatic decrease in the flow of drugs and the incidence of crime in this nation's small towns and large cities. Investigation, interdiction, and even arrest do not seem to deter criminal activities, especially those that yield such a high return on investment.

Prison and loss of money, property, and other assets are sanctions that, if severely applied, are effective deterrents. If these measures cannot be successfully imposed because the criminal justice system is unable to accommodate the volume, their basic deterrent impact is lost.

Similarly, there is no deterrent effect to drug testing to screen job applicants and employees if there is no policy specifying actions for positive tests or if existing policy sanctions are not applied.

Intervention

There appears to be cautious hope for intervention strategies that identify youthful drug users early enough to modify their behavior through social pressure, psychological treatment, and legal deterrence. Intervention is often thought to be successful with first-time offenders, but that phrase is frequently a misnomer. The youth is probably just "first-time caught," posing a stronger challenge to intervention programs.

Treatment

Treatment of drug abusers continues to be subject to academic and practical debate. Proponents of treatment cite cost-effectiveness, although it appears that for many addicts treatment must be applied repeatedly and for lengthy periods of time. The many varieties of addiction require as many varieties of treatment, and some addicts may simply be untreatable. The practical problem with treatment is its critical lack of availability nationwide.

Prevention

Given the proven limitations of other efforts, the best hope for reducing drug abuse, and thus reducing crime, appears to rest with prevention. Experts are researching educational approaches to steer adolescents away from activities that will bring them into contact with the criminal justice system. Currently, the methods of prevention are diverse and, for the most part, unproven. They encompass education, the reinforcement of family values, athletics, decision-making skills, the threat of certain and severe sanctions, and alternative choices. Fundamental questions—who should teach what and when they should teach it—still remain largely unanswered.

The DARE Program

One prevention program that police agencies are involved in is *Drug Abuse Resistance Education (DARE)*, which began in Los Angeles and is spreading to police agencies throughout America. This program places trained police officers in elementary and junior high schools. One focus of the DARE program is to build trust between the schools and the police. Through DARE, students learn that:

- Real friends will not push them into trying drugs and alcohol.
- Contrary to popular myth, the majority of their peers do not use these substances.
- Being grown-up means making their own decisions and coping with problems in a positive way.
- They can assert themselves in the face of peer pressure.

DARE encourages youngsters to feel good about themselves. The curriculum is organized into 17 classroom sessions, conducted

A police officer involved in "hands-on" drug education with schoolchildren as part of a Beverly Hills Drug Abuse Resistance Education (DARE) program.

by police officers trained in the DARE concept. Various teaching techniques are used, among them group discussions, role-playing, workbook exercises, and question-and-answer periods. The DARE program encourages student involvement. The following is a brief summary of the DARE curriculum. (DeJong, 1986, pp. 3–4)

1. *Practices for personal safety.* The DARE officer reviews common safety practices to protect students from harm at home, on the way to and from school, and in the neighborhood.
2. *Drug use and misuse.* Students learn the harmful effects of drugs if they are misused, as depicted in the film *Drugs and Your Amazing Mind.*
3. *Consequences.* The focus is on the consequences of choosing to use alcohol, marijuana, and other drugs. If students are aware of those consequences, they can better decide how to behave.
4. *Resisting pressures to use drugs.* The DARE officer explains different types of pressure that friends and others exert on students to get them to try alcohol or drugs, ranging from friendly persuasion and teasing to threats.
5. *Resistance techniques: way to say no.* Students rehearse the many ways of refusing offers to try alcohol or drugs—for example, simply saying no as often as necessary, changing the subject, and walking away or ignoring the person. They learn to avoid situations where they might be subjected to such pressures.
6. *Building self-esteem.* Poor self-esteem is one of the factors associated with drug misuse. Students learn to see their own positive qualities and discover ways to compliment others.
7. *Assertiveness: a response style.* Students have certain rights—to be themselves, to say what they think, to say no to offers of drugs. They learn to assert those rights confidently without interfering with others' rights.
8. *Managing stress without taking drugs.* Students learn to recognize sources of stress in their lives and to develop techniques for avoiding or relieving it, including exercise, deep breathing, and talking to others. They learn that using drugs or alcohol to relieve stress causes new problems.
9. *Media influences on drug use.* The DARE officer reviews strategies seen in the media to encourage tobacco and alcohol use, including testimonials from celebrities and pressure to conform.
10. *Decision-making and risk-taking.* Students learn the difference between bad risks and reasonable risks, how to recognize the

The DARE Program (*Continued*)

choices they have, and how to make a decision that promotes their self-interest.

11. *Alternatives to drug abuse.* This session points out that drugs and alcohol are not the only way to have fun, to be accepted by peers, or to deal with feelings of anger or hurt.
12. *Alternative activities.* Sports or other physical fitness activities are good alternatives. Exercise improves health and relieves emotional distress.
13. *Officer-planned lessons.* The class is given a special lesson tailored by the DARE officer to that particular class.
14. *Role modeling.* A high school student selected by the DARE officer visits the class, providing students with a positive role model. Students learn that drug users are in the minority.
15. *Project DARE summary.* Students summarize and assess what they have learned.
16. *Taking a stand.* Students compose and read aloud essays on how they can respond when pressured to use drugs and alcohol. The essay represents each student's DARE pledge.
17. *Assembly.* In a schoolwide assembly, planned in concert with school administrators, all students who participated in DARE receive certificates of achievement.

The President's Drug Report

It has become clear that there are two ways to influence individuals in their decision to use illicit drugs. The first method of influence is moral persuasion and information. The second approach attempts to make the individual fear the penalties and consequences of using illicit drugs. Generally, the education/persuasion strategy has been thought to reduce demand and the consequences strategy is thought to reduce supply. Both strategies are important in preventing drug abuse. In the National Drug Report, President Bush made a number of recommendations pertaining to education, community action, and the workplace.

- Implement firm drug prevention programs and policies in schools, colleges, and universities. Such programs and policies will be a condition of eligibility for receipt of federal funds.
- Develop model alternative schools for youths with drug problems. Federal assistance to local education agencies will promote such development.

- Develop media outreach activities that deal with the dangers of using illegal drugs, particularly crack, and with drug-impaired pregnancies. Provide federal support for these programs.
- Create a national program to mobilize volunteer efforts to fight drugs.
- Implement Executive Order 12564 to ensure a drug-free federal workforce. Put in place drug-free workplace policies in the private sector and state and local government, including clear penalties for drug use, and drug testing where appropriate.
- Establish a demand-reduction working group to coordinate and oversee implementation of the national drug control strategy. This group will consider demand-related drug policy issues that are interdepartmental in nature. It will not deal with operational decisions or have line authority or responsibility.

Summary

In recent decades, drug abuse in the United States has become a serious social problem. The use of narcotics and other dangerous drugs has not only reached epidemic proportions but also has led to the commission of other crimes. The federal Controlled Substances Act places chemical substances under five schedules based on their medical use, potential for abuse, and dependence liability.

Narcotics—opium derivatives or synthetic substitutes—are used to relieve pain, suppress cough, and cure diarrhea. Narcotics can be smoked, sniffed, or injected intravenously. Any relief obtained from them, whether psychological or physical, can result in short-lived euphoria.

A number of organizations bring drugs into the United States. These organizations vary in structure, operations, size, sophistication, clientele, area of operation, and product. A penchant for dealing in cash and the desire to get the cash into the legitimate economy pervade the drug-trafficking organizations. Money laundering may be tracked to identify drug traffickers. Organizations involved in drug trafficking include Colombian drug cartels, La Cosa Nostra and the Sicilian Mafia, Asian organized crime groups, Jamaican posses, outlaw motorcycle gangs, California street gangs, and foreign nationals.

Money laundering masks the existence, nature, and disposition of monies obtained from the profits of the sale of illicit drugs. Drug dealers use a number of individuals, known as smurfs, who make deposits at different banks below the required reporting amounts. Law enforcement officers consider money laundering one of the most difficult areas of drug trafficking to understand and penetrate.

To effectively curtail drug trafficking, intelligence must be collected. Police agencies, regardless of their size, should gather, analyze, and disseminate drug intelligence. All appropriate federal, state, and local drug information pertaining to drug trafficking and drug production should be shared with law enforcement agencies.

Many American communities are inundated with drugs, crime attributed to drugs, and even more fearful acts of violence caused in part by illicit drugs. These acts of violence are associated with street-level drug dealing, specifically crack cocaine. Much of the violence can be attributed to street gangs. A drug addict's body changes physiologically until the drug is required for normal functioning. An addict develops a tolerance for the drug taken, so dosages must be increased to obtain the desired effect.

There are two basic models for responding to chemical substances. The disease or public health model defines substance abuse as a disease to be prevented or treated like any other health problem. The moral-legal model defines alcohol and other psychoactive drugs as either legal or illegal and attempts to control availability through penalties.

Investigative techniques basic to all crimes should be used, in addition to specialized techniques unique to drug investigations. These can include the use of informers, buy/busts, drug stings, and other investigative techniques.

The first phase of a drug case is receipt and verification of information. The drug investigator learns who is involved in illegal drug activity. Information can be received from various sources, including the investigator's organization, other law enforcement agencies, and informants.

A valuable part of any drug investigation is legal assistance. Since drug laws are complex, numerous legal technicalities could nullify months of investigations. Drug investigators need to follow investigative guidelines developed by the prosecutor's office. Any questions, either legal or on a specific tactic, should be posed to the prosecutors.

Investigators should examine records and documents maintained by other agencies within their geographic area, from federal agencies, and from private organizations. Informers must be used cautiously. The management of informers is based upon their involvement in the investigation. In drug-buy activities, the investigator and/or the informant make contact with the suspect. Local law enforcement is most effective in controlling drugs on the street level, which helps curtail other crimes that are a by-product of street drugs.

Police have developed strategies to curtail drug activities taking place at crack houses. Local police also keep street dealers and drug users on their toes with saturation, inundating an area with police officers.

In 1990 the state of Georgia imposed an excise tax on marijuana and controlled substances, whether they are real or counterfeit, held, possessed, transported, transferred, used, consumed, sold, or offered for sale in violation of state laws. In 1989 the Tampa Police Department established the Quick Uniformed Attack on Drugs (QUAD) unit to suppress drug sales at the street level.

Federal legislation allows drug investigators to discontinue the operations of arrested drug dealers. The asset forfeiture law permits investigators to seize any property constituting or derived from drug trafficking.

Law enforcement agencies are beginning to recognize the importance of drug prevention programs. For example, the Los Angeles Police Department initiated the DARE program to help elementary and junior high students say no to drugs.

Key Terms

asset forfeiture
black tar
buy/bust
cocaine
crack
crack house
designer drugs
Drug Abuse Resistance Education
drug addiction
drug dependency
fentanyl
lysergic acid diethylamide (LSD)
marijuana
methamphetamine
money laundering
morphine
narcotics
opium gum
Papaver somniferum
PCP
saturation
smurfs
withdrawal syndrome

Review Questions

1. What is the Controlled Substances Act?
2. What items are indicators that a drug or other substance has a potential for abuse?
3. What is the main source of narcotics?
4. Describe two drugs that are often abused.
5. Describe two drug trafficking organizations.
6. Why is drug intelligence important?
7. Describe money laundering.
8. Define the terms *drug dependence, drug addiction*, and *withdrawal syndrome*.
9. Discuss the two basic models for responding to chemical substances.
10. Discuss some of the police department records and reports that could assist in a criminal investigation.
11. Discuss some of the federal agencies that are involved in drug investigations.
12. What should a drug investigator be concerned with when dealing with informants?
13. Describe drug buys.
14. Explain asset forfeiture.
15. Describe the DARE program.

References

Abadinsky H: *Drug Abuse: An Introduction.* Chicago, IL: Nelson Hall, 1989.

Brown L: "Strategies for Dealing with Crack Houses." *FBI Law Enforcement Bulletin,* vol.57, no. 6, 1988.

Caroll P: "Operation Pressure Point: An Urban Drug Enforcement Strategy." *FBI Law Enforcement Bulletin,* vol.58, no. 4, 1989.

Chaiken MR, Johnson BD: *Characteristics of Different Types of Drug-Involved Offenders.* Washington, D.C., National Institute of Justice, 1988.

Controlling Drug Abuse: A Status Report. Washington, D.C., General Accounting Office, 1988.

DeJong W: "Project DARE: Teaching Kids to Say No to Drugs and Alcohol." *National Institute of Justice,* 1986.

Dickerson C: "Drug Stings in Miami." *FBI Law Enforcement Bulletin,* vol.57, no. 1, 1988.

Drugs of Abuse. Washington, DC: U.S. Government Printing Office, 1988.

Drug Trafficking: A Report to the President of the United States. Washington, DC: U.S. Department of Justice, 1989.

Florez CP, Boyce B: "Laundering Drug Money." *FBI Law Enforcement Bulletin,* vol.59, no. 4, 1990.

Introduction to Drug Investigation. Savannah, GA: Georgia Police Academy, n.d.

Liska K: *Drugs and the Human Body,* ed.3. New York, NY: Macmillan Publishing Co. 1990.

Managing Drug Investigative Activities. Gaithersburg, MD: International Association of Chiefs of Police and Drug Enforcement Administration, n.d.

Moore MH, Kleiman M: "The Police and Drugs." *Perspective on Policing.* Washington, DC: National Institute of Justice, September 1989.

Morley CH: *Asset Forfeiture: Tracing Money Flows through Financial Institutions.* Washington, DC: U.S. Department of Justice, 1989.

National Drug Control Strategy. Washington, DC: U.S. Government Printing Office, 1989.

Narcotics Investigator's Manual. Gaithersburg, MD: International Association of Chiefs of Police and Drug Enforcement Administration, n.d.

Pace DF, Styles DF: *Handbook of Narcotics Control,* Englewood Cliffs, NJ: Prentice-Hall, 1972.

Reducing Crime By Reducing Drug Abuse. Gaithersburg, MD: International Association of Chiefs of Police, 1988.

Smith RL, DePolis T, Hatcher B, Cuesta J: "Tampa, Florida: One City's Successful Drug Enforcement Initiative." Unpublished paper, 1990.

CHAPTER 19

Special Investigations

The various types of criminal cases an investigator may encounter require special training and understanding. No textbook can cover every type of crime that an investigator will come across during his or her career. Most criminal investigators are generalists, so they need to develop the skills and knowledge to perform all kinds of criminal investigation. This chapter will consider art theft, arson, domestic violence, computer crime, white-collar crime, organized crime, and terrorism.

Art Thefts

During the early morning hours of March 18, 1990, the biggest art theft in history was committed. Boston's Isabella Stewart Gardner Museum lost art estimated at $200 million, but its true worth is incalculable. Stolen artworks are getting record prices. After drug trafficking, art theft is the second largest international crime committed today. Interpol, the international police agency, sends out approximately 200 notices a year of the most spectacular cases. This compares with 10 to 20 theft notices in the 1940s. Only 10 percent of art thefts are solved.

During the 1970s, art theft became a problem for both Europe and the United States. Because of the seriousness of the problem, the FBI, the New York Police Department, and the Philadelphia (Pennsylvania) Police Department have all hired art theft specialists. The investigator's written report should include the following information: "Name of artist; medium, such as oil on canvas, oil on wood panel, etc.; size (give the vertical measurement first); and any date or signature and its location on the art object. Also note the

The main foyer of the Isabella Stewart Gardner Museum in Boston—site of the biggest art theft in history.

presence and location of any museum or exhibit tabs, stock numbers, or any other written information appearing on the reverse side of the canvas." (Mason, 1979, p. 19)

When citizens ask for advice on how to deal with an art theft, the following suggestions may be helpful.

- Report the theft to the local police.
- Do not disturb the scene of the crime. Try to keep it as you found it until the police arrive.
- Consider publicizing the theft through local news media.
- Report the theft to your insurance company and insist that photographs and a description of the missing treasures be forwarded to pertinent dealers, museums, and auction houses.

Due to the great financial losses resulting from art thefts, the FBI in 1979 implemented the **National Stolen Art File** (NSAF) at FBI headquarters in Washington, D.C. This computerized index of stolen and recovered art serves as a central repository of data and photographs of art reported stolen to local law enforcement agencies. The NSAF also maintains information and photos of art that has been recovered but whose origin or ownership is unknown or in question.

For artworks to be included in the National Stolen Art File, specific criteria must be met. The FBI's laboratory division defines an art object as a "two or three dimensional object that was created by, or created under the direction of, an individual considered by the art community to be an artist or designer." (McPhee, Spitzer, and Sundin, 1983, pp. 18–19)

The NSAF collection is limited to paintings, prints, and sculptures. Law enforcement agencies submit a photograph of the art object, with a complete stolen art data sheet (obtained from the FBI) to the FBI lab. The information is entered into the NSAF computer, which lists each art object by the artist's name, its title, and its description. The search retrieves images that can be viewed on a monitor.

The FBI has approximately 5,000 art objects on file and plans to expand the list and improve the system's accuracy and speed. The National Stolen Art File provides police agencies with an important tool for investigating art theft.

Arson

On March 25, 1990, a Cuban refugee in an illegal New York City social club started a fire that burned 87 people to death. The club patrons were primarily Hondurans and Jamaicans who frequented the club for social activities. The arsonist set fire to the establishment by pouring gasoline in various locations and putting a match to the flammable liquid. He was distraught over an altercation with his girlfriend. This was the greatest number of deaths in one fire in the United States in thirteen years.

Arson has become a serious problem in America. The New York arson case made international news, but not all arsons are even discovered. The crime of arson leads to billions of dollars of property loss annually. It also raises insurance premiums, increases medical expenses, and results in a loss of tax dollars. In 1978, Congress classified arson as one of the eight index crimes in the FBI's Uniform Crime Report.

Bodies are covered along the sidewalk in front of New York's Happy Land Social Club following the arson fire that claimed 87 lives. In September 1991 a judge sentenced Julio Gonzalez, the convicted arsonist, to 174 concurrent jail terms of 25 years to life.

The Uniform Crime Report defines **arson** as "any willful or malicious burning or attempt to burn, with or without intent to defraud, a dwelling house, public building, motor vehicle or aircraft, personal property of another, etc." Approximately 100,000 arson offenses are reported yearly. The national clearance rate is usually around 16 percent. Arson is usually committed by white males under the age of 25, although, of course, it knows no ethnic, gender, or age boundaries.

Arson is a difficult crime to investigate and prove. Factors that can be used to establish the crime of arson include the type of fire, its point of origin, the type of building structure, the time of day, the owner of the building, individuals associated with the property, the market value of the property, the amount of insurance on the property, whether the building was occupied, and whether there was a recent sale or title change of the building. (Rider, 1980, p. 11) An exhaustive investigation may be required to establish that arson has been committed.

Motives

It may be difficult to build an identifiable motive from the ashes of a fire. The National Fire Academy lists the following basic motives for people who set fires. (Stickevers, 1986, pp. 2–3)

1. Frauds for direct gain (insurance) and indirect gain (to eliminate competition).
2. Pyromania.
3. Crime concealment (murder).
4. Vanity (e.g., security guards for employment, or a hero who wants to save a victim).
5. Spite/revenge (in work, love, or religion).
6. Civil disorders, revolutions, and political activity.
7. Actions of juveniles, adolescents, or children (ranging from gang activities to curiosity).

Figure 19–1 illustrates the typical psychology of arsonists.

FIGURE 19–1: Psychology of the Arsonist

	The Torch (Professional Arsonist	**The Self-Starter** (Failing Businessman, Troubled Spouse)	**The Sparkler** (Pyromaniac)
Thought Patterns	Cool, rational, calculating	Somewhat rational, calculating	Compulsive urge Irrational, more-or-less calculating
Degree of Planning	High	Less than Torch, but varies from considerable to very little	Varies
Types of Hits	For profit To cover other crimes To commit murder	For profit To cover other crimes To commit murder	To burn, without regard for consequences
Motivation	Money, revenge	Money, revenge	Revenge, sexual gratification
Employer	Organized crime. Failing, legitimate businessman	Self	Self
Clues	"Professional Job." Few clues. Past record of criminal involvement in burned establishments.	High debt. Poor credit rating. High insurance. Evidence of marital problems.	Series of seemingly unconnected fires. No suspicious clues. Same person seen at several fires. Evidence of sexual gratification.

Source: Adapted from MJ Palmiotto, *Critical Issues in Criminal Investigation*, 2d ed. Cincinnati, OH: Anderson Pub. Co., 1988, p. 143.

Arson for Profit

The goal of arson for profit is to burn structures for the fire insurance. This kind of arson is not only widespread but difficult to prove. Arson investigators may have to initiate fire investigations months after the building has been burned. They must review all available information and reports to identify every fire included in the scheme, The sources of fire data include police-fire records, local newspapers, state fire marshals, the Insurance Crime Prevention Institute, insurance adjusters, and informants. The following clues indicate positive circumstantial evidence that the fire was set for the purpose of insurance fraud. (Walsh, 1979, p. 19)

- Presence of incendiary material.
- Multiple origins of fire. (Arson must be a total loss to be profitable.)
- Location of the fire within the building. (The roof is suspicious, because many insurance adjusters will declare a total loss once the roof is destroyed.)
- Suspicious hours or holidays (no witnesses).
- Building that is vacant or being renovated.
- Recent departure of occupants.
- Removal of objects (woodwork, plumbing, etc.)
- Property for sale or recently sold.
- Previous fire.
- Building is overinsured or insurance has recently been obtained.
- Habitual claimants.

The Investigation

The investigator must determine whether there is anything unusual about the fire scene. Has anything been added, or is something missing from the area that normally would be present?

Normally, a fire investigation begins outside the building. A cursory investigation of the outside of the structure can often disclose an external fire origin. The investigator has to examine the entire structure of the building, photograph all external evidence, take notes, and preserve evidence. When proceeding into the building, the investigator should try to determine if entry was forced.

An important aspect of the investigation is the evaluation of how the fire spread. Smoke, char, burn patterns, and other indicators allow the investigator to reconstruct the fire. After determining where the fire started, the investigator should concentrate on the ceiling, retracing the heat flow downward. Burn patterns can indicate the direction of the fire spread and may be observed on structural elements, wall surfaces, or furnishings. The arson investigator should consult with experts to eliminate accidental causes of the fire—for example, shorts in electrical wires. (Palmiotto, 1988, pp. 147–148)

Domestic Violence

Family violence became an issue in the late 1960s, when the general public became aware of the frequency of child abuse. Domestic violence evolved to include any violence between couples. "**Spouse abuse** is usually defined as acts of violence between sexual partners, married or unmarried, who are living together," according to Nancy Loving in *Responding to Spouse Abuse and Wife Beating: A Guide for Police* (1980). In this definition, one partner intentionally uses physical force against the other. Loving writes, "Wife beating is a form of spouse abuse in which a woman is subjected to a pattern of recurring assaults by her husband or boyfriend." (pp. 3–4)

Assault is a major cause of injury to women in America. Approximately a third of murders of females are committed by husbands or boyfriends. Nationwide, approximately 16 percent of all murders involve a family relationship. The extent of domestic violence between spouses is unknown, because neither law enforcement nor social service agencies have maintained accurate records of violence

This specialized family investigation unit handles cases of domestic violence.

between spouses. Researchers in *Behind Closed Doors: Violence in the American Family* believe that approximately 50 to 60 percent of all couples use violence in their marriage. Violent acts include throwing things; pushing, shoving, or grappling; hitting with fists; beating up; threatening with a knife or gun; and using a knife or gun.

The Attorney General's Task Force on Family Violence recommends that all police agencies establish family violence as a priority response and require officers to file written reports on all incidents. (1984, pp. 17–18) Police officers should:

- Process all complaints of family violence as reported criminal offenses.
- Presume that arrest, consistent with state law, is the appropriate response in situations involving serious injury to the victim, use or threatened use of a weapon, violation of a protection order, or other imminent danger to the victim. If an arrest is not made, the officer should clearly document his or her reasons in the incident report.
- Provide the victim and the abuser with a statement of the victim's rights. The officer should inform both parties that any person who uses force to physically injure a household member has violated the law. Victims should be told that they have the right to be protected from further assault and abuse, to press criminal charges against the abuser, and to obtain an order of protection from the court.
- Take a written statement from the victim in order to assist in the effective criminal prosecution of the offender. The statement should indicate the frequency and severity of prior incidents of physical abuse by the assaulter, the number of prior calls for assistance, and, if known, the disposition of those calls.
- Complete a written report documenting the officer's observations of the victim, the abuser, visible injuries, weapons present, and any other facts significant to the abuse situation. When possible, the officer should photograph any personal injuries or property damage sustained by the victim.
- Interview the parties separately so that the victim can speak freely without being inhibited by the offender's presence.
- Instruct the abuser to leave the premises if an arrest is not made. If the victim chooses to leave, the officer should stand by long enough for the victim to remove personal and necessary belongings.
- Inform the victim about a shelter or other appropriate victim assistance services if available in the community.

- Arrange or provide transportation for the victim to a shelter, medical treatment facility, or victim assistance agency.
- Remove dangerous weapons for a reasonable period of safekeeping. Standard law enforcement procedures require custody of any weapon used in committing a crime.
- Verify the existence of an order of protection at a central warrants unit if the offense involves the violation of such an order.
- Provide the victim with an information card that specifically notes the officer's name, badge number, report number, and follow-up telephone number.

During the initial investigation of a domestic violence call, the responding officers should obtain such specific information as the nature and extent of injuries, use of force or weapons, threatening language or actions, nature of the conflict leading up to the violence, history of past conflicts and violence and previous police interventions, legal status of the relationship, civil injunctions now in effect against the assailant, and alcohol or drug abuse problems of the assailant. (Loving, 1980, pp. 95–96)

Generally, police departments do not conduct follow-up investigations of domestic violence cases. However, the Baltimore County Police Department has established a spousal abuse unit within the criminal investigation division. Its duties are summarized as follows. (Goolkasian, 1986, p. 149)

- Identifying repeat offenders (batterers).
- Maintaining an accurate file on all repeat offenders, including prior offenses, court proceedings and dispositions, and prior counseling received.
- Reviewing the quality of reports for prosecution purposes and for any additional investigation that may be needed.
- Conducting follow-up investigations.
- Arresting offenders when appropriate.
- Assisting the patrol division in case preparation as needed.
- Identifying households where domestic violence is common or members are prone to assaults on the police.
- Notifying precinct stations of violent households in their area (especially if the family has moved from one area to another).
- Providing or coordinating victim assistance with social services by being in contact with both victims and batterers, as well as civic organizations and public interest groups, to inform them of the services available to help them.
- Following all cases through all prosecutory stages.

Computer Crime

Computer abuse has probably existed since the invention of computers in the 1940s. The first recorded computer abuse was in 1958. The first computer crime identified and prosecuted in a federal court occurred in Minneapolis in 1966 and involved bank records altered by computer. Currently there are no accurate statistics on computer abuse. Victims often attempt to protect their image by not reporting losses.

During the 1980s, there were countless debates over how to define computer crime. Conly distinguishes among three concepts. (1989, p. 7)

Computer abuse encompasses a broad range of intentional acts that may or may not be specifically prohibited by criminal statutes. Any intentional act involving knowledge of computer use or technology is computer abuse if one or more perpetrators gained or could have gained or one or more victims suffered or could have suffered loss.

Computer fraud is any crime in which a person uses the computer either directly or as a vehicle for deliberate misrepresentation or deception, usually to cover up the embezzlement or theft of money, goods, services, or information.

Computer crime is any violation of a computer crime statute.

All known cases of computer crime involve at least one of the following four roles. (Parker, 1989, p. 2)

1. *Object.* Cases include destruction of computers or data or programs contained in them or of supportive facilities and resources (such as air-conditioning equipment and electrical power) that allow them to function.
2. *Subject.* A computer can be the site or environment of a crime or the source of or reason for unique forms and kinds of assets lost (such as a pirated computer program). A fraud perpetrated by changing account balances in financial data stored in a computer makes the computer the subject of a crime.
3. *Instrument.* Some methods of crime are complex enough to require the use of a computer as a tool or instrument. A computer can be used actively (for example, to automatically scan telephone codes to make unauthorized use of a telephone system). It can also be used passively (for example, to simulate a general ledger in planning and controlling a continuing financial embezzlement).
4. *Symbol.* A computer can be used as a symbol for intimidation

or deception. This could involve an organization falsely claiming to use nonexistent computers.

Computer crime can be divided into four categories.

- The introduction of fraudulent records or data into a computer system.
- The unauthorized use of computer-related facilities.
- The alteration or destruction of information or files.
- The stealing, whether by electronic means or otherwise, of money, financial instruments, property, services, or valuable data.

Computer crimes can also be categorized by types of information and by information-processing loss: modification, destruction, disclosure, and use or denial of use. These classes define acts that are "intrinsic to information such as changing it, extrinsic to information such as changing access to it, and external to information by removing or copying it." (Parker, 1989, p. 31)

Various computer abuse studies have identified categories in several dimensions.

- By ways in which information loss occurs: loss of integrity, confidentiality, and availability.
- By the type of loss: physical damage and destruction from vandalism, intellectual property loss, direct financial loss, and unauthorized use of services.
- By the role played by computers: object of attack, unique environment and forms of assets produced, instrument, and symbol.
- By the type of act relative to data, computer programs, and services: external abuse, masquerading, preparatory abuse, bypass of intended controls, passive abuse, active abuse, and use as a tool for committing an abuse.
- By the type of crime: fraud, theft, robbery, larceny, arson, embezzlement, extortion, conspiracy, sabotage, espionage, and more.
- By modus operandi: physical attacks, false data entry, superzapping, impersonation, wiretapping, piggybacking, scavenging, Trojan horse attacks, trap-door use, asynchronous attacks, salami techniques, data leakage, logic bombs, and simulation.
- By skill required: physical skills (scavenging, spying, masquerading, entering false data, and theft) and programming skills (system scavenging, eavesdropping, scanning, piggybacking and

tailgating, superzapping, Trojan horse attacks, virus attacks, salami attacks, trapdoor use, logic bombs, asynchronous attacks, data leakage, pirating, and use in criminal enterprises).

These classifications are grouped into extensive explanations and models of computer crime, which can be effective investigative tools. Computer crimes should be investigated with methods similar to those used to investigate traditional crimes such as robbery or burglary. Criminal investigators should understand methods of computer abuse and know where to get information pertaining to computers to assist in conducting the investigation. Sources include college professors, computer students, consultants, and other law enforcement personnel and agencies. The key question pertaining to computer crime is: How was it committed? The National Institute of Justice describes in detail 17 methods of computer abuse. (Parker, 1989, pp. 9–25)

Eavesdropping and Spying

Eavesdropping and spying are two methods of achieving essentially the same goals—obtaining information illegally.

Eavesdropping involves wiretapping and monitoring radio frequency emissions. Few wiretap abuses are known, and no cases of radio eavesdropping have been proven outside of government intelligence agencies. Case experience is probably so scarce because industrial spying and scavenging are easier, more direct ways for criminals to obtain the required information. On the other hand, these passive eavesdropping methods may be so difficult to detect that they are frequently used but never reported. These abusive methods are described in the news media far more than they deserve: nevertheless, the opportunities to pick up emanations from isolated small computers and terminals, microwave circuits, and satellite signals continue to grow.

Eavesdropping should be assumed to be the least likely method used in the theft or modification of data. Detection methods and possible evidence are the same as in the investigation of voice communication wiretapping.

Spying consists of criminal acquisition of information by covert observation. For example, shoulder surfing involves observing users at computer terminals as they enter or receive displays of sensitive information such as passwords. A gang of juvenile delinquents in Atlanta using binoculars obtained passwords in this fashion. Frame-by-frame analysis of video recordings to pick up personal identification numbers (PINs) being entered at automated teller machines (ATMs) is also feasible.

One way to prevent both eavesdropping and spying is electronic shielding. It uses a Faraday grounded electrical conducting shield against eavesdropping and physical shielding from view against spying. Investigators must observe the acts and capture equipment for evidence.

Scanning

The process of presenting sequentially changing information to an automated system to identify those items that receive a positive response is called **scanning.** This method is usually used to identify items that receive a positive response—phone numbers that access computers, user IDs, and passwords that facilitate access to computers, as well as credit card numbers that can be used illegally to order merchandise or services through telemarketing.

The perpetrators of scanning are mostly malicious hackers and potential computer system intruders. Many computer systems can deter scanners by limiting the number of access attempts. Trying to exceed these limits results in long delays meant to discourage the scanning process. Identifying the perpetrators is often difficult. It usually requires the use of a pen register or dialed number-recorder (DNR) equipment in cooperation with communications companies. The possession of a demon program may constitute possession of a tool for criminal purposes, and printouts from demon programs may be used to incriminate a suspect.

Masquerading and Playback

In **masquerading,** a person assumes the identity of an authorized computer user by acquiring identifying items, knowledge, or characteristics. Physical access to computers or terminals and electronic access through terminals to a computer require positive identification of an authorized user. The authentication of identity is based on something the user knows, such as a secret password; some physiological characteristic of the user, such as fingerprint, retinal pattern, hand geometry, keystroke rhythm, or voice; and a token the user possesses, such as a magnetic stripe card, smart card, or metal key.

Anybody with the correct combination of identification characteristics can masquerade as another individual. One clever masquerade occurred when a young man posing as a magazine writer called on a telephone company claiming that he was writing an article about its computer system. He was given a full and detailed briefing on all the computer facilities and application systems, information he used to steal over $1 million worth of telephone equipment from the company.

Playback is another masquerade and occasional piggyback method. User or computer responses or initiations of transactions are surreptitiously recorded and played back to the computer as though they came from the user. Playback was suggested as a means of "jackpotting" ATMs by repeating cash-dispensing commands through a wiretap. This fraud was curtailed when banks installed controls that placed encrypted message sequence numbers, times, and dates into each transmitted transaction and command.

Masquerading is one of the most common activities of computer system intruders. It is also one of the most difficult to prove in court. When an intrusion into the victim's computer takes place, the investigator must obtain evidence identifying the masquerader at a terminal as performing the acts that produced the events in the computer. This task is doubly difficult when network weaving connections through several switched telephone systems interfere with pen register and DNR line tracing.

Piggybacking and Tailgating

Piggybacking and tailgating can be done physically or electronically.

Physical **piggybacking** is a method for gaining access to areas where access is limited by electronically or mechanically locked doors.

Electronic piggybacking can take place in an on-line computer system. When a terminal has been activated, the computer authorizes access, usually on the basis of a protocol (a secret password, token, or other exchange of required identification and authentication information).

Tailgating involves connecting a computer user to a computer in the same session as and under the same identifier as another user whose session has been interrupted. This situation happens when a dial-up or direct connect session is abruptly terminated and a communications controller (concentrator or packet assembler/disassembler) incorrectly allows a second user to be patched directly into the first user's still-open files. The problem is exacerbated if the controller incorrectly handles a modem's data-terminal-ready (DTR) signal.

Many network managers set up the controller to send DTR signals continually so that the modem quickly establishes a new session after finishing its disconnect sequence from the previous session. The controller may miss the modem's drop-carrier signal, allowing a new session to tailgate onto the old one.

Electronic door access control systems are frequently run by a microcomputer that produces a log showing time of access for each individual gaining access. Human guards frequently keep equivalent logs. Investigators can detect unauthorized access by studying journals and logs and by interviewing people who may have witnessed the unauthorized access.

False Data Entry

One of the simplest, safest, and most common methods used in computer abuse is **false data entry,** also known as data diddling. Anybody associated with or having access to the processes of creating, recording, transporting, encoding, examining, checking, converting, and transforming data that ultimately enter a computer can change these data. Trusted, authorized computer users engaged in unauthorized activities are often the culprits.

Examples of data diddling are forging, misrepresenting, or counterfeiting documents; exchanging valid computer tapes or disks with prepared replacements; falsifying keyboard entries; failing to enter data; and neutralizing or avoiding controls. Potential perpetrators hold various kinds of occupations.

Superzapping

Superzapping derives its name from Superzap, a macro or utility program used in most IBM mainframe computer centers as a systems tool. Any computer center that has a secure operating mode needs a "break-glass-in-case-of-emergency" program that will bypass all controls to modify or disclose any of the contents of the computer.

Many Superzap types of programs for sale and in the public domain are available and necessary for micros as well. Computers sometimes stop, malfunction, or enter a state that cannot be overcome by normal recovery or restart procedures. Computers also perform unexpectedly and need attention that normal access methods do not allow. In such cases, a universal access program is needed. This situation parallels using a master key if all other keys are lost or locked in the enclosure they were meant to open.

The investigator can detect superzapping by comparing the current file with father and grandfather copies of the files, where no updates exist to account for suspicious changes.

Scavenging and Reuse

Obtaining or reusing information that is left in or around a computer system after processing is called **scavenging.** Simple physical scavenging could mean searching trash barrels for copies of discarded computer listings or carbon paper from multiple-part forms.

More sophisticated methods of scavenging include searching for residual data left in a computer or computer tapes and disks after execution.

Trojan Horses

The **Trojan horse** is the covert placement or alteration of computer instructions or data in a program so that the computer will perform unauthorized functions but still perform most or all of its intended purposes. The Trojan horse program, which can be the carrier of any abusive acts, is the primary method used for inserting instructions for other abusive acts, such as logic bombs, salami attacks, and viruses. It is the method used most often in computer program-based frauds and sabotage.

Instructions may be placed in production computer programs so that they will be executed in the protected or restricted domain of the program, giving the user access to all of the data files assigned for the program's exclusive use. Programs are usually constructed loosely enough to allow space to be found or created for inserting the instructions, sometimes without even extending the length or changing the check sum of the infected program.

Computer Viruses and Worm Attacks

A set of computer instructions that propagates versions of itself into computer programs or data when it is executed within unauthorized programs is a **computer virus.** The virus may be introduced through a program designed for the purpose (called a *pest*) or a Trojan horse. Hidden instructions are inserted into the computer program, the data, or the computer hardware the victim uses. The hidden virus propagates itself into other programs when they are executed, creating new Trojan horses. It may also execute harmful processes under the authority of each unsuspecting computer user whose programs or system have been infected.

A **worm attack** is a variation in which an entire program replicates itself throughout a computer or computer network. The best protection against viruses is to frequently back up all important data and programs, maintaining multiple backups for up to a year to allow for recovery from infected backups. The perpetrators, detection, and evidence are the same as for the Trojan horse attack.

Salami Techniques

An automated form of abuse using the Trojan horse method or secretly executing an unauthorized program that causes the unnoticed or immaterial debiting of small amounts of assets from a large number of sources is the **salami technique** (taking small slices without noticeably reducing the whole).

Other methods must be used to remove the acquired assets from the system. For example, in banking the accounting system of programs for checking accounts could be changed (using a Trojan horse) to randomly transfer 10 or 15 cents from each of a few hundred accounts to a favored account where the money can be withdrawn through authorized, normal methods. No controls are violated because the money is not removed from the system; small fractions of the funds are merely rearranged.

The success of the fraud is based on the idea that each checking account customer loses so little that it goes unnoticed. Many variations are possible. The assets may be an inventory of products or services as well as money. Few reported cases are known.

Trapdoors

When developing large application and computer operating systems, programmers insert debugging aids that provide breaks in the code for insertion of additional code and intermediate output capabilities, much as scaffolding and temporary braces are used in building construction. Operating systems are designed to prevent unintended access and insertion or modification of code. But, programmers sometimes insert codes that allow them to compromise these requirements during the debugging phases of program development and later during system maintenance and improvements.

Programmers often have unexecuted, redundant, or incomplete instructions and unused data or parameters in their program codes. These facilities are **trapdoors** that can be used for Trojan horses and such direct attacks as false data entry. Normally trapdoors are eliminated in the final editing, but sometimes they are overlooked or intentionally left in to facilitate future access and modification. Some unscrupulous programmers introduce trapdoors for later compromising of computer programs. Designers or maintainers of large, complex programs may also introduce trapdoors inadvertently through weaknesses in design logic.

Investigators should always assume that the computer system and program are not secure from intentional, technical compromise. However, these intentional acts usually require the expertise of the very few technical people who have the skills, knowledge, and access to perpetrate them.

Logic Bombs

A set of instructions in a computer program, executed at appropriate or periodic times in a computer system, that facilitates the perpetration of an unauthorized, malicious act is a **logic bomb.** In one case, secret computer instructions were inserted into the computer operating system, where they were executed periodically. The instructions would test the year, date, and time clock in the computer so that at a specified time on a specified day the time bomb, a type of logic bomb, would trigger the printout of a crime confession on all 300 computer terminals on-line, causing the system to crash.

A logic bomb can be programmed to trigger an act based on any specified condition or data that may occur or be introduced. Logic bombs are usually placed in the computer system using the Trojan horse method.

Asynchronous Attacks

Most computer operating systems function asynchronously, based on the services that must be performed for the various computer programs they execute. For example, several jobs may simultaneously call for output reports to be produced. The operating system stores these requests and, as resources become available, performs them according to an overriding priority scheme. Therefore, rather than executing requests in the order they are received, the system increases its efficiency by performing them asynchronously based on resources available. **Asynchronous attack** techniques take advantage of this system design element.

Data Leakage

A wide range of computer crime involves the removal of data or copies of data from a computer system or computer facility. This part of a crime, **data leakage,** offers the greatest risk of exposure. The perpetrators' technical act may be well hidden in the computer, but to convert it to economic gain, they must get the data out of the computer system. Output is subject to examination by computer operators and other data-processing personnel who might detect the perpetrators' activity.

Data leakage is probably best investigated by interrogating data-processing personnel who might have observed the movement of sensitive data. Investigators could also examine the operating system's usage journal to determine if and when data files were accessed. Trojan horse, logic bomb, and scavenging methods should be investigated when data leakage is suspected.

Computer Piracy

The copying and use of computer programs in violation of copyright and trade-secret laws is often called computer **piracy.** Malicious hackers commonly engage in piracy, sometimes even distributing pirated copies on a massive scale through electronic bulletin boards.

Investigators can most easily obtain evidence of piracy by confiscating suspects' disks, the contents of their hard disks, paper printouts from the execution of the pirated programs, and pictures of screens produced by the pirated programs.

Simulation and Modeling

A computer can be used for planning, data communications, or control in a criminal enterprise. Like any other business, complex white-collar crimes often require the use of a computer. A planned method for carrying out a crime can be modeled or a crime can be regulated by computer to help assure its success. (See the next section of this chapter for more discussion of white-collar crime.)

Figure 19–2 lists the potential perpetrators, methods of detection, and kinds of evidence in various types of computer crime.

Theft of Computers

The theft, burglary, and sale of stolen microcomputers and components are increasing dramatically, a severe problem because the value of the contents of stolen computers often exceeds the value of the hardware taken. Computer larceny is becoming epidemic, in fact, as the market for used computers expands.

Investigation and prosecution of computer larceny follow accepted criminal justice practices, except for proving the size of the loss when a microcomputer worth only a few hundred dollars is stolen. Evidence of far larger losses (for example, programs and data) may be needed.

FIGURE 19–2: Detection of Computer Crimes

	Potential Perpetrators	Methods of Detection	Evidences
Eavesdropping	Communications technicians and engineers Communications employees	Voice wire tapping Observation Tracing sources of equipment used	Voice wire tapping evidence
Masquerading	All computer users Hackers	Audit log analysis Password violations Observation Report by person impersonated	Computer audit log Notes and documents in possession of suspects Pen register and DNR records Witnesses Access control package exception or violation reports
Piggybacking and Tailgating	Employees, former employees, vendors' employees Contracted persons Outsiders	Access observations Interviewing witnesses Examination of journals and logs Out-of-sequence messages Specialized computer programs that analyze characteristics of on-line computer user accesses	Logs, journals, equipment usage meters Photos, voice, and video recordings Other physical evidence
False Data Entry	Transaction participants Data preparers Source data suppliers Nonparticipants with access	Data comparison Document validation Manual controls Audit log analysis Computer validation Reporter analysis Computer output comparison Integrity tests (e.g., for value limits, logic consistencies, hash totals, crossfoot and column totals, and forged entry)	Data documents Source Transactions Computer-readable Computer data media Tapes Disks Storage modules Manual logs, audit logs, journals, and exception reports Incorrect output control violation alarms
Superzapping	Programmers with access to Superzap programs and computer access to use them	Comparison of files with historical copies	Output report discrepancies

(continued on next page)

FIGURE 19-2: *(Continued)*

	Computer operations staff with applications knowledge	**Discrepancies noted by recipients of output reports** **Examination of computer usage journals**	**Undocumented transactions** **Computer usage or usage or file request journals.**
Scavenging	Users of the computer system Persons having access to computer or backup facilities and adjacent areas	Tracing of discovered proprietary information back to its source Testing of an operating system to discover residual data after job execution	Computer output media (page numbers and vendor) Type font characteristics Similar information produced in suspected ways in the same form
Trojan Horses	Programmers having detailed knowledge of a suspected part of a program and its purpose and access to it Employee technologists Contract programmers Vendors' programmers Computer operators	Program code comparison Testing of suspect program Tracing of unexpected events or possible gain from the act to suspected programs and perpetrators Examination of computer audit logs for suspicious programs or pertinent entries	Unexpected results of program execution Foreign code found in a suspect program Audit logs Uncontaminated copies of suspect programs
Salami Techniques	Financial system programmers Employee technologists Former employees Contract programmers Vendors' programmers	Detailed data analysis using a binary search Program comparison Transaction audits Observation of financial activities of possible suspects	Many small financial losses Unsupported account balance buildups Trojan horse code Changed or unusual personal financial practices of possible suspects
Trap Doors	Systems programmers Expert application programmers	Exhaustive testing Comparison of specification to performance Specific testing based on evidence	Computer performance or output reports indicating that a computer system performs outside of its specifications
Logic Bombs	Programmers having detailed knowledge of a suspected part of a program and its purpose and access to it	Program code comparisons	Unexpected results of program execution Foreign code found in a suspect program

FIGURE 19–2: *(Continued)*

	Employees Contract programmers Vendors' programmers Computer users	Testing of suspect program Tracing of possible gain from the act	
Asynchronous Attacks	Sophisticated advanced system programmers Sophisticated and advanced computer operators	System testing of suspected attack methods Repeat execution of a job under normal and safe circumstances	Output that deviates from normally expected output or logs containing records of computer operation
Data Leakage Crimes	Computer programmers Employees Former employees Contract workers Vendors' employees	Discovery of stolen information Tracing computer storage media back to computer facility	Computer storage media Computer output forms Type font characteristics Trojan horse or scavenging evidence
Program Piracy	Any purchasers and users of commercially available computer programs Hackers	Observation of computer users Search of users' facilities and computers Testimony of legitimate computer program purchasers Receivers of copied programs who testify to whom they have given copies	Pictures of computer screens while pirated software is being executed Copies of computer media on which pirated programs are found Memory contents of computers containing pirated software Printouts produced by execution of pirated programs
Simulation and Modeling	Computer application programmers Simulation and modeling experts Managers in positions to engage in large, complex embezzlement Criminal organizations	Investigation of possible computer usage by suspects Identification of equipment	Computer programs Computer and communications equipment and their content Computer program documentation Computer input Computer-produced reports Computer and data communications usage logs and journals

Source: Adapted from *Computer Crime: Criminal Justice Resource Manual*. National Institute of Justice, 1989.

The Typical Computer Criminal

Computer-related crimes have a broad impact on victims from large financial institutions to individuals. Offenders can range from trusted employees to common criminals who have discovered a new tool for achieving criminal goals.

Traditional criminals have found computers as indispensable as legitimate businesspeople. Drug dealers and child pornographers maintain computer files for their illegal activities. Computers are also used in such crimes as embezzlement. Computer-related crimes can be committed by any person who has access to a computer.

The typical computer law violator has the following characteristics. (Bequai, 1983, p. 43)

- The violator is between 15 and 45 years old.
- The violator is usually male, although women are increasingly entering the field.
- Experience ranges from the highly experienced technician to a professional with little or no technical experience.
- The offender normally has no previous contact with law enforcement.
- The offender targets both government and business.
- The offender is usually a bright, motivated individual who is ready to accept the technical challenge.
- The offender fears exposure, ridicule, and loss of stature with the community.
- The majority of cases are one-person shows, although conspiracies of two or more criminals are surfacing.
- The offender appears to deviate little from the accepted norms of society.
- The offender usually holds a position of trust within the company and has easy access to the computer systems.
- The offender is usually on guard, is the first to arrive and the last to leave the office, and takes few or no vacations.
- The offender justifies his or her criminal acts by considering them a game.

Investigating Computer Crimes

Approaches to investigating computer-related crimes vary. One police officer notes that it involves 90 percent traditional police work and 10 percent technical computer skills.

Investigations of computer-related crime require a considerable investment of time. Depending on the type of case, estimates for a thorough investigation range from four months to one year. In cases involving the use of communications systems and bulletin boards, considerable time must be spent on electronic surveillance. Because criminals in those cases use computers to communicate quickly among themselves and because search warrants in computer-related cases are complicated, a considerable amount of investigative work must occur before warrants are issued.

In situations where surveillance may not be required because the crime occurred in the past (for example, embezzlement), often large quantities of computer data must be reviewed for evidence. Investigating an 18-year-old who had defrauded area investors out of $1 million, criminalists in Jefferson County, Colorado, analyzed more than 80 computer diskettes and produced 11 notebooks of evidence.

Investigation of computer-related crimes involves interaction with victims. Often victims familiar with their own computer systems are asked to assist investigators. When businesses are victimized, investigators must use the victims to determine the role the computer plays in the organization and to identify the persons who have access to the computer system. Victims may provide considerable technical support as well.

The very private nature of computer-related crime often necessitates a proactive approach to its investigation, whether it is monitoring computer bulletin boards or speaking routinely to local schools and businesses. A proactive investigation also reaps a return in increased prevention. (Conly, 1989, pp. 18–20)

The criminal investigator should comprehend computer operations well enough to obtain evidence and information. It is important for the investigator to be familiar with computer equipment in use, the number of people involved in the crime, the kind of peripheral equipment present (telephones, printers, and modems), and the type of paper records kept. The most frequently used pieces of apparatus are pen registers and dialed number recorders, as criminals often use the telephone lines to commit computer-related crimes.

Also, investigators should know what to expect at the crime scene so they can consult with experts from other investigative agencies, universities, and the private sector. Knowledge of new technology is important for conducting the crime-scene search. Being familiar with the intricacies of the case can prevent errors in conducting the search and investigation.

The Secret Service provides guidelines for the search of a crime scene in a case involving personal computers. (Conly, 1989, p. 21)

- Learn as much as possible about the occupants of the crime scene, including the number of residents and their employment and educational backgrounds. The intent is to establish which occupants could have committed the crime. If only one resident knows anything about computers, the likelihood of any other resident's committing the computer crime is reduced.
- Review the records of all phone lines to the crime scene.
- Explore the possibility of developing an informant.
- Observe the habits of the suspect(s).
- If phone abuse is involved, use DNR to collect evidence. DNR records will not be sufficient evidence of the suspect's involvement if anyone else could have committed the crime.

Most public police agencies do not yet have computer crime investigative units. However, the Federal Law Enforcement Training Center (FLETC) in Glynco, Georgia, offers training in computer crime to federal, state, and local investigators. Computer crime investigative units usually have the following responsibilities. (McEwen, 1989, p. 18)

- Investigate all crimes in the city in which computers are the object of attack.
- Investigate all crimes in which computers are the vehicle for the commission of criminal acts.
- Investigate all telecommunications crimes and thefts of telecommunications services.
- Provide technical assistance to other departments and city units in support of their investigations.
- Develop public, private sector, and law enforcement agency relations in areas associated with crimes involving computers.
- Respond to requests for public appearances and speeches in areas such as computer crimes, computer and data security, and computer ethics.

White-Collar Crime

Edwin Sutherland coined the term **white-collar crime** in a 1939 address to the American Sociological Society and defined it as "a crime committed by a person of respectability and high social status in the course of his occupation." (Sutherland, 1949, p. 2) This broad definition covers every aspect of white-collar crime, including embezzlement, industrial espionage, and bribery of both public and private sector officials.

A Handbook of White-Collar Crime provides a more elaborate definition: "White-collar crimes are illegal acts characterized by guile, deceit, and concealment—and are not dependent upon the application of physical force or violence or threats thereof. They may be committed by individuals acting independently or by those who are part of a well-planned conspiracy. The objective may be to obtain money, property, or services; or to secure businesses' or personal advantage." (U.S. Chamber of Commerce, 1974, p. 3)

Elements

There are five principal elements of white-collar crimes and abuses. (Edelhertz, 1977, pp. 21–25)

1. Intent to commit a wrongful act or to achieve a purpose inconsistent with law or public policy.
2. Disguise of purpose or intent.
3. Reliance by the offender on ignorance or carelessness of victim.
4. Voluntary victim action to assist the offender.
5. Concealment of the violation.

Intent

In every white-collar crime or related abuse, it is usually clear that the offender knows he or she is involved in an activity that is wrongful or very much in a gray legal area, whether or not the offender is aware of a particular statute's being violated. The intent may be to avoid something required by law (such as disclosing acts that would make a particular transaction undesirable for the victim) or to deceive the victim by some explicit and affirmative deceitful conduct. Intent is usually inferred from the behavior or statements of the subjects of investigation and from the presence of the remaining four elements of white-collar crime.

Disguise of Purpose

This second element involves the character of the offenders' conduct or activity in implementing the plan. When a common crime is committed, the wrongful intent is followed by some overt implementing act, such as an armed attack, that is clearly observable. In a white-collar crime, the offenders deliberately avoid force or the threat of force. Instead they employ disguise, the facade of legitimacy with which they cover the actions that implement the scheme.

Disguise may be written or oral. In a bank, for example, the loan officer who creates a fictional borrower—complete with promissory note, a purported borrower's financial statement, and perhaps a false background check on the nonexistent borrower—has created a facade of reality intended to deceive other bank personnel and bank examiners so they will believe that they understand the transaction they are approving or reviewing. In white-collar schemes, pieces of paper are not what they appear to be, even when they bear all indications of legitimacy.

Oral disguise is usually employed in combination with written materials, as in the case of con games such as pigeon drops or merchandising frauds where an oral sales pitch is made to induce a signature on a document that imposes obligations on the victim without indicating the misrepresentations made to obtain the signature.

Reliance on Victim's Ignorance

While intent and disguises clearly originate with and are controlled by the white-collar offender, reliance on the victim's ignorance or carelessness is based on the offender's perception of victim susceptibility. Offenders will not go forward unless they think they can depend on the victim's inability to perceive deception.

Voluntary Assistance from Victim

The successful execution of a white-collar scheme is not fully under the control of the scheme operator. He or she must induce the victim to voluntarily undertake some act. This element is most important, because measures designed to prevent inadvertent victim cooperation may be more effective than other deterrents.

Voluntary victim action involves the victim who will be defrauded of money or property, but it may also involve an intermediate victim—such as the government agency that accepts a land or securities registration statement from prospective individual buyers, or the accounts payable officer who approves a voucher for payment on the assumption that the facts in the voucher are accurate.

Concealment

The ideal white-collar crime, from the offender's point of view, is one that will never be recognized as a crime. For example, in a charity fraud, small amounts are taken from large numbers of victims, none of whom has a big enough stake to pursue the matter even if he or she suspects fraud. In antitrust or price-fixing cases, coconspirators make every effort to convince the public, regulators, and law enforcement agencies that normal market forces, rather than illegal agreements, determine the prices they pay.

Some investment frauds are predicated on the perpetrators' assumption that they can use the scheme proceeds to make a killing on some speculative investment, square accounts with their victims, and thus prevent the day of reckoning.

Bribes, Kickbacks, and Payoffs

The criminal offenses of bribes, kickbacks, and payoffs occur between businesses, between business and government, and between both public and private sector management and labor officials. These criminal activities can involve almost anyone in an organization who has the authority to purchase supplies, make personnel decisions, and make recommendations that pertain to the overall operation of the organization. This might include police officers, clerks, politicians, and chief executive officers of companies. Almost any aspect of operations can be open to bribes, kickbacks, and payoffs, including government contracts, insurance needs, purchase of supplies, and personnel matters.

There are numerous reasons why bribes, kickbacks, and payoffs exist. In some communities, they are a way of life. In some businesses, they are standard operating procedures. Some common methods for arranging kickbacks and other payoffs follow. (*A Handbook of White Collar Crime*, 1974, pp. 16–17)

- A pipeline contractor decided to facilitate acquisition of easement rights, certain permits, and labor peace by paying $110,000 to municipal and union officials. Plans were made to cover up the payoffs by a series of bogus work orders and invoices.
- Engineering consultants favored with state contracts were called upon to make substantial campaign contributions. Contractors and consultants were given to understand that if they did not contribute, they would not receive future work.
- An investigation revealed that small-loan companies used three principal tactics to bribe state officials so they would grant licenses, changes in location, and the like: control and misuse of a trade association, informal planning and cooperation among the companies involved, and individual action. Since the bribes amounted to substantial amounts, the companies paying them had to make the expenditures appear as legitimate deductible expenses paid by check. They also had to raise cash for the bribes. The solution was to remit checks to lawyers for nonexistent services. These payments (minus income tax payments and an honorarium) were returned to the companies, which used the cash to pay off officials.
- An engineering firm received a contract from a turnpike authority after agreeing to put a relative of the authority's chairman

on the payroll and to permit the relative to acquire 50 percent of the firm's stock.

Credit Card Fraud

Credit card fraud costs American consumers and businesses millions of dollars each year. Credit cards are obtained by a variety of means. They can even be counterfeited using legitimate account numbers and names of cardholders, which are obtained from the carbons generated when the cards are used for purchases. The carbons can be gotten from trash cans or unscrupulous salesclerks. A *Handbook of White-Collar Crime* delineates a variety of card schemes. (U.S. Chamber of Commerce, 1974, pp. 34–35)

- A merchant and a holder of a lost or stolen credit card agree on a "purchase" of a $500 television set. The credit card transaction proceeds in the normal way, except in lieu of the TV set the unauthorized cardholder receives $250 from the merchant, who in turn collects $500 from the card issuer. The store owner may eventually sell the set at a cash discount to another merchant or an out-of-town friend.
- After purchasing major appliances with a fraudulently obtained credit card, the buyer fences them for 30 percent of their retail value.

A document analyst working on a credit-card fraud case

- A waiter or gas station attendant imprints two sets of charge slips: one for the current transaction and one he or she fills in later, forging the cardholder's signature.
- A cashier raises the $7.00 total on a credit card slip so that the sum reads $70.00.
- A waitress presents a bill for $50 and receives cash, which she pockets. Using a lost credit card, she accounts for the bill by preparing a charge slip for $50 and forges the cardholder's signature.
- A card is treated so that carbons of the charge slips are not imprinted.
- A stolen credit card is presented to a bank for a cash advance.

Says a well-known credit card defrauder: "I gave [stolen cards to] a lot of prostitutes. They can use the card in the man's name as the wife, and they work them for two days and split the fee fifty-fifty down the line. Sometimes I had six to seven people working different credit cards."

When cards become unsafe, operators often give them to cooperative merchants or employees, who turn them in to the issuer to collect the recovery reward. Or a hot card is dropped on the sidewalk or in a terminal, perhaps to be spotted by a passerby who may try to use it, get caught, and be blamed for its previous unauthorized use as well.

Embezzlement

Embezzlers take money or property entrusted to them and convert it to their own use. Victims include businesses, financial institutions, and pension funds.

Embezzlers usually steal petty cash, materials, products, or tools. A simple embezzler is a sales clerk who steals from the cash register and tampers with the customer's receipts. Bank tellers, loan officers, bookkeepers, and company presidents can do more monetary damage to a company than a sales clerk. An embezzler is trusted with money. In one case an embezzler skimmed money collected from a direct mail solicitation. Another example of embezzlement is when white-collar employees pad their expense accounts.

Investigating White-Collar Crime

White-collar crime comprises a wide variety of criminal offenses, among them false advertising, fraud, tax evasion, welfare fraud, and bankruptcy fraud. Figure 19–3 is a link diagram depicting an actual welfare case and Figure 19–4 depicts the flow of events in a bankruptcy fraud.

FIGURE 19-3: Link Diagram of Welfare Fraud

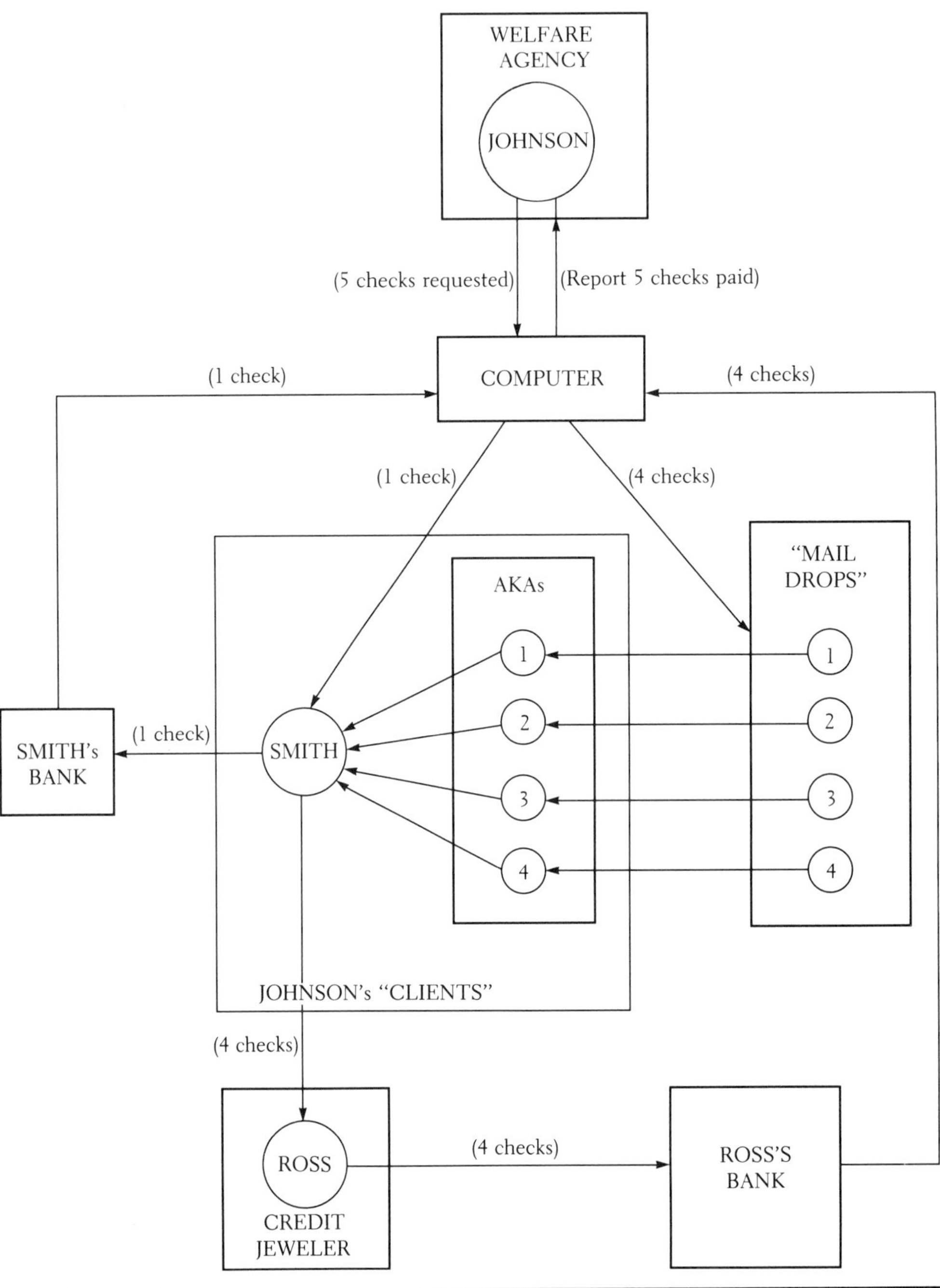

Source: H. Edelhertz, *The Investigation of White-Collar Crime: A Manual for Law Enforcement Agencies,* April 1977.

FIGURE 19–4: Time Flow of Events in a Bankruptcy Fraud

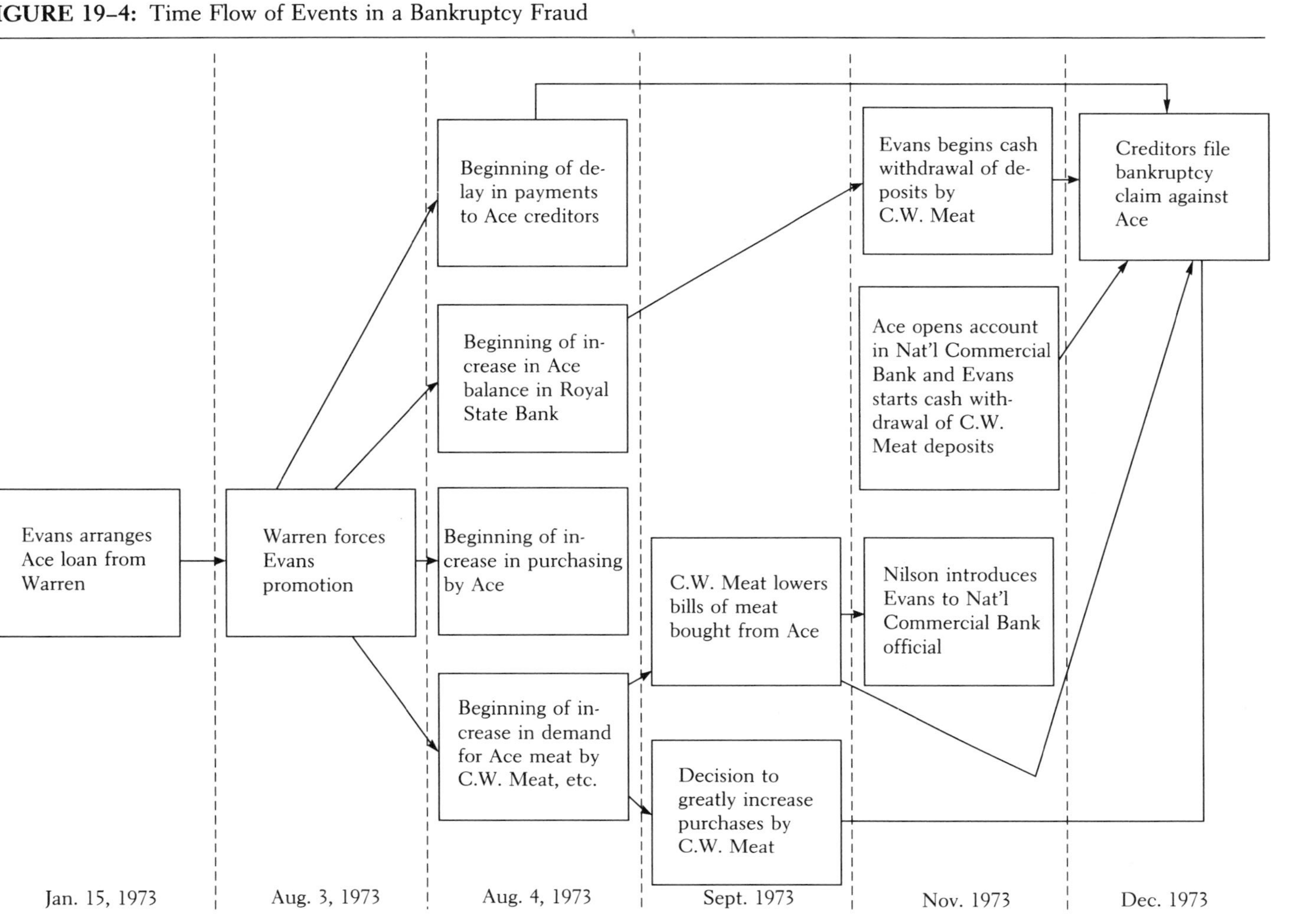

Source: H. Edelhertz, *The Investigation of White-Collar Crime: A Manual for Law Enforcement Agencies,* Washington, DC: U.S. Government Printing Office, April 1977.

The investigation of white-collar crime requires imagination, patience, and a clear comprehension of the numerous approaches that are employed in the investigative process. At times it is difficult to focus on a specific crime. Investigators should try to obtain information that can be geared to achieving solutions in addition to the primary goal. The government study on white-collar investigation gives some examples of additional remedies. (Edelhertz, 1977, pp. 121–122)

- An investment fraud investigation is facing difficulties under a local larceny statute. But the case might be moved forward under a local false pretenses statute or under mail fraud statutes.
- A police investigation of an auto repair fraud may not yield evidence that convinces the prosecutor she or he can show guilt beyond a reasonable doubt. But the prosecutor may have enough evidence to meet a civil burden of proof and thus commence civil action or may refer the case to the state attorney general's office or a municipal consumer protection office, which can take civil action to protect victims or take appropriate injunctive action.
- A local municipal consumer protection office that is primarily engaged in mediating complaints by consumers against merchants may, in the course of gathering facts to support its mediation/restitution efforts, develop evidence that indicates a potential for criminal prosecution. The office can refer its evidence and findings to an investigation or prosecuting agency that has criminal jurisdiction.

White-collar crimes usually operate over a period of time, without specific beginnings and endings. Evidence obtained may not solve a current criminal investigation but may assist an investigator in the future. Investigative techniques should be considered an inventory that can "(1) help to identify what evidence should be gathered, (2) show the different ways in which investigators can better accomplish conventional investigatory tasks when working in this field, and (3) be a roadmap and guide for the analysis and organization of evidence for maximum attractiveness and utility to prosecutors or other litigators." (Edelhertz, 1977, p. 122)

Organized Crime

In 1983, the President's Commission on Organized Crime called it "the most serious problem in America today." (Kaufman, 1983, p. 20) There are numerous definitions of organized crime. A useful one is this: "**Organized crime** is a continuing criminal enterprise that rationally works to profit from illicit activities that are in great public demand. Its continuing existence is maintained through the use of force, threats, and/or the corruption of public officials." (Albanese, 1989, p. 5)

The FBI states that "Such organizations are involved in every conceivable type of crime, including extortion, pornography, labor racketeering, bribery, and murder." (Kaufman, 1983, p. 20) Organized crime consists of two or more persons who engage in such activities as the supplying of illegal goods and services (e.g., vice, loan sharking) or predatory crime (e.g., theft, assault).

There are five general types of criminal activities that fit into these definitions of organized crime. (Abadinsky, 1990, p. 3)

- *Racketeering.* Groups of individuals that organize more than one of the following types of criminal activities for their combined profit.
- *Vice Operations.* Individuals who operate a continuing business providing illegal goods or services such as narcotics, prostitution, loan sharking, and gambling.
- *Theft/Fence Rings.* Groups of individuals who engage in a particular kind of theft on a continuing basis—such as fraud and bunco schemes, fraudulent documents, burglary, car theft, and truck hijacking—and associated individuals engaged in the business of purchasing stolen merchandise for resale and profit.
- *Gangs.* Groups of individuals with common interests or backgrounds who band together and collectively engage in unlawful activity to enhance their group identity and influence—for example, youth gangs, outlaw motorcycle clubs, and prison gangs.
- *Terrorists.* Groups of individuals who combine to commit spectacular criminal acts, such as assassination and kidnapping of public figures, to undermine public confidence in the established government for political reasons or to avenge some grievance.

The term *organized crime* cannot be restricted to any one specific crime group. Joseph Bonanno, a noted crime figure of the 1960s, described the many faces of organized crime: "The Kefauver Committee assumed the Mafia was a monolithic organization that controlled crime in America. Such a body, as defined by the Committee, doesn't exist. Organized crime embraces a lot of people—not just Sicilians, but Jews, Irish, Puerto Ricans, Cubans, Blacks, Anglos, you just name it." (Kaufman, 1984, pp. 422–423)

Regardless of their ethnic makeup, organized crime groups operate outside the control of mainstream America. They violate governmental regulations and business and criminal laws. They function through conspiracies that work to gain control over specific fields of activity, both legitimate activities such as garbage collection and criminal activities like narcotics sales, gambling, loan sharking, and prostitution.

The Mafia

The organized crime group that receives the most attention is the Mafia. In 1951 the Kefauver Committee claimed that the Mafia controlled the most lucrative rackets in America's largest cities. A 1957 meeting in Apalachin, New York, led to the conviction of 20 organized crime figures.

The President's Task Force on Organized Crime indicated that there was a core of 24 groups operating as criminal monopolies in our bigger cities and that their membership was primarily of Italian descent. (1967, p. 6)

In 1963, Joseph Valachi testified before the U.S. Senate Subcommittee on Investigations that an organization involved in criminal activity existed nationwide. Valachi's testimony was the first time that anyone openly admitted the existence of an organized criminal conspiracy in the United States. The name of this criminal organization, according to Valachi, was La Cosa Nostra (LCN). (Albanese, 1989, p. 43)

The "pizza connection" case grew out of an FBI investigation into the Bonanno crime family of La Cosa Nostra. Working in cooperation with Italian police agencies, the FBI uncovered a conspiracy that involved the importation of heroin and money laundering by Sicilian Mafia members in the United States. This investigation led to the indictment of 35 members of the Sicilian Mafia in 1984. The scope of this operation was worldwide. Members of the Sicilian Mafia operated in Brazil, Spain, Switzerland, Sicily, and Canada, and throughout the United States.

The relationship of the Sicilian Mafia with LCN has been described by Italian police officials as one of "common interest" in narcotics trafficking and money laundering, where each group needs the other. "The relationship is very precise, equal, and built on respect for each other; the common denominator is the ability to make money together." (McWenney, 1987, pp. 6–10)

FBI organized crime investigators in New York have concluded the following about the Sicilian Mafia/American LCN relationship.

- The Sicilian Mafia operates in the United States as a separate criminal organization, specializing in heroin smuggling, with first allegiance to its "family" in Sicily.

- Prior to initiating a major heroin smuggling operation, the Sicilian Mafia obtains the sanction of certain American LCN families (for example, the Gambino family in New York and the DeCavalcante family in New Jersey).
- The Sicilian Mafia pays a monetary tribute to the American LCN family (up to $5,000 for each kilo of heroin smuggled into the United States).

The Sicilian Mafia has been active in the United States for decades. The LCN grew out of it. Currently, the Sicilian Mafia controls the worldwide heroin distribution network. Its relationship with the American LCN appears to be excellent, and it is developing contacts with black and Colombian criminal groups.

Outlaw Motorcycle Clubs

Traditional organized crime is estimated to have 2,500 to 3,000 members, while the Big Four motorcycle gangs have approximately 8,000 members. The Hell's Angels, Outlaws, Pagans, and Bandidios have moved through four stages. (Abadinsky, 1990, p. 217)

- Rebellious and antisocial activity is random and nonutilitarian.
- A police response causes less committed members to drop out. Members of weaker clubs either disperse or join the stronger clubs.
- The remaining clubs are able to exercise discipline and control over their membership, particularly over violence, which now changes from random and nonutilitarian to instrumental.
- The leadership uses organizational skills and the ability to intimidate for utilitarian criminal pursuits, and the group becomes a fully committed criminal organization.

Outlaw motorcycle clubs are involved in the manufacture and distribution of synthetic drugs, prostitution, motor vehicle theft, gun-running, gambling, loan sharking, fencing, and murder for hire.

Prison Gangs

Prison gangs developed in the California prison system in the 1960s. They have spread to 32 states and the federal system. Prison gangs are conceded to control narcotics within most prisons and even have influence over the distribution of drugs on the street. This is primarily due to their willingness to use violence. (Palmiotto, 1988, p. 120)

Asian Criminal Groups

Like the Mafia and La Cosa Nostra, members of the Chinese Triad and the Japanese Yakuza organizations can trace their origins back hundreds of years. These Asian criminal groups are involved in illegal activities such as narcotics trafficking, gambling, and prostitution. They corrupt public officials in pursuit of their criminal activities and are willing to use violence toward potential victims and witnesses. They also adhere to a code of silence. Generally, law enforcement officials lack sufficient information to make accurate assessments of their criminal activities. This is primarily due to ethnic insulation from mainstream America.

Even the simplest crimes or acts of violence are difficult to solve because of the language barrier and because law enforcement agencies have communications with the Chinese community. The law enforcement community has to establish new methods of dealing with Chinese criminal groups. (Kaufman, 1984, p. 455)

- Exchange of intelligence with other agencies.
- International criminal history checks (the DEA's posts in Southeast Asia are very helpful).
- Organizational intelligence charting.
- Improved community relations.

In testimony before the President's Commission on Organized Crime, Raymond Chenault of the Oakland (California) Police Department made the following comments on Chinese organized crime.

- In extortion or physical threats leveled at Chinese, the target is the victim's family in Hong Kong. This demonstrates the strong ties criminal groups in the United States enjoy with criminal operatives in Hong Kong.
- The Tsong organization has a decision-making hierarchy, the committee of elders, which numbers anywhere from four to seven people.
- Gang members are grouped together according to criminal specialty (one group for prostitution, one for heroin, one for gambling). Gang members may eventually graduate to become members of the Tsong.
- Tsong usually use the Chinese restaurant with which they are affiliated not only as a meeting place but also as a money-laundering facility. (Kaufman, 1984, p. 464)

Investigating Organized Crime

Since many organized crimes are conspiracies, they are not reported by the victim. Generally, investigations are initiated by a tip or a suspicion. They are lengthy and tedious and require surveillances and reviews of financial records. A common technique used in an organized crime investigation is a financial analysis. There are three types of financial analysis: the bank-deposit method, net-worth method, and expenditure method. These methods are used to determine a suspect's total assets by comparing assets with reported taxable income. (Albanese, 1988, pp. 109–110)

Another method of collecting information against organized crime figures is electronic surveillance. Title III of the Omnibus Crime Control Act authorizes federal law enforcement officers to eavesdrop on conversations of criminal suspects, provided they obtain a warrant first. Investigators of organized crime also use pen register surveillance to record the telephone numbers dialed by the suspect.

In *Critical Issues in Criminal Investigation*, Kip Schlegel discusses the poor performance of electronic surveillance in organized crime investigations: "Criminal conspiracies often take an inordinate amount of time to complete. The plans for their execution generally take place in a variety of locations, some of which can be detected by bugs, others not. Thus electronic monitors tend to pick up fragments of criminal activity at best. It is very difficult to piece these fragments together, and to do so requires the same techniques used in investigating other pieces of information: witnesses are sought in an effort to gain insight into the information picked electronically. Finding witnesses and employing informants are, of course, both expensive and time consuming." (Palmiotto, 1988, p. 103)

Probably the confidential informant is the most effective tool for organized crime investigations. Usually an informant cooperates with law enforcement authorities in exchange for immunity from prosecution or a reduced criminal charge.

Undercover investigators infiltrate organized crime groups to collect sufficient evidence to make arrests and prosecute. The success of the undercover method is debatable. (Albanese, 1989, p. 114)

Terrorism

The FBI defines **terrorism** as "the unlawful use of force or violence to intimidate or coerce a government, the civilian population, or a segment thereof, in furtherance of political or social objectives." (Webster, 1986, p. 11)

Terrorist groups are involved in numerous activities, depending upon their political ideology, technological sophistication, and the resources available. Terrorist activity usually varies from region to region, and investigators should become familiar with the behavior patterns of the terrorist group or individual under study. According to Chris Hertig, actions that terrorists are involved in include "bombings, arson, assassination, kidnapping (removing the hostage from the immediate area), hostage-taking, aircraft hijacking, bank robbery, thefts from military or police arsenals, armored car robbery, product tampering, industrial sabotage, and miscellaneous propaganda efforts." (Palmiotto, 1988, p. 237)

The Los Angeles Police Department is one of the few agencies to create a full-time unit to combat terrorism. The LAPD's Anti-Terrorist Division (ATD) was established in 1983 under rigid, court-ordered guidelines regarding what groups or individuals should be targeted for investigations and what constituted a terrorist activity. The ATD is divided into four units: surveillance, investigative, legal, and intelligence analysis.

The intelligence analysis unit provided the lead in innovative techniques in the fight against terrorism. (Gates, 1989, p. 2)

- *Threat assessments.* Operations-oriented reports containing information on major events, visiting dignitaries, planned demonstrations, and other activities that may be targeted by terrorists.
- *Officer safety bulletins.* Interdepartmental memos regarding terrorist threats, such as new weapons or tactics, that reflect directly on the police officer working the street.
- *Briefing papers.* Reports covering key world and national situations involving terrorism that could ultimately affect the city of Los Angeles.
- *Intelligence analysis.* Translating intelligence data into meaningful investigative conclusions for effective case management.

The Anti-Terrorist Division defines terrorist acts as: "Unlawful actions which can reasonably be expected to result in death, serious bodily injury, or significant property damage and which are intended to have such results to further societal objectives, to influence societal action, or to harass on the basis of race, religion, or national origin." (Gates, 1989, p. 2)

Analysis examines raw intelligence data to uncover possible terrorism trends and furnish feasible management of the investigation. The analysis gives purpose and guidance to intelligence data, fills investigative gaps, and recommends additional investigative avenues. Trend analysis produces data to assist in decisions pertaining to current and future terrorist activities.

Investigators can use the information obtained to make decisions about specific operations or follow up on recently developed leads. Case analysts search for similarities and differences in a wide variety of investigations. To be successful, analysts must develop rapport with investigators, building trust and confidence.

The analysis process is important in the crusade against terrorism. As the investigator collects information, the analyst provides a comprehensive image of the case and can help interpret the meaning of divergent pieces of information. An important aspect of the analysis process is to provide a strong base for decision making.

Terrorist activities require investigative techniques similar to those for organized crime. The investigator must perform the following activities: identify coconspirators; identify all aiders and abettors; pursue all unapprehended parties; apprehend all persons wanted in connection with an incident; investigate all arrestees to disclose associations, past history, and potential for cooperation; upgrade preventive surveillance to secure additional information on suspects; and pursue kidnappers immediately after the incident to discover the location of the hostage and the terrorist. (Palmiotto, 1988, p. 239)

Summary

The investigation of crime can require special training and understanding for the various types of criminal cases an investigator can encounter. Most criminal investigators are generalists and need to develop the skills and knowledge to perform all kinds of criminal investigation.

During the 1970s, art thefts became a problem for both Europe and the United States. Since they result in great financial losses, the FBI has established a National Stolen Art File, a computerized index of stolen and recovered art. The NSAF serves as a central repository of data and photographs of art reported stolen to local law enforcement agencies. All art objects that are investigated by law enforcement agencies should be searched through NSAF.

The offense of arson is defined by the Uniform Crime Report as "any willful or malicious burning or attempt to burn, with or without intent to defraud, a dwelling house, public building, motor vehicle or aircraft, personal property of another, etc." Factors that can establish the crime of arson include the type of fire, its point of origin, the type of building structure, the time of day of the fire, the owner of the building, individuals associated with the property, the market value of the property, whether the property was overinsured, whether the building was occupied, and whether there was a recent sale or title change of the building. An exhaustive investigation may be required to establish that arson has been committed.

Family violence became an issue in the late 1960s with increased public awareness of child abuse. Spouse abuse and wife beating also became recognized as serious problems. The Attorney General's Task Force recommended that all police agencies establish family violence as a priority response and require officers to file written reports on all incidents. During the initial investigation of a domestic violence call, the responding officers should obtain specific information such as the nature and extent of injuries and the use of force or weapons.

Computer crime has existed since the 1940s. Computer crimes can be categorized by types of information and by information-processing loss: modification, destruction, disclosure, and the use or denial of use. These classifications are grouped into extensive explanations and models, which can be effective tools for investigation of computer crime. Investigators of computer crimes should understand methods of computer abuse and know where to get the information pertaining to computers needed to conduct the investigation.

White-collar crime is an illegal act characterized by guile, deceit, and concealment rather than physical force. The investigation of white-collar crime requires imagination, patience, and a clear comprehension of the numerous approaches employed in the investigative process. At times it is difficult to focus on a specific crime. White-collar crimes do not have specific beginnings and endings, and they usually operate over a period of time. Evidence obtained may not solve a current criminal investigation but may assist an investigator in the future.

The President's Commission on Organized Crime in 1983 called it "the most serious problem in America today." The FBI defines organized crime as "criminal organizations whose primary objective is to obtain money through illegal activities." Many varieties and combinations of criminal groups fit into the organized crime definition. Regardless of their ethnic makeup, organized crime groups operate outside the control of mainstream America. They violate governmental regulations and business and criminal laws. They function through conspiracies that work to gain control over specific fields of activities, both legal and illegal (for example, narcotics, gambling, loan sharking, and prostitution).

Since many organized crimes are conspiracies, they are not reported by the victim. Generally, investigations are initiated by a tip or a suspicion. Investigations of organized crime activities are lengthy and tedious and require surveillance and reviews of financial records. The confidential informant is probably the most effective tool in organized crime investigations. Usually an informant cooperates with law enforcement authorities in exchange for immunity from prosecution.

The FBI defines terrorism as "the unlawful use of force or violence to intimidate or coerce a government, the civilian population, or a segment thereof, in furtherance of political or social objectives." Terrorist groups are involved in numerous activities, depending on their political ideology, technological sophistication, and resources available. Terrorist activity varies from region to region.

Investigators should become familiar with the behavior patterns of the terrorist group or individual under study. In working terrorist cases, investigators must identify coconspirators; identify all aiders and abettors; pursue all unapprehended parties; apprehend all persons wanted in connection with an incident; investigate all arrestees to disclose associations, past history, and potential for cooperation; upgrade preventive surveillance to secure additional information on suspects; and pursue kidnappers immediately after the incident to discover the location of the hostage and the terrorist.

Key Terms

arson
asynchronous attack
computer abuse
computer crime
computer fraud
computer virus
data leakage
eavesdropping
embezzler
false data entry
logic bomb
masquerading
National Stolen Art File
organized crime
piggybacking
piracy
playback
salami technique
scanning
scavenging
spouse abuse
spying
superzapping
tailgating
terrorism
trapdoors
Trojan horse
white-collar crime
worm attack

Review Questions

1. What suggestions should an investigator give citizens who ask what to do in the event of an art theft?
2. What is the National Stolen Art File?
3. Name the seven basic motives the National Fire Academy lists for people who set fires.
4. Name six clues that indicate positive circumstantial evidence that a fire was set for insurance fraud.

5. Define spouse abuse.
6. What are the duties of a spousal abuse unit?
7. Distinguish among computer abuse, computer fraud, and computer crime.
8. What are the four categories of computer crime?
9. Explain these types of computer abuse: eavesdropping, masquerading, piggybacking and tailgating, superzapping, scavenging, Trojan horse, salami technique, logic bomb, trapdoor, asynchronous attack, and piracy.
10. What is the profile of the typical computer law violator?
11. Explain the five principal elements of white-collar crime.
12. Describe some of the most common methods for arranging kickbacks and other payoffs.
13. Define organized crime.
14. Explain the influence of the Sicilian Mafia on organized crime.
15. Explain the function of the Anti-Terrorist Division of the LAPD in fighting terrorism.

References

Abadinsky H: *Organized Crime*, ed.3. Chicago, IL: Nelson-Hall, 1990.

Albanese J: *Organized Crime in America*, ed.2. Cincinnati, OH: Anderson Publishing Co., 1989.

Attorney General's Task Force on Family Violence. Washington, DC: U.S. Government Printing Office, 1984.

Bequai A: *How to Prevent Computer Crimes: A Guide for Managers*. New York, NY: John Wiley and Sons, 1983.

Conly C: *Organizing for Computer Crime Investigation and Prosecution*. Washington, DC: National Institute of Justice, 1989.

Edelhertz H: *The Investigation of White-Collar Crime*, Washington, DC: U.S. Government Printing Office, 1977.

Gates D: "The Role of Analysis in Combating Modern Terrorism." *FBI Law Enforcement Bulletin*, vol. 58, no. 6, 1989.

Goolkasian G: *Confronting Domestic Violence: A Guide for Criminal Justice Agencies*. Washington, DC: U.S. Government Printing Office, 1986.

A Handbook of White-Collar Crime. Washington, DC: U.S. Chamber of Commerce, 1974.

Kaufman I: *Organized Crime: Federal Law Enforcement Perspective*. Washington, DC: U.S. Government Printing Office, 1983.

Kaufman I: *Organized Crime of Asian Origin*. Washington, DC: U.S. Government Printing Office, 1984.

Loving N: *Responding to Spouse Abuse and Wife Beating*. Washington, DC: Police Executive Research Forum, 1980.

Mason DL: "Art Theft Investigation." *FBI Law Enforcement Bulletin*, vol. 48, no. 1, 1979.

McEwen JT: *Dedicated Computer Crime Units*. Washington, DC: National Institute of Justice, 1989.

McPhee JB, Spitzer T, Sundin, RP: "The National Stolen Art File." *FBI Law Enforcement Bulletin*, vol. 52, no. 3, 1983.

McWenney S: "The Sicilian Mafia and Its Impact on the United States. *FBI Law Enforcement Bulletin*, vol. 56, no. 2, 1987.

Palmiotto MJ: *Critical Issues in Criminal Investigation*, ed.2. Cincinnati, OH: Anderson Pub. Co., 1988.

Parker DP: *Computer Crime: Criminal Justice Resource Manual*. Washington, DC: National Institute of Justice, 1989.

President's Commission on Law Enforcement and Administration of Justice: *Task Force Report: Organized Crime*. Washington, D.C.: Government Printing Office, 1967.

Rider AO: "The Firesetter: A Psychological Profile." *FBI Law Enforcement Bullentin*, vol. 55, no. 6, 1986.

Stickevers J: "The Investigation of Fatal Fires: Views of Fire Investigators." *FBI Law Enforcement Bulletin*, vol. 55, no. 8, 1986.

Sutherland E: *White Collar Crime*. New York, NY: Dryden Press, 1949.

Walsh R: "Inner-City Arson." *FBI Law Enforcement Bulletin*, vol. 48, no. 10, 1979.

Webster W: "Terrorism as a Crime." *FBI Law Enforcement Bulletin*, vol. 55, no. 5, 1986.

CHAPTER 20

The Police/Prosecutor Relationship

Police officers have the responsibility of preparing criminal investigations for trial. Since **prosecutors** represent the state against criminal offenders and the police apprehend offenders on behalf of the state, the police officer's responsibilities can be closely identified with those of the prosecutor. When a criminal violation is discovered the police investigate, make arrests when appropriate, and file a complaint for prosecution. The prosecution then has the responsibility to bring the case to trial. A criminal case can be closed without prosecution for several valid reasons. (Bennett and Hess, 1987, p. 486)

- The complaint is invalid.
- The prosecutor declines after reviewing the case.
- The complainant refuses to prosecute.
- The offender dies.
- The offender is in prison or out of the country and cannot be returned.
- No evidence or leads exist.

Case Preparation

Law enforcement officers investigating crimes should use all available resources to obtain information about the crime and the offender's involvement in it. Criminal investigators need to search the crime scene, interview victims and witnesses, collect evidence, and have the evidence analyzed.

Investigators should be able to obtain legal assistance from the prosecution in complicated cases or if they lack knowledge about a specific criminal violation. Investigators should collect information that allows the prosecutor to make a sound decision as to whether the case should be prosecuted or filed. All written police reports that relate to the crime should be submitted to the prosecutor, including arrest, follow-up, and supplemental reports. Statements made by the suspect should be in writing; if tape-recorded, a written summary of statements should be included. Summaries of interviews with victims and witnesses should be written. All fingerprint, handwritten, or ballistics findings should be attached to the complaint. The investigator should corroborate statements made by suspects and verify statements of witnesses and victims. (De Ladurantey and Sullivan, 1980, pp. 423–424)

When the prosecuting attorney decides to prosecute the case, he or she must know what evidence to present, what witnesses to call to testify, the strengths and weaknesses of the case, and the kind of testimony the criminal investigator can provide. To prepare a case for court, the investigator must:

- review and evaluate all evidence, positive and negative,
- review all reports on the case,
- prepare witnesses,
- write a final report, and
- hold a pretrial conference with the prosecutor.

Case Screening

The prosecutor has discretionary power to either prosecute or not. A number of factors play a role in the decision whether or not to bring charges. (*Screening of Criminal Cases*, n.d., pp. 2–3)

- Does the prosecutor think the individual is guilty?
- Is the case likely to result in a conviction?
- Will the time and effort spent on the case be justified if a conviction is obtained?
- Is there pressure from another agency or division of government?
- Will a conviction make it appear that the prosecutor is being heartless?
- Is the prospective defendant someone well known in the community so that the resulting publicity would impose a more severe penalty than justified?
- Would the resulting sentence be too severe for the crime committed?

- Is this an area in which juries are disinclined to convict?
- Would it be better to wait until the offender commits another offense with a stronger set of facts for the prosecution?
- Would the perpetrator be valuable as a witness in another trial or against parties involved with him or her?
- Will the judge who will probably hear this case be favorable?
- Even if the possibility of a conviction is slim, should the case be pursued because the defendant appears to be guilty of other offenses for which he or she was not charged?
- Should the case be prosecuted in spite of doubtful outcome because civil rights are involved?
- Can this case be transferred to another court or to another agency for civil penalties?

Outside influences can also be a factor in the prosecutor's decision whether to prosecute, among them the police, the trial court, the defense counsel, and public opinion.

The Police

Police arrests set the outer limits of prosecution. The prosecutor is generally limited by those cases that are actually presented by the law enforcement agencies within his or her jurisdiction. Since the police practice discretion in their arrests, they selectively determine which cases come to the prosecutor's attention.

It is therefore important that the prosecutor's office establish rapport with law enforcement agencies, particularly with regard to arrest policies. The quantity and quality of the evidence in a case will normally depend on the police as well as the procedures used to obtain it. A decision not to prosecute is often based on shortcomings in this area. Also, the charging decision is usually relegated to the police for minor offenses.

The Trial Court

The attitudes of the court affect the decision to prosecute. The prosecutor's decisions have a strong tendency to conform to the court's predispositions.

Defense Counsel

Often the defense counsel influences the prosecutor's decision by pointing out weaknesses in the case and possible mitigating circumstances. Negotiations between the defense counsel and the prosecutor determine whether a charge will be reduced, dropped, or not initiated in the first place.

Public Opinion

The news media, civic organizations, individuals, and political groups exercise influence on the policies of the prosecutor. It may be wise not to pursue an unpopular case, even if the evidence is weighty enough to assure conviction. In contrast, when a heinous crime is committed but the evidence is weak, the public tends to expect a speedy arrest anyway. But prosecutors must try to resist this pressure.

Police Liaison with Prosecution

The President's Commission on Law Enforcement in 1967 discovered that most police forces received limited legal assistance from the prosecutor's office. The report's American Bar Foundation (ABF) researchers paint a bleak picture: "While private counsel representing a business client would believe it to be of the utmost importance to consult fully with his client, prosecutors commonly proceed on the assumption that the police not be consulted." The ABF concluded "A prosecutor who understood the problems of the

Police officers complete a district attorney's case report.

police . . . could better decide what issues are in greatest need of clarification." (1967, p. 65)

In the early 1970s, because of procedural due process and the application of the exclusionary rule to the states, the duties and powers of the police changed fundamentally. The National Advisory Commission on Criminal Justice Standards and Goals recommended the following standards relating to the prosecution function: "The prosecutor should endeavor to establish and maintain at all times a relationship of mutual confidence and cooperation with the police. In some places, especially where large staffs are involved, a useful device has been developed in having the prosecutor and the police department each designate one staff member as a coordinated **liaison** officer through whom all interoffice matters are cleared." (1973, p. 248)

This standard means that prosecutors should not only provide the police with legal advice but also maintain open communications with them. Both the prosecutor and the police have to make the other aware of their administrative problems and even help develop solutions for these problems. Problems that may be common to both the prosecutor's office and the police agency include unnecessary court appearances by police officers, advising officers of the disposition of their cases, providing officers with the reasons for unfavorable dispositions, getting each other's assistance for case preparation, and dealing with uncooperative or poorly prepared prosecutors and police officers.

The standard also requires that prosecutors assist police departments in training officers: "Many of the problems which plague the police—and indeed the public—in recent years can be traced to mistakes of the police, often entirely inadvertent, in carrying out such routine duties as securing warrants, making arrests, executing warrants, interrogating persons in custody, and conducting line-ups for identification purposes. . . . It is imperative that every patrolman on the beat be trained carefully as to the limits of police authority." (National Advisory Commission on Criminal Justice Standards and Goals, 1973, p. 248)

In addition, the Commission advises that prosecutors should evaluate police reports and assist the police in revising forms. One prosecutor who has taken this to heart is the district attorney for the Atlantic Judicial Circuit, which covers several rural counties in southeast Georgia. The district attorney, a former police officer, realized that some police officers were avoiding writing essays about specific crimes because they were poor writers. His office developed an arrest report (Figure 20–1) that all officers must complete if they want their arrests prosecuted.

FIGURE 20–1: Arrest Report

Atlantic Judicial Circuit

REPORT OF ARREST

Instructions:
Attach Supporting Documents and Forward to D.A.'s Office.

__________ DEPARTMENT, __________, GA.

DATE OF REPORT __________

Name of Defendant __________

Address __________

Sex _____ Race _____ DOB _____ SSN _____

Charged With __________

Place Crime Committed __________

Victim __________

Address __________ Telephone Number __________

Date of Crime _____ Time _____ Date of Arrest _____

Arresting Officers __________

Investigating Officers __________

Did Defendant Make Statement? Yes ____ No ____ Written ____ Oral ____ To Whom ____
(Attach copy of statement)

Physical Evidence Available __________

Scientific Reports: Was evidence sent to crime lab Yes _____ No _____
Other reports(circle): Autopsy Hospital Physician Other _____

SUMMARIZE WHAT EACH WITNESS CAN TESTIFY TO (Attach any written statements by witnesses)

Prosecuting Witness - Name __________

Address __________ Telephone Number __________

Witness No. 1 - Name __________

Address __________ Telephone Number __________

Witness No. 2 - Name __________

Address __________ Telephone Number __________

Witness No. 3 - Name __________

Address __________ Telephone Number __________

Witness No. 4 - Name __________

Address __________ Telephone Number __________

Source: District Attorney, Atlanta Judicial Circuit, Hinesville, Georgia.

The completed arrest report helps the prosecutor for the case decide whether more information is needed to prosecute. The report is an excellent training method to get police officers to obtain pertinent evidence and information to prosecute a criminal case successfully.

Benefits of an Improved Relationship

A positive relationship between the prosecutor and police agencies is beneficial to both units and can only assist the criminal justice process. "A formal system for obtaining feedback can help the police manager spot trouble within the organization on the matter of investigative performance and evaluate the relative effectiveness of units and individuals. . . . Police feedback to the prosecutor can provide important suggestions concerning operating policies, procedures, and practices, as prosecutor performance." (Cawley et al., 1977, pp. 108–109)

Two-way communication between the police and the prosecutor can improve criminal investigations and the successful prosecution of cases. Input from the prosecutor's office to the police can assist in case screening, case management, and follow-up investigations. Ways to improve the relationship between the police and the prosecutor include feedback and case disposition analysis systems, improving investigative quality, and assigning liaison responsibility. (Cawley et al., 1977, pp. 109–120)

Feedback and Case Disposition Analysis Systems

One of the most important questions to ask in developing a case disposition feedback system is: What does a chief or manager need to know in order to improve the investigative effort? The police administrator needs to know, at a minimum:

- the disposition of the case,
- why the case was rejected for prosecution, or
- why a case submitted by the prosecutor resulted in a dismissal.

Other questions to be asked concerning feedback systems are:

- What does the police manager have to know to effectively manage?
- Who else has to know?

- What do people do with the information they receive?
- When is the process subjected to evaluation and rethinking?

Improving the Quality of Investigations

Police investigators must first identify the prosecutor's need for information. They must carefully gather all the available evidence, evaluate the facts at their disposal, make arrests where warranted, and present the evidence upon which the charge is made.

The prosecutor must then evaluate the evidence and accept or reject the case on the basis of the facts presented. If he or she accepts the case, the prosecutor formally charges the defendant in the manner prescribed by the court that has primary jurisdiction over the offense within the geographic area in which the crime was committed. When the case is called for trial, the prosecutor presents it and attempts to prove beyond a reasonable doubt that a crime did in fact take place and that the defendant committed it.

Through the experience gained in court, the prosecutor is in the best position to identify the elements of information that are needed to present and substantiate the charges.

Identifying mutual priorities for police and prosecution is another important step in improving investigative quality. Enforcement priorities are set to address major concerns of the community. Emphasis may also be placed on those crimes that generate other crimes, such as those related to narcotics and organized drug distribution systems or high-stakes gambling operations.

A clear understanding of and agreement with police priorities will help the prosecutor's office gear up for more effective prosecution of these crimes. Agreement on priorities will increase the combined impact of the police/prosecutor relationship. Mutual priorities are preferable because of the progress that can be made by both police and prosecutors toward achieving their goals. Interactive goals will bind the two elements into a more professional, cohesive, and unified organization in the interests of justice in the community.

Assignment of Liaison Responsibility

Increased activity to strengthen the liaison between police and prosecutors has been promoted by the relatively new concept of the police legal adviser. A legal adviser is an attorney who can be a civilian, a police officer, or a prosecutor. He or she performs services that require special skills such as assisting police administrators in police planning, community relations, department legal

A prosecuting attorney and a police officer discuss an upcoming case.

problems, and advising officers on legal issues arising out of specific cases.

The record-keeping function of a legal liaison unit should not be minimized. The unit is a perfect place for the compilation and clarification of data from case feedback forms that is so important to the interactive relationship between the police and prosecutor. Here data can be quantified, problems identified, and solutions developed.

Model System for Developing Effective Liaison

A system for creating a productive liaison between the police and the prosecutor begins with commitment. There is the initial approach, periodic meetings, agreement on a systems approach, determination and management of information needs, design of forms, setting of priorities, and consideration of special needs.

- *Commitment.* The first and most important element in developing an effective liaison between police and the prosecutor's office is the commitment to do so by the chief executives of both agencies.
- *The initial approach.* To begin to develop an effective police/prosecutor liaison, someone has to take the first step. An initial contact needs to be made on an executive-to-executive level.
- *Monthly meeting.* A firm schedule for meetings of the two executives should be established.

- *Systems approach.* Only if both the police and the prosecutor view themselves as interlocking parts of the same system can any improvement in their relationship be expected.
- *Investigative information needs.* To achieve the goal of prosecuting a higher percentage of the cases presented for consideration, the police must provide all the information the prosecutor's office needs to evaluate the prospects of presenting each case to the court.
- *Management information needs.* Proper management cannot take place without detailed knowledge of the operations of the unit to be managed.
- *Joint utilization forms.* From the previous step, the informational needs can be transcribed as entries on experimental forms. The forms should be tested to see if they satisfy the informational needs of everyone concerned.
- *Prosecutorial priorities.* The two chief executives should clarify and reach agreement on their priorities for prosecution.
- *Special needs and remedies.* A good rapport between the police and the prosecutor has been instrumental in setting up several potentially effective types of special units. For example, joint investigator/prosecutor teams can be established for such crimes as narcotics trafficking, vice, and organized crime. Also, deputy prosecutors could be assigned to specific geographic areas or specific investigative units, as after-hours resources to agencies. (Cawley et al., 1977, pp. 119–120)

Since the 1970s there has not been much written about the police/prosecutor relationship. This does not necessarily mean that the parties do not perceive the relevance of a good working relationship. It may simply mean that an informal process of cooperation and communication is in place and working. Another reason for the lack of information concerning police/prosecutor relationships may be that written policies could come under the scrutiny of defense attorneys.

Summary

Police officers have the responsibility of preparing criminal investigations for trial. Since prosecutors represent the state against criminal offenders and the police apprehend offenders on behalf of the state, the police officer's responsibilities can be closely identified with the prosecutor's. Investigators should be able to obtain legal assistance in complicated cases or if they lack knowledge about a specific criminal violation.

The prosecutor has discretionary power to either prosecute or not. A number of factors play a role in the decision-making process, including the police, the trial court, the defense counsel, and public opinion.

The President's Commission on Law Enforcement in 1967 discovered that most police forces received limited legal assistance from the prosecutor's office. Because of procedural due process and the application of the exclusionary rule to the states, the duties and powers of police had fundamentally changed. A positive relationship between the prosecutor and the police agencies is beneficial to both and can only assist the criminal justice process. Two-way communication between the police and the prosecutor can improve the success of case prosecution. Input from the prosecutor's office to the police can assist them in case screening, case management, and follow-up investigation.

Key Terms

liaison
prosecutor

Review Questions

1. Describe the importance of case preparation.
2. Describe the importance of case screening as it relates to the prosecutor's discretionary authority.
3. What are some of the factors that play a role in the decision whether or not to prosecute?
4. Why is police liaison with prosecution important?
5. What are some of the benefits of an improved relationship between the prosecutor and the police?

References

Bennett W, Hess KM: *Criminal Investigation*, ed. 2, St. Paul, MN: West Publishing Co., 1987.

Cawley DF, Wasserman R, Miron HJ, Mannello T, Araujo W, Yale H: *Managing Criminal Investigations*. Washington, DC: U.S. Government Printing Office, 1977.

De Ladurantey JC, Sullivan DR: *Criminal Investigation Standards*, New York, NY: Harper and Row, 1980.

National Advisory Commission on Criminal Justice Standards and Goals: *Courts*. Washington, DC: U.S. Government Printing Office, 1973.

President's Commission on Law Enforcement and Administration of Justice: *Task Force Report: The Police*. Washington, DC: U.S. Government Printing Office, 1967.

Screening of Criminal Cases. Chicago, IL: National District Attorneys Association, n.d.

CHAPTER 21

Investigative Trends

The United States is going through social and cultural changes. Our country has an aging population and an increasing population of blacks, Hispanics, and Asians. In the future, minorities and women may have more wealth and influence in American society than white males. Blue-collar America, with its factory workers, is giving way to service and technological industries. "Muscle work" seems to be decreasing while the need for educated workers increases.

According to an *FBI Law Enforcement Bullentin*, "It is simple-minded to blame crime on poverty. There are plenty of societies in which poverty does *not* produce crime. . . . It is equally witless to assume that millions of poor, jobless young people—not part of the work-world culture and bursting with energy and anger—are going to stay off the streets and join knitting clubs." (Toffler, 1990, p. 3)

The family where the father goes to work while the mother stays home to raise the children is fading from the American scene. The impact of the increase in two-career couples, childless couples, and divorce must be felt by society. One consequence has been an increase in singles and loners and a breakdown of social bonds. Increased mobility and loosening of support systems have lessened social constraints. The opinions of family, friends, and neighbors have less impact than they once did.

Violent and criminal behaviors have long been held in check by social disapproval, but "Law enforcement professionals starting out now face approximately 25 years of a society that is confused, rent with conflict, struggling to find a new place in the world, and bombarded by destabilizing technological changes and economic swings." (Toffler, 1990, p. 5)

Computers

Criminal investigators are becoming computer-literate as the computer becomes an essential investigative tool. Criminal records and pertinent information about suspects and informants will be more efficiently and quickly obtained. With computerized communications systems, an investigator in a motor vehicle has rapid access to records anywhere in the United States. Information provided by computers will assist criminal investigators in the decision-making process.

The federal government and most states will soon have automated fingerprint systems in operation, saving time and manpower. With the aid of lasers that can locate fingerprints on wood surfaces, clothing, and concrete blocks, automated fingerprint systems will allow criminal investigators to solve crimes that in the past were unsolvable. Even when an investigator found fingerprints at the crime scene, it was often too time-consuming to manually locate the fingerprints of the suspect, but now they can be found in minutes or even seconds.

Report Processing

To eliminate duplication, investigators can type their reports on a word processor, which will store them in the computer's memory. A hard copy can be produced whenever necessary. It may be possible through **optical character readers** (OCR) for a computer to read and record handwritten information, which can be retrieved as needed. Also, investigators may use an **integrated image system** to record documents into the computer memory. An electronic digitizing video camera is interfaced with a computer. The camera focuses on a document and scans and digitizes the image electronically. Then the computer processes the image into the memory.

John Probert writes that, in the future, investigators will only have to radio or telephone their reports and the computer will:

- automatically record and type the report in correct grammatical style and spelling.
- position and type the appropriate information for the computer memory and on the proper report form.
- check vehicle registration and owner for verification and accuracy.
- ask, by voice communication, for additional information if the

This Riverside, Illinois, lieutenant accesses the computerized Area-wide Law Enforcement Radio Terminal System (ALERTS) for up-to-the-minute data on local criminal activity. Computers in vehicles assist patrol officers in conducting investigative work at the crime scene.

officer forgets any essential details. The computer will also be programmed to say why the data are needed (if asked).

- accept the report in any order and rearrange the data in proper sequence according to the report form.
- automatically distribute the report to the proper authorities for review and disposition.
- scan the report to determine if all the elements necessary to establish a crime are present and enumerate the statutes to be considered for prosecution. (Palmiotto, 1988, p. 29)

Analysis and Profiling

Criminal investigators can use computers to trace crime trends and analyze them. Crime analysis focuses on groups of events rather than isolated incidents. When crime-prone locations have been identified, crime analysis can make the best use of investigative time.

The FBI's behavioral science unit uses crime pattern analysis to profile rapes, arsons, extortions, and other violent and nonviolent offenses. The BSU uses criminal profiling as a law enforcement tool. The FBI defines the profiling process as "an investigative technique by which to identify the major personality and behavioral characteristics of the offender based upon an analysis of the crime(s) he or she has committed." (Douglas and Burgess, 1986, p. 9)

The profiling process generally involves seven steps.

1. Evaluation of the criminal act itself.
2. Comprehensive evaluation of the specifics of the crime scene(s).
3. Comprehensive analysis of the victim.
4. Evaluation of preliminary police reports.
5. Evaluation of the medical examiner's autopsy protocol.
6. Development of the profile with critical offender characteristics.
7. Investigative suggestions predicated on constructions of the profile.

Criminal personality profiling is a method for narrowing the scope of an investigation. Profiling does not identify the offender, but it can indicate the type of individual who possesses the characteristics related to a specific crime. Criminal profiling provides skilled investigators with another tool to be used in crime solving. An investigator needs to be computer-literate to effectively perform profiling or crime analysis.

With an increase of computers in workplaces and in the home, computer crime will be on the increase. Law enforcement agencies either have to hire employees trained in the computer field or provide their officers with computer training. Criminal investigators should be familiar with the characteristics that typify computer-related crime and criminals. (See Chapter 18 for more details.) (Parker, 1989, pp. 8–10)

- *Low visibility.* Most computer crimes that are detected are found by accident or by routine audits.
- *Victim reluctance to report incidents.* The publicity can damage their reputations or they do not believe the law enforcement community can solve the offense.
- *Potential for enormous losses.* Million-dollar losses have been reported.
- *Can be committed over long distances.* Telecommunications capability is worldwide.
- *Can be committed in as little as three milliseconds*
- *Low risk of discovery and prosecution.*

- *Persons prosecuted are not severely punished.* Some authorities believe the odds of going to jail are one in 22,000.
- *Discovery of losses does not reveal how the offense was actually committed.*
- *Prosecution difficult under existing laws.* Traditional offenses must often be charged.
- *Establishing time of offense may be impossible.*
- *Obtaining physical evidence is difficult,* since it becomes partially electronic in nature.
- *Evidence issues.* Originality and hearsay exceptions are at issue.
- *Explaining technological crimes to juries is difficult.* Doubt is easier to plant when the concepts are hard to comprehend.

Private Security Connections

The 1990s may be regarded as the decade of cooperation and recognition that the missions of public law enforcement and private security have similarities. Crime can be prevented and controlled only when public law enforcement, the private police, and their clientele willingly work toward the same goals. The police cannot solve crime without public support.

Realistically, the police need all the help they can get. They also need to recognize that the private sector of policing may have more expertise, access to more knowledge, and more information about a specific crime than a public law enforcement investigator and agency. For example, can public investigators make a case against a toxic-waste or computer-crime offender? Criminal investigators can learn much from investigators who work in the private sector.

Post and Kingsbury list ten functions that both law enforcement and private police perform. (1977, p. 473)

- Prevention,
- Protection,
- Enforcement,
- Detection,
- Investigation,
- Deterrence,
- Emergency services,
- Reporting,
- Inspections, and
- General services.

Private investigators may be concerned with theft, fraud, vandalism, burglary, background checks, and pre-employment checks, as well as undercover work. For example, a private investigator working undercover on behalf of the Royal Canadian Mounted Police infiltrated a drug ring in Ontario. (Shearing et al., 1980, pp. 177–178)

Another reason for cooperation between public and private police is that private police accomplish a significant amount of investigative activities, including credit card fraud, check kiting and forgery, embezzlement, employee theft, shoplifting, and computer hacking.

Law enforcement and private police must recognize one another as equals in crime prevention and the need to cooperate and exchange information to solve criminal cases. Petty jealousies and a false superiority are detrimental to crime-solving.

Research Methods

A variety of research methods should be considered when investigating crime. Five useful forecasting methodologies are scenarios, the Delphi technique, the cross-impact matrix, relevance trees, and technology assessments. (Tayofa, 1990, pp. 203–206)

Scenarios

In research, a **scenario** encompasses four essential characteristics: it is hypothetical, summarized, multifaceted, and factually based. A scenario must be based on fact. It should be a carefully researched, realistic representation of a sequence of events. The best scenarios are not one-dimensional. Rather, they depict at least three conceivable outcomes: the best case, the worst case, and the most likely case of the forecast alternative futures.

All of the suppositions and limitations inherent in the presentation must be outlined. The most valuable scenarios present possible, probable, and preferable futures. The scenario method is ideal for criminal investigators because it lends itself to complex situations, such as serial murder or rape.

Delphi Technique

A structured group process that maximizes the likelihood of reaching consensus and identifying disagreement is called the **Delphi technique**. Essentially, this method involves anonymous structured exchanges among a panel of experts who receive controlled feedback and statistical group responses between rounds of propositions posed by a moderator using a series of mailed questionnaires.

The strength of the method for law enforcement results from

its precision and ability to circumvent impediments to decision-making in conventional group settings. Its weakness results from the need to use experts and the time required to conduct a conventional Delphi study, typically six to eighteen months.

Cross-Impact Matrix

In the **cross-impact matrix**, the probability of one forecast event can be adjusted as a function of its potential interaction with all other forecast events. This feature is particularly useful because the forecasts that emerge with other methods are frequently one-dimensional. That is, they view events in isolation and ignore factors that might be mutually reinforcing or mutually exclusive.

Relevance Trees

Used to analyze situations in which distinct levels of complexity can be identified in a hierarchy, **relevance trees** present a hierarchical structuring of detailed relationships. The process directs attention to the critical nodes and branches of the relevance tree and highlights the most cost-effective pathways to completion of a project. The method is most like the program evaluation and review technique. Figure 21-1 is a relevance tree for a homicide investigation.

Technology Assessment

With a variety of forecasting and analytical tools, **technology assessment** anticipates and evaluates the potential impact on a society of emerging technological developments.

Reports from the Office of Technological Assessment should be of interest to law enforcement personnel. Criminal investigators, for example, might well benefit from the findings presented in the OTA publication *Science, Technology and the Constitution.*

Technology

Although technological advances in law enforcement occur slowly, technology continues to be developed to assist police officers and criminal investigators in solving crimes. Law enforcement will reap the benefits of new technology developed for the space program, national defense, and the private sector.

Biometrics

Computers are revoutionizing police work. In the near future, police will be able to run a complete criminal check on a suspected offender, including fingerprints, from their vehicles. Lawrence K.

FIGURE 21–1: Relevance Tree

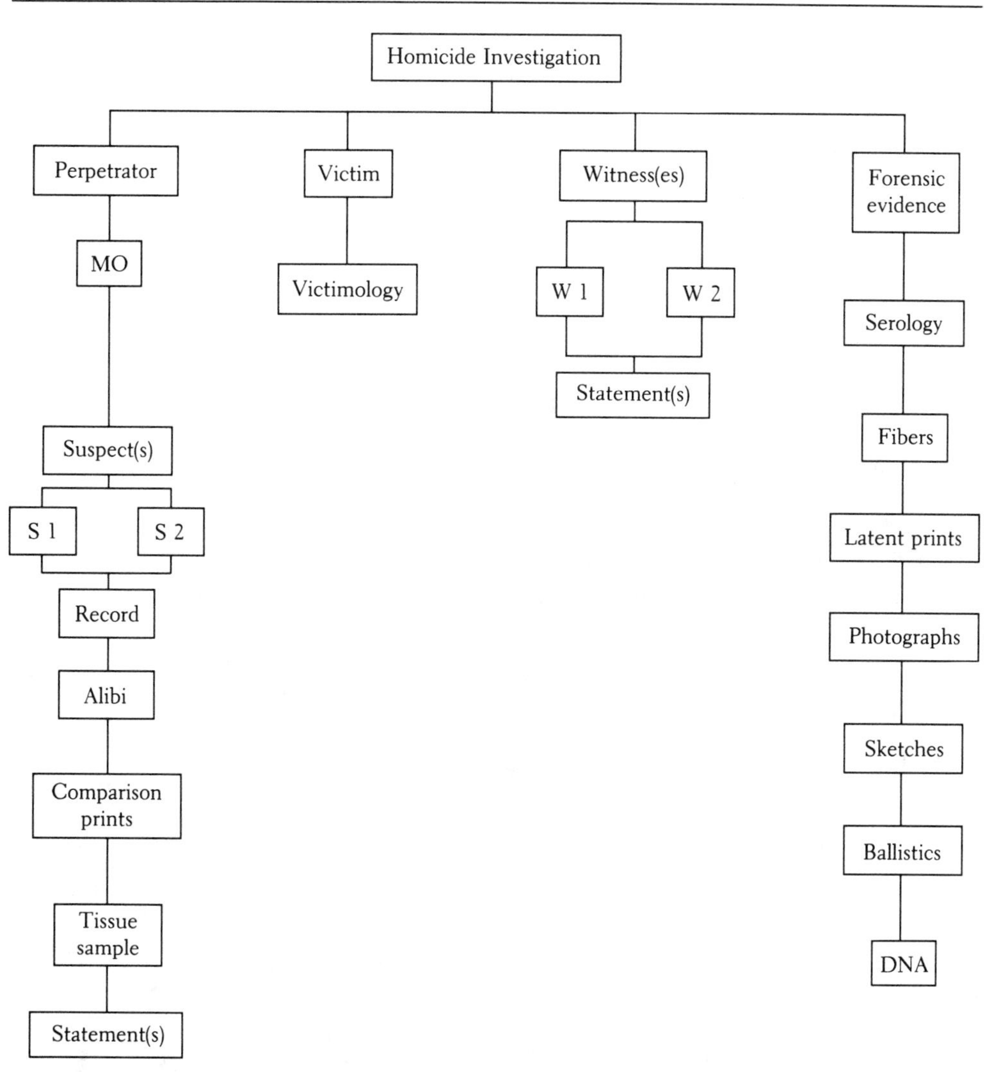

Source: Reprinted with the permission of Merrill, an imprint of Macmillian Publishing Company, from *Criminal Investigation: Essays and Cases,* 1990, p. 207, by James N. Gilbert. Copyright © 1990 by Merrill Publishing Company.

York, assistant director of the FBI's identification division, is enthusiastic about developments in fingerprint identification: "In 20 years, I expect that all systems will incorporate automatic classification of fingerprints, perhaps based on the application of neural nets. Ten-print live scan devices will take high-quality fingerprints without ink. These images will then be transmitted electronically from large numbers of remote locations to local, state, and national levels for entirely automated searches." (Gardner, 1990, p. 59)

Experts in the identification field believe that fingerprints will be only one method of identifying individuals. Within the next few decades, DNA could develop into a reliable method of identifying specific human beings by their body products.

Biometrics, physical or behavioral characteristics of a human being, can be used to identify a specific person. In a few years a specific individual's eye, voice, handwriting, or even touch on a typewriter may be used for identification purposes. **Retina scanning** may have the most promise. Other means of biometric identification may offer even more advantages for identifying specific individuals.

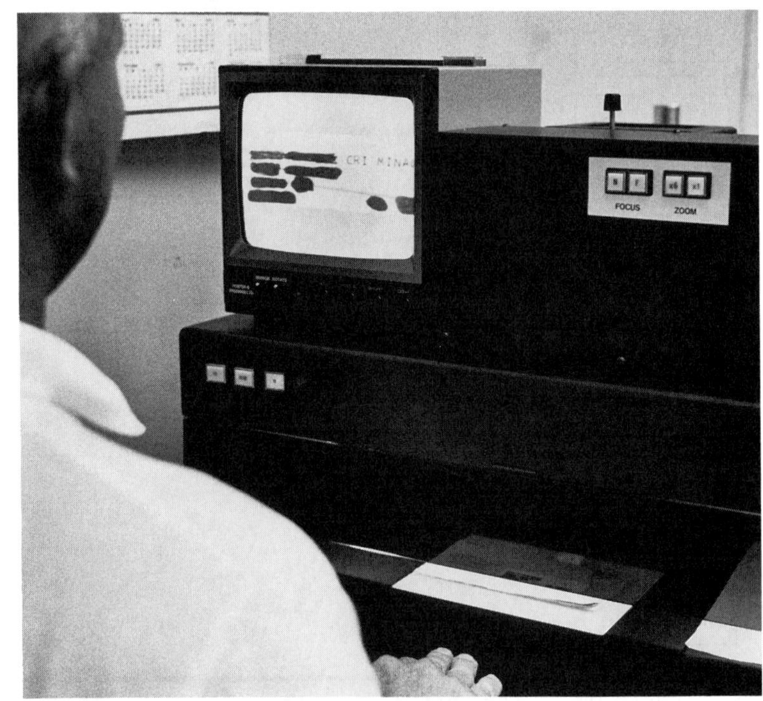

The Video Spectral Comparitor is a state-of-the-art investigation tool. Using infrared radiation to selectively filter out various wavelengths of light, the device has many applications. These include detecting fingerprints, scanning for gunshot residue, and, in this photograph, "seeing through" blockages on documents.

Predictions

Although it is difficult to accurately predict new technology that could aid law enforcement personnel, it is possible based on current trends to make a few projections. Technological predictions include the following. (Gardner, 1990, pp. 59–61, 89)

- The battle against illegal drugs and other contraband will be bolstered by laser devices, already under development, capable of probing cargo containers and similar receptacles for hidden compartments.
- Quicker, simpler, and less expensive drug-screening tests will probably be developed for use as part of routine prisoner processing. The tests should be more accurate and more substance-specific than those currently available.
- Police training will become more realistic as new generations of interactive video training aids, with advanced "branching" capabilities, come on line. The new programs will allow trainers to present a wide array of realistic, on-screen responses to test the student officers' role-playing decisions. "Shoot/don't shoot" training will be only one facet of these expanded practice scenarios.
- Small television cameras for unmanned surveillance of high-crime areas and traffic problem spots could see even greater use.
- As prisons continue to overflow, police agencies may assist corrections personnel in electronically tracking individuals "doing time" at home. This will require the development of portable monitoring equipment that can be carried in patrol vehicles.

LARS

Technology such as the LoJack Auto Recovery System (LARS) is currently being studied by police departments. LARS is a system that helps the police locate stolen vehicles and their thieves. A homing device about the size of a stick of butter is installed in the owner's vehicle. If the vehicle is reported stolen, the homing device becomes activated and a signal is transmitted. Police vehicles are fitted with four-phase antennas and a tracker. Picking up a series of beeps, the tracker will display a lighted compass and an illuminated strength meter that informs operators when they are nearing the stolen vehicle. To gain public acceptance, the police would have to put tracking devices in their automobiles. (Nilson, 1990, pp. 36–37)

Video Cameras

Another area where technology can help in investigations is the use of video cameras. Some departments have mounted video cameras in their patrol vehicles. Videos can be used when interviewing witnesses, victims, and suspects. Videos can be used at the crime scene and to tape the entrance to and exit from the crime scene.

Video cameras can be helpful in case management and case preparation. When they are used in court, the jury and judge can see what the crime scene looked like immediately after the crime. They can see the suspect at the time of arrest and compare this with his or her appearance at the trial. The attitude and comments of the suspect, victims, and witnesses after the crime can be reviewed.

Bias Crimes

In recent decades, certain groups have begun requesting that the police thematically investigate criminal violations against them. In 1990 the federal government mandated that the FBI begin collecting bias-crime data. **Bias crimes** are hate crimes committed against a specific ethnic, racial, religious, or sexually oriented group. They include attacking homosexuals, painting swastikas on synagogues, and burning crosses on the lawns of black families.

At least twelve states monitor bias crimes, and more will probably follow. Some law enforcement agencies have created investigative units that handle bias crimes. There is also a movement to prosecute violent crimes against women as violations of their civil rights. Criminal investigators can probably expect that in the future violent crimes against certain groups of people will be considered civil rights violations.

Summary

Criminal investigators are becoming computer-literate. The federal government and most states will soon have an automated fingerprint system in operation. Investigators can type their reports on word processors, which store them in memory and produce a hard copy whenever necessary.

In the future, criminal investigators will use computers to trace and analyze crime trends. Crime analysis focuses on groups of events rather than isolated incidents. Police agencies will also need to train investigators to work on computer crimes. With an increase of computers in workplaces and in the home, computer crime will be on the increase.

The 1990s may be regarded as the decade of cooperation and the recognition that the missions of public law enforcement and private security are similar. Criminal investigators need to recognize private investigators as equals and to cooperate and exchange information to solve criminal cases.

Various research methods should be considered when investigating crime, including scenarios, the Delphi technique, the cross-impact matrix, relevance trees, and technology assessment. Technology will continue to be developed to assist police officers and criminal investigators in crime solving. Biometrics, LARS, and video cameras are among the innovations that have already had an impact. Law enforcement will reap the benefits of new technology developed specifically for the space program, defense, and the private sector.

Bias crimes—hate crimes against a group of specific ethnic, racial, religious, or sexual makeup—seem to be increasing. At least twelve states monitor bias crimes and the FBI maintains statistics on them.

Key Terms

bias crimes
biometrics
cross-impact matrix
Delphi technique
integrated image system
optical character reader
relevance tree
retina scanning
scenario
technology assessment

Review Questions

1. What do the Tofflers predict about crime?
2. What is an automatic fingerprint system?
3. What are some of the advantages of a computer in police work and criminal investigations?
4. What is profiling?
5. What characteristics typify computer-related crime and criminals?
6. How can law enforcement and private security cooperate in the investigative process?
7. Discuss some of the research methods crime investigators should consider.
8. Discuss how technological advances in law enforcement can assist the investigative process.
9. What are bias crimes?

References

Douglas JE, Burgess A: "Criminal Profiling: A Viable Investigative Tool Against Violent Crime." *FBI Law Enforcement Bulletin*, vol. 55, no. 12), 1986.

Gardner GS: "Future Tech." *Police*, vol. 14, no. 6, 1990.

Nilson DW: "Vehicle Recovery: New Technology Captures Chicago's Attention." *Law and Order*, vol. 38, no. 2, 1990.

Office of Technological Assessment: *Science, Technology and the Constitution*. Washington, DC: Office of Technological Assessment, 1987.

Parker D: Computer Crime: Expert Witness Manual. Washington, DC: National Institute of Justice, 1989.

Post RS, Kingsbury AA: *Security Administration: An Introduction*. Charles C. Thomas, 1977.

Probert J: "Computers and their Effects on Investigative Procedures" in Palmiotto MJ, *Critical Issues in Criminal Investigation*, ed. 2, Anderson Publishing Co., 1988.

Shearing C, Farnell MB, Stenning PC: *Contract Security in Ontario*. University of Toronto, 1980.

Tayofa WL: "Further Research: Implications for Criminal Investigations" in Gilbert JN, *Criminal Investigation: Essays and Cases*. Merrill Publishing Co., 1990.

Toffler A, Toffler H: "The Future of Law Enforcement: Dangerous and Different." *FBI Law Enforcement Bulletin*, vol. 59, no. 1, 1990.

INDEX

Photo Credits

p. 4. Historical Pictures Service/Stock Montage
p. 6. *A Short History of Law Enforcement,* Charles C. Thomas Publisher
p. 9. Courtesy of the Georgia Public Safety Training Center
p. 11. Courtesy of the Metro-Dade Police Department, Florida
p. 21. Courtesy of the City of Rochester, New York
p. 26. Courtesy of the Hamilton County Sheriff's Department, Ohio
p. 29. Courtesy of the Aurora Police Department, Colorado
p. 41. Courtesy of the Connecticut State Police Department
p. 45. Courtesy of the Georgia Public Safety Training Center
p. 46. Courtesy of the Stark County Sheriff Department, Ohio
p. 49. Courtesy of the Georgia Public Safety Training Center
p. 52. AP/Wide World Photos
p. 60. Courtesy of the Federal Bureau of Investigation
p. 67. Courtesy of the United States Postal Service
p. 69. Courtesy of the Bureau of Alcohol, Tobacco and Firearms
p. 80. MGA/Photri © Spencer Grant
p. 82. Courtesy of the Aurora Police Department, Colorado
p. 91. Courtesy of the Federal Bureau of Investigation
p. 100. Courtesy of the Quick Uniformed Attack on Drugs (QUAD) unit, Tampa Police Department, Florida
p. 112. Courtesy of the Hamilton County Sheriff's Department, Ohio
p. 127. Courtesy of the Aurora Police Department, Colorado
p. 138. Courtesy of the City of Beachwood, Ohio
p. 140. Courtesy of the Ohio Peace Officer Training Academy
p. 170. AP/Wide World Photos
p. 189. Courtesy of the Hamilton County Sheriff's Department, Ohio
p. 190. Courtesy of the Aurora Police Department, Colorado
p. 193. Courtesy of the Connecticut State Police Department
p. 195. Courtesy of the Ohio Peace Officer Training Academy
p. 198. (*Top and bottom*) Courtesy of the Connecticut State Police Department
p. 200. Courtesy of the Connecticut State Police Department
p. 204. Courtesy of the City of Rochester, New York
p. 206. Courtesy of the Connecticut State Police Department
p. 209. (*Left and right*) Courtesy of the Connecticut State Police Department
p. 210. Courtesy of the Connecticut State Police Department
p. 220. Courtesy of the Federal Bureau of Investigation
p. 226. Courtesy of the Metro-Dade Police Department, Florida
p. 228. Courtesy of the Ohio Peace Officer Training Academy
p. 228. Courtesy of Life Codes Corporation
p. 235. Courtesy of the Ocean County Sheriff's Department, New Jersey
p. 236. Courtesy of the Federal Bureau of Investigation
p. 238. Courtesy of the United States Postal Service
p. 252. UPI/Bettmann
p. 256. Lyle Shook Collection
p. 258. Courtesy of the Ohio Peace Officer Training Academy
p. 265. Lyle Shook Collection
p. 275. Courtesy of the Georgia Public Safety Training Center
p. 277. Courtesy of the Ohio Peace Officer Training Academy
p. 280. Courtesy of the Fort Pierce Police Department, Florida
p. 287. Courtesy of the City of Rochester, New York
p. 291. Courtesy of the City of Rochester, New York
p. 301. AP/Wide World Photos
p. 302. UPI/Bettmann
p. 307. AP/Wide World Photos
p. 318. Courtesy of the Ohio Peace Officer Training Academy
p. 343. Courtesy of the Aurora Police Department, Colorado

p. 345. Courtesy of the Ohio Peace Officer Training Academy
p. 345. Courtesy of the City of Rochester, New York
p. 348. Courtesy of the Fort Pierce Police Department, Florida
p. 369. UPI/Bettmann
p. 374. Courtesy of the Connecticut State Police Department
p. 393. Courtesy of the Ohio Peace Officer Training Academy
p. 394. UPI/Bettmann
p. 404. Courtesy of the Chatham County Sheriff's Department, Georgia
p. 407. Courtesy of the Chatham County Sheriff's Department, Georgia
p. 414. Courtesy of the Savannah Police Department, Georgia
p. 429. Courtesy of the Stark County Sheriff Department, Ohio
p. 429. Courtesy of the Stark County Sheriff Department, Ohio
p. 430. Courtesy of the Stark County Sheriff Department, Ohio
p. 432. Courtesy of the Stark County Sheriff Department, Ohio
p. 436. UPI/Bettmann
p. 462. Courtesy of the Quick Uniformed Attack on Drugs (QUAD) unit, Tampa Police Department, Florida
p. 466. Courtesy of the Beverly Hills Police Department, California
p. 475. Isabella Stewart Gardner Museum, Boston, MA
p. 477. UPI/Bettmann
p. 480. Courtesy of the Aurora Police Department, Colorado
p. 502. Courtesy of the Aurora Police Department, Colorado
p. 523. Courtesy of the Chatham County Sheriff's Department, Georgia
p. 528. Courtesy of the Chatham County Sheriff's Department, Georgia
p. 534. Courtesy of the Illinois Criminal Justice Information Authority
p. 540. Courtesy of the Ohio Peace Officer Training Academy